MUSIC IN CANADA

Capturing Landscape and Diversity

ELAINE KEILLOR

McGill-Queen's University Press

Montreal & Kingston • London • Ithaca

© McGill-Queen's University Press 2006
ISBN-13: 978-0-7735-3012-6   ISBN-10: 0-7735-3012-6 (cloth without cd)
ISBN-13: 978-0-7735-3177-2   ISBN-10: 0-7735-3177-7 (cloth with cd)

Legal deposit fourth quarter 2006
Bibliotheque nationale du Québec

Printed in Canada on acid-free paper that is 100% ancient forest free (100% post-consumer recycled), processed chlorine free

This book has been published with the help of a grant from the Canadian Federation for the Humanities and Social Sciences, through the Aid to Scholarly Publications Programme, using funds provided by the Social Sciences and Humanities Research Council of Canada.

McGill-Queen's University Press acknowledges the generous support of the Canada Council for the Arts, which in 2005 invested $20 million in writing and publishing throughout Canada, for our publishing program. We also acknowledge the financial support of the Government of Canada through the Book Publishing Industry Development Program (BPIDP) for our publishing activities.

Library and Archives Canada Cataloguing in Publication

Keillor, Elaine, 1939–
Music in Canada : capturing landscape and diversity / Elaine Keillor.
May be accompanied by a compact disc.
Includes bibliographical references and index.
ISBN-13: 978-0-7735-3012-6   ISBN-10: 0-7735-3012-6 (book)
ISBN-13: 978-0-7735-3177-2   ISBN-10: 0-7735-3177-7 (book and compact disc)
1. Music – Canada – History and criticism.   I. Title.
ML205.K385 2006   780'.971   C2006-901632-1

Typeset in 10.5/14 Warnock Pro with Myriad Pro
Book design and typesetting by zijn digital

Dedicated to the memory of John Churchill

Contents

Vignettes

Acknowledgments

Through the years I have been indebted to many who have aided me in exploring the musical expressions to be found in Canada. My mother first awakened my interest in Canadian music by telling me about her teacher W.O. Forsyth and showing me piano pieces written by him. At the University of Toronto my dissertation advisor, Carl Morey, encouraged me to further pursue this interest in Forsyth. As his research assistant I combed the Toronto *Globe and Mail* for items about Canadian musicians and music-making. Soon I was preparing entries for the forthcoming *Encyclopedia of Music in Canada*. When I began teaching at Carleton University, I was responsible for Canadian music courses that had been introduced at the Department of Music by John Churchill in 1968. Much of this book has grown out of the stimulating discussion with and research done by undergraduate and graduate students at Carleton University. With financial assistance from the Department of Indian Affairs, the Social Sciences and Humanities Research Council of Canada, the government of the Northwest Territories, and Carleton University, I have been able to undertake fieldwork trips to learn from the First Peoples about their musical expressions. Many of these experiences came together in the work undertaken by the Canadian Musical Heritage Society in 1982. I owe much of my understanding and knowledge of Canadian music to my fellow editors in the Society, including John Beckwith, Robin Elliott, Clifford Ford, Frederick Hall, Helmut Kallmann, Marie-Thérèse Lefebvre, and Lucien Poirier.

As this book was taking shape, a number of my colleagues have provided valuable guidance by reading portions. I wish to particularly acknowledge William Echard, Paul Litt, Del Muise, and Deirdre Piper. I am indebted to Clifford Ford for digitizing many of the examples, and to numerous librarians and museum directors who kindly provided information and fulfilled requests for photographs. The Interlibrary Loan staff at Carleton University cheerfully tracked down a wide variety of books and essays. In addition I appreciate all the assistance I have received at the Music Division of Library and Archives Canada and the Archives of the Canadian Museum of Civilization.

In the final stages of preparation of this book, I wish to thank anonymous readers for their comments and criticisms. Lukas Ridgeway and Lucian Badian Editions kindly assisted in preparing digitized images. I am extremely grateful to Ruth Pincoe for her editorial expertise to produce the final version. My thanks is extended to the staff at McGill-Queen's Press for the final stages of production. The financial assistance of an anonymous donor and the grant from the Aid to Scholarly Publications Program administered by the Humanities and Social Sciences Federation of Canada made this publication a reality. Only with the constant encouragement and emotional support of my husband, Vernon McCaw, have I been able to carry this project through to its completion.

Elaine Keillor
Ottawa, 2006

MUSIC IN CANADA

1   Exploring the Sounds of Canada

More than ever before, it seems, Canadians are concerned with questions of identity, and musical expression – a powerful communication force – can be an important source of information about the Canadian ethos. Ninety percent of human communication is non-linguistic. While music can involve language, it also relays non-textual messages that we respond to on several levels. On a sensory level, performers and listeners take in musical sound through the body and receive kinaesthetic and immediate stimulation of feelings and memories associated with that sound. These responses are influenced to some degree by cultural conditioning, including the geographical spaces in which the earlier feelings were formed. We constantly take in information from the geographical space.

Our culture determines which sounds we consider as music and which we hear as noise. Indeed, some languages do not have specific words for the phenomenon that John Blacking has called "humanly organized sound," referred to in English as "music." Our culture conditions our minds to interpret and our bodies to respond to specific sensory messages in a particular way. An individual's initial reactions are based on learning from others, but through exposure, that individual may come to accept a wide variety of sounds as music, particularly if there is an opportunity to experience many different types of sound. Thus, a wide variety of musical expressions can become a defining aspect of a particular culture. These musical sounds influence what that society believes about music, and determine behaviour, or, as Christopher Small would say "musicking" – "To music is to take part, in any capacity, in a musical performance, whether by performing, by listening, by rehearsing or practising, by providing material for performance (what is called composing), or by dancing" (Small 1998, 9). Musicking even encompasses activities of ticket sellers, stage managers, roadies, cleaners, etc., that contribute to the creation of a musical performance and its consumption by the community.

The Sounds of Canadian Music

The aim of this book is to trace relationships between production and consumption of musical performances as they have evolved in Canada, and to explore links between these relationships and our conception of and behaviour about musicking. During the 1990s, the United Nations rated Canada as the best country worldwide in which to live in terms of basic human needs, but in 1995, another UN survey of ninety countries ranked Canada last in terms of presentation and promotion of its own culture. This low rating may have been due in part to the fact that many Canadians are simply not aware of their cultural wealth in areas such as music.

Our observations about the functions served by music remained, for the most part, of only passing interest until the 1950s when Helmut Kallmann, then music librarian at the Canadian Broadcasting Corporation (CBC), began a painstaking study of Canadian music. In the course of his research, Kallmann tracked down many composers, both historical and contemporary, and where possible obtained copies of their compositions for the CBC Music Library. Since the publication of his landmark study *A History of Music in Canada 1534–1914* (1960), two other histories (Ford 1982 and McGee 1985) have appeared. In 1970 Kallmann was appointed head of the newly created Music Division at the National Library of Canada (now Library and Archives Canada [LAC]). Prior to that date the LAC had no program for the systematic collection of data on music and musicians in Canada. Indeed, at one time copyright permissions for music in Canada were handled by the Department of Agriculture, and from 1895 to 1923 publications of Canadian music were regularly deposited, not in Canada, but at the British Museum!

The centennial celebrations in 1967 stimulated much exploration of Canada's history as a nation and its more ancient past, and many Canadian musicians and dancers were showcased across the country. Around that time, the first Canadian music history courses appeared at l'Université de Montréal (in 1966, taught by Maryvonne Kendergi) and at Carleton University (in 1968, taught by Willy Amtmann). After searching through a number of standard music reference books for Canadian content, John Beckwith wrote "About Canadian Music: The P.R. Failure"

(1969). This caught the attention of Floyd S. Chalmers, who realized the need for systematic research on and presentation of the music of Canada. His foresight and generous monetary support resulted in the formation of a team led by Helmut Kallmann, Gilles Potvin, and Kenneth Winters to prepare the *Encyclopedia of Music in Canada (EMC)*.[1] With increasing knowledge of and interest in Canadian music came a need for published copies of the music referred to in EMC. The Canadian Musical Heritage Society (CMHS) was founded in 1982 to locate, select, edit, and publish Canadian compositions written prior to 1950.[2]

Books published since 1980 cover a wide range of musical activity in Canada, from twentieth-century composers to reference books on popular, folk, and country music, rock, and jazz.[3] Among collections of essays on Canadian music, *Canadian Music: Issues of Hegemony and Identity* (1994), edited by Beverley Diamond and Robert Witmer, is particularly important as it includes a number of articles from obscure sources and English versions of important French writings as well as new essays. In her incisive, analytical examination of the three histories of Canadian music (by Kallmann, Ford, and McGee), entitled "Narratives in Canadian Music History," Diamond underlines Kallmann's lead, followed by Ford and McGee, in recognizing that a history of music in Canada must be compiled and written from a different perspective than that used for European countries; such a history must be socially based so that music is considered within the Canadian circumstances of the time. Through a detailed statistical analysis of these histories, Diamond demonstrates that music considered to be complex, urban, and sophisticated is valued more highly while "simple, rural, unsophisticated" music receives short shrift (Diamond and Witmer 1994, 160).

Categorization and Terminology

HISTORICISM AND PRESENTISM

My historical overview of Canadian musicking is the first history of Canadian music that makes an attempt to at least touch on the full range of sounds that have and are being heard within the borders of the country. Accordingly guidelines are needed to establish specific umbrella terms to refer to different kinds of music. I have based this volume on two orientations developed by anthropologist George W. Stocking: "historicism" and "presentism." Historicism is an attempt to understand the past for its own sake; presentism concerns studying the past in order to understand the present.

The categorization of different types of music has been a feature of European tradition and other cultures for more than a thousand years, but the terminology used for such categorization is constantly changing. Terms are used loosely and often have different meanings in different parts of the world. Terminology used in Europe and the United States has had an important impact on Canada; different meanings of a given term are often in conflict with one another, and some take on yet another meaning in a Canadian context. A full study on this issue is yet to be done, but we can trace a few broad outlines in order to lay groundwork for terminology used in subsequent chapters.

EUROPEAN CLASSIFICATION

In Europe until around 1800, music was generally subdivided according to function: the terms "church" and "chamber" covered music created for the elite of the Christian church and members of the nobility. Music that was transmitted orally – today usually called "folk music" – was used by those who did not read Western musical notation, but was also considered the common property of everyone. European composers such as J.S. Bach, Haydn, and Beethoven regularly incorporated folk tunes into their compositions or based melodic and rhythmic material on folk models. With the rapid changes brought about by industrialization, the rise of the bourgeoisie, and new political and social ideals exemplified in the French Revolution, composers such as Mozart aimed to write music that would appeal to people of all classes. These new developments enlarged the potential audience for notated compositions, which in turn had an impact on the rapidly growing business of music publishing. In the 1790s, as the piano became a symbol of gentility desired in every home, music publishers began to make a sharper distinction between keyboard music written for connoisseurs and that intended for amateur performers, who required technically undemanding pieces with diatonic harmonies, light textures, clear structures, and simple melodies. Composers wrote sonatas and sonatinas for pianists of modest abilities, but most amateur music consisted of dances, song arrangements, simple variations, fantasias on familiar songs or arias, and descriptive character pieces sometimes related to current affairs. In 1802 the Zurich music publisher Hans Georg Nägeli began a series of publications that was to include "classic" keyboard music of the early eighteenth century by J.S. Bach and G.F. Handel and contemporary piano music aimed at connoisseurs.[4] We can note the fluctuation in meaning of the term "popular" with regard to Beethoven's Piano Sonata, op. 27, no. 2 ("Moonlight"), a "classical" work that met

Nägeli's requirements for a "connoisseur" sonata: the first movement has also become a "popular" hit. Here, "popular" describes a creation that has a wide audience, but it does not necessarily refer to the style or genre of a specific piece of music.

CATEGORIZATION IN THE UNITED STATES

In his study of "highbrow" and "lowbrow" in the United States, Lawrence Levine traced the application of these two terms to a sacralization of specific cultural expressions.[5] Initially the United States, in glorifying democracy and a classless society, celebrated events that mixed the two types of cultural expression. Gradually, however, creative expressions from northwestern Europe became particularly favoured in theatres frequented by the wealthier members of American society.[6] The phrenology of the day supported the view that certain people were superior due to their high brows, and accordingly music by German composers was particularly glorified while Italian operas were seen as music for the masses.[7] Musical expressions from other cultures, including Asia, Africa, Eastern Europe, and the North American First Nations, were seen as noise rather than music (Levine 1988, 220). An article written in 1918 for the *New Orleans Times-Picayune* underlines these expressions as unmusical because they are prominently rhythmic: a "down in the basement, a kind of servants' hall of rhythm. It is there we hear the hum of the Indian dance, the throb of the Oriental tambourines and kettledrums, the clatter of the clogs, the click of Slavic heels, the thumpty-tumpty of the negro banjo, and, in fact, the native dances of the world" (Levine 1988, 221). Along with the sacralization of certain kinds of expressions, there was a rigid hierarchy of the meaning of culture. Sacralized expressions, considered the best, were to be appreciated only by educated intellectuals.[8] It was widely believed that the masses could not appreciate "true culture," but that a musical pap derived from the "amateur music" publications that proliferated through the nineteenth century could be provided for them.

The sacralization and the hierarchical meaning of culture led to an even greater gap between what was considered amateur and professional. An observer writing in the *Atlantic Monthly* in 1894 noted: "Amateur has collided with professional, and the former term has gradually but steadily declined in favor; in fact, it has become almost a term of opprobrium. The work of an amateur, the touch of the amateur, a mere amateur, amateurish, amateurishness – these are different current expressions which all mean the same thing, bad work" (Levine 1988, 140). This view differed significantly from European thinking. Participation in musicking was seen as open to all who wished to participate, regardless of their economic class. State support of institutions such as opera houses and symphony orchestras meant that the average person could afford to attend performances.

VIEWS OF FOLK MUSIC

Throughout the late eighteenth and the nineteenth centuries, Europeans also developed different views about folk music. Publishers, particularly in English- and German-speaking countries, realized there was a large market for arrangements of folk songs. Many composers, including Haydn and Beethoven, fulfilled commissions for arrangements of Scottish and English folk songs. Interest in folk songs was fuelled by German-speaking literary figures for whom "the folksong movement came to symbolize nationalist aspirations in Europe and the British Isles ... through the 19th century."[9] However, Europeans considered people who created and continued the original folk music as innocent, uneducated entertainers rather than "real musicians." These shifting ideas from the United States and Europe undoubtedly found their way to Canada. In the chapters that follow, I will illustrate how neither sacralization nor a hierarchy of culture became absolutely predominant in Canada, although there were individuals, often in influential positions, who held these views. Certain musical repertoire did become sacralized, largely through influences of the European conservatory system. European ideas about the role of the state in encouraging a country's cultural expressions gradually infiltrated Canada during the twentieth century and into the twenty-first. Meanwhile, because of the isolation of much of the Canadian population, older ideas of musicking persisted in the sense that music was a necessary part of human activity.[10]

"POPULAR" AND "REFINED" MUSIC

Throughout this book, I use the term "popular music" loosely to refer to products that are – or have been in a specific period – approved of by a large audience, often through widespread transmission, and promotion. For musical expressions that do not receive such widespread transmission and promotion, but that often, through time, become definitive markers of a particular culture, time, and space, and for a wide range of European and European-derived music, I will use the term "refined."[11] I retain the designation "popular" to refer to forms of music-making that, at one time or another, were considered popular by the public at large. Accordingly jazz is included in these "popular" expressions. This delineation is used only to help organize very diverse materials that in many cases overlap, as can be readily heard in the wide variety of sounds produced within Canada.

Sounds of Music across Canada

VIGNETTES

Canada encompasses a huge geographical area in which many different cultural heritages co-exist and amalgamate. It is difficult for a single historian to provide a balanced picture of such a complex situation, particularly because music is primarily an aural phenomenon that left few verifiable traces before the early 1900s. We do, however, have scattered records of musicking in small communities across the country, a number of which are described in the course of this book. The "vignettes" placed throughout the text provide snapshots of chronological developments or musical experiences in a particular location; each one can also be seen as representative of similar developments or experiences in communities across Canada. These parallels might be separated not only geographically but also chronologically. For example, a feature of musical life seen in Nova Scotia in the early 1800s may not have appeared in Manitoba communities for another hundred years.[12]

There are many important aspects that I will not address in any detail. These include the individual lives of musicians, the role of gender particularly for women making music publicly before 1900, the relationships between class and economic status and musicking, the developments in various music businesses including instrument making, publication, media, and technology. Even a particular area of musicking such as experimental music performance will only be referred to in passing (Waterman 2005). All of these areas are awaiting thorough studies both regionally and nationally.

RECORDINGS

Because this study is concerned with exploring *sounds* heard in Canada over the past four hundred years, the experience of listening to examples is an important element. As recording technology did not become a reality until the last decade of the nineteenth century, we have no recordings of musicking in Canada before that date; unfortunately many recordings made ca. 1890–1925 are either unplayable or unavailable in commercial format. In addition, many Canadian creations, both notated and orally

A Village in Southwestern Ontario

I recall a great variety of music-making during the 1940s and 1950s in the tiny southwestern Ontario village (population about 200) where I grew up. Choirs, gospel quartets, and vocal solos played a major role in the four churches. One church prohibited musical instruments, but the other three encouraged instrumental music in services and other church events. There were fine fiddlers in the vicinity and country music was heard at square dances in the town hall. At least once a year, the community organized an evening entertainment ranging from excerpts of Shakespeare's plays to skits from minstrel shows, interspersed with popular songs, traditional fiddle music, and piano solos ranging from Chopin to the "Glow Worm."

My mother was a music teacher so our house resounded with music prescribed by the Toronto Conservatory of Music: mainly works by European composers such as Bach, Beethoven, and Chopin, with the occasional piece from the Americas (works of Edward MacDowell or Heitor Villa-Lobos). Canadian music, except for pedagogical pieces by Boris Berlin and Clifford Poole, was rare. Students performed the repertoire they were learning at various local functions. Local musicians also met regularly in various homes for an evening of Haydn trios and other chamber works: two of the instrumentalists had been members of an opera orchestra in the former Yugoslavia and relished the opportunity to play chamber repertoire, and wind players from a neighbouring town that had a band were always available.

Children's songs were heard in the school yard, and other folk songs were learned not only in piano arrangements but also from neighbours who came from Central Europe. We heard – and in some cases learned – these songs working in tobacco fields or hoeing vegetables. Songs and dances also played a major role at weddings of our European neighbours, and in time this music broadened the musical horizons of the largely English- or American-based material of average Canadian weddings.

Most homes had a radio, and people often sat down to listen. Some tuned in to broadcasts of the New York Philharmonic Orchestra, the Telephone Hour, the Metropolitan Opera, and the Toronto Symphony, while others listened to country musicians such as Don Messer and variety shows such as the Happy Gang. The radio and the nickelodeon at the ice cream shop kept us informed of the latest popular tunes, which were then rendered by local musicians at functions ranging from strawberry socials to school graduations. Many of these tunes were American, but those by Guy Lombardo and His Royal Canadians were particularly appreciated. Guy Lombardo came from London, Ontario, and his band, consisting of family members and other musicians was one of the most popular dance bands of all time.

Village residents attended musical events at larger centres in the area. One larger town of 20,000 had a Women's Music Club that presented a concert series of solo artists and perhaps touring operatic production from Toronto. During a week-long visit in the early 1950s the New York City Opera gave eight different operatic productions in London, Ontario. London had had an orchestra since the late 1930s and there were several concert series: the Community Concerts provided a range of leading (usually non-Canadian) artists while other series featured local organists, rising young artists sponsored by a women's club, a summer festival of Cleveland Orchestra concerts, and special events at the University of Western Ontario. The inauguration of the Stratford Festival of Canada in 1953 provided opportunities to enjoy not only live theatre but also musical events. Excursions to many of these events were organized by the village, and it was not unusual to see a favourite square dance caller and fiddler climbing on the bus to hear violinists such as Mischa Elman play in London!

transmitted, have never been recorded.[13] Because of these major limitations, the music examples referred to in this book are largely selected from those available in recent recordings or reissues.[14]

The Theses of Landscape and "Rubbaboo"

In an interview broadcast on the CBC, Murray Adaskin commented that Darius Milhaud could instantly recognize the compositions written by the Canadians in his summer classes of the late 1940s and the 1950s without prior knowledge of their nationality.[15] What was it that signalled "Canadian" to him? In his foreword to Greg Potter's book *Hand Me Down World: The Canadian Pop-Rock Paradox*, Randy Bachman commented that, for him, each Canadian rock band had a distinct sound, while successful bands in the United States had a dozen or more clones that were indistinguishable from one another. Bachmann attributed the distinct identity of bands such as Rush, BTO, Trooper, and Cowboy Junkies to the types and varieties of music that individual musicians heard as they were growing up in Canada. Radio was an important factor but cultural heritage of their communities – Jewish, Mennonite, Ukrainian, etc. – also played a significant role (Potter 1999, ii).

LANDSCAPE
Characteristics of terrain and quality of light have a direct influence on the work of painters and other visual artists. Art critic Corinna Ghaznavi

(2002) has written: "Canadian identity is deeply entrenched in ideas of land and landscape. Canadiana is full of images of loons, lakes and vast spaces vacant of people. We drown in images of Niagara Falls. The Group of Seven looms" (86).[16] In her assessment of folklore development in Canada, Carole Henderson Carpenter uses settlement and landscape characteristics to point out major differences from the United States. In Canada, settlers of one culture tended to remain in groups, and areas of settlement were often further defined by geography (1979, 100). During the past two decades there have been some attempts to systematically apply theories of landscape influence to music created within a specific area, but in descriptions of musical movements in Canada, reference is often made to regional areas that are strongly demarcated by differences in terrain. Is there any evidence to indicate commonalities among the regional musics created in Canada? If so, how has this come about, and of what does it consist? How did Milhaud and Bachmann recognize it?

RUBBABOO

Another commonly recognized characteristic of Canada is multiculturalism. Although only officially recognized in federal government policies of the last quarter of the twentieth century, many cultures have inhabited the global space now known as Canada since time immemorial. Different cultures created forms of musickings that varied greatly, and this variety has continued to grow as members of almost every culture in the world chose to make Canada their home. Inevitably Canadians partake of many musical experiences, and through their relationships with one another they participate in and blend different forms. As early as 1862, the term "rubbaboo" was applied to this type of musical blending.[17] The exploration of the sounds of Canada through the following chapters document rubbaboos of many types, created long before the concept of world music became current in the 1980s.

The Song of Duke Redbird

Looking back on my early experiences with music, I realize that there was no distinction made between types of musical expressions (except by a few individuals who had conservatory-based ideas of what "good music" was supposed to be). Most people were not concerned with this canonization, but they did have distinct views of what constituted a good performance, be it a violin solo by Fritz Kreisler or a fiddler's rendition of *Big John McNeil*. It is impossible to highlight every type of music heard or performed in Canada within the confines of a single book. My attempt with this book is rather to document examples of some of the vast cornucopia of musics to be found. It is up to individual readers to continue this exploration, particularly in the ways that musics brought from other parts of the world are adapted and blended within the Canadian mosaic to create new rubbaboos. Duke Redbird's song "I Am a Canadian,"[18] celebrates the diversity of this land and the activities of average Canadians in their relationships with one another.

> I'm a lobster fisherman in Newfoundland
> I'm a clambake in P.E.I.
> I'm a picnic, I am a banquet
> I'm mother's homemade pie.
> I'm a few drafts in a Legion hall in Fredericton
> I'm a kite-flyer in a field in Moncton
> I'm a nap on the porch after a hard day's work is done.
> I'm a snowball fight in Truro, Nova Scotia
> I'm small kids playing jacks and skipping rope
> I'm a mother who lost a son in the last great war
> And I'm a bride with a brand new ring
> And a chest of hope
> I'm an Eastener
> I'm a Westerner
> I'm from the North
> And I'm from the South
> I've swum in two big oceans
> And I've loved them both
> I'm a clown in Quebec during carnival
> I'm a mass in the Cathedral of St. Paul
> I'm a hockey game in the Forum
> I'm Rocket Richard and Jean Beliveau
> I'm a coach for little league Expos
> I'm a baby-sitter for sleep-defying rascals
> I'm a canoe trip down the Ottawa
> I'm a holiday on the Trent
> I'm a mortgage, I'm a loan
> I'm last week's unpaid rent
> I'm Yorkville after dark
> I'm a walk in the park
> I'm Winnipeg gold-eye
> I'm a hand-made trout fly
> I'm a wheat-field and a sunset

Under a prairie sky
I'm Sir John A. Macdonald
I'm Alexander Graham Bell
I'm a pow-wow dancer
And I'm Louis Riel
I'm the Calgary Stampede
I'm a feathered Sarcee
I'm Edmonton at night
I'm a bar-room fight
I'm a rigger, I'm a cat
I'm a ten-gallon hat
And an unnamed mountain in the interior of B.C.
I'm a maple tree and a totem pole
I'm sunshine showers
And fresh-cut flowers
I'm a ferry boat ride to the Island
I'm the Yukon
I'm the North-West Territories
I'm the Arctic Ocean and the Beaufort Sea
I'm the prairies, I'm the Great Lakes,
I'm the Rockies, I'm the Laurentians,
I am French
I am English
And I am Metis
But more than this
Above all this
I am a Canadian and proud to be free

2   Traditional Musical Expressions of the First Peoples

By at least 14,000 years ago humans were living throughout the land that today we know as Canada, and by 1400 C.E. there were a number of cultures established across the country. Each of these cultures integrated musical expressions into their daily lives according to their needs and belief systems, which in turn were interdependent on an economic foundation closely tied to climatic and geographical characteristics of the area; it has become customary to group cultures sharing common characteristics together into regions.[1] The following review is subdivided into eight geographical regions, largely determined by language families and traditional economies (see figure 2.1): Northwest Coast, Western Subarctic, Plateau, Plains, Eastern Sedentary, Eastern Nomadic, Maritime, and Arctic. It is important to recognize, however, that there are no clear lines dividing one region from another. I will discuss one or two cultures from each region in some detail, with the understanding that musical practises are not necessarily similar for other cultures in that region. Spellings and terms are, as far as possible, based on designations chosen by the cultures in question; common names used in the past appear in brackets, and translations are given in parentheses.[2]

Northwest Coast Region – Kwakwaka'wakw [Kwakiutl]

Of the seventy or so Aboriginal languages spoken in Canada today, more than half are found in British Columbia. These languages belong to the strikingly different groups of Athapaskan, Azteco-Tanoan, Salishan, and Wakashan (Dickason 1992, 33),[3] and their variety reflects the diverse origins of these communities. The main cultural groups along the Northwest Coast (north to south) are: Tlingit, Haida, Nisga'a, Gitxsan, Haida,

Figure 2.1   Map of Canada showing Aboriginal linguistic areas, the eight geographical regions used for discussion of First Peoples' Music, and the approximate location of some cultures.

Tsimshian, Haislan/Henaaksiala, Oweekeno, Nuxalk [Bella Coola or Coast Salish], Heiltsuk [Bella Bella], Kwakwa̲ka̲'wakw [Kwakiutl], Nuu-cha-nulth [Nootka], Shíshálh, Sliammon, Dakelh [Carrier], Wet'suwet'en, Homalco, Klahoose, Squamish, Halq'emeylem, Sto:lo, Hul'qumi'num, Pacheenaht [Nootka], Semiahmoo, Straits Peoples, and Makah (Coull 1996, x). The language of the Kwakwa̲ka̲'wakw belongs to the Wakashan family, whose material culture indicates strong links with Oceanic Polynesian peoples. When George Vancouver sailed into Kwakwa̲ka̲'wakw territory in 1792 there were some 100 'na̲'mima (families) living in large rectangular wooden houses in about thirty communities. Surrounded by bountiful forests, these wood-working peoples created a "carpentered world" (Vastokas 1992, 27). Cedar, the tree of life, was essential for the economy, providing material for dug-out canoes, feast dishes, bent boxes, ceremonial houses, and totem poles, as well as fibres for clothing, baskets, and rope. Each 'na̲'mima was derived from a first Chief, and the origin story explaining his identity (as one of the Transformers, such

Figure 2.2   Kwakwaka'wakw (Kwakiutl) dancers, Alert Bay, Vancouver Island. Photograph by J. Barnard

as Killer Whale, or a supernatural being, such as Wolf, Grizzly Bear, or Thunderbird) was told in songs, dances, and theatrical presentations that were owned by each woman, man, and child in the ranked system of the *'na'mima*.[4] The Kwakwaka'wakw use music to verbally relay values, morals, and traditions of their culture, and each performance of a song "is a symbolic reenactment of crucial behavior patterns upon which the continuity of a culture hangs" (Teskey and Brock 1995, 53).

KWAKWAKA'WAKW WINTER CEREMONIAL (POTLATCH)

Winter ceremonials were connected with events such as the opening of a new *gukwzi* (Big House) or raising of a totem pole, a birth, coming of age, marriage, death, or to honour a great deed or right an old wrong. These gatherings, attended by up to several thousand people lasted up to a month and required much preparation. Hosts provided gifts for each guest as well as accommodation and food, and hired a composer to create new songs. In the nineteenth century these gatherings came to be referred to as potlatches.[5] Music plays a major role throughout the gathering. Guests arrive in boats singing paddle songs and are greeted in song by the host. Musical and theatrical events are performed each day and evening in the *gukwzi*. Those involving myths and dances connected to a specific matrilineal lineage (such as Killer Whale, Sun, Grizzly Bear, or Thunderbird) can only be performed by members of that lineage. A song could be obtained only by inheritance, marriage, or commissioning. The songmakers conceived songs through dreams, visions, or spiritual trance, and through learning a song, dance, or ritual, an individual could experience the originating vision. Elaborate masks, inspired through dreams of a myth or a supernatural being were also used in dance presentations. Because of the importance of the number four, each song and dance was done at least four times. The main part of the potlatch began with a Mourning Song to remember those departed since the last *'Tseka* season, followed by the Cedar Bark complex, possibly the *hamat'sa,* and then the *Tla'sala* (Peace Dance Song) and the Feast Song.[6] Totemic crest songs were also presented by the host and important guests, and on some occasions lullabies were sung.

The main dance complexes are the responsibility of Kwakiutl dancing societies (Padfield 1991, 15). The song master of each society was an expert musician and composer; he and his assistants sing the required repertoire with absolute accuracy and create new material as required. They also provided accompanying instruments, such as *t'amidzu* (cedar logs or planks) and the *tamyayu* (batons). "During the dance the song master and his assistants sang the song while the people beat time with sticks as they danced around the room ... Some ... kept watch during each dance and announced publicly when a mistake had been made in the dancing ... The 'Word Passer' ... assisted the song master and acted as a prompter, having memorized the songs made by the maker for each new dancer ... The drum beater, 'Hotluliti' or 'Obeyed by All' was a director of ceremonies for each dancing society" (Hawthorn 1979, 41). Mythological beings are portrayed with brightly painted cedar masks regarded "as objects of immense power" that could transform their wearers (Padfield 1991, 17). The supernatural impact is increased with "the masked dancers stepping, then crouching and hopping to the syncopated, percussive beat of the song, the bark fringes swaying, the masks turning with birdlike jerks, and then the jaws snapping in resounding staccato" (Padfield 1991, 17). Complicated arrangements of tunnels, props, ropes, and boxes are also used to create special effects. The potlatch ends with a Farewell Dance in which everyone participates after removing the crest head pieces to signal a return to the everyday world. Other dances may also be inserted before the giving of gifts and the final feast. In performance, each dance is identified with an account of how it was received to justify the dancer's right to perform it. Otherwise the potlatch host could be challenged.

The giving of a potlatch was a socially recognized means of enhancing the reputation – which was directly related to the magnitude of the potlatch, the amount of food prepared, and the volume of gifts – of the host. In 1896, Maquinna (ca. 1835–1901), a Nuu-chah-nulth chief compared the potlatch to the White man's bank: "We are Indians, and we have no such bank; but when we have plenty of money or blankets, we give them away to other chiefs and people, and by-and-by they return them, with interest and our heart feels good" (Petrone 1983, 70). The potlatch is strongly linked to identity in its reiteration through song and dance of the lineages of the participants, and the history of their clans.

KWAKW_AKA_'WAKW ŚONGS

Kwakw_aka_'wakw crest songs and some hamat'sa songs are lyrical in nature, but the lyrical love/mourning[7] songs are sung in falsetto with a fast vibrato meant to imitate crying. Ritual and potlatch songs often have a recitative-like declamatory style with elevated language. Pitches for each text are fixed and there is no improvisation; a limited number of pitches are used, and often the chanting line centres on a single pitch while the chorus sings a lower undulating melody. Rhythmic organization is complex with three or four durational values and varying rhythmic layers. "The Kwakiutl's use of jagged rhythms has been compared to the 'steady, yet broken beat of the sea,' an appropriate simile since the tribe is known for its fishing skills and knowledge of the sea. The rhythms ... contain a great deal of contrast, including triplets and syncopation as well as repetition. Constant drumbeats precede and underlie but do not strictly coincide with vocal melodies" (Teskey and Brock 1995, 42). The range of most songs – about a major 6th, with some special songs extending to an octave – is wider than that of other Northwest Coast groups, but more restricted than those found in many other North American Indigenous cultures. The most common intervals are a minor 2nd and an untempered major 3rd. It has been suggested that the predominant melodic movement – an undulating pattern with a downward tendency – imitates the cry of a seagull (Teskey and Brock 1995, 43). The many vocables in children's songs are often the phonetic sounds from which new songs grow, and vocables also serve to keep stressed syllables and meaningful words on accented musical beats. Ceremonial songs include both vocables and meaningful words. Songs consist of several sections, some of which may recur in a rondo-like pattern (for example, Introduction AB AC AC'AD AE), with the recurring section often attached to vocables. Repeated patterns are usually varied melodically or rhythmi-

The *Hamat'sa*

During the *'Tseḵa* (Red Cedar Bark Dance, the primary winter ceremonial complex) dancing societies enact mythic and visionary encounters with supernatural beings in ancestral theatrical ceremonies and songs that they possess. One of the most important of these is the myth of Baxwbakwalanuxsiwe', the Ogre who lives at the north end of the world. This cannibal lives with many servants in a mountain dwelling; those possessed by him become *hamat'sas* with the same desire to eat human flesh. George Hunt has translated Baxwbakwalanuxsiwe' as the first one to eat man at the mouth of the river. The *hamat'sa* ceremony, which comes from the Awik'inuxw people of Heiltsuk (Rivers Inlet), was added in the nineteenth century to restore young initiates returning from the land of supernatural beings to society.

The role of the *hamat'sa* (Man Eater) – the guiding and initiating spirit – is traditionally taken by the son of a chief. After spending several weeks in the forest, the young initiate returns to the village, whistles tentatively as he approaches the dance house, and makes a dramatic entry through the smoke-hole in the roof into the midst of the villagers seated around the perimeter of the house. The *hamat'sa* song usually consists of four verses with a refrain indicating the tonal centre. The singer is accompanied by a loud rhythm beaten on a log and a drum. This complex, syncopated rhythm often consists of groups with five pulses plus a longer cadential pattern at the phrase ends. A rapid rhythm signifies that the *hamat'sa* is violently possessed by the spirit, while a slower rhythm indicates the taming of the initiate. Rhythm, words (called "the walk of the song), and gestures are all related; the words guide hand motions, and the rhythm is connected with foot and leg movement. Specific masks and whistles are associated with Baxwbakwalanuxsiwe' and his associates, and interjections such as "hap" or "we-yu-pa, we-yu-pa" signify the Ogre or his associates eating. Movements of the masks are indicated by other syllables, such as "hem" for opening and closing the beak (Reid 1981, 246). A more upright posture and a slower rhythm portrays the human side of the initiate *hamat'sa*, and the dancer also extends his arms like the wings of a bird, again according to the words of the song. During the fourth strophe while circling the fire the dancer indicates in actions that he wishes to be fed (Reid 1981, 247).

The whole purpose of this elaborate presentation is to portray a transformation of death into life and present the Kwakwaka'wakw view of their place in creation. The ritual emphasizes the mouth of the river where the salmon gather; the purifying season of winter, the use of sacred rather than public names, the counter-clockwise direction of the dances, and the metaphorical switching of sex achieve a complementarity. These presentations also teach societal values, warning against unacceptable sexual practises through a re-enactment of a woman's marriage to Baxwbakwalanuxsiwe' and by the socialization of the *hamat'sa* into adult society (Reid 1981, 252). As Vastokas underlines, the whole performance, with specific songs and instruments, is a microcosm of the Kwakwaka'wakw universe (see Vastokas 1992, 24)

cally. Some songs have a strophic structure in which musical material is repeated with a varied text. Defining elements of a song, such as short motifs or phrases, may be varied and repeated many times. Phrases or melodic lines generally end with a descent or a flattening of an extended or repeated pitch.

INSTRUMENTS

Drumming to accent the beat, a basic ingredient of all performances, was done on planks and a log, plus a lead drum (originally a rectangular wooden box suspended from a rafter and beaten with a fist wrapped in cedar bark). Following the introduction of the gambling game, the Kwakwaka'wakw began to use circular single-headed drums made of hide stretched over a wooden frame and beaten with a padded stick. These drums became more common after First Nations ceremonials, including the potlatch, were banned by the Canadian government in 1885. Over the next fifty years, masks, rattles, and boxes holding ceremonial and dancing outfits were confiscated and scattered around the world.[8] Musical instruments lost in this way include *hamat'sa* wooden rattles (carved like skulls) and rattles made of copper (an important symbol of wealth). Potlatches continued underground, often with reduced props. There were also cedar whistles with reeds (used in the *Tla'sala*) and bellow whistles (concealed in a dancer's outfit). Wooden whistles (*madzis*) with finger holes, several shafts, and reeds produce a strong, clear, eerie sound, particularly when several pitches sounded together; these instruments were used to announce the return of the *hamat'sa* and particular whistle sounds are associated with specific characters in presentations. The Kwakiutl consider their whistles and drums not as musical instruments but rather as ways to reproduce the voice of the spirits and to underline the rhythm of the dance and the polyphonic songs of the chorus (Reid 1981, 187). Rattles, however, are considered musical instruments. The sound of round or oval shamans' rattles provided direct contact with the supernatural. Held in the left hand, this rattle calms the initiate, and also announces the entry of each dancer. Some rattles are engraved with a representation of a spirit and painted in the traditional colours of white, red, and black (Reid 1981, 188).[9] The cedar was viewed as a supernatural power and a way to the sky, and bundles of shredded cedar bark were used as decoration on the powerful rattles used to calm dancers.

Musical instruments of the Tlingit, Haida, Tsimshian and Halq'emeylem were influenced by interior groups who made rattles using clusters of deer hoofs. The Tlingit, Haida, and Tsimshian have suspended puffin beaks, animal teeth and claws, or shells on rings that were shaken to the beat of the dance or worn by dancers on their ankles. Most whistles were made of wood and cord, sealed with pitch, but prior to contact, a few southern cultures had end-blown flutes with finger holes. Haida argillite flutes with six finger holes found in museum collections may be similar to those made in the pre-contact period. Bull-roarers (a flat stick attached to the end of another stick that was whirled, producing a booming noise) were used to represent supernatural beings. In many cases, these instruments were associated with specific dances, and major differences in dances are found even among various groups of the Kwakwaka'wakw.

Western Subarctic – The Dogrib

The Dene peoples developed an economic system in the Deh-cho (Mackenzie River) drainage system on the tundra stretching south to Lake Athabasca, north to a point near the Mackenzie Delta, west to the present Alaskan border and east across the Barren Grounds to Hudson Bay. Languages of the Dene cultures of the Western Subarctic belong to the northern Athapaskan family: east of the Mackenzie River, these include Denesuline [Chipewyan], Tłicho [Dogrib], Gwich'in, Dehcho [Slavey], Dene Tha', Hare, Mountain, Yellowknife; to the west are the Han, Tanana, Tutchone, Kaska, Taku River Tlingit, Tagish, Champagne-Aishihik, Tahltan, and Sekani. In a terrain of massive rock outcrops interspersed with boreal forest and thousands of lakes and a climate notable for short summers and long winters, the Dene moved from one temporary or semi-permanent camp to the next following an annual cycle based on fish runs, caribou migrations, and the availability of small game. Some Athapaskan groups in the far west built subterranean dwellings but most travelled in small groups of one or two extended families, living in tipis about five metres in diameter made of cariboo skins supported by wooden poles. Most groups had no complex chief-clan hierarchy, but marriages were regulated by two or three matrilineal or patrilineal clans; for example the Tanana had three matrilineal clans (Laguna 1995, 23).

The Dogrib (Tłicho) led a nomadic existence in the area between Great Slave and Great Bear Lakes. Meetings with other small family groups were marked by dancing and feasting. In 1789 Alexander Mackenzie described a dance in which both men and women formed a circle.[10] During the twentieth century, there was a gradual shift from unaccompanied Tea Dance songs to songs accompanied by drums, and new forms of dances accompanied by drums and traditional-sounding melodies continue to be introduced (see appendix A). Today, during a *Toghà Dagowo* (all night dance), Dogribs perform a *Tadǫʔa t'a dagowo* (Tea Dance) without drum accompaniment; men (some of whom sing the song) and women face inward around a circle and move clockwise. The men, empty handed, use energetic steps and arm movements while the women do a side shuffle.

Individuals who have shamanic powers beat a round, single-headed snare drum with an unpadded stick.[11] These drums are used by singers/drummers to accompany specific dances and are also played during a complex guessing hand game that was played at gatherings, to settle disputes, or as recreation during caribou hunting expeditions.

Dogrib dances take place at night. The drum-dance songs have either a single or a double beat. Songs for dances are performed by a group of two to eighteen male singers/drummers who stand at the edge of the dancing area. Each drummer/singer has a repertoire of fifty to several hundred songs, and the groups are taught or led by an elder. The songs have a monophonic texture. If many dancers participate, the same song is repeated in a circular fashion for half an hour or more. Some songs come from prophets; others are given as messages for the community by celestial beings who visit in dreams or visions (Beaudry 1992). For the Prayer or Prophet Song (*nadats'e ti zhi*) singers bow their heads; the drum beat is slower and lighter and there is no dancing. Dance songs include the drum dance (*Eye t'a dagowo*), in which dancers move clockwise around a circle in single file, the couples or partners' dance (*Lila nats ʼI to t'a dagowo*), and a lady's choice circle dance with men on the outside and women on the inside moving similarly to the drum dance.[12] In the line dance or fast partner dance (*Nake k'e dagowo*) lines of men and women move forward and back.

Because the Dogrib traditionally lived in small family groups, much of their expressive culture consists of dances and songs performed by one or two people. For example, the solo Ptarmigan Dance imitates the actions of the bird. Dogribs also recited stories in which references to an individual or animal were realized with a song (*cante fable*), a practise found in many different cultures. As part of the transition to adulthood,

A Dogrib Gambling Game

Many of the Aboriginal cultures in Turtle Island (North America) developed some form of guessing or gambling game. Stewart Culin (1907) has subdivided these games into four categories: four-stick, stick, hidden-object, and hand. The stick and hand forms involve objects, some of which have special markings. Hidden-object games concern an object hidden in one of four types of places. In hand games the object is held in the hand, and location guesses involve one of two or one of four choices. While data is still lacking for many areas, Lurie has concluded that in Canada, the hand game is found west of the Red River, while the moccasin game (a form of hidden-object) appears largely east of that area (Helm and Lurie 1966, 90). Guessing was indicated with hand signals, possibly because these games were played between groups speaking different languages. The Dogrib hand game has the largest and most complex series of hand signals on record and can also involve the largest number of players; for example, a player might indicate the location of the hidden object in the left or right hand of each of twenty men on the opposing team simultaneously. Two types of songs are used in the hand game *idzi*. One is a chant sung by the drummers during the game. "In syncopation with the drum beat, the singers repeat one tone. At times the leader rises to the third above, in an unpredictable and evidently improvisatory play on two notes" (Helm and Lurie 1966, 27). The other is a melodious tune sung by the hiders (*idzi*-men) without drum accompaniment, during the game, at the end of a game or a round, or while the drummers heat the drumheads to restore proper tone (27).

For an *udzi* game each team facing each other will have an equal number of men. Each man of the active playing team hides an object in one of his fists. The single guesser on the opposing team indicates by means of a hand signal simultaneously where every player has hidden the object. While he is considering and doing that guess, the drummers of the active team vigorously sound the drums and expound with heads thrown back the one- or two-note chant to try to distract him. Their kneeling fellow team members with the hidden objects sway the upper parts of their bodies in rhythm with the drum beat. After the guess is made, the men open their fists to reveal the location of the objects and a tally with sticks is made of the correct guesses. If the active team remains in that position, their men go into a crouch to reshuffle the location of the objects, while the members of the opposing team quietly watch. If that team loses because of an accurate guess, the opposing team becomes active and receives the drums to continue the process. Today these games are usually used for entertainment, but in the past they were often used to settle disputes. (A portion of an *udzi* game can be seen at www.native-drums.ca.)

young persons spent a period of separation from the group during which they received a song from the spirit of an animal or an insect. Individuals carried these songs for the remainder of their lives and used them as a source of strength in difficult moments. Other personal songs of the Dogrib fall into two categories. *Ets'elà* (Love songs) are either teasing songs that make people laugh or more personal expressions of longing or sorrow. *Ndè ghǫ shį ts'et'į* (Love of the Land songs) are often sung while working (for example, cutting up meat in the barrens).[13]

The Dogribs have a stock of musical gestures. For example, an individual might put words and vocables to the tune of a Tea Dance to create a personal song. These songs often have two main phrases repeated in various patterns (such as ABB' ABB' or ABA'B'); melodic contours begin on or leap up to a 5th above the resting tone and then gradually descend. Songs have a circular structure in which any point may be selected as an end. Some dance songs are sung in a pulsating, nasal tone in a medium to high register for projection.[14] Personal songs, lullabies, and story songs are sung with a more even, non-nasal tone. Dance songs use few lexical words and have vocables at the beginning and end of musical phrases.[15] Love songs have more meaningful texts, but contextual information about the song's origin is needed for full comprehension. The few musical instruments used by the Dogribs in their traditional nomadic life style include rattles, hand-held drums, and a whistle made from a bird wing or a green willow branch; conical rolls of birchbark (similar to those found in the Maritime Region) were also used to call animals while hunting.

Western Athapaskan cultures also held potlatch-type ceremonies lasting several days, with feasting, gift giving, costumes, singing, and drum dancing. The most important ceremony was the Feast for the Dead (also known as the Stick Dance or *Hi'o*) to honour a deceased relative. "Each relative of those memorialized is supposed to compose his or her own eulogy for the whole group to sing, but those unskilled may have another 'put the song in her (or his) mouth' and as many as thirty songs have been composed for one celebration ... Mourning songs, are sung by a chorus of men, the women dance in place" (Laguna 1995, 53). Dances of several different types are accompanied by one or several drums. Dances involving a number of people move in multilayered circles (somewhat similar to the Dogrib) but movements for line dances are similar to those described by Mackenzie. In the Stick Dance, a pole, brought in at the beginning of the festivities, is danced around the village while twelve sacred "Stick Dance Songs" are performed at the main meeting place. After the pole is re-installed, the entire assembly dances around it clockwise, repeating the syllables "hee-yo" in various musical phrases, through the night. At the end, the pole is broken up and thrown into the river.

Plateau

The sharply demarcated environmental zones of present-day western British Columbia – grasslands ending abruptly at river terraces, forests on mountain slopes, and high alpine meadows –supported a complex hunter-gatherer culture that incorporated wealth, private ownership of key resources, hereditary élites, intense trading, slavery, polygyny, high population densities, and a seasonal sedentary life style. There were Salishan-speaking tribes –the Senijextee [Lake; now located in the United States], the Okanagan, the Nlaka'pamux [Ntlakyapamuk, Knife, or Thompson], the Secwepemc [Shuswap], the St'at'imc [Lillooet], and the Tsilhqot'in (Chilcotin) – plus the Ktunaxa (Kutenai, Kootenay), speaking a Kootenayan language that may be a branch of the Algonkian-Wakashan family. Through the spring, summer and fall, kin-related bands traversed valleys and mountains on foot, gathering roots and berries and fishing for salmon in the major rivers. They had lodges for summer use and met at gathering places to celebrate the mid-summer solstice with dancing. In the fall and winter they hunted large and small game. Winters – a time for social gatherings, dancing, feasts, games, and story-telling – were spent in pithouses in permanent locations. Each group had several male chiefs designated to make specific decisions for the community as a whole. While land was generally held in common, some fishing stations were considered private.

Each animal, bird, insect, plant, etc. was seen as a being with a soul; prayers or songs were performed by women harvesting plants and by successful hunters and fishermen. There were also ceremonies to celebrate the first harvest of berries and roots and the first run of salmon. Sprits of nature communicated with the people through three categories of songs: personal guardian spirit and curing songs; songs given by the earliest ancestors; and songs passed through prophets from the Old One (Wickwire 1983, 87). Youths received their own protective guarding songs in a dreamlike state induced by fasting, running, sweating, swimming, and dancing, during which a spiritual being taught the song to the initiate and advised on its use (in hunting, fishing, gathering, gambling stick-games, illness, or other trouble).[16] Men and women undertook long periods of training to obtain curing powers. Teit describes how a Nlaka'pamux shaman used his curing powers:

[The shaman] kept up his song which had been given to him by his guardian spirit and sometimes he imitated the latter both by voice and gesture. At intervals he turned his song into a conversation with his spirits, which was unintelligible to the listeners. Sometimes shamans improvised this song. While he was singing, he gesticulated sometimes with his arms and sometimes with his body, while he kept time with his feet. Sometimes he would break into a kind of dance in which he went through many jerking and jumping motions with his body and legs. He also blew on the body of the patient and repeatedly made passes over it with his hands. Sometimes, shamans, after singing their songs, thereby invoking the aid of their spirits, immediately proceeded to remove the disease by sucking. (Teit 1900, 362)

During puberty training adolescents performed songs given by their ancient ancestors while dancing around a fire shaking deer hoof rattles and addressing the Dawn of the Day (Teit 1900, 311–18), and an ancient song was used in the sweathouse to request purification, relief from pain, or success in hunting (Teit 1914, 310–11). A mourning song thought to have been given by the bear was sung whenever a bear was killed,[17] and a special mourning song was used when twins were born.[18] Both male and female war songs included prayers to the sun. The men, dressed in feathers, paint, and full armament, danced in a counter-clockwise circle, accompanied by drums, imitating a battle, with each participant creating the sound of his guardian spirit. After the men departed, the women, also painted, wearing armaments, and carrying wooden spears, were led by an elder representing the war chief in a counter-clockwise circle dance, throwing out the spears, then pulling them back (Teit 1915–21, VI.M.114, 144).

Songs given by the Old One (the Chief of the Dead or Chief of the Land of Souls) were transmitted by prophets "male or female who had died (visited the spirit-land) and then had been reborn on earth" (Wickwire 1983, 92). The texts of these songs often included instructions on behaviour in difficult times and strength in adversities. Other "given" songs were for specific birth, death, and other life cycle events. In Teit's designation "lyrical songs" expressed personal feelings and emotions and had an acknowledged composer; these songs were often created by women and sung during puberty rituals or while harvesting roots and berries (Teit 1915–21, VI.M.155). "Going home" songs were sung by groups returning from an expedition (VI.M.72, 97). The melodies of Plateau songs consist of three or four different pitches, often moving downward through an interval between a major third and a fourth. Musical structure usually consists of two phrases that are repeated (ABABAB) often with small variations. Vocables often imitated the sounds made by animals or birds, such as "hwa" for a bear. In mourning songs the vocable "ŏ" (comparable to "oh!" or "alas") sung to descending four-note gestures conveys the sound of crying. Songs for stick-games (gambling games somewhat similar to the Dogrib Hand Game) use the vocables "ho! ha! hau!"[19]

Percussion instruments used for occasional accompaniment include drums made of birch bark or boards, hide, basket bottoms, or bark kettles. A rasp made from a serrated stick and a bone scraper was used for war dances. Sticks were used as rhythm instruments, and in stick games were struck on boards. Rattles made of deer hooves were used for specific songs, and in puberty ceremonies were tied around the arms and legs. Children played imitations of bird calls on small three- or four-holed flutes made from bones of larger birds (Teit 1915–21, VI.L.27).

Plains – The Cree

The variety of cultures whose economic survival depended on the bison included languages of several families: the northern Athapaskan-speaking Sarcee, Dunne-za [Beaver], Algonkian-speaking Nehiyaw [Cree], Saulteaux [Plains Ojibwa], Atsina [Gros Ventre], Siouan-Catawba Hidatsa, Siksika [Blackfoot], Kainah [Blood], Peigan, and Siouan-speaking Assiniboin, Dakota, Nakota, and Lakota. Small bands or hunting groups of Cree[20] moved from parkland to grassland, travelling in summer by canoe and in winter by snowshoes or toboggan. They lived in conical or dome-shaped lodges, wore clothing made from animal skins, and made tools and weapons from wood, bone, hide, and stone. Religious life was based on spirits who revealed themselves in dreams, and each individual was responsible for his actions. A yearly cycle of thirteen moons was ruled by the seasons. While leaders were selected to direct hunts and raids, there was no tradition of inherited leadership. During the summer, larger groups gathered for socializing, exchanges, and ceremonies.

The most important occasion for dancing and singing was the annual Thirst (Sun) Dance, often held around the summer solstice. The purpose of the Thirst Dance is to pray for rain and to obtain personal strength. Drums begin at a medium fast pace and dancers, each with a whistle in his mouth, must keep perfect time to the drum beats; singing and drumming are kept up continually through the dance. At the conclusion gifts are distributed among the aged and needy and there is a magnificent feast (Dion 1979, 36–41). Preparations for this major event include ceremonies associated with Medicine Bundles, songs for each object in the bundles, and practise sessions for the Thirst Dance songs. Plains songs are typically monophonic, with the women singing an octave higher than the men. Male singers normally produce a tense vocal tone with pulsations on longer notes and frequent glissandos at the middle or ends of phrases. Often a leader sings the first phrase and everyone joins in on the repetition. The general melodic contour, consisting of two to four or more phrases, some of which are repeated, usually begins in a high register and descends through plateau-like steps to the final, lowest pitch. There are usually about five pitches spread over the range of a tenth; intervals close to major seconds and minor thirds are common. Rhythm accompaniments, played by a drum or rattle, include an unaccented steady beat, an accented one-two beat, and a tremolo.

Plains cultures had various societies that looked after specific ceremonies and provided fellowship and entertainment. The Cree had a Thirst Dance Society, a Cree Prairie Chicken Society, a Buffalo Dance Society, a bachelors' Witigo Society, and the women's Elk or Wapiti Society. Sometimes specific musical instruments, such as rattles, were used only for songs of one society. After the Cree obtained horses (possibly in the early 1700s) and adopted the pound for hunting bison, a Horse Dance was performed at the summer gathering. Riders trained their horses to follow a lead horse moving to the beat of the drummers and singers. Periodically the dance maker called a halt for the pipe to be smoked and passed around, after which another leader began a new series of songs (Dion 1979, 45–6). Male dances not connected with societies include the Bear Dance (in which dancers clad in bear skins danced on their knees) and the Chicken Dance (a pre-sunrise dance imitating the prairie chicken) (Dion 1979, 48, 44). In the Tea Dance everyone danced where they stood, but gradually the *pee-tchi-tchi* developed into a circle formation with the men on one side and women on the other (Dion 1979, 54).

Mitewok (Medicine Dances) took place during the rutting moon and were followed by the Ghost, Give Away, and Calumet (peace pipe) dances. The drum used for these dances was "made by hollowing out a length of log a foot or more in diameter and about two feet in length. Rawhide is stretched tightly over the open ends" (Dion 1979, 49). The low hollow sound blended well with Medicine chants. Shaking tent or curing rituals were performed only by properly trained shamans using a rattle called a *sisikwanis*.[21] The Ghost or Spirit dance was performed during the night to commemorate those who had departed. Dancers (including children) often carrying Burdens (containing an article of a departed loved one) moved in single file while four singer-drummers sat along the north wall

A Cree Drum

The Cree use several types of drums: some have double heads, but most are single-headed, hand-held drums with or without snares. (For descriptions on how drums are made and a video documenting the creation of an Ojibwe drum, see www.nativedrums.ca.) Crafters of drums use wood and hide available in the surrounding particular terrain. Traditional knowledge about drum construction includes the types of wood that are appropriate and the specific construction methods for each type; for example, the procedure for birch differs from that for balsam. Hides are chosen from the species of animals that inhabit the area, and are usually prepared by women. Once again, some hides are better than others; for example, a drum crafter in a particular locale might prefer deer hide to caribou because it might withstand climate changes more readily.

The sound of a drum is a complex combination of the fundamental tone, various harmonics, and inharmonic partials produced when the skin of the drum is struck. Snares attached over or under the membrane make the sound even more complex. The Cree drum with a snare under the membrane manipulated by the thumb gives a sound that can effect the singing voice of the player. This drum is normally held with the left hand grasping the handle and the thumb under the loop of the tuning strings. To obtain the best sound, it may be necessary to sprinkle water on the hide and

brush it in before playing. The basic sound – produced without engaging the tuning strings – is a low humming tone with faint upper partials, but when the tuning strings vibrate against the underside of the drum head, the basic tone is amplified with a buzz tone an octave lower. The number of harmonics vary according to the tension of the hide, the rhythm and speed, plus the manipulation of the tuning strings.

A version of the Round Dance Celebration – a ritualized victory celebration held after a successful hunt or skirmish – takes place at Moberly Lake, B.C. in late fall. At this event, the Cree drummers/singers present songs based on the fundamental tone to which their drums have been tuned by means of heating and cooling. The most common rhythm is a long-short, long-short pattern. "In this rhythm, the thumb pulls the tuning strings on the long beat and releases slightly on the short beat, with the richest array of harmonics and partials occurring just as the strings are released between the beats ... Striking the centre of the drum produces more harmonic partials, while the areas of the periphery of the head produce more inharmonic partials when struck" (Pearson 1987, 22). For the dance, men and women join hands and move slowly clockwise around a large circle using a sideways shuffle step that matches the rhythm of the drums. "The drum is said to be the sound of the Earth's heart beat, which rises up to link the heart beats of the people" (Pearson 1987, 22).

of the dwelling. "Each leader of four singers had his own songs; he could use three of these before he called a halt" and allowed another group of singers/drummers to take over (Dion 1979, 51). The Give Away dance lasted for several days; at the end of a song the dancemaker picked out a gift and, to the accompaniment of a new song and drum accompaniment, approached an individual, who danced in turn before accepting the gift. The Calumet Dance *oskitchy*, only performed by elders, belonged to a specific individual for life. Each individual also had personal songs, one obtained as a puberty rite and others used for various life rituals. Cree held regular practise sessions, using a rattle rather than drums, to refresh their memories and teach songs that accompanied each dance and ceremony. One-hole whistles were made from a bird's wing bone. The Cree also discovered the principle of the mouth bow and could create drones and melodies by manipulating overtones.[22] Some tribes, including the Assiniboin, used rasps.

Eastern Nomadic – Ojibwe

The Algonkian-speaking Woodland groups known as Anishinaabeg[23] inhabiting the large area of boreal forest stretching from southern grassland and mixed hardwood trees north to the tundra include Cree, Algonquin, Montagnais/Naskapi or Innuat, and Atikamekw. While the forest, interspersed with lakes and waterways, is an essential underpinning of these cultures, groups closely allied with the Wendat [Huron] also developed agricultural skills, growing corn, beans and squash. The Ojibwe (Chippewa), were initially centred around present-day Sault Ste Marie on Lake Superior, where there was a bountiful supply of fish and wild rice.[24] Politically independent bands each had a chief selected on the basis of hunting or shamanic prowess and hunting territories. For much of the year bands dispersed into family hunting units but congregated at larger gatherings during spring and summer. Society was divided into clans, each identified by a symbol or totem (*Do-daim*). Hunters and gatherers took only what they needed from the forest and offered paeans of gratitude to Gitche Manitou (The Great Spirit). Manidog[25] (spirits) inhabited everything: evil was personified as a mythical cannibalistic giant known as Winebojo, both a trickster and a teacher for the use of plants. Boys aged twelve to fourteen underwent a vision process before they were accepted as adults (see Johnson 1976, 127).

Many songs and dances were associated with important events.[26] The Pipe of Peace Dance was performed at least once each spring for renewal and regeneration of peace.[27] Songs and often dances also marked important life ceremonies: Naming Ceremony, First Kill of a Boy (with dances representing a hunt or enacting the habits and conduct of game animals), Marriage, and Feast of the Dead (held each autumn to honour those who had died in the previous year. Thanksgiving ceremonies were held at the first flow of sap in the spring and in late fall before families departed to isolated wintering habitats; smoking of the pipe and offerings to Kitche Manitou were followed with a dance and chants embodying the theme of survival (Johnston 1976, 144). One form of the Festival of the Dog was limited to warriors; the other, open to everyone, reminded participants of famine and survival through dance. The evening before a war party set out, a drum summoned the village to a War Dance (see Johnston 1976, 146–7), and a Victory Dance (see appendix A) was held after a victorious return. Other dances include the Deer Dance, the Snow-shoe Dance, the Begging Dance, and the Partridge Dance, each of which involved specific movements, songs, and accompaniment by rattles and or drums. For the Ojibwe "songs were the utterances of the soul ... Most were of a personal nature composed by an individual on the occasion of a dream, a moving event, a powerful feeling" (Johnston 1976, 148). Songs arrived in dreams or during a puberty fast, and could be used for a variety of purposes, ranging from war dances and doctoring to moccasin games.[28] Many were strophic, with tunes consisting of several different sections (such as A B C D E) one of which might be repeated.

Drums used in the *Midéwiwin* (Medicine Dance) include the "grand-father" (a water drum made from a tall, hollow log) and a smaller "little boy" (the membrane of which is tied down with seven stones signifying the seven fires, prophecies, or teachings),[29] both of which are struck with non-padded beaters. The curved stick beater represents the head and eye of a loon (Densmore 1979, 96). Single-membrane hand drums, frequently painted according to designs received in a dream, are played with padded or non-padded drumsticks at the distal end. Other double-membrane drums have specific drumsticks, one of which is made from a loop of cedar branch. The drum for the moccasin game has snares held in place by short sticks and is beaten in a strong-weak pattern. The Drum Dance – which the Ojibwe in legend received from the Dakota through Turkey Tailfeather Woman around 1877 – uses a large double-membrane drum that became the symbol of the sacred Drum Religion. Several rattles used only in *Midéwiwin* meetings are made by attaching a stick handle to a container made of hide (moose scrotum), wood, animal horn, or birch bark and filled with pebbles, buckshot, small bones, or corn kernels. Skin-covered disc rattles are made from a wooden circle, extended to form a handle. Rattles are also made from fish skin or animal and bird parts,

End-Blown Flutes

In the literature the terms of whistle and flute are used somewhat indiscriminately; however, whistles usually have no finger holes. The term flute usually refers to an end-blown duct instrument, held vertically, with a whistle mouthpiece, similar to a European recorder. This type of flute is widely distributed among Aboriginal cultures of North America. In Canada they are found in the Maritime, the Eastern Sedentary, Eastern Nomadic, Plains, Plateau, and Northwest Coast regions. Flutes without a whistle mouthpiece are found in some cultures present in the United States, but within Canada, these instruments only appear in the southernmost part of the Plains region.

Each region has myths about the origin and importance of the flute. The Plains Sioux "Sound of Flutes Legend" relates the use of the flute in love medicine. It describes the instrument's origin in the sound created by the wind blowing through holes made by a woodpecker in a cedar tree, and explains the reason for the bird's head carved on the end of the flute (Conlon 1983, 8). In the Mi'kmaq tale "The Indian Who Became a Mi'kmwesu" Glooscap (Kluskap) gives a magic flute to an ugly person who, through learning how to play the flute, is transformed into a handsome man (Diamond, Cronk, and von Rosen 1994, 78). Other epics describe a Mi'kmaq flute (*pipukwaqn*) two and a half feet long, made of elder wood with six finger holes. In the Northwest Coast region the Makah played a cedar flute with six finger holes during the Klokali midwinter celebra-

tion (Densmore 1939, 103). In the Plateau region, Nlaka'pamux (Thompson), and N'kamapeleks (Okanagan) used long flutes with six holes to serenade girls at night and also to give signals for horse-stealing raids. In the Plains and Eastern Nomadic areas many love songs were sung or played on the flute; a young man courted a woman by playing the flute and the woman might return the favour by singing the song. Some groups, such as the Ojibwe, also used flutes for signalling and in specific ceremonies. While Iroquoian cultures mainly used the flute as a courting instrument, it also played a role in the Little Water Ceremony (Tooker 1978, 460).

End-blown flutes vary in length from forty centimetres to almost a metre. They normally had six finger holes and an external block – a piece of wood attached to the outside of the flute – to direct air into the chamber. In the Plains region, the external block is often carved in the shape of a bird, and the flute is referred to as the "bird on the roost." Other terms for the block include "saddle" and "rider" (Conlon 1983, 24). In Eastern regions, the external block is usually carved in the shape of an animal (Diamond, Cronk, and von Rosen 1994, 86). Because young men used flutes for courting purposes or for signals during wars or raids, players often tried to imitate the songs of birds; the body of the flute and the external block might be carved in the shape of a bird or a bird's head and painted. The most important sound quality was the strong warble produced by the lowest fundamental pitch of the instrument. Some scholars claim that flutes with this external block construction are unique to North America (McAllester 1980, 307; for a detailed description of the construction of these flutes see www.nativedrums.ca.)

Because flutes were made from materials that deteriorated quickly, few examples made prior to 1900 have survived. In the early twentieth century, traditional usages of the flute began to disappear, and the instrument went into serious decline. Extant recordings of traditional flute music indicate that flute melodies were derived from melodies that were sung (Conlon 1983, 56). Most melodies were based on pentatonic or hexatonic scales with contours of descending undulations through small intervals to the lowest tone of the instrument; a few melodies began with a large leap upwards. Rhythm for the most part was free and unmetred. Many players deliberately tried to imitate bird calls by using ornamental devices such as glissandi, turns, and trills. Since 1970 there has been a significant revival of interest in constructing and playing the flute. The Mi'kmaq flute can be heard on *Mi'kmaq Chants*, KCD 0001. Iroquoian flutes are used on *Caught Between Two Worlds: David R. Maracle*, SCD 5261. Jody Gaskin and Jani Lauzon use mostly Plains flutes.

and some, carved out of wood, represent specific totems. A rattle made of deer hoofs was used to transmit news from one group to another. Whistles and flutes were used for transmitting signals, and hunters also used animal callers. There is considerable variety in the shape, construction, and decoration of rattles and drums throughout the Eastern Woodland. Some drums were quite large and had snares with pieces of bone or teeth attached across both membranes.[30]

Eastern Sedentary Region – The Neutral and Wendat Nations

The economy of the area comprising present-day Ontario and a portion of the St Lawrence valley was based on agriculture, supplemented by hunting and fishing. Here, in fields surrounding the buildings of palisaded settlements, cultures including the Wendat [Huron], Petun [Tobacco], Neutral, and Mohawk cultivated the "three sisters" – corn, beans, and squash – as well as tobacco. They made maple syrup and gathered apples, berries, and nuts, and evidence of pottery in this area dates back some 3,000 years. In 1626 the Neutral nation occupied twenty-eight towns and "several hamlets of seven or eight cabins [longhouses], built in various parts convenient for fishing, hunting and agriculture" (Jury 1977, 3).[31] Bark-covered longhouses constructed with bent poles lashed with roots and vines to form a rounded roof might accommodate several families with up to 200 persons. Father Bressani praised the Neutrals as having "exceedingly acute vision, excellent hearing, an ear for music and a rare sense of smell" (Jury 1977, 7). The *Jesuit Relations* contains references to their love of feasts and dances that were often combined with the games of lacrosse. Shamans were skilled in the application of herbs and other natural remedies for disease and encouraged the use of sweat-houses with singing to prevent illness. The Feast of the Dead, an elaborate ceremony lasting several days, was held every ten years. Several villages took part in placing the bones of the dead in a communal burial pit (Jury 1977, 16), and lamentations, sung by the women were an integral part of the proceedings. By the early 1640s the population of Neutrals was already diminishing due to deaths from diseases brought to North America by the Europeans.

Fragmentary French documentation from the early contact period indicates some musical practises. Men had important personal songs called *adònwe'* which were used for empowerment while hunting, fishing, in council meetings, at feasts, and as the last song before death. Singing feasts – *atouronta ochien* – were probably held at different times throughout the year depending on the purpose and occasion (Grabell 1990, 37). These feasts, held in the communal longhouse, might last up to twenty-four hours. A host who wished to display his goodwill might have a traditional set of dances, accompanied by songs usually led by two chiefs, each carrying a tortoise-shell rattle. Singing feasts were also an important element of the naming of a chief. Tortoise-shell rattles could be used by shamans in medicine ceremonies. Other idiophones include sticks beaten against pieces of bark, or a fist struck on the ground. The descriptive titles of the seventy-eight traditional Wendat songs recorded by Marius Barbeau in 1911 – such as Amusement, Amusement Songs around a kettle, Pipe, Snake Dance, Ceremonial Song of Welcome (see appendix A), Canoe, Cradle, Song in a Myth, Invitation to Dance, Dance for Women, Vision, and Lyric songs (Sargent 1950, 175) – seem to indicate that some might be remnants of songs and dances used in singing feasts. Others may have been connected with life cycle events or everyday activities such as canoeing.

The songs have one to three sections, each of which might be repeated with variations. Some sections are largely based on one pitch used in a recitative-like manner, while other sections are more lyrical with undulating lines descending toward the end of the phrase. Some songs have a fast tempo, while others are quite slow. Most melodies consist of five or fewer pitches within the range of an octave. Accompaniment patterns

The Iroquoian Calendrical Cycle

Because the Iroquoian economy was based on agriculture, the yearly cycle of events revolved around the growing season, beginning with the Midwinter ceremonies, held over an eight-day period roughly corresponding to late December and early January. During this ceremony Stirring Ashes is done by the two moieties, each of whom stirs the ashes of the other's fire with long wooden paddles, singing a special set of songs (Foster 1974, 117). Curing Rites – done over the next two days for medicine societies such as False Face, Husk Face, Bear, Otter, Eagle Dance – are followed by the most important sacred rite of all, the Great Feather Dance. Songs for this rite are variable and change according to the spirit forces appropriate to the occasion. Men's personal chants of adònwe' (ató:wé), a Sacred Rite, are sung individually with accompanying dances. The Skin Dance, one of the Four Sacred Rites, belongs to the Creator and is done for his amusement (Foster 1974, 153):

The [water] drum and a cloth bag containing the horn rattles are placed on the bench ... the four performers and the men in Indian dress leave the longhouse by the men's (eastern) door and repair to the cookhouse nearby. Here they receive instructions, and a few 'practise' songs are sung. They then re-enter the longhouse and take their places, the lead singer with his back to the men's stove, the speaker standing by the south side of the bench. [The assistants to the lead singer straddle the bench holding their rattles.] Meanwhile, the ... men are lining up at the men's entrance. The lead singer gives a loud tense whoop kúh, which has the purpose of "getting the Creator's attention" ... and the singers commence a song set. Three songs are sung with the dancers still outside, each punctuated by a whoop. On the fourth song, which has a slower beat, the men enter and begin to dance counterclockwise about the bench. After several more dances the remainder of the assembly joins in. The step is similar to that of the Great Feather Dance. (Foster 1974, 157)

The last of the Four Sacred Rites is a long version of the Bowl Game (a betting game scored with bean counters), played between the moieties on the final day of the Midwinter ceremony. Other dances – such as the Eagle Dance (based on the Plains Calumet form probably obtained from the Pawnee in the eighteenth century – may be included) (Foster 1974, 120).

The next ceremony, Our Sustenance Dances, takes place shortly after Midwinter. At the Seneca Longhouse this includes four dances – the Woman's Shuffle, Standing Quiver, Corn or Bean Dance, and the Squash Dance – that are often performed at subsequent ceremonies through the remainder of the year: the Bush Ceremony, Maple Festival, Seed Planting, After Planting, Strawberry Festival, Raspberry Festival, Green Bean Festival, Little Corn, Green Corn, and finally the Harvest Festival. Other components of these ceremonies include the Great Feather Dance, and a variable number of other elements.

A specific set of songs accompanies each ceremony and each has its own length, number of strophes, and tempo.

In fact, an Iroquoian can identify an individual song belonging to a set, such as the Standing Quiver (the first social dance to be performed) even if he has never heard that particular song before because all songs in a set have a particular melodic or rhythmic gesture. There are three types of step styles: stomp, fish, and side-step shuffle. For the stomp, the right foot leads and the left foot is shuffled up to meet it; the feet must hit the floor according to the beat of the song. In the fish step, each foot hits the floor for two or more consecutive beats. For the side shuffle, a women's step, the right foot shuffles first, followed by the left. (See the Iroquois Language and Songs site, www.collections.ic.gc.ca/language for a description of twenty-one dances and sound clips of the songs.)

differ from one section to the next: some have a tremolo-like rhythm played on a rattle, while others have specific beats, some of which are sub-divided. Other Iroquoian cultures have these musical characteristics. The Six Nations – Onondaga, Oneida, Cayuga, Seneca, Mohawk, and Tuscarora – settled in the south-western Ontario area in the eighteenth century.

Maritime – the Beothuk, the Mi'kmaq, and the Maliseet

The area of present-day Newfoundland and the Maritime provinces is the region of longest continuous contact with Europeans, beginning with Norse settlements ca. 1000.[32] Even before Jacques Cartier's arrival in 1534, Native Peoples were suffering from epidemic diseases brought by the Europeans against which they had no immunity. By 1640, the Mi'kmaq (Micmac) and Maliseet population was diminished by half.[33] As more Europeans arrived to exploit the rich fishing stocks, the Beothuks were forced into the interior of Newfoundland where, cut off from shellfish, an important part of their diet, they tried to survive on caribou migration and other mammals. Before her death from tuberculosis in 1829, Shanawdithit, a woman considered to be the last pure Beothuk, recounted some details of Beothuk culture, but the only surviving evidence of musical expressions – one- and two-holed whistles plus small pebbles and seeds likely used in rattles – comes from archaeological sites.

The Mi'kmaq and the Maliseet are closely related and there are many cultural similarities. Mi'kmaq territory covers the Gaspé peninsula, northern and eastern New Brunswick, all of Nova Scotia, Prince

Edward Island, and parts of Newfoundland. Maliseet (Malecite) territory extends from the St John River in western New Brunswick into Quebec. The Maliseet, however were primarily an interior culture and cultivated small plots of corn, while some 90 percent of the Mi'kmaq diet came from the sea.[34] The size of social groups varied according to season: in winter small groups worked together, but in summer larger groups congregated.[35] They lived in wigwams made of birch bark on a pole frame with a fire in the centre; larger wigwams, holding ten to 12 people, were oval shaped, and had two fires. Each group had a *saqamaw* (Mi'kmaq) or *sakom* (Maliseet) who was highly respected in the community and a *kinap* (Mi'kmaq) or *ginap* (Maliseet) who looked after defense. A son with sufficient ability and personality might inherit one of these titles from his father. The Mi'kmaq also recognized a Grand Chief who lived at present-day Amherst (now resident at Chapel Island), where council meetings of the seven Mi'kmaq districts were called to discuss issues of common concern (Leavitt 1995, 108).

Kluskap (Glooscap) is the central figure of both the Mi'kmaq and Maliseet interpretation of the world; history is divided into three eras.[36] The Mi'kmaq belief system – expressed through their Algonkian language, songs, rituals, and oral traditions – is based on the medicine wheel, an ancient symbol representing the four grandfathers, four winds, four directions, four stages of life, and the balance of mind, body, heart, and spirit (Leavitt 1995, xvi). The Mi'kmaq also developed a pictographic system that was likely used to represent words; in 1677 Le Clercq noticed children making marks with charcoal on birch-bark as he spoke (Schmidt 1995, 5), and it is possible that shamans (*puoin* in Mi'kmaq; *motowolon* in Maliseet) used this system for mnemonic aids for cures, rituals, and songs. Both male and female *puoins* usually carried a medicine bag (Leavitt 1995, 107), and since shamans were a main target of Jesuit missionaries, these medicine materials were replaced by leaflets of Christian songs and biblical passages in hieroglyphics. Writing in 1845 Kauder reported that "there is no other song in their language, if you except a few war songs, than ecclesiastic, pious songs" (Catholic Church in the Wilderness 1868, 252).

Information on pre-contact dances is scarce. Silas Rand referred to *neskovwadijik* as an important "feast and mystic dance" during which the chief used a specific song and dance step (1850, 14). Rand also noted that "war songs," (a term seemingly applied to any traditional Mi'kmaq song) differed from other songs in "words and tune" (1894, 238). One of the Kluskap stories includes a description of a dance in which men and women moved together in a circle "according to the custom" and each man "places his female partner in front of himself" (Rand 1894, 276). The dancers kept time with a musician who stood in the middle of the circle beating "with a stout stick upon his *cheegumakun* (piece of birch)." *Kojua*, the signature dance of the Mi'kmaq, is realized in different ways according to gender and age group. Additional accompaniment for songs was provided by rattles either woven like baskets or made from deer-claws and rawhide; turtle shells were particularly important since Turtle was Kluskap's uncle and the thirteen plates on his shell represented the lunar year of thirteen moons (Leavitt 1995, 68). Rhythm accompaniments were created by beating on a piece of bark, a tree, or a kettle. There are various descriptions in the literature of the *jigmaqn (ji'kmaqn)*, a unique Mi'kmaq instrument; the form used today is a slap-stick made from a piece of white ash split into layers along the grain and held together at one end by a leather binding. "The player slaps the *jigmaqn* against the palm of one hand to accompany a dance or song" (Leavitt 1995, 75). There is some controversy as to whether the Mi'kmaq had membrano-phone drums prior to European contact (see Diamond, Cronk, and von Rosen 1994, 76). Flutes (*pipukwaqn* in Mi'kmaq; *pipiqat* in Maliseet) are a prominent feature in mythology and were presumably used in pre-con-tact times; Rand describes "peepoogwokun" as "a wind instrument of any kind, as a flute, horn or trumpet" (1894, 361), and the Mi'kmaq also had a type of horn used to call animals in hunting.

The Arctic

Until about 200 BCE the area above the tree line stretching from the west-ern Arctic coastline through the Northwest Territories, Nunavut, north-ern Quebec, and Labrador was first inhabited by Paleo-Eskimos and the Pre-Dorset culture. Following a warm spell around 1000 the Thule, the direct ancestors of today's Inuit, gradually replaced the Dorsets. The Thule developed a sophisticated technology including the *kayaks* and *umiak* (larger open, hide-covered boats) to hunt sea mammals, sleds pulled by dogs, *ulus* (semicircular knives used by women), fine bone needles and thimbles, and the bow-drill for working bone and ivory. The Thule also brought pottery-making skills, but gradually switched to more durable pieces made of soapstone. Permanent houses had stone walls, with hide stretched over whale bones and jaws, covered with turf; while snow-houses (igloos) and hide-covered tents were used as temporary dwellings. *Inuksuit*[37] (rocks piled to represent humans) were used not only as trail markers but also to funnel caribou into an area where the hunters waited. Changes made to accommodate the cooling of the climate between 1200 and 1850 resulted in the variety of Inuit cultures known in the Arctic today (McMillan 1995, 257–69): Ungava (northern Quebec), Baffin Land, Caribou, Iglulik (Iglulingmiut), Sadlermiut, Copper, Netsilik, and Inuvialuit (Yukon and Mackenzie Delta).

In *The Central Eskimo* (1888),[38] Franz Boas notes the major role of musical expression in a description of calls made by drivers to sled dogs, and a section on poetry and music includes twenty-three transcriptions in Western musical notation (Boas 1964, 240–50) indicating the use of songs in stories (*cante fable*), personal songs ("every man has his own tune and his own song," 241), and songs used with games. Boas also describes songs used in drum dances, in which a male drummer danced on the spot, swaying his upper body and striking the *kilaut* (drum) with his wrist. Songs, often satirical in character, were performed by a chorus of women. Boas notes strophic structures (varying in length according to the text) and the interjection of the neutral syllable *"aja"* to keep the rhythm and delineate units. Repetition of musical phrases were iterative (sectionalized repetition) or reverting (variation of previous material), but short songs were through-composed. The importance of rhythm and text in a language dependent on prefixes and suffixes influenced the use of recitative-like passages with words enunciated on the same pitch. The range of melodic contours might be as small as a second or as wide as a tenth, usually beginning with a leap followed by undulating or plateau levels; many examples had a descending contour in the final phrase. Most melodies were based on a pentatonic scale (A G E D C) with the final pitch on the tonal centre; another common scale form had six notes (E D C B A G).

Generally speaking, Boas's observations hold true throughout the Eastern Arctic, with some variation in terminology, drum usage, and gender participation. Pelinski has verified multi-part singing in drum songs among the Caribou Inuit, usually in parallel fourths or fifths: the drumbeat gradually increases in speed from a proportion of 1:4 between song and drumbeat to 1:1 at the end, or remains steady throughout in the proportion of 1:1, 1:2, or 1:4. The drummer (*qatiurtuq*) follows the *imik* (rhythm) of the song. There are two different styles for hitting the drum (*kilaut*) with the beater (*katuk*): in *tuqaqpuk* the beater strikes the drum frame on the perpendicular; in *anaupaa*, the drummer slides the *katuk* along the frame below to above. Rasmussen describes the Iglulik using a *kei-is-ou-tik* (drum) almost a metre in width, made of caribou skin stretched across a wooden hoop or whale fin and fastened with sinew, while a *kentoon* (beater) was about twenty-six centimetres long. The drum, held in the left hand, was rotated in a fan motion and struck on the rim up to 160 strokes per minute. Each Iglulik man has a song partner whom he challenges with the beauty of his songs.

The Copper Inuit used the drum dance to honour members of the family, to express gratitude, and to welcome and bid farewell to visitors. Each community had one *kilaun* (drum) about a metre across and with a sixteen-centimetre handle of poplar attached by sinew. The beater (about 35 centimetres long) was covered with seal skin. Both men and women used the drum, holding it above the head and hitting the rim, or lowering it between sections and tapping the middle. The drum represented the ring around the sun and was a good omen. A woman began the dance while the drummer started the song and a chorus, led by the father or the wife joined in. A distinction is made between *pisik* (where the words fit exactly with the drum beat) and *aton* (where the tempo is slower and the performer wears a hat and possibly mitts).[39] Special apparel might include a cap with a loon's beak, since the loon was considered the bird of song. Seances might be held after a drum dance, with songs to control the weather or to release seals. The Netsilik drum (*kelaudi*) has a wooden hoop covered by caribou hide and a handle. It is struck by a small wooden club covered with seal-skin. The male dancer wears a cap and gloves; a women's chorus keeps time with the dancer. Songs were composed by men, women, or children in a solitary place and those that included riddles were highly valued. The lead dancer would hand the drum to his song partner *iglua* for the next dance. Songs were also used in drum duels to settle disputes; each disputant composed songs to state his case with ridicule and amusement and the community would judge (Cavanagh 1982, 34–45). A variety of sound was created by flicking a fingernail against the upper teeth. West of Hudson Bay there is some evidence of a whistle flute, and in the east, goose-feather quills (*suluk*) were used. In all areas, there were buzzers and bull-roarers, mostly used by children.

In the Eastern and Central Arctic traditional songs of *pisitt* and *ajajait* can be further sub-divided into men's and women's songs. *Hamaaq*, a man's song sung after catching five bearded seals, can also be used as a drum song; *qamna*, a more general term, refers to songs sung by men. Women who had borne children sang *Qangmaaq*. The texts for these songs use a language of their own; for example the word *niggi* takes the place of *siquqtijjuti*, used in speech (Green 1983). Text can also serve to determine whether a song was created before or after contact with the *Qallunaat* (White people); for example, the word *sullulik* (gun) is found in songs of the post-contact period.

The Inuvialuit culture of the far western Arctic is distinctively different. There are some solo dances with one drum, but group drumming

Inuit Throat-Games

Inuit games developed to test the control and strength of breath are often referred to as "throat singing," but the Inupiat term *ka*, meaning "the one who fell," probably comes from the fact that the winner is the one who lasts the longest without bursting into laughter. (Nattiez has proposed calling them "vocal games" since many are not limited to throat sounds.) Through much of the Eastern Arctic these games are collectively referred to as *katajaitt (katajjaq)*, but there are many different types. Some use specific words or vocables and some are performed by only one person, but most are played by two people facing one another. The games are usually performed by women and girls but youths learned them too; children normally learned the games from their grandmothers, and men used them in a form of competition. While there is more documentation for the eastern and central areas than the western area, it appears that, according to earlier descriptions, these games were part of a circumpolar complex (Nattiez 1983).

A vocal game has three layers of expression: a textual or morphemic layer consisting of meaningful words, words for which meanings have been lost, and vocables, such as *ama, ama*; a melodic layer; and a third layer consisting of vocal timbre and quality and the use of the breath. When performed by two people facing each other, usually about six inches apart, the leader "selects a syllabic-rhythmic context in which pitch and respiration patterns are alternated by each performer," but sometimes "rhythmic contexts are created exclusively by certain breathing patterns set to vocables" (Charron 1978, 246). Performers inhale and exhale rhythmically, usually in canon with one another, producing a range of sounds from voiced to voiceless pitches. "When the glottis is almost closed, the vocal cords are set in vibration and modulate the air stream to produce a voiced sound; when the glottis is sufficiently open, so that the vocal cords are no longer set in motion, a voiceless sound is produced by the air stream" (Charron 1978, 251). Various methods, including a basin or other utensil used to reflect the sound, were employed to amplify the voiceless sounds;

The Iglulik refer to these vocal games as *pirkusirartuq*, but other cultures often label a game by the first word used. In performances where a story is told, the text is enunciated in a precise rhythm. On other occasions, the same pattern of alternating exhaled and inhaled sounds is done by the two performers in canonic form. A game might include gestures and actions; for example, in the *qiarpalik*, (which refers to the peritoneum of the seal), the performer must keep her balance while lowering and raising her body with different gestures. The *qatipartuq (qatsivaaq)* always uses the refrain vocables *hapapi, hapapi, hapapiha*. The *quananau* incorporates the sound of a baby carried in the special hood of a woman's garment. Texts such as *haangahaaq* or *marmartuq* are like tongue twisters, and similar material exists in juggling songs primarily created by females. (For a variety of vocal and other games with detailed notes by Jean Jacques Nattiez, see *Canada: Jeux vocaux des Inuit*, Ocora CD, HM 83.) Other games that include songs are hide-and-seek, the string game during which the performer creates a figure out of string, a juggling competition between two persons, skipping, and enumerative songs incorporating actions. (Recorded examples of some of these are included on *Inuit Iglulik Canada: Museum Collection Berlin* CD 19.)

One of the objectives of these games is to imitate the environmental soundscape including sounds heard indoors (babies, pups, boiling water) and outdoors (wind, geese, the Northern Lights, waves). These games stimulate imagination and creativity and provide linguistic practise. The versatility required for performance has made this form of traditional Inuit music increasingly popular since 1980.

and dancing is more common. The square-shaped dance-house *kashim (kasig)* built in the centre of the village was mainly underground. The traditional drum has a narrow wooden frame (about four cm), usually covered with the skin from the belly of a female caribou, and a handle made of caribou antler. The beater, a long slender unpadded stick, is used for two different strokes: one lightly touches the underframe; the other strikes both frame and membrane together with more force. Groups of four or more drummers/singers provide the music for dances.

The dancers, often wearing gloves with appendages for each finger, dance out stories, using more movement than found in eastern Inuit cultures. Four categories of motion dancing are recognized among the Inuvialuit: (1) for women – arm movement while standing stationary, sitting, or squatting; (2) for men – energetic actions and changing steps co-ordinated with the "soft" and "loud" beats of the drums; (3) for men and women; (4) for a partner.[40] The fourth category dates from the early twentieth century, influenced by performances of the waltz and other European-based dances. The songs for partner dances are traditional and the movements resemble the motions of the other three categories rather than those of Caucasian couple dances.

Drums and voices are the primary musical instruments; the voice is pre-eminent, as drums are used only to accompany singing or dancing. The Eskimo fiddle, *tautirut*, is a type of zither that resembles an instrument found in northern Finland (Diamond 2001h, 1275) or the three-string *fidla* of the Orkney Islands. Canadian versions consist of a somewhat triangular box with a bridge, a tail piece, and a hole on the top over which one to three sinew strings are attached with pegs. Short bows are made of sinew or a whalebone strip stretched between two ends of a curved wooden stick, but the strings could also be struck with a stick. Within the period of written documentation this instrument was used mainly to accompany dances, playing tunes primarily of Scottish origin. As Donald Whitbread commented: "The Eskimos found it better to manufacture their own version [of fiddle], and what they lacked in quality, they make up for by the ability to produce music under any conditions and music which had perfect timing and melody" (1953, 83). It is possible that tunes sung for dances were adapted by the fiddlers.

The personal songs (*pisitt, pisiq* is the singular) composed singly or for drum dances express emotions or relate favourite stories. The texts of Inuit songs are much more meaningful than those of Amerindians, but context remains important to obtain the full meaning. Both those blessed with shamanic abilities and ordinary individuals have songs to address spirits, to affect the weather, to cure illnesses, among other purposes, but it is not expected that every person would have the ability to drum dance or chant in public. The performance of songs is intended to convey information or express a sense of solidarity and respect for each person in the community. Well-crafted songs are highly regarded and passed down through generations, and when sung in public, the performer states the name of the composer (who could be either male of female). The wide variety of songs used for entertainment include juggling songs and string game (cat's cradle) songs. Some Amerindian and Inuit cultures could create a wide variety of designs by manipulating a loop of sinew with their fingers. Each design usually had a song to accompany its creation. Musical expressions were and remain a constant factor in how the peoples of the Arctic relate to their geographical space and their everyday activities.

Elements of Aboriginal Musical Heritage

MELODIC CONTOURS

Even within single cultures there is no uniform type of melody, rhythm, or structure to be found. Because of the richness of each individual culture and the need for music to accompany almost all activities, each community developed a wide range of musical expressions. The melodic contour examples given in Appendix A have been chosen to represent some common characteristics and major differences found from region to region. Since the majority of Aboriginal musical expressions are monophonic, all eight examples present a single melody line. Melodic ranges vary from one region to another; for example, melodies found in the

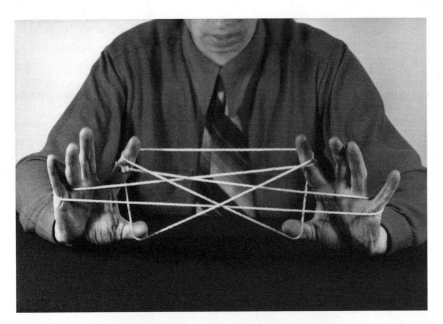

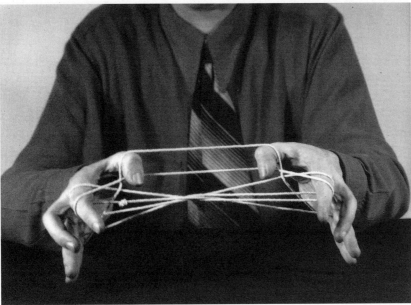

Figure 2.3 Examples of Inuit string figures created while singing songs. Canadian Museum of Civilization 99770 and 99771. These photographs were taken under the auspices of Marius Barbeau at the National Museum some time during the 1920s.

Plains region extend well over an octave, while melodies of the Northwest Coast, Maritime and Eastern Nomadic regions have a more undulating contour. Melodies from all regions usually begin on or leap up to a high point and then gradually descend to a tonal centre.

LANDSCAPE AND RUBBABOO

If we attempt to apply landscape theories to these musical expressions, we might account for regional variations with reference to topographical differences from one region to another. For example, the wide range of melodies found in Plains cultures could be related to vastness of space visible in their particular landscape. Russell Wallace of Tzo'kam comments:

Landscape plays an important role in the way songs are composed. On the coast you see mostly water and really have no need with the mountains for sustenance. The songs for Coastal Salish people would be low in key and would not venture very far from the root note. However, inland you have many mountains and you would choose places to live that are high enough to see any travellers coming ... The Interior Salish songs should then begin high and work their way down in pitch ... Leroy Joe says ... "Lilwat music is right from the land; it is the people, the trees, water, life." (www.nativedrums.ca)

With regard to the rubbaboo thesis, there is considerable evidence of the existence of borrowing and mixing of traditions. For example, just prior to European contact, the Haida were in the process of adapting Tsimshian songs and dances, and Haida songs accompanying the most important dances use words from the Tsimshian language (Dawson 1881, 127). Other evidence of adaptations has been pointed out in the preceding discussion. Yet there are also commonalities among these musickings that sets them apart from music heard in other parts of the world. The rhythmic complexity and the often forced vocal production made these musical expressions sound very strange indeed to persons coming to Canada from Europe.

3 Music the French Brought to Canada

By the early 1400s the rich supply of fish off the west coast of the Atlantic had attracted European fishermen, and the goal of finding a trading route to the East spurred further exploration. In 1498, Jean Cabot attempted to found a colony that could serve as a trading station between England and Asia, and further attempts were made by the Bristol Company of Adventurers in 1503 and 1504. Meanwhile, Basque, Portuguese, and French boats had made Newfoundland fish a common commodity in western Europe.

The accounts of Jacques Cartier give us the first details about music in Canada. Records of his 1534 and 1535 voyages describe music making by both Europeans and First Nations: "*Et voyons une partie des femmes qui ne passèrent, lesquelles estoyent jusques aux genoux dans la mer, sautans et chantans ... et tous les hommes se mirent à chanter et danser en deux ou trois bandes, et faisans grands signes de joye pour nostre venuë.*[1] In 1535 Cartier made his way up the St Lawrence as far as Hochelaga (the site of Montreal), where he commanded the playing of trumpets and "autres instrumens de Musique" (Cartier 1865, 54); the two priests in Cartier's party – Dom Guille Le Breton and Dom Antoine – probably celebrated the sung masses he describes. Seven Psalms of David and the Litany were performed in 1536 at Stadacona (the site of Quebec City). In 1603 Henri IV of France named Pierre du Gua de Monts, a Huguenot, as lieutenant-general of New France with the rights and privileges of creating a colony. Among the passengers that left Le Havre in 1604 were two Roman Catholic priests, a Huguenot minister, and two cartographers: Jean de Biencourt (Baron de Poutrincourt) and Samuel de Champlain. After a devastating winter at Île Sainte-Croix, the remaining colonists moved to the Bay of Fundy where they founded the settlement of Port-Royal. During the winter of 1606 Champlain established *l'Ordre de bon temps*. The French folksong *À la claire fontaine* (see figure 3.3) was sung at the first ceremony of *l'Ordre*, and Lescarbot noted that at ceremonies of *l'Ordre* there were always twenty or thirty Aboriginal men, women, and children "who observed our style of service."

Through the following decades, French settlements became more concentrated in the area now known as Quebec. Quebec City was founded by Champlain in 1608 as a trading post and missionaries soon followed (Recollets in 1619, Jesuits in 1625, and Ursulines in 1639). Montreal was founded in 1642 as a missionary colony, and by 1673 had a population of 1,500 and an annual fur-market that drew 800 canoes from the interior. Quebec City, however, remained the centre of the French empire in America. From 1663 on a governor-general, an intendant responsible for civil administration, and an administrative council of clergy and government officials ran New France as a royal province for Louis XIV. Three forms of musicking were incorporated into the social fabric of New France and Acadia: religious music, French folk songs, and current notated music from France. All three were, to some extent, interwoven with musical expressions of the First Nations.

Religious Music

Much of the activity concerning religious music centred around the Roman Catholic liturgy, particularly the mass.[2] Extant references to a sung mass in Canada probably refer to a basic form using well-known Gregorian chant settings. In seventeenth-century France – and by extension New France – it was still customary to sing chants in the Gregorian style. In the 1630s religious music was likely limited to Gregorian chant, but *The Jesuit Relations* for 1644 informs us that "at vespers, some psalms were chanted in *faux-bourdon*" (Thwaites 1959, 26: 117), and an account from December 1645 states "we began on the Day of St Thomas to sing in four voices."[3] These ceremonies depended on the availability of liturgical books. Extant books brought from France include missals, breviaries, and chant books of graduals, antiphonaries, psalters, vesperals, and processionals, either in large choir book format or condensed versions.[4] Sacred music played a large role in Catholic educational institutions; more than fifty volumes of sacred music from institutions established by the Ursulines, Augustines, Sulpicians, Jesuits, and the Quebec Seminary have survived. Each religious community had its own rule and constitution which included the practise of the chant.[5]

Marc Lescarbot

New arrivals to Port Royal in 1605 included the historian, poet, and lawyer Marc Lescarbot (ca. 1570–1642). Following the model of the ideal Renaissance humanist-courtier described in Baldassare Castiglione's *Il Libro del cortegiano* (1529), Lescarbot was skilled in music and poetry. To celebrate Poutrincourt's return to Port Royal in 1606, Lescarbot created a theatrical *réception* (modeled on a similar spectacle he wrote for a visit of the papal legate to his hometown of Picardy). "After many difficulties ... M. de Poutrincourt reached Port Royal on November 14th [1606] where we happily received him with a ceremony absolutely new on that side of the ocean ... Since it was written hastily in French rhymes I have placed it among my *Muses of New France* under the title of 'Théâtre de Neptune'"(Lescarbot 1968, 2: 340–1). Lescarbot's *réception* consists of mimed scenes interspersed with verse, and includes two cues for music: a trumpet call and the song "Vray Neptune" at the end, accompanying Neptune's arrival in a barque with an entourage of Tritons and Mi'kmaqs; one verse was sung in French, another in Mi'kmaq.

> *Vray Neptune donne nous*
> *Contre tes flots asseurance,*
> *Et fay que nous poissions tous*
> *Un jour nous revoir en France*
> [True Neptune, grant us / protection against they billows / and grant us that we may all / meet again some day in France.]

Lescarbot also mentions the celebration of a mass with music composed by Poutrincourt, but unfortunately none of this music has as yet come to light. Lescarbot describes singing and dancing that served to lessen the tedium of the days. The colonists may have had musical instruments or used mouth-music (humming or singing). Popular dances from France, such as *Bransles de Bourgogne*, could well have been heard at Port-Royal. Lescarbot took a keen interest in the culture of a local band of Mi'kmaqs (called Souriquois).

One day [1606] going for a walk in our meadows along the river, I drew near to Membertou's cabin, and wrote in my tablet-book part of what I heard ... in these terms: Haloet ho ho hé hé ha ha haloet ho ho hé, which they repeated divers times. The tune is also in my said tables in these notes: re fa sol sol re sol sol fa fa re re sol sol fa fa. One song being ended, they all made a great exclamation, saying Hé-é-é-é! Then they began another song, saying, egrigna hau egrigna hé hé hu hu ho ho egrigna hau hau hau. The tune of this was: fa fa fa sol sol fa fa re re sol sol fa fa re fa fa sol sol fa. Having made the usual exclamation, they began yet another in these words: Tameja alleluyah tameja dou veni hau hau hé hé. The tune whereof was: sol sol sol fa fa re re re fa fa sol fa sol fa fa re re." (Whitehead 1991, n.p.)

Membertou, *saqamaw* of this group, was a highly respected elder who had seen Cartier during one of his trips to Canada. If Lescarbot's transcription is correct, *egrigna* is a Mi'kmaq word, the meaning of which is now lost. However, words such as *alleluyah* and *dou veni (tu veni)* may indicate that Mi'kmaqs were already incorporating elements from the mass into their own chants as words of power.

The "half-Basque" language of some of the First Nations in the area noted by Lescarbot probably indicates a long relationship with Basque fishermen.

RELIGIOUS MUSIC AMONG FIRST NATIONS

According to French accounts, the First Peoples found European religious music pleasing. This attraction may have been partially due to common features shared by monophonic liturgical melodies and First Nations traditional musical expressions. When De Monts' fur monopoly was revoked in 1607, eight men were left to hold Port-Royal while Poutrincourt endeavoured to find new colonists. One of Poutrincout's passengers on his return voyage in 1610 was the Jesuit Father Jessé Fléché. That same year Fléché negotiated a *Concordat*[6] between the Grand Council of the Mi'kmaqs and the Pope. Among other issues, this agreement provided for the translation of the liturgy – including chants – into the Mi'kmaq language. The Mi'kmaq had the right to use their own language in mass and to have priests who could speak, read, and write the Mi'kmaq language. To this day Mi'kmaqs use biblical passages and hymn texts prepared by priests (particularly Chrestien Le Clercq) before 1689.[7]

In their religious services, the Jesuits incorporated elaborate processions and spectacle as well as music to attract First Nations to the Roman Catholic faith. By 1655 the Gloria, and the Credo were sung in Wendat using plainchant (Gallat-Morin and Bouchard 1981, 42), and pilgrimages to Sainte-Anne-de-Beaupré (which, according to the *Jesuit Relations*, began around 1656) likely included musical performances in Latin, French, and First Nations languages. The *Te Deum* was sung to celebrate important occasions such as a royal birth, a saint's day, the signing of peace treaties (including the treaty of 1666 between the French and Iroquois), or the arrival of a new governor.

Regardless of frequent wars and ambushes, the various orders continued to work diligently among the First Nations. One result was that Roman Catholic music became a vital part of their culture and observers frequently praised their singing. For example, at the main mission to the Abenaki in Saint-François-de-Sales, two-part singing was introduced by 1685. In 1699, Father Vincent Bigot wrote: "The women in particular have very beautiful voices, as gentle yet stronger than the voices of the French women. The men's choir sings the bass, when we sing a motet in three or four parts, and each of the other parts are sustained by several women's voices, which blend perfectly and do not sing in the least out of tune, when the song is repeated after a pause" (Dubois and Gallat-Morin 1995, 84). In 1751, the Superior of the Hôtel-Dieu in Quebec praised the singing at the Abenaki missions:

All the villages we know of are Christian, and there are two Missions towards Trois Rivières and another towards Acadia ... They have had Missionaries who have translated into their tongue the Gloria in excelsis, the Credo, the proses and hymns of the Church, so that they understand everything they sing. We had the satisfaction of hearing them in our Church, where their missionary came to sing Mass. What is most agreeable is that they form two choirs; the men on one side and the women on the other; the men begin the Kyrie with strong and full voices, the women repeat the second with soft but brilliant voices, and all sing in perfect tune in all of the plain chant tones. Then they continue with the Gloria, the Credo, and at the Elevation with hymns or motets in parts. (Dubois and Gallat-Morin 1995, 85–6)

In France musical instruments were often used in religious services. The *vielle* referred to by Father Paul Le Jeune in the *Relations* of 1636 (probably a hurdy-gurdy) was used to provide music for dancing and would not likely have been used in church. By 1640 Mother Marie de Saint-Joseph, an Ursuline nun, was teaching young First Nations girls to sing and to play the viol. A letter of 1640 tells us that she had a beautiful voice and led the choir (*Les Ursulines de Québec* 1863: 41). One of her First Nations students, the twelve-year-old Agnes Chabdikowechich, became especially proficient on the viol and was called upon to play during religious services (letter XII). By 1645 a violin and a transverse flute were heard at the Christmas mass in Quebec City, and by 1646 at least two violins were available. From June 1647 on, high mass was sung at Quebec every Sunday and Feast Day.

By 1654 the Wendat were singing important parts of the mass such as the Gloria and Credo in their own language, and on occasion were likely accompanied by instrumentalists of their culture. Maisonneuve (the founder of Montreal) played the lute, an instrument that may also have been used for sacred music. The presence of such instruments and evidence of increasing vocal skills indicate that more ambitious sacred music, such as French motets for one or two voices could be undertaken. All of this changed in 1659, however, with arrival of François de Laval as bishop of Quebec. Laval apparently took a dim view of the elaborate musical performances of the Ursulines.[8] In the Quebec Seminary (later

Jesous Ahatonia

Catholic missionaries who came to New France to convert Native Peoples to Christianity discovered *cantiques* (sacred songs the vernacular language used for personal devotions) to be a particularly effective tool. The first extant example of a newly created *cantique* for use with the First Nations – known as *Jesous Ahatonia* (*HACM*–1; *CMH2*, 2–3) – is in the tradition of the *cantique en français sur des timbres* [a song based on an existing melody]. It is thought that Jean de Brébeuf (1593–1649), one of a group of Jesuits who established missions among the Iroquoian-speaking Wendat (Hurons) near Georgian Bay, wrote the Iroquois text relating the Christmas story with imagery relevant to the Wendat experience and then developed the melody, the opening of which resembles the French song *Une jeune pucelle*. After the destruction of the Wendat communities (largely due to rivalries between First Nations brought on by the fur trade), a small number of Wendat and some surviving French made their way to Lorette, just north of Quebec City. Those survivors kept the carol alive in the oral tradition for more than a century until the text and tune were written down by Père Jean de Villeneuve, a priest at Lorette from 1747 to 1794. This version, with a French translation, was published in 1913 by Ernest Myrand. John Steckley found a reference to *Jesous Ahatonia* in the *Jesuit Relations* of 1668: near Quebec City, a fourteen-year-old Wendat girl was gravely ill and kept asking her mother when Christmas would come. The evening before her death, Jesuits came to visit her and sang "When Jesus is Born" (*Globe and Mail*, 20 December 1986, A11).

Université de Laval, founded by Laval in 1663) instruction in Gregorian chant was compulsory as a necessary requirement to create the "New Church" in New France based on missionization.

In 1664 Laval wrote to the Pope describing services in Quebec City: "There is here a basilica built of stone; it is great and magnificent. Divine service is celebrated in accordance with the bishops' ceremonial. Our priests, our seminarists, as well as ten or twelve choir boys, attend regularly. On great feasts, Mass, Vespers, and Benediction in the evening are magnificently sung in music of various hexachords and modes, and organ sweetly mixed with voices wonderfully adorn this musical harmony" (Dubois and Gallat-Morin 1995, 63). That same year Laval instituted a new feast day, *La sainte famille*. Since portions for the Proper would not have existed in France, it is likely that existing material was adapted for the first celebrations of the new feast. The two settings used most frequently for the Ordinary in this celebration were the *Messe royale* by

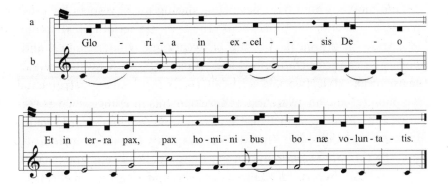

Figure 3.1   The opening of the Gloria of *Messe bordeloise*: (a) as published in the *Graduel romain à l'usage du diocèse de Québec*, Québec: J. Neilson, 1800; (b) as transcribed by Charles Bourque.

French composer Henry Du Mont and the *Messe bordeloise*, a mass composed in measured and ornamented plain chant (see figure 3.1). By 1684 a newly-composed Prose (or Sequence) for *Sacrae Familiae*, traditionally attributed to Charles-Amador Martin (1641–1711) was in use. There are at least five extant manuscript copies[9] of his composition (Amtmann 1975, 120), and it was published in *Le graduel romain* (1800), the first Canadian publication with music (*HACM*–3; *CMH2*, 4–12).

URSULINES AND AUGUSTINES
Regardless of Laval's personal musical tastes, surviving manuscripts and publications from the Ursulines and the Augustines indicate that a wide range of sacred music was performed. Extant chant volumes include the *Graduale romanum juxta missale* (Paris 1668), the *Antiphonarium juxta breviarium romanum* (Paris 1670), and the *Psalterium monasticum* (1683) (Pinson 1989, 6). There are also printed volumes of French polyphonic masses and magnificats, collections of *noëls* and *cantiques spirituels*, motets, and cantatas by well-known European composers including Nicholas Bernier, André Campra, Marc-Antoine Charpentier, Elizabeth Jacquet de La Guerre,[10] and Jean-Baptiste Morin. The archives of the Monastère des Augustines de la miséricorde de Jésus (l'Hôtel-Dieu de Québec) and the Monastère des Ursulines de Québec (both founded in 1639) hold manuscripts of some 120 motets (Schwandt 1981); some of these have been attributed to French composers including Michel-Richard Delalande, but a number that have no concordances in collections in France may have been composed in Canada.

These motets would have been sung during mass, vespers (or other offices), benediction, or processions. The texts are scriptural, scriptural paraphrase, or liturgical. A group of twenty anonymous motets, antiphons, and canticles transcribed and edited by Erich Schwandt reveals the use of solo style, two solo voices alternating with choir, instrumental "symphonies" and an awareness of developments in France, such as recitative and virtuosic or melismatic passages, metre changes, and markings for mood and speed. In style they are similar to the French *air de cour*. The *Cantate Domino* in figure 3.2 has a dance-like character with tempo indications, several changes of metre, and long vocal melismas.[11] The use of triple metre with running eighth-note passages is a prominent feature of tonally conceived eighteenth-century French motets (Schwandt 1996, 71). An elaborate Christmas motet, *Magnus Dominus* (HACM–2; CMH2, 13–16) is scored for SATB chorus with treble and bass solos and was probably accompanied by organ.

Such works would have been performed in the largest churches of Quebec City and Montreal, but heard only occasionally in parish churches. Parish churches often had two singers who were laymen or perhaps musicians employed by the local *seigneur*. We even have documentation of a few names: notaries Ameau at Trois Rivières and Jean-Baptiste Pothier at Lachine in 1686; a school teacher Jean-Baptiste Tetro at Boucherville in 1703; and a notary Pierre-Georges Guelte at Repentigny in 1767 (Pinson 1996, 31). Trained boy choristers, if available, were possibly used for two- or three-part settings. By 1756 there were eighty-eight parishes of which about twenty had a school, a convent, or both, where instruction for boys and girls included plainchant and musical notation.

Mère Marie-Andrée Regnard Duplessis de Sainte-Hélène (1687–1760), an Augustinian nun who arrived in Canada in 1702, compiled *les Annales de l'Hôtel-Dieu de Québec*, documenting the period from 1639 to 1716. Her *Musique spirituelle où l'on peut s'exercer sans voix* (1718), is "the first treatise on the theory and practise of music to have been undertaken in North America" (Schwandt 1988, 51). The text proceeds from basic information to more complex matters: "*1*. the scale; the three clefs; transposition (by change of clef); *2*. the accidentals and their effects; *3*. the staff; the notes and their values; their arrangement into measures; *4*. the *agréments du chant* [ornaments]; *5*. singing in tune; chords and arpeggios; fugues; *6*. rests; the symphony (i.e., improvised or composed preludes); *7*. tempo and *mouvement*; the *notes inégales*; the conductor's role" (Schwandt 1988, 52). A revealing passage on singing style for various circumstances, confirms the major role of the members of the orders, particularly female, in providing vocal and instrumental music for diverse situations: "One

Figure 3.2 *Cantate Domino*, a motet found in the archives of the Ursulines; digitized by C. Ford from Schwandt (1981).

ought to sing: In choir: *lentement, posément et gravement*; At the hospital: *vite*, that is, *fervement*; In the parlour: *legerement* and as if in passing; At recreation: *gayement et gracieusement*. The Superior conducts all this music. She sets the tempo. She calls for transpositions, provides accompaniments, furnishes the symphonies, and beats time. Provided that one is careful to follow her directions and to respond to the slightest cue, the concert will be so harmonious that it will charm every observer" (Schwandt 1988, 52–3).

ORGAN BUILDING AND ORGAN MUSIC

In 1657 there was an organ at the Jesuit Chapel in Quebec City, but little is known of how it was used. Laval figures prominently in written documentation of early organs in New France as the instigator for making good instruments available. In his *Mémoires sur la vie de Mgr de Laval* Bertrand de Latour states that Laval brought an organ from Paris in 1663: "On this model a mechanically gifted cleric made organs for several churches, solely in wood, which produce an agreeable sound" (Gallat-Morin and Bouchard 1981, 23). If a skilled woodworker could copy the construction of a French organ, the same was true of stringed instruments such as violins and guitars. Archeological excavations in Quebec City have confirmed the presence of guitars in New France (Gallat-Morin and Guimont 1996, 53).

Organs were present in several churches, and among extant printed books from New France is Guillaume-Gabriel Nivers's *Livre d'orgue contenant cent pieces de tous les tons de l'église* (1667). A fascinating manuscript collection, now known as the *Livre d'orgue de Montréal*, contains 398 pieces grouped according to church mode or liturgical function. The six masses, eleven Magnificats, and three Te Deums reflect encyclicals issued in 1662 and 1670 that lay out rules for organists.[12] This manuscript includes almost every type of French organ music of the period: homophonic pieces, *pleins jeux*, *préludes*, *dialogues* on the *grand jeu*; two, three and four-part pieces, duos, trios, fugues, and *récits*.[13] The manuscript was brought to New France by Jean Girard (1696–1765), a Sulpician who became schoolmaster and organist at Notre-Dame in Montreal in 1724. It is thought that Girard, a student of Nicolas Lebègue, copied out some of the pieces and obtained other manuscripts before leaving France (Gallat-Morin 1987, xiii). Many of the pieces lack concordances in France and the only composer that has been identified is Lebègue.

The organ at Montreal's Notre-Dame church was obtained before 1705 and had one manual (probably divided at the middle so two different registrations could be used) with seven stops. In 1721 Paul Jourdain dit La

Brosse of Montreal agreed to make a seven-stop organ with *voix humaine* for the Cathedral in Quebec. A document from 1721 lists six sheets of vellum, six pounds of copper, ebony, brass wire, sheepskins, and sixty-eight pounds of tin – presumably materials for the manufacture of this organ – shipped from the King's warehouse to La Brosse (Gallat-Morin and Bouchard 1981, 25). In 1753 documentation concerning a new organ that would become the Positif at the Cathedral outlines efforts to curtail costs but not to omit the *trompette* stop. This organ was to resemble the most beautiful in Paris (at Petits-Pères, Saint-Médéric, and Saint-Eustache). Jollage, a former organist to the King of Poland, tried out the organ before it was shipped to New France and declared it an outstanding instrument; unfortunately the organ was severely damaged in the bombardments of 1759 (Gallat-Morin and Bouchard 1981, 27).

French Folk Music

OLD WORLD ROOTS OF NEW WORLD SONGS

When Marius Barbeau reflected on his experiences recording more than 4,000 French folk songs and collecting another 3,000 versions of texts, he estimated that nineteen out of every twenty songs he heard had arrived in New France between 1608 and 1673 (Barbeau 1935, 4). Barbeau analysed this rich repertoire according to the regions from which French immigrants came. Between 1608 and 1634 immigrants from Honfleur, Havre, and St Malo settled around Quebec, Charlevoix, and the Gaspe. The folk songs of their descendants consist largely of ballads, narratives, and *complaintes* that flourished in Normandy and northern France. After 1642 many immigrants from La Rochelle settled in Trois Rivières and Montreal; their musical roots were in the Loire valley and their heritage was of southern France where lyric songs predominated. Barbeau points out that the themes of these songs "are clear-cut and tersely developed" and suggests that they were likely adopted and polished by the *jongleurs errants* or *jongleurs de foire* who flourished in the provinces of the Loire River and northern France (Barbeau 1935, 6).[14] Modern folklore researchers use the wide variety of literary themes and motives to categorize these monophonic songs.[15]

The repertoire of the Acadian population, who came largely from Poitou, was different again. Massignon has subdivided the 1,264 songs and 415 melodies in her collection as follows: *grands chansons* (on elevated topics); historical; religious; themes of popular imagery; on a soldier's life; on that of a sailor; about criminals; love; *pastourelles*; sentimental shepherds; marriage; lullabies; children's songs; dance songs;

Figure 3.3 *À la claire fontaine*: The melody and French text are from Gagnon's *Chansons populaires* (Montreal: Beauchemin, 1865)

A la claire fontaine m'en allant promener.
J'ai trouvé l'eau si belle que je m'y suis baigné..
    Refrain: Lui y'a longtemps que je t'aime, jamais je ne t'oublierai.
J'ai trouvé l'eau si belle que je m'y suis baigné.
Sous les feuilles d'un chêne je me suis fait sécher.
Sur la plus haute branche le rossignol chantait.
Chante, rossignol, chante, toi qui as le coeur gai.
Tu as le coeur à rire, moi, je l'ai t'à pleurer.
J'ai perdu ma maîtresse sans l'avoir mérité.
Pour un bouquet de roses que je lui refusai.
Je voudrais que la rose fût encore au rosier.
Et que le rosier même fût à la mer jeté.

[English translation by Elaine Keillor: By the clear fountain I walked one day. / The water looked so cool I bathed without delay. / *Refrain: For many years I've loved you, in my heart you'll stay.* / Beneath an oak tree I dried myself that day. / High up a nightingale produced a song gay. / Sing, silly bird, with your heart so gay. / My heart is broken, so please go away. / I've lost my mistress and I cry all day. / I refused to give her roses in a bouquet. / Yet I wish that rose was on the bush today. / And the rosebush into the sea thrown away.]

enumerative songs; occupational; rituals; drinking; anecdotal; comical; and of local origin (Massignon 1962, 365). According to Massignon, most of these songs – including *Le roi Renaud, Les anneaux de Marianson, La belle enfermée dans la tour,* and *Le mariage anglais* – were brought to North America by settlers in the seventeenth century.

The first documentation of a French folk song sung in Canada is for *À la claire fontaine* (see figure 3.3). This song is a *laisse*[16] that can have an imbricative form – that is, the second line of one verse becomes the first line of the next. The 220 Canadian versions and 126 versions collected in France include many different tunes and a variety of texts. There are usually references to a nightingale (a bird not found in America) and a bouquet of flowers. Ernest Gagnon, the first important collector of French Canadian folk songs, wrote: "Depuis le petit enfant de sept ans jusqu'au viellard aux cheveux blancs, tout le monde, en Canada, sait et chante la 'Claire Fontaine.' On n'est pas canadien sans cela" (Gagnon 1865, 3). The tune given in figure 3.3 is from Gagnon's *Chansons populaires* and one of the most widely known for this text.

Many of the folk songs heard in New France, including *À la claire fontaine*, date back to medieval times. Laforte (1997) has identified 353 folk songs in more than 12,000 versions dating to 1200 or earlier, and Kelher has discovered melodic families based on contours and prominent intervals. For example, in the first phrase the interval of a third is commonly filled in and followed by a leap of a fifth. There is often a drive to a high point (a sixth or an octave above the lowest note) and then a descent toward the lowest pitch (frequently the tonal centre). This arch contour – typical of Western European melodies – is strikingly different from contours found in traditional First Nations musical expressions. Musical characteristics also confirm the antiquity of many of these folk melodies. More than half of the tunes identified by Laforte have only four, five, or six different pitches. Where there are seven pitches, the notes usually conform to a modal scale (Dorian, Phyrgian, etc.), with the melody beginning on the fifth and ending on the tonal centre.[17] In more than half of these folk songs (all of which have a *laisse* structure) the text is set syllabically; if we include songs that have no more than two notes slurred on a syllable, the percentage might be as high as 83 percent (Laforte and Kelher 1997, 1: 61). The remaining songs contain melismas lasting anywhere from three to twenty-nine pitches. Most have a duple metre (usually 2/4 or 6/8), but four percent have a triple metre (Laforte and Kelher 1997, 1: 62). Some have fluctuating metres (such as 2/4 and 3/4), and a few are free and irregular.

LES COUREURS-DE-BOIS

The people who sang these melodies in New France found themselves in circumstances quite different from those in France. Kelher points out that the melody used for the refrain of a *laisse* is often quite different from the main melody. Because many of these songs were used for paddling, it seems likely that the texts and tunes for these refrains may have originated in Canada By the latter half of the seventeenth century, the French traders found that the furs brought to the main centres by Native

Peoples were not sufficient to meet European demands. The solution was for traders to travel inland along the rivers and lakes, find hunters willing to provide the skins, and bring the pelts back to the main centres for shipment to France. Thus a new occupation – the voyageurs or *coureurs-de-bois* – emerged. Since their work required intimate knowledge of the waterways and survival skills for living off the land, it is not surprising that many of them were of mixed heritage (First Nations and French). Many travellers remarked on the beauty of old French songs heard floating across the water. In the early nineteenth century Hugh Gray wrote:

They strike off singing a song peculiar to themselves called the voyageur song: one man takes the lead and all the others join in chorus. It is extremely pleasing to see people who are toiling hard, display such marks of good humour and contentment although they know that for a space of more than 2,000 miles their exertions must be unremitting, and their lives very poor ... The song is of great use; they keep time with their paddles to its measured cadence, and by uniting their force, increase its effect. (1809, 155)

Other accounts give the exact speed of paddling: fifty strokes in a minute (McMillan 1983, 20). Songs with a two-phrase structure were sung by a leader and answered by the other paddlers; sometimes the leader sang the main lines, and the rest answered with the refrain. New refrains, often added to songs that lacked them, were usually unrelated to the song text, and some were simply vocables. For example, *Les trois beaux canards* (the French-language song most frequently collected in Canada), has a number of refrains that refer to paddling, the best known being "En roulant ma boule" (Creighton and Labelle 1988, 40). Sometimes sound that appear to be vocables are actually imitations of First Nations words.

TUNES FOR DANCING

The textual richness and structural variety found in French folk songs brought to Canada by French settlers during the seventeenth century have only been touched on, but the tunes on which these texts were hung continue to resound in Canada wherever French tradition is strong. Many of these tunes have a dance-like character and, when no instruments were available, were performed as mouth music (in French, *turluteux*) to accompany dancing. In the early twentieth century some round dances were still accompanied with vocal sounds, much as they had been in Europe three or four hundred years ago. A soloist sang the main strophes and the directions, while everyone joined in the chorus (*rondeau*). These dances often included gestures such as sowing seed.

The violin was the most common instrument for accompanying dances, but there were other possibilities. The Acadians came largely from Poitou, an area famous for instrumentalists and dancers. Settlers likely brought oboes in three sizes (*dessus, taille,* and *basse*) that were often played as a group along with a *cornemuse*[18] on the melody. Military units introduced fifes[19] and drums, instruments that had been added to French military units in 1545. In Europe it was common for a dance musician to play an end-blown flute with one hand and a two-headed drum with the other. This combination, or a drum alone, was often called *tambourin,* a term found in descriptions of dance music played on ships coming to Acadia (Dôle 1995, 214). Mère Jeanne-Françoise Juchereau de St-Ignace (1650–1723) described a group of militia arriving at Quebec City in 1711, impatient for battle: "their days were spent fortifying the city, and their nights in entertainment, dancing and singing, such that on occasion the citizens of Quebec were unable to sleep" (Courville 1998, 18). We can assume that military musicians gladly provided music for various informal dances.

Notated Musical Traditions from Europe

The seigneurial system applied in New France from the early days of settlement effectively divided society into classes. The folk songs and dance music discussed above constituted the main musical repertoire of the *habitants* (tenants of the *seigneurie*). As the colony grew and became much more self-sufficient, musical resources and repertoire gradually increased beyond the staples of church and folk music. For example, the fife and drum players who arrived with the Carignan-Salières regiment in 1665 would have known military marches of the day and probably adapted them for use in New France; when *habitants* took over the defence needs of the colony, folk tunes were likely added to the mix. Some *habitants* may also have had opportunities to hear more elaborate musical productions at official residences or seigneurial houses. Well-educated members of the upper class would have been cognizant of current literary and musical productions in France. For example, as early as 1645 the audience for a play (probably Corneille's *Le Cid*) presented at Quebec included a group of First Nations (Thwaites 1959, 28: 251). Somewhat later Church officials tried to contain such secular presentations in New France; in 1694 a performance of Molière's *Tartuffe* was banned.

PRIVATE LIBRARIES IN NEW FRANCE

The bishop could not, however, prevent the addition of such works to private libraries of officials and seigneurs. Gilles Proulx (1987) has itemized the contents of private libraries in Quebec City from inventories drawn up after the deaths of their owners: some one hundred of these titles are of music. Louis-Guillaume Verrier (1690–1758), a law teacher and attorney general of the Superior Council of New France, owned ten music books, including Bodin de Boismortier's pastoral *Daphnis et Chloé*. François de Chales, inspector for the Compagnie des Indes, owned books of menuets and *vaudevilles*.[20] François-Étienne Cugnet (1688–1751), a lawyer, merchant, and director of the Domaine d'occident for New France, left about fifty musical scores among which are several cantatas and some drinking songs, including *Nouvelles parodies bachiques*. Copies of and references to *Ribon-Lully: parodies bachiques sur les airs et symphonies des Opera* (1696), a collection that includes selections by Lully, have been found, and Lully's operas and ballets appear in other anthologies known to have been used in New France. The Intendant Claude-Thomas Dupuy (1678–1738) owned a large collection of music including operas by Lully and vocal and instrumental music by leading composers of the day such as Corelli, Campra, and Clérambault.[21] A copy of Michel Pignolet de Montéclair's *Principes de musique* (1736), a singing method with music selections, was found in the library of a Quebec City merchant. François Mion had a particularly interesting collection of musical scores. Born in Versailles, he and his brother Charles-Louis had been choristers at Sainte-Chapelle and were trained by Nicolas Bernier. François came to Quebec City as a soldier in 1722, and gave private music lessons before his appointment as King's scribe at the Quebec City shipyard. Publications in his library included operas and ballets composed by his brother; a group of anonymous manuscripts suggests that François may also have been a composer (Gallat-Morin and Pinson 2003, 357–8).

A number of ecclesiastics also owned secular music books. Daniel-Guillaume de La Colombière Serré, chaplain of the *Hôpital général* in Quebec City and organist there from 1704, played treble and bass viol, and the Mother Superior asked him to take harpsichord lessons so that he could accompany the nuns' singing. Apparently the chaplain subsequently taught harpsichord using the works of Jacques Champion de Chambonnières (Gallat-Morin and Pinson 2003, 157). There was a copy of Hotteterre's treatise on flute-playing (1741) in the Seminary Library, bound with methods for flageolet, bassoon, drum, and serpent[22] and musical works by Couperin and Rameau. By the early eighteenth century it had become more common to use secular tunes in settings of sacred texts. The archives of the Hôtel-Dieu held a copy of *Histoire de l'ancien et du nouveau testament avec le fruit qu'on en doit tirer: le tout mis en can-*

tiques, sur des airs choisis (1713), a two-volume collection of hymns set to airs from operas by Lully, Campra, and Lully's son.

MUSICAL INSTRUMENTS IN NEW FRANCE

The same instruments were often used for both sacred and secular music. The two violins used to provide dance music at the wedding of the daughter of M. Couillar, seigneur of Espinay, to Jean Guion on 27 November 1645 might well have been heard the next day during church services. The first documented ball in Canada took place at the home of Louis Théandre Chartier de Lotbinière on 4 January 1667, but the Jesuit writer gives no information about the dances or the instruments (Thwaites 1959, 43: 324).

Prior to 1700 only a few references confirm the presence of violins, viols, lutes, guitars, transverse flutes, spinets, organs, and drums, but after that date, more documentation is available. Merchants carried large quantities of *bombardes*,[23] a pocket instrument used for individual enjoyment or for accompanying dances. Archeological evidence indicates that the hundreds of *bombardes* exported to New France were used mainly as items for trade with the Native Peoples. In the early 1700s, there are also references to spinets and even a few harpsichords. Viols were imported, but were also made in the colony, along with violins and possibly guitars.[24] Library inventories also fill out the sketchy picture of musical instruments in New France. A letter of 1692 from François Vachon de Belmont, missionary, lutenist, and later superior of the Sulpicians in Montreal requests that his organ and harpsichord be sent from Paris (Gallat-Morin and Bouchard 1981, 18). Jacques Raudot and his son Antoine-Denis Raudot, intendants from 1705 to 1711, presumably had musical instruments available as they held regular concerts at their residence, and Claude-Thomas Dupuy, intendant from 1725 to 1728, owned two bass viols, a portable spinet, and a twelve-stop cabinet organ with wind chest and bellows.

With such instruments at hand, solo keyboard and viol music would have been frequently heard, and ensembles organized to play trio sonatas, with two violins, probably a bass viol on the lowest string part and a harpsichord, spinet, or lute filling in the figured bass. Music books known to have been present in New France contain arrangements from operas, including many duets which could have been accompanied by a dessus viol and a keyboard or stringed instrument to realize the figured bass. In a letter of 18 December 1748 Madame Bégon describes Messieurs de Longueil, Noyan, Céloron, and Lantagnac meeting for lunch and singing together until eleven in the evening. Apparently their singing was so

Balls in New France

In France the ball was a favourite form of entertaining, and officials who came to New France established the same practise in their new surroundings (Voyer and Tremblay 2001, 28). Writing in 1722, Bacqueville de La Potherie remarks on the number of dances held in New France from the end of Advent and to the end of Carnival time, and comments that the women love to dance and do it well (30). Indeed, it was necessary for members of the upper classes to be skilled in dancing; J.-C. B. (Sieur de Bonnefons), who was in New France from 1751 to 1761, soon discovered that the main winter activities were sleigh riding or skating during the day and balls in the evening, but not knowing how to dance, he was not invited to the balls. He began lessons and spent the remainder of 1752 attending society balls (31). On the occasion of a wedding, balls were often held on five successive nights. Dancing masters taught the current dances, often using a small pocket fiddle (*poche*) to play the tunes. *Jesuit Relations* for 1655 documents one *poche* in New France and there is also evidence of dancing masters: Louis Renaud of Montreal taught dancing from 1739 on (Gallat-Morin and Pinson 2003, 387), and François Moine dit Bourguignon taught in Quebec in 1756. (Interestingly Moine dit Bourguignon's lodgings were in the home of the merchant Charles Berthelot, who owned a copy of Hotteterre's treatise *Principes de la flûte traversière* with many dance tunes.)

Madame Bégon's correspondence of 1748 to 1753 relates details of numer-ous balls, which by that time were held even during the penitent seasons of the Church year. In 1748 she describes a ball given on 8 December by Madame Verchères that lasted all night; the next evening there was a ball at Madame Lavaltrie's, and by 11 December two more had taken place at the homes of Madame Bragelogne and Madame Beaulac. In a letter of 19 December 1748, Madame Bégon's comments that everyone was learning to dance. A month or so later, describing a ball on 21 January 1749, she writes: "There was a great deal of drinking at M. De Lantanac's dinner last evening. Everyone had difficulty danc-ing the minuet ... I have a bad headache from these follies that went on to early morning" (Bégon 1972, 70; my trans.). Around 1770 Pierre de Sales Laterrière wrote: "Never have I known a nation to dance like the Canadians. They have their French country dances and minuets which they intermingle with the English dances. During the winter which lasts eight months, they pass the time with cooking suppers, dinners and having balls" (Voyer 1986, 32; my trans.). Three years earlier Madame Brooke described a ball where twenty-seven *contredanses* were used. "One does not have a meal in Canada without the violin. What a race of dancers!" (Voyer 1986, 37; my trans.).

The only dance named by Madame Bégon is the minuet, but country dances of the English court tradition – which were adopted by the French court in 1705 and subsequently modified – have been found in extant manuscripts of New France; Voyer has argued that French *contredanses* were introduced

etc.

Figure 3.4 *Les Ormeaux*, a contredanse found in a manuscript of contredanses owned by Pierre-René Boucher de la Bruère; this dance is also published in *Pot-pourri françois de contre-danses anciennes tel qu'il se danse chez la Reine* (Paris, n.d.). The first staff (ending with "etc.") is the tune that appears in the manuscript; the remaining three staves show the published version. Both are digitized by C. Ford.

in New France before English-style country dances. Pierre-René Boucher de la Bruère, a soldier who fought on the Plains of Abraham, owned a notebook containing sixty-one *contredanses français* (see figure 3.4). This book, probably used by a dancing master, gives an incipit of the tune and instructions for the steps and pattern of the dance; the tune incipits were obviously written from memory as there are variants with Parisian concordances.

Charles Berthelot, a Quebec merchant, owned a copy of Hotteterre's treatise, *Principes de la Flûte traversière* that was bound with a 300-page manuscript containing menuets, musettes, tambourins, and contredances for wind instruments, most of anonymous origin. The Berthelot manuscript is now held by the Musée de

l'Amérique française at the Séminaire de Québec. The paper dates from ca. 1742, and most of the tunes are of anonymous origin. Gallat-Morin has identified more than fifty menuets as being from publications of Esprit-Philippe Chedeville, Sr, and another group from his brother's publication (2003, 368–9). Some thirty dances also appear in the *Recueils de pièces, petits airs, brunettes, menuets* published by Blavet ca. 1750. Other concordances include publications of Toussaint Bordet, Jean-Baptiste Anet dit Baptiste, Michel Corrette, Jean-Christophe Naudot, Jean-Jacques Rippert, and Jean Pantaléon Leclerc. Some of these menuets, musettes, and tambourins are arrangements from popular works such as Rameau's *Menuet de l'Europe galante* and Couperin's *Les vandangeuses*. There are also arrangements of vaudeville songs such as *La Confession* and parodies from Lully's operas including *Thésée*. Regardless of how this manuscript came to New France and who copied it, the contents indicate that society attending balls along the St Lawrence River heard much the same repertoire as their counterparts in Paris.

lovely that passers-by stopped to listen (Bégon 1972, 48).[25] Unfortunately we are not told what they were singing.

Despite frequent remonstrances of the clergy against dancing and other leisure pursuits, members of New France's elite pursued many of the same activities as their counterparts back in France. Yet these French pastimes and practises were grafted on to a way of life not drastically different from that of the Iroquoian farmers in Cartier's time. Trapping, hunting, fishing, and long wilderness journeys were a regular part of Canadian life. The canoe was still the principal means of transportation, although a crude road from Quebec to Montreal was completed in 1734. Having learned to build habitations like forts, with walls two to four feet thick and large double-flued chimneys to accommodate both fireplaces and iron stoves (introduced to the colony in 1668), people enjoyed the winter with sleigh and skating parties outside and dancing in halls that occupied the entire ground floor of larger homes. In the last days of New France, while Intendant François Bigot gave lavish dinner parties and balls, hard times, unemployment, and food shortages were the lot of farmers and labourers.[26]

Thus musical sounds heard in New France were similar to those in the mother country, and the Canadian landscape probably had little influence on their shape. On the other hand, long-distance travel on inland waterways led to adaptations of folk songs, and missionaries in Acadia and New France created rubbaboos in their work with the First Nations. Were these sounds also influenced by First Nations musical traditions? There are hints that some missionaries adapted Amerindian music, but this type of rubbaboo has not yet been confirmed.

4   Music the British Brought to Canada

The British Conquest

By the early 1700s France controlled an area stretching from Newfoundland to the prairies, north almost to Hudson Bay, and south through the Ohio and Mississippi valleys to Louisiana, with a population of some 70,000 colonists. Britain had more than a million colonists, and skirmishes between the two competing powers had been going on for the past century. An account of the siege of Louisbourg in 1745 includes a brief musical reference: a week before the surrender, the conquering British had "celebrations, with violin, flute, and vocal music, plus a generous allowance of rum, in honour of the birthday of King George II" (Baker 1978/1995, 57). Another more poignant reference is to 141 Acadians who sang *Faux plaisirs, vains honneurs* (see figure 4.1) as they were marched to a British ship on 10 September 1755.[1] The text of this song, now known as *La cantique des Acadiens*, was written down ca. 1791 and first published by Gustave Lanctôt in 1929. The music of the refrain was transcribed by Gérard Morisset in 1932.

Four years later, the British conquest was over. Montcalm reached Quebec with two regiments and won several victories, but in July 1758 British troops recaptured Louisbourg and under Wolfe were advancing down the St Lawrence. By the time they reached Quebec City, 1,400 farms along the St Lawrence had been destroyed and eighty per-cent of Quebec City lay in ruins. Wolfe had trained soldiers while Montcalm's forces were half militia, trained only in bush fighting. The battle of the Plains of Abraham lasted fifteen minutes; Wolfe was killed and Montcalm survived only long enough to surrender Quebec. The British held Quebec for a second battle in 1759 and secured Newfoundland from the French in

Figure 4.1 *Faux plaisir, vains honneurs,* now known as *La cantique des Acadiens.*

1762. With the Treaty of Paris in 1763 "Canada"[2] – an area stretching from the Detroit River to the Gaspé and north to Lake St John on the Saguenay – was ceded to Britain. Of their once vast empire, France retained only the islands of Saint-Pierre and Miquelon. Nova Scotia comprised Acadia and lands to the north including the islands of Cape Breton and St John (Prince Edward Island). Newfoundland included the Magdalen Islands, Anticosti, present-day Labrador, and most of what is now known as the Quebec North Shore. The remainder of present-day Canada was divided between the First Peoples and Rupert's Land, a vast territory controlled by the Hudson's Bay Company extending to the Pacific and south into the American West.

In 1760, the Euro-Canadian population of these new British colonies was about 88,000, of whom 24,000 were Anglophone. The vast franco-phone majority (64,000) was made up of Acadians who were returning to their ancestral farms and *habitant* farmers along the Ottawa and St Lawrence rivers. Trappers and fur-traders with a heritage of several generations in North America chose to remain rather than leave for France, and many French soldiers also opted to settle in Canada. Traders from the other North American colonies swept into Nova Scotia and Quebec to seek their fortune, and their success likely gave rise to hopes of revolutionaries in the Thirteen Colonies that Canada would join their cause. The Americans captured Montreal in 1775, but retreated in 1776 after the arrival of British reinforcements. That same year the population of Halifax doubled with the first influx of Loyalists. By 1780 Loyalists were settling in the Niagara Peninsula, and during that decade some 50,000 merchants, professional men, clergymen, clerks, shopkeepers, farmers, artisans, schoolteachers, labourers came across the borders, along with hundreds of Blacks who had been attached to British colonial aristocrats and plantation owners. Boatloads of settlers, particularly from Scotland, where the English had recently asserted their rule over the Highlands, also transplanted their music to Canada.

British Band Music

Wherever British forces were stationed, there were resident musicians. Military regiments needed instrumentalists to play the various signals, and as in French forces, these musicians played fifes and drums. The *Articles of Agreement of the Royal Artillery* (1762) stipulated that regimental bands must include two trumpets, two french horns, two bassoons, and four hautbois (oboe) or clarinets,[3] although it is doubtful that all British regiments acquired all ten musicians immediately. Fife and drum bands remained a part of the Canadian scene through the nineteenth century, as is evident from a newspaper account of the funeral for General Gabriel Christie, Colonel Commandant of the 1st Battalion, 60th Regiment on 20 January 1799: "The 60th Band, Drummers and fifers had also Crapes, Sword Knots, and Gloves – The Instruments trimmed, and all the Drums muffled" (Bourassa-Trépanier and Poirier 1990, 120). Some regiments, however, had larger complements of musicians as a variety of instruments appear frequently on extant concert programs. The 1762 *Articles* stipulated that the musicians "must also be capable to play upon the violoncello, bass, violon and flute, as other common instruments" (Farmer 1912, 57). In colloquial British usage a group of wind instrumentalists combined with strings and percussion was referred to as a "band" rather than an orchestra, and this terminology became common in Canada where regimental band string and wind players joined local instrumentalists to provide music for dancing, church services, concerts, theatrical events, and even circuses. Indeed regimental bands dominated music performance in Canada up to 1900 and beyond. Nineteenth-century American visitors to Canada enjoyed the military music that was no longer part of their daily lives at home. Bernhard Silliman, a chemistry professor at Yale University describes his return to Quebec City after an excursion to Chaudière Falls:

It was ... dark when we landed ... and just as we passed through the perfectly dark arch of the Prescot gate ... a flash like lightning, illuminated the upper town, and was instantly followed by the thunder of the evening gun. It needed but little help from the imagination to make us believe that we were entering a fortress of the dark ages; and the grand flourish of martial music, which immediately burst upon our ears, with the full swell and deep intonation of bugle-horns, clarionets, and trumpets, and other wind-instruments, was well adapted to increase the illusion. (Silliman 1822, 92)

Because bands were so involved in Canadian musical life it is not surprising that we have original Canadian compositions for band dating from 1791, in the form of manuscripts scored for keyboard. Due to the wide range of instruments in bands, composers usually wrote band works for keyboard so conductors could arrange the material as required. The *Royal Fusiliers' Arrival at Quebec* by Charles Voyer de Poligny d'Argenson (HACM–4; CMH22, 208–9) is an example of this practise. Band conductors also arranged popular tunes of the day, including French Canadian folk songs. John Mactaggart, a visitor to Canada in the late 1820s wrote: "Our military bands in Canada pay much attention to these *airs,* a thing which charms the Canadians. In cases of war, they will be doubly valuable; although none of them are of a martial nature, they will nevertheless serve to rouse some of the noblest of faculties of the mind" (1829, 1: 255). Mactaggart includes twelve strophes *Petite Jeanneton* (the maid in the well) with an English prose translation. The repertoire of nineteenth-century civilian bands was much the same but also included hymn tunes and folk songs popular in the community.

Music for Dancing

Newspapers, provide more direct evidence of the role of music in social events post-1764. The most frequent events involving musicians were the assemblies and balls held in Quebec City and Montreal. Beginning in 1765, newspaper announcements indicate that an *assemblé* (dancing assembly), attended by about 100 people, took place almost every second week during the winter season.[4] The dancing – which consisted mainly of four groups of country dances, sometimes preceded by a minuet – began at 7:00 p.m. Newspaper accounts indicate that the Band of the 24th Regiment, conducted by Francis Vogeler and Frederick Glackemeyer (two well-known professional musicians in Quebec City) provided music for dancing assemblies during the years 1789 to 1791. An anecdote from a 1786 issue of the *Gazete de Montréal*, however, indicates that there were different types of musicians and dances: "Few days ago one zealous overmuch, reprobated his neighbour for being at a Dancing Assembly. The neighbour plead the example of King David in excuse: But, replied the other, David only danced a minuet, to a divine tune, played on the harp; whereas, ye now dance jiggs, reels, hornpipes and country-dances, to profane tunes, played on guitars, violins, flutes, hautboys and fiddles; nay ye even dance pantomines, to the tune Orpheus played for the devil, when he charmed back his wife" (Bourassa-Trépanier and Poirier 1990, 9).

After 1771 some events, given by upper-class families or associations and attended by up to 300 people, were distinguished as balls. The evening opened with five minuets followed by English country dances for twenty-five couples, each dance lasting about an hour.[5] Meanwhile the remaining guests were served Madeira wine, warm water with sugar, and condiments. After a supper at about 11:30 p.m. several ladies might entertain the gathering with a song. Then the dancing resumed and continued until 5:00 a.m.[6]

Dances of the Eighteenth and Nineteenth Centuries

MINUETS
One of the main differences between an assembly and a ball was the inclusion of a minuet. In France the minuet was a slow dance in triple metre with an emphasis on elegant and complex step patterns. At the French court minuets were done one couple at a time, in order of social rank; in colonial Williamsburg it was used at formal occasions to delineate social order (Feyock 1995, 211), a practise that presumably also occurred in Canada. After the French Revolution, the minuet fell into disfavour because of its association with the corrupt French court.[7]

COUNTRY DANCES
In both England and France ca. 1730–1770 a series of minuets were followed by country dances that became quite popular and were spread through much of Europe by publications and dancing masters. "Country dance" is a generic term referring to dances derived from English round and chain dances that entered the court repertoire of Elizabeth I. John Playford's *The English Dancing Master* (1651), the first published collection of country dances, went through eighteen subsequent editions, the last published in 1728, containing a total of almost nine hundred dances.[8] Playford provided both the tune and floor pattern for each dance (see figure 4.2).[9] The tunes have a binary structure with metres of 2/2 (4/4) or 6/8. Each section was repeated as necessary for each couple to perform the required figure(s).

SCOTCH REELS
By the 1760s three new dance genres – the Scotch reel, the cotillion, and the jig – had become popular in sophisticated English circles. Merry

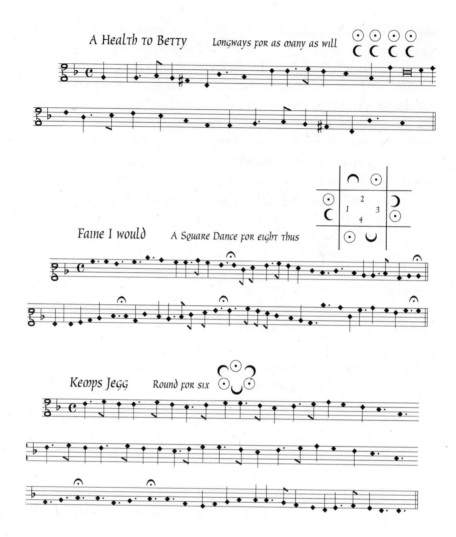

Figure 4.2 Digitized transcriptions of three dances found in John Playford's *The English Dancing Master*, with diagrams for the formations of the dancers; men are represented by a crescent, women by a circle with a dot.

Feyock describes two forms of the Scotch reel: "the simple longways done in reel (common) time" and "complex dances for two, three, or four people who would alternately 'reel' – dance an extended figure eight pattern around and by each other – for a certain amount of music and then 'foot it': dazzle the onlookers with a variety of fancy steps more or less in place. Some reels seemed to be improvised on the spot; some were more carefully choreographed. Occasionally, they probably featured changing patterns like jigs, All, however, involved a complex set of steps and a lot of stamina" (Feyock 1995, 212–3).

COTILLIONS AND QUADRILLES

Originally derived from English square formations, cotillions were later modified by French dancing masters. Four couples face each other in a square: the dance itself consists of a series of movements called "changes"[10] and "the figure" – the basic choreography that distinguished one dance from another (Feyock 1995, 213). The cotillion was being danced in Quebec by 1767. In France some forms of cotillions were called quadrilles: elaborate dances for sets of four, six, or eight couples. The quadrille usually consisted of five distinct parts or figures, named for the original country dances that made up the standard quadrille; these names were retained even when new quadrille music was composed: *Le pantalon, L'été, La poule, La pastourelle* (or *Trénis*), and *Finale* or *Galop* (Buckman 1978, 135).[11] The French quadrille was introduced into England in 1815 (Voyer and Tremblay 2001, 53), but the dance may have reached Canada even earlier. In an 1806 advertisement Antoine Rod, a dancing master in Quebec City lists steps and figures for English country dances, reels, and cotillions (Voyer and Tremblay 2001, 52); by 1821 he claimed to know the ballroom dances used at the King's Theatre Opera House in London and could "teach and explain the *Quadrille, Cotillon, Scotch, Irish* and *Waltz* steps, *menuet* and *Strathspeys* connected with the different manners of dancing it" (53).

The many variants of quadrilles and lancers (a derivative dance) that developed during the nineteenth century became the basis of square dances; it became customary to have a "caller" to announce the different combinations of figures during the dance. Different formation dances also intermingled with one another, and there are numerous local variants found in Canada. Quigley summarizes the dances in one area of Newfoundland: "Although the organization of the Reel is somewhat different from the Square Dance and Lancers, the structural system is closely related. All three prescribe floor designs and dancer direction, using individual, partner, two couple, and whole group interactions. Despite their symmetrical repetitive forms, each contains a progressive sequence of distinctive figures, beginning with two couple interactions and culminating in whole group patterns. In the Reel however, the join together and exchange partner movements are incorporated throughout the dance, rather than only in the final section (1985, 45).

JIGS, STRATHSPEYS, AND CLOG DANCES

The terms "jig," "hornpipe," and "reel" were used to refer to specific steps in country dances. In the sixteenth century, a jig (or jigg) was a vigorous solo dance for men, particularly associated with Scotland.[12] Jigs are by one person or a couple. Regular jig tunes consist of two eight-bar sections; irregular tunes, used in set dances, have sections of unequal length. Single jigs are in 6/8 with a quarter-eighth-note rhythm; double jigs have six eighth notes to the bar. Slip jigs or hop jigs are in 9/8 with a steady eighth-note rhythm; promenades alternate with stepping. The strathspey is a form from northern Scotland in "Scots measure" (quadruple metre, with a dotted-eighth-sixteenth-note rhythm or the reverse. Solo clog dances was a less vigourous form that developed in northern England. In clog dances the arms are raised and the head and body are tilted forward to preserve balance. The stepping is sometimes executed over crossed sticks or swords, as in the Scottish sword dance. Tap dancing is derived from this form of clogging.

HORNPIPES

The hornpipe is a solo dance indigenous to Scotland, Wales and known in England since the sixteenth century. During the seventeenth century, dancing masters used hornpipes in longways country dances. Early hornpipes were in 3/2, but later dances are in 4/4 (or 2/4) with two repeated sections of four (or eight) bars. The main difference between a jig and a hornpipe is that the hornpipe has sixteen steps while the jig has fourteen; skilful dancers could alternate between the two dances. In Ireland jigs were distinguished from reels by the number of accents to the bar.

Old Dances in a New Country

All these dances were introduced into Canada in the eighteenth century and remain an integral part of our culture, along with their music. The Métis are some of the most vibrant exponents of dances such as the Handkerchief Dance, the Reel for Four, and Drops of Brandy. They learned these from their Scottish and French forebears, sometimes with an Aboriginal touch.[13] Dancing was an integral part of Canadian life for all levels of society. Visitors remarked on the frequency and the numbers of participants. An account from Quebec City in the 1840s indicates that current dance crazes from Europe crossed the Atlantic to Canada:

At one end of the ball-room was the regimental band, whence the lungs of some dozen or so strong-built soldiers, assisted by the noisiest possible musical contrivances, thundered forth the quadrilles and waltzes. It was a gay sight; about eighty dancers were going through a quadrille as I entered the room; the greater number of the gentlemen were in their handsome uniforms of red, blue and green ... Then there were the [French] Canadian gentlemen, with their white neckcloths and black clothes, generally smaller and darker than their English fellow-subjects and much more at home in the dance ... There is one thing in which the [French] Canadian ladies certainly excel, that is dancing; I never saw one dance badly, and some of them are the best waltzers and polkistes I have ever seen in a ball-room. (Warburton 1846, 91–3)

The waltz originated in the German-speaking areas of Europe and by 1793 had spread to Paris. It created a scandal when introduced in England in 1812, but only eight years later advertisements for waltz instructions were appearing in Canadian newspapers. Similarly the galop and the polka, popular dances in England during the 1830s, are included in the *Canadian Ten Cent Ball-Room Companion and Guide to Dancing* (1871).[14]

Although they were denounced by strict Protestant denominations and Roman Catholic priests, various versions of all these dances made their way across the country to new settlements and Hudson Bay Company posts. The mistress of the house might be refused Absolution and the Holy Sacrament for allowing fast dances in her home, but most parish priests had little success in banning the practise.[15]

Fiddle Music

If no regimental band or local musicians were available, people either made do with humming, "tuning," or "jigging" the dance tunes (singing abstract vocables or nonsense lyrics) or they used whatever instrument was available. Alfred Domett finished Christmas day near Woodstock, Upper Canada, in 1833 by dancing with the young ladies of the household to the music of a jaw's harp (McMillan 1983, 70). The most common instrument was the fiddle: John Robert Godley describes a scene on the steamboat travelling between Quebec and Montreal: "All evening there was wonderful fiddling and dancing of jigs among Canadian boatmen and the Irish emigrant girls. The former are quite French in their love of festivity" (1844, 1: 92). This dance music – performed by fiddlers – laid the foundation for the rich fiddling traditions of Canada. Philip Stansbury describes a fiddler who played for a farm-house dance at Williamsburg near Cornwall, Upper Canada, in 1821. "A venerable grey-headed fiddler 'the bard of olden times' kept up the never-ceasing screeches and saws, and beat time with his right foot, his head nodding in unison, so

Figure 4.3   *Red River Jig*, a Métis step dance tune, as transcribed by Roy Gibbons (1981).

Figure 4.4   *La grande gigue simple* as transcribed by Roy Gibbons (1981).

Figure 4.5   *The Illumination*, a Scottish fiddle tune written in 1781 by William Marshall.

forcibly, that the glasses of the sideboard, may be said to have answered the place of a cymbal. The ladies, not at all deficient in beauty, and their faces glowing beneath graceful straw-hats instead of head dresses, and the gentlemen, not a whit the more disliked for their lofty persons and heroic broad shoulders, acted their parts with engaging ease, simplicity and good humour" (Stansbury 1822, 156).

Tunes used to accompany dancing came from continental Europe and the British Isles. The three main streams of fiddling repertoire and style that came to Canada during this period were Scottish, Irish, and French. Many Scottish employees of the Hudson's Bay Company brought fiddles with them; records of the trading posts include countless references to evenings of "dancing and singing," usually with members of First Nations cultures present. Métis fiddling, a mixture of Native, French, and Scottish traditions, grew from encounters in the fur trade, while French Canadian fiddling fused elements of Scottish-Irish repertoire and style with French tunes. Two tunes often heard today probably date back to the 1700s. *The Red River Jig* (see figure 4.3), a step-dance tune particularly associated with Métis fiddlers, is a variant of the well-known Québec tune *La grande gigue simple* (see figure 4.4) (Gibbons 1981, 82). Some scholars suggest that this melody was originally a European hornpipe. Both tunes share common features with *The Illumination*, a Scottish fiddle tune written in 1781 by William Marshall (see figure 4.5). The Marshall tune may have required scordatura tuning because of its bagpipe-like usage of the lowered seventh and other tricky passages. Certainly both Canadian tunes given here use scordatura tuning as indicated. The tune *Drops of Brandy (Le brandy, La danse du crochet, The Hook Dance)* was used for a Scottish line dance. Additional evidence that original fiddle tunes were created in Canada during the eighteenth century can be found in the Berthelot manuscript; the title of one tune – *Menuet de l'Hôtel-Dieu*, named for the first hospital in Quebec (Courville 1998, 22) – may indicate that this is an original Canadian composition.

In the late 1700s immigrants from Irish, English, and German backgrounds added their fiddle traditions to the mix. Specific mixtures of these elements varied according to settlement patterns, but four main fiddling traditions – French Canadian, First Nations and Métis, Scottish Cape Breton, and Down East[16] – can be identified before the establishment of Ukrainian and Country traditions in the early twentieth century. As yet, thorough investigation of regional differences in fiddling has been limited, and there are often lacunae in considering important aspects such as bowing techniques.[17] Prince Edward Island (PEI) can serve as a case study as three of the main fiddling streams are present.[18]

Fiddling in Prince Edward Island

In other parts of Canada there is a strong tradition of fiddle contests but the PEI Fiddlers' Association discourages such events. Because individual fiddlers are encouraged to continue their own traditions, the process of homogenization seen elsewhere has not occurred here, and the relationship between fiddling and dancing has also been preserved. Ken Perlman's careful research of fifty-eight fiddlers in Prince Edward Island, including 480 different tunes, is a rich resource, as is his two-CD set *The Prince Edward Island Style of Fiddling* (Rounder CD 7015–16): *Fiddlers of Western Prince Edward Island* features Acadian-Québécois fiddling; *Fiddlers of Eastern Prince Edward Island* demonstrates the Gaelic inspired Cape Breton style.

Island repertoire includes locally composed tunes, but most of the reels, jigs, strathspeys, marches, waltzes, and airs arrived from outside sources. Tunes brought by the first waves of settlers and travelling musicians or learned from tune books were passed down orally from generation to generation. Musicians who could read musical notation taught other fiddlers, and after about 1950, fiddlers picked up new tunes from recordings and radio broadcasts. Tunes were often reshaped and rhythmically transformed to serve for particular dances: "For example, hornpipes, strathspeys and marches (moderate-tempo tunes with irregular rhythms) were often recast as reels (fast tunes with regular rhythms). Similarly, many old pop songs or traditional songs were pressed into service as jigs, waltzes or 'set-tunes' (polka-like dance tunes)" (Perlman 1995, 35). Regardless of the broader aspects of style all Island fiddlers aim to play tunes accurately as known in the community from memory, with an infectious rhythm, a proper tempo for the dance, and with a sweet, smooth sound.

BOWING AND CLOGGING

To obtain this sound fiddlers use a powerful modified "saw stroke" – one stroke per note – with occasional slurs. In fast tunes they use only a small portion of the bow to avoid arm fatigue. The Scottish style has a gritty sound, similar to a bagpipe, produced by short bows near the tip with the bow tilted toward the player. Down East bowing (based on Irish) is the smoothest of all, with the bow tilted away from the player, and the violin tilted almost perpendicular to allow ready access to the fourth string. Players influenced by French and Acadian styles use more of the lower portion of the bow.

Players are almost always seated so they can execute a highly stylized foot-tapping routine that features a strong heel-stomp on the main beats and a stronger toe-stomp on the off beats. French Canadian clogging has more accentuation and fiddlers of Acadian and Scottish streams have a complex pattern for reels, where the heel of one foot alternates with the toe of the other. (Quebec fiddlers use a heel-heel-toe-toe pattern; Cape Breton fiddlers tap four beats with the same part of the foot for strathspeys and alternate heel and ball for reels [Dunlay and Reich 1986, 18].) Scottish and Acadian traditions produce an eighth-and-two-sixteenths rhythm with a heel-toe-toe pattern.

SCORDATURA AND ORNAMENTATION

Acadian and Scottish styles are strongly influenced by the bagpipe heritage of much of their repertoire; a number of Scottish fiddlers were also pipers and used the same repertoire for both instruments. (Contrary to general belief, piping was not banned by the Disarming Acts of 1746–48; see Gibson 1998, viii.) Double stops are used to create drones, increase volume, and ornament the tune. Perlman has identified several categories of double stops used by Island fiddlers: open neighbour strings, anticipated stopped strings (stopping the neighbour string early and playing it with the melody string), doubled open strings, and fingering forms (Perlman 1996, 25). Island fiddlers also use a number of different scordatura (cross-tuning) including: A–D–A–E (high bass), A–E–A–E (high bass and counter), and G–E–A–E (high counter), particularly when two or more fiddlers play together (Dunlay and Reich 1986, 17; Perlman 1996, 26).

The strong Celtic tradition of ornamenting a tune with short decorative notes is imitated by Island fiddlers with noting-hand ornaments (grace notes) and bowing inflections. Ornaments are produced by slurring one or more quick notes off the same bow stroke before the main melody note (Perlman 1995, 38). Perlman has noted two ornamental techniques unique to PEI: reverse grace notes created by momentarily releasing the finger pressure without actually lifting it off the string, so that the open string sounds briefly; a hard scratchy vibrato produced by a combination of vibrato in the noting-hand and bearing in with the bow (38). Bowing inflections include snaps (a Scottish rhythmic device often notated as a sixteenth plus a dotted eighth), created by quick pairs of alternate-direction bow strokes, and cuts (called birls in piping) that consist of three quick notes in the time of a quarter note, played with down-up-down bows. Suppressed strokes are used as syncopation: "On a strong beat of a tune, the fiddler manipulates the bow in such a way that a `scratching' sound is heard instead of a pure note. As the tune goes by, the weak-beat note rings, but the strong beat sounds empty. This creates the impression that the weak beat note has been accented (syncopated), and the strong beat note omitted altogether" (39).

EAST AND WEST

With such a variety of special techniques each fiddler develops a unique quality, but there are also distinctions in repertoire and approach in the eastern and western areas of the Island. In the east, where Gaelic influence is strongest, there are more Scottish tunes, played at a moderate tempo and with considerable ornamentation. In the west there is more Acadian influence; tempos are faster and there are frequent bow-driven syncopations. (See Diamond 2000a for a discussion of the Acadian fiddler Anastasia Desroches.) Whatever the style or repertoire, this music was provided for an evening's entertainment consisting of "square sets" (square dancing) interspersed with solo dances, known as step-dancing.

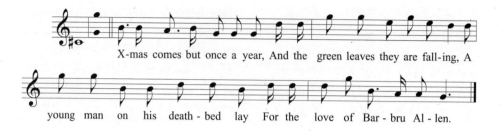

X-mas comes but once a year, And the green leaves they are fall-ing, A young man on his death-bed lay For the love of Bar-bru Al-len.

Figure 4.6   Barbara Allen, transcribed from a performance by Mary Galbraith on Folkways FE 4312 (reissued on *A Folksong Portrait of Canada*, Mercury 769748000-2: CD2-17)

Christmas comes but once a year
And the green leaves they are falling,
A young man on his death bed lay,
For the love o' Barbru Allen.

"Get up, get up," her mother said,
"Get up and go and see him."
"O Mother, Mother dear, do you mind
   yon day
You told me for to shun him."

"Get up, get up," her father said
"Get up and go and see him,"
"O Father, Father dear, do you mind
   yon day
You brought out your gun to shoot him."

Slowly, slowly, she got up,
And slowly she got on her feet
And slowly to his bedside went
And she said "young man you're dying."

"O yes, O yes, I feel very sick,
But I think that you could spare me,
One kiss from your ruby, ruby lips" he said,
"And name me, Barbru Allen."

"One kiss from me you never will see
If I saw your heart's blood flying,
For in the garden walking one day,
You slighted Barbru Allen."

"A kiss from you, I was ever true,
And I am not denying,
I gave a rose to the ladies there
But I still loved Barbru Allen."

"Look up, look up, at my bed head,
And there you will see hanging
A watch and chain, a diamond ring,
That I bought for Barbru Allen."

"Look down, look down, at my bed foot,
And there will you see lying,
A napkin stained with my hot blood,
That I shed for the love o' Barbru Allen."

I won't look up at your bed head
There to see a-hanging
A watch and chain, a diamond ring
That he bought for Barbru Allen

He turned his pale face to the wall
And death came to him creeping
O "Mother, Mother dear," he said to her
"Be kind to Barbru Allen."

She went out for a morning walk,
She saw a corpse a-coming,
The birds of the air, they seemed to say,
"Hard hearted Barbru Allen."

"O Mother, Mother, dig my grave,
And dig it long and narrow
For the love that died for me today,
I will die for him tomorrow."

One was buried in St Paul,	They grew so high, so very very high
The other in Mary's Tower,	That they could grow no higher,
And out of her grave grew a red, red rose,	They twisted at the top, to a true lovers knot
And out of his a brier.	And there they remain forever.

Vocal Folk Music

BALLADS

The British brought a wide variety of orally-transmitted vocal music. British traditions, like the French, included a storehouse of tales from distant times organized into verse and hung on tunes. Most of these songs were known as "ballads."[19] Many of the oldest English-language ballads are referred to as "Child ballads" because they appear in Francis James Child's five-volume collection *The English and Scottish Popular Ballads*.[20] The tunes for ballads with four-line strophes can be organized in different combinations: two different phrases (AABA, ABBA, ABAB, AA'A"B); three different phrases (AABC, ABBC, ABAC); four or more different phrases (ABCD, ABCDE, etc.). Many English tunes have five (or fewer) pitches, and two pentatonic forms (C–D–F–G–A; C–D–E–G–A) are found frequently. Some tunes have a sixth pitch forming a hexatonic scale. Tunes of seven pitches are usually based on Ionian, Aeolian, Dorian, or Mixolydian modes.

Of the seventy-seven Child ballads collected in Canada by 1980, *Bonny Barbara Allen* (Child 84) is found most frequently (Doucette and Quigley 1981, 10). At least one version has been collected in every province except PEI, and although there are textual differences all the Canadian versions tell essentially the same story[21] as presented in the version transcribed from a performance by Mary Galbraith (see figure 4.6) who learned the ballad in Ireland before coming to Saskatchewan in 1915.

BROADSIDES

By the seventeenth century, printing was well-established in England and publishers had discovered there was a profit to be made in single broadsheets of the text (and sometimes the tune) of a ballad. To fill the demand, publishers hired poets to versify current events of the day, which were fitted to existing tunes. The regular scansion and obvious rhyme schemes set these journalistic broadside ballads apart from the older Child ballads.[22] Tunes are often based on a seven-note scale and have a wider range than the older ballads. Many broadsides were passed on orally; some

Broadside Ballads about Canada

The earliest known separate broad-side publication – "England's Honour Revived," published in the fall of 1628 – recounts naval battles fought by the British in their conquest of the St Lawrence settlements that same year. According to the text, the only wounded Englishman was "one who was a Trumpeter ... a bullet shot ith'hand." The ballad was to be sung to "King Henrie's Going to Bulloyne," a popular tune of the day. Canada was the subject of several eighteenth-century broadsides associated with the Seven Years War. The capture of Louisbourg, celebrated in one broadside, inflamed patriotic sentiment and sparked the publication of several more. A well-known lament on the death of General Wolfe (see figure 4.7) was written shortly after the battle of the Plains of Abraham and first published in Dublin by John Lee. A number of versions of broadsides about Wolfe have been collected in Canada (*CMH3*, vi).

Figure 4.7 General Wolfe, a broadside published in Dublin, Ireland, by John Lee (fl. 1778–1803), also published in *CMH3*, 3

printed texts also found their way to Canada. Emigrants brought broadsheets with them and we have letters from Canadians requesting friends or relatives travelling to Britain to pick up the latest broadsides. Broadsides published in England often recounted exploits of British military or naval heroes in Canada.

OTHER BRITISH FOLK SONGS

In addition British settlers brought lyrical folk-songs, *cante fables* (stories containing songs), fairy tales, animal fables, proverbs, riddles, and children's game songs. Lyrical folk-songs express a mood related to love, work, protest, religious sentiment, entertainment or parties, or a particular life style. Many of these songs are in the poetic and musical structure described for songs of Irish provenance. One of the most beautiful, *She's Like the Swallow*, has inspired many arrangements and new compositions. Settlers often sang these songs while working on the many tasks involved with establishing their homes in a new and unfamiliar terrain. For example, *N uair nighidh tu* (When You Wash) is one of a number of milling frolic songs (sung while scrubbing and pounding newly woven wool cloth) regularly sung by Gaelic-speaking settlers.[23]

Many of the countless references to Canadians singing songs of oral provenance involve French Canadian songs sung by boatmen and voyageurs. Thomas Moore tried to capture the essence of this musical tradition in *A Canadian Boat Song* (HACM–7; CMH3, 4–10). Such songs were not only sung on the water; by the late 1700s they were also heard as after-dinner entertainment in homes. John Bigsby, a nineteenth-century traveller, describes an intriguing performance with a First Nations influence:

The guests at the wine table now joined the ladies for coffee, when one of the Miss M'Gillivray called to Mr. M–, and insisted upon his singing a wild voyageur song, "Le premier jour de Mai," playing the spirited tune on the piano at the same time with one hand. Thus commanded, Mr. M– sang it as only the true *voyageur* can do, imitating the action of the paddle, and in their high, resounding, and yet musical tones. His practiced voice enabled him to give us the various swells and falls of sounds upon the waters, driven about by the winds, dispersed and softened in the wide expanses, or brought close again to the ear by neighbouring rocks. He finished, as is usual with the piercing Indian shriek. (Bigsby 1850/1969, 1: 119)

Singing songs from oral transmission occurred in many locales and on many different occasions, and the selections rendered had a remarkable breadth. The occasion of the following description was a wagon-ride from Hamilton to Brantford in 1833 with the driver, a retired army officer, a tailor, and the writer:

Graham ... was in high spirits all the way, and sang patriotic or sentimental songs with his usual vigour, imitated cats caterwauling, dogs barking and growling, nightingales singing, bugles and French horns blowing etc. till the driver was perfectly astonished .... Graham's songs aroused what music there was in the soul of our driver, who from repeated potations of whiskey whenever we stopped, was getting fast intoxicated and he accordingly struck up a long woeful Ballad, which he sung in a doleful monotonous whine, containing about 50 stanzas or thereabouts. The tailor too amused us by striking up in the most solemn style some Methodistical hymns, which he chanted with great unction, seriously. (Domett 1955, 33)

Church Music

The above description indicates that religious songs were also part of the English tradition of orally transmitted vocal music. Although some British emigrants were Roman Catholic, the majority of Loyalists and English or Scottish emigrants were connected with Protestant traditions of Christianity. The British ruling class were almost all Anglican, but other sections of society belonged to denominations descended from Calvinist thought.[24] Both Catholics and Anglicans had a tradition of training musicians for church services, but the average Protestant congregation required assistance for musical participation. In Britain, this need had been met by lining out: each phrase of the psalm was sung by a leader or precentor and repeated by the congregation. The practise of lining out continued in Canada as late as 1845, according to this description of a church service in Fergus, Canada West: "There was no organ or choir then. William Rennie was precentor and sat in a little enclosure of his own in front of and beneath the pulpit. He got the pitch by the tuning fork and used to sing alone the first line of the psalm or paraphrase (there were no hymns used at that time) before the congregation joined in. He was the only one to stand, for the congregation sat while singing but stood during prayer" (Farquharson 1983, 11). An instrument such as a cello was sometimes used to support the melody; the instrument in figure 4.8 has labels on the neck indicating pitches, possibly to assist the player.

Singing schools, a tradition that originated in Scotland and spread to the Thirteen Colonies, were a more effective method of training congre-

Figure 4.8
A nineteenth-century cello
probably used for "lining
out" or supporting the
congregation in hymn
singing. Keillor House
Museum, Dorchester, New
Brunswick. Photograph
by Diane Nicholson. The
labels on the neck of
the instrument indicate
pitches.

gations. Compilations of hymn tunes that included a section on musical
notation and rudiments served as textbooks for the numerous singing
schools that sprang up.[25] Classes lasting about three hours were usually
held during the winter, sometimes in a local tavern. Teachers led voice
exercises by rote and taught simple elements of music notation. Hymn
tunes were learned from the selected text or from manuscripts. At the
end of the instruction period the class gave a concert consisting of hymns
and anthems.[26] Undoubtedly Loyalists who poured into Canada brought
both books and a desire for singing schools, not only as a way to learn
music, but also as a social institution. From 1764 to 1772 James Lyon
served as a Presbyterian pastor in the area around Truro, Nova Scotia,
and he may well have also tried to improve the congregational singing,
using his own publication, *Urania* (named for the Greek muse of astron-
omy) as the textbook.[27]

When published books were not available, hand-written manuscripts were created. The practise of writing moralistic texts to be sung to psalm tunes came from Scotland. "Mary Miller Her Book" (1766), a small music notebook at the Colchester Historical Museum in Truro, contains thirteen psalm tunes: the tunes are written on five-line staves in fa-so-la notation, and nine are in two parts. There are also a number of child-like coloured drawings (Vogan 1991, 251). Judith Humphrey's note book (1813), a collection of twelve psalm tunes, each with a secular verse, was used in the area of Simcoe (in Haldimand County, Upper Canada); each page is decorated with fraktur art and the music is written in fa-sol-la notation on a five-line staff (Beckwith 1987, 10). One of the tunes in this collection, "Abbey" (see figure 4.9), is found in the Scottish Psalter of 1615. The secular text reads: "Love heightened to a mutual wish / And Sympathetick Glow / Of courting her A dearer self / Joys exquisite bestow." As with the tune "Abbey," sacred music was not always tied to a sacred text or a sacred event. Sacred music might be heard at band concerts in the parks on a summer evening or at theatrical or musical programs. Before 1870, if an average household owned any printed music, it was likely a compilation of hymn tunes that were sung in three- or four-part harmony or played on the piano or parlour organ, instruments found in many Canadian homes.

Concerts and the Stage

British bureaucrats and tradesmen who came to Canada were accustomed to attending occasional concerts or theatrical presentations. Under the French regime such activities were frowned upon by the Roman Catholic clergy, but the new British order quickly took effect. In Quebec City a public theatrical presentation was advertised in November 1765. Five years later there was a subscription series of concerts and by the 1780s there was a concert every second week during the winter season. By the 1790s there were twenty-four subscription concerts as well as various single events (Bourassa-Trépanier and Poirier 1990, 16) and similar activities were beginning to take hold in Montreal and Halifax.

MUSIC AT CONCERTS

Entertainment in the assembly rooms of taverns covered a wide spectrum from jugglers, magicians, and actors, to dancers and musicians, but by the 1790s these walls were echoing to sounds as sophisticated as any heard in the major European cities. For example, the program of a concert in the British Tavern in Halifax on 15 January 1793 reflects cur-

Figure 4.9 "Abbey" from Judith Humphrey's Book (1813) in fa-sol-la notation; a modern transcription by John Beckwith is given below.

rent European repertoire[28] from Vienna, Mannheim, and Paris: a grand overture and a symphony by Haydn, two "favorite quartets" and a trio by Ignaz Pleyel, a trio by Franz Kotzwara, an overture by Antonin Kammel, a "much admired quartet" by Jean Baptiste Davaux, an overture by Johann Christian Bach, and an overture by Lord [Michael] Kelly.

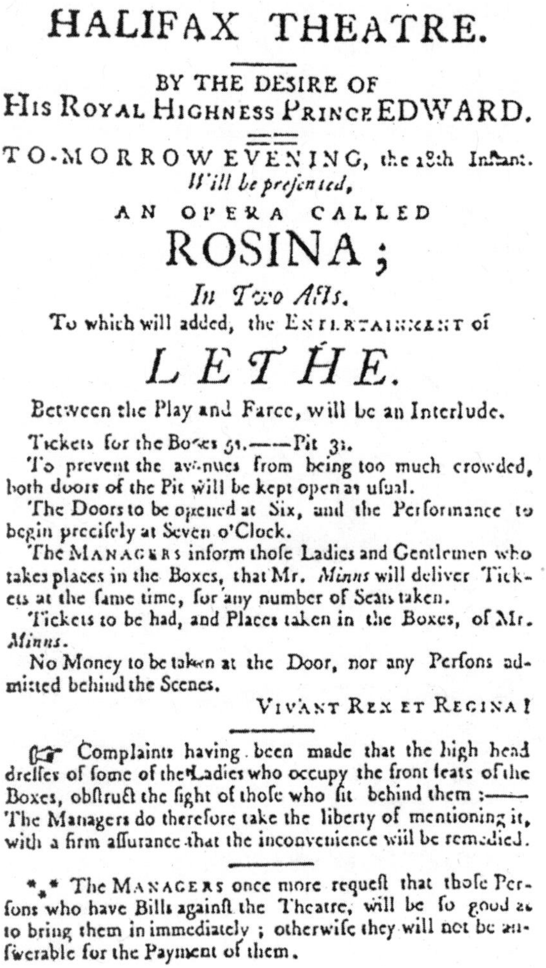

HALIFAX THEATRE.

BY THE DESIRE OF
His Royal Highness Prince EDWARD.

TO-MORROW EVENING, the 18th Instant.
Will be presented,

AN OPERA CALLED

ROSINA ;

In Two Acts.

To which will added, the ENTERTAINMENT of

LETHE.

Between the Play and Farce, will be an Interlude.

Tickets for the Boxes 5s.——Pit 3s.

To prevent the avenues from being too much crowded, both doors of the Pit will be kept open as usual.

The Doors to be opened at Six, and the Performance to begin precisely at Seven o'Clock.

The MANAGERS inform those Ladies and Gentlemen who takes places in the Boxes, that Mr. *Minns* will deliver Tickets at the same time, for any number of Seats taken.

Tickets to be had, and Places taken in the Boxes, of Mr. *Minns.*

No Money to be taken at the Door, nor any Persons admitted behind the Scenes.

VIVANT REX ET REGINA!

☞ Complaints having been made that the high head dresses of some of the Ladies who occupy the front feats of the Boxes, obstruct the fight of those who fit behind them :—— The Managers do therefore take the liberty of mentioning it, with a firm assurance that the inconvenience will be remedied.

. The MANAGERS once more request that those Persons who have Bills against the Theatre, will be fo good as to bring them in immediately ; otherwise they will not be answerable for the Payment of them.

By 1800, thirty-seven theatrical presentations had taken place in Halifax. Three of these were ballad operas: *The Devil To Pay* (1731) by Charles Coffey, *The Ladies Frolic* with music by William Bates and Thomas Arne, and *The Poor Soldier* (1783) by William Shield. Among sixteen comic operas produced in Halifax during the 1790s are William Shield's *Rosina*, S. Storace's *No Song No Supper* (1790), Charles Dibdin's *The Padlock*, S. Arnold's *The Castle of Andalusia*, and Thomas Linley's *Duenna* (Hall 1983, 303–5). Shield wrote the overture and some of the songs for *Rosina* (see figure 4.10); the rest of the music he arranged from works by other composers. The overture was also played in Quebec City in 1788, and some selections were also done in Halifax before the complete performance in 1795.

Figure 4.10   A notice in the *Halifax Royal Gazette and Advertiser* of 17 March 1795 for a performance of William Shield's *Rosina*.

From extant newspaper notices we know that in Halifax at least seventeen different overtures, ten concertos, sixteen symphonies, and fifteen chamber works were performed in the 1790s (Hall 1983, 291). An examination of similar data from Quebec City for this decade documents twelve symphonies (including Haydn's "grande symphonie in D" and a symphony by Thomas Arne), fifteen overtures (including one of Gluck's *Iphigénie* overtures), eighteen concertos (including a piano concerto by Mozart), and about nine works for string quartet, string quintet, or *harmonie*. In Quebec there is more representation of French opera overtures but also works of Corelli, Handel, and Charles Avison. A fairly complete rendition of Handel's *Messiah* – the first of many performances this work was to have in Canada – was given in Quebec City on 26 December 1793. Many instrumental concerts included vocal selections (songs, duets, operatic arias, and glees), and a musical entertainment in Quebec City on 14 January 1790 included a vocal solo "by a young Chippaway." The English expected singers to be versatile. "In addition to ballads ... and patriotic songs, singers had to be ready with Italian operatic arias and songs, patter songs, solos, duets, catches, and glees" (Mates 1962, 120).

PRODUCTIONS ON STAGE

By the 1780s full theatrical productions were a vital part of cultural activities. These evenings usually consisted of two plays (two to five acts) and a short one- or two-act afterpiece. Many plays included musical numbers and other productions which were primarily musical.[29] Before 1789 all theatrical productions in Montreal and Quebec City were in English, presumably because of the influence of the Roman Catholic clergy, but some French Canadians participated in these events. The first Théâtre de société was formed in Montreal around 1789 and the second appeared in Quebec City. The majority of these productions were cast from local talent, with orchestras drawn from regimental bands and local musicians. Undoubtedly the visits of Prince Edward Augustus, the son of George III to Quebec City 1791–94 and Halifax 1794–1800 (see figure 4.10) affected the standard of musical entertainment; the Prince kept a fine band of musicians; some of whom were recruited from German-speaking countries in Europe (Hall 1989, 255). They joined members of regimental bands for concerts and operatic performances. Excellent local musicians were also available. For example, Frederick Glackemeyer (1759–1836), who came to Quebec in 1777, taught viol, bass viol, violin, and piano, and imported music and instruments. Jonathan Sewell Jr. (1766–1839), who came from a Loyalist family, was a skilled violinist and lawyer. He came to Quebec City in 1789, and a year later formed a string chamber group that performed quartets and quintets by Mozart and Haydn during the 1790s.

THE OPERAS OF JOSEPH QUESNEL

Canada's first original opera was composed and staged in this stimulating milieu. Joseph Quesnel (1746–1809) was a native of Saint-Malo who travelled widely as a sailor, wrote extensively and played the violin. In 1779 he was captured by the British off the coast of Nova Scotia while in command of a French ship loaded with supplies for the rebel forces in the Thirteen Colonies. After his release he settled near Montreal, set up business as a merchant, and married a French Canadian woman. With

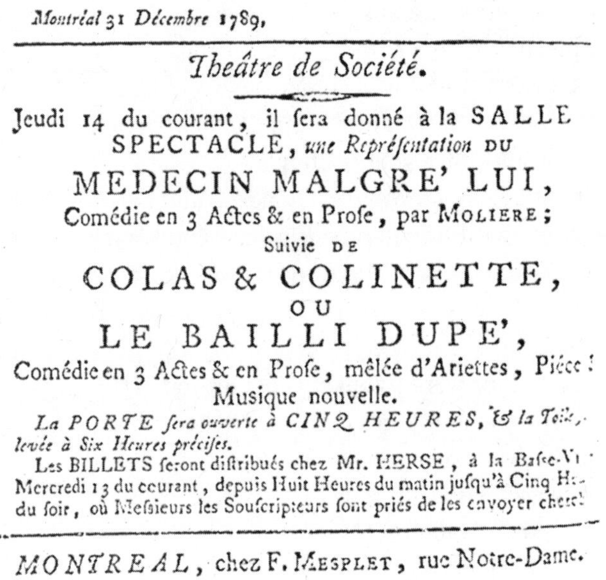

Theâtre de Société.

Jeudi 14 du courant, il fera donné à la SALLE
SPECTACLE, *une Repréfentation* DU
MEDECIN MALGRE' LUI,
Comédie en 3 Actes & en Profe, par MOLIERE;
Suivie DE
COLAS & COLINETTE,
OU
LE BAILLI DUPE',
Comédie en 3 Actes & en Profe, mêlée d'Ariettes, Piéce !
Musique nouvelle.
La PORTE fera ouverte à CINQ HEURES, & la Toil.,
levée à Six Heures précifes.
Les BILLETS feront diftribués chez Mr. HERSE, à la Bafce-Vi '
Mercredi 13 du courant, depuis Huit Heures du matin jufqu'à Cinq H:.
du foir, où Mefsieurs les Soufcripteurs font priés de les envoyer chez!

MONTREAL, chez F. MESPLET, ruc Notre-Dame.

Figure 4.11
An advertisement for the
premiere of *Colas et
Colinette* on 14 January
1790 in Montreal.

past experience as an actor he was soon put to use in the newly-formed theatrical society, and on a visit to Europe in 1789, he probably attended theatrical presentations. On his return to Canada he completed *Colas et Colinette*, a *comédie mêlée d'ariettes*; the first performance in Montreal on 14 January 1790 (see figure 4.11), was followed by a second on 9 February, and productions in Quebec City in January 1805 and 1807. In the first production the role of Colinette was sung by a young man because the influence of the Roman Catholic clergy prevented the participation of women in French Canadian theatres, but after the successful première, Quesnel and his fellow actors mounted a spirited defence of their stage activities.

Undoubtedly Quesnel drew on stock eighteenth-century elements; the two main characters are strikingly similar to those in Jean-Jacques Rousseau's *Le Devin du village* (1752) and the plot[30] reflects values of the period, but Quesnel manages to fill out these stock characters with skilfully written music. The solid, rhythmically firm music sung by the upright Dolmont contrasts with the chromatic, slithery material of the Bailiff. Colinette has graceful, ingratiating melodies, but she is obviously more than a simple-minded country girl. Colas sings folk-like strophic songs in the early part of the opera, and his straightforwardness comes through particularly in his duets with the Bailiff (see *HACM–8*; *CMH10*, 1–6). The opera ends with a vaudeville, typical for the period, in which the characters each give their view of events in a solo stanza before the final chorus.

John Neilson, an important publisher in Montreal, wanted to publish the complete opera, but because *Colas et Colinette* had been produced as an afterpiece, there was no overture. Neilson published the libretto in 1808, but unfortunately Quesnel died before completing the overture. Only the vocal parts and the second violin part have survived in manuscript. In 1963 Godfrey Ridout reconstructed the orchestral parts and wrote an overture based on themes from the opera – a practise rarely found before the 1820s. Ridout's version was first performed in 1963 at a Ten Centuries Concerts in Toronto. A truncated recording was made in 1968 and a performance was broadcast on CBC Television. On 3 December 1808 the *Courier de Quebec* announced the production of a new opera by Quesnel. It is not known whether *Lucas et Cécile* was performed during Quesnel's lifetime; there is no libretto and only the vocal parts have survived. John Beckwith's restoration of this fascinating work, completed in 1989, has seventeen numbers including several trios in which each character is musically delineated (Beckwith 1991) and the work ends with a modified vaudeville for which Quesnel wrote a rhyming couplet for each character. This restoration was performed in Toronto by Tafelmusik in 1994 and more recently in Montreal (Robert 2000, 68). Quesnel was also said to have written songs, duos, motets, quartets, and symphonies, but sadly none of these works have been found. However, his two operas establish Joseph Quesnel as a worthy composer to lead off the contributions made by Canadians through to the present day.

A great deal of British music in a wide variety of genres was transplanted to Canada. Some of it was transformed to a degree in its new landscape. Substitutions of Canadian terms and place names gradually occurred in oral texts of songs. Probably the tunes also changed slightly in the new surroundings due to Aboriginal and French influences. It seems likely that if the voyageur style of singing with a final Aboriginal 'whoop' was being used by an English-speaking Canadian singing a song in the French language, these vocal characteristics were possibly used in English-language songs as well. The rubbaboo was occurring in the intermingling of dance forms and the tunes that accompanied them. Possibly other adaptations occurred in the performances of larger-scale works such as operas and instrumental works because of the Canadian circumstances.

5 Expanding Settlements before Confederation

Major political changes occurred with the arrival of more and more settlers. In 1769, Britain separated Prince Edward Island from Nova Scotia and created provinces of Cape Breton and New Brunswick. The fur trade retained economic importance, but in 1821 intense transcontinental rivalry coupled with a declining demand for furs forced the North West Company, operated by French-speaking bourgeoisie in Montreal, to merge with the Hudson's Bay Company. In the later 1700s Canada gradually began to export wheat, first to the West Indies and then to Britain and southern Europe. The timber trade, centred in Quebec City, the Ottawa Valley, and the Eastern Townships grew rapidly after 1806, due to Napoleon's continental blockade. In Lower Canada, even without immigration, the francophone population was doubling every twenty-five years, but the rising value of forest products and a massive wave of British immigrants made an impact. By 1831 Quebec City was almost evenly divided between the two language groups, and a decade later Montreal was more than sixty percent anglophone. In both cities, business was dominated by anglophone merchants. Changing economic conditions and demographic shifts in both Lower and Upper Canada led to political tensions that erupted in the rebellions of the 1830s.

The creation of Upper Canada in 1791 reflected settlements of Loyalists and military officers, but after the War of 1812 American immigration was formally halted. New immigrants from Britain settled in small communities from the Ottawa River to the head of the Great Lakes, with few schools, hospitals, or local government structures; opposition to a British oligarchy finally erupted in 1837. Lord Durham's proposal for a single province of Canada and other measures led to a common commercial system and responsible government. By 1850 canal traffic was booming and soon new industrial centres were developing along an expanding railway network, ending a dependence on water routes and enforced isolation in winter. Settlers were conscious of their cultural heritage: for example, in 1858, the population of Bancroft was listed as: 24 English, 41 Irish, 30 [French] Canadian, 18 Scotch, and 31 German. In such a community, music of one culture was heard, learned, and performed by other ethnic groups, creating what became known as a musical rubbaboo. The Earl of Southesk,[1] travelling through Hudson's Bay Company territories in 1859–60 described a visit to the school of the Sisters of Charity in Fort Garry on 6 June 1859 with Dr. Rae:

We had the pleasure of seeing a few of the pupils, whom Sister C– very obligingly sent for, asking them to give us some specimens of their progress in music. Two nice-looking dark girls of fourteen first came in, and played several pieces on a piano-forte, – which, I confess, it surprised me to see in this remote and inaccessible land; then two pretty little fair-haired children took their place, and, like the others, played in a pleasing and very creditable manner ... Fort Garry was amply provided with churches, for besides the two greater edifices known as the cathedrals, there was a large place of worship for the Presbyterians, who formed a numerous and important body ... Though the Presbyterian psalms and hymns were not in use, it was easy to see that the Scottish race prevailed in the congregation – the tunes and the manner of singing so forcibly recalling the sober, deliberate fashion of my own country, that I could scarcely believe myself thousands of miles away in the innermost heart of America. (Southesk 1969, 33)

With increasing numbers of merchants and family businesses came the availability of more music and musical instruments. Performances took place not only in wealthy homes but also at kitchen parties held whenever someone skilled on the fiddle or in humming dance tunes was available. Musical activities, both sacred and secular, also took place in churches, and events of fraternal organizations such as the Masons. Where there were military bands, there might be summer concerts in the park and skating in the winter. Sometimes a single skilled musician (often a band leader or choral conductor) became a catalyst for a considerable development of activity, even in very small communities.

Pre-Confederation Music Publishing

The *Graduel romain*, published by John Neilson in 1800, has 645 pages of text and chants in square notation; within two years Neilson also published the *Processional romain* (1801) and the *Vespéral romain* (1802).

Music at Sharon

David Willson (1788–1866) came from an Irish Presbyterian background in New York state and in 1801 settled with his family about fifty kilometres north of York. He initially became a member of the Society of Friends (Quakers) but due to a number of differences with Friends testimonies, he broke away to establish a new sect. (For further information on David Willson, his relationship with the Society of Friends, and the community of Sharon, see Schrauwers 1993). By 1817 Willson had begun to incorporate congregational singing into the meetings for worship of his sect; because he saw music as a spontaneous expression of the Inner Light, he wrote new texts for thousands of hymns that were sung to a specific set of melodies using a 'lining-out' process. In 1819 a small girls choir from the community's school was performing at each service. By this time, the sect was known as the Children of Peace.

The first meeting house (completed in 1819, later known as the Music Hall) was a square building with barrel organ (see figure 5.1) on a platform in the centre, around which musicians were seated. The organ was built by Richard Coates (1778–1886), who also organized a small band to accompany the choir. Coates remained active in the community as a music teacher and bandleader through the 1820s; of the seven organs he is known to have built in Canada, three were for the Children of Peace. The barrel organ has 133 pipes and four stops, covering a compass of 37 notes. The player pumped the bellows with the left foot

Figure 5.1   The first barrel organ (1820) built by Richard Coates for the Children of Peace. Sharon Temple Museum, Sharon, Ontario, photograph by Elaine Keillor.

while turning the crank of the barrel with the left hand. Of the barrels Coates pinned two are extant, each containing ten tunes (see Appendix D). *In the Cottage* (see figure 5.2) is often identified as an English folk song, but it has also been found in French sources such as Ségur 1866. It was likely included at Willson's request and based on a printed source from the United States. *Angel's Song/Hymn* (see figure 5.3) was written by Orlando Gibbons. Unfortunately a second barrel organ, also built by Coates,

Figure 5.2 *In the Cottage*, a barrel organ tune heard at Sharon, ca. 1820, transcribed by D.F. Wright (1967) and revised by Ann Schau (1983).

that contained secular tunes is not extant. Around 1848 Coates built a third organ for the second meeting house: a keyboard instrument with a tracker action, a 49-note manual, and four ranks of 188 wooden pipes.

The most remarkable structure created by the Children of Peace is the Temple (built 1825–32), a three-tiered symmetrical "wedding-cake" structure used for fifteen special services a year, in which music played an essential role. At the sound of a trumpet members formed a procession led by the band and the choir. The band entered by the east door and climbed "Jacob's Ladder" to the musicians' gallery on the second floor, and played while the congregation took their places (men on one side, women on the other) and the choir assembled around a central ark singing one of David Willson's "Songs for the Altar." It is likely that in the 1820s the choir and band were performing the seventeen anthems found in the Coates manuscripts.

Willson developed friendships with local reformers, such as William Lyon Mackenzie, and the band and choir performed at numerous local secular events, particularly political rallies. Mackenzie himself commented on the music he

Figure 5.3 *Angel's Song*, a barrel organ tune heard at Sharon, ca. 1820, transcribed by D.F. Wright (1967) and revised by Ann Schau (1983).

heard at Sharon: "I found some of the singers in the chapel practising their hymns and tunes ... Two young men had bass-viols, and the full-toned organ aided their music" (1833, 123); this and two descriptions dating from 1829 and 1831 indicate that for over two decades the band included both string and wind instruments (see Schau 1983 20–21) (see table 5.1). By the 1830s newspaper accounts indicate that the Sharon Band was playing arrangements of folk tunes, songs and dance tunes. Among the folk songs noted in these accounts and found in music books associated with Sharon are *The Bush Aboun Traquair* – a Scottish folk tune originally published in William Thomson's *Orpheus Caledonius* (1725) – and the English song *A Frog He Would a-Wooing Go/The Lovesick Frog* (Schau 1985, 26). A concert of the Sharon band described by *The Colonial Advocate* in 1834 refers to *The Bush Aboun Traquair* and a political song on the Irish tune *Rodney's Glory* (Schau 1985, 28).

In 1844 the band requested new instruments to further improve the performance standard and they also urged the sect to adopt a style of congregational unison singing. From 1846 to 1848

Table 5.1 Instrumentation of the Sharon Band given in writings by William Lyon Mackenzie, based on items from the *Colonial Advocate* quoted in Schau 1983, 20–21.

1829	1831	1833
1 violin	violins	
2 cellos	cellos	
1 flageolet[a]		
2 octave flutes[b]	octave flutes	1 octave flute
2 German flutes[c]	German flute	
2 clarinets	3–4 clarinets	3 clarinets
1 bassoon	2 bassoons	1 bassoon
		1 keyed bugle[d]
2 concert horns	French horns	2 French horns
		1 trombone
		1 drum

NOTES

[a] a type of keyed recorder

[b] probably a recorder

[c] a side-blown transverse flute, somewhat larger than a fife

[d] probably a form of signalling horn made of copper or brass with a wide conical bore. Various versions were known in the nineteenth century, some of which had a key to lower the pitch, thus increasing the range of available harmonics.

Daniel Cory, a music teacher from Boston, gave systematic training in singing. Band membership fluctuated; in the early years it was made up solely of men, but later several women were added (*Make a Joyous Noise* 1992, 10). Women members in the 1860s included flute players Martha Reid and Ellen Lundy, Hannah Graham and Hannah Willson on cornets, and Anne Doan on ophicleide (Schau 1983, 19–20). In 1860, after the purchase of a set of silver instruments (at a cost of $1,500) the band became known as the Sharon Silver Band. Some newspaper reports refer to it as the oldest and best civilian band in the country. Like many bands in the nineteenth century, the Sharon band gradually moved toward an all-wind instrumentation. The band functioned as a marching band as well as an instrumental ensemble, playing alone or with the choir and sometimes the organ.

According to extant descriptions, vocal forces heard at Sharon included three- or four-part mixed choir (either unaccompanied or doubled by organ or instruments), three- or four-part women's or men's choirs, and men's or women's unison choruses accompanied by organ or instruments, and solo voices with instrumental accompaniment. Volumes in the Coates Collection and Ira Doan's Book (a manuscript of flageolet parts from 1830), confirm that the Sharon band played hymns and possibly some accompaniments for anthems. The seventeen anthems in the Coates volumes are extended choral settings, some of which have several choruses, solo or ensemble sections, and instrumental accompaniment. The Sharon choir probably also sang anthems from various Canadian and American hymn-tune collections used at Sharon (Schau 1985, 22).

A considerable repertoire of secular music – found in Ira Doan's Book, Hester Hannah's Book (a bound collection of printed music), and the Keyboard Book (a handwritten manuscript of music for harmonium, melodeon, or piano) – includes selections from English ballad and comic operas, keyboard arrangements from oratorio selections, British military band music, quadrilles, waltzes, marches, quicksteps, solo songs and duets, some glees, and folk tunes. The Sharon musicians used a small keyboard instrument – probably a melodeon or a harmonium – to play accompaniments for concerts in neighbouring communities; the Sharon Temple Museum presently houses several Canadian-made reed organs and pianos known to have been used in the community up to the 1880s. Popular glees for unaccompanied male voices include *Melting Airs* by English composer William Hayes and *Drink to Me Only with Thine Eyes*. In Hester Hannah's Book there are some keyboard arrangements of glees and a large number of solo songs with piano accompaniment (some of which have flute parts or alternate accompaniments for harp or guitar). Another keyboard piece included is the German waltz tune *Ach, du lieber Augustin*, under the title *Buy a Broom*.

The community of Sharon drew on American, English, Scottish, Irish, and German musical traditions for their repertoire, and in the mid-nineteenth century Sharon was the place to hear the most current music; every year the band leader travelled to Boston to note down the latest repertoire by ear. The band continued to give concerts throughout the region into the 1870s, but with changing political and economic conditions the foundation of the beliefs of the sect gradually dissipated. By 1889 the Children of Peace ceased to exist.

Around the same time, the first Canadian collections of hymn tunes and anthems, intended for Protestant sects, began to appear. Some were published in languages of First Nations peoples (Ojibwe, Montagnais, Cree, etc), and almost all included an introductory section with instructions on how to sing and how to read musical notation. Sacred music books produced by specific denominations did not appear until the 1870s (see Appendix C).

The first edition of Stephen Humbert's *Union Harmony: British America's Sacred Vocal Musick* appeared in 1801.[2] The didactic purpose of this collection – the earliest Canadian tune book – is underlined by the inclusion of a secular part-song *Singing School* (HACM–17; CMH5, 85). Humbert wrote a total of twenty-two tunes and nine anthems that appear in various editions of *Union Harmony* (Beckwith 2002, 29). *Nouveau Receuil* (1819), compiled by Jean-Denis Daulé (1766–1852), includes 201 musical items published in a separate volume as *"Airs notés."*

SOLMIZATION SYSTEMS

The music instructions included in many of these collections use one of several solmization systems including Lancashire sol-fa (similar to the fa-sol-la system), shape notes (buckwheat), and ziffern (a numerical system), but the most frequent was the round note notation.[3] The introduction to *The Canadian Church Harmonist* (1864) includes explanations of the fa-sol-la system and the latest version of an Italian system (do-re-mi-fa-sol-la-si), both beginning at middle C, as well as a numerical system for the major scale pointing out the semitones (3–4 and 7–8) in the two tetrachords. The heritage of these systems is still evident in Canada today. A "fixed-doh" system (where *doh* is C) is used predominantly in Francophone areas, while a "movable-doh" system (where *doh* is the tonic of the key) is used elsewhere.

The numerous singing schools, taught by resident or itinerant musicians across Canada in the late eighteenth century and through the nineteenth centuries, grew out of a movement to improve performance of the traditional psalm tunes and to repress an ornamented folk style of singing. These schools formed the backbone of music education in Canada and laid the foundations for a rich tradition of choral societies still evident today. Canadian tune books were used not only for didactic purposes but also for church services and for secular enjoyment (Farquharson 1983, 34), as in this description of a gathering in a farmhouse near Owen Sound (Canada West) ca. 1850:

The pleasure and strengthening these Sunday afternoon gatherings brought was very real, as the isolation and limitations of life in the bush pressed heavily upon the spirits of the pioneers. When cold weather came again and before the snow was too deep for easy travel, many of those who came to the Sunday services came to the William's home on certain mid-week evenings to sing, under Margaret's direction, both secular and religious songs, and to increase their musical knowledge. These singing classes, that in later years were to involve many more persons than the few who first met together to express their feelings in song and to learn to sing "in parts," were a form of recreation that enriched the lives of early Canadian settlers. (Farquharson 1983, 59–60)

Jean-Denis Daulé's *Nouveau Receuil*

Jean-Denis Daulé (1766–1852), a composer and amateur violinist, was ordained as a priest in Paris, and came to Quebec in 1794. His *Nouveau Receuil*, published in 1819, a collection of vernacular French texts, includes 201 "Airs notés" published in a separate volume. There is no text with the melodies (Beckwith 2002, 9), but like other collections used in New France, Daulé includes melodies from the works of Lully and more recent French and Italian composers, such as François Joseph Gossec, André Grétry, Étienne Méhul, and Giovanni Pergolesi, as well as folk songs and vaudeville airs (Beckwith 2002, 30–5). The reality of Quebec as a British colony is reflected by English tunes such as "God Save the King." The most interesting Canadian tune is *Cantique no. 79* (see figure 5.4), the melody of the vaudeville ensemble in Joseph Quesnel's opera *Colas et Colinette*. Beckwith hypothesizes that Daulé either knew Quesnel personally or had heard the operetta in a Quebec production, since the tune had not yet been published (2002, 12). The twenty-three tunes designated *"airs nouveaux"* may have been composed by Daulé; Theodore Molt's *Lyre Sainte* includes one of Daulé's airs, attributed to him, as does Louis Bouhier's *Trois cents cantiques anciens et nouveaux* (Beckwith 2002, 13). Beckwith observes that the harmonizations and accompaniments are similar to those used by the New England School composers.

Figure 5.4 *Cantique no 79* from Jean-Denis Daulé's *Nouveau Receuil* (1819); the tune comes from the vaudeville at the end of Joseph Quesnel's opera *Colas et Colinette*.

Music Organizations

The American composer Lowell Mason had considerable influence on notated repertoire used in North America. Mason favoured European music and adaptations and taught this repertoire in his Boston singing-schools.[4] Some of his publications include portions of large-scale choral works by composers such as Handel and Haydn. In Canada these works became known through Mason's publications and also through Canadian collections, such as J.P. Clarke's *Canadian Church Psalmody* (1845), which contains a tune from Haydn's *Creation* and three tunes adapted from Handel. Acquaintance with portions of larger choral works and occasional newspaper references to performances of oratorios such as Haydn's *Creation* or Handel's *Messiah* stimulated groups in smaller communities to do likewise. Music organizations, usually pulled together by an energetic and knowledgeable church organist or bandmaster, were often short-lived as key musicians moved to another town, rivalries flared, and the day-to-day struggle of running a voluntary organization overwhelmed its leaders. Nevertheless large-scale organizations became more evident and active throughout the nineteenth century in both urban and rural areas.

There were three societies in Halifax: the New Union Singing Society (1809), the St Paul's Singing Society (1819), and the Amateur Glee Club (1836). The Halifax Harmonic Society, founded in 1842, drew 38 players and singers to weekly rehearsals under the direction of John St Luke (a former ballet master of the Theatre Royal, Bristol, England) and performed Haydn's *Creation* at its first concert, 31 January 1843. Until its demise in 1850, the Society presented sacred works by Handel, Haydn, and Mozart in the Harmonic Hall. The organization was revived in 1858 under E. Jeans. Other music organizations in Nova Scotia include the Lunenberg Harmonic Society (founded December 1828) and societies in Antigonish and Pictou.

In Saint John, by 1801 Colin Campbell was advertising violins, fifes, an Aeolian harp, and fashionable music for sale. A Music Academy (possibly only a teaching establishment) was set up in 1822 by the Irishman Arthur Corry, and a Philharmonic Society was established in 1824. Another Irish immigrant formed the Catch and Glee Club in 1833. Like many Presbyterian churches, St Andrew's Kirk did not allow musical instruments in services, but one of its members, Alexander Lawrence, formed a Sacred Music Society in 1837. Under Weisbecker, a former regimental bandmaster, this Society performed selections from works by Handel, Haydn, and Mozart until at least 1845. Stephen Humbert formed a Sacred Music Society that gave its first public performance in 1840. In 1854 organist Theodore Wichtendahl formed a Harmonic Society with twenty-three singers; during the 1855–56 season they presented seven concerts of excerpts from operatic and sacred works, but Wichtendahl resigned his $75-a-year post in 1857 (after a dispute with the executive concerning an orchestra) and a new director failed to keep the Society active.

Musical life in Quebec City continued to depend mainly on musicians from the garrison and well-educated amateurs. The Société harmonique de Québec was particularly active during the years 1819–21 and 1848–57. In its early years, under the direction of Frederick Glackemeyer, Société performers joined with church choirs and singers to give concerts. Every Sunday the regimental band marched to the Holy Trinity Anglican Cathedral (erected in 1804). Stephen Codman arrived from England in 1816 and served as Cathedral organist for the next thirty-six years. In 1833 Adam Schott (son of the founder of the German publisher B. Schott's Söhne) formed the Société Sainte-Cécile, a student orchestra, at the Séminaire de Québec. The group was transformed into a band in 1836 and remained active until the late 1960s (CMH21, vii). In 1849 the young Antoine Dessane (1826–73) arrived in Quebec City with his wife, who was an excellent singer. Dessane became organist at the basilica and ran a busy music studio, and the couple also promoted concerts. The Société harmonique, founded by Dessane, gave many concerts at the new Académie de musique, and even produced several operas including Boieldieu's *Dame Blanche* and Adam's *Si j'étais Roi* (Michaud 1933, 74).

Montreal depended largely on regimental bands and local musicians. In 1837 Jean-Chrysostome Brauneis II (1814–1871), who taught guitar, harp, violin, voice, and theory, tuned pianos, and imported instruments, formed a short-lived Société de Musique. In 1856 François Benoit (1824–77) formed the Société musicale des montagnards canadiens,[5] a male choir of thirty voices. In 1864, Joseph Gould formed the 100-voice Mendelssohn Choir and remained conductor until its demise in 1894.

Some of the earliest descriptions of music in the new settlement of York (later Toronto) can be found in Elizabeth Simcoe's diary for 1796.[6] By 1818 the population of York had grown to 1,000 and Mr Maxwell's violin was heard at most occasions requiring music. At St James Anglican Church Mr Hetherington played the psalm tunes on a bassoon until the establishment of a permanent choir (accompanied by clarinet, bassoon, and string bass) in 1819. Some twenty years later, however, church music was still not of the highest order, according to Anna Jameson: "If the sympathy for literature and science be small, that for music is less. Owing to the exertion of an intelligent musician here, some voices have been so

Stephen Codman

Stephen Codman (ca. 1756–1852) was an English organist, teacher, and composer who had studied with John Christmas Beckwith and William Crotch. He arrived in Quebec City in 1816 to assume the post of organist at Holy Trinity Anglican Cathedral, where he served for the next thirty-six years. Aside from his duties at the cathedral, Codman was involved in a number of musical productions. He organized a benefit performance for the Quebec Emigrant Society; this concert of sacred music, presented on 26 June 1834, involved 174 musicians: "A chorus of 111 singers was supported by an orchestra of over 60 players, composed of 10 first violins, 12 second violins, 4 violas, 6 cellos, 1 bass, 8 flutes, 4 each of clarinets, bassoons, horns, and trumpets, 1 each of trombone, serpent, and bass horn, and 2 drums" (Kallmann 1960, 82). The program included selections for solo voice, vocal ensemble, and chorus from sacred works by Haydn, Mozart, Handel, Cherubini, Rossini, and J.C. Beckwith, and Codman played his own Invocation and an organ concerto by William Crotch. According to the *Quebec Gazette* of 27 June, "the signal success of the exertions of the whole corps of amateurs and professional gentlemen, was the subject of universal praise. Not only the pieces in which the grand and imposing strength of the whole orchestra was displayed, but the different concertos, and particularly that of Mr. Codman on the organ, who exhibited his distinguished professional talents to the best advantage, gained the warmest approbation of all present. The effect of the different solos, too, and particularly those by the young ladies, excited general applause" (quoted in Kallmann 1960, 83). Some of the instrumentalists may have come from the Société Sainte-Cécile, a student orchestra, at the Séminaire de Québec.

far drilled that the psalms and anthems at church are very tolerably performed; but this gentleman received so little general encouragement that he is at this moment preparing to go over to the United States. The archdeacon is collecting subscriptions to pay for an organ which is to cost a thousand pounds; if the money were expended in aid of a singing school, it would do more good" (Jameson 1839/1923, 69). Both W. Warren, the organist in 1837, and his successor Dr Edward Hodges (1796–1867) moved to the United States, and the next cathedral organist, Mrs. Gilki(n)son, resigned after her salary was reduced from £100 to £50 in 1848.

A Toronto Musical Society was organized in 1835 and a Harmonic Society gave concerts in 1840. Various organizations known as the Toronto Philharmonic Society were active in the years 1845–50, and 1853–5;

the following comes from an announcement of a Society concert on 23 April 1847: "The Members will be assisted in the vocal and Instrumental departments by several Amateurs, and by the Band of the 81st. Regiment under the direction of Mr. Crozier. The Choruses will be accompanied on a new Organ of great power and richness of tone, which has been lent for the occasion, and erected in the hall, by the builder, Mr. Thomas, of this city. J.P. Clarke, conductor, will preside at the Organ" (quoted in Sale 1968, 72). The first half of the program included symphonies by Mozart and Beethoven[7] and "The marvellous works" from Haydn's *Creation*. After the intermission the audience heard another Beethoven symphony, the chorus "Worthy is the Lamb," and the Hallelujah chorus (arranged for full military band!) from Handel's *Messiah* (Sale 1968, 72). In any case the 1847 Philharmonic program is the most ambitious, in terms of symphonic music, heard in Canada before 1850.[8]

Mid-Century Entertainment

MUSIC IN HOMES AND SMALL COMMUNITIES

By the 1850s, occasional concerts had become social highlights; one example is Mrs Widder's *soirèe musicale* in Toronto on 12 March 1844 (see Guiguet 2004). The bulk of musical activity consisted of orally-transmitted traditions and musical entertainments created from written sources in the home. While we have little written documentation of such activity, references in diaries, letters, and travellers' accounts suggest that it was very extensive. Anglophone and francophone folk-song heritages were supplemented by traditions from a variety of other cultures, and some folk songs referring to specific Canadian events, locales, or people date back to the early decades of the nineteenth century. The lumber camps, where men signed up for several months of the year, provided optimum conditions for the creation and transmission of folk songs. These camps usually had weekly entertainment nights at which each man told a story or performed a song or an instrumental piece, and since men went to different camps each year, songs and music circulated through the lumber camps and into the wider community.

In Canada there was no clear division situating orally-transmitted musics in rural areas and notated, mainly European, musical forms in urban areas.[9] Oral traditions, particularly those associated with dancing, were celebrated in urban centres, while performances of European and European-derived genres such as chamber music and larger choral works occurred in rural and urban locales; both trends have continued into the twenty-first century. In 1830, Pierre de Sales Laterrière spoke of Canadi-

Figure 5.5   *Mozart's Waltz* as notated in the Allen Ash Fiddle Manuscript. Digitized version by C. Ford.

ans as the most dance-loving nation on earth (1830, 133), and described *les habitants* going from place to place in *carioles* for rounds of parties and dancing, a custom followed to some degree by the *bourgeoisie*. While the Roman Catholic clergy railed against dancing, priests were seen as advocates rather than rulers (Laterrière 1830, 139). Puritan-derived ideas about dancing as a criminal pastime were stronger in some anglophone Protestant sects but dancing remained an important social activity, particularly at barn raisings, weddings, and other important occasions. People who could play dance tunes on portable instruments such as fiddles, harmonicas, or accordions were much in demand.

Many of these musicians did not read music notation but picked up tunes from the notated European canon aurally. For example, in 1820, Allen Ash (1800–1890), a fiddler of Newcastle (Ontario) began to compile a manuscript of fiddle tunes; one of these tunes, entitled "Mozart's Waltz" (see figure 5.5) is based on melodies from the first and third of Mozart's *Sechs Ländlerishe* (1791), K 606.[10] J.J. Bigsby, a traveller in the 1840s, describes hearing tunes from Rossini operas in the backwoods by the River Malbaie near present-day Percé:

During the day of coffee-coloured fog ... I was reading in a little bed-closet ... when I suddenly heard, within the house, two or three short delicious strokes of a fiddle-bow, succeeded immediately by a masterly execution, on one of Amati's best violins, of "Nel Silenzio," that mysterious and mournful air in [Meyerbeer's] "Il Crociato [in Egitto]," which again instantly ran off into one of the gay galloping melodies of Rossini.

Such music in a hut! – such wild capriccios, and passionate complainings, in the murky air of an American wilderness, astounded me. Rushing to see whence it came, I found in the living-room (kitchen, &c.) of the house, playing to the family and some gossips, a slender, pale young man, in corduroy and fustian. I need not say that the violin did not cease; but that the musician received a reward ... He was ... a London artist, named Nokes, on a free ramble through the Western world, and subsisting on his violin. (Bigsby 1969, 1: 232–3)

Hamnett Kirkes Pinhey (1784–1857) came to Canada in 1820 and built a two-storey log cottage at Horaceville (now part of Kanata) on the Ottawa River. Musical entertainment likely took place in a large parlour that neighbours called "the ballroom." Documentation associated with Pinhey's house includes three bound volumes of sheet music for voice and piano, each with a woman's name on the flyleaf. The first volume, *A Miscellaneous Collection of Songs, Ballads, Canzonets, Duets, Trios, Glees & Elegies* (London: Clementi, 1798), was likely brought from England when the family emigrated. The second volume, *A Collection of Favorite Waltzes Selected & Arranged for the Piano forte or Harp* by F.L. Hummell, originally belonged to the Edgecombe family of Lachine, Quebec and is dated 1822 on the flyleaf; this volume includes one of the many printed versions of the well-known *A Canadian Boat Song* by Thomas Moore (HACM–7; CMH3, 4–10) as a glee for three voices with piano accompaniment. The third volume contains a variety of sheet music, probably dating from the 1830s (Elliott 1997, 1–2). The contents of collections such as these were played and sung not only in private homes but also in public spaces such as Mechanics' Institutes.[11]

TOURING COMPANIES

In addition to "home made" entertainments, some Canadian communities occasionally hosted touring productions; one of the earliest of these, the Hermann and Company of the Royal Conservatory of Munich, gave concerts in Saint John and Halifax in 1832. A "company" might be only a group of three or four musicians, and this period also saw the birth of one-man shows consisting of music and anecdotes. Henry Russell (1812–1900), a popular British songwriter and performer, visited Toronto in 1833 and wrote several songs on Canadian subjects, including *The Canadian Sleigh Song* (CMH3, 28), which he popularized through solo recitals in the United States and later in Britain.[12] Resident and touring companies usually presented shortened English adaptations of operas along with a farce or melodrama. In August 1840, Mr and Mrs Seguin and their small ensemble gave English versions of Mozart's *The Marriage of Figaro*, Rossini's *The Barber of Seville*, *La Cenerentola*, and *La gazza ladra*, Auber's *Fra Diavolo*, Bellini's *La Sonnambula*, and the first act of Weber's *Der Freischütz* with "the greater portion of the original music preserved" (CMH10, vi). In 1853, Luigi Arditi's New York-based Artists' Union Italian Opera Company presented full productions of Italian grand operas in the original language: Montreal audiences saw Donizetti's *Lucrezia Borgia*, *Lucia di Lammermoor* and *La Favorita*, and Verdi's *Ernani*, while Bellini's *Norma* was presented in Toronto (CMH10, vi).

With the development of railways in the early 1850s Canadian communities became accessible for touring artists. Newspapers and magazines regularly published items about famous artists of the day – including singers Jenny Lind and Adelina Patti, pianists Sigismund Thalberg and Anton Rubinstein, and violinists Ole Bull and Henri Vieuxtemps – and music lovers flocked to their Canadian concerts. On 21 and 23 October 1851, Jenny Lind sang to an audience of one thousand at St Lawrence Hall in Toronto. As was typical for such concerts during the nineteenth and the early twentieth centuries, Lind toured with a company of three or four musicians, each of whom presented a solo or two on the program.[13] In 1850 and 1852 centres from Montreal to Toronto were favoured with concerts given by the Germania Musical Society (known as "the Germanians").[14] Their repertoire included the first eight symphonies by Beethoven, three Haydn symphonies, overtures by Mendelssohn, Mozart, and Weber, and Mozart's *Jupiter* and *Haffner* Symphonies. In June 1850 they gave nine concerts in Montreal over two weeks, then moved on to Kingston (a city of 12,000) to present a program that included the overture to *Der Freischütz*, a march by Mendelssohn, an arrangement of Styrian melodies, and two galops. A review of this event comments on a performance of the duet from Donizetti's *Linda di Chamonix* played by oboe and flute ("we are familiar with the vocal version, and it should have been sung"), and continues: "Their greatest defect ... is an absence of a sufficient number of violins. The works of Mozart, Haydn, Cimarosa, and even of Rossini, are sealed books to them, constituted as the society is [of 22 performers] ... In the florid school of Verdi, Donizetti ... they are at home, but where would they be if they attempted the overture to *Figaro* or *Tancredi*? ... Take them as they are; the Germanians are the best set of musicians that ever visited Canada; and it is worth a journey to Toronto to hear them play again" (quoted in Keillor 1997, 56). The Germanians returned in 1852 with a group of twenty-five performers. While none of the Toronto programs included a complete symphony, on 28 June 1852 they played the last movement of Beethoven's Symphony no. 5.

As indicated by the above review, Canadian audiences were acquainted with standard European works and local orchestras (often heavily supplemented by band players) performed this repertoire. For example, the overture to Mozart's *La Clemenza di Tito* and one of Beethoven's *Leonora* overtures were performed in the legislative council chamber in Fredericton on 1 August 1844, and Quebec City heard Mozart's Symphony no. 40 in 1857. Some visiting performers also wrote about their impressions of Canada and its musical life. For example, in 1862, the American pianist Louis Moreau Gottschalk gave a concert (using a Chickering piano) in Kingston, "a pretty town more animated than most of the others in Canada" (1964, 87); in 1864 he described Toronto as "smaller than Montreal, it has the advantage of being more animated; its society more hospitable and European" (1964, 223).[15] Gottschalk's references to women in audiences and as amateur musicians underline the expectation that ladies were expected to be knowledgeable about and competent in music, a view reflected in evidence about music used for home entertainment.[16]

Notated Canadian Compositions

We know that many local dance tunes and original Canadian folk songs were created during the first six decades of the nineteenth century, but it is almost impossible to date this orally-transmitted material. Up to about 1830 the situation is not much better for notated music. Life in a largely frontier society left little time for composition, and facilities to print music were almost non-existent. Some musicians turned to publishers in the United States or Europe, but many works existed only in manuscript; few have survived to the present day.

BAND MUSIC
Band music was a constant feature of Canadian life in communities where there were garrisons, and by 1820, citizen bands were also developing. These bands had ten to forty musicians[17] and they usually played music either arranged or composed by the bandmaster. For example, Frederick Glackemeyer wrote *Châteauguay March* for a performance in 1818; Jean-Chrysostome Brauneis I wrote *Grand Overture of Quebec* for the installation of the Duke of Richmond and Lennox as the Governor-in-Chief

Louis Moreau Gottschalk in Canada

The following quotations are from *Notes of a Pianist*, Gottschalk's descriptions of his travels in North, Central, and South America between 1857 and 1868 (Gottschalk 1964). His limited time in Canada included visits to cities and towns in Quebec and Ontario.

From Montreal to Lachine, 5 July 1862:
At the invitation of three officers of the Scots Guards we went in a canoe as far as Alvarge Island ... We sang in chorus the quartet from Rigoletto. (82)

Quebec, 6 July 1862: At Montreal, L'Ange déchu by Kalkbrenner is the object of attraction. The blind pianist Letendale is very polite to me. La Belle, the organist ... paid me very obsequious attention ... The pieces played in English at the theatre are translated from the French. (82) ... I improvised with great success, at my concert, on the air, "A la claire fontaine." I heard them whistling several of my pieces in the streets. (83)

Quebec, 8 July 1862:" Saw the internment of a sergeant ... A detachment of the Seventeenth rifles of the artillery gunners and one hundred sergeants, with staff officers accompanied the body, which was placed on a gun carriage. The music was singular. The drummers beat a roll that lasted one bar; then a rest for one bar, and a blow of the bass drum on the weak part of the bar; then a harmony of eight bars in the minor mode, played by flutes in minor thirds. It was melan-choly and mournful and filled you with profound emotion. I followed them for a quarter of an hour, not being able to tear myself away from the melancholy charm of this strange music. The sound of the bass drum in countertime, the rests alternating with this lugubrious roll, the plaintive melody of the flutes, and the slow rhythm marked by the tread of the soldiers produced an effect I had never before imagined. (84)

Quebec, 9 July 1862: Review on the Esplanade ... The band is large, and played "Dixie," which is very popular here, not only on account of its melody, which is very original, but because, being the air adopted by the Confederates ... After the review, the band played "God Save the Queen" [and] "Rule Britannia." (84)

Montreal, 1864: I am back from the concert ... The hall [in spite of rain] was well filled, and the ladies, elegantly dressed, produced a beautiful effect as seen from the stage. The parterre is generally occupied by those who care less for being seen than for listening to the music. They applauded with enthusiasm, and listened with an attention that singularly contrasted with the noise made by some elegant English officers. (201)

Toronto, 11 May 1864: I will mention an improvement over our concerts at Montreal, which is that conversation, if there was any, took place in an undertone that permitted the music to be heard

Toronto, 12 May 1864: One of the [garrison] officers ... introduced me into the mess-room where the officers take their meals. A piano in one corner, two oratorios of Handel, and lying in another corner, as if it was ashamed of being found in such good company, my humble Cradle Song. (225) ... Heard in a music store the Fantasia on La Muette, played by a charming young girl, Miss C., an amateur, with most remarkable strength and clearness. I record this fact because it is the first case of native talent I have met with in Canada. (225)

St Catharine[s], 13 May 1864: Concert, notwithstanding the rain. There were fifty persons who applauded like five hundred, and for whom we played as if, in place of thirty dollars of receipts, we had received three hundred. (227)

1 November 1864: In Bellevue (Canada) the "Grand Italian Opera Company" gave *Lucrezia.* In the supper scene, when Madame Testa comes to the "Vaso d'oro," she says that the gold and silver vase of the Borgia amounted to a blue china pitcher of water and two tumblers. The Canadian audience, who did not understand a bit of Italian, nor of the opera, put up with the glass for the "Vaso d'oro" (cup of gold), but Madame Testa, on seeing the *Brindisi* sung with this singular cup, was taken with a fit of laughter that was caught by Orsini and Gennaro. The audience, thinking that the laughter was part of the opera, thought the scene marvelously played, and laughed till they cried, and the opera of *Lucrezia* ended amid the applause of the hall. (230–31)

of British North America, 27 February 1819. Like many other such compositions of the time, neither of these works has survived. We do, however, have a flute manuscript (ca. 1850) connected with the Longueil Band that contains thirty-one tunes, most of which are not original Canadian works.[18] Band repertoire often consisted of arrangements of patriotic or popular tunes. Antoine Dessane's *Pas redoublé sur les airs de Vive la canadienne et God Save the Queen* (HACM–33; CMH21, 1–8), scored for wind octet,[19] makes effective use of motives from both tunes as bridge and counter-melody material. His quick march (1865) was likely written for St Jean-Baptiste Day.

VOCAL MUSIC

Compositions for voice with piano were very popular in this period. Most parlour songs were strophic settings of contemporary poems in either French or English with simple accompaniments, a limited vocal range, regular four-bar phrases, and predominantly diatonic harmonies. Songs incorporating vocal techniques from opera and oratorio and a demanding piano part were called art songs or *chansons lyriques*. The first published

Figure 5.6 Cover of *The Band: A Selection of Fashionable Dances for the Pianoforte …
as performed by the military bands*. Lithograph engraving by W.C. Chewett. Toronto:
Nordheimer, n.d. Library and Archives Canada, Negative NL 22079.

art song by a Canadian composer, Stephen Codman's *The Fairy Song* (HACM–10; CMH3, 40–47; printed in England, *ca.* 1827), has a largely through-composed structure in which the setting closely emulates the text. Codman's brilliant vocal writing reflects the demands of contemporary European works such as Weber's *Oberon*. Antoine Dessane's strophic setting of *Le Grillon* (HACM–13; CMH7, 106–9) reflects the influence of European strophic songs of the period; the second and third versos of Alphonse Lamartine's poem are printed at the end of the music, and the extensive piano introduction and accompaniment are independent of the syllabic vocal line. Samuel P. Warren's *The Wings of Song* (published 1866; CMH3, 77–80) is an effective strophic setting of an English translation of Heinrich Heine's well-known poem.

While Canadian composers set many texts by European poets, this period also saw the emergence of Canadian texts, particularly for patriotic songs. John F. Lehmann's[20] *The Merry Bells of England* (1840; HACM–11; CMH3, 11–13) is one of the first examples of independent music publication in Canada. The text concerns birthday celebrations for Queen Victoria and the strophic setting in C major with regular four-bar phrases and the vocal line doubled by the piano is typical of parlour songs published in contemporary magazines. The first broadsides for New Year's Day were published in Quebec newspapers in 1797, and by 1830 newspapers were also publishing typeset or engraved music for St Jean-Baptiste Day (June 24). *Le drapeau de Carillon* (HACM–12; CMH7, 40–1) by Charles Wugk Sabatier (1819–62) first appeared on 1 January 1858 in the *Journal de Québec*, and was frequently reprinted in other newspapers; Octave Crémazie's text celebrates Montcalm's victory at Fort Carillon in 1758 (CMH7, xvi), and Sabatier's strophic setting opens with a pseudo-canonic introduction followed by a broken-chord accompaniment under the vocal line.

A. & S. Nordheimer of Toronto, the first Canadian firm to specialize in music publishing, began printing music in 1844. J.P. Clarke's[21] *Lays of the Maple Leaf, or, Songs of Canada*, published by Nordheimer in 1853, is a cycle of seven songs scored for solo voice, duet, and chorus. The glee of this cycle, *Emblem of Canada* (HACM–15; CMH17, 55–9) has a three part structure consisting of a piano introduction, tenor and bass solos, and a four-part male chorus; solo lines are supported by subtle piano chords and the tenor melody is only doubled by the piano in the chorus.

SACRED MUSIC

Two tunes in Mark Burnham's *Colonial Harmonist* (1832)[22] are worthy of note: Burnham's tune *Hermitage* (HACM–18; CMH5, 129) which has a four-staff format with the melody in the tenor; and William Arnold's tune *Daniel Street* (1807), which is renamed *Canada* (*CMH5*, 130). *Sacred Harmony* (1838) – the most widely used tunebook in Upper Canada – was compiled by Alexander Davidson,[23] who followed some of Burnham's practises; Thomas Clark's *Chillendon* (1815) appears in Davidson's collection without attribution as *Port Hope* (*CMH5*, 91a–b), a title likely chosen in honour of Davidson's hometown. Sometimes a tune lacking attribution to a composer indicates a composition by the compiler. For example, *York New Church* (*HACM*–20; *CMH5*, 136) was composed by William H. Warren for inclusion in *A Selection of Psalms and Hymns* (1835); here again the main melody is in the tenor. As keyboard accompaniment for hymns became more common, publishers began to print hymn tunes in a two-staff format; two examples of this practise are L.E. Rivard's *Confie au plus tendre des pères* (*HACM*–22; *CMH5*, 168) from *Chants évangéliques* (1862), and G.W. Linton's *Just As I Am* (*HACM*–23; *CMH5*, 185) from *The Vocalist* (1865). Because tune books and hymn books were frequently found in Canadian homes, the harmonic style had a strong impact on listeners. Most collections published before 1840 have characteristics associated with the first New England School, but introductions to later collections denounce the florid settings of such publications and recommend that congregations sing plain four-part settings.

There must always be, in Congregational singing, a harsh, 'jangling' confusion of sound, so long as the air is sung indiscriminately, by men, women, and children, – a few, indeed, imagining that they sing the Bass, when they are only growling out the air in a gruff under-tone. We would urgently say to all – Take the trouble to study the parts proper to your voice. Then, and not till then, there will be pleasing harmony. Let the voice come from the chest, – not from the nose or throat. Let not the plaintive air be rattled, nor the cheerful tune drawled, and adhere strictly to your own part; sing it as it is written – without any grace notes or ornamental flourishes whatever. (*The Presbyterian Psalmody*, Montreal, 1851; quoted in *CMH5*, xi)

In response to such criticisms, compilers moved toward homophonic and homorhythmic settings based on the harmonic conventions of the major-minor key system. Florid singing was reserved for the more highly trained singers in the choir who sang motets and anthems. Antoine Dessane's setting of *Panis angelicus* (*HACM*–16; *CMH2*, 65–74), written for the Benediction of the Blessed Sacrament is a case in point, with a homophonic choral texture, fugal entries, and an independent organ accompaniment. J.P Clarke's anthem *Trisagion* (*HACM*–24; *CMH2*, 161–3) includes solo and florid sections supported by a constant organ accompaniment. As Clifford Ford points out: "In the Catholic churches of Quebec, composers gave much of the musical interest to the accompaniment – usually the organ – and wrote few a cappella settings. This is possibly due to a low priority placed on the cultivation of church choral singing and the dominance of the organ in church musical life there. Outside Catholic Quebec the situation is often reversed where the organ is relegated to accompaniment while the choir takes the central role" (CMH20, xi). This contrast in accompaniment can be readily seen in two Christmas pieces: J.P. Clarke's *A Canadian Christmas Carol* (HACM–25; CMH5, 152), composed in 1853 and published in *Anglo-American Magazine*, has a simple accompaniment and a brief introduction based on the first line of the tune. The *Kyrie* from J.J. Perrault's *Messe de Noël* (HACM–26; CMH20, 12–15), completed in 1860, is based on two popular carols and has a much more complex organ part: the Kyrie eleison uses the tune *Silence ciel* in a fugal manner; the Christe section is a homophonic setting of the tune *Venez divin Messie*.

KEYBOARD MUSIC

The increasing availability of keyboard instruments created a greater demand for organ and piano music. Frederick Glackemeyer's *Marche* (HACM–5; CMH4a, 13–5), composed in 1807, is classical in style and was probably intended as an organ solo for a special service in Quebec City. J.C. Brauneis II's[24] piano solo *Marche de la St-Jean Baptiste* (HACM–28; CMH1, 29–31) is a patriotic piece honouring the St-Jean de Baptiste Society founded in 1834. Most keyboard music of this period, however, was either intended for dancing or inspired by dance idioms (see Appendix E), and dance music was also played for personal enjoyment. Women were expected to be accomplished musicians, but society frowned on their professional involvement, so women composers often published their work under pseudonyms. The earliest available published composition by a Canadian woman is the *Canada Union Waltz*[25] (HACM–27; CMH1, 15–17); the "Canadian Lady" who wrote it may be Josephte Desbarats Sheppard, an accomplished musician of Quebec City who had other works published subsequently in New York (Lefebvre 1991, 30). A.H. Lockett's *Centenary or Fancy Fair Polka and Galop* (HACM–29; CMH1, 18–19) is an example of European dances modified into elegant couple dances during the 1830s.[26] G.W. Strathy's *Magic Bell Polka* (HACM–30; CMH1, 47–9) was published by Nordheimer in 1852.[27] Folk tunes also found their way into dance music. Dessane used five folk songs in his piano composition *Quadrille canadien* (HACM–31; CMH1, 94–8).[28]

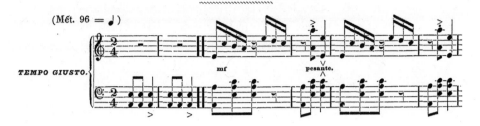

STADACONÉ.

DANSE SAUVAGE POUR PIANO.

(Mét. 96 = ♩)

TEMPO GIUSTO.

Figure 5.7   The opening of the original edition of *Stadaconé* by Ernest Gagnon, published in Montreal in 1858 by John Lovell.

Ernest Gagnon's[29] well-known collection *Chansons populaires du Canada* contains more than 100 folk tunes that he transcribed from oral renditions. In addition to his work with French folk traditions Gagnon also took a sincere interest in the music of First Nations. His *Stadaconé: danse sauvage pour piano* (see figure 5.7) (*HACM*–32; *CMH1*, 105–10) is named for an Iroquois village at the present site of Quebec City.[30] In a letter to Thomas-Étienne Hamel written in 1864, Gagnon comments: "In *Stadaconé* I have incorporated certain stylistic aspects of native music. These included melodic and rhythmic repetition, open fifths, and marked accentuation patterns" (quoted in Smith 1989, 36). Gagnon apparently made a band arrangement of *Stadaconé* that was performed in 1862 by the Regiment of Quebec. According to Beaurival the "Indians were suitably impressed by the performance, and they ... recognized familiar elements of their own music in Gagnon's composition" (quoted in Smith 1989, 37). Gagnon's *Stadaconé* is a good example of the rubbaboo theory, and it may be the first North American example of purposely merging elements of First Nations music with notated music apart from earlier sacred efforts.

A CANADIAN HERITAGE

During this period musicians in Canada were composing in a number of genres. Few orchestral and chamber works have yet been found,[31] but judging by the music that has survived, these compositions were not merely pale imitations of music produced in Europe; Canadian composers were beginning to express their own heritage, looking to Canadian landscape for titles and texts of song, and incorporating a variety of traditional musics in their own creations. Much of the repertoire produced by Canadian composers can bear comparison with similar works produced in Europe. One reason for this is that knowledgeable settlers chose to make Canada their home, and these musicians laid a foundation on which future developments could grow.

6 Forging a Nation with Music: 1867–1918

On 1 July 1867 New Brunswick, Nova Scotia and Canada united to become the Dominion of Canada, a result of initiatives begun at Charlottetown in September 1864. One of the main forces in forming a nation was to improve economic conditions through massive public expenditure on railways that would link sparsely populated areas and open up rich terrain for agricultural and timber development, and the Intercolonial Railway clause of the Constitution Act played a crucial role in Canada's development. The "last spike" of the all-Canadian route, built by the Canadian Pacific Railway Company, was driven on 7 November 1885. This railway had a profound effect on the settlement of the Canadian west and the development of cities such as Winnipeg and Vancouver. While there were many issues for this new country to address, it was recognized that some amenities for cultural expressions were needed, and gradually buildings for theatrical events began to appear. Documentation concerning musical activity for communities across Canada exists in printed sources, but much detailed research is still waiting to be done.

The Music Clubs

During the post-Confederation period music clubs provided an important forum for Canadians to hear and create music and to learn about a wider range of musical expression. In many cases these clubs played a pivotal role in the development of younger musicians. Club programs usually consisted of a talk given by a member or a visitor on a composer or a group of composers with musical illustrations. For example, in 1884, the students' music club at the Collège Sainte-Cécile at Joliette, Quebec,

Ottawa in the 1870s

Writing in 1871, Charles Roger described changes in Ottawa, which at that time had a population of 21,000: "Ottawa is, we repeat, making rapid progress, covering a space of three miles in length and about as many in breadth but having no good place of amusement – no theatre, nor any proper Music Hall" (1871, 52–3, 88). Her Majesty's Theatre, completed in 1856, was dilapidated. The Rink (also called the Ottawa Music Hall) was used for music, skating, and dances, but the collapse of temporary galleries in 1876 ended its use for concerts. In 1869, the Gowan family opened a small hall on Sparks Street (Keillor 1988, 123) and in 1874 enlarged it to a capacity of 1,500. Gowan's Opera House, seating more than 1,000, with stage carpentry and scenic painting by the staff of Booth's Theatre, New York, opened on 1 February 1875 with a performance of Balfe's *The Bohemian Girl*. That same year, New Edinburgh opened a Music Hall. Two years later, the *Institut canadien français* erected a 1,200 seat theatre on York Street.

Musical events sponsored by churches, patriotic societies, or the *Institut canadien français* often involved a parade followed by a concert consisting of band selections, piano, vocal, and instrumental solos, and the occasional duet or glee. Signor Raineri conducted the 60th Regiment Band, and J.C. Bonner organized the Ottawa Brigade Garrison Artillery, The Governor General's Foot Guards Band, also organized by Bonner, performed for functions at Rideau Hall and elsewhere in the city. Their repertoire included operatic selections such as the overture to Verdi's opera *Nabucco* plus the usual mixture of marches and dance tunes. Bands sponsored by associations, companies, and church organizations usually gave programs consisting of marches, hymn tunes, quick steps, waltzes, and quadrilles, interspersed with the occasional song or instrumental solo (Keillor 1988, 122–3). The *Canadian Ten-Cent Ball-Room Companion and Guide to Dancing* (1871) specified how to set up a dance evening and recommended a band of piano, cornet, violin, and cello (7). An 1871 advertisement for J. Gowan's quadrille band (organized in 1857) claims that their eighteen to twenty performers are "all capable of rendering their parts in first class style in any new piece of music at sight" (Keillor 1988, 120).

Band members, both military and civilian, often supplemented the orchestras of travelling companies that presented variety shows and sometimes operas and operettas. In the late 1860s the Bateman and the Holman opera troupes performed Balfe's *The Bohemian Girl* (1843), and in July 1869 The Holman English Opera Company gave Offenbach's *La grande duchesse de Gerolstein* (1867) and *La belle Hélène* (1864), Balfe's *Statanella* (1858) and *The Enchantress* (1845). On 20–21 June 1871, the Grand English Opera Company presented Flotow's *Martha* (1847) and Auber's *Fra Diavolo* (1830). The latter work and Donizetti's *Lucrezia Borgia* (1833) were presented by the Italian Opera Troupe on 15–16 July 1872. Probably none of these were complete performances, since a reviewer described the presentation of Lecocq's

La fille de Madame Angot (1872) by Grau's Grand Opera on 26 October 1874 as the first full opera given in Ottawa. The Holman Company returned to Ottawa to open Gowan's Opera House in 1875 with performances of The Bohemian Girl, Bellini's La Sonnambula (1831), Auber's Fra Diavolo, Offenbach's La Grande Duchesse and Lischen und Fritschen, Rossini's Cinderella (1817), and Donizetti's L'Elisir d'Amore (1832). The first performance of Gilbert and Sullivan's HMS Pinafore in Ottawa, given by the Martinez English Opera Company of Boston on 20 January 1879, was swiftly followed by a local production in April and productions by two other touring companies during the same year.

W. Warren's vocal and instrumental classes of classical music, begun in 1872, became the Musical Union in 1879 (132). The Ottawa Choral Society, formed in 1865, became the Ottawa Philharmonic Society in 1870. In 1875 the Ottawa Choral Union, a chorus of 120 and a small orchestra performed selections from Haydn's Creation, but the conductor, who had not been paid his full fee, left in 1876. A new choral society was organized in 1878. Canadian artists included Ottawa in their itineraries. In 1871, a reviewer commented that a concert given by Elena Waters, with violinist Frantz Jehin-Prume and his wife, mezzo-soprano Rosita del Vecchio, "drew the fullest house of any concert this season" (129). Jehin-Prume returned to Ottawa with Calixa Lavallée on 21 September 1875, and with Guillaume Couture on 6 March 1876. In 1879, shortly after completing three years of study at the Paris Conservatoire, Alfred De Sève appeared in Ottawa to an enthusiastic reception (Keillor 1988, 130).

The Mendelssohn Quintette Club of Boston (founded 1849; Ryan 1899/1996, 20) made annual visits to Ottawa, and was occasionally joined by local performers; in 1874 E.J. Butler of the Ottawa Ladies' College joined them to play Haydn's Piano Trio in G major. The following year a reviewer described their performance of the "Bridal Procession" from Wagner's Lohengrin as "very fresh and bold" (Keillor 1988, 129). Like most Europeans, Canadians became familiar with standard orchestral literature through arrangements. When the Beethoven Quintette Club of Boston came to Ottawa in 1875 they were asked to include the Andante and Allegro from Beethoven's Symphony no. 7 in the program. A few months earlier the Boston Philharmonic Club played the Overture to Rossini's Tancredi along with Mozart's Piano Quartet in G minor.

heard a lecture on Beethoven given by Edmond Dubé (Locat 1994, 57). The article on music clubs in the second edition of the *Encyclopedia of Music in Canada* lists sixteen women's musical clubs across Canada: twelve of these were founded in the two decades following 1889, the year that the Duet Club of Hamilton was formed, and ten of the sixteen are still active today. On Thursday 25 November 1909, the Yorkton Amateur Musical Association presented a varied program of songs, chamber music, and choral and orchestral pieces.[1] The sixty-five members of this group held rehearsals every Wednesday in the Town Hall. In 1914, the Halifax Ladies' Musical Club (founded 1905) devoted all of its activities to a study of German music. Medicine Hat, Alberta, a community of around 6000 in 1914, supported the Saturday Musical Club whose object was "to promote an appreciation of good music, to help one another and be helped by taking an active part in the work of the club and to promote good fellowship" (Keillor 1997, 61). Members, both men and women, met every second Saturday afternoon, and were fined if not present! This club also devoted several of its 1914 meetings to German composers, along with musical illustrations by Mr. Stride's Orchestra and other members of the Club. Sometimes recordings were played on a Victrola. As with many of the women's music clubs, the Medicine Hat group began to sponsor concerts by touring artists; for example, in 1918 pianist Leopold Godowsky presented a program that included works by Schubert. By 1900 there were eight women's musical clubs in Toronto, a number of which provided their members with opportunities to perform and to broaden their musical knowledge. In many cases, as in Medicine Hat, these societies also began to sponsor solo and chamber music recitals by professional musicians (Elliott 2001, 1209).[2] Occasionally music club programs included compositions by Canadian composers such as Calixa Lavallée, W.O. Forsyth, Gena Branscombe, and Clarence Lucas.

Emma Albani

Emma Albani (1847–1930, née Lajeunesse) from Chambly, Quebec was probably the best known nineteenth-century Canadian artist, with huge successes in Europe and Britain. After reports of her triumphs abroad, Canadians finally had a chance to hear her on 13 February 1883 (Vachon 2000, 33) when she appeared with the renowned Adelina Patti and Her Majesty's Opera Company in a performance of *Lucia di Lammermoor* at the Grand Opera House in Toronto. A month later, she was in Montreal for a concert with her ensemble: singers Jessie Dickerson, Signor Caravatti, and Signor Mierzwinski, flautists Signor Ciampi-Cella and Signor

A. Carreno, pianist Mme Carreno.[3] Albani made subsequent Canadian appearances in 1889 and 1890, when she was performing with the Metropolitan Opera in New York. In 1892 she brought her operatic troupe to Montreal for performances of *Les Huguenots* by Massenet and Wagner's *Lohengrin*. She appeared at major centres in Canada usually with several other soloists, such as violinist Frantz Jehin-Prume, and in 1896 she made her first trans-continental tour from Halifax to Victoria with Canadians mobbing her train at each stop. Similar tours followed in 1901, 1903, and 1906. Albani is said to have composed a twenty-five-page grand duo at the age of eight and later a sonata. Unfortunately, of her entire output, only one sacred vocal work has been located.

Music in the Schools

The rise of music clubs was due in part to increased opportunities for music education in the last three decades of the nineteenth century, and the clubs in turn helped to improve standards of music teaching. In order to perform, amateur musicians needed access to music teachers, published music, and instruments. Earlier in the century, all of these might have been provided by the same person, but gradually more specialization began to appear as some teachers concentrated on one or two areas of instruction while others operated music stores for the sale of publications and/or instruments. Singing schools still played a role in training people to read basic music notation. Music was taught in some private schools, particularly those for girls; for example, by 1834 schools operated by several orders of sisters in Quebec included piano and vocal instruction in the curriculum (Green and Vogan 1991, 5). However the quality of music education in schools usually depended on the initiative of individual teachers such as Henry Frost, who taught in a small school in York County (now in Ontario) between 1835 and 1850 and prepared a set of twelve manuals covering the rudiments of music notation through to three- and four-part songs (Green and Vogan 1991, 47).

Egerton Ryerson's Common School Act (1846) included vocal music in the list of required subjects (Green and Vogan 1991, 50), and since it was to be taught by non-specialist teachers, music training was provided in the normal schools. Initially Ryerson selected the Wilhem-Hullah method using a fixed doh (Green and Vogan 1991, 51–2) and Henry Sefton (music master at the Toronto Normal School from 1858 to 1882) prepared *Three-Part Songs* (1869) and *A Manual of Vocal Music* (1871) to adapt this method for Canadian schools. When Ryerson retired in 1876 vocal music ranked ahead of most optional subjects, but "art surpassed music in 1880;

drill surpassed it in 1889, and temperance and hygiene in 1909. As an optional subject, it was dependent upon the whim of board, principal and teacher" (Green and Vogan 1991, 62). John Curwen's Tonic Sol-fa method[4] was brought to Canada by British immigrants. There are records of its use as early as 1865 for singing classes in Victoria, and it appeared in some Ontario centres around 1869. From then until the early 1900s periodic debates arose as to which of the two systems was better. Alexander Cringan, a proponent of the Tonic Sol-fa system, came to Toronto in 1886; he was soon appointed music director for the city schools, and from 1901 to 1931 was music director at the Toronto Normal School. Cringan prepared a number of manuals using the Tonic Sol-fa system, usually combined with the music staff, and in 1913 he established a music summer-school program to upgrade teachers and train music supervisors. Throughout Ontario, however, music education was still largely a token gesture provided only at the elementary level. In Halifax Jacob Norton was appointed music instructor for the school system in 1867, but this position was abolished in the early 1880s due to financial constraints, and was not reinstated until 1919. Norton and W.O. Perkins, however, did publish a school music text entitled *The Dominion Songster* (1870). The first community to appoint a music teacher in New Brunswick was Moncton in 1905, and occasional postings gradually appeared in other centres. In Prince Edward Island and Newfoundland, some music instruction was offered by the church schools; the Methodist church favoured vocal music, while the Roman Catholic schools often encouraged orchestras or bands.

In British Columbia some Anglican churches – and after 1898 the Salvation Army – organized brass bands that performed for church services and community entertainments. Music was taught in the schools operated by the Sisters of St Ann, and in New Westminster, after 1865, they offered piano instruction. In British Columbia, John Jessop, who had attended the Toronto Normal School and admired Ryerson, was appointed the superintendent of education in 1872; in his annual report he wrote: "A knowledge of vocal music is of more practical value than mathematics" (Green and Vogan 1991, 95). However the reality, as in Ontario, was that only about a quarter, or at most half of the students actually received music instruction. In Winnipeg, music instruction in the schools began in 1890. Classes were based on *The King Edward Music Readers*, a series of school music books prepared by Laurence H.J. Minchin, the Winnipeg music supervisor, for schools in western Canada that were eventually adopted in Manitoba, Saskatchewan, Alberta, and British Columbia. Unlike Ontario, where music was limited to elementary schools, music appears in 1892 as a subject in the "Programme of Studies" for high schools in Manitoba (Green and Vogan 1991, 84). This aim was not generally carried out, but where expertise and leadership were available, glee clubs and choirs were organized, usually as extra-curricular activities at the secondary level. In Brandon, Superintendent White recommended that the schools be closed so school children could attend a concert given by the St Paul's Symphony in 1911 (Green and Vogan 1991, 86); and in British Columbia, by 1914 the Victoria High School had an orchestra.

Canadian Conservatories

Most families who wanted a music education for their children had to turn to the wide variety of private music teachers; some had high credentials while others were of dubious quality.[5] Some teachers who were serious about their profession concentrated on a single instrument or on voice. By the 1870s, one result of this specialization was that teachers began to band together to form studios offering instruction in several instruments; occasionally such studios were entitled conservatories. The nineteenth-century concept of a conservatory was largely based on the Paris Conservatoire, and a number of Canadian musicians who had studied there dreamed of establishing a similar institution across the Atlantic.[6] In 1868 musicians in Quebec City, including Ernest Gagnon, founded the Académie de musique de Québec (AMQ) with the aim of raising the level of teaching by administering examinations and granting diplomas in all of the areas of music study. While the provincial government contributed token funding in the first few years, the AMQ has remained an independent institution. Elsewhere in Canada an increasing demand for music instruction led to the formation of private conservatories along the lines of the Leipzig Conservatory of Music, where a number of Canadian musicians had studied.[7] Former students of British institutions such as Trinity College, the Royal Academy of Music, the Royal College of Music, and the Guildhall School of Music also established private institutions based on British structures.

A number of American institutions, including the New England Conservatory of Music, the Oberlin Conservatory of Music, and the Peabody Institute were established during the 1860s.[8] The American institutions placed much emphasis on educating the musical community at large through lectures and recitals that were open to the public. From these various European, British, and American influences, Canadian institutions for musical studies evolved in communities where there were groups of teachers.[9] The availability of competent teachers made it possible for more Canadians to consider a career as a professional musician.

Kathleen Parlow

Kathleen Parlow (1890–1963), who was born in Calgary, received her music training in the United States and in Europe. First she moved to San Francisco to study with Henry Holmes, a pupil of Spohr. After successful performances as a prodigy in England, she was offered several scholarships, (including one with Ysaye in Brussels), but finally chose to study with Leopold Auer at the St Petersburg Conservatory, where she enrolled in 1906. Parlow was the first foreigner to be admitted to the Russian conservatory system (Parlow 1961, 13–4). After an outstanding international career as a soloist, she returned to Canada where, for the last three decades of her life, she made a significant contribution as soloist, chamber musician, and teacher. If she had been born a few years later, she would have been able to study in Canada with Elaine Dudley Smith, who came to Calgary in 1907. Smith was also active in Calgary's first symphony orchestra and for many years conducted her own string orchestra (Dempsey 1994, 102).

The first Canadian institution to offer instruction in a wide range of instruments, voice, and music theory was the Toronto Conservatory of Music (TCM), which opened in 1886 with a staff of some fifty teachers in fifteen different disciplines; by the end of the first quarter there were 283 students (Jones 1989, 82), and by 1887 professional training was available for foreign languages, public school music, piano tuning, and hygiene. From the beginning the TCM offered a combination of class and private instruction, so that the cost of studies depended on individual students' choices of teachers, courses, and type of instruction. Following the practise of some American music institutions, in 1888 the TCM affiliated with the University of Trinity College so that work by advanced students could be recognized at the university level. In its early years the TCM also established syllabi of required repertoire and initiated a graded examination system.[10] The TCM was initially headed by Edward Fisher (1848–1913), and over the years featured many fine teachers on its roster, including Humfrey Anger, who developed an outstanding theory program after his appointment in 1892. In 1947, when a royal charter was granted in recognition of its wide influence, the TCM became the Royal Conservatory of Music (RCM). This institution has had an immense impact on musical development in Canada, and is presently the largest national integrated conservatory in the world.[11] A number of other similar organizations arose in Toronto prior to 1918. The Toronto College of Music (1888–1918), founded by F.H. Torrington (1837–1917), laid an emphasis on organ and orchestral instruments; by 1890, it had 400 students, a faculty of fifty teachers, and an affiliation with the University of Toronto. The Metropolitan College (later School) of Music began in 1893; two years later, with W. O. Forsyth (1859–1937) as its director, it offered instruction in piano, violin, voice, teacher training, musical kindergarten, and theoretical subjects. In 1912 it was absorbed by the Canadian Academy of Music (1911–24). Another important multi-teacher school was the Hambourg Conservatory of Music (1911–51), which became an influential meeting place for musicians, visual artists, and writers.[12] These institutions provided a systematic environment for music education and they also encouraged chamber music and orchestral playing through sponsorship and organization of groups. For example, the members of the Toronto String Quartette taught at the city's music institutions (Logan 1913b, 142).[13]

The feud that developed in the late 1890s over a national examination system indicated a developing sense of Canadian nationalism. By 1879, Trinity College in England had established an external examination system; the Royal Academy and Royal College of Music followed suit in 1881 and 1889 respectively. To prevent duplication, the Royal Schools of Music in Britain set up an Associated Board which, from 1895 on, provided examinations outside of Britain. However, when the Associated Board offered to set up a nation-wide examination system in Canada, leading members of several Toronto institutions united against this intrusion.[14] One result was the formation of the Associated Musicians of Ontario, which opposed the introduction of British examinations into Canada. At its preliminary meeting on 23 February 1899, this body unanimously voted in favour of "practical examinations in music under the auspices of the University of Toronto," and in a draft to the Senate of the University in January 1900, stated that:

It has been estimated that there are 75,000 students of music in the province of Ontario. Every village and even the remotest township contains a greater or lesser number of persons engaged in music study ... The universal interest in the study of music throughout the province has been reached through the musical desires of the people themselves, and the guidance and indefatigable efforts of the teachers, musicians and music schools. No government or municipal assistance has been proffered or received beyond the teaching of sight singing in a rudimentary way in some localities; no university has offered inducements or degrees which have affected the study of practical music; no philanthropist has established facilities for its encouragement; no colleges of professional chairs have been endowed; no provincial music schools instituted; no national course of training for teachers; no provincial certificates. Yet in the absence of these stimulating aids no other of the arts has so flourished or become to such an extent the object of popular attention. (Jones 1989, 131)

Although the University did set up some practical examinations in 1901, the following year there was a decision to leave performance and theory examinations in the domain of the TCM, which had been operating them for fifteen years. Indeed, by 1898 the TCM had established examination centres in thirty cities and towns across Ontario and Manitoba (Jones 1989, 132).

Montreal also had several teaching institutions. The Dominion College of Music/Collège de musique Dominion (founded in 1894 and affiliated with Bishop's University in 1895; Gordon 1991) administered practical and theory examinations as well as a bachelor of music and later a doctorate, through to the 1940s in various centres across Canada and the United States, but its activities as a teaching institution ended in 1899.[15] A Conservatorium linked to McGill University was opened in 1904 with financial assistance from Lord Strathcona. Charles A.E. Harriss, the director of the McGill Conservatorium, had been largely responsible for providing a foothold in Canada for examinations of the Associated Board of the Royal Schools of Music. The Conservatorium laid out requirements of music degrees at the bachelor and doctoral levels. On a recommendation from Harriss that a full-time professor of music be appointed, this position in 1907 was given to Harry Crane Perrin, formerly the organist of Canterbury Cathedral in England. Perrin organized an examination system in fifty centres across the country, thus detaching the McGill system from the Associated Board, and he also set up McGill's first symphonic ensemble. The Conservatoire de musique de Montréal was formed in 1895 to fulfil the needs of Montreal's Francophone population; this institution provided free tuition, but was closed by the government in 1900 because its funds were raised through a lottery (Becker 1983, 21). The Conservatoire national de musique et de l'élocution, founded in 1905 by Alphonse Lavallée-Smith (1873–1912), granted diplomas in music, diction, elocution, drawing, and painting, but instruction only began after 1928. In 1951, it affiliated with the Université de Montréal.

Many other studios blossomed into conservatories, usually of short duration. Exceptions include the Mount Allison Conservatory (founded 1885 and now part of Mount Allison University), the Halifax Conservatory of Music (1887–1954), the London Conservatory of Music (1892–1922), the Hamilton Conservatory of Music (1897–1965), and the Mount Royal College Conservatory of Music and Speech Arts (established in Calgary in 1910). Some of these institutions set up examination systems that were influential within a limited geographic area.[16] Although the various examining bodies were in competition with one another, the establishment of guidelines concerning repertoire and editions and a systematic guide for instruction and evaluation proved invaluable for music teachers in private studios. Comments of the examiners provided much-needed direction and helped prominent musicians to grasp a more holistic view of the musical development across Canada; for example, in the course of a forty-day examining tour in 1909, J.W.F. Harrison of the TCM travelled over 6000 miles to examine in twenty Canadian communities!

Musical Instrument Manufacturing

The demand for musical education came about in part because people owned or had purchased musical instruments. The demand for musical instruments in turn led to further development not only of importation but also of manufacture. Since keyboard instruments had become a status symbol for the home, and everyone wanted one for the parlour, many new Canadian manufacturing firms built pianos and parlour organs.

The rise of keyboard instruments, however, was preceded by the manufacture of pipe organs, an important industry that has continued to the present day. In Montreal, Jean-Baptiste Jacotel established an organ business in 1821 that was carried on as Jacotel and Fay after 1832. There were a number of individual builders including Watson Duchemin in Charlottetown and Samuel Warren (1809–1882), an American who established himself as an organ builder in 1835 and by the 1860s had become Quebec's most prominent organ builder.[17] Joseph Casavant built his first organ around 1840, and his sons, who studied organ-building in France, established the world-renowned firm of Casavant Frères in 1879. To meet the demand for parlour instruments, many companies produced reed cabinet organs. The melodeon was a domestic-sized reed organ in which air is moved by suction produced by pumping the pedals alternately. These instruments were being produced in Canada by the late 1840s. The harmonium, usually a more complex reed organ with several stops for preset combinations of reeds, used the compression principle for its air movement. Both of these instruments were favoured because they were easier to keep in tune. Prior to 1918, some sixty companies were active at various times from Victoria (Bagnall & Co. 1863–85) to Nova Scotia (Acadia Organ Co. 1878–82).[18] By 1902 it was possible to purchase a pump organ through Eaton's catalogue, and thousands were subsequently sold at prices ranging from $29.50 to $76. The cabinet organ began to lose favour as a parlour instrument, however, because of the need to pump

Musical Instruments Move Westward

Many Canadians brought musical instruments with them as they moved farther west. The following account is from the diary of a member of the "Overlanders of '62," a group of 138 men from the Queenston and St Thomas area of Canada West who travelled by cart to the Cariboo gold fields in 1862:

After supper some went fishing, some shooting, while many others were amusing themselves playing on different kinds of Brass Instruments, claranetts (sic), fluits (sic), violins and a Concerteenia (sic), and some 2 or 3 groups were gathered together singing over a few favourite pieces of Vocal Music which wiled away the hours of the Evening till bed time as merrielly and pleasant as though we had been in some grand concert hall, of the first fashion of Modern times in a[n] Eastern City ... an association of musicians [was]... formed on the trail with a membership of 32 ... At Edmonton, the largest post in the area which is now Alberta and Saskatchewan, the musicians on July 25 gave a concert to a crowded house 'in the Musical Hall. (quoted in McCook 1958, 21)

In his memoirs, William Moberly, a member of the survey team for the new railway, described Christmas Day, 1871, and subsequent evenings in the camp at Eagle Pass in the Kootenays: "Several of the men were good musicians and singers and having brought with them a fiddle, a flute and an accordion, the long winter evenings were very enjoyably spent" (quoted in Graham 1945, 156). Travelling in the 1880s through what is now rural Saskatchewan, E. Roper was amazed to find young women who could not only milk cows but also sit down at the piano to play and sing very competently (Roper 1891, 30). Pianos were much more difficult to transport than smaller instruments but many women from England or eastern Canada would not consider settling in the Canadian West unless they could bring their keyboard instruments. As a child, Emily Carr was told about the first piano brought to British Columbia, probably around 1851, for the household of Edward E. Langford, a bailiff for the Puget Sound Company. After sailing around Cape Horn, the ship landed at Esquimault Harbour and the piano was carried along a rough bush trail from Esquimault to Langford (Smith 1958, 5). Louisa McDougall's parlour organ was transported by oxcart to Edmonton in 1879. A report from Birtle, Manitoba, published in the *Musical Courier* of 1888 provides a vivid picture of keyboard instruments in this Western community:

On his arrival here in 1882 your correspondent found only one miserable little melodeon and two pianos in the whole place. In 1883 our Methodist friends advanced a step and invested in a very fair reed organ; the English church people shortly after following suit. The same year witnessed a large increase in the town, not only of musical instruments, but of talent. In 1884 the Presbyterians, following the good example of the other churches, purchased a good reed organ. The town could then boast of seven organs and eight pianos. Towards the end of this year we organized the "Birtle Musical and Dramatic Club." From then till the spring of 1887 things went smoothly, new organs and fresh talent appearing every month or two. Early in the spring of 1887 the Presbyterians substituted a small but good "pipe organ" for the reed organ they had hitherto used. (quoted in Kallmann 1960, 167)

the bellows and because, compared with the piano, it lacked expressive variety.[19] Even though piano tuners were few and far between, pianos made their way into parlours, taverns, and other gathering places.

The 1851 Canadian census lists four individual piano builders or companies in Toronto, ten in Montreal and three in Quebec City. A number of organ companies moved into piano manufacturing, and many new piano companies were formed. There were some 240 different brand- and stencil-name pianos made in Canada between 1816 and the end of the twentieth century (Kelly 1991, 126). Many firms catered to local markets, and some existed for only a short period before they merged with stronger establishments, but while in existence each firm advertised the excellence of their particular products.[20] The Bell Piano and Organ Company of Guelph began making melodeons in 1864 and by the 1890s Bell instruments were to be found in the residences of Queen Victoria and the Sultan of Turkey as well as many homes in North America, Europe, and Australia. By 1902 – when the first Canadian branch of the Piano and Organ Workers Union was formed at the Bell plant – the company claimed to have produced 100,000 instruments. In 1934 Bell declared bankruptcy and its assets were acquired by Lesage Piano Ltée. of Ste Thérèse-de-Blainville, Quebec. W. Doherty & Company, a furniture and music store in Clinton, Ontario, manufactured its first organs in 1875. By 1900, they offered 74 models of organs, and around 1905 they began manufacturing pianos. By 1913, grand pianos were introduced and Doherty products were being shipped around the world. In 1920 the business was bought out by Sherlock-Manning Organ Company of London. Among the most highly regarded Canadian pianos ever produced are those of Heintzman & Company.[21] By 1888, Heintzman was building a thousand pianos a year, and in the 1900s the company established more than twenty retail centres selling pianos, other instruments, accessories, and music across Canada.[22] One of the companies taken over by Heintzman was the Nordheimer Piano & Music Company. When the Nordheimers opened their Toronto shop in 1844, they sold music books, square pianos, and sewing supplies. They began manufacturing their own pianos in 1886 and continued in business until they were bought out in 1927. The Mason & Risch Company of Toronto was in business from 1871 to 1972; from about 1914 into the 1950s they had a perennial contract for pianos with the T. Eaton Company. Lesage Pianos in Quebec was founded in 1891 when Lesage bought the Canadian Piano Company; during the 1930s they bought up the assets of a number of other companies, and they survived until 1986.[23] Around 1854, R.S. Williams opened a shop in Toronto where he sold imported square pianos as well as his own mandolins, banjos, guitars, violins, and later brass instruments. By 1888 he had taken over the Canada Organ and Piano Company in Oshawa and had moved his whole operation there. This expanded instrument factory operated until 1932.[24] The last surviving piano business in Canada, the Sherlock-Manning Piano Company, founded in Clinton, Ontario, in 1890, went out of business in 1988.

By the late nineteenth century new technology made it possible to transmit music. Recording devices developed by Edison became available in the late 1880s[25] and Canadians began to record music. By 1900 the E. Berliner company in Montreal was releasing commercial recordings (Moogk 1975). In November 1879 a telephone was first used to transmit a concert at St James' Hall in Ottawa to "a number of ladies and gentlemen in the offices of the Dominion Telegraph Company" (Keillor 1997, 63). For households that could not yet afford a Victrola, enterprising owners of Canadian telephone companies such as Robert Wightman provided concerts of recorded music for their subscribers on Sunday afternoons (Keillor 1997, 64). Another popular music-making device was the player piano (see figure 6.1).[26] Between 1906 and 1925 models were offered by almost every major piano manufacturer in Canada. An extension to the player piano was the nickelodeon, a device operated by paper rolls that, when a nickel was inserted, produced a variety of sounds including snare and bass drums, tambourines, whistles, xylophones, and banjo. Nickelodeons could be found in restaurants, ice-cream parlours, pool halls, and saloons. All of these new inventions allowed Canadians access to a wider range of music. While they may have reduced the number of performers, the size of audiences for live musical presentations increased.

Permanent Performing Organizations

Many of the performing organizations through this period were choral groups and bands. (See appendix F for a list of prominent choral groups.) While most choirs gave occasional performances of large-scale oratorios,

Figure 6.1   Advertisement for the Williams Piano Co., suggesting that Canadian businessmen should relax with one of their player pianos (*Canadian Magazine Advertiser*, October 1910, p. 43).

particularly *Messiah* and *The Creation*, some ventured into opera and operetta, and others, such as the Mendelssohn Choir of Montreal, concentrated on a cappella works. Performances of oratorios, cantatas, and even operettas (particularly the ever-popular Gilbert and Sullivan works), usually accompanied by piano and or organ, were given by church choirs at special events.

A concert presented by the Société des symphonistes de Montréal (founded by Guillaume Couture in 1878) on 4 March 1880 included Mozart's Overture to *Don Giovanni* and Beethoven's Symphony No. 1 and Violin Concerto. After he became conductor of the Montreal Philharmonic Society, Couture combined the two organizations to perform what was becoming standard repertoire for Canadian choral societies: Beethoven's *Christ on the Mount of Olives*, several of Handel's oratorios, Haydn's *Creation* and *The Seasons*, Mendelssohn's *Elijah* and *St Paul*, and Schumann's *Das Paradies und die Peri*. In 1895–6 the two organizations joined forces with the first Montreal Symphony Orchestra (founded in 1894), for concert performances of Wagner's *Flying Dutchman* and *Tannhäuser* – the first complete presentations of these works in Canada. Couture often imported Boston musicians (and on occasion the entire Boston Festival Orchestra) to provide the high standard of musicianship he wanted, a practise that was followed by conductors of other established organizations when pickup orchestras proved unreliable. For example, the Toronto Mendelssohn Choir gave performances with the Pittsburgh Symphony Orchestra under Victor Herbert (between 1902 to 1907), and with the Theodore Thomas (Chicago) Symphony Orchestra under Frederic Stock (between 1908 and 1912). For such visits, the choir gave two or three concerts; the "guest" orchestra included an orchestral number in the concerts and sometimes presented a complete symphonic program as well.[27]

These occasions provided opportunities to hear professional orchestras and gave a spur to efforts to form local orchestral organizations. Large-scale non-competitive choral festivals stimulated these efforts. In 1903 Charles A. E. Harris organized a "Cycle of Musical Festivals" in fifteen centres across the country (see appendix G). The event required two years of preparation – training existing choral organizations, forming new choruses, and learning repertoire – in each centre, and Festival concerts involved the Montreal Symphony Orchestra, the Chicago Symphony Orchestra, the Minneapolis Orchestra, and the Portland/Seattle Orchestra. On occasion, pick-up orchestras – made up of local band members and string players employed by choral organizations – in turn became the nucleus of a more permanent orchestral group. There were

The Victoria Philharmonic Society

By the late 1850s, for example, music was an essential element of daily life in Victoria. "There were voices and instruments: Mrs. Mouat, with the piano brought out with her from England; Mr. Augustus Pemberton, lately arrived from Ireland with his flute; Mr. B. W. Pearse, with his violin; I [Bishop Cridge] did what I could with my cello ... Christ Church had a barrel organ and three barrels ... Before long ... a keyboard was adapted to this instrument, and the organist played it at the morning and afternoon services" (quoted in Smith 1958, 7–8). A Victoria Philharmonic Society was formed in 1859 with forty members, each of whom paid five dollars for enrollment. The first concert, presented on 10 May 1859, took place in the upper storey of the Assembly Rooms, heated by wood stoves and lit only by candles, and was reviewed in the *Gazette*. Tickets for the three-hour program cost $2.50.

The concert opened with selections from Maria Padilla by the band of H.M.S. Tribune, followed by the National Anthem ... The anthem was not given with as full effect as some of the choruses later in the evening, when the amateur performers had gained greater confidence. Mr. Arthur T. Bushby then sang the "Village Blacksmith," with taste and good effect. A chorus of Rossini by the society, and a French romance by Mme. Ballagny followed, succeeded by the "Indian drum," fairly rendered by Messrs. Potter, L. Franklin and A. T. Bushby. A solo on the clarionet was then given by Master John Bayley, and enthusiastically encored. Mr. Crowley gave an aria of Verdi with good effect. This was followed by "Sabbath Morn," sung by eight voices very creditably. A French duet by Mme Ballagny [a French opera singer resident in Victoria] and Mr. Crowley was then given, when the first part concluded with the Prayer from Moses in Egypt – the most successfully rendered piece on the programme. Selections from Rigoletto by the band, opened the second part, followed by the ballad "Thou art gone from my gaze," so effectively rendered by Mme. Hotier as to call forth an encore. The Society then gave the "Phantom Chorus" from Sonnambula, followed by an aria from the same opera by Mr. S. Franklin, rendered with correctness and tasteful expression, but somewhat lacking in vigor. "Le Muletier de Toledo," was next sung by a young lady who, in her charming timidity unconsciously so accelerated the time of the piece as to call forth the display of quite unusual powers in articulation and prolongation of sound. The song was vociferously encored. The "Liberty duo" from Puritani was finely rendered by Messrs. Crowley and L. Franklin, and followed by "La Trompette de Marengo," in which Mme. Ballagny made up by piquant effects for some slight variations from the design of the composer. A solo on the violin succeeded .... Mr. Bushby then sang "Could you cast me aside," very sweetly and effectively ... The concert closed with "Spring's Delight," by eight voices. (Quoted in Smith 1958, 11)

Harry Walker

The fact that permanent orchestral organizations appeared first in the midst of the still sparsely populated Canadian mid-west was due in large part to the activities of individual musicians such as Harry Walker (1840–1911). Walker was appointed a bugler in the Red River Expedition of 1870. He played flute, piccolo, cornet, and concertina, among other instruments, and led a series of bands in the west, often writing original compositions or making arrangements for them (Lobaugh 1997, 80). In the early 1870s Walker led several bands in the Winnipeg area and at Fort Battleford, the major headquarters of the North West Mounted Police. When the police headquarters moved to Regina, Walker moved there with the band, and he also formed a dance orchestra consisting of flute, cornet, violin, and cello, with himself on the piano. By 1887 he was training a brass band in Qu'Appelle. The following year the Regina City Council persuaded him to return to the community of 1,000 as bandmaster for both a civilian band and the Mounted Police Band. There Walker produced a series of concerts, presenting selections from Verdi's operas, dances, marches, vocal solos, and his own compositions. His string orchestra was kept busy for dance engagements. All this continued until 1906 when he moved to Winnipeg (Lobaugh 1997, 88).

many such attempts across the country: in London, Ontario (population under 12,000) between 1875 and 1878, the London Musical Union performed two Haydn symphonies, Mozart's Overture to *Die Entführung*, and Beethoven's *Romanza in F*, op. 50 (Keillor 1997, 59); around 1895, Charlottetown had a fifteen-member orchestra conducted by Henry W. Vinnicombe; the present Regina Orchestra claims to be a direct descendent of the orchestra that first accompanied the Musical and Dramatic Society in 1898; and a small orchestra formed in Calgary in 1891 became the Calgary Symphony Orchestra of 1913.[28]

The program for the first concerts of the Société symphonique de Québec (SSQ) on 31 August and 1 September 1903 (under the direction of Joseph Vézina) included overtures by Mendelssohn, orchestral suites by Massenet, Gounod, Bizet, and Grieg, and settings of Canadian folksongs for choir and orchestra by Ernest Gagnon (Bernier 1977, 50–1). Earl Grey, Canada's Governor General from 1904 to 1911, inaugurated a competition for Canadian symphony orchestras,[29] and in 1907 the trophy and $780 was awarded to the SSQ for its performance of a program of works by Gounod (*Marche religiuse*), Ed Missa (*Scènes mexicaines*), Saint-Saëns (*Une nuit à Lisbonne* and *Danse macabre*), and Vézina (his new work *La brise*). Even in these early years, while the SSQ performed larger works, such as Mozart's *Jupiter Symphony* and the early Beethoven symphonies, there was a strong commitment to Canadian compositions. Supported by subscription campaigns and gifts, the SSQ managed to survive the difficult years of the First World War, and presented concerts each year, often including large-scale choral works with local choirs (*CMH16*, vi). Provincial funding of $200 annually from 1904 was raised to $400 in 1922. Although the competition initiated by Earl Grey was open to orchestras across Canada, those situated some distance from Ottawa could not afford to take part. This dilemma led to the formation of an Edmonton festival in 1908 with thirty participants. The Edmonton festival became an annual event and was quickly followed by similar endeavours in Regina (1909), Winnipeg (1918), Vancouver (1923), and Nanaimo (1928).

During the first two decades of the twentieth century, there were symphony orchestras operating in Halifax, Montreal, Ottawa, and Toronto. By 1885 the Haydn Quintette Club, augmented by bandsmen, was performing orchestral repertoire in Halifax. The Halifax Symphony Orchestra, conducted by Max Weil, flourished from 1897 to 1908,[30] and in 1901 presented a "Grand Wagner Concert." The orchestra formed by Donald Heins in 1905 at the Canadian Conservatory – eventually known as the Ottawa Symphony Orchestra – won the Earl Grey trophy three times, but folded in 1927 when Heins moved to Toronto. In 1906 Frank Welsman formed a Toronto Conservatory Symphony Orchestra with Bertha Drechsler Adamson as concertmaster; two years later, with the backing of several businessmen, this ensemble became the first Toronto Symphony Orchestra (TSO). Between 1908 and 1918 the TSO established a professional standard of performance and presented a broad, although somewhat conservative, repertoire.[31] Its demise in 1918 was caused by factors that particularly affected many Canadian musical organizations during the First World War: the loss of personnel due to war service, casualties, and too often, deaths; and the curtailment of travel for artists due to the war conditions.

Canadian Compositions 1867–1918

Canadian composers rarely had the opportunity to hear performances of their large-scale works unless they had a close association with an orchestra. The one exception to this was the SSQ, which frequently presented Canadian works. The increase in oratorios, and chamber works, and orchestral compositions written during this period is partly due to the number of Canadians who studied at foreign institutions such as the

Leipzig Conservatory,[32] the Paris Conservatoire, and the New England Conservatory. For example, extant manuscripts show that to fulfill composition requirements at the Leipzig Conservatory, W.O. Forsyth (1859–1937) wrote a short chamber work and also planned an orchestral Suite in E minor. It seems that only the *Romanza* (*CMH8*, 121) of this proposed suite was completed; it was premiered in Leipzig by the 134th Regiment Orchestra under Alfred Jahrow on 5 December 1888, and after Forsyth returned to Toronto, the work was performed by Torrington's Orchestra with the composer conducting. The first Canadian orchestral work to be performed in Europe, however, was likely a piece by Calixa Lavallée (1842–91). There are records of the performance of a "symphony" or "suite" during the time that Lavallée was a student at the Paris Conservatoire (1873–75), and the cover of the score of his *Ouverture: Patrie* (*HACM*–66; *CMH15*, 1–24) is annotated "Paris, 12 August 1874." The sectional form of this work is typical of suites written in Europe at that time.[33] In 1873 Guillaume Couture (1851–1915) left for France to study with Théodore Dubois at the Paris Conservatoire, and on 15 May 1875 his *Rêverie*, op. 2 (*CMH8*, 46–90),[34] was premiered by the Société nationale de musique under Édouard Colonne. Canadian orchestral works were rarely published, either in Canada or abroad, but Couture's *Rêverie* was published that same year by E. et A. Girod in Paris, and in 1899 *As You Like It Overture* by Clarence Lucas (1866–1947) was published in London.

CHORAL WORKS

A number of larger choral works were commissioned for particular occasions and there were good choirs available to perform such ambitious compositions. One example is a cantata written by Lavallée to a text by Napoléon Legendre in honour of the visit of Marquis de Lorne and Princess Louise to Quebec City. For the performance on 11 June 1879, Lavallée assembled nearly 300 musicians from four choirs and bands in Québec City and brought in string players from Montreal, Ottawa, and the United States to augment the orchestra (Barrière 1999, 28). According to an enthusiastic review, the musical climax involved a simultaneous presentation of *God Save the Queen, Vive la canadienne*, and *Comin' thro' the Rye*. Unfortunately, like many other works by Lavallée, a manuscript for this cantata has not yet been located. *Daniel before the King* (*HACM*–40; *CMH18*, 55–67), a dramatic sacred cantata by Charles A.E. Harriss, was first performed in Montreal on 19 April 1880 under the direction of Guillaume Couture. This multi-movement work includes solo recitatives and airs, and a variety of choral numbers including sections for double chorus.[35] In 1892 the Toronto Choral Society with orchestra and soloists performed the cantata *Gulnare, or The Crusader's Ransom* (*CMH18*, 8–27)[36] by Francesco D'Auria (1841–1913), an Italian-born conductor, voice teacher, and composer who was active successively in Toronto, Winnipeg, and Vancouver from the late 1880s. Clarence Lucas wrote in a wide range of genres, and like Couture, he had studied with Dubois at the Paris Conservatoire. His effective Christmas cantata *The Birth of Christ* (*CMH18*, 28–53)[37] was composed for the Apollo Club, Chicago, and first performed there in 1902.

Eva Rose York (1858–1938) was born in western Ontario and studied at Woodstock College and at the New England Conservatory of Music. She formed the Belleville Philharmonic Society, and on 11 January and 30 May 1887 this organization performed her oratorio *David and Jonathan*, probably the first oratorio written by a Canadian-born composer. The May concert also included one of her compositions for orchestra. Unfortunately no trace of her manuscripts has been found. By 1890 York was living in Toronto where she was editor of the *Musical Journal* and taught music, but little is known of her life after 1913. The first extant Canadian oratorio is *Caïn* (*CMH18*, 117–39), composed by Alexis Contant (1858–1918) and scored for five soloists, choir, and full orchestra.[38] This work was first performed on 12 November 1905 at the Monument national in Montreal. Contant was the first major composer to be entirely Canadian-trained. Largely self-taught, he studied for several months with Lavallée in Boston. Contant wrote a second oratorio entitled *Les deux âmes* (1909; *CMH18*, 141–55) and three masses with orchestra.

The First World War affected the careers of several Canadian composers. Guillaume Couture completed his largest work, a religious lyric poem in three parts entitled *Jean le précurseur* (*CMH18*, 156–225; *CMH15*, 25–55) in 1911, but due to the outbreak of war, the proposed 1914 premiere never took place; the work was finally performed in 1923.[39] Ernest MacMillan (1893–1973) completed *England, an Ode* (*CMH18*, 246–74) in a German prison camp where he was interned from 1915 to 1918 as an "enemy alien." The work, scored for two soloists, a chorus divided in four to ten parts, and orchestra, was written to fulfill part of the requirements for a D Mus degree from Oxford University. The premiere in England in 1921 was quickly followed by a performance with the Toronto Mendelssohn Choir. Aside from his obvious grasp of contrapuntal skills, the music shows that MacMillan was aware of contemporary currents in composition. The harmonies are often quite Wagnerian or dissonant, and some passages introduce augmented chords and whole-tone scales.

Canadian composers continued to create shorter sacred works including motets, anthems, and hymns. *The Canadian Anthem Book* (Toronto,

1873) contains, among other items *Blessed Be the Man that Provideth* (HACM−34; CMH2, 175−7), an impressive verse anthem by John McCaul (1807−86), then president of King's College (later University of Toronto). John Medley, a choirmaster at the Anglican Cathedral in Fredericton, composed at least thirty-six sacred choral pieces and a number of hymns (Cooper 1990, 35). Effective anthems, such as *This Is the Day* (1874; HACM−35; CMH2, 205−9), show his skill as a melodist and his use of melodic and rhythmic motives to unify the composition. Other examples of shorter choral works include the verse anthem *Lead, Kindly Light* (HACM−39; CMH9, 3−8) by Charles A.E. Harriss. Among Canadian hymns we find *Will He Not Come Back* (HACM−41; CMH5, 225) by J.M. Whyte, who wrote many similar hymns connected with the temperance movement, and *Soldats du Christ* (HACM−42; CMH5, 231) by L.E. Rivard, whose militant style is reminiscent of the well-known *Onward Christian Soldiers*. For the Roman Catholic liturgy Couture wrote the motet *Sub tuum* (1877; HACM−36; CMH9, 189−202); his sensitive, diatonic antiphonal style avoids theatrical aspects and is more reminiscent of Gregorian settings. Achille Fortier (1864−1939) composed the two-voice motet *O Salutaris hostia* (HACM−38; CMH9, 234−8) in 1895 as part of a mass with orchestral accompaniment that is otherwise not extant. Ernest Gagnon's *Venez, Divin Messie!* (HACM−37; CMH2, 103−5) is an example of the tradition of *cantique de missions* – religious songs based on well-known tunes written to attract Huguenots back to the Roman Catholic Church in the seventeenth century. These *cantiques* became popular among Roman Catholics and Gagnon's collection, published in 1897, could be viewed as an extension of his work with folk music. Some secular works written in this period also have a folklore basis. Examples include *La canadienne, chanson à repondre* (1916; CMH18, 5−6) by Léo Roy (1887−1970) and *An Indian Lullaby* (1906; CMH18, 210−13) by Augustus Vogt (1861−1926), composed for the women of the Toronto Mendelssohn Choir.

OPERETTA AND OPERA

In the 1860s we find the first evidence of operatic composition since Quesnel's productions. These include three operettas by Célestin Lavigueur (1830−85); Mr. Nelson's *The Haymakers* (1869), which was performed twice in Toronto; and *La conversion d'un pêcheur de la Nouvelle-Écosse* (1884; CMH10, vi) an "opérette canadienne" by Jean-Baptiste Labelle (1828−98) about the merits and drawbacks of Confederation. Clarence Lucas wrote five operas – *Semiramis* (Sidthorpe Wells, 1884), *Arabia* (1886), *Anne Hathaway* (Monk Lewis, 1887), *Puff & Co.* (J. Bengough,

1889), and *The Money Spider* (1897) – but his greatest success was with his musical, *Peggy Machree* (1904). Calixa Lavallée wrote three light operas: *TIQ – The Indian Question Settled at Last*, (1865–66), *Lou-Lou* (1872, now lost), and *The Widow* (1880). *TIQ*[40] is the first Canadian operetta based on a plot concerning First Nations issues, and Lavallée made an attempt to incorporate genuine musical characteristics of the Sioux Nation. *The Widow* (*HACM*–44; *CMH10*, 55–87)[41] was composed in the same year that Lavallée wrote *O Canada* for the St Jean-Baptiste celebrations, just before his third and final departure for the United States. During Lord Dufferin's tenure as Governor General, F.A. Dixon (1843–1919) wrote several librettos and children's plays for Rideau Hall; his librettos include *The Maire of St Brieux* (1875; *CMH10*, 11–5), an opera by Frederick W. Mills, and *Pipandor* (1884), a three-act comic opera by Susie Frances Harrison (1859–1935), and *Canada's Welcome: A Masque* (1879; *CMH10*, 17–26) by Arthur A. Clappé (1850–1920).[42]

The growing popularity of Gilbert and Sullivan operettas encouraged Canadians to create their own parodies or original works. Among the parodies were *Bunthorne Abroad; or, the Lass that Loved a Pirate* (Toronto, 1883) by J.W. Bengough, and a "musical and dramatic burlesque" of the Riel uprising *The 90th on Active Service or, Campaigning in the North West* (Winnipeg, 1885) by George Broughall, who adapted tunes by Arthur Sullivan, and Stephen Foster. Broughall also produced *The Tearful and Tragical Tale of the Tricky Troubadour; or, The Truant Tracked* (1886), an adaptation of Verdi's *Il Trovatore* (*CMH10*, vii). William Henry Fuller, who emigrated to Canada around 1870, wrote *HMS Parliament, or, The Lady Who Loved a Government Clerk* (1879), a brilliant parody of *HMS Pinafore* (using Sullivan's music) based on current Canadian politics; the production opened in Montreal and eventually toured to thirty towns and cities from Winnipeg to Halifax.[43] The most frequently performed unique work was the "entirely new and original Canadian military opera" *Leo, the Royal Cadet* (*HACM*–45; *CMH10*, 88–110)[44] by Oscar F. Telgmann (1855–1946) with a libretto by George F. Cameron. The situation and characters are drawn from the Royal Military College of Canada in Kingston and the plot traces Leo's career at the College, with affectionate spoofs on local characters such as the College's professors of German and French, and at the end, Leo returns a hero from the Zulu War of 1879 to his true love Nellie (see figure 6.2).

Those living in towns or cities with an "opera house" had occasional opportunities to see grand opera. Throughout this period, touring companies gave performances of staple works by Rossini, Verdi, Gounod, Massenet, and even Wagner.[45] With relatively frequent performances

Figure 6.2   Cast of a performance of *Leo, the Royal Cadet*, Grand Opera House, Kingston, Ontario. Queen's University Archives, PG-K 149-3 C.1.

of major operas, it is not surprising that some Canadian composers also tried their hand at through-composed theatrical works. Charles A. E. Harriss composed the two-act *Torquil* (1896; *HACM*−46; *CMH10*, 111–40), a "Scandinavian dramatic legend" as a concert work without action or scenery. Performances with soloists, chorus and orchestra conducted by the composer took place in Toronto, Ottawa, and Montreal in 1900 as a benefit for a patriotic fund to aid Canadian soldiers in the Boer War (*CMH10*, xiii). Approximately half of the twenty-three numbers are set as choral episodes representing Scandinavians, Christian monks, Icelanders, and priests of Odin. Harriss uses a wide range of styles, and his effective chromaticism is obviously influenced by Wagner. "The Happy Birds," an air sung by Maida, a Christian woman held in captivity, has non-harmonic tones and altered chords in the accompaniment.

Joseph Vézina wrote three operettas: *Le Lauréat* (1906), *Le Rajah* (1910), and *Le Fétiche* (1912). The libretto for *Le Fétiche* (*HACM*−68; *CMH10*, 180–202), written by Alex Villandry and Louis Fleur, is based on a serious indigenous theme: the early eighteenth-century conflict between the Iroquois and the French settlers in the Lake Champlain area. With his long experience as a band master and symphonic conductor, it is not surprising that Vézina's orchestration is colourful and imaginative. The accompaniment of "J'ai pour maison," an air sung by the trapper Pérusse, mimics the gliding movement of snowshoes. The opéra-comique *Gisèle* (ca. 1911) by Alphonse Lavallée-Smith (1873–1912) also has a Canadian story. The action takes place in a Quebec village in 1911, and the plot concerns the Montreal Opera Company. Gisèle is in love with Albert Leroux, an opera singer, but both realize that he must leave Canada in order to further his career. While Leroux is away, Gisèle's grandfather tries to make her marry another man but Gisèle is determined to wait. Leroux finally returns with the news that he can remain in Canada because a new opera company has been formed in Montreal (*CMH10*, xvi). Like Vézina's operettas, this work was enthusiastically received at its premiere in 1924.

ART SONG

Although *I am waiting for thee* (1867; *HACM*–52; *CMH3*, 154–6), by Edwin Gledhill (1830–1919), with text by Edward B. Shuttleworth, is much like a parlour song, composers such as W.O. Forsyth and Clarence Lucas were familiar with the tradition of German *Lied* and the French *mélodie*. This heritage can be heard in *Serenade* (1905; *CMH14*, 79–80) by Gena Branscombe (1881–1977), the text of which is the first verse of a poem by Robert Browning. The rhythmic treatment of the words is imaginative and distinctive, and the ending, where the voice rises to the dominant of F major while the pianist plays the closing notes, is effective. Canadian composers of art songs continued to hone their skills in making the piano accompanist a true partner with the voice in setting the mood and conveying the text. E. Blain de St Aubin (1832–83), who moved to Canada in 1857 and was active in Québec City and Ottawa, used his own text (including some amusing Quebec colloquialisms) for *Vir' de bond mon ami Pierre* (1882; *HACM*–59; *CMH7*, 120–1). Ernest Lavigne (1851–1909) set *Novembre* (1882; *HACM*–60; *CMH7*, 188–1) to a text by the Canadian poet Faucher de Saint-Maurice. Calixa Lavallée's *Andalouse* (1886; *HACM*–63; *CMH7*, 144–53) is a favourite coloratura concert song with a Spanish flavour in the bolero idiom. In his own day Achille Fortier (1864–1939) was compared favourably with Fauré. *Mon bouquet* (1892; *HACM*–65; *CMH12*, 81–5), a setting of the sonnet by Canadian poet Louis Fréchette, uses an irregular metre (5/4) and its sophisticated harmonies are reminiscent of Duparc. In *Le Souvenir* (1907; *HACM*–82; *CMH7*, 177–81), Guillaume Couture sets the four stanzas of Lionel Nastorg's poem in a continuous and variational manner.

CHAMBER MUSIC

The balance between voice and piano to be found in art songs is similar to good chamber music writing. Repertoire from this period includes not only works for instruments such as violin or cello with piano, but also innovative piano trios. This trend may be partially due to a true distinction between orchestral pieces and works intended for smaller performing forces that developed toward the end of the nineteenth century.[46] Edward B. Manning (1874–1948)[47] was born in Saint John (according to his marriage certificate) and played the second violin in the Mozart String Quartette of Saint John, New Brunswick. His Piano Trio (early 1900s?; *HACM*–90; *CMH11a*, 1–50) is an effective three-movement work with striking themes and well-chosen late-Romantic harmonies. The particularly effective string writing is probably due to his own intimate knowledge of the instruments. Like the composers of the Second New England School (Amy Beach, George W. Chadwick, Frederick Converse, Arthur Foote, Edward Macdowell, and John Knowles Paine), Manning was strongly influenced by Brahms as a model of musical style.[48] Alexis Contant's Piano Trio (1907; *CMH11a*, 51–101) was premiered in an all-Contant concert given at the Monument national in Montreal on 12 November 1907. The three movements are in different keys, and there is much modulation within each movement. The texture of the first movement is particularly striking; all the main melodies are played by the strings until the recapitulation, where the piano finally bursts forth *fortissimo* with the opening theme. The final movement is linked rhythmically to the jig tradition of Quebec folk music.

KEYBOARD MUSIC

Much of the keyboard music created by Canadian composers in this period – such as dances and marches – is purely functional, but there are a number of short character pieces, the majority written in a conservative but competent idiom based on European models. Prior to 1950, the Canadian keyboard composition best-known internationally was Lavallée's study *Le papillon* (1874?; *HACM*–49; *CMH1*, 212–9), which was selected by the Paris Conservatoire as required repertoire, and was subsequently published by thirty different firms. Branching out beyond short descriptive pieces, some composers tried their hand at classic structures such as the fugue. The earliest extant piano sonata is likely a four-movement work by Byron C. Tapley of Saint John (published 1909; *CMH6*, 105–17). While Tapley's approach suggests that he had little if any exposure to sonatas by Mozart or Beethoven, it does show his awareness of the form. Healey Willan (1880–1968) came to Canada in 1913 to replace Humfrey Anger at the Toronto Conservatory of Music. His *Introduction, Passacaglia and Fugue* (1916; *HACM*–113; *CMH4a*, 97–120) was composed for the Casavant organ at St Paul's Anglican Church. The arresting, dramatic, and chromatic fantasia-like introduction is followed by a passacaglia built on a ground bass of eight bars. Eighteen contrasting variations unfold over this recurring line using various contrapuntal techniques, distinct rhythmic motives, dynamic gradations, and metrical changes in the tradition of J.S. Bach, Max Reger, and Joseph Rheinberger. The closing fugue is created from a subject based on the first half of the passacaglia theme.[49]

MODERN INFLUENCES

A few piano pieces composed before 1920 reveal a hint of modern harmonies and techniques. Debussy's piano music was beginning to be heard in Canada, particularly through recitals being given by Mrs. Walter Coulthard in Vancouver and by Léo-Pol Morin of Montreal. This influence can perhaps be seen in the shifting metres and final pentatonic scale of W.O. Forsyth's *Prelude* (*CMH6*, 50–52). In *Tintamarre* (published in 1911; *HACM*–87; *CMH6*, 58–62) Humfrey Anger (1862–1913) uses parallel streams of tone clusters to express the idea of the French word for "din." This work also predates several works usually cited for the first use of several consecutive seconds on the keyboard.[50] In Montreal Alfred La Liberté (1882–1952), who had studied in Berlin, headed a small avant-garde group of musicians. La Liberté was a close friend of Scriabin and had some of the composer's manuscripts in his possession. Presumably it was these that Rodolphe Mathieu (1890–1962) studied thoroughly before composing his *Trois préludes* (1912–15 for piano, later transcribed for orchestra; *HACM*–118, 119; *CMH6*, 190–5; *CMH8*, 199–214). *Prélude no 1, Sur un nom,* the first "legitimate" atonal Canadian work, is based on an opening gesture of four pitches with a tritone in the centre. Like Scriabin, Mathieu avoids piled-up thirds, instead building chordal aggregations of biting sevenths or ninths. *Prélude no 2* (1914) is indebted harmonically to Wagner and features *ostinato* figures reminiscent of those found in Debussy's piano music. The pointillistic texture of the orchestral verison of *Prélude no 3, Une muse* (1915) is seemingly metreless; upper woodwinds alternate in short, agile gestures while the strings provide a background cloud of sound. These modernistic compositions reveal that some Canadian composers were responding to the changing circumstances of the twentieth century and adapting their musical expressions accordingly. At the same time they periodically linked their compositional process to the landscape realities of Canada and drew on the mixtures of musical traditions to be found within the country.

Popular Music in the Nineteenth-Century Scene

Prior to 1800 there are passing references in Western musical history to a specific type of music preferred by a large segment of the population but it was only during the nineteenth century that a genre of popular music clearly emerged. Timothy Rice has pointed out that artificial divisions arising in Europe were linked to nationalist strategies of the day (Rice 2000, 2). Nevertheless, the concept of a refined music enjoyed by the cultivated, literate, or monied classes – as opposed to folk music used by the rural peasant class and popular music used by the urban working middle class – had ramifications in North America. In the United States a division between "highbrow" and "lowbrow" began to develop (see chapter 1); lowbrow – or popular – music is characterized by short duration, use of familiar materials, and immediate accessibility to large audiences. This music – usually used for dancing, entertainment, or as background sound – might be seen as taking over the role played by ritual, and ritual musics survive in the form of group participation in hymns or carols, nationalistic, political, or militaristic anthems, and marches, or songs for colleges or sports teams. Much of this music circulated in oral form as well as printed notation; the popular music genre developed from an intermingling of elements from diverse sources.

As noted earlier, Canadian bands modelled on their British counterparts played folk song arrangements, marches, dances of the day, hymn tunes, overtures, and operatic arias. The British brass band movement had a working-class base, and although class distinctions were not as rigid in Canada (particularly after the uprisings of the 1830s), the band and amateur choral movements that emerged from the singing school tradition can be seen as a means to encourage lower classes to develop aesthetic norms of bourgeois society. In European cities of the early 1800s "popular" concerts (a development of the "pleasure garden" tradition) included dance music and selections from symphonic and operatic literature. In earlier years, such performances might have been held in coffee houses or taverns that had a music licence, but around 1850 two new venues – the dance hall and the music hall – emerged in Britain; modified forms of both were adopted in Canada. The earliest music halls (ca. 1825) provided food and convivial singing entertainment led by the owner for working-class audiences. By the 1850s British music halls had a platform at one end and the entertainment included professional acts.[1] Audiences of several hundred sat at tables, were served drinks, and occasionally participated in the entertainment by singing the choruses of songs and engaging in verbal interplay. As entertainment became the main *raison d'être*, platforms developed into real stages with a proscenium arch and the music halls became variety theatres.

European music publishing grew by leaps and bounds in the nineteenth century. As more people became familiar with well-known "hits" by composers such as Haydn, Mozart, Beethoven, Schubert, and Mendelssohn, acquired pianos or parlour organs, publishers ran short of material within the modest capabilities of their clientele. This gap was soon filled by composers writing within the prevailing norms at a more simplified level. Publishers soon discovered that one of the best ways to popularize these new pieces, modeled on folk, street, or comic songs, drawing-room ballads, instrumental dances and salon pieces, was to have recent publications performed by artists in the variety theatre circuit perform, announcing "being sung by "..." on covers of subsequent editions. Popular "amateur" music from both Britain and the United States made its way to Canada. Obviously not everyone who sang or played Foster's *Old Folks at Home*[2] could read musical notation or had even seen the sheet music. This song, and many others like it, quickly became part of an oral repertoire akin to folk music.

Canadian Folk Songs of the Nineteenth Century

THE FRENCH HERITAGE

In the nineteenth century, *À la claire fontaine* was sung in French-speaking homes by young and old, boatmen sang it on the rivers, and in the 1860s sled drivers in the far north sang it to their dogs. Changes in the text reflecting everyday experiences of Canadian settlers likely began to appear in folk songs as early as the 1700s, and many folk songs originating in the nineteenth century also reflect new economic and political realities. *Vive la canadienne* – set to the tune of *Par derriér' chez mon père*, an earlier folk song in the *laisse* tradition – may be one of the earliest folk songs with an all-Canadian text.[3] *Un canadien errant*, another Canadian song from the early nineteenth century, is still popular today. Antoine Gérin-Lajoie wrote the poem in 1842 when he was a college student at Nicolet. The text, structured as a *laisse* and set to the tune of *Par derrière chez sa tante*, describes a rebel in the uprisings of 1839 and his subsequent banishment from Canada, a topic many could relate to. The song soon became well known and was published in the *Charivari canadien* in 1844. *L'engagé de Bytown*,[4] another French folk song known from Acadia to francophone Ontario, describes the situation of a young couple when the man signs up to serve in the military. Other French folk songs that have both tune and words of Canadian origin include *Mon canot, Les canayens sont la!* and *Vie penible des cageux*.[5]

THE LUMBER CAMPS

Edward Ives has argued that the new folk-song tradition centred in the lumber camps is distinct from other working song traditions (such as sea shanties sung by sailors) and local traditions (largely sustained by women singing "old-fashioned" songs while spinning, sewing, cooking, or looking after children). These lumber camps held up to eighty men who signed up to work in the woods from October through to March. The men did not create songs for their work, but on Saturday nights, after six days of hard work, they relaxed with card games, reading, conversation, singing, and step-dancing, and in some camps each man was required to contribute to the entertainment. According to Angus Enman of Spring Hill, PEI:

Saturday night, you see, when you'd come into the camp after supper you had to tell a story or sing or dance. If you didn't, they'd ding you; they'd put the dried codfish to you ... They had these old dried codfish and two or three would throw you down and whale you with it ... Hit you! Hard! Yeah. You take one of them old Cape Bretoners, great big old Scotchmen; or them Dutchmen, one of them big buggers from River Herbert, Nova Scotia ... If you couldn't sing, you could tell a good story [or] perhaps you could dance. Oh, yes, somebody he'd go round: "Now boy, come on. Do what you're going to do." (quoted in Ives 1977, 19)

Songs created by loggers circulated from camp to camp, and also passed into local traditions. Numerous examples of Canadian folk songs connected with the lumber industry can be found in collections such as Béland 1982, Fowke 1970, and Ives 1989. *Les raftsmen* (see figure 7.1) orig-

Figure 7.1 *Les raftsmen*, as sung by Jon Bartlett and Rika Ruebsaat.

Là ous-qu'y sont, tous les raftsmen? (bis)
Dans les chantiers y sont montés

Chorus:
Bing sur la ring! Bang sur la rang!
Laissez passer les raftsmen,
Bing sur la ring! Bing bang!

Et par Bytown y sont passés,
Avec leurs provisions achetées.

En canots d'écorc' sont montés,
Et du plaisir y s'sont donné.

Des "porc-et-beans" ils ont mangé
Pour les estomacs restaurer.

Dans les chantiers sont arrivés
Des manches de hache ont fabriqué.

Que l'Outaouais fut étonné,
Tant faisant d'bruit leur hach' trempée.

Quand le chantier fut terminé
Chacun chez eux sont retourné.

Leur femmes ou blondes ont embrassé,
Tous très contents de se retrouver.

inated in a lumber camp in the Ottawa Valley some time before 1867. Anglicized expressions in the text reflect the usage of both English and French in the camps. It is likely that the creator of *Les raftsmen*, unaware of the poetical rules of the *laisse*, used a structure he was familiar with through the many folk songs he knew.[6]

Among lumbering songs in English are *Hogan's Lake* – which describes the daily routine in a lumber camp and refers to Daniel McLachlin (died 1872), an Ottawa Valley lumber baron – and *How We Got Up to the Woods Last Year*. Both songs use previously existing tunes, a common practise in the lumber camps. The tunes of lumber camp songs came from older folk songs, dance tunes, hymn tunes, or current popular songs music halls or variety theatres; a few tunes are original.[7] The texts are arranged in four-line strophes with a rhyme scheme.[8] As with earlier broadsides, the narrator put emphasis on his participation in the story and songs often relate a recent tragedy. *Peter Emberley* created by John Calhoun, tells of the death of a young fellow worker from Prince Edward Island who was fatally injured in the lumber woods near Boiestown, close to the Miramichi River. The text is written as if Emberley is singing his death lament, and Calhoun borrowed a couple of fourteen-syllable lines from the ballad *Mary Hamilton* ("Little did my mother know ..."). Calhoun asked Abraham Moon [Munn?] to put a tune to his text; the melody is an old Irish ballad with a typical A B B'A' form. *Peter Emberley* has become one of the most popular Miramichi folk songs.

Many of these new songs sung in the lumber camps filled the function of a newspaper; details checked against contemporary accounts are usually accurate, even after several generations of oral transmission. For example, *The Wreck of the Asia*[9] relates the tragic loss of a Canadian ship and the lives of more than 200 passengers and crew in Georgian Bay on 14 September 1882, and includes information about the location, time, and individuals on board. The song was sold on the streets of Orillia, Ontario, and circulated in lumber camps.

OTHER CANADIAN FOLK SONGS IN ENGLISH

The Poor Little Girls of Ontario is unusual in that it gives a woman's point of view on the changing conditions as men headed first to Northern Ontario and then to Western Canada in search of better employment in the 1880s. The song became extremely popular throughout much of Canada, as women created different versions referring to their own local situations, and in some cases, attached a different tune to the text.[10] One of the major differences in both subject and quantity noted in comparisons of English-language folk songs created in Canada and the United States is the general lack of interest in murder ballads on the Canadian side. *John R. Birchall* is almost unique in the Canadian canon of folk song. The story recalls a famous Ontario case in which Birchall was tried for murder in 1890 and sentenced to be hung. He maintained his innocence up to his execution, at Woodstock, Ontario, but meanwhile wrote his story for the Toronto *Mail* and the New York *Herald Tribune* to raise money for his wife.[11]

It is not surprising to find macaronic folk songs (that have words from two different languages) in Canada (see Posen 1992). The use of English words in a French song was noted above in *Les Raftsmen*, and the song *I Went to Market* uses both languages almost equally. Gaelic words also appear in English songs; for example *Young MacDonald* has a Gaelic chorus, and Fowke suggests that the song is based on a waulking or milling song (Fowke 1973, 206). Acadians often made their own French ver-

Chanson de Louis Riel

Louis Riel (1844–85) is remembered as a great leader in the struggle of the Métis people for their rights against the influx of settlers first in the Red River Settlement and later in what became Saskatchewan, and to this day, Métis often drink a toast before singing *Le chanson de Louis Riel*. This song is also known as *L'adieu de Riel* and *La lettre de sang* (N-20 vol. 2 of Conrad Laforte's catalogue). Philip Thomas (1993; 1995) published extensive textual analyses of some thirty versions, and concluded that the folk song attributed to Louis Riel is a variant of a song known in Eastern Canada as *La lettre de sang, La chanson du guerrier, Chanson du régiment, La vie la plus esclave, Sur le champ de bataille,* or *Sur un champ de bataille*. He further suggests that Riel may have learned this song in Quebec in the early 1860s (Thomas 1993, 18). The textual elements that Thomas found in most versions include the location on the battlefield, the lack of pen or ink, the narrator cutting himself to use blood as ink, writing a letter in blood, his mother's receipt of the letter, and her urging the family to pray for their brother. In Western Canadian versions the text is in Michif French (a mixture of Cree and French). All the tunes associated with these texts belong to the same family, with a jig-like 6/8 metre and a gentle rising and undulating melodic contour peaking just past the mid-point; most versions are hexatonic.

The Western Canadian versions, however, reveal the blending of several cultures to form a "rubbaboo." Métis people were involved in the fur trade and came in close contact with Scots in charge of trading posts. It is common to find highland bagpipes, a fiddle, and a Native drum played together at Métis gatherings (see the video *Métis Summer*). Versions of *Chanson de Louis Riel* sung by Joseph Gaspard Jeannotte and other Métis have a strathspey rhythm (dotted eighth–sixteenth) or its reverse (the Scotch snap). Singers who accompany

Figure 7.2 *La Lettre de sang* as sung by Mme Albert Leblanc, Rogerville, New Brunswick.

Figure 7.3 *Chanson de Riel* as sung by Mme François McKay, St-Eustache, Manitoba.

themselves on a fiddle often add extra beats to the 6/8 bars in a fashion noted in Métis fiddling (Lederman 1987, 12–3).

The overall structure of the Western Canadian versions also shows Indigenous characteristics. In Acadian and Quebec versions, the text consists of eight-line strophes with the tune sung straight through on each repetition (see figure 7.2). Métis versions begin with a two-line strophe, then shift to four-line strophes. The opening melody of the two-line section appears irregularly and is usually varied (see the incomplete repetition form in figure 7.3).

Research into the predominant structure of traditional songs of the Plains Indigenous peoples in the nineteenth century reveals a gradual change to what is now often referred to as incomplete repetition (Keillor 1998, 26). This melodic structure opens with a phrase (A) followed by a new phrase or several phrases (B) which may be repeated with variants; A only recurs if there is a full rendition. If Riel was responsible for the song now known as *Chanson de Riel*, his return from Eastern Canada in the 1860s might have coincided with the development of this new incomplete repetition form.

Figure 7.4   Four men with musical instruments (mandolin, fiddle, accordion, guitar) and a child on a sailboat, Talbot Lake, southwest of Hinton, Alberta, 1914. Glenbow Archives, Calgary, NA-471-1.

sions of English songs; *Où vas-tu, mon petit garçon* is a French variant of Child no. 3, *The False Knight upon the Road*. Other Acadian songs include First Nations words, as in *Le vieux sauvage* (Fowke 1976, 73).

SONGS IN WESTERN CANADA

Riel's second rebellion was put down quickly because the government sent out troops on the new railway being built to the west coast. The railway – an important symbol, particularly for Western Canada – often appears in Canadian folk songs. *Drill Ye Tarriers, Drill*, sung to the tune of a music hall song, describes the building of the CPR. A song known as the *C.P.R. Line* appeared in many publications (including the *Family Herald*). *C.P.R. Line* uses the tune of *Rock Island Line*, and was in turn modified for *The Grand Hotel*, a Western Canadian lumbering song about loggers on a spree at Vancouver's Grand hotel (Thomas 1979, 123). Canadian government advertisements lured many settlers to travel west by train. *Life in a Prairie Shack* (set to the tune of *Life on the Ocean Wave*) is a vivid description of the drawbacks of the sod huts they built as their first protection from the elements.

In 1896 many loggers joined transients from all over the world in the Yukon Territory, dreaming of instant wealth, and singing the folk song *Klondike!* The chorus mentions Moodyville, a sawmill community close to north Vancouver, and references to a "five-pound note" and "quid" indicate that the author of the words may have been British. By 1898 Dawson, a town at the mouth of the Klondike River created by the Gold Rush was the largest community north of Seattle and west of Winnipeg, with a population of 30,000, telephones, electricity, and a flourishing entertainment industry of saloons, dance halls, and variety theatres. A French folk song *Le Klondike* describes the lure of the gold fields and the mirage of quick wealth; the final verse warns listeners to stick to their books, learn to speak English, then find wealth up north (Payant 1998, 121).

FOLK SONG TRANSCRIPTIONS

Some folk songs became popular not only through oral transmission but also through publication. While song texts were often published in newspapers and magazines, the nineteenth century saw the beginning of transcription and publication of vocal and instrumental folk materials. Little research has been done in this area but the example of John Burke in Newfoundland provides a good example. Burke apparently started by transcribing songs from the oral tradition, occasionally reworking them for publication. Then he began to publish his own songs, inspired by local events, as broadsides. His *The Kelligrew's Soiree* (1904) has become a folk song in its own right (Taft 1990, 58), and is included in *Old-Time Songs of Newfoundland*, first published by Gerald S. Doyle in 1927.[12] Carrie Grover's *A Heritage of Songs* (1973) illustrates the range of orally-transmitted vocal material in her own Nova Scotian home. Her collection includes Child and broadside ballads, sea shantys, lumbering songs, hymns, Black songs (some religious in nature), songs from popular entertainments such as minstrel shows and vaudeville, plus published songs from the nineteenth century. As a fiddler, Grover also carried on oral instrumental traditions.

Fiddling in the Nineteenth Century

Fiddlers' repertoire continued to grow as new dances were introduced. Along with the development of French Canadian, Scottish, Irish, and Métis styles were many individual traits within each tradition and regional variations. This individuality was supported by circumstances of isolation and self-teaching. Many of the old tunes continued to be used or transformed while new tunes were learned and created. Many of the

Figure 7.5 The opening bars and the chorus of *Peek-a-boo* by William J. Scanlan

new tunes added to the fiddling repertoire came from popular songs of the day. The tune *Peek-a-boo* (see figure 7.5) by the American songwriter William J. Scanlan (1856–89) was played by fiddlers from the Ottawa Valley area to the West Coast and possibly beyond, and the Canadian Musical Library edition was immensely popular. Fiddlers play the chorus of this song, a waltz in 3/4 metre; the verse portion, is in 4/4.

In Quebec pre-nineteenth century tunes such as *La bastringue* or *La danse du barbier* were still heard along with *La grande gigue simple;* here a *gigue* (or jig) referred to a tune in binary rhythm – often a reel used for solo step dancing– rather than in 6/8 as in other areas of Canada. In the nineteenth century, reels, marches, and galops became more prevalent while many hornpipe, strathspey, and bourrée tunes gradually declined. The waltz did not enter traditional Québécois repertoire until the early twentieth century; older twentieth-century fiddlers (for example, Louis Boudreault from Chicoutimi) never played waltzes (Bouchard 1997, n.p.). Québécois dance practises also had an impact on the tunes. Since the Québécois did not particularly follow musical phrases but danced on the beat regardless of the phrase length, it is not unusual to find tunes that do not fall into regular sixteen-beat phrases, and the absence of callers in many regions allowed these irregular structures to develop (Bouchard 1997, n.p.). Even French Canadian fiddlers who regularize phrases still put a strong accent on the first beat and usually emphasize all the strong beats to create the characteristic Québécois swing. By the mid-nineteenth century the button diatonic accordion was becoming popular and many fiddle tunes were adapted for that instrument.

Unique traditions in Newfoundland continued into the latter part of the twentieth century. Individual strains of the tune were referred to as the first "turn" and second "turn." As in Quebec, the length varied considerably and turns might or might not be repeated. Although English and Irish influences are generally considered the strongest, Newfoundland fiddling terminology differs from that used in Ireland and elsewhere in Canada: a single jig is a 2/4 tune with the accent on the down beat; a classic jig is the 6/8 version; and double or Irish jig tunes have quarter–eighth divisions (Osborne 2002, 66).[13] The tunes and the way a fiddler plays them are influenced by dance traditions. In addition to solo step dancing, Colin Quigley has identified a number of traditional group dance forms. Square dances are local variations of the plain quadrille, and the lancers quadrille is widely known; both emphasize facing-couple figures. The reel, cotillion, or old eight is an alternation of standard changes with a distinctive figure that is similar to the running set (where each couple leads a set by dancing one of several figures with each of the other couples in turn), but has a clockwise circular movement leading to the left (Quigley 1995).

Métis and Native fiddling continued to develop through the nineteenth century. Regional differences depended largely on the strength of French Canadian or Scottish roots in a particular area, and these influences were mixed with Native elements in dance forms. For quadrillles, a circular (rather than a square) formation was used. The Rabbit Dance is a popular variant of an English longways dance; for the chase in this dance, Mishler has identified the lady as a rabbit and the man as a lynx (1993, 82), and the tune he transcribes – used by the G'wichin and identified as *Chase the Squirrel* – has similarities to *The Jacket Trimmed in Blue*, played by Métis fiddler Mel Bedard (Dorion-Paquin 2002, 115).

New Cultures on the Canadian Scene

Some of the Italians who settled in Canada through the 1800s were musicians. For example, Charles Augustus Sippi became manager of the Nordheimer Music Company; his brother George was a violinist, organist, music teacher, and composer. Most Italians loved to sing, and played plucked instruments such as guitars and mandolins. *A Storm on the Lake* (1884), a programmatic piano piece by William Horatio Clarke (*CMH1*, 237), describes a group of Italian musicians on board the yacht "Oriole" in the Toronto harbour singing a barcarolle and playing a delicate accompaniment. Italians sang both operatic arias and a wide range of oral folk music: hundreds of traditional and street ballads, lullabies, work songs, serenades, religious songs, funeral lamentations, nursery rhymes, and riddles have been recorded from Italian-Canadians, but research on this rich tradition has only recently begun (Del Giudice 1994).[14]

The thousands of Mennonites who left Ukraine to settle in Manitoba spoke Low German and held strong religious beliefs, including an opposition to military service. They brought a rich tradition of choral singing that has continued to the present day. Wesley Berg observes: "The music of the church consists of Lutheran chorales contained in a hymnal reprinted in the style of the first German hymnal prepared for the Mennonites of Polish Prussia in 1767, sung to melodies transmitted in an oral tradition going back to the late eighteenth century. The melodies are melismatic ... and rhythmically amorphous as a result of several centuries of oral transmission and are led by a group of song leaders singing in a slow, stentorian vocal style" (2001b, 1238). Mennonites also brought a rich tradition of secular song: of lullabies, singing-circle games, street and village songs, and ballads (Klassen 1989).

A group of Ukrainian immigrants settled in a colony at Edna, in block settlements where local cultural-educational associations supported a retention of language, song, and dance (Cherwick 2001, 1241). They contributed different melodic contours, pitch organizations, and instruments to Canada's mix of musical cultures: two of their string instruments – the *cymbaly* (hammered dulcimer) and the *bandura* (a plucked instrument with about thirty strings) are unique to their culture. As Bloom points out, unlike their counterparts who remained in Russia, Ukrainians in Canada have retained the older types of instruments and the traditional Kharkov style of *bandura* playing (Bloom 1982, 27). George Lyon has noted that the Ukrainian *bubon* (a frame drum) is played in a manner somewhat similar to that of the Irish *bodhran* and First Peoples' hand drums; the *bubon* adds a specific rhythmic layer, analogous to that found in some First Nations musical traditions (Lyon 1999, 38). Such similarities aided acculturations that subsequently developed as musicians from different cultures in Western Canada performed together.

A group of Doukhobors settled first on the prairies, but in 1905, moved to southern British Columbia where they established a new self-contained community. Their rich tradition of vocal music is based in the Russian language (see Peacock 1970). Sacred music consists of psalms (*psalmi*) and hymns (*stikhi*), while secular music includes traditional songs (*pesni*) (Mealing 2001, 1268). Doukhobors refer to their rich repertoire of orally-transmitted psalms and hymns as the Living Book. In *We've Concluded Our Assembly* (Peacock 1970, 105–10) – a song often sung to close a *sobranya* (assembly)[15] – a soloist leads off and is joined by groups of men and women, each singing in several parts. There may be as many as six different vocal lines in this homorhythmic choral texture: one group sings the original psalm in octaves, while the rest improvise lines often at intervals of a third, a fourth and a fifth from the melody – a practise that retains elements of medieval European styles that now survive only in Canada (see figure 7.6) According to some informants, *We've Concluded Our Assembly* was created on the Canadian prairies ca. 1930, and the melodic contour may have been influenced by a non-Russian hymn style, possibly an interdenominational hymn sung in the Canadian prairies both as a secular folk song and in church services. *A Mosquito Wanted to Marry a Fly* (Peacock 170, 132–3) is a typical example of the Doukhobor two-part, largely homorhythmic secular song tradition. The lower voice sings the main melody and the upper voice sings a counter melody; the main melody begins at a high point, descends and gradually returns to the starting pitch, a pattern opposite to the Western European profile found in Canadian folk songs with English or French texts.

Figure 7.6   A Doukhobor choir of the Lundbreck-Cowley area in a sobranya ceremony, with salt and a loaf of bread on the centre table. Photograph by Kenneth Peacock at Lundbreck, Alberta. Canadian Museum of Civilization K64-58.

The last half of the nineteenth century saw the immigration of large numbers of Chinese men, brought over initially as miners and in the 1880s for railway construction. In spite of hardships and legal barriers, the Chinese community grew; families established laundries and restaurants and held on to their traditions – including music – as best they could. Photographic evidence attests to the presence of Chinese orchestra and opera performances by the 1890s (Diamond 2001g, 1095); by the early 1900s two theatres in Vancouver's Chinatown, in large part supported by the Yip Sang family, presented Chinese opera. Existing documentation from the 1890s indicates that instruments indigenous to China found their way to Canada. In the mid 20th century, even in centres where the Chinese community was relatively small, ensembles of *erhu* (bowed fiddle), *bianqing* (stone chimes), *dizi* (side-blown flute), *xiao* (end-blown flute), *pipa* (plucked lute), *qin* (board zither), and *ban* (clappers) were fairly common and likely had been for decades.[16] Chinese oral repertoire includes vocal and instrumental court music, which probably dates back a thousand years or more, Buddhist chanting, and folk songs from many parts of China. Although Chinese musical traditions include much variety, melodic contours have a strong descending tendency, and

Figure 7.7 *Echoing Mountain, Whispering Bird*, an *erhu* solo as performed by W.F. Kwan and transcribed by Mai-yu Chan.

Figure 7.8 *Picking Tea*, a mountain Hakka folk song from central China, as transcribed by Mai-yu Chan. English translation: "The sun rises, big and round; birds sing across the sky; bring your baskets up to the north mountain when the dew on the grass is still wet. Walking steadily we approach the tea plantations, and meeting our neighbours and co-workers we nod and exchange greetings."

melodies are frequently based on a pentatonic scale as can be seen in the transcriptions of two melodies recorded in Canada (see figures 7.7 and 7.8). Chinese communities in Canada have formed opera companies to present several types of operas, and have formed choirs that sing multi-part settings of folk songs. Instrumental traditions have also been preserved.

Published Popular Music

In the early days of settlement, music publications found in homes were usually collections of hymn tunes, but with the advent of the railway, a wider variety of "popular" sheet music and books found its way into communities across the Canadian West. Many were instrumental dances, such as the waltz and the two-beat polka; the first examples of these dances published in Canada appeared in 1846. Western Canadians may well have enjoyed *The Nor' West Mounted Police Waltzes* (CMH22, 30), written by Sergeant George B. Crozier (1814–92), a bandmaster and music teacher who came to Belleville, Ontario, in 1871 as organist at St Andrew's Church and music director of Albert College. Sheet music available for purchase in Canada included an ever-increasing variety of songs from European, American, and (after 1840) Canadian publishers. Charles Hamm has described this song literature as "people's music" based on a "musical vocabulary understood by everyone" that would "reach the broadest public" (1983, 233). Some were modeled on English strophic songs, with a refrain line ending each verse, a sentimental text, and often a dedication to a young woman (234). Others were modelled on Irish songs (such as Thomas Moore's *Irish Melodies*), with texts about nostalgia for lost youth and happiness (235). Musical influences include the pentatonic melodies of Irish songs and folk songs and elements of Italian opera, such as graceful melodic lines, expressive appoggiaturas, and arpeggiated accompaniments. Some Canadian songs seem to be structurally modelled on Stephen Foster's "plantation songs,"[17] with solo verses and a chorus in three- or four-part harmony. The tune of Foster's *O Susanna* was used for a song by Blacks escaping to Canada.[18]

Another prevalent influence in Canadian song writing is a march-like idiom of nationalistic songs. Alexander Muir's *The Maple Leaf For Ever* (HACM–53; CMH3, 83–4)[19] has solo verses of eight line strophes (alternating seven and eight syllables) and a rhyme scheme of *abcbefgf*; the chorus is in three-part harmony (two tenors and bass). In response to a movement to establish lacrosse as the national game of Canada in the 1870s, Henry F. Sefton[20] arranged an "old English melody" for *Lacrosse,*

Canadian Sheet Music

Most of the approximately 25,000 pieces of sheet music published for or in Canada between 1849 and 1950 can be classified as popular. George Washington Johnson (1839–1917) wrote the text of *When You and I Were Young, Maggie* in honour of his wife who had died a year after their marriage, and published it in his collection *Maple Leaves* (Hamilton, Upper Canada, 1864). James Austin Butterfield (1837–91), an English emigrant, was so moved by the poem that he set it to music, and self-published it in Indianapolis in 1866. The song had a second surge of popularity in 1922 with a version titled *When You and I Were Young Maggie Blues*. One of about eighty songs by Robert S. Ambrose (1824–1908), an organist and music teacher in Kingston and Hamilton, is a setting of *One Sweetly Solemn Thought* (HACM–55; CMH3, 110–2), a sacred poem by American poet Phoebe Carey (1824–71). The song was published by Nordheimer in 1876 and went through many editions as its popularity soared. Both of these songs have regular four-bar phrases, a hallmark of "people's music."

In the 1870s and 1880s people often had their collections of sheet music bound together in volumes. These collections – with broadsides next to a piece by Handel or Mozart, followed by a popular comic song from a variety show – provide a fascinating and revealing snapshot of musical tastes of the day. For example, a volume owned by a family in the Ottawa valley includes four Canadian publications: Crozier's *Nor-West Mounted*

Figure 7.9   The cover of *La belle canadienne* by New Brunswick composer Braybrooke Bayley, published as sheet music by A. & S. Nordheimer.

Police Waltzes; La belle canadienne, a "new dance" by New Brunswick composer W. Baybrooke Bayley (see figure 7.9); *March Brillante* by Charles D. Blake; and *Only a Pansy Blossom*, a "waltz song" dedicated to F.H. West, by Frank Howard, "of Thatcher, Primrose and West's Minstrels." For more information and examples of sheet music in Canada, see *Sheet Music from Canada's Past* on the Library and Archives Canada website (www.collectionscanada.ca/sheetmusic/index-e.html).

Our National Game (HACM–54; CMH3, 91–3); the text is by James L. Hughes (1846–1935). Here a solo verse is followed by a four-part chorus, and the internal and end-rhymes create a readily memorable lilt.

By 1830 some newspapers in French Canada were publishing type-set or engraved music. Specialized newspapers, journals, and magazines devoted considerable space to the "romance" (parlour songs) and its sub-types (CMH7, vii). From 1860 on the most important sources for Canadian songs in French were the *Echo du cabinet de lecture paroissial, Le Canada musical, L'album musical, Le Canada artistique, Le Piano-Canada,* and *Le passe-temps.* Like English songs of the period, most of the songs were written as "people's music" and many of these periodicals printed new versions or arrangements of songs that had become popular in earlier newspaper editions. One of the most frequent was *Le drapeau de Carillon* (1858), a solo song with music by Charles Wugk Sabatier and words by Octave Crémazie (CMH7, 40). The text recounts Montcalm's victory at Fort Carillon in 1758. Subsequent editions and arrangements of this song include an English version by David Bispham in the American periodical *The Etude* (August 1919).

Chant national O Canada (HACM–58; CMH7, 59–61) was first heard on 24 June 1880. Calixa Lavallée (1842–91) initially wrote the music as a march, and the French words added by Adolphe-Basile Routhier. The tune opens with an outline of the tonic triad (G major), and in Arthur Lavigne's publication (1880) the strophe and chorus are presented in four-part largely homorhythmic harmony. The song achieved immediate popularity among francophone Canadians, and in 1901 a literal English translation was made. *O Canada* did not, however, gain wide acceptance in anglophone Canada until Robert Stanley Weir prepared a second translation in 1908. At least twenty-five different English versions appeared between 1906 and 1933; the English text accepted by Parliament for Canada's national anthem in 1980 is a modified version of Weir's original words.

Music of Black Canadians

Blacks have been resident in Canada since the beginnings of European settlement. Many Blacks came as slaves with the French and later the Loyalists, and some freedmen, known as Black Pioneers, also found their way to Canada. The Maroon Blacks of Jamaica who fought for the British in the American War of Independence were settled in poor plots in Nova Scotia, and Black refugees from the United States arrived during the War of 1812–14. From 1830 to 1869, the underground railway shuffled Blacks across the border, mostly into southwestern Ontario.

These people brought a rich variety of musical traditions rooted not only in their African heritage but also in their experiences in North America. One fundamental song type is a call or cry, often ending with a falsetto whoop. Cries were sung as work songs, for selling goods, or for dance music. Often several were strung together to tell a story, as in *No More Auction Block for Me,* a freedman song known in Nova Scotia. A common slave shanty *Blow, Boys, Blow,* about a slave ship on the Congo River ("Yankee ship coming down the river, Blow boys! Bully boys blow!"), was recorded from Arthur Fauset of Nova Scotia in the 1920s. Another tradition is the Saturday night "Frolic," [21] a time for singing and dancing during which cries may have been sung with instrumental accompaniment in a form that became known as the "blues." The instrument (a banjo or guitar) played an introduction, continued under the voice, and also played interludes between the cries. The accompaniment kept the singer on definite pitches and established a rhythm; eventually vocalists added a short dance in the instrumental interludes.

Many Blacks who came to Canada were members of Protestant sects, particularly the Baptists, and had adapted hymns into two styles: spirituals and jubilees. Spirituals are choral antiphonal songs with a slow tempo and a broad line, somewhat akin to the sorrowful cries, but without accompaniment. Nathaniel Dett (1882–1943) recalled: "My grandmother sang spirituals with a very beautiful but frail soprano voice; but, to the ears of her grandchildren, educated in northern white schools and used mostly to the hymns of the northern white churches, these primitive Negro songs sounded strange, weird and unnatural. Yet they were never without a certain fascination" (quoted in Spencer 1991, 94). The vigorous jubilees were joyous powerful statements of Christian faith and the possibility of a better life in heaven, if not on earth. Jubilees called "Coming out" or "rising" hymns are sung after baptism; *Hallelujah Tis Done* was particularly popular among Nova Scotian Blacks. Although Black settlements in Canada in the nineteenth century were considerably smaller and more scattered than those in the United States, Canadians had the opportunity to hear touring groups, usually from the southern United States, singing spirituals and jubilees. [22]

Popular Entertainment in the Nineteenth Century

Most entertainments included some form of music; travelling actors, acrobats, magicians, and circuses brought bands or hired local musicians. Much of the music they chose or created was modelled on songs by the popular English entertainer Henry Russell; the seventy-five or so songs written during his North American sojourn include strophic ballads, simple, sentimental songs, and melodramatic pieces that drew heavily on Italian opera. All three of these song types were used both in variety shows (later minstrel shows), and Wild West shows.

MINSTREL SHOWS

The minstrel show, created by white Americans for the amusement of other white Americans, grew out of stage portrayals of Blacks in English comic opera. With the success of such acts, music publishers in the United States began to produce "nigger songs" that portrayed Blacks as comical and illiterate (Hamm 1983, 183). Verses were strung together in a rambling fashion with no sequence of events, and the lively dance-like tunes often had a pitch inventory of five notes or less. Two types of Black impersonations emerged: Gumbo Chaff or Jim Crow, a ragged plantation or riverboat hand, and Zip Coon, a citified northern dandy with exaggeratedly elegant clothes and manners. In 1832, American actor Thomas Rice blackened his face with burnt cork and incorporated the song of a Black dancer that he had heard on the streets of Cincinnati into his skit; his act and the song *Jim Crow* became an instant hit. The popularity of blackface impersonations led to minstrel shows that were completely based on these stereotyped portrayals. The first blackface minstrel shows consisted of "nigger songs" and virtuoso dances, comic sketches, mock sermons in dialect, and instrumental pieces. Members of the troupe, who played fiddle and banjo, bones, tambourine, were arranged in a semicircle with bones and tambourine at either end. Most performers were white males, usually from the northern United States, in blackface. Hundreds of minstrel groups were formed prior to 1860.

The first part of the show was based on the urban Black dandy, and the second on the southern plantation slave. The music, almost invariably in duple metre, was adapted from traditional Anglo-American folk songs, published popular songs, and Italian opera; before the American Civil War, none of it was based on the music of Black slaves or freedmen. In the 1850s, older dialect tunes were replaced by a three-section show consisting of a set of popular and sentimental ballads of the day, an "olio" (a potpourri of dancing and musical virtuosity, with parodies of Italian opera, stage plays, and touring European vocal groups), and a walk-around. Most elements linked with Blacks were in the walk-around, an ensemble finale that included songs, instrumental music, and dance.

Minstrel shows were a popular entertainment form in Canada for more than seventy-five years, and on an amateur level elements of blackface continued to appear until the early 1950s. By the 1870s Canadians were forming their own minstrel troupes, one of which was the Gowan Brothers of Ottawa. Canadians were also exposed to a somewhat more genuine Black musical expression as Blacks themselves formed minstrel troupes, and producers, following in the footsteps of Ned Harrigan and Tony Hart, who employed Black performers in place of whites in black-face for their productions in New York. One notable exception to the all-male minstrel show is a script called *The Lillie Whytes* by Canadian author Louisa Alberta Griffin-Brownlee (1859–?), written for eight female musicians, singers, and dancers and one male interlocutor. The suggested instruments are banjo, ukelele, guitar, mandolin, ukelele-banjo, violin, tambourine, and bones or castanets, and the instructions include the following statement: "It is essential that after each item on programme, – be it song, speech, joke, dance, musical exhibition, etc. – a few bars of music shall be played by the Orchestra or Pianist."[23]

Around 1920 the production of minstrel shows shifted from professional to amateur companies.[24] In communities where no one knew a Black resident, the mask of blackface allowed criticism of local politics and foibles without racist intent, and the continuation of minstrel skits into the latter part of the twentieth century might be seen as an expression of nostalgia.

REVUE AND VAUDEVILLE

Elements of minstrel entertainment appeared in other variety entertainments such as revues and vaudevilles made up of a mixture of self-contained acts involving music, dancing, acrobats, jugglers, magicians, and animal acts. The major difference between vaudeville and revue was that in revues the same performers appeared in several different numbers. As in minstrel shows songs or instrumental numbers achieved great popularity on the vaudeville or revue circuit as production companies, increasingly based in New York, sent out troupes to perform in theatre chains across the continent in both the United States and Canada.

WILD WEST SHOWS AND RODEOS

The other uniquely American form of entertainment that arose in the nineteenth century was the Wild West show. P.T. Barnum included First Nations performers and their dances in his shows as early as 1843, and elements of the cowboy rodeos[25] also began to play a major role. Between the 1880s and the 1930s more than one hundred Wild West shows toured in Europe and North America (Farnum 1992, 11). By 1880 the bison – the underpinning of the traditional economy of the Plains people – had largely been destroyed. As their traditional ways of life were shattered by the open range industry, many First Nations men became cowboys; some participated in the shows as skilled horsemen and presented staged performances of their songs and dances. First Nations culture took another major blow with the government banning of the potlatch in the Northwest and Plateau areas in 1884, and of the Sun (or Thirst) Dances of the Plains region in 1895. Some of these rituals were continued clandestinely, in spite of police raids, arrests, and fines, and First Nations also learned that a "celebration" on holidays such as Christmas or the first of July allowed them to perform many of their traditional songs and dances in a new framework. On such occasions, it was handy to be able to make a quick switch to a current popular waltz or two-step if the police happened to appear.

The Wild West shows thus contained elements that became significant popular expressions in the twentieth century. Country music has its origins in folk songs or newly-created songs of the American cowboys from Appalachia. Through the cowboy experience this repertoire developed into "western music," sung by cowboys first among themselves and later in the professional rodeos that came with the collapse of trail herd industry in the early 1890s. This new music was formed from a mixture of elements including traditional folk songs, Amerindian riding songs, and published popular songs that had passed into the oral tradition. The theme of landscape appears frequently as texts were adapted to relate to the Plains area of North America. The traditional dances and songs that First Peoples were allowed to perform, either in public events such as Wild West shows or in their own rodeos and holiday celebrations, became the basis of the powwow movement.

The two wars that enclose this period left drastic worldwide political, economic, social and technological alterations in their wake. These years also saw women playing significant roles outside the home and an increase in linguistic tensions that further entrenched anglophone and francophone Canadians as two solitudes. Within Quebec, musicians no longer crossed linguistic borders as readily as before, and although some national bridges were established in the 1950s and 1960s, the Canadian music industry became largely structured as two distinct units, one serving anglophone Canadians and the other serving francophone Quebec. Women who taught music in their homes did not face major barriers, but performers and composition students were considered dilettantes rather than serious musicians.[1] Another effect of wartime and the years after was that the skills of workers formerly employed by piano makers were much in demand in the factories making telephones, automobiles, and airplanes; this plus the stock market crash of October 1929 ended most Canadian piano manufacturing.

The Depression had a significant impact on Canadian life. Between 1930 and 1940, unemployment rates never fell below ten percent, and as early as 1931, wages for those who did have jobs took a dramatic plunge. Large numbers of rural Canadians, particularly in the Prairie provinces where drought conditions ravaged farm economies, moved to cities in an attempt to find work. During these times, women who had jobs were considered as cheap labour or seen as taking jobs away from men. Musicians, although for the most part paid poorly if at all, were much in demand during the Depression and the war years, and they played a vital role in helping Canadians, even briefly, to forget their many problems. Many were able to adjust the use of their skills in a rapidly changing economy.

With the rise of the film industry musicians employed in the minstrel and vaudeville scene faced limitations. Some found work providing music and sound effects for silent movies. Large movie houses often had small orchestras or theatre organs, while smaller theatres had only a pianist, or perhaps a chamber group. Thousands of musicians, however, lost these jobs with the arrival of the talkies in 1927.

Permanent Orchestras of the 1920s and 1930s

In various centres across Canada groups of theatre musicians were banding together to play more challenging music. Canadians heard symphonic repertoire played by US orchestras, such as the New York Philharmonic, on radio broadcasts, and choral organizations continued to bring in professional orchestras for large choral works. These US orchestras often gave orchestral concerts as well. For example, in March 1929, the Cincinnati Symphony Orchestra under Fritz Reiner, came to Toronto for performances with the Toronto Mendelssohn Choir; on Saturday afternoon, 13 March, Toronto audiences heard a suite from Handel's *Water Music*, Beethoven's Symphony no. 8, Debussy's *Prélude à l'après-midi d'un faune*, a suite from Stravinsky's *Petrouschka*, and a suite from Alfredo Cassella's ballet *La Giara*. By the end of the 1920s Canadian musicians were anxiously looking for opportunities to perform. Of the present nineteen orchestras comprising the Organization of Canadian Symphony Musicians, at least seven were formed during the 1930s.

In Montreal several orchestral organizations were formed in the 1930s. The first of these grew out of a group of unemployed musicians who presented a series of orchestral concerts (Prower 1964). The Montreal Concert Orchestra (later the Montreal Orchestra) was formed at the instigation of clarinetist Giulio Romano with Douglas Clarke, a British musician and director of the McGill Conservatorium, as honorary conductor (Potvin 1984, 24).[2] After Clarke was appointed dean of the music faculty of McGill University in 1930 he was able to draw on the limited collection of scores and parts at McGill. Performances took place at His Majesty's Theatre on Sundays at three p.m. – the same time as the New York Philharmonic broadcasts! (Prower 1964). During the first season, 1930–31, the Montreal Orchestra gave a series of twenty-five concerts, but this number was gradually reduced to ten between 1936 and 1941. The seventy-odd orchestral musicians earned an average of fifteen dollars per concert (plus performing fees for the occasional CBC broadcasts). "Throughout the existence of the orchestra the conductor received no remuneration whatever" (Bishop 1974, 6).

Orchestras in Victoria

During the forty-odd years between 1899 and the founding of the Victoria Symphony Orchestra in 1941, a number of orchestras were formed in Victoria. The following timeline provides an overview of these ensembles.

16 March 1899: The orchestra (35 members) for a Philharmonic Concert plays the overture to Mozart's *Die Zauberflöte*, Schubert's *Rosamunde Entr'acte* and Haydn's *Farewell Symphony*. As the Victoria Philharmonic Society, this group also played Haydn's *Surprise Symphony* and several works by Mendelssohn.

1900–1914: These years saw the appearance of the Cecilian Orchestra, the Wickens' Orchestra, and the St Andrew's Presbyterian Church Orchestra. During the 1914–15 season concerts were presented by the Victoria Symphony Orchestra (45 members), the Victoria Amateur Orchestra (30), and Miss Ethel Lawson's String Orchestra.

5 May 1918: A concert given by the Red Cross Orchestra is reviewed as "the finest exposition of orchestral music yet given in Victoria" (McIntosh 1994, 331).

30 November 1921: A concert by the Victoria Symphony Orchestra (65 members) includes Beethoven's Symphony no. 1 and J.S. Bach's concerto for two violins (McIntosh 1994, 331).

1924: A Philharmonic Society Symphony Orchestra reappears. The Victoria Orchestral Society ("the lineal descendant of the Red Cross Orchestra") plays Haydn's *Oxford Symphony*, Mozart's Symphonies nos. 40 and 41, conducted by W.A. Willen, who also led the Cowichan Amateur Orchestral Society in Duncan (McIntosh 1994, 335).

1930s: Active orchestras include the Coliseum Little Symphony Orchestra, the Victoria Philharmonic Society (58 members), and the Victoria Little Symphony. School orchestras during these years include the Victoria High School Orchestra and a city-wide junior orchestra.

8 January 1931: The Victoria Junior Symphony (53 members) plays Haydn's *London Symphony* (McIntosh 1994, 337).

1935: The Victoria Musical Arts Society presents Bach's Concerto in D minor for three pianos, Mozart's concerto for three pianos, and Bach's concerto for two violins (McIntosh 1994, 342).

1941: The Victoria Symphony is founded by Melvin Knudson.

With Clarke's British bias and his connection to the English-language McGill University, Montreal's francophone population felt a need for their own orchestra. Clarke's alleged refusal at the end of the 1933–34 season "to provide more openings for conductors and soloists from Quebec" (Potvin 1984, 24) led to the resignation of some committee members and plans for a new orchestra. In November 1934 the Quebec government announced a grant of $3,000 for the creation of la Société des Concerts symphoniques de Montréal (SCSM) and an inaugural season of six concerts in the 1,200-seat hall of the École supérieure le Plateau. The soloist for the first concert, presented on 14 January 1935, was Canadian pianist Léo-Pol Morin, and the program included an arrangement of Lavallée's *Le Papillon*.[3] When Wilfrid Pelletier[4] took over as conductor at the fifth concert, one of his conditions was the establishment of the Matinées symphoniques pour le jeunesse, a series of Saturday afternoon concerts for school children. The admission charge was ten cents, and Pelletier designed special programs that included analysis and commentary. The success of this venture led to similar programs in other orchestras including the New York Philharmonic (Potvin 1984, 45).

In Toronto, the New Symphony Orchestra was organized by violinist Louis Gesensway and flutist Abe Fenboque, two theatre musicians who wanted "some respite from the steady grind of playing commercial theatre music for silent movies and vaudeville shows." Together with Luigi von Kunits they assembled an orchestra, and on 23 April 1923 gave their first one-hour "twilight" concert in Massey Hall (Schabas 1994, 101).[5] In 1927 the library, charter, and name "Toronto Symphony Orchestra" (TSO) were given to the Symphony Association.[6] In 1928, the TSO inaugurated a series of twenty-five Sunday radio concerts broadcast on the CNR trans-Canada network from Halifax to Vancouver (Wood 1937, 9).

By 1912 Saskatoon, a city of 25,527 had two opera houses, four good bands, two good orchestras, a Philharmonic Society, and an Amateur Operatic Society (Leeper 1981, 91). There had been attempts to form a permanent orchestra in 1909, 1913, and 1924, but with the arrival of radio, the venture became more feasible. By 1927 Quaker Oats was subsidizing a radio orchestra and most of the musicians also played in the Saskatoon Orchestral Society (Leeper 1981, 10). In 1931 Arthur Collingwood, the first incumbent of the chair of music[7] at the University of Saskatchewan, inaugurated a lecture series illustrated with live performances of the orchestra (Leeper 1981, 11). In 1933 the Saskatoon Symphony Orchestra (as it was now known) launched its own regular season of two concerts, the proceeds of which went to the music fund for the purchase of scores and parts (Fricker 1933, 43).[8]

The present Vancouver Symphony Orchestra dates back to a group of musicians from the Capitol Theatre Symphony Orchestra who "provided music before and during the movies and played free concerts on Sunday evenings in the park above English Bay beach" (Becker 1989, 6). Allard de Ridder, who was asked to conduct this group in 1930, "personally guaranteed the players' wages with his life savings, a sum of $1,500 that was later returned to him" (6). During his tenure, which lasted until 1941, Ridder expanded the size to eighty musicians, and in 1938 formed the Vancouver Junior Symphony Orchestra to train young musicians.

The Rise of Radio

Through the 1920s and early 1930s signals from a proliferation of new radio stations, particularly in the United States, were heard in Canada. Radio broadcasts played an important role in the support of orchestras in Toronto, Montreal, and Saskatoon, and a semi-public radio network operated by the CNR sponsored an All-Canada Symphony Hour. Because commercial messages were initially prohibited in Canada, commercial interest in Canadian radio was relatively weak. Radio was, however, used for public service and educational purposes.[9] In 1924 the CNR placed radio receivers on their trains and built two transmitting studios in Ottawa and Moncton. Five years later, a transcontinental CNR network of studios was complemented by those of the CPR. With the Depression the CNR abandoned broadcasting in 1931 and the CPR in 1932. In 1928 the Mackenzie King government appointed a Royal Commission under John Aird, to study broadcasting in a number of countries; their report, submitted in September 1929, recommended the establishment of a national system. The Canadian Broadcasting Act (1932) created the Canadian Radio Broadcasting Commission (CRBC), and the Bennett government appointed Hector Charlesworth[10] as chairman. By Christmas 1932 the first CRBC broadcasts were reaching Canadian homes, many of which were in rural areas with no regular local newspapers or magazines. Live-to-air programs carried current events, a wide variety of spoken-word programs, and or course music across the country, and it soon became clear that radio was indeed a medium that could bring Canadians together and present Canada to the world. After the creation of the Canadian Broadcasting Corporation in 1936 in a revision of the Broadcasting Act, new powerful stations at strategic locations provided better reception; soon Canadians were tuning into *Hockey Night in Canada* and *The Happy Gang*, a daily noon-hour entertainment show.

By the end of the 1930s, the annual licence fee was dropped in favour of regular parliamentary grants to support the operation. CBC broadcasts played a crucial role in ending isolation in Canada, establishing a sense of unity, and counteracting an ever-increasing US influence.

From the beginning, the CBC was a vital force for support of music and musicians in Canada. In 1939 Samuel Hersenhoren was given responsibility for preparing incidental music for many CBC programs. Hersenhoren initially used standard works by Hollywood studio composers, but soon became familiar with Canadian composers and their music. In 1940 he prepared fifty-two *Canadian Snapshots*, each featuring a Canadian composer. For *Young Canadian Composers*, broadcast on 30 December 1941, he conducted performances of orchestral works by seven composers,[11] and subsequently recommended that Canadian composers be hired to write incidental music for radio. John Weinzweig describes the importance of this support:

The young Canadian Broadcasting Corporation and the newly created National Film Board were mobilized for the war effort and they reached out to enlist our writers, poets, painters, and composers ... Prior to my assignment, background music was supplied by silent film stock, offering music for every situation ... [a] scriptwriter for radio plays, Alister Grosart ... complained to the CBC network director that he was tired of hearing Respighi's *Pines of Rome* played for just about every dramatic and undramatic situation.

Writing music for radio plays was an experience that taught me to meet deadlines, sharpen my orchestral craft, respond to dramatic situations with brevity, to be prepared for those last-second cuts in the script, and frequently, to say good-bye to a great music cue, and as well, to stay clear of complex fugal activity behind voices. (Weinzweig 1996, 79)

Music as a Tourist Attraction

The CBC and the National Film Board, however, were not the first important patrons of Canadian arts in this period. This role had been foreshadowed by the CPR. With a mandate to populate Western Canada, the CPR hired painters, artisans, and photographers for a publicity campaign aimed at immigrants and tourists. Between the 1880s and the late 1920s the CPR also built a chain of hotels from Quebec City to Victoria in which tourists could break their journeys.[12] The involvement of the CPR in Canada's arts and traditional cultures began with the appointment of John Murray Gibbon as advertising agent.

John Murray Gibbon and the CPR

John Murray Gibbon (1875–1952), a CPR employee based in Britain, first encountered French Canadian folk songs on a cross-country publicity tour for editors of European newspapers. He began writing his own lyrics for these tunes – turning *Auprès de ma blonde* into *Along the Wide St Lawrence* (Kines 1988, 20) – and he also wrote verses about Canada which he set to traditional European tunes (including "Quebec" to a seventeenth-century French dance tune, "A Song of Manitoba" to the English tune "The Ploughboy," and "The Mountie," to an eighth-century Welsh air; Kines 1988, 22). This tour made him aware of the role of the railway in Canada's growth as a nation, and Canadian history, particularly social aspects and the blending of cultural traditions, became one of his chief interests (24).

Gibbon returned to travel in Canada each summer and by 1910 he had bought property in British Columbia. In 1913 he moved to Montreal as general publicity agent for the CPR. Visits to US cities where he heard orchestral concerts and opera and visited art galleries and museums brought him to recognize the flow of Canadian artistic talent moving south for lack of recognition and opportunity in Canada, and he began to plan ways "to entice 'the cultured elite of Canada, authors, artists, professors [and] musicians' to remain" (Kines 1988, 40). His extensive cultural efforts, which encompassed music, art, literature, and even film, were supported by the CPR as a component of the railway's public image.

Gibbon often travelled on horseback to areas not yet within the reach of the railway, and in 1924 became involved with the newly formed Trail Riders of the Canadian Rockies, a group dedicated not only to trail riding but also to historical sites and First Nations culture (Kines 1988, 59). These interests were soon linked with the CPR publicity machine in an annual tour package that included evening singsongs around a campfire and an elaborate "powwow" on the final night. With his knack for writing new lyrics for old songs, he created several songbooks that are still in use. Harold Eustace Key (founder and director of Montreal's Mendelssohn Choir) led the evening singsongs on a portable harmonium, and Gibbon recruited Wilf Carter, a cowboy singer associated with the Calgary Stampede, to entertain riders along the way. At the other end of the musical spectrum Gibbon arranged chamber music performances by the Hart House Quartet, and a trio consisting of Murray Adaskin (violin), John Adaskin (cello), and Louis Crerar piano and harmonium. This trio grew out of the Banff Springs Hotel Quintet, and as the Toronto Trio, worked for the CPR across the country for twenty years; they were often joined by soprano Frances James (Kines 1988, 86–9).

When British adjudicator Hugh Robertson told Gibbon that children's choirs in Canada did not have songs with which they could identify, Gibbon became involved. G. Roy Fenwick, the supervisor of school music for Ontario, sponsored *Northland Songs No. 1* (1936), a selection of Gibbon's songs on Canadian themes arranged by Harold E. Key. A second folio about the nine provinces arranged by Ernest MacMillan followed in 1938, and the following year, Ryerson Press published Gibbon's *New World Ballads* (1939). Gibbon based subsequent radio programs and war efforts on these mate-rials: for Montreal's tercentenary celebra-tion he presented a musical history of the city, and for the fourth victory loan campaign in 1943, he wrote the lyrics for a wartime hit, *Back the Attack*, with music by Murray Adaskin (Kines 1988, 169). After retirement he was commissioned to write a history of nursing in Canada; the songs that nurses sang to their patients, collected during his research, were published in *Nursing Songs of Canada* (1946). For additional details on Gibbon's activities in the arts during these years, see Kines 1988.

MARIUS BARBEAU AND CANADIAN FOLK MUSIC

Marius Barbeau (1883–1969) studied anthropology and ethnology at Ox-ford (1907–1910) and on his return to Canada became a staff ethnologist at the National Museum under Edward Sapir (1884–1939). In 1914, Franz Boas had encouraged Marius Barbeau to research not only Indian lore but also his own folk heritage. Barbeau made his first field recordings in 1916, using wax cylinders and an Edison gramophone, and by 1920 had accumulated 3,000 recordings from the Charlevoix and Gaspé regions of Quebec. With the assistance of Édouard-Zotique Massicotte, a Montreal archivist and folk song collector, Barbeau organized the first presenta-tions of folk music in a concert hall setting, the "Soirées du bon vieux temps," held on 18 March and 28 April 1919.[13] Barbeau first met John Murray Gibbon through Margaret Gascoigne, a composer who was writ-ing accompaniments for a group of French Canadian songs Barbeau had collected.[14] As a student at Oxford Gibbon had encountered Pre-Rapha-elite and Fabian ideas about the value and use of folklore, including doc-trines of national romanticism and the universality of folk music, which could also serve "as a vehicle to unite those from different cultures who employed it in mutual experience" (Kines 1988, 104). Kines argues that it is reasonable to assume that Barbeau, who was at Oxford only a few years later, had also been exposed to these ideas and that this made it easier for him to share Gibbon's efforts to develop and promote Canada's folk arts. "Together, they formed a powerful union for the transposition of the revival idea to this country" (105). Their collaboration extended over a variety of areas. For example, part of Barbeau's research on the Kootenay and Stony Indians was used in *Indian Days in the Canadian Rockies* (1923), a book used as propaganda for CPR-sponsored "Indian Days" celebrations at Banff (see figure 8.1). When the Chateau Frontenac's Chambre canadienne – a replica of a traditional habitant home was destroyed by fire, Barbeau provided Gibbon with photographs and a three-page essay to assist in its re-construction. Wanting a performance of French Canadian folk songs for the opening of the new wing in 1926, Gibbon contacted Charles Marchand,[15] who agreed to perform, using Gibbon's new translations written in colloquial English. After the event, on the encouragement of Fred Jacobs (of the *Toronto Mail and Empire*) who felt that "if Ontario people could hear those folk songs, there would be more accord between the two provinces" (Kines 1988, 107), Gibbon began preparations of the collection *Canadian Folk Songs (Old and New)*.[16]

THE QUEBEC FOLK SONG AND HANDICRAFT FESTIVAL, 20–22 MAY 1927

Gibbon organized the first Quebec Folk Song and Handicraft Festival in 1927 to launch the tourist season at the Chateau Frontenac, once again working closely with Barbeau. Realizing that most visitors would come by train, he aimed his promotion at New York, sponsoring a concert by Juliette Gaultier[17] presented in New York's Town Hall on 10 April 1927. Gaultier sang groups of Inuit and Nuu-chah-nulth materials accompanied only by a drum, and habitant songs sitting at a spinning wheel accompanied by a viole d'amour (Kines 1988, 112). Musicians included in the festival included Harold Eustace Key (billed as director of music) and guest artists Gaultier, Marchand, Ernest MacMillan, Healey Willan, the Hart House Quartet, Jeanne Dusseau, J. Campbell McInnes, and Rodolphe Plamondon. Gibbon's historical interests and musical knowledge is also evident in plans for the festival; to illustrate medieval roots of some French Canadian folk songs, he wrote

[Plamondon] is certainly a great artist. I found that he was familiar with some of the Troubadour songs, and it occurs to me that we could strike a very interesting note if we began our Friday concert with a group of those songs, introducing "L'Hirondelle, messager de l'amour" as an instance of a case where there appeared to be traces of a survival ... this would give a sort of 'cachet' to the professional concert elements, which I think would impress the highbrows ... Plamondon has been feeling rather out of the picture in Canada after his success in Europe, and I believe this opportunity of showing what he can do would give him a new spirit. (quoted in Kines 1988, 114)

Other musical events included a full choral high mass at the Basilica featuring the boys choir La petite mâitrise de Notre-Dame and a group of Wendat of Lorette performing songs learned from the Jesuits in the seventeenth century. By this time Marius Barbeau had collected and recorded some 6,000 folk songs from the St Lawrence River Valley, many of which were used as sources for the five major concerts. In addition to performances by Plamondon and Gaultier, the Hart House String Quartet premiered Ernest Macmillan's *Two Sketches for Strings*;[18] their concert also included paraphrases on the chansons *Joli coeur de rose* and *Dans Paris il y-a-t'une brume*, by Toronto-based composer Leo Smith, and Oscar O'Brien composed a sonata for cello and piano based on *Dans les prisons de Nantes* for the occasion.

OTHER CPR ARTS INITIATIVES

The CPR was one of the earliest sponsors of Canadian music competitions. In 1927 CPR President E.W. Beatty announced five composition prizes, all for works based on French Canadian folk melodies.[19] The winning works performed in Quebec City in May 1928, included an orchestral work by Arthur Cleland Lloyd of Vancouver, Ernest MacMillan's *Six Bergerettes du bas Canada*, and Claude Champagne's *Suite canadienne*. Other winners were Irvin Cooper and Alfred E. Whitehead of Montreal and George Bowles of Winnipeg. New compositions were also commissioned for subsequent CPR festivals.

During the 1929–30 season Gibbon and Harold E. Key (director of the CPR department of music) organized a six-concert cross-Canada tour of British and Canadian music.[20] The performers travelled by train and presented programs at the CPR hotels in Toronto, Winnipeg, Regina, Calgary, Vancouver, and Victoria. The railway also sponsored a number of radio programs. Gibbon's thirteen-week series *Musical Crusaders*, broadcast from Toronto in 1930. featured tenor Stanley Maxted and soprano Frances James and was heard over a network of fourteen US stations. In 1938 Gibbon presented *Canadian Mosaic*,[21] a series highlighting folk songs from various immigrant groups, many of which were arranged by Ernest MacMillan and Bernard Naylor (Lazarevich 1988, 53), and his book of the same title, published that year, included the work of many Canadian artists he had hired in the past.

New Sounds in Canada

While the availability of radio broadcasts and recordings introduced Canadian musicians and composers to a wider range of repertoire, live

The CPR Festivals

After the success of the first Quebec Folk Song and Handicraft Festival, Gibbon organized sixteen similar events across Canada. The first "Highland Gathering: Scottish and Music Festival," held in early September 1927, included two concerts presenting music in historical sequence from thirteenth-century lowland Scottish and Gaelic ballads to songs from the era of Mary, Queen of Scots, providing an accurate musical frame for the games, Highland dancing, and bagpiping competitions (Kines 1988, 117). A "Stoney Indian" program of "Old Time Indian Songs and Dances" included First Nations songs and dances (see figure 8.1). Gatherings over the next four years each included a ballad opera: *The Jolly Beggars* (based on songs by Robert Burns) in 1928; Healey Willan's *Prince Charlie and Flora* in 1929; Willan's *The Ayreshire Ploughman* in 1930; Ernest MacMillan's *Prince Charming* and a repeat of Willan's *Prince Charlie* in 1931.

Old Time Indian
Songs and Dances

HIGHLAND
GATHERING
BANFF. ALBERTA
Banff Springs Hotel
Sept. 4, 1927

The Stoney Indian Programme
September 4th, 8.30 p.m.
Banff Springs Hotel

Four Drummers will announce the coming of:

Chief Hector Crawler (Chief White Head) -- Who enters alone--others follow. Chief Crawler extends his hands in benediction.

George Maclean---makes an announcement that these two songs are part of a ritual which have never been given before.

Chief Crawler --Medicine Song
Song of the Sun.

George Maclean (Walking Buffalo)---Outlines the meaning of the Buffalo Song and Dance which he performs.

Enos Hunter (Spotted Eagle)---dances alone in The Deer Dance; others join in.

George Maclean---The Nest Song

Mark Panssette (Savage Hunting Eagle)---with two children in the Prairie Chicken Dance.

Entire Group--Thirst Song--(with whistles) Part of the SUN DANCE

Mrs Maclean and Mrs. Crawler---Lullaby.

Entire Group---Parting Song.

Figure 8.1 *The Stoney Indian Programme* presented during the Highland Gathering at Banff, 4 September 1927.

Music for the 1928 Folksong and Handicraft Festival in Quebec included, the thirteenth-century pastoral play *Le jeu de Robin et Marion* by Adam de la Halle. Wilfrid Pelletier wrote an overture and led the performers. Gibbon asked Willan to provide and arrange music for a ballad opera to Louvigny de Montigny's libretto *L'ordre de bon-temps* (based loosely on Champlain's society founded in 1606). The New Canadian Folk Song and Handicraft Festival (held three weeks later in Winnipeg at the CPR Royal Alexandra Hotel) featured more than 400 performers representing nineteen nationalities (Kines 1988, 121). The first Old English Yuletide Festival took place at Victoria's Empress Hotel in December 1928.

January 1929 saw the Vancouver Sea Music Festival, which included *Bound for the Rio Grande* by Frederick William Wallace, an operetta based on English sea shanties. Performers included Danish baritone Poul Bai singing Viking songs, John Goss singing sea shanties, and a Welsh male choir. The Great West Canadian Folksong–Folkdance and Handicrafts Festival, held in Regina in March 1929 included music of Romanian,

Czech-Slovak, English, Yugoslav, Scottish, Métis, Ukrainian, Dutch, German, Italian, French Canadian, Hungarian, Swedish, Polish, Irish, Danish, and Icelandic origin. Stars included a group of Hungarian settlers from Esterhazy and 200 Ukrainians from Saskatoon (Kines 1988, 123). The English Music Festival in Toronto in November 1929 featured Ralph Vaughan Williams' folk opera *Hugh the Drover* with an orchestra conducted by MacMillan as well as Morris, country, and sword dances, and a recital by English cellist Felix Salmond. The year ended with premieres of two ballad operas at Victoria's Yuletide Festival in December: *Indian Nativity Play* by Alexander Ramsay and *Christmas with Herrick* by Healey Willan and Gibbon, using Herrick's lyrics, with arrangements by H.E. Key.

A Sea-Music Festival, also in Victoria, in January 1930 included re-mounts of *The Order of Good Cheer* and *Bound for the Rio Grande* as well as the premiere of MacMillan's *Three French-Canadian Sea Songs*. A Calgary Festival at the Palliser Hotel in March 1930 presented a Welsh miners' choir, a dance program that included Ukrainian, Scottish and Irish dancers plus square dancing. Through these later years, however, Barbeau apparently became somewhat disillusioned with the Quebec festivals in particular; Gibbon organized the 1930 Quebec event entirely on his own (Kines 1988, 125). As Lazarevich argues, these festivals were much more than tourist attractions or CPR publicity vehicles; with First Nations groups demonstrating their skills and paintings on loan from the National Gallery of Canada, attendees were learning about their cultural traditions. "This was the beginning of the idea of nation-building – that the arts and cultures of Canada can serve as unifying elements and as a means of communicating across cultures" (Carruthers and Lazarevich 1996, 6).

concerts were still important. For example, Pablo Casals gave the first of his many Canadian performances in Montreal on 18 October 1915. The Cincinnati Symphony Orchestra played Stravinsky's *Petrouchka Suite* in 1926, and Stravinsky first appeared in Canada in 1936 when he conducted *Petrouchka*, and *The Firebird* with the Toronto Symphony Orchestra. These earlier works do not have the bitonal sonorities, varying metrics, and cellular structures of *Sacre de printemps*, which was not performed in Canada until the 1960s. Radio broadcasts of the NBC Symphony under Toscanini and the New York Philharmonic under Damrosch also steered clear of Stravinsky, although they did broadcast music by Walton, Vaughan Williams, Prokofiev, and Shostakovich; Sibelius remained a staple in both Canada and the United States. Other composers visiting Canada during this period include Vincent d'Indy (1921), Milhaud (1922),

John Weinzweig and New Music

At the age of nineteen John Weinzweig decided he wanted to be a composer. He had discovered music through folk songs of his Jewish and Italian friends, mandolin repertoire learned at a summer camp, piano lessons, and an extra-curricular music program of Harbord Collegiate Institute in Toronto. In 1934 he was admitted to the Faculty of Music at UofT. At that time, examinations were the only requirements for a degree; lectures and tutorials were optional. The faculty included Leo Smith (harmony and history), Healey Willan (counterpoint), and Ernest MacMillan (orchestration). Teaching was based on rules or facts rather than sounds. Weinzweig asked persistent questions when his work came back with red marks, but never received satisfactory answers. He completed the requirements for a B. Mus. degree by studying scores at the Toronto Public Library.

Since further studies in Europe were impossible, he went to the Eastman School of Music in Rochester, where, for the first time in his studies, he was asked to write an essay on a piece of music – Stravinsky's *Sacre de printemps*; the orchestration and rhythm were a revelation. A second revelation came with Berg's *Lyric Suite*, but he was unable to find much more information about dodecaphonic technique, and requests to instructors at Eastman were rebuffed. In spite of all this, Weinzweig completed *Spasmodie* (1938); this eighteen-bar piano piece was the first dodecaphonic Canadian composition. In 1939, after Weinzweig returned to Toronto, he and a group of composers and performers formed the Canadian Friends of New Music that "envisioned a library of contemporary and Canadian music, whose contents were selected by voting and on the basis of live performances" (Weinzweig 1996, 82).

Bartók (1927), and Ravel (1928) (Potvin 1988, 148). Some musicians were curious about newer sounds. In Montreal, Rodolphe Mathieu left the avant-garde path to promote the career of his son André, but he held frequent all-Canadian concerts in his studio. In Toronto the Vogt Society, formed in 1936 to promote contemporary composition, heard piano works by Arnold Schoenberg performed by the Chilean-born pianist Alberto Guerrero. Some works written during these years reflected discoveries of new music, but difficult economic times and the lucrative publishing market for popular music, meant that Canadian composers of refined music had even more difficulty in obtaining publication.

The Hart House String Quartet,[22] formed in Toronto in 1923 by Géza de Kresz, Harry Adaskin, Milton Blackstone, and Boris Hambourg, undertook extensive tours in North America, and had a broadcast contract with the CNR radio network; after 1938 they were heard on CBC Radio. In 1925 they gave the Canadian premiere of Bartók's Quartet no. 1, and Ravel, who made his US debut as a pianist with the quartet in 1928, described them as the finest he had worked with. European tours in 1929, and 1936–37 earned rave reviews, and their extensive repertoire included works by Delius, Dohnanyi, Hindemith, Kodály, Prokofiev, Schoenberg, and Vaughan Williams. Their last performance, broadcast by the CBC, took place at Hart House on 26 April 1946.

MacMillan, Willan, and Champagne

During his multifaceted career Ernest MacMillan (1893–1973) matured from a precociously talented child organist into a distinguished elder-statesman of Canadian music. In 1914 he was in Paris pursuing musical studies; while he was in Bayreuth attending performances of Wagner operas the First World War was declared; he spent the war years as an Allied civilian prisoner, first in Nuremberg, and then at the Ruhleben prison camp near Berlin. His musical activities there included preparing musical scores, giving lectures, conducting an orchestra and choir, and completing the doctorate of music requirements for Oxford University.[23] After his return to Canada, MacMillan was active as an organist, pianist, and teacher, and he was an examiner for the Toronto Conservatory. He became a close friend of Marius Barbeau, and accompanied him on collecting trips to British Columbia. While MacMillan was clearly a gifted composer aware of new trends, his ever-increasing conducting duties severely limited his time. Beginning in 1923, he presented annual performances of Bach's *St Matthew's Passion* with an augmented Toronto Conservatory Choir. In 1931 he was appointed conductor of the Toronto Symphony Orchestra and also conducted frequently in the United States. He served as dean of the Faculty of Music, University of Toronto from 1924 to 1952, and in 1942 he succeeded Herbert A. Fricker as conductor of the Toronto Mendelssohn Choir.

MacMillan recognized the limitation of folk song as an inspiration for art music: "We cannot by [thinking] produce a national music: all we can do is to create an atmosphere in which a strong musical personality can express itself creatively and naturally ... [Art] has a way of emerging at the most unexpected places" (quoted in Kallman 1996, 18). But Kallmann also points out that MacMillan "made no mention of one of the main reasons for the retarded development of composition in Canada: the lack of Canadian music schools or teachers familiar with and devoted to the new compositional techniques of Hindemith, Schoenberg, *Les Six* of France,

Figure 8.2   Godfrey Ridout, Leo Smith, John Weinzweig, and Healey Willan surround Ernest MacMillan seated at the piano in his studio at the Toronto Conservatory of Music, ca. 1942. Photograph courtesy of Freda Ridout.

Bartók, or Stravinsky. This undoubtedly *was* one of the main reasons for the slow development of contemporary music in Canada" (18).

Healey Willan's appointment as organist-choirmaster of St Mary Magdalene in Toronto in 1921 was recognized as a perfect fit, with his interest in and love for an Anglo-Catholic style of church music.[24] His association with this church, its musical traditions, and its choir, for which he wrote many motets and other liturgical pieces, lasted until his death in 1968. The eighth-century text of *Fair in Face* (1928) (*HACM*–97; *CMH*25, 136–8), comes from the responsories for an office of Our Lady. Willan's setting uses changing metres to approximate the free rhythm of plainchant, and the contrapuntal texture highlights long, flowing lines in the lower parts. The text of *Rise Up, My Love, My Fair One* (1929) (*CMH*25, 139–41), is from the Song of Solomon; cadential points are marked by plagal-like harmony with the bass falling a second, and the vocal lines of individual parts form rich seventh chords that are not resolved according to nineteenth-century harmonic practise. The text of *Hodie, Christus natus est* (1935) is a celebratory setting of a Christmas antiphon.[25]

A PROGRAMME OF

CANADIAN MUSIC

will be broadcast in the National programme this evening at 7.30.

HARRY ADASKIN
(*Violin*)

FRANCES ADASKIN
(*Pianoforte*)

Danse Canadienne, No. 1;
Reminiscence ; Danse
Canadienne, No. 2
Hector Gratton

Sonata, E Minor
Healey Willan

Tambourin .. *Leo Smith*

Danse Villageoise
Claude Champagne

Figure 8.3
Notice of a recital of Canadian music, broadcast 22 August 1930, that appeared in the *Radio Times* (BBC), London, England.

If for many years MacMillan and Willan were the most influential voices in the music scene of anglophone Canada, their Quebec counterpart was Claude Champagne (1891–1965).[26] In 1918, the young composer, showed his orchestral score *Hercule et Omphale* (*CMH15*, 56–78) to Alfred La Liberté, who found funds for him to study in Europe. Champagne spent most of the 1920s, in Paris at the Conservatoire and Vincent d'Indy's Schola Cantorum; both *Hercule et Omphale* and *Suite canadienne* were performed in Paris to high praise. Returning to Montreal in 1928, he quickly became involved with improving music training at home. He prepared five solfège training manuals, and from 1932 to 1941 taught harmony and composition at McGill University. Most of the major francophone composers of the next generation worked with Champagne,[27] who had little time for his own composition until the 1940s, at which point he turned his attention to orchestral music. His well-known *Danse villageoise* (1929) (*HACM*–91; *CMH23*, 168–94) – initially scored for violin and piano, and later arranged for larger instrumental forces in three different forms – is written in the style of Quebec fiddle tunes but uses only original material.[28] It is one of five compositions heard in a recital of Canadian music by Frances and Harry Adaskin broadcast on the BBC, 22 August 1930 (see figure 8.3).

Colin McPhee and the Music of Bali

Colin McPhee (1900–64) was raised in Toronto where he studied at the Hambourg Conservatory. He was known as an outstanding pianist, but from an early age he was fascinated with musical sound:

When I was 12, I wrote a piece for children's percussion band with a few strings etc. I had various ideas for effects but at the end, on the last two chords, two plates had to be dropped and smashed. The effect was not so good, but I was thinking of frail china splintered on marble. Ten years later when I wrote a full-blown piano concerto [*Second Piano Concerto*, performed with the New Symphony Orchestra, Toronto, in 1924] ...I had in the scherzo, a place where one percussion man had to shake a number of those little Chinese glass wind-chimes that one hung on the verandah in the summer. This was never performed, to my disappointment the conductor thought it nonsense. (Oja 1984, 3)

One of his few surviving early compositions is *Four Piano Sketches* (1916); the fourth of these, *Silhouette* (*HACM*–115; *CMH6*, 267) is written in the tradition of the nineteenth-century character piece, but McPhee's experimentation with piano sonorities is evident in the careful pedal markings of the final bars. After further studies in the United States and Paris he spent the late 1920s in New York, where he met Henry Cowell and Aaron Copland, and was involved in concerts at Greenwich Village organized by Edgard Varése. McPhee first heard Balinese music in 1928 on newly-released recordings by the German Odeon company. Enthralled by these sounds, he travelled to Bali to learn more about this music. He discovered that "in Bali, music is not composed but rearranged" (McPhee 1935, 165), and began a procedure of making transcriptions of Balinese music for Western instruments and composing links between passages, creating what Mueller has called "a montage-like structure" (1983, 204); his chamber work *Pemoengkah* was based on this procedure.[29]

McPhee had used neoclassicism, folk influences, and excessive dissonance, none of which satisfied his needs, but in Bali he found an aesthetic where music was a part of the daily life of the people. Returning from Bali in 1935, he renewed his friendship with Mexican composer Carlos Chávez. "I suddenly had the idea, partly suggested by Carlos Chávez, of writing an orchestral work utilizing materials I had collected in Bali. 'Come to Mexico City,' he said, 'write it, and I will play it with the orchestra'" (Oja 1990, 101).[30] Using a concerto concept as in his previous large works, McPhee scored a "nuclear gamelan" of two pianos, celesta, xylophone, marimba, glockenspiel, and two Balinese gongs against a standard symphony orchestra.[31] Regardless of quotations from Balinese compositions, McPhee insisted that this work was his own. "The cross-rhythms, irregular ostinatos, sectional structures, and layered textures of *Tabuh-Tabuhan* all appeared in McPhee's work from the late 1920s. In subsequently incorporating materials and techniques from Bali, he did not simply tack on exotic effects but found in the music of the gamelan traits common to his own personal voice ... It is one of the earliest attempts by a Western composer to meet the East on its own terms" (Oja 1990, 116). *Tabuh-Tabuhan* had its premiere in Mexico City on 4 September 1936 with the Orquesta Sinfónica de México under Chávez, who also promoted the work to five other conductors.[32] McPhee's work was enthusiastically received by critics. The Balinese people revere McPhee as the person who documented their traditions and helped them to survive. In his later years McPhee was invited by Malm to help establish a centre for ethnomusicology at the University of California in Los Angeles (UCLA), and some scholars argue that he is the "inventor" of minimalism.[33]

The Voices of Younger Composers

During the late 1930s and early 1940s a number of young Canadian composers found their unique voices in composition. Some of them took advantage of the number of outstanding musicians resident in North America at the time. Barbara Pentland (1912–2000) studied at Juilliard in New York and was influenced by Renaissance counterpoint; she returned to Winnipeg to write virile, intervallically based works such as *Rhapsody 1939: The World on the March to War Again* (CMH6, 268–77). During her studies at McGill University Violet Balestreri Archer (1913–2000) completed several orchestral compositions, and in the early 1940s went to New York for lessons with Béla Bartók who inspired her to incorporate folk-based materials (Lenoir 1980, 149). She also pursued graduate studies at Yale University, where she took every course given by Paul Hindemith. Meanwhile, Jean Coulthard (1908–2000) was searching out instruction – in Vancouver studying with Arthur Benjamin (1939), and in New York with Bernard Wagenaar (1945) – and she also sent her works for criticism to Copland (1939), Schoenberg and Milhaud (1942), and Bartók (1944). Nadia Boulanger – one of the European musicians who spent the war years in the United States – taught Jean Papineau-Couture (1916–2000) at the Longy School in Cambridge, Massachusetts (1941–43). A strong supporter of Stravinsky, her many Canadian students received a rich appreciation of his approaches.

Weinzweig described 1941 as a year of discovery for Canadian concert composers. Henry Cowell asked him to assist Lazare Saminsky (a composer, author, and mathematician who had studied with Rimsky-Korsakov) with a cross-Canada tour to meet Canadian composers in order to gather material for a forthcoming book, *Living Music of the Americas* (1949). It is significant that Saminsky, an outside observer, noted the influence of landscape and the mixing of musical heritages that gives Canadian composers a distinctive voice. "He observed that our landscape painters were closely followed by our composers who were discovering their country through its aboriginal and Franco-Anglo folklore" (Weinzweig 1996, 80). Saminsky also rewarded Canadian hospitality by arranging a concert of music by "Young Canadian Composers" – Pentland, Ridout, Applebaum, Gratton, André Mathieu, and Weinzweig – in New York under the sponsorship of the American League of Composers on 11 June 1942 (80).

During this period, most musicians had to use their own resources to develop compositional and performing skills beyond the limited resources available in Canada. One major exception was the Banff School of Fine Arts (later the Banff Centre), established in 1933 as an extension program of the University of Alberta under a grant from the Carnegie Foundation of New York (Hockenhull 2001, 18). Located in Banff National Park, and surrounded by spectacular mountain scenery, the Centre has, over the years developed theatres, galleries, visual art, and recording studios, hosting senior artists from around the world. Over the years, Programs expanded to include dance and opera (1953), the International String Quartet Competition (1983), and a special First Nations program (1990s).

9   From *A Rag Time Spasm* to *I'm Movin' On*

By 1900 New York had become the centre of the entertainment industry in North America. America's first musical "smash hit" *The Black Crook*, which opened at Niblo's Garden in 1866, included more than a hundred chorus girls (who appeared in one scene with black tights and no skirts!) laying the groundwork for lavish spectacle and hit songs. Between 1855 and 1900 theatres on or near Broadway produced eighty-three operettas and seventy-two other musical shows. This vibrant theatre scene encouraged composers to write songs[1] they hoped would be used in musical comedy, vaudeville, or revues, setting the stage for Tin Pan Alley, the music publishing centre in New York's theatre district that produced large runs of vocal sheet music and marketed their products aggressively.

The Impact of Technology

The establishment of this New York mecca of music publishing in the 1890s and early 1900s coincided with innovations in distribution made possible by new technology. In the 1890s Franz Boas, James A. Teit, and Alexander T. Cringan all used phonographs to record traditional songs of Canada's First Nations, and the first Canadian commercial recordings were released by the E. Berliner company in Montreal in 1900.[2] In these early years, strong solo voices were best for recording. Canadian artists such as Emma Albani, Pauline Donalda, and Joseph Saucier, and two tenors – Harry Macdonough and Henry Burr – had extensive careers in the United States.[3] Ensembles were more difficult to record, but Canadian examples include the first record of the Belleville Kilties Band in 1902. Cornet virtuoso Herbert L. Clarke (1867–1945) made many recordings as soloist and leader of the Sousa Band. These years also saw a recognition of recordings as a learning tool; in 1918, Quebec pianist Emiliano Renaud developed a pedagogical series called Renaud-Phone-Piano-Method. In French Canada there was a steady market for local products but most other Canadian musicians had to record for foreign companies.

The appearance of the player piano, or pianola, is discussed in chapter 6. Piano rolls of current popular songs provided effortless musical recreation at home and a uniform standard for piano rolls adopted by four manufacturers in 1905 contributed to a huge demand. Within a decade player pianos accounted for fifty-six percent of the piano production and sales (Théberge 1997, 28). The musically democratic player piano became linked to the "notion of universal accessibility to culture that would later become an essential component in the consumer mythology associated with the phonograph and radio" (Théberge 1997, 29). The first commercial radio station[4] in Canada was established in Montreal in 1919 and by 1928, there were sixty stations operating in Canada. In terms of cost and space radio was even more "musically democratic," and with recordings it became the dominant medium for determining popularity during the twentieth century. Charles Seeger argues that the mechanical music industries have promoted the consumption of music in all kinds of styles, popular, folk, and classical, producing a profound levelling effect on American musical taste (1977, 229). Technology also allowed the development of modern popular music that became the core of "middlebrow" or middle-of-the-road taste. As emerging radio stations strived to create a distinctive niche, a sandwich structure with "highbrow" and "lowbrow" categories developed in the 1920s.

Musical Forms

Most folk songs and published Canadian popular songs of the nineteenth century have a strophic form, with each stanza followed by a short refrain. Regular four- or eight-bar phrases are repeated either immediately or after a contrasting phrase. Common phrase patterns include AABA, ABBA (of Irish provenance), and ABAC (music-hall songs). In published songs sixteen-bar sections consist of two eight-bar phrases with an open-closed (antecedent-consequent) harmonic and melodic relationship. Influenced by developments in the United States, refrains were extended into a "chorus" often sung by a group. Verbal forms of the text (rhyme scheme, line length, and stanza structure) also affected the sequence and repetition of musical materials.

Published and orally transmitted instrumental music of the nineteenth century usually consists of eight- or sixteen-bar sections or "strains."

Common forms include two sections (each repeated) with a common tonal centre, and three sections arranged in an ABA pattern, with a contrasting tonal centre in B. Series of two-section themes were often strung together (for example, in a collection of five or six waltzes), or combined in patterns (such as ABA/CD, ABA/CA, or ABA/CDC). All of these vocal and instrumental structures carried over into the twentieth century and can be found in popular music.

Canadians in Tin Pan Alley

It is not surprising that popular songs reflected technological advances of the early twentieth century. Inspired by J.A.D. McCurdy, who on 22 February 1909 flew the first powered airplane in Canada, Alfred Bryan, a native of Brantford, Ontario, wrote *Come Josephine in My Flying Machine* (1910) which was set to music by Fred Fisher. The words and music of *Oh! What a Difference Since the Hydro Came* (1912) (CMH14, 230) are by Claud L. Graves, a printer working in London, Ontario, from 1907 to 1922.[5] The dominant dotted-eighth/sixteenth rhythm may reflect Scottish heritage in the London area.

Geoffrey O'Hara (1882–1966), known as a fine pianist and organist in Chatham, Ontario, had a varied and successful music career. His musical background includes performances with Black residents in Chatham, and around 1913 O'Hara made recordings of First Nations music in the United States. In 1904 he joined the Dockstader's Minstrels and later sang in operettas in New York. He performed in the Lyceum vaudeville circuit and Chautauqua productions.[6] His compositional output included fourteen operettas and more than 500 songs. His first big hit, *Your Eyes Have Told Me* (1913) (CMH14, 239)[7] was sung by Al Jolson and recorded by Enrico Caruso. *K-K-K-Katy* (HACM–107; CMH14, 217–8),[8] written in 1918 on a visit to Kingston, Ontario, became one of the biggest hits of the First World War; it was published in New York by Leo Feist (selling one and a half million copies), and recorded by eleven artists, and used in the movies *The Cockeyed World* (1929) and *Tin Pan Alley* (1940).

Popular patriotic songs written by Canadians during the First World War include *Good Luck to the Boys of the Allies, When Your Boy Comes Back to You, I Want to Kiss Daddy Good Night, When They Wind Up the Watch on the Rhine*, and *For the Glory of the Grand Old Flag*. The composer of *We'll Never Let the Old Flag Fall* (CMH14, 212), Michael F. Kelly (ca. 1882–1916) from Saint John, was a bandmaster of the 132nd Overseas Battalion; this song, with text by Albert MacNutt sold more than 100,000 copies in the year after its release in 1915. Gitz Rice (1891–1947), a member of the Princess Patricia Comedy Company (formed to entertain the soldiers) wrote a number of songs including *Dear Old Pal of Mine*, *Keep Your Head Down, Fritzie Boy!*, and *Some Day I'll Come Back to You*, which became a big hit for Henry Burr; Rice has also been credited for *Mademoiselle from Armentieres*, but his authorship is unsubstantiated. *Jesus, Tender Shepherd, Lead Us*, by Hattie Rhue Hatchett, a musician in the Black community of North Buxton, Ontario, was a popular sacred song just after the end of the war.

Under the pseudonym "Raymond Roberts" Ernest Seitz (1892–1978) came up with the perfect tune for Eugene Lockhart's show song *The World Is Waiting for the Sunrise* (*HACM*–108; *CMH14*, 253–5) in 1919.[9] This sentimental ballad, written for a war-weary world, is one of the most successful works produced in Canada. It was recorded by more than a hundred artists including Billie Holiday, Chet Atkins, Fritz Kreisler, and Duke Ellington, and in 1923 a band leader in Pittsburgh changed the rhythm to a fox trot (Hutton 2000, 46).[10] In June 1940, Luigi Romanelli, the orchestra leader at Toronto's King Edward Hotel, adopted it as the theme for his orchestra and radio program (partly because *O Sole Mio* was no longer acceptable when Canada was at war with Italy).

William Eckstein[11] began his career as an accompanist for silent films in 1906 first at Lyric Hall and then the Strand in Montreal (which because of his drawing power was the last house in Montreal to switch to talkies).[12] In 1919 "Mister Fingers," as he became known, accompanied singer Gus Hill in the first live radio broadcast in Canada on Montreal radio station XWA (later CFCF) (Gilmore 1989, 78). By 1923 his Strand Trio was recording for His Master's Voice, Apex, Okeh, and Victor. Eckstein wrote a number of popular songs including: *Goodbye Sunshine, Hello Moon* (1919), which was included in *Ziegfield Follies* and *Lest You Forget* (1922) (*CMH14*, 247) with lyrics by Sam Howard. The fox trot *Won't You Meet Me at Murray's* (*CMH14*, 233) is characterized by chromaticism in both melody and harmony and phrases of varying length often beginning on the second beat.[13] His ragtime hit, *"S'Nice"* (1923) (*CMH14*, 250) also features irregular phrasing, and off-beat accents in the piano introduction continue throughout the song.[14]

The Rise of Ragtime

There is no agreement on the origin of the term "ragtime" but the style is undoubtedly related to practises associated with musical expressions of Black Americans. Black slaves sometimes parodied European dances to an accompaniment of syncopated tunes played on a fiddle or a banjo.

Whites often watched these high-stepping, vigorous "walkarounds," and in later years the most inventive couple received a prize, frequently a cake. By the 1890s the "cakewalk," a white imitation of the strutting, high-kicking dance with syncopated music, was an important part of the minstrel show. By the late nineteenth century some Blacks had the opportunity to play and even to own pianos and organs. When Black women played European-derived music, such as hymns, they often created "ragged" or syncopated accents with the right hand against a steady, straight rhythm in the left.

The music associated with the term "ragtime" is mostly for piano and may be a derivative of "jigtime" a type of piano dance music in the northeastern United States. Ragtime is modelled on European-derived duple-metre marches and sectionally constructed dance tunes. Sections or strains of sixteen bars are played twice. Many rags have four strains (AABBCCDD), but some have three or five. The left hand plays a "boom-chuck" pattern (a bass note on the beat and a chord on the off-beat) with variations at the end of inner phrases; the right hand plays a melody featuring off-beats. Scott Joplin's *Maple Leaf Rag* (named for the Maple Leaf Club[15] Missouri) appeared in 1899, and the first of many Canadians rags – *A Rag Time Spasm* (1899) by W.H. Hodgins and *The Cake Winner* (1899) by G.A. Adams – appeared the same year. Willie Eckstein and pianist Harry Thomas (1890–1941) collaborated on *Delirious Rag*,[16] and in 1916 Thomas made Victor Talking Machine Company's first ragtime recording (*Delirious Rag* on one side, *Classical Spasm* on the other). C. Joseph Lamb (1887–1960), another major composer of ragtime, wrote his first rags, including *Walper House Rag* (1903), and *Rapid Rapids Rag* (1905) while he lived in Berlin (Kitchener, Ontario). Rags by Montreal theatre pianist Jean-Baptiste Lafrenière (ca.1875–ca.1911) include *Raggity-Rag* (1907) (CMH22, 194), *Taxi Rag*, and *Balloon Rag*. Vera Guilaroff (1902–76) often played duets with Eckstein and replaced Thomas as a silent movie pianist at Montreal's Regent in 1919. She wrote several compositions influenced by the ragtime idiom and was best known as a popular entertainer in ragtime and early stride style. She was the first woman in Canada to record Black-influenced music.

Some Canadian ragtime musicians were of Black heritage. Shelton Brooks,[17] a self-taught musician, became an outstanding pianist and vaudeville entertainer. His ragtime-influenced songs are brash, sexually suggestive, and perfectly suited the changing social context of the early twentieth century. *Some of These Days* (1910)[18] became a big hit and was used by Sophie Tucker as a theme song for some five decades of her career. *Darktown Strutters' Ball* (1917), another Brooks hit, was frequently

Nathaniel Dett's Views of Black Music

Robert Nathaniel Dett (1882–1943) began his musical career by taking piano lessons in Niagara Falls, Ontario. In his autobiography he relates that both his parents were educated and musical. His mother played the piano, sang, and was active in local concerts. Dett learned to play by ear, by listening to his mother and his two older brothers who were already taking piano lessons with "an English lady named Mrs. Marshall." One day Mrs. Marshall heard him at the keyboard, and asked his mother's permission to give him lessons free. "After my first teacher I had several others who seemed to teach me nothing at all ... Olivia Willis Halsted at his Conservatory in Lockport [USA] ... was my first teacher to throw light upon the serious study of music ... At the end of the year, I was able to give a recital (Beethoven, Chopin, Schumann, MacDowell) ... At the recital I also played some things that I had composed and these were very well received indeed" (Spencer 1991, 91–3).

Dett's early works include *After the Cakewalk – March Cakewalk* (1900) and *Cave of the Winds* (CMH22, 249) (see figure 9.1), a "march and two step" published in 1902; the syncopated rhythms of the latter work indicate that he was aware of the rhythmic idioms associated with Black music. Dett later wrote: "Negro music was merely 'rag time' – something to be amused at, danced to, employed as a ready made missile of ridicule if not actual ill will against Negro citizens. At that time, to talk with colored people about Negro music was to embarrass them, since the general attitude of the public toward such music was mildly contemptuous" (Spencer 1991, 94). He decided "that if a form of song were evolved which contained all the acceptable characteristics of Negro folk music and yet would compare favorably in poetic sentiment and musical expression with the best class of church music ... it would save to the Negro and his music all the peculiar and precious idioms, and as a work of art would summon to its interpretation the best of his intellectual and emotional efforts" (Spencer 1991, 36). In 1913 Dett's "spiritual anthem" *Listen to the Lambs* (1913) (CMH9, 58) won one of two prizes for a composition on a Negro theme awarded by the Music School Settlement for Colored People in New York; in 1919 it was performed in a memorial service in Hamilton, Ontario, for Canadian soldiers killed in the First World War. This piece and other spiritual anthems, including *I'll Never Turn Back No More*, and *Oh, Holy Lord*, are still frequently performed (particularly by the Nathaniel Dett Chorale of Toronto). Willis James argues that: "No Negro has been able to achieve comparable distinction as a choral writer of Negro songs" (1995, 232). Dett was a master at arranging spirituals and writing music infused with Black idioms. The *Juba Dance* from his piano suite *In the Bottoms* is likely his most frequently performed instrumental work. ("Juba" is a Black joyous dance of the southern states.) Dett received a bachelor of music degree from the Oberlin Conservatory of Music (1908), had further studies in the United States and Europe, and became a professor at Hampton Institute.

Cave of the Winds

March and Two Step.

R. Nathaniel Dett.

Figure 9.1   Opening page of *Cave of the Winds* by Nathaniel Dett.

used in revues. In 1923 Brooks toured Europe playing in musical shows and vaudeville (Robbins 1969, 26). Lou Hooper (1894–1977) was born in North Buxton, Ontario, of Black, Irish and Cree heritage. By age twelve he was performing in the Hooper Brothers Orchestra throughout Michigan. He earned a Bachelor of Music degree in 1920 and moved to Harlem where he taught piano and theory, accompanied singers (including Bessie Smith and Paul Robeson), recorded extensively as an arranger, leader and sideman, and toured with revues. In 1932 he moved to Toronto where he formed another Hooper Brothers Orchestra of Black musicians. By 1933 he was playing with the Canadian Ambassadors in Montreal where he accompanied Billie Holiday. He organized the Hooper Southern Singers to perform spirituals and Stephen Foster songs, played in various jazz groups, and continued composing. In 1975 he joined the faculty of the University of Prince Edward Island, and his ballet *The Congo* was staged in 1976.

Ragtime slowly disappeared from the scene with the popularity of dance bands and jazz groups beginning in the 1920s, but after the publication of *They All Played Ragtime* (1950) by Rudi Blesh and Harriet Janis, original ragtime composers and performers were sought out. Hooper was often called upon, and Joseph Lamb gave his final public performance in Toronto at Club 76 on 8 October 1959. The Ragtime Society, founded in Toronto in 1962, helped to focus international attention on the style, and a number of Canadian musicians include rags in their repertoire and have written new examples.

The cakewalk was one of a number of Black dance movements imitated by the Caucasian majority of North America: others include the buck (tap dancing), pigeon wing (arm movements), breakdown (heavy-footed and rough), blackbottom (included hand clasping or embracing), shimmy (highly suggestive and sensuous), truck (shuffling), jump (elements of buck and the juba), and jitterbug (acrobatic). Many of these terms were later applied to various derivative dances. Another dance that became popular after 1920 was the twisting, improvisational Charleston. These Black-inspired dances were very different from sedate European-derived dances (such as the waltz or the one step) and the faster, syncopated music they required permeated revues, vaudeville, and dance halls.[19]

Entertainment and Popular Songs

The Dumbells, a soldiers' comedy group, was formed during the First World War near Vimy Ridge under the direction of Merton Plunkett (1888–1966). The original members were baritone Al Plunkett, comedian

Figure 9.2.
Cover of Dumbell's song
Shall I Have It Bobbed or Shingled (1924), by Robert
Patrick Weston, from the
Dumbell's revue, *Ace High*.

Ted Charters, female impersonators Ross Hamilton and Allan Murray, pianist and music director Jack Ayre, tenor Bill Tennent, and bass-baritone Bert Langley. By August 1917 the Princess Patricia Comedy Company had largely become part of The Dumbells. After their first shows more members, including some instrumentalists were added. Back in Canada, they reorganized as a vaudeville troupe with an orchestra that included some of the best dance-band musicians of the day. Their 1919 revue *Biff, Bing, Bang* opened in London, Ontario and they were soon booked for a cross-country tour.[20] Later revues included such popular songs as *Canada for Canadians* (by Albert Edward "Red" Newman), *Winter Will Come*, Albert Plunkett's *And Her Mother Came Too, Come Back Old Pal, It's Canada, the Land for Me, K-K-K-Kiss Me Again, Li'l Old Granny Mine, Shall I Have It Bobbed or Shingled* (see figure 9.2) *She Must Be A Wonderful Girl, Shufflin' Along*, and *Yum-Yum-Yum-Yum*.

Guy Lombardo and His Royal Canadians

The Lombardo Brothers Concert Company (see figure 9.3) was formed in London, Ontario, around 1915. The original members – violinist Guy Lombardo (1902–77), Carmen Lombardo on flute and saxophone, Lebert Lombardo on trumpet or piano – were often joined by a friend or two when they played for community socials. Carmen occasionally played with a band in Detroit that used slower dance tempos (rather than the fast, snappy "businessman's bounce") and the Lombardos' new arrangements based on slower tempos soon became their most requested numbers. By 1924 the band had engagements in Ohio and were known as Guy Lombardo and His Royal Canadians. During an extended engagement, the owner of the Claremont in Cleveland, advised Lombardo to shift to a softer sound with less emphasis on the beat. Around the same time, Guy began to create medleys of several tunes strung together with a bridge based on a Scottish strathspey rhythm (dotted eighth–sixteenth). The Royal Canadians had a unique sound; saxophonists based their sound on Carmen's flute-like vibrato, trumpeter Lebert aimed for a singing sound (like an Italian opera singer), and the drummer used a subtle beat. Soon WTAM of Cleveland was broadcasting the Lombardo sound for an hour every day, and by 1927 the band had engagements in Chicago and a broadcast on WBBM. In response to these broadcasts, sponsors came forward for programs in Chicago and St Paul's (KSTP).

In 1929 Lombardo and His Royal Canadians began a thirty-year stint at the Roosevelt Grill in New York. The size of the orchestra varied but there was a core of two trumpets, trombone,

Figure 9.3 The Band of the Lombardo Brothers, ca. 1917–1924. Lenore Stevens Keillor Fonds, Library and Archives Canada.

three saxophones (no baritone), three clarinets, two pianos (providing rippling background), guitar, tuba, and drums. In 1930 the band began a weekly Robert Burns Panatella Cigar show on NBC radio, picking a new song for a hit each week, some of which were by the Lombardos themselves. Carmen was the most prolific writer with over 200 songs, all of which reflect the successful Lombardo formula: somewhat saccharine harmonies touched with chromaticism, graceful Italianesque melodies, an occasional nod to ragtime and a recurring strathspey idiom. Compositions by Carmen include *Seems Like Old Times, Sweethearts on Parade* (written with Charles Newman, 1928); John Jacob Loeb, Carmen's most frequent collaborator, wrote lyrics for *Boo-Hoo* (1937), *A Sailboat in the Moonlight* (written with Guy Lombardo, 1937), and *Get Out Those Old Records* (1951). In 1933, comedy teams were added to the Lombardo broadcasts. The success of the band continued through and after the Second World War, and between 1953 and 1977, they sold more than 450 million records. Although they were criticized for their "sweet" or commercial sound, their successful formula kept them at the top of the charts for many years. *Auld Lang Syne*, a fixture since their early years in London, remained in their repertoire and from 1954 on, was a feature of their New Year's Eve broadcasts.

Guy Lombardo and his Royal Canadians were not the only Canadian artists in the US top achievement charts. Other Canadians to make their way to the top include Henry Burr and Harry Macdonough, vaudeville singer May Irwin (1862–1938), Toronto-born singer and actress Beatrice Lillie (1894–1989), Winnipeg-born singer and actress Deanna Durbin (1921), and Toronto-born tenor Harold Jarvis (1866–1958) who had his greatest recording success in 1914 with *Beautiful Isle of Somewhere*. Radio played a crucial role in the success of Guy Lombardo's band in the United States; in Canada the emphasis was placed on live music, rather than recordings.[21] Many of the featured groups were dance bands, often connected to large hotels across the country. Mart Kenney and his Western Gentlemen were formed in 1932 in Alberta, and over the next decade played for more Canadians than any other band. Kenney played saxophone and clarinet and sang while Art Hallman played saxophone and wrote many of their arrangements.[22] The band remained mainly in Western Canada until 1940 when they appeared at the Royal York Hotel in Toronto. From 1943 to 1945, their radio broadcasts were carried in the United States and Britain (Ginsburg 1998, 69). Their signature tune, *The West, A Nest, and You*, was a waltz by Billy Hill and Larry Yoell, and their country flavour comes across in songs such as *Take Me Back to My Boots and Saddle*. Although the Kenney band was undoubtedly influenced in name and sound by Lombardo, their more prominent country and western stylings greatly influenced the type of dance music Canadians preferred.

Robert Farnon and Percy Faith were involved in *The Happy Gang*, an influential daily program broadcast out of CBC Toronto from 1937 to 1959, and both had influential international careers. Robert Farnon (1917–2005), musical director for *The Happy Gang*, played trumpet and wrote arrangements for Percy Faith's orchestra. During this time he also wrote two symphonies.[23] By 1943, he was conductor of the Canadian Band of the Allied Expeditionary Forces.[24] After his arrival in England in 1944, he did numerous shows for the BBC, many of which included his own compositions (Stephens 1993, 43); his show themes include *Melody Hour* (1946), and his film scores include *Captain Horatio Hornblower*. As resident conductor and arranger for Decca, he worked with leading musicians including Bing Crosby, Tony Bennett, Vera Lynn, and Lena Horne (Stephens 1993, 44). Some of Farnon's compositions, including *Lake of the Woods* and an atmospheric tone poem based on *À la claire fontaine*, were inspired by Canada. *Jumping Bean* (1947) has often been used as a signature tune and *The Peanut Polka* illustrates his understated humour.

Percy Faith (1908–76) began as an organist for silent films in Toronto. He wrote arrangements for several CBC shows including *Music by Faith* (which featured Farnon on trumpet) and *The Happy Gang*. His popular song *Cheerio (I'm Going to See the King and Queen)* (CMH14, 236) dates from 1939. By 1940 he was writing arrangements for US shows and recording mood music, and from 1950 to 1976 he was Columbia's most cherished arranger and conductor. His dreamy orchestral settings, like music for films, are written as background music for relaxation and romance, but the influence of George Gershwin is evident in his preference for peppy, quasi-Latin percussion and complex syncopation. Highlights include an arrangement of Waldyr Avecedo's *Delicado* (1952) with Stan Freeman playing amplified harpsichord and his own *Theme for Young Lovers* (1960), and *A World of Whispers* (1967), with text by Paul F. Webster. Faith made a vital mark as an instrumental stylist. Using elements of jazz and even rock – for example, the rock-derived triplet patterns in *Summer Place* – he expanded the popularity of easy listening. The compositions and arrangements of Lombardo, Farnon, and Faith were the first of many Canadian contributions to what has been called "easy listening," or "adult contemporary" music. Canadian musicians seem to have a knack for blending elements from various sources into a compromise acceptable to a wide range of listeners.

In 1939, two weeks after the death of her husband, Ruth Lowe wrote *I'll Never Smile Again*, a song that captured the mood of the early weeks of the Second World War. Tommy Dorsey heard a broadcast of Faith's version of the song in Toronto and arranged for its publication. In addition to Dorsey's recording. Lowe's song has been recorded more than a hundred times. Lowe also wrote the lyrics for *Put Your Dreams Away*, which Frank Sinatra used as his theme for twenty-five years (before he switched to Canadian-born Paul Anka's *My Way*). In 1948, assisted by the Rhythm Pals, Elisabeth Clarke, a Canadian nurse, had a hit with *There's a Bluebird on Your Windowsill*.

Popular Music in Quebec to 1950

In the early twentieth century the francophone population of Quebec gradually shifted from a mainly rural to an urban society. Folk music remained a part of most households, but cities offered other forms of musical entertainment. Musical acts at Sohner Park between 1891 and 1919 presented by French or American (usually New Orleans) artists included songs, vaudeville, and operetta. In 1906, Joseph-Ernest Ouimet[25] introduced "motion pictures and illustrated chansons" at his Ouimetoscope (*CMH12*, viii); he bought illustrated Tin Pan Alley songs, had them translated, and hired local musicians to perform them. In addition to providing background music, pianists or orchestra in the cinemas gave a short concert consisting of symphonic overture, an operatic aria or romance, and a popular march or waltz. After this, the players took a break while the organist accompanied the short comedies, travel films, and cartoons before returning to play the score for the main film, "worked out as meticulously as though it were for a ballet" (*CMH12*, viii).

Madame (or La) Bolduc (1894–1941, née Marie Travers), the first popular singing star to emerge in Quebec, grew up in the Gaspé playing violin, harmonica, jaw's harp, and singing with her family. She left home at age thirteen to work as a domestic in Montreal, married, and began to raise a large family, but with her husband often out of work, she accepted a paid job accompanying the singer Ovila Légaré on a recording. This led to appearances in *Les veillées du bon vieux temps*.[26] Bolduc was heard as a violinist in these concerts, which were also broadcast on radio, but in 1927, after enthusiastic response to her appearance as a singer, she was invited to create her own songs. Recordings of *La cuisinière* and *La ser-*

vante released on the Starr label sold 12,000 copies. She wrote many more songs and became known largely as an interpreter of her work, appearing in concerts in Quebec and French Canadian areas of the New England states. Some of her songs are variants of folk songs, and many of the texts are quite personal and concern the everyday lives of ordinary Quebecois. She uses language of the street with reckless verve and almost always includes humour and a note of optimism. Bolduc used gigues and reels to create an individual style of mouth music, and she became famous for her *turluter.*[27]

In the 1930s French-language radio stations were too weak to reach rural areas so rural Quebeckers mostly heard English-language stations that played country music, with ensembles featuring fiddles and singers glorifying cowboy life, open spaces, and sentimental views of the family – themes that, even in English, resonated strongly. By the 1940s singers such as Roland Lebrun, Marcel Martel, and Willie Lamothe were writing French songs in a similar vein. Roland Lebrun (1919–80), born in Amqui, Quebec, sang his new francophone country songs to his fellow soldiers during the Second World War,[28] and on his return was dubbed "le soldat Lebrun." Many considered him the male counterpart of Madame Bolduc, because his songs spoke to ordinary people struggling with everyday life. His career developed through publications and radio broadcasts (CMH12, ix) but many of his lyrics – such as *La prière d'une maman* (CMH12, 72) – seemed outdated after the war. Most Quebec homes had a copy of *La bonne chanson*, a collection of familiar folk songs and newer songs approved by Abbé Charles-Émile Gadbois. Although usually known as a compact book of favourites, the full edition of *La bonne chanson* consists of ten albums, published between 1937 and 1955 (Maître 1993, 53), containing some 500 songs emphasizing the country, patriotism, the Christian life, and nature. Gadbois spread these songs through recordings, festivals, and his radio station CJMS ("Canada je me souviens").[29]

Quebec Fiddling

Fiddle music was a vital part of Quebec traditions, and with the availability of recording technology many of the finest fiddlers have been documented. One of these, Joseph Allard (1873–1947), won many fiddling competitions in the United States and Quebec, and in 1928 began recording for RCA Victor. His remarkable technique was influenced by Irish and American elements, and his repertoire included not only hundreds of folk tunes but also some sixty of his own. Jean Carignan (1916–88) listened to Allard in Montreal between 1927 and 1931, adopted a light supple bow stroke, and learned material recorded by Irish fiddlers such as Michael Coleman, and Scottish violinist J. Scott Skinner.[30] From 1930 to 1937 Carignan was principal fiddler of George Wade and His Corn-huskers, a popular Toronto-based country-style dance group consisting of violins, string bass, banjo, guitars, accordion, harmonica, trumpet and saxophone who toured across Canada. Carignan modified his style for this group, emphasizing the melody and reducing ornamentation and variation. Tiring of constant travel, he returned to Montreal to earn a living mainly by driving a taxi. He also worked with several dancers, and during the 1950s he began an association with the Feux follets dance troupe, with whom he toured Europe. In the 1970s Yehudi Menuhin sought him out for television appearances as a soloist with symphony orchestras. Carignan, who never learned to read music readily, learned classical concertos by rote and claimed that he played everything exactly as he heard it on recordings. Krassen contests this statement:

Everyone admires his dazzling virtuosity, but from traditional Celtic points of view, his playing is full of inaccuracies, improper phrasing, and eclectic and inappropriate techniques ... Even in his nominally Irish and Scottish selections, there is a French-Canadian sense of phrasing. His beat is never quite the light and subtle rhythms of the fiddlers from Sligo or the intensely restrained and precise patterns of the Scots. In all his playing the buoyant and exuberant pulse of French Canada comes through. The other telling feature in Carignan's performance is his application of classical techniques. In his French-Canadian selections, these uses are minimal and mainly involve slightly more complex bowings than would be common ... In the Irish selections, the classical touches are probably most intrusive ... Carignan's classical technique though clearly formidable is of the homemade variety and here again he must be considered an artist of the "folk." (Krassen 1974, 42–3)

Folk Traditions in Anglophone Canada

Collections of Canadian folk songs that appeared after 1900 (Hutton, 1906; Mackenzie 1909; Creighton 1932; Greenleaf 1933) created a new awareness of the rich heritage of English-language folk traditions, and in turn inspired singers to create their own material. Wade Hemsworth (1916–2002) was one of the most important traditional folk singers of the pre-1950 generation, and a number of his songs have become Canadian folk anthems. Hemsworth was heard in many radio broadcasts and festivals, and the NFB used two of his songs for animation shorts.[31] His

Don Messer

Don Messer (1909–73) was basically self-taught; he began playing for dances as a child and learned to read music while working in Boston. After his return to Canada in 1929 he formed Don Messer's Lumberjacks, a group of about nineteen musicians – including the singing lumberjack Charlie Chamberlain – broadcast on radio. Messer also toured the Maritimes with the Backwoods Breakdown. By 1934 he was heard on radio six days a week, and in 1939 he became musical director and orchestra leader for CFCY in Charlottetown. Don Messer and His Islanders recorded hundreds of tunes, toured cross-country and became ever more popular. By 1956 they were broadcasting television programs based on "old time" music with a wide array of fiddle tunes, dances, songs stressing family values, and touches of big band jazz. "Don had appealed to ethnic groups by playing their music and promoting their dances" (Sellick 1969, 68). When the CBC cancelled *Don Messer's Jubilee*

in 1969, demonstrations, protests, and headlines burst out across Canada. (Sellick 1969, 93). Many Canadian fiddlers were influenced by Messer's style and repertoire. He emphasized the melody and left elaboration to the accompanying instruments. His straight-ahead style became synonymous with the Down East style. "To the extent that his values and ideas regarding music and dance in the past and present were congruent with those of his peers, both musicians and listeners, he functioned as a community spokesperson ... Messer played an integral part in acting out the Canadian musical identity of his time. To this day, the fiddle is fundamentally more important to country music in Canada than in the USA: in part, because fiddle music is traditional in many of the European-derived ethnic groups that make up the older portions of the Canadian cultural mosaic; in part, because fiddle music transcends language barriers; and in part, because of Messer's legacy as a star of Canadian country music" (Rosenberg 1994, 31).

songs are based on Canadian tales or experiences, and many incorporate varied musical influences and French, Yiddish, or Mohawk words. *The Blackfly Song* (1949) describes his trials as a hydro worker in northern Ontario. Other well-known songs include *The Wild Goose, The Log Drivers' Waltz, The Land of the Muskeg and the Shining Birch Tree, The Story of the I'm Alone*, and *The Log Jam Song*. During this period, Canadian fiddling traditions were enriched by new strains from the Ukraine and from regional American styles. The Red River style of fiddling is considered to have been established by Andy DeJarlis (1914–75), who recorded more than forty albums and composed more than 300 tunes; his theme song was *Blueridge Mountain Home*.[32]

Country Music

After 1928, recording companies increasingly merged into large conglomerates, and Canadian branches mainly pressed recordings from elsewhere, usually the United States (Barr n.d. www.capsnews.org); the major exceptions were the folk and country artists and the recordings for the francophone market cut in Montreal by RCA Victor of Canada. Although some cowboy songs were recorded as early as 1919, the heyday of cowboy music was the 1930s. Ranch hands, often of First Nations cultures, had been creating and singing their own songs for at least five decades but the music industry did not give serious consideration to musicians from this genre until the early 1920s. Perhaps as a reaction to burgeoning technological dominance in the cities, record companies realized that people wanted to hear the down-to-earth sounds of fiddlers, string bands, gospel singers, yodelers, and balladeers. This music was labelled "hillbilly" until the term "country" gained wider acceptance around 1945. Two personas – the mountaineer and the cowboy – appeared in vaudeville, accompanied by mandolin, upright bass, banjo, fiddle, and guitar, and carried over into Hollywood films, presented as a self-burlesque or as dignified with traditional values of morality and stability. The cowboy, symbolizing freedom and independence, was added to the mix, in the 1930s with a steady stream of cowboy imagery from Tin Pan Alley writers. A number of Canadians played key roles in the development of the country genre.

Bob Nolan (1908–80; born Robert Clarence Nobles in Point Hatfield, NB) joined his father in Arizona after the First World War. By 1927 he was writing songs and had busked his way out to California. In 1931 he joined Leonard Slye (later Roy Rogers) and fiddler Bob Nichols as the tenor and yodeller in the Rocky Mountaineers. In 1933 he formed the Sons of the Pioneers with Slye, Tim Spencer, and fiddler Hugh Farr. Their polished style was characterized by well-crafted romantic songs, a fusion of smooth harmonies, and hot fiddling with touches of jazz-like instrumentation. Nolan wrote many of his 1,200 songs for this group, including *Tumbling Tumbleweeds* (*HACM*–110)[33] and *Cool Water*. Nolan stayed with Sons of the Pioneers until 1949 and continued to record until 1957.

Wilf Carter (1904–96), born in Nova Scotia, heard a group of Swiss yodellers as a boy and worked to master the technique. He heard and learned many songs in the lumber camps, then moved to Alberta in the 1920s where he became a working cowboy and performed in his spare time. Carter began radio broadcasts from Calgary in 1930, and in 1932 released his first record (*My Swiss Moonlight Lullaby* and *The Capture of Albert Johnson*). In 1935, under the name "Montana Slim" he became host of a radio show in New York. A serious car accident hampered his career in the 1940s, but he resumed touring and singing in the 1950s. A number of his hundreds of songs, including *The Yodeling Cowboy, Midnight the Unconquered Outlaw, Calgary Roundup,* and *The Fate of Old Strawberry Roan* have been covered by other singers. Hank Snow (1914–99), another Nova Scotian, left home at age twelve to work as a fisherman. He soon picked up guitar and was learning songs from Jimmie Rogers recordings. By 1933 Snow had his own radio show out of Halifax, and his first recording in 1936 consisted of his own songs. Live tours gradually extended into the United States and by 1950 he was a regular at the Grand Ole Opry in Nashville; his first major success that year was *I'm Moving On.* Other hits through the 1950s and 1960s include *The Rhumba Boogie* (1952) and *Tangled Mind* (1957).

Canadian Jazz to 1950

Canadians first heard the kind of music that became known as jazz (or jas) in vaudeville shows that included all-Black groups. In 1914 the Creole Band appeared in Winnipeg, and by 1917 the term "jazz" was used in descriptions and advertisements of this music.[34] At this time, jazz ensembles usually consisted of piano, cornet, clarinet, and percussion; the music was played with slapstick humour, as loud and as fast as possible (particularly when whites imitated Black musicians). Saxophone ensembles were sometimes heard in vaudeville and the saxophone soon became strongly associated with jazz. One of the earliest saxophone groups – the Six Brown Brothers (Tom, Fred, Vern, William, Alex, Percy) from Ottawa – began a twenty-five year career in 1908 (See Vermazen 2004). Tom, the key member of the group, performed in blackface and created humorous effects on his instrument. Popularity was such that by the 1920s there were numerous other "Brown" groups. The original Browns made some thirty-five recordings of rags, blues, pop songs, and excerpts from Broadway shows including two pieces by African-Canadian Shelton Brooks: *Darktown Strutters' Ball* and *Walkin' the Dog.* The Original Winnipeg Jazz Babies (see figure 9.5), a group of seven teenagers, each playing two or more instruments, first appeared in 1919 (two years after the first commercial release by the Original Dixieland Jass Band), and in the following years, introduced jazz to many centres in Western Canada, but a Winnipeg musicians' union ruling that made jazz players ineligible for membership indicates a rising resistance to the sound. In spite of this, jazz played by local musicians was heard mainly in Western Canada.

Figure 9.4   Morgan Brothers Syncopated Jaz Band. *Calgary Herald*, 15 December 1917, p. 8. "'Jazz' in the new government. Election night at The Plaza. Full and complete returns to be announced between each musical selection or dance."

In Vancouver George Paris, a Black athletic trainer, was admitted to the musicians' union and in 1917 organized a jazz band for the Patricia Hotel. Paris had been directly exposed to contemporary Black American popular culture through his travels as a fight manager, and in retrospect can be identified as Canada's first true jazz musician (Miller 1997, 57). A number of musicians from a small community of Black Americans in Alberta managed to play in integrated bands. Pianist Shirley Oliver played in Tipp's Orchestra, a band specializing in "hot-dance" tunes, and in 1926 opened his own music studio in Edmonton. Arthur Daniels was one of a number of Black Canadians who performed in Calgary's vaudeville and theatre shows. Montreal was a vibrant hub for Black musicians through the 1920s and 1930s (the era of prohibition in the United States). Although individual musicians only spent two or three years in the city, the succession of Black musicians playing genuine jazz gave others an opportunity to learn from them. Barred from the hotels, they worked at the Terminal Club, Café St Michel, and Rockhead's Paradise. Local record companies took advantage of their presence to fill a demand for recordings of Black jazz and blues artists.

ROYAL ALEXANDRA HOTEL
Friday, September 12

DANCING
8.30—1

DANCING
8.30—1

Gentlemen - 75c
Ladies - - 50c
War Tax included

MUSIC GIVEN BY SIX ARTISTS OF SYNCOPATION

Figure 9.5   The Original Winnipeg Jazz Babies, Dance at Royal Alexandra Hotel, 12 September 1919. From left: Cecil Taylor, Oliver Thomas, Leo Martin, Ab Templin, Sam Friedman, W. Green, Sam Rosefield. Cecil H. Taylor Collection, Provincial Archives of Manitoba, N. 14782.

BIG BANDS, SWING, AND BEBOP

In the 1920s Toronto was slow to accept the new sounds of jazz, but through the 1930s there were growing pockets of enthusiasts. By 1921 Luigi Romanelli had established a dance orchestra – violin, piano, saxophone, harp, drums, and bass – at the King Edward Hotel; his excellent musicians and top-rate arrangements of the latest songs soon made it the premier band in the city (Ginsburg 1998, 27). In 1936 Horace Lapp, a pianist in Romanelli's band, was asked to form the Imperial Room Orchestra for the Royal York, and this group became known for their radio broadcasts as well as their stints at both the Royal York and the Banff Springs Hotels (Ginsburg 1998, 29). Groups of Black musicians – such as the Wright Brothers and Cy McLean's band – played a stronger jazz-based idiom, but until 1947 Blacks were not admitted to these hotels and were shut out of the musicians' union in Toronto (Ginsburg 1998, 84). In the early 1940s Clement Hambourg's recording studio on Bay Street in the Gerrard Street Village attracted young musicians such as pianist Norm Amadio, trumpeter Gordon Delamont, Moe Koffman, Hagood Hardy,

Ron Collier, and Norman Symonds for bebop jam sessions. By the 1950s, jazz musicians from Paris, New York, London, or Los Angeles knew that in Toronto, the House of Hambourg (as it became known) was the place for jam sessions after their gigs at the Colonial or the Town Tavern.

Support for Canadian Music

Many Canadian musicians – influenced by Canadian spaces, aware of the newer sounds, and influenced by mixture of musical heritages – were involved in developing popular music genres, but apart from the CBC there was little infrastructure to support their efforts. Unless they travelled abroad there was little opportunity for them to be known or heard beyond their local areas. Even in the 1940s, however, there was a growing movement to build support for Canadian music. An anonymous editorial in the *Canadian Review of Music and Other Arts* comments on the need for a "Ministry of Cultural Affairs":

Plans are being laid for wide social reforms, for the re-establishment of men and women in civilian life, for the turning over of war industries to the production of civilian goods, and for the reconstruction of ravaged cities and countries. Artists and craftsmen will play a vital role in making possible "the bright new world" when peace comes ... it is vitally important that artistic activities be given purpose and direction now. Canada has no lack of skilled craftsmen and artists, but there never has been any centralized direction of their work. (1943, 2/1: 6)

Canada contributed much to the defeat of fascism in the Second World War, at great cost, but unlike Europe and other areas in the world, North America was not in ruins. Canada was in an advantageous position with its mining potential, forestry industry, hydro power, uranium deposits, vast reserves of oil and gas plus manufacturing and financial know-how. With a world-wide demand for resources, foreign capital poured into the country along with a postwar wave of immigration mainly from Europe. After the rationing of the war years, Canadians revelled in consumer goods and full employment, bolstered with unemployment insurance, family allowances, old age pensions, and later, universal health insurance. Government funding of the arts was established and the new medium of television led to significant changes in all areas of performance. The centennial celebrations of 1967 – including Montreal's Expo '67 – the largest extravaganza to date, showcased Canadian performers and composers across the country.

Music Education

Prominent teachers working largely in private studios could provide a solid musical foundation for students – some of whom went on to further studies and even international careers – and they made contributions to Canadian concert music. Yvonne Hubert (1895–1988), born in Belgium, came to Montreal in 1926 and in 1929 founded the Alfred-Cortot Piano School. Gifted students gravitated to her studio, and a number became well-known teachers or internationally recognized pianists.[1] Greta Kraus (1907–98) arrived in Toronto as a refugee from the Nazis in 1938. Known in Vienna as a consummate musician, pianist, and Lieder coach, she promoted the harpsichord in recitals and broadcasts and founded the Toronto Baroque Ensemble (1956–63). Her performances and teaching established a foundation for the lively early music scene existing in Canada today.[2] Quebec-born Lyell Gustin (1895–1988) came to Saskatoon in 1912 and in 1920 established the Lyell Gustin Piano Studios. He was soon known for the interpretation classes and recitals at which his students performed and for monthly soirées at which students read plays by Shakespeare, Ibsen, Shaw, and O'Neill, played piano reductions of symphonic literature, and discussed art with painters such as Ernest Lindner and Robert Hurley. In 1924 Gustin founded the Saskatoon Musical Art Club to promote accompanying and chamber music, and he was also a leader in promoting professional status for music teachers.[3] Gladys Egbert (1896–1965) another well-known piano pedagogue, came to Calgary as a child in 1903; she opened her studio in 1914 after studies in England and New York.[4]

Soprano Pauline Donalda (née Lightstone, 1882–1970), born in Montreal, began a distinguished career in Europe by 1904. In 1937 she returned to Montreal to teach, and founded the Opera Guild (1942–69) to provide experience for young singers. Ernesto Vinci (1898–1983), a proponent of *bel canto*, emigrated to Canada in 1938; he taught in Halifax and from 1945 to the early 1970s in Toronto.[5] Well-known violin teachers include Kathleen Parlow, Géza de Kresz, Elie Spivak, and Francis Chaplin (1927–1993), who was born in New Brunswick and came to Brandon in 1966. Thomas Rolston, Jean Cousineau, and Claude Létourneau first introduced Canadians to the Suzuki method for teaching violin around 1965. Tommy Reilly (1919–2000), from Guelph, Ontario, became the world's leading classical harmonica player.[6] Some thirty concert works were specifically written for Reilly's chromatic harmonica, and he also recorded film and television soundtracks, including *Those Magnificent Men in their Flying Machines* (1965), and *Midnight Cowboy* (1969). Clarinettist Avrahm Galper (b. 1921 in Edmonton) developed his own pedagogical approaches and published several books and articles.[7] These and many other teachers across Canada raised standards of music education, but major changes were also implemented at the conservatory and university levels.

The Conservatoire de musique du Québec,[8] a network joining seven music schools in the province of Quebec, was founded in 1942; under the leadership of Wilfrid Pelletier, Claude Champagne, and Jean Vallerand, this institution had a major impact on teaching and performance. In 1950 the new music department at l'Université de Montréal joined those at McGill (1920) and Laval (1922). Until the mid-1940s, however, only music composition was recognized at the university level, and even then, training was minimal. In 1945 the bachelor of music at the University of Toronto was a three-year degree (reduced to two for applicants holding an associate degree from the TCM). Students had difficulties in finding composition teachers. In 1946, after sessions with Leo Smith and Ernest MacMillan, Murray Adaskin finally found fruitful guidance as a private student with John Weinzweig (Lazarevich 1988, 138). Through the 1950s and 1960s, however, universities in Canada laid foundations – in part, following American models – for comprehensive music faculties distinct from conservatories. Arnold Walter (1902–73) had obtained advanced European training before he escaped the Nazis and came to Canada. In 1945 he was named vice-principal of the senior school at the TCM, and in 1952, was appointed director of the music faculty at the University of Toronto. New developments included an opera department and special-ists (beginning with Harvey Olnick in 1954) were appointed to estab-lish musicology as a discipline. In 1955 Walter introduced the theories of Carl Orff to North America, and in collaboration with Doreen Hall, prepared English versions of Orff's manuals on music education. In 1959 Walter established the first electronic music studio in Canada. Many of the first instruments installed were invented and manufactured by Hugh Le Caine (1914–77), a musician from Ottawa who, around 1945, created Sackbut, the first voltage-controlled music synthesizer. In 1964, Univer-sity of Toronto opened the Edward Johnson Building – the first building in Canada designed specifically for professional music study (Chandler 1990, 17) with room to accommodate a large library made up of music holdings at the University, holdings of the former TCM library, and vol-umes from Edward Johnson's personal collection; this library has since become the largest music library in Canada and now includes the Snider-man Recording Archives. A bachelor of music in performance was first offered in 1966–67.

The University of Toronto example proved to be a stimulus for music programs at other universities. In 1965 the Canadian Association for Uni-versity Schools of Music (CAUSM; after 1981 Canadian University Music Society) held its first meetings in 1965 with representatives from thirteen universities.[9] A "Curricular Standards" document issued by CAUSM in 1969 placed musicology in a senior position, encouraged other areas, and included courses in ethnomusicology, computer music, and Canadian music.[10] At last it was possible for Canadians to receive music education in a full range of musical disciplines – composition, education, perfor-mance, music librarianship, musicology – in their own country. There were no full programs for ethnomusicology, jazz, or popular musics, but

Figure 10.1   Montreal Women's Symphony Orchestra, 1941. Canadian Musical Heritage Society Fonds, Library and Archives Canada.

such programs were not offered in universities outside of Canada at the time either.

Opportunities for Performance

While Canadian orchestras established before the Second World War managed to survive, there were still few opportunities for women outside of community orchestras. In 1940, partly in response to this situation, Madge Brown and violinist Ethel Stark provided funding to form an orchestra of seventy-five women (Vézina 2000, 29). The Montreal Women's Symphony (see figure 10.1), conducted by Stark, gave about ten concerts a season, presenting eclectic programs that included works such as Strauss's *Tod und Verklärung* and Schoenberg's *Verklärte Nacht*; they also premiered Violet Archer's *Sea Drift*. The Women's Symphony was the first Canadian orchestra to perform in New York, and their concert on 22 October 1947 at Carnegie Hall received glowing reviews. The present Thunder Bay Symphony Orchestra was founded in 1960 as the Lakehead Symphony Orchestra by René Charrier and Douglas Dahlgren. A

Verna Jacobson in Rouyn-Noranda

Rouyn-Noranda, a town near the Ontario-Quebec border in the Abitibi-Témiscaming region was one of many communities where orchestras and choirs were formed during the mid-1900s. Verna Jacobson arrived in 1957 to take over a class of piano and theory students and encourage chamber music; soon she was conducting choirs at the Anglican church and the English-language high school. By 1959 these groups wanted to tackle larger choral works with orchestra. The Rouyn-Noranda Symphony Orchestra and Cantata Singers (see illustration) gave their first public concert on 22 April 1960. Orchestra members came from the local band and chamber groups, some of whom travelled from Kirkland Lake (about 100 kilometres), for rehearsals and performances. For works only available in piano-vocal scores Jacobson wrote her own arrangements. The performance, held in the community centre, was a huge success. After this start, the group broadened their activities to include more challenging repertoire and concerts in other northern centres. The spring concert of 1961 included Vivaldi's *Gloria*, an orchestral suite by Gluck, *Dance of the Clowns* by Rimsky-Korsakov, *Valse Triste* by Sibelius, *Romanza* by Granados, and Rossini's overture to the *Barber of Seville*. The following December they played works by Mozart, Smetana, Copland, and Josef Achron, and excerpts from Handel's *Messiah*. The program for 6 May 1962

Figure 10.2   The Rouyn-Noranda Symphony Orchestra and Cantata Choir, conducted by Verna Jacobson, early 1960. Photograph from Verna Jacobson.

included the Easter section of *Messiah*, Haydn's Symphony no. 94, the scherzo movement from Beethoven's Symphony no. 3, and the march from Bizet's *Carmen*. The enthusiasm for musical performance in northern communities is evident in the number of musicians they have pro- duced: examples from Ontario include conductor Mario Bernardi, pianist and musicologist Paul Helmer, and violinist Terrence Helmer, all from Kirkland Lake, and pianist William Aide from Timmins. Unfortunately the mining business is fickle; as resources decline, people move on to economic opportunities elsewhere. By the mid-1960s the Rouyn-Noranda Symphony Orchestra had become a memory.

string quartet-in-residence program provides core professional players and training, and the orchestra gives school programs and tours to other northern centres.

Because the only available training for orchestral musicians was through participation in community or school orchestras, Canadian instrumentalists lacked opportunities to prepare for professional careers. Walter Susskind, who came to Canada in 1956 as conductor of the TSO, had been involved with the National Youth Orchestra Association of Great Britain; he began to gather support for a similar training orchestra in Canada, and in 1960 the National Youth Orchestra of Canada (NYOC) was launched. Each year, about a hundred young musicians are selected from auditions across Canada for intensive summer workshops and training followed by a series of concerts. By 2001, thirty-seven percent of all orchestral musicians in Canada were NYOC alumni, and many others were performing in orchestras throughout the world.

When the National Arts Centre – encompassing spaces to accom- modate opera, concerts, theatre, and venues for gatherings – opened in 1969, the National Arts Centre Orchestra (NACO), conducted by Mario Bernardi, was the only state-supported orchestra in North America. This classical-sized orchestra of forty-four players specializes in late Baroque and Classical repertoire with some forays into the twentieth century, particularly works commissioned from Canadian composers. To ful- fill its mandate the NACO travels across Canada and has made tours to Europe, the United States, Mexico, and Asia. Foreign critics praise their accomplished ensemble playing, rhythmic buoyancy, and supple melodic shading.

The formation of the Opera School at the Toronto Conservatory of Music in 1946 was an important development. Arnold Walter hired Nico-

Beatrice Carmichael in Edmonton

By the 1930s touring companies could no longer afford to transport sets and musicians over long distances, but Canadian centres were still hungry for the operatic offerings that had been available in earlier years. The Edmonton Civic Opera Society (1935–71) was one of the most ambitious of a number of local operatic productions in communities across Canada. Beatrice van Loon arrived in Edmonton in 1920 as leader of an all-women "novelty" act for vaudeville and variety shows, for which she played violin and sang ballads and arias. She soon won the love of a local dentist, and by November of that year had become Mrs J.B. Carmichael. She joined the newly formed Edmonton Symphony Orchestra, and in 1933 she conducted this ensemble in its final concert (Berg and Paulson 1997, 33). Meanwhile, an orchestra she formed at the University of Alberta gave regular radio broadcasts, performed at university functions, and in the late 1920s joined the University Glee Club to perform light operas. Beatrice Carmichael was a prominent supporter of the Edmonton Women's Musical Club, and in 1932 was asked to organize a concert performance with orchestra of Gounod's *Faust*. After this success and concert presentations of Mascagni's *Cavalleria Rusticana* and Bizet's *Carmen* in 1933–34 (Berg and Paulson 1997, 34) she proposed the formation of an opera company. The Edmonton Civic Opera Company was founded in 1935 to produce one grand opera and one lighter work each season; the success of these productions is reflected in an increase to three and then four performances plus a matinee. The war years, however, had a major impact on productions: material for sets was limited and the size of the orchestra and chorus was reduced. New organizations emerging after the war included a new Edmonton Symphony Orchestra in 1952 and the Alberta Opera Society (after 1966 the Edmonton Opera Association) in 1958. However, it was Mrs. Carmichael's Civic Opera Society that was asked to stage a production of *Carmen* during the week-long dedication of the new Jubilee Auditorium in 1957, an appropriate choice since the Society was "the only stable, continuing organization in Edmonton devoted to the production of classical music" from 1935 into the early 1950s (Berg and Paulson 1997, 44).

las Goldschmidt and Herman Geiger-Torel, both refugees from Nazism with extensive experience in European and American opera houses, for the project, and in 1947 the performances of Smetana's *The Bartered Bride* drew raves from public and press (Morey and Schabas 2000, 18). The success of further productions led to the formation of the CBC Opera Company in 1948. These CBC productions drew on the expertise and advanced singers of the School, and demonstrated a growing appetite for live professional opera. In February 1950 the first Toronto Opera Festival presented multiple performances of *La Bohème, Rigoletto, Don Giovanni*, and that same year Torel formed Opera Backstage, a small group that toured across the country presenting operatic excerpts with piano accompaniment.

When the University of Toronto refused to accept financial responsibility for a second Opera Festival, Goldschmidt and Torel set about finding backing for a professional company. In 1950 a charter was granted to the Opera Festival Association (now the Canadian Opera Company [COC]).[11] The next fifty years saw productions of 119 operas, eighteen of which went on tour, with a repertoire ranging from Monteverdi through to Leos Janácek and Benjamin Britten. The COC has helped to establish the careers of many Canadian singers, set designers, choreographers, musicians, and composers: productions of Canadian works include *Red Emma* (Gary Kulesha), *Guacamayo's Old Song and Dance* (John Oliver), *The Luck of Ginger Coffey* (Raymond Pannell), *The Golden Ass* (Randolph Peters), *Louis Riel* (Harry Somers), *Dierdre* (Healey Willan), and *Heloise and Abelard* (Charles Wilson).

The establishment of the COC played a crucial role in the careers of young singers trained in Canada, particularly since tour management systems, like movie theatres, were in the hands of US companies. Community Concerts and the National Concert and Artists Corporation controlled concert series in more than 150 centres across Canada, and most of the profits left the country; these agencies occasionally added Canadian artists to their roster, but placed them in the lowest pay brackets with exhausting tours. The Women's Musical Clubs provided assistance and performance opportunities for young artists (Elliott 1997). For example, contralto Portia White, from Truro, Nova Scotia, received assistance from the Halifax Ladies' Musical Club for her early professional training and engagements, and the Nova Scotia Talent Trust was formed to help defray expenses for her New York debut on 13 March 1944. Rave reviews led to another New York engagement and a contract with Community Concerts. However, she received little financial return from a long gruelling tour of Central and South America, and many believe these hardships led to her subsequent ill health and forced cancellation of performances planned in Europe and elsewhere. The duo piano team Reginald Bedford and Evelyn Eby made an extensive tour for Community Concerts but after expenses were paid, there was only enough left to buy a new tea kettle (personal communication).

CBC/Radio Canada initiated a number of competitions to assist young performers. Each year more than 200 contestants performed on *Singing*

Stars of Tomorrow (1943–56), *Nos futures étoiles* (1947–57), or *Opportunity Knocks* (1947–57), and a number went on to enjoy outstanding careers.[12] The standards of the CBC National Radio Competition for Young Performers, established in 1959, are equal to other international competitions, and judges may not award first or even second prizes if these standards are not reached. Winners of this competition form a "who's who" of Canadian concert artists. The Canadian Music Competitions / Concours de musique du Canada was formed in 1970 to establish a high-level hierarchical system of provincial and national competitions, providing valuable preparation for the rigours of international competition.

Major changes in the period between 1945 and 1970 affected Canadian performers. Violinist Steven Staryk (b. 1932) received most of his training in Toronto and by his early teens was playing in the Promenade Symphony Orchestra, the CBC Symphony Orchestra, and the Hart House Orchestra. At age twenty-four he joined the Royal Philharmonic Orchestra as concertmaster, and over the following decade was concertmaster of Amsterdam's Concertgebouw Orchestra and the Chicago Symphony Orchestra. Making occasional visits to Canada for recitals he was concertmaster for the CBC Symphony Orchestra on the Stravinsky recordings. His repertoire included works by Rodolphe Mathieu, Jean Papineau-Couture, André Prévost, and Harry Somers. From 1982 to 1986 he was concertmaster of the Toronto Symphony, but devoted most of the latter part of his career to chamber music as a member of Quartet Canada (1976–81) and in recitals with pianist John Perry. Staryk's career illustrates that in spite of the important role of the CBC there was still a need to work abroad to develop skills and launch a career. The development of a growing infrastructure of educational institutions, concert halls, and promotion organizations, however, allowed more Canadian artists to pursue careers in music, and possibly make an international mark while remaining in Canada. The career of pianist Glenn Gould (1932–82) is an interesting example. After a few years on the international circuit and a huge success with his 1955 recording of Bach's *Goldberg Variations*, Gould became a world icon. He ended his concert career in 1964, but continued to record and broadcast for the rest of his life, and through all these years he lived in Canada.

The Massey Commission and the Canada Council

Apart from Quebec, where the Institute of Music and Dramatic Arts was established in 1942, the prevailing view was that the arts were an expensive luxury. On the other hand Canadians gratefully accepted generous donations from the Carnegie, Rockefeller, and Guggenheim foundations to set up libraries, buy musical instruments, and endow university scholarships, a situation that, along with proliferation of American books, periodicals, and concert series, increased US influence in Canada. Finally, in 1950, after much pressure from the Canadian Arts Council (formed in 1945), the Royal Commission on National Development in the Arts, Letters and Sciences, chaired by Vincent Massey, began hearings. One submission after another stated that while there were many talented Canadians in the arts, they could not fully develop their careers or earn a living in their own country because of a weak professional infrastructure overly dependent on the United States.[13] Canada was largely dependent on universities to promote development in culture, and lagged far behind smaller countries such as Belgium and Australia in cultural exchanges. Canadian composers had a particularly precarious existence. Music publishing in Canada was limited, and most firms were branches of British or US companies with no interest in Canadian works. The four Canadian orchestras capable of playing difficult symphonic literature – Vancouver, Winnipeg, Toronto, and Montreal – all had financial problems, and even if they were willing to perform Canadian repertoire, there was no library or other source of Canadian scores and parts. There was also a general resistance to contemporary music because Canadians had little opportunity to hear international works dating from the early twentieth century.[14] In answer to all these concerns, the Massey Commission recommended the creation of a public body that combined the features of a government agency and a private foundation; on 28 March 1957 the Canada Council Act received royal assent. The early years of the Council saw an explosion of creative activity.[15]

The Canadian League of Composers

The Canadian League of Composers was essentially formed by John Weinzweig and a group of his former students (after timely prodding from Weinzweig's wife, Canadian writer Helen Weinzweig) on 3 February 1951. One important decision was to make professionalism – regardless of aesthetic outlook – the main criterion for membership. In the first five years, the League membership increased from the initial eight charter members (Murray Adaskin, Louis Applebaum, Samuel Dolin, Harry Freedman, Phil Nimmons, Harry Somers, Andrew Twa, John Weinzweig) to thirty-six. Performances of member's works was an important priority, and the first concert sponsored by the League on 16 May 1951 in Toronto presented compositions by Weinzweig.[16] In 1952 the League hired the Toronto Symphony Orchestra – even though they only had fifteen dollars in the bank and the orchestra's fee was $4,500! The concert, conducted by Geoffrey Waddington, was well received and financially successful, and concerts in other Canadian cities followed. The Canadian Music Associates was formed to produce concerts in centres such as Hamilton, Ottawa, Kitchener, London, Montreal and New York but this group became inactive in 1958 due to lack of funding. La société de musique canadienne, a Montreal-based concert committee, was active between 1959 and 1969. In 1955, to underline a desire to be seen as a professional composers' association with a broad view, both Healey Willan and Claude Champagne were made honorary members.

The Canadian Music Centre

The League had accumulated a collection of scores from member composers and deposited some at the Toronto Public Music Library, but a better resource centre was needed for scores and recordings. In 1957 Weinzweig and John Beckwith prepared a proposal for Canada Council to fund a library of Canadian music, and two years later the first office of the Canadian Music Centre (CMC) was established in Toronto. Branches have since opened in Montreal, Vancouver, Calgary, and Sackville, NB. Associate composers, chosen by application and selection, have the right to deposit their works with the Centre which makes scores and parts available for loan or purchase. In addition to promotional work, the Centre acts as a liaison between composers and publishers, commissioning agencies, performing organizations, and recording companies. The John Adaskin Project, an important initiative of the CMC to involve young people in Canadian music, began as a series of week-long composer-in-the-classroom sessions in the Toronto area in 1963. Many of the composers involved created works for and in collaboration with the students. In 1968 the CMC issued a catalogue of Canadian pedagogical works.[17] One of the most popular works is R. Murray Schafer's *Statement in Blue* (1964), a graphic score that introduces the technique of controlled improvisation and the concept of art as process rather than a fixed product. Schafer's *Threnody* (1967), a moving statement on the destruction of war, and *Epitaph for Moonlight* (1968), based on coined words of elementary students, are also frequently performed.

Composers as Canadians in an International Context

One of the earliest events featuring Canadian composers was a Symposium on Canadian Contemporary Music in Vancouver in 1950. Works by thirty-three composers[18] were presented in five concerts (one choral, three chamber, and one symphony orchestra) by the best musicians in Vancouver. Many of the works were written in the 1940s and reflected a wide range of contemporary styles including English, American, atonal and twelve-tone influences. During the 1950s Garant, Morel, and Tremblay organized several concerts of contemporary music in Montreal. A concert in 1955 included five works of Webern and Garant's *Nucléogame* (1955).[19] Musique de notre temps, formed in Montreal in 1956, was the first of many organizations to create a place for contemporary music and to educate audiences about current musical directions.

In 1960 the Canadian League of Composers was involved in the International Conference of Composers that took place in Stratford, Ontario. The conference grew out of a discussion in 1958 with Louis Applebaum (director of music at the Stratford Festival) and a group of American composers (including his former teacher Roy Harris) during a visit to Russia exploring exchanges between the Stratford Festival Company and ensembles in the Soviet Union. After much planning, delegates from thirty-five different countries descended on Stratford.[20] Louis Applebaum wrote: "We hoped to create an environment in which serial, tonal, electronic, and conventional approaches to composition all could be expounded and defended without embarrassment ... [this conference] has given a self-respect that is vital and hard to come by. This was achieved simply and effectively by having music by Canadian composers scheduled, criticized, and accepted on the same terms and by the same standards applied to music by the renowned guests" (Beckwith and Kasemets 1961, viii–ix). The CBC broadcast the concerts, interviews, and discussions across Canada, and distributed broadcast material to about sixty other national broadcasting systems. The impact is summed up in a review by American critic Alfred Frankenstein:

The composers I especially liked number exactly thirteen. Of these, three (Varèse, Rochberg, and Cage) are American; one (Hamilton) British; one (Blomdahl) Swedish; one (Schiske) Austrian; two (Maderna and Berio) Italian; one (Badings) Dutch; and four (Joachim, Anhalt, Freedman and Weinzweig) Canadian ... In 30 years' activity as music critic for US newspapers, the only Canadian composer I had ever heard of was Healey Willan, whose choral works are often performed in the US. That there was a Canadian League of Composers was completely news to me ..., and that these composers practise all manner of styles and media was an even more striking revelation. That Canada has excellent performing musicians is, of course, a fact of which we in the US are well aware, but only by hearsay; actually to experience the elegant work of the CBC Symphony and the Stratford Festival Orchestra, of vocal soloists like Mary Simmons and conductors like

Walter Susskind and Victor Feldbrill is something else again, and very rewarding. In short, what this festival did was put Canada on the map, musically speaking, for those of us who came from the nineteen foreign countries. As a result of it, I have no doubt but what Canadian orchestral and chamber music will figure more and more prominently on international programmes and Canadian music take its proper place in the international scheme of things. It is obviously past high time for such a development. (quoted in Beckwith and Kasemets 1961, 170)

In August 1961 Mercure organized the Semaine internationale de musique actuelle / International Contemporary Music Week in Montreal, during which works by contemporary composers including John Cage, Karlheinz Stockhausen, Mauricio Kagel, Christian Wolff, Iannis Xenakis, and Toru Takemitsu were heard. This event gave composers an opportunity to assess international currents and allowed audiences to place Canadian works within a broader international context. As Lefebvre states, this event "put an end to European hegemony in Québec's music production and gave rise to new artistic thinking" (2001, 1151).

International influences seemed particularly evident in the Toronto new music scene. Between 1952 and 1964 the CBC Symphony Orchestra gave concerts of mostly twentieth-century repertoire, including many works by Canadians.[21] When R. Murray Schafer returned to Toronto from Europe and the Middle East, he linked up with Toronto-based composers to found Ten Centuries Concerts in 1961. For about six years this organization presented imaginative programs – for example, combining medieval music with a reconstruction of Quesnel's *Colas et Colinette* and Stravinsky's *Histoire du soldat*.[22] Udo Kasemets, a composer of Estonian heritage and a devotee of John Cage, presented "happenings," the first of which was a concert devoted to Charles Ives. From 1965 to 1968 a loose ensemble of musicians, actors, painters, and dancers performed at the Isaacs Gallery in Toronto; a week-long festival in 1968 included Kasemets, Lowell Cross, and David Behrman from Toronto, along with visual artists Marcel Duchamp, Gordon Mumma, and David Tudor. Such groups, devoted almost exclusively to contemporary music, gave composers an outlet for performances of their works, and with the commissioning system of the Canada Council in place, composers might even realize an appropriate fee.

New Directions in Composition

In 1946, the CBC announced a series of seventeen music broadcasts with the following statement:

Orchestral and instrumental music in Canada has not developed in any single, strong direction and there are few works which can be said to be characteristic of the century. This is not to say that Canada possesses few serious composers but rather that their completely different environments and personalities are portrayed in their music. This is inevitable in any country as large as Canada whose cities are widely dispersed and where many ethnic groups live surrounded by great sweeping plains and forests, mountains, whose peaks are hidden in the clouds and whose climate varies from the humid semi-tropics to the perpetual arctic cold. (Quoted in Weinzweig 1996, 84)

Internationally there was much factionalism in musical directions with a major split between those who supported serial techniques developed by Schoenberg, Berg, and Webern, and those who dismissed this approach. In the postwar years, the consistency and continuity of centuries-old traditions in Europe were shattered by political events and a new social awareness. In Paris, Milan, Cologne, Aix-en-Provence, and Darmstadt, new traditions of exploration, experimentation, questioning, and challenging emerged from the vantage point of what Kasemets has called "the immediate NOW."

The turmoil of both wars ensured that what had been concurrent series of national traditions – German, French, Italian, Russian, etc., although always feeding on each other – became a cosmopolitan arena, a new tradition of modernism. The wars and dictators had made artistic geography obsolete. The movers of the '20s and '30s – Varèse, Schoenberg, Stravinsky, Bartók, Hindemith – had moved to the United States. New inventors – Stockhausen, Boulez, Maderna, Berio, et al. – took over the European scene. American-born originals – Ives, Ruggles, Cowell, Thomson, Cage, Harrison – had an uphill struggle to be accepted as creative forces, but then eventually established themselves as leaders of a movement characterized by its freedom from conventions and appreciation of uniqueness. (Kasemets 1991, 31)

The hallmark of Canadian composition in these years was a wide divergence of styles. Composers inclined to follow serial or aleatoric practises were seen as more avant-garde, while those who developed idioms out of late romantic ideals were seen as more conservative. Sometimes division spilled over into who was a pupil of whom, rather than recognizing that a good teacher should allow a student to find one's own particular voice.

Barbara Pentland's *Studies in Line* (1941), a set of four piano studies, is a musical rendition of four abstract designs. When Pentland joined the music department at UBC in 1949, she became more appreciative of the discipline of serialism. *Octet for Winds* (1948), her first strictly serial work, was really an extension of the intervallic techniques she had been using for the past decade. On a visit to Darmstadt in 1955, she heard the music of Anton Webern for the first time, and became truly convinced of the possibilities of this technique. *Symphony for Ten Parts* (1957) illustrates Webern's impact in its conciseness of structure, imaginative and delicate sonorities. Pentland was first introduced to serialism by John Weinzweig while they were teaching at the TCM. Weinzweig's approach to serial technique can be seen in *Divertimento no. 1 for Flute and Strings* (1946);[23] the strings play ostinato patterns while the flute presents the set. The twelve individual pitches are presented in his "add-one-and-go-back" process, which allows a gradual spinning out of melodic gestures and allows occasional departure from the strict order of pitches.

When Harry Somers (1925–99), a former student of Weinzweig, went to Paris to study with Milhaud in 1949, he was suprised to learn that writing in a serial idiom was forbidden.[24] In *North Country* (1948) Somers had established his own musical idiom that involved extended tonality contrasted at times with serial technique. The sparse texture and long soaring lines of this string orchestra piece evoking central and northern Ontario has long been considered a hallmark of a distinctive Canadian idiom. Later Somers wrote a number of works for voice. *Twelve Miniatures* (1963) for piano (harpsichord), flute (recorder), and cello (viola da gamba) reflects the development of performance on early instruments in Canada, but the texts are Japanese haiku translated into English. Somers continued along these lines in *Evocations* (1966); the first song of the set incorporates the call of the quintessential Canadian bird, the loon.

In 1967, Somers received a commission from the Canadian Opera Company for the full-scale opera *Louis Riel*. This three-act music drama is scored for twenty-six soloists, full orchestra, and prepared electronic tape. Mavor Moore's libretto – which includes four different languages (English, French, Cree, and Latin) with French translations by Jacques Languirand – explores issues still endemic in Canadian politics through the fate of Riel, a Métis leader caught in a web of rivalries between French and English, the fears of the First Nations, and the rapidly changing Canadian West. Musical approaches include quotations of First Nations and folk music, atonal-abstract materials, diatonic ironic versions of nineteenth-century styles, and for the more surrealistic moments, electronic sounds. Most pitches and rhythms are fully scored, but there is some use of graphic notation and aleatoric writing. The poignant *Kuyas*, a Cree lullaby for voice, flute and percussion sung by Marguerite at the opening of act 3, is often performed in concerts and recitals.[25] Somers's interest in folk traditions and music is also evident in *Songs of the Newfoundland Outports* (1968), his intricate setting of songs recorded and transcribed by Kenneth Peacock.[26]

Oskar Morawetz (b. 1917) came to Canada in 1940 to escape Nazism and obtained a doctorate at the University of Toronto, where he taught from 1946 to 1982. A self-taught composer with extensive knowledge of European music, he developed an idiom largely rooted in late romanticism. His style is characterized by expanded tonality and polytonality in a contrapuntal texture of motivically generated melodies; his effective orchestration and Slavic-infused rhythms can be heard in *Carnival Overture* (1946).

At the time of his death in 1966, Pierre Mercure was preparing the television production of R. Murray Schafer's *Loving/Toi* (1965). This "audiovisual poem" about love between the sexes in Canada's two official languages combines prepared tape and live performance. The score, in graphic and conventional notation, includes roles that are sung, spoken, and danced. The non-linear, surrealistic story line uses a stream-of consciousness technique, and the singers are personae in the allegorical sense, rather than individual characters. This work contains many elements that Schafer continued to pursue in subsequent musical theatrical works that extend the ideas of Wagnerian music drama. *Son of Heldenleben*, a commission from the Montreal Symphony in 1968, illustrates two main traits of Canadian composition in the subsequent decades: humour and musical quotation.[27]

One of the most performed Canadian works of the second half of the twentieth century is Godfrey Ridout's *Fall Fair* (1961), an orchestral piece that evokes an annual event in many small towns of Canada, with original tunes that have a folk-like character. Ridout describes the two main themes as "a country-fiddle figure" and a "lop-sided waltz" (Bradley 1982, 125–6), and his syncopated rhythms and off-beat accents are reminiscent of big band jazz. Polish-born Harry Freedman (1922–2005), another of Weinzweig's students, began his musical career as a jazz musician while studying art in Winnipeg. His scores are often infused with jazz idioms (such as augmented fourths) and inspired by painting. *Toccata for Flute and Soprano* (1968), an exuberant work incorporating scat singing, was written for his wife, soprano Mary Morrison, and Canadian flutist and composer Robert Aitken. Both these pieces have a clear North American stamp, and demonstrate that Canadian compositions in this period reflect influences of geography and incorporate rubbaboo elements in their blending of different kinds of sounds.

Directions in Quebec

Varying influences can be found as well in the compositional approaches of francophone Canadian composers. In Quebec, folk-based compositions were largely rejected, and Claude Champagne emphasized the need for symphonic compositions. The third movement of his *Concerto for piano and orchestra* (1948), entitled "Fiesta," captures a mood of *joie de vivre* in a brilliant dialogue between piano and orchestra. Champagne's imaginative *Quatuor à cordes* (1951), perhaps influenced by his students' interest in recent musical developments, is more intervallically conceived and explores the use of different metres simultaneously.

The musical languages of François Morel, Clermont Pépin, Pierre Mercure, Serge Garant, Roger Matton, Gilles Tremblay, André Prévost, and Jacques Hétu were more imbued with the essence of Stravinsky, both rhythmically (his *Rite of Spring* period) and structurally (his neo-classicism). Jean Papineau-Couture (1916–2000) studied with Nadia Boulanger and became an influential composition teacher in Montreal. His works are structuralist in approach and feature contrapuntal writing. The polyphonic concept of harmony establishes tonal centres, but from time to time, he adapted other approaches, including serial technique. In the latter part of his career he became more concerned with timbre and sonorous resources (Gagné et al. 1990, 101).

Serge Garant (1929–86), an influential performer and conductor, helped to make Montreal audiences aware of the latest musical trends in Europe and the United States and blended these in his own composition. In 1951 he attended classes in analysis given by Olivier Messiaen in Paris, and on his return to Canada, gave the first Canadian performances of piano works by Messiaen, Webern and Boulez. In *Pièce pour piano no. 1* (1953) Garant combines serial technique with aleatoric practises and direct playing on the piano strings to create new sonorities. In 1966 Garant founded Le société de musique comtemporaine du Québec, a Montreal new music society that performs a range of contemporary chamber works. With *Trois huit* (1950), a work for piano or harpsichord, Gilles Tremblay (b. 1932) introduced "sound for sound's sake" into francophone Canadian composition,[28] and this concept became an increasingly constant element. It even appears in the title of François Morel's *Deux études de sonorité* (1952–4); the rhythmic second *étude* explores the sound palette by exploiting various registers of the piano. Morel's *Antiphonie* is a modal exploration of the different sonorities created between two instrumental groups.[29] This fascination with sound can be seen in relation to the French concern for language. André Prévost's *Soleils couchants* (1953) is a choral setting of an evocative poem by Paul Verlaine.

In the late 1940s Pierre Mercure (1927–1966) was associated with painters, writers, and dancers later referred to as *automatistes*,[30] and had been writing works strongly influenced by Stravinsky and Messiaen. After studies with Luigi Dallapiccola at Tanglewood in 1951, he rejected strict serial writing for its lack of artistic flexibility. His neo-classical *Divertissement* (1957) for string quartet and orchestra opposes the sonorities of the two groups. In 1958–59, looking for new sonorities and strongly influenced by American popular music and jazz, Mercure worked with Pierre Schaeffer at the Groupe de recherches musicales in Paris. His orchestral work *Triptyque* (1959) takes its structure from visual arts: the third movement is a retrograde of the first, a procedure also used by Papineau-Couture in *Pièce concertante no. 1* (1957). From 1959 to 1962, Mercure explored the sonorities of electronic music. In his last major work *Lignes et points* (1964), a theme and eight variations for orchestra, he largely uses graphic notation to show relationships between music and geometric shapes, creating acoustic sounds similar to those formed electronically.[31] Mercure wrote many radio drama scores and he played a major role as the first producer of television music for Radio Canada; significant programs include a broadcast of Berg's *Wozzeck*.

Electronic Music and Instruments

Magnetic tape was invented just prior to the Second World War, but the technology was not reliable enough for recording music until after 1945. Meanwhile, several Canadians were involved in electronic sound production experiments parallel to developments elsewhere. Two electronic instruments – the thérémin and the ondes Martenot – were invented before 1930, and a number of Canadian composers, particularly francophones, used these instruments in major works; the best known example is Champagne's *Altitude* (1959). Filmmaker Norman McLaren, who joined the NFB in 1940, was drawing sound tracks directly on the films; his small strokes and blobs created a wide range of percussive rhythms.[32] In 1949, Louis Applebaum was exploring Osmond Kendall's drawn sound technique.[33]

Huge Le Caine (1914–77), a young science student at Queen's University interested in electronic sound, met Morse Robb, an inventor in Belleville who had developed the wave organ in 1926.[34] In 1937 LeCaine designed an electronic organ with more subtle control. He joined the

National Research Council (NRC) in 1940 to work on the development of radar, but also continued his experimentation with sound, and in 1945 produced Sackbut, the first monophonic electronic instrument – now called a synthesizer. Sackbut had a touch-sensitive keyboard, a portamento glide strip, modulation control for vibrato and timbre, and limited voltage control. It could produce glides between notes and bend pitches, and it had more subtlety of timbral control than any synthesizer produced before 1990.[35] LeCaine also developed a Touch Sensitive Organ, with volume controlled by how deep the keys were depressed. His Multi-Track Tape Recorder (1953) could accommodate several tapes at once and had a keyboard to control the speeds (Keane 1984, 62).[36] These and other instruments invented by LeCaine were used in electronic music studios in the University of Toronto, McGill University, and in Jerusalem. "Perhaps the most important aspect of Le Caine's designs for his instruments was the 'playability' that he took care to build into them. His ideal was to enable nuance-filled expressive performance. Touch sensitivity was an essential ingredient in this, and was used in keyboards, mixers, and other components, applied mechanically, electronically, and through light sensitivity" (Lanza 2002, 46). LeCaine, a nuclear physicist, wrote fifteen electroacoustical compositions; *Dripsody* (1955), a classic, is considered a landmark in electronic music. One December night, LeCaine recorded the fall of a single drop of water and "created a rhythmic pattern by splicing together copies of the original recording of the water drop (occupying about 1/2-inch of tape). Also, he used the multi-track to re-record the water drop at various speeds (and thus, at various pitches) and then spliced these copies together to create a rising pentatonic scale pattern. In all, only 25 splices were made" (Keane 1984, 63). These electronic developments soon had an impact in many different genres of music, as electronically-produced sound provided the background for many musical expressions from 1950 on.

The Hit Parade

The decade of the 1950s saw worldwide changes in popular music. A large teenage population with money to spend bought music that spoke to their needs, and producers quickly found that they were not satisfied with sentimental love songs against a background of dreamy strings. Canadian Gisele Lefleche (b. 1927), a talented pianist, violinist, and singer, played a key role in popularizing the sentimental songs of the early 1950s; as Gisele MacKenzie she first performed with the Bob Shuttelworth Band then as lead singer on the television show *Your Hit Parade* (1953–7), and later on her own show on the NBC network. Her top hit *Don't Let the Stars Get in Your Eyes* was released in 1952, the same year that television sets first appeared in Canada. The music business was also expanding. By 1954 Capitol Records of Canada had pressed five million discs.[1] In 1957, CHUM, a Toronto radio station, began publishing a hit parade chart, largely dominated by what large US record companies were pushing, and that remained Canada's top singles chart until 1983.

In the United States, music played an important role in the emerging civil rights movement, and strict boundaries between recordings made for the "race" market and those made for the dominant majority began to break down. By 1956, a new exciting sound had emerged: the young Elvis Presley's blend of country music with gospel and rhythm and blues. Rock 'n' roll was based on a strong lead singer, who also played guitar, and a back-up band of guitar, drums, and string bass. Young Canadians became enamoured with this sound and journalists unanimously labelled the first rock 'n' roll concert at the Montreal Forum in the autumn of 1956 as "infernal and barbarous" (Lacoursière and Bizier 1980, 23). By the early 1960s, a new major influence was making itself felt: the Liverpool sound of the Beatles: while their music includes rock elements the Beatles expanded their sound to include rockabilly, rhythm and blues, and sentimental ballads. Elements of refined music in their performances include a string quartet (for McCartney's *Yesterday*, 1965) and a trumpet solo (in the accompaniment for McCartney's *Penny Lane*, inspired by J.S. Bach's second Brandenburg Concerto); the bilingual text of McCartney's *Michelle* was an important model for Canadian musicians. Their 1967 album *Sgt Pepper's Lonely Hearts Club Band* (Capitol SMAS-02653) has been called the first rock "concept album," with all the songs organized around a central theme; instrumentation stretches the limit of the accepted rock sounds, with a string orchestra, a brass band, kazoos, a group of clarinets, and a calliope. Influences from India are heard in *Within You Without You*. Other breaks from standard style include the triple metre verse and duple beat chorus of *Lucy in the Sky with Diamonds*. For North American and Western European audiences, all of this signalled that this music was for listening as well, and the album opened the door to electronic instruments and electronic manipulation of sound (for example multitracking, splicing of tape fragments, the tapes played backward, and synthesizers) that subsequently played an important role in popular music. No rock band could escape the influence of the Beatles, and in Canada clones proliferated. Young people heard this music on portable and car radios as well as vinyl recordings, and by 1967 portable cassette tape recorders provided even greater accessibility.

Popular Canadian Folk Music

Links between this music and the past include pre-war folk music expressions and elements of music hall and older styles of English song. By 1950 more than half of Canada's population lived in urban areas, but folk music traditions were very much alive and had in fact been strengthened through radio broadcasts and the work of folklorists. Marius Barbeau was continuing to collect and publish French Canadian songs, *La bonne chanson* encouraged families to sing older songs at home, and the *Family Herald and Weekly Star* printed a weekly column of "Old Favourites."[2] The major published collections of folk songs compiled by Helen Creighton, Edith Fowke, Edward Ives, MacEdward Leach, Louise Manny, and Kenneth Peacock, appearing through the 1960s and 1970s are one result of popularizing folk music through live performances, radio broadcasts, and recordings. Some of these collectors hosted their own radio or television programs: from 1947 to 1961 Manny hosted a weekly show on CKMR (Newcastle, N.B.) featuring the songs she was collecting from Miramichi lumbermen; Creighton, who had recorded more than 4,000 songs in English, French, Gaelic, Mi'kmaq, and German in Nova Scotia and Prince Edward Island, made guest appearances on both radio and television from the late 1940s on; Edith Fowke hosted *Folk Sounds* (1963–74) and *Folklore and Folk Music* (1965) on CBC radio; John Jeannotte hosted a CBC radio folk music series during the 1950s and 1960s. Alan Mills (1913–77), began his career in a vocal quintet and also sang minor operatic roles. He was the star of the Montreal CBC radio programs *Folk Songs for Young Folk* (1947–59) and *Songs de chez nous* (1952–5). His own contemporary folk song *I Know an Old Lady Who Swallowed a Fly* (1951) was performed by Burl Ives among other singers. In 1952 his first of several recordings for Folkways was released.[3] Marius Barbeau undertook occasional promotions of folk-song performance;[4] by 1955 he was assisting Sam Gesser with *Folksongs*, a weekly CBC television program, and this led to further collaboration with Moses Asch of Folkways Records.[5] Through the late 1950s and early 1960s Folkways produced many Canadian recordings and promoted such performers as Hélène Baillargeon, Tom Kines, Alan Mills, Alanis Obomsawin, and Stanley G. Triggs (see appendix H).

Tom Kines was one of many performers who sang at coffee houses or *boîtes à chansons*. While radio stations and record stores were blaring out *Billboard* magazine's designated top forty, Canadian singers and bands were playing these venues, the most important of which were in Quebec City, Montreal, Ottawa (Le Hibou), Toronto (in the Yorkville region) and a few scattered across the west. With luck, they might realize twenty-five or even fifty dollars for a gig. Performers such as Ian & Sylvia, Gordon Lightfoot, Joni Mitchell, Buffy Saint-Marie, Neil Young, David Clayton-Thomas, Anne Murray, The Guess Who, The Stampeders became known by performing a folk song or two along with their own songs. By the end of the 1960s those who managed to finance their own recording could sell as many as 100,000 copies even if their music was not broadcast on the main radio stations. The rise of folk festivals[6] added another element to the mix. In 1958, Louise Manny began presenting local performers at the Miramichi Folk Festival. Two years later, Ruth Jones, a folk music supporter from Orillia, worked with many of the Yorkville performers in Toronto to organize the first Mariposa Festival.[7] An all-Canadian lineup at Mariposa in 1961 included O.J. Abbott, Jean Carignan, Alan Mills, Jacques Labrecque, the Travellers, and Ian & Sylvia. The annual Mariposa Folk Festival underlined the bridge between traditional folk songs to contemporary song writing. From the early years, programs pre-

Tom Kines, the Song Pedlar

Thomas Kines (1922–94) began singing and playing in choirs and orchestras in his community of Roblin, Manitoba, and learned folk songs from his Irish grandfather, who had sung in logging camps. At the University of Manitoba he appeared in Gilbert and Sullivan operettas, and in the Canadian Navy he often entertained his fellow sailors with songs. After the war he became head of the administration of the Canadian Legion, but continued singing and acting on CBC Radio and in NFB films. He also appeared as tenor soloist in oratorios and Lieder recitals, and was guest soloist for the Toronto Bach Society, the Montreal Bach Choir, the Ottawa Choral Society, and the Montreal Consort of Viols. He was a founding member of the Tudor Singers, an Ottawa madrigal group. His interest in the music of Elizabethan England led to research on songs connected with Shakespeare's plays and the discovery that a number of Elizabethan songs had passed into oral transmission. He taught himself to play the lute in order to perform these songs and songs by Robert Burns, interspersed with an ever-widening range of Canadian folk songs, all usually linked by a theme. His first commercial recording, *Maids and Mistresses* (1960) was followed by offers from Folkways, for whom he recorded *Popular Songs of Shakespeare's Time* and *An Irishman in Americay* among other albums; he also recorded Canadian folk songs for RCA Victor.

Kines's career as a broadcaster began in 1959 with the radio series *Puttin' On the Style*, and he appeared on television; later series include *The Song Pedlar* (1960–70) and *Folk Fair* (1977–79). On these programs, which he researched and hosted, he interviewed not only folk collectors but also some of their informants (guests included Edith Fowke, O.J. Abbott, Helen Creighton, Kenneth Peacock, and Lennox Gavan). His appointment as head of Care Canada gave Kines the opportunity to travel and perform abroad, and to learn about folk musics of the world. He sang Gaelic songs on a BBC program, collected some twenty-one musical instruments of non-Western cultures, and recorded music of these cultures, examples of which were broadcast, with explanations, on subsequent radio shows. Kines relished Canada's rich and varied folk music heritage and considered himself a "purveyor of songs" or a "song pedlar" – somewhat like a seventeenth-century ballad monger. In an interview for the *Ottawa Citizen*, 17 April 1965, he said, "I mess around with them a little bit, rewrite them, put them in settings, present all kinds of stuff which couldn't really be called folk-music." This approach and his performances of his own songs provided a role model for other performers. At the same time he refused to commercialize his music. In the same interview, he commented: "Take Burl Ives ... who's had 15 years at the top and is thoroughly commercial now. I couldn't look myself in the eye if I had to sing some of the junk he sings now to keep his record sales up." This information was gathered from the Tom Kines Collection, at Carleton University, School for Studies in Art and Culture; this collection is described by Paula Conlon in *Canadian Folk Music Journal* 22 (1994), 50.

Figure 11.1
Poster for concert of
Canadian folk musicians
at Town Hall, New York,
20 October 1962.

sented a broad variety of folk traditions found in Canada, including First
Nations music, fiddling and bluegrass, Black musics such as blues and
gospel, francophone groups, and other cultural traditions, such as those
of India. This multicultural emphasis has remained a characteristic of
folk festivals in Canada.[8]

ShBoom: Canadian Influence on American Pop

Juliette (b. Juliette Sysak in Winnipeg, 1927), one of the first Canadian
television stars began her career singing on radio out of Vancouver. Her
first television appearance was in 1954 and by 1956 she had her own CBC
show, which became very popular and ran until 1967. Her back-up, the
Rhythm Pals, were among the first Canadian groups to appear on US television; their recordings with Juliette include W. Lassiter's song *I Caught
the Bride's Bouquet*. The Crew Cuts,[9] one of the first white groups to perform Black rhythm and blues hits, remained active until 1963; their big-

Table 11.1   A comparison of *ShBoom* recorded by the Chords and the Crew Cuts

	Chords (1953)	Crew Cuts (1954)
structure	8-bar periods of two 4-bar phrases 4-bar introduction 4-bar extension (vocables) after first period	8-bar periods of two 4-bar phrases 4-bar instrumental introduction ninth period shortened to 7 bars no four-bar extension.
instrumentation	guitar, string bass, drums with saxophones on the solos opening: 2 bars a cappella plus 2 bars instrumental 6th and 7 periods instrumental with tenor sax improvisation.	swing-style dance band: saxophones, brass, rhythm section, and kettledrums. occasional instrumental fills between lines of text band plays behind the vocables of 5th and 6th periods dramatic pauses broken by kettle-drum glissando
vocals	group sings all periods solo bass on the bridge.	different solos (no bass) on first 4 periods group sings last 7 periods vocables changed to "sh-boom" or "la, la, la."

gest hit was their cover of the Chords' *ShBoom* (1954), a rhythm and blues song. The Black vocal harmony of the Chords, influenced by work songs, gospel singing, and barbershop quartets, was referred to as "doo-wop" for the "race" record market. A comparison of the two versions of this song (see table 11.1) demonstrates the Crew Cuts approach that turned *ShBoom* into a hit record. While the tempo and the lyrics are the same in both versions, "[t]he roughness of the original recording is smoothed over, and as their very name suggests, the Canadian group managed to establish a clean-cut, wholesome image which allowed them to 'cross-over' both the border and the pop market and to achieve commercial success" (Grant 1986, 117). In other words, the Crew Cuts incorporated a modicum of Black-based traditions without antagonizing their largely white-based audience. Other successful Canadian doo-wop groups include the Four Lads;[10] their first big hit, *The Mockingbird*, was followed by two songs by Robert Allen and Al Stillman (*Moments to Remember* and *No, Not Much*). Their schmalzy clean-cut barber-shop harmonies feature tenors rather than lower voices. The Diamonds[11] covered some Black groups using a more edgy sound than that of other white groups.

Their cover of the Gladiolas' *Little Darlin'* (Maurice Williams) released in 1957 has a strange mixture of rhythm and blues with calypso-like percussion.[12] Their original *The Stroll* (1958) began a major dance craze. The Beau-Marks,[13] a Montreal quartet that combined vocal and instrumental skills, influenced the make-up of pop groups through the following decades, and had several hits including *Clap Your Hands.*

In the late 1960s a number of Canadians played key roles in groups that influenced trends in popular American music. David Clayton-Thomas (b. Toronto 1941) became known for the range of songs that he attacked with gusto. Influenced by the eclectic range of musics and styles of Toronto's Yorkville, he fused jazz with rock.[14] *Brainwashed* (1966), written and recorded in Yorkville with The Bossmen features a rock guitar section with jazz piano and is considered the foundation of what became known as jazz rock fusion, and he had a big hit with *Spinning Wheel* (1969) with the US group Blood, Sweat & Tears. Lovin' Spoonful[15] – with Toronto guitarist Zal Yanovsky – scored with *Do You Believe in Magic* (1965). Denny Doherty (b. Halifax 1940) performed in various groups with Yanovsky among others, but his major work was with two seminal folk-rock groups: The Mugwumps, and the Mamas and the Papas.[16] In 1971 he resumed a mainly solo career in Canada. Steppenwolf[17] played a menacing hard rock that became known as heavy metal,[18] with a deafening volume – an absolute rejection of the peace and love ethos –made possible by power chord strumming and maximum sustain created by electric instruments and amplification. Mashmakhan[19] had a big hit with Pierre Sénécal's *As the Years Go By* (1970), which begins with a Hammond organ and became popular in Japan.

Canadian Singer-Songwriters

A tradition of singer-songwriters rooted in folk song creation has remained particularly strong in Canada, and the 1950s saw the rise of several influential artists. Paul Anka (b. 1941 in Ottawa) had his first major hit with *Diana* (1957).[20] Musicians that developed their musical abilities in the "peace and love ethos" of the coffee houses and *boites à chansons* include Ian and Sylvia Tyson. Ian Tyson's *Four Strong Winds* (1961), with folk and cowboy song roots, became an international hit. Sylvia Tyson (born Fricker) included folk songs from the collections of Edith Fowke (such as *Mary Anne* and *Un Canadien errant*) in her early Yorkville appearances, and she continued to create a distinctive sound with this repertoire after she joined Tyson.[21] *You Were On My Mind* (1965) was covered by musicians of San Francisco pscheldia and folk-rockers of Los

Angeles. Gordon Lightfoot played in jazz bands in Toronto during the 1950s and for a short time in Los Angeles before he joined *Country Hoe-down*, (a CBC television show starring Tommy Hunter) in 1960, but after hearing Ian & Sylvia he saw the possibilities for the combination of folk and country. Lightfoot began writing his own songs which soon became well known; *For Lovin' Me* was covered by Peter, Paul & Mary in 1965. Much of his inspiration came from the Canadian outdoors – for example, *Steel Rail Blues* came out of an eighteen-hour train trip to Moosonee (Jennings 1997, 85) – but gradually he moved from country-tinged songs to pop-ballads. His *Canadian Railroad Trilogy* was a CBC centennial commission;[22] in the tradition of train songs, it has distinct sections with contrasting tempos, metres, and moods, each of which reflects the spatial nature of a region of Canada. The wholeness of the country is suggested through subtle variations of melodic gestures in the initial descending line of the opening.

Québécois Popular Music in the 1950s and 1960s

The French language and tradition played a major role in the develop-ment of francophone popular music, particularly because of the stress on the final syllable of multi-syllable words and a tradition of musical struc-tures that were less square or formal that came from fiddle tunes not closely tied to a six- or eight-beat pattern. Links with the development of cabaret songs (*chanson rive-gauche*) in post-war France were nourished in cabarets and *boites à chansons* such as Faisan Doré in Montreal and Chez Gérard in Quebec City. A common language led to influences of Cajun, zydeco, and First Peoples styles, particularly evident in instru-mental combination such as accordion and fiddle.

In the 1940s Marcel Martel (1925–99) learned Lebrun's songs and was soon writing his own country-flavoured material which he began record-ing in 1947.[23] His songs have a rockabilly mode with steel guitar solos (as in *Le rock 'n roll du Père Noël*), and he claimed to be the inventor of the "cowboy québécois," with vocal effects such as sliding and swelling on each word group (for example, in *Allo ma prairie*). *Mon amour du rock 'n roll* is a loose version of Presley's *Hound Dog*. Willie Lamothe (1920–92) was influenced by Lebrun and Wilf Carter and wrote cowboy-type songs that incorporated Tyrolean yodelling. *Je chante à cheval* (CMH12: 74) presents a solitary cowboy on the Canadian prairies with a yodel ending each verse and tongue-clicking to imitate hoof beats. In later recordings, instrumental accompaniment expanded beyond the guitar; *Rock cowboy rock* and *Rock 'n roll à cheval* were recorded with the Cavaliers des Plaines

(Bobby Hachey, guitar, and Fernand Thibault, violin). In the early 1970s he had a popular TV program called *Le Ranch à Willie*. He was known as the "king of the Québécois cowboys," and sold over a million records in the United States alone.

Félix Leclerc (1914–88) wrote his first songs as a student, and after a variety of jobs (a rich source for later songs), made his first appearance as a *chansonnier* on the CBC in 1939.[24] His blues-influenced *Le Train du nord* (1950) became particularly popular. Leclerc cited Madame Bolduc as an influence, but he also drew on a range of crooner and cabaret influences particularly in France after 1950 (wearing a checked lumberjack shirt and playing a guitar). Many of his songs had recurring references to nature, but after the 1970 October crisis, he turned to social comment and protest; *L'Alouette en colère* describes the plunder and dispossession of Quebec (Tétu de Labsade 2001, 401), and *Un soir de février* (1972) deals with the aftermath of the British conquest. He became an inspiration for younger generations of Quebec chansonniers concerned with issues of identity and Quebec nationalism. Gilles Vigneault (b. 1928 in Natashquan) was largely influenced by Léclerc and also used themes of nature and landscape, particularly of his birthplace on the North Shore; *Mon Pays* (1965) captures the growing feelings of identity based in Québécois language, heritage, and landscape.

Quebec musicians followed developments in American music, particularly the strong presence of Black musicians in Montreal playing blues, gospel, and jazz. The accented second and fourth beats (the backbeat of gospel and rock 'n roll) blended with Quebec's strong affinity for layers of rhythms in Latin music and the 1960s funk of James Brown had an important impact. Interestingly, these influences, particularly 1950s rock 'n roll, crept into western canadien (Quebec country music). Léo Benoit had a great success with *Le rock 'n roll dans l'lit* (1958) as music to listen to, not for dancing. New couple dances, such as rock, cha-cha, and samba and line dances such as ya-ya and pinto, were accompanied by guitar, bass, and drum set (often electric and amplified) rather than the fiddle and accordion used for the more traditional square dances and jigs. The Beau-Marks, formed in 1958, the first of many new dance bands, sang in English, but by 1962 there were many francophone groups. The Mégatones had the widest influence, with Fender guitars and use of echo and reverberation effects, but other successful groups include the Jaguars (whose *Mer-Morte* became a classic), the Hou-Lops, and the Majestiks. The invasion of the Beatles in 1964 was followed by vocal groups called *yé-yé*, connected not with dance but with the popular music world of spectacle. In November 1964 Les Classels appeared at the Quebec Coliseum playing white instruments and dressed in white top hats, tails, and white wigs. Between 1964 and 1968 the Sultans produced a high level of music influenced by the Beatles and Rolling Stones, but infused with their own unique contagious humour. Other *yé-yé* groups include Chancelliers, Lutins, Christine et ses Copains, and Bel Canto.

New vocal groups were able to build on a *pop québécoise* that developed in the mid-1950s. By 1957 a Radio-Canada competition for Canadian songs in French had produced Michel Louvain as a pop music star, and an increase in recordings and air play supported francophone crooners such as Pierre Lalonde, Dean Edwards, Yvan Daniel, and Norman Knight. In the 1960s, the popular vocal music world in Quebec split into two largely opposed camps: the *yé-yé* groups, who were modelled on anglophone American trends, and the *chansonniers*, whose music and use of language tended towards France. *Jeunesse d'aujourd'hui*, a program launched in 1962 to present young Quebec singers to teenage audiences, worked on the cover system: all the songs were French versions of the American/British hits. In hindsight, L'Osstidcho, a concert combining music and theatre (monologues, improvisation, and comedy) presented in Montreal in the summer of 1968, represented a completely secular manifestation of popular culture in a society that was only beginning to separate church and state:[25] "The show, often referred to as an anti-concert, featured Robert Charlebois, Louise Forestier, Yvon Deschamps, Mouffe, and musicians from Le Jazz libre du Québec in a partially improvised mixture of music, monologue, and theatre. This type of performance was unheard of in the *chansonnier* tradition, and the combination of the local vernacular, the presence of several performers, and electrified instruments makes the event a point of crystallization for popular music" (Morrison 2001, 1158).

Charlebois (b. 1945 in Montreal), labelled "Superfrog," performed in joual,[26] wearing a Montreal Canadiens hockey sweater, and accompanied by a jazz-rock group. A number of vocal duos (such as the Satellites, Lionel et Pierre, and the Rythmos) had produced songs in joual, a few of which were recorded in the early 1960s, but Charlebois managed to combine elements of French heritage with popular American musics into a genuine expression of Quebec that was both poetic and musical. He became the touchstone for all future development of popular music in francophone Canada.

The first festival of traditional music of Quebec at l'Université de Québec à Montréal in December 1973 led to the rediscovery of fiddlers Carignan and Pitou Boudreault and accordionist Philippe Bruneau. La bottine souriante, one of the many groups performing up-dated traditional music, first appeared in 1976 and continues to present lively vocal and instrumental arrangements that draw on jazz, tex-mex, New Age, and even refined music. Musicians recording in Quebec during the 1970s benefited from a new attitude that considered recording an art in itself. The album was seen as a total entity, somewhat like the Beatles' *Abbey Road*. The first Quebec example is Jean-Pierre Ferland's album *Jaune* (1970), which contains such classics of new Québécois song as *Quand on aime on a toujours vingt ans, Le petit roi,* and *Le chat du café des artistes.*

Popular Musicals

The twentieth century saw an increase in repertoire from American musical theatre, which by the 1920s was centred in New York along with the song writers of Tin Pan Alley. In a model developed by New York-based composers such as George Gershwin, Jerome Kern, Irving Berlin, and Richard Rodgers, songs, dances, and choruses were treated as insertions into the drama, but this changed with *Oklahoma* (Rodgers, 1943), in which individual character development takes place during musical numbers and catchy tunes and rousing dance numbers are woven into the story. This newer model was followed by the creators of one of Canada's most successful musicals. *Anne of Green Gables,* based on Lucy Maud Montgomery's 1908 novel, began in 1956 as a television production with book and lyrics by Don Harron, music prepared by Norman Campbell, and orchestration by Phil Nimmons. In 1965 the Charlottetown Festival commissioned Harron and Campbell to prepare a full-length musical, the success of which made it an annual fixture of the Festival. The show has toured across Canada and had successful runs in London, New York, and Japan. In 1967 Galt MacDermot (b. 1929 in Montreal)[27] completed the music for *Hair* (book by Gerome Ragni and James Rado), a bold and innovative musical that incorporated rock and dealt with controversial issues of the day, including the war in Vietnam, the younger generation's challenge to long-established values, and the emergence of a "hippie" counterculture. The stage version of *Hair* started a major controversy with its use of nudity, and many of its songs made the hit parade.[28]

Mid-Twentieth Century Jazz

In the 1940s the popularity of jazz began to wane; swing, as played by big bands led by Lombardo, Duke Ellington, Glenn Miller, Count Basie, and Woody Herman remained popular, but touring costs inevitably led to the emergence of smaller groups playing bop jazz.[29] The essence of this style is an insistent four beats to a bar played by the double bass and, rhythmic layers, frequently subdividing the beat into triplets and adding off-beat accents, played by the drummer on ride cymbal, hi-hat, snare, and bass drums, and additional on- and off-beat punctuation by the piano. The harmonic vocabulary, including altered ninth, eleventh, and thirteenth chords and chromatic melodies set bop apart from swing. Although bop has little popularity with the general public, many Canadian musicians have worked in and developed this form of jazz. Oscar Peterson (b. 1925, Montreal) is considered an outstanding representative of the second bebop generation. By age 15 he had his own program, *Fifteen Minutes Piano Ramblings*, on CKAC in Montreal, and by 1945 was appearing on CBC programs such as *The Happy Gang*. In the mid-1940s he worked with Johnny Holmes' orchestra and by 1948 his trio (bass Ozzie Roberts and drums Clarence Jones) was broadcasting from the Alberta Lounge in Montreal. After a sensational New York debut as an unannounced guest in *Jazz at the Philharmonic* at Carnegie Hall on 18 September 1949, he built an international career, performing and recording as a soloist and with his trio.[30] Through all these years he kept Canada as a home base. In 1958 he moved to Toronto where he founded (1960) and taught (1960–64) with Butch Watanabe, Ed Thigpen, Ray Brown, and Phil Nimmons, at the Advanced School of Contemporary Music. In the 1960s he published four volumes of piano exercises and solos. His *Hymn to Freedom* (1962) is frequently performed. Each section of his *Canadiana Suite* reflects a region of Canada.[31] Some critics consider Peterson to be the greatest jazz pianist ever with his knowledge of harmony, sense of structure, and independence of hands creating a strong rhythmic swing.

Maynard Ferguson (b. 1928, Verdun, Quebec) was also raised in Montreal and played in his brother's band, the Montreal High School Victory Serenaders with Peterson on piano. In the early 1940s he was heard regularly on CBC radio, and by 1945 had formed his own band, playing stints in both Toronto and Montreal and the occasional pre-concert warmup for touring bands led by Count Basie, Duke Ellington, Woody Herman, and the Dorsey Brothers. These musicians noted his high-register trumpet and in 1948 he joined the Boyd Raeburn orchestra in the United States. He recorded many titles with the Charlie Barnett and Stan Kenton orchestras and as a studio musician for Paramount recorded many film soundtracks. Over time he formed several small groups, using a number of musicians from Montreal. The musical direction of these bands varied from rock and bop to traditional swing, funk, and commercial pop (Megill and Demory 2001, 227). Although he also played flugel-horn, bass trombone, French horn, as well as hybrid horns he designed for the Horton-Leblanc company, he is best known as a trumpet player, covering the entire range with a controlled, full-throated tone and centred pitch, and using his high register ability judiciously, making certain that the notes have meaning in a compositional context. Other Montrealers who built careers largely away from Canada include Paul Bley (b. 1932), an early proponent of electric keyboards in the late 1960s. Bley mainly leads his own groups in collective improvisation, but has also created epigrammatic pieces and has a reflective approach to piano solos, thinking "in melodic shapes and rhythmic thrusts" (Kallmann 1992, 131).

Toronto-born Gil Evans (1912–88)[32] became known for charts in which he drew on elements from Louis Armstrong, Ellington, and Charlie Parker, combined with aspects of classical and swing techniques. He was a great admirer of the Toronto-born composer Robert Farnon and aimed for the same subtle effects, particularly Farnon's sense of space and airiness; his horn players used a lightweight tone and legato lines, with few hard, sudden attacks. Moe Koffman (Toronto, 1928–2001) was one of the first Canadian jazz musicians to adopt bebop in the early 1940s, initially as an alto saxophonist, and later on flute. The album *Blues à la Canadiana* made by his Quartette (which included guitarist Ed Bickert) introduced *Swingin' Shepherd Blues* and clearly established the flute as a jazz instrument. For more than thirty-five years Koffman was the booking agent for Toronto's major jazz venue George's Spaghetti House; his quartet (or quintet) performed throughout North America, often with Dizzy Gillespie, and at international jazz festivals. Tumpeter and flugelhornist Kenny Wheeler (b. Toronto 1930), another bop musician, studied first with John Weinzweig and then moved to London, England, where he continued his career. From 1959 on he played regularly with John Dankworth's groups, often with fellow Canadians Art Elleston and Ian McDougall, and has become highly regarded in the European jazz scene as both a performer and a big band composer. Since the 1970s he has regularly appeared in North American jazz festivals, and has taught at the Banff Centre since the early 1980s.

Lenny Breau (1941-84), the son of the country singer Lone Pine, grew up in the Maritimes and later in Winnipeg, where he worked with jazz pianist Bob Erlendson and was house guitarist for the weekly CBC program *Music Hop*. Breau's country music finger style opened up new melodic and harmonic possibilities for jazz guitar, and he explored the harmonic potential with partial chord tones and harp-harmonics that rivalled and sometimes even surpassed the range of a keyboard instrument (Anderson 2000, 8, 34). In the early 1960s he performed with singer Don Francks and with his own trio or quartet in Winnipeg and Toronto, and accompanied jazz musicians such as Peter Appleyard and Glenn McDonald and folk/pop singers Malka and Anne Murray. During his last ten years, he performed mainly in the United States. Many of Canada's top jazz musicians felt a need to go to the United States for continued development, but Canada also benefited by outstanding jazz emigrants. One of these was pianist Linton Garner (1915–2003)[33] who appeared on the Vancouver jazz scene in 1972. Garner moved to Montreal in the 1960s and also worked in Toronto (Grove 2000, 250).

First Nations Make Their Contemporary Mark

Through the first half of the twentieth century, First Nations musical expressions were either prohibited or severely restricted; government bans of the Northwest Coast potlatch (1884) and the Prairie Sun or Thirst Dance remained in effect until 1951. To circumvent these legal restrictions, gatherings were organized on major white holidays such as Christmas and July 1 with versions of round dances or two-steps ready if police or government officials appeared.[34] In the mid-1940s First Nations and Métis veterans returned from war to find their people denied suffrage and not considered as citizens. Through connections made during military service, these men began to forge cross-cultural links. Many became involved in the pan-Indian development of powwows begun in the United States.

Phonographs and radios provided First Peoples with access to a wider range of musics. Country music in particular appealed to their aesthetic sense, with its descending melodic contours, reiteration of single pitches, and textual themes (family, hard work, the rambling man, prison, fate, and religion) that had relevance to their own musical expressions and lives. During the 1960s Mi'kmaq Willie Dunn and Nehiyaw (Cree) Buffy Sainte-Marie were singing their own songs and folk songs in coffeehouses and on folk music circuits. Buffy appeared at the Mariposa Festival in 1964, and the following year her anti-war *Universal Soldier* became a big hit for Donovan. In the 1970s, Buffy Sainte-Marie was expressing Native viewpoints with her song *He's an Indian Cowboy in the Rodeo* and material prepared for the television program *Sesame Street*. By the late 1960s, David Campbell, Winston Wuttumee, and Shingoose (Ojibwe Curtis Jonnie) were writing songs that presented First Nations perspectives to a multi-cultural public, often using humour, a strategy highly valued in their parent-cultures. Shingoose has said: "My influences were the Beatles and the Stones, like everybody else. When you start to get more responsible and see your people suffering, there is an awakening. What makes me different, if I am different? It leads to a mingling of tra-

The Powwow

Dances at powwows were based on traditional dances and music of the Central Plains traditions that originated among the Ponca, Omaha, Pawnee, and Sioux. The powwow, a complex that includes functions of honouring, entertainment, social prestige, and identity, maintains a flexibility that allows expression of regional and tribal differences. By the late 1880s two distinct forms, Northern and Southern began to emerge. Canadian groups mainly followed the Northern form, during which music is sung at a higher pitch and dancers move in a clockwise formation. The Plains area has remained the stronghold of powwows. While the powwow has not been accepted in many parts of Canada, by the 1980s a circuit of powwows was in place across southern Canada, followed by drummer/singer groups and the dancers. By the 1950s a sharp distinction – in terms of tempo, steps, and costume – between straight and fancy dancing was established. Men wore feathered outfits in a tailored style for traditional dances, and more lavish costumes for fancy dances (such as the grass dance or the Prairie Chicken dance). Women's traditional outfits were based on older regional styles in buckskin or cloth, but some dances, such as the Jingle and Shawl dances require special dress. Straight traditional dancing has slower tempos and more dignified steps, while the fancy dances have fast tempos and flamboyant movements.

Powwows are usually held on a weekend and begin with the Grand Entry of flags, veterans, elders, and all of the participating dancers, each attired for their particular gender category and age group. A Flag Song, usually in a native language, is followed by an invocation. A Veterans' Song or Victory song usually comes at this point, and honour songs and dances may be inserted at various points in the proceedings to honour individuals, the organizing committee, or the deceased. Specific dances – such as the Round Dance which uses a basic side step, or the Intertribal Dance where a basic toe-heel step is used – are done by everyone. Contest Dances have specific styles: men's dances include Straight, Traditional, Grass, and Fancy; women's include Traditional, Fancy Shawl, and Jingle. At competitive powwows there are also age categories for each dance. Songs used for each dance style vary between regions and tribal groups. Powwows may include Exhibition or Special dances, such as the Sneak-up, Crow Hop, Buffalo, or Hoop Dances, and some ladies' choice dances with male-female partners known as Two-Step or Rabbit Dances, usually accompanied by forms of love songs.

Early on in the powwow movement, dance types came north from the United States, while the best songs were said to be provided by singers from the Canadian Plains. As many as eight singers/drummers sit around a large powwow drum (often a bass drum from an instrumental band placed sideways) resting on a blanket on the ground or hung from songposts. In the northern parts of Saskatchewan and Alberta, singers use individual hand-held drums. Now women may sit at the drum, but before about 1935 they were restricted to sing-ing. The structure of the typical powwow song consists of a lead (sung by a soloist), a second (a repetition by all singers), a first chorus (sung by everyone) ending with vocables, and a second chorus (sung by all) with four to six downbeats or honour beats; the final ending of the second chorus completes one strophe or push-up. Four push-ups are required but more may be sung. Drumbeats depend on the dance. Patterns include a steady one-two beat, a beat accented on one, a beat accented on two, and a ruffle or roll used for the men's fancy dances. The vocal sound is produced at the back of an open mouth and throat, and quality is judged according to range and volume. The typical contour of a powwow song is predominantly descending over a wide range, similar to the traditional Plains-style songs. For more information and videos of various powwow dances, see www.nativedrums.ca and www.native-dance.ca.

ditional and contemporary. It's conceptual, rather than a sound" (Taylor 1993, C-1).

Ronnie Hawkins (b. 1935 in Arkansas) came to Canada in 1961 and has helped many Canadian artists and groups including Bobby Curtola, John Kay (later of Steppenwolf), as well as members of the rockabilly group The Band. This group (Rick Danko, bass guitar, Levon Helm, drums, Garth Hudson, organ, Richard Manuel, piano, and Robbie Robertson, guitar) began as The Hawks, a backup band for Ronnie Hawkins in 1961. In 1965 they left Hawkins and later changed their name to The Band. Hawkins's new backup group, Crowbar, recorded *Oh, What a Feeling* (1971), consid-ered a quintessential musical expression of Canada. A tension between individual and group solidarity, a continuing aspect of Canadianism, is evident in the sound of The Band. Each player was encouraged to present his views, but at the same time The Band had a certain tautness. The resul-tant sound has jagged edges on a slick angular core. Even their recording procedures (in basements and rented houses) connect them more with the folk music scene than the milieu of sophisticated studio bands.

Robbie Robertson spent the summers on his mother's Six Nations Reserve near Brantford, where "he learned the customs of his moth-er's people and got his first exposure to music, a 'rural' style ... played on guitars, fiddles and mandolins" (Jennings 1997, 24). Back in Toronto, he listened to blues from CKAC, Nashville, and recordings of Ronnie Hawkins. As a member of The Suedes he opened for Hawkins band,[35] and soon after, joined the Hawks. Robertson crafted meaningful songs, full of an outsider's observations, influenced by folk music heard in Yorkville and an interest in the history and culture of the southern United States. The album *The Band* (1969), for which he also did most of the engineering, contains his *Up On Cripple Creek* and *The Night They Drove Old Dixie Down*, a study of the American Civil War from a Canadian point of view. In *Acadian Driftwood*, a statement about being a Canadian in the United States, Robertson imagines himself as an Acadian telling his story to descendants, stressing that it is the little people who are trampled by events, a theme he developed in projects exploring Native heritage. Robertson has commented that his guitar style was based on pickings his uncles used on the Six Nations Reserve. He has consciously delved into his Aboriginal heritage and his songs often reflect this heritage with references to traditional musics, powwow material, and the assistance of other Aboriginal musicians.

New Anglophone Directions

The Travellers, Canada's first professional folk song group, began singing at Jewish youth gatherings and moved on to bring a message of peace and brotherhood to various leftist organizations. Their Canadian version of Woody Guthrie's *This Land Is Your Land* (1955) became an unofficial anthem. They appeared on television and toured coast-to-coast performing Canadian folk songs collected by Fowke and Creighton, and paving the way for later contemporary folk and protest music. Many songs of the 1960s and 1970s were protests against situations in and policies of the United States. The Guess Who's misogynistic anti-Yankee *American Woman* (1970), performed by Burton Cummings, Randy Bachman, Garry Peterson, and Jim Kale of Winnipeg, emerged on an Ontario tour. With their exceptional ability to write hit singles (*These Eyes, Laughing, Undun, No Time, Hand Me Down World, Share the Land, Clap for the Wolfman*), the Guess Who "opened the doors internationally for the Canadian music industry in Canada" (Einarson 1995, 10). They were able to remain in Canada absorbing pop trends, refining and filtering them through a keen understanding of rock music history and experience, "and play back at Americans a sound that was at once new and familiar" (Einarson 1995, 12). Much of their success was grounded in Winnipeg, a relatively isolated city where teens supported local bands that covered a wide spectrum of styles. There was also a unique guitar tradition centred around Lenny Breau, Randy Bachman, and Neil Young. Later in the 1970s Bachman left The Guess Who to form Bachman-Turner Overdrive specializing in hook-laden, heavy-metal songs with trucker imagery.

The Music of Joni Mitchell

Joni Mitchell was born Roberta Joan Anderson in Fort Macleod, Alberta, in 1943. Her career took off in 1970 with *Big Yellow Taxi*, and she participated in The Band's final concert in 1976. Portrayed as a major figure in the folk movement, she was the first female songwriter to create a large body of work. "Up until that point I still looked and sounded like a folk-singer because I hadn't a band that could play my music. Folk-rock was what's happening. I came in seeming like a folk-singer but really what I was doing was more like Schubert. I was developing the art song" (Enright 2001, 25). Like Cohen, Mitchell came out of a literary tradition, and she recognizes Cohen songs such as *Suzanne* as an early influence (Enright 2001, 30). Musically Mitchell sees her development coming first from her early exposure to piano music (and her frustration with a teacher who did not encourage her creativity), and she developed her own ukulele and guitar tunings and technique. Her first album was a concept album with a schematic continuity, and she has always taken full control of the production of her recordings; she was one of the first to include full texts with her albums.

Mitchell feels that her innovative approaches to music come from her initial training as a painter, where her original voice was encouraged. Working mainly with jazz musicians since the late 1970s, she follows her response to sound rather than a series of rules. In part, she believes that this is in the nature of being a woman. "If a woman has a problem and she tells it to a woman, the woman sympathizes. If a woman has a problem and she tells it to a man, he wants to resolve it. Sus[pended] chords are unresolved chords. If you go from an unresolved chord to an unresolved chord to an unresolved chord, I think it bugs men. But my life has been unresolved, so these chords suited my disposition emotionally; they depicted my life" (Enright 2001, 27). In her interview with Michael Enright, Mitchell comments on her use of the sophistication of classical composition along with elements of folk music, the folk singer-songwriters, dance music, and black rock n' roll. "You know, African rhythm and blues meets Ireland with its rhythms. I was trying to hybrid so many things and keep them all going" (Enright 2001, 27). In addition to discussing this rubbaboo, Mitchell underlines her need for humour that comes across in both her lyrics and her painting. In her experimental 1975 album *The Hissing of Summer Leaves* she combines elements from the legitimate art-song, folk-song, with jazz, and rock elements. The title song of her next album *Hejira* (1976) demonstrates the fusion that she was trying to develop; she considers the album as a song cycle, "unified by the theme that 'time-honoured notions of tradition have been lost to the siren song of change'" (Briscoe 1997, 196). The title is the Arabic word for "flight," and the ostinato in the lower line suggests a continuum and insistence for change that provides a ground for her song-speech lines of varying length. The song ends without a clear sense of tonal centre, a perfect example of her exploration of shifting unresolved sounds.

Neil Young (b. 1945) began performing in the Toronto coffee house scene, and in 1966 he went to Los Angeles where he formed Buffalo Springfield.[36] Two years later he went solo with Crazy Horse as his backup group. With Crosby, Stills, and Nash – which recorded Mitchell's *Woodstock* for the soundtrack of the film – he continued to produce thoughtful songs on current situations. His first big hit was *Heart of Gold* (1972). Young experimented with elaborate stage shows, new styles and video. His path as a solo artist and a group member is, perhaps, a part of his Canadian heritage. In groups he emphasized vocal harmony with sophisticated major sevenths and altered chords, often dwelling on the flattened seventh of the key (as in rock). Melodies feature non-chord tones, particularly suspensions, rather than harmony notes, and he developed a sophisticated, layered approach to rhythm (Fetherling 1991, 135). Although the phrase structure is balanced, like Cohen, he uses a recitative style following rhythms of speech, so the texts are clear. Fetherling points out that while Young had much more rock influence than Lightfoot, Cohen, Mitchell, or Robertson, his voice still "sounds like the wind on the Prairies" (Fetherling 1991, 136). Murray McLauchlan (b. 1945, born in Scotland) has a passionate love for Canada but remains aloof from the issues of Canadian quotas. In his autobiography he acknowledges college radio stations as a determining factor in the discovery of many Canadian artists. After American folksinger Tom Rush recorded two of his songs in the late 1960s, McLauchlan released his first album on Finkelstein's True North label, and had a series of hits in the 1970s, beginning with *Farmer's Song*, a commentary about New Yorkers who don't know who produces their sustenance.

Stompin' Tom Connors (b. 1936 in Saint John) deals with some of these issues in a country style, building his career with no radio airplay before 1970. His distinct if eccentric brand of plain-speaking, hard-rhyming, East coast blue-collar-cowboy nationalism won him a fervent following in bars, lounges, and fairgrounds across Canada. His intriguing songs are rooted in Canadian realities: *Bud the Spud, Sudbury Saturday Night, The Hockey Song, Snowmobile Song, Tillsonburg, Poor Poor Farmer,* and *The Don Messer Story*. The "core" Connors sound is produced by bass and acoustic guitar (Echard 1994, 14), but Latin elements, a snare drum (in *Sudbury Saturday Night*), and sounds symbolizing Inuit culture (in *Muk Luk Shoo*) go far beyond typical American country music. In 1971 he co-founded Boot Records to promote Canadian artists and he helped to launch the careers of guitarist Liona Boyd[37] and the Canadian Brass.

Anne Murray (b. Springhill, N.S., 1945) is one of a number of musicians to build an international career while remaining in Canada. Her well-supported mezzo voice, inimitable stylings, and choice of fine, frequently Canadian, material ensured continued success after her first international hit with *Snowbird* (1970).[38] In pop and country categories she anticipated both k.d. lang and Shania Twain, and she is part of the rich Maritime musical continuum that includes Don Messer, Wilf Carter, Hank Snow, Stompin' Tom Connors, Rita MacNeil, and the Rankin Family. Kate and Anna McGarrigle combine French-Canadian and Irish folk music traditions with instrumental skills on piano, banjo, guitar, and accordion. They first gained recognition in 1972 with *Heart Like a Wheel*; other well-known songs include *Love Over and Over* (1982). Their performances are clearly an extension of the kitchen party, and their sound is strongly influenced by traditional French-Canadian music of the St Saveur area (Regenstreif 1997, 49). Terry Jacks, a leader and rhythm guitarist on the CBC's *Music Hop* show in Vancouver, teamed up with his wife Susan to perform in a coffee house in Blubber Bay. As the Poppy Family they sold two million copies of *Which Way You Goin' Billy* (1969), and in 1970 *That's Where I Went Wrong* topped French charts in Quebec as *Le Bateau du Bonheur*. Gino Vanelli came from a musical family (his father played in the Maynard Ferguson Band); his big hits include *People Gotta Move* (1974) and *I Just Wanna Stop* (1978), which was written by his brother Ross. He has also used symphony orchestras, as in his successful album *Brother to Brother* (1979). Vanelli and the McGarrigles are among the many Canadian musicians who have created new rubbaboos from musical strains found in landscapes of the country.

Problems of Promotion

Many Canadians musicians went to the United States to establish their music careers because there were few good Canadian recording studios, no major Canadian-owned record labels, and no Canadian business managers. Radio play was determined by American hit lists and there was little support for touring schedules or venues.[39] When Bobby Curtola (b. 1944 in Thunder Bay) failed to interest a recording company, he formed Tartan Records and undertook his own management. His *Fortune Teller* (1962) is one of a number of hits from the 1960s, and two of his songs made the country charts in 1990. As more Canadian songs were covered internationally, some Canadian artists were able to earn a decent living from royalties[40] while remaining in Canada. However, many Canadian musicians were not identified as such in Canada because much of their music had American or universal themes. Through the 1950s, support for Canadian musicians increased. Recording companies or branches of international labels established in Canada (Dominion, Quality, Decca, Capital Records of Canada, Columbia Records of Canada) increased the possibility of Canadian record releases and television opened up other opportunities. The coffee house circuit provided venues where musicians not only gained live performing experience but also heard a variety of musics –a major factor in the mixing of different types and traditions, which is a cornerstone of Canadian production.

Organizations also directed more attention to Canadian accomplishments. The Canadian Record Manufacturer's Association (later the Canadian Recording Industry Association) was formed in 1963 by ten record companies who slowly began to sign and record Canadian acts. Band recordings were made across the country in tiny studios on basic equipment, and small independent labels were emerging, but Canadian recording artists and labels had a difficult time breaking into national hits. *RPM Music Weekly*, founded in 1964 by former policeman Walt Grealis, published articles on Canadian talent and the recording industry and radio programming surveys. A national chart in each issue brought singular attention to Canadian artists for the first time. Grealis provided valuable information for the Canadian Radio-Television Commission (CRTC) which was formed under new broadcast legislation in 1968, and he designed the MAPL logo indicating Canadian music, arrangement, performer, lyrics that appears on most popular Canadian recordings. All these efforts were stimulated by a rise of nationalism with the 1967 Centennial celebrations and the Montreal Expo.

In 1964, Walt Grealis published the results of his first year-end *RPM* poll to choose notable Canadian artists and in 1970 the first RPM Gold Leaf Awards were presented in a ceremony in Toronto (Melhuish 1996, 20).[41] After the formation of the Canadian Academy of Recording Arts and Sciences in 1974 the Awards were expanded to the whole music industry; in 1971 they became the Junos, in honour of Pierre Juneau. Meanwhile, under chair Pierre Juneau, the newly formed CRTC introduced a CanCon policy that required thirty per cent Canadian content on AM radio. The resulting demand for Canadian material to fill quotas stimulated the recording industry to sign more Canadian artists, and this in turn led to more professional recording studios and better engineering. New companies emerged and in 1975 the Canadian Independent Record Production Association was formed. Canada was the first nation to place a communication satellite in geostationary orbit (the Anik A-1 in 1972).[42] With improved radio and television reception, First Peoples musicians had more opportunities to hear current popular musics and were inspired to create their own, particularly in communities where powwow rock groups and country singers flourished.

The showcasing of minority heritages during centennial events led to continuing broader interest. For example, Toronto's Caribana, first mounted in 1967, has been staged annually ever since and has become the largest outdoor party in North America, and from the beginning, music has been an important focus.[43] Martin has commented that popular culture can help to foster a sense of place where the myths and images that form the basis of identity, loyalty, and nationhood can be created (Martin 1995, 13). Lehr points out that in *Four Strong Winds* Ian Tyson "captured the vastness and melancholy of the Canadian West" (Lehr 1994, 276); Tyson has been able to express real regional contrasts of Canada as "intra-national – east-west – not international – north-south" and to reveal fundamental differences from the US north-south rural-urban models (Lehr 1994, 277). Canadians also express these differences with place names; country musician Rick Neufeld was pressed to change the title of his *Moody Manitoba Morning*, written in the early 1970s, to "Moody Minnesota Morning." He refused, with the result that the song was a success in Canada but failed to become popular south of the border (Lehr 1994, 275). Government attempts to protect Canada's fledgling pop music industry include the Maple Music Junket, launched in 1972 to promote Canadian pop recordings in Europe.

In 1970 *Rolling Stone* observed that Canada "was notorious for virtual non-support of its own talent." Canadian legislators were concerned with two pertinent axes of articulation (Wright 1994, 283) The first axis was the relationship between the music community and the musical scene concerning different musical practises within a geographical space. Will Straw has defined community as a relatively stable population group "whose involvement in music takes the form of an ongoing exploration of one or more musical idioms said to be rooted within a geographically specific historical heritage" (1991, 373). The concept of musical scene concerns a "cultural space in which a range of musical practises coexist, interacting with each other within a variety of processes of differentiation, and according to widely varying trajectories of change and cross-fertilization" (Straw 1991, 373). The second axis has boundary management strategies concerning group identification within and outside boundaries. These boundaries are articulated by a group's definition of themselves; in order to do this, the group, like a single human being, requires the presence of the Other (Martin 1995, 6). In much of Canada, the Other had been the founding colonial countries of France and Britain, or after the 1790s the

United States. Thus, boundaries created on national, regional, and even local levels indicate to outsiders that the group within is unique in terms of history, language, customs, and musical expressions. The Canadian situation is more complex in that there are at least four separate yet interlocked cultural spaces (Maritime, Quebec, Ontario, and the West), and within each space, multiple musical communities participate in numerous musical scenes.[44]

The CRTC's 30 percent CanCon ruling was not welcomed by all musicians, and many remained ambivalent. Musicians who had major successes abroad in the late 1960s did not want this success to be seen as government meddling. The first wave of successful popular musicians came from the vibrant Yorkville coffee house scene in Toronto, where a strong folk music tradition fed into the creation of the contemporary singer-songwriter. Bernie Finkelstein convinced bands that they needed to produce their own material. In turn, Wright has argued that their success rode on the coattails of US folk singing (Woody Guthrie and Pete Seeger) as carried on by Bob Dylan (1994, 289). For many musicians, "folk was a medium perfectly suited to express what they, as Canadians, were seeing in the world around them." While Canadians were aware of both Dylan and Burl Ives, a folk music tradition well ensconced in Canada was for the most part a much more rooted authentic form than that widely heard in the United States. In 1972 Bruce Cockburn attempted to articulate another aspect of the sound Canadians produced:

I think a lot of the songs that are being written are distinctively, if not obviously, Canadian. Playing something close to American music but not of it. I think it has something to do with the space that isn't in American music. Buffalo Springfield had it. Space may be a misleading word because it is so vague in relation to music, but maybe it has to do with Canadians being more involved with the space around them rather than trying to fill it up as Americans do. I mean physical space and how it makes you feel about yourself. Media clutter may follow. All of it a kind of greed. The more Canadians fill up their space the more they will be like Americans. Perhaps because our urban landscapes are not yet deadly; and because they seem accidental to the whole expanse of the land. (Wright 1994, 291–2)

Fetherling also tried to elucidate this elusive Canadian sound that became prominent in Canadian anglophone music of the 1970s; in his opinion it is a "sincere gentleness" that gets its true flavour when combined with a sense of isolation, reflecting the loneliness of the landscape. Musically this sound is often created with simple instrumental acoustics placed against complex vocal progressions. Canadians have reacted to the five singer-songwriters that Fetherling discusses – Lightfoot, Cohen, Mitchell, Robertson, and Young – in a unique way (Fetherling 1991, 10). All five leaned more toward the longer album songs (rather than three-minute one-hit wonders) that allow greater depth of lyrical and musical exploration. Jennings points to a strong Maritime flavour in spite of the regional nature of Canada's music, and Joni Mitchell has described her own and Neil Young's music as having "a lot of Prairie in [it] ... I think both of us have a striding quality to our music which is like long steps across flat land" (Jennings 1997, 240). The important role played by the Black heritage has been increasingly recognized: "The blues ... run through Canadian music as distinctly as the sound of a train whistle in the Rockies. From Vancouver's Powder Blues Band to the Maritimes' own Dutch Mason Blues Band, the music has enjoyed a long-standing national following ... Add up these Prairie, Maritime, folk-based, bluesy, traditions, combine them with writerly lyrics that express the loneliness of wide-open spaces, the shifting feeling of the changing seasons and the grandeur of the great outdoors, and you come up with something that might be called the Canadian Sound. Actually [it has] flourished in the shadow of the giant American neighbour to the south" (Jennings 1997, 241).

12 Refined Music in Canada and Abroad

The final three decades of the twentieth century saw increasingly rapid change, nationally and internationally, as Canadians dealt with issues concerning energy, the environment, free trade, and deficits. Increasing cutbacks had a major impact on funding for cultural and education programs; while the success of Canada Council initiatives had resulted in a wealth of gifted artists, there was insufficient activity in Canada for all to earn a living wage. At the same time, artists from many different fields were developing skills relevant for the electronic age. By 1980, changing conditions had led to a realization that a new examination of the arts in Canada was needed. Composer Louis Applebaum and writer-publisher Jacques Hébert were appointed co-chairs of a Federal Cultural Policy Review Committee with a mandate to investigate the situations and needs of those involved in Canadian culture. While the Applebaum-Hébert Report (1982) confirmed some conclusions of the Massey Commission (1951), it took a more pragmatic approach.[1] Interestingly the issue of national identity was not included. More than a decade later an independent report – *An Economic Case for Government Support* (1995) – underlined the importance of government support over the previous twenty years for Canada's vibrant musical scene.

Government response consisted of efforts to funnel more private funding into the arts coupled with a decrease in cultural spending, particularly for the CBC, the NFB, and the Canada Council. In the controversy over public versus private arts funding it became clear that the economic value of the arts was recognized at lower government levels (Keillor 1998, 365), but provincial and municipal arts councils were limited by budget cuts and federal regulations.[2] But beyond economic arguments for continued state support to ensure a strong music industry lay a need for

Canadians to become more aware of their own music, to recognize the many strains of their musical heritage and celebrate the increasing international recognition of Canada's unique sound.

Developments with International Impact

In 1965, R. Murray Schafer, one of a number of composers influenced by Cage's ideas about environmental sound, joined the Centre for the Study of Communications and the Arts at Simon Fraser University, where he and his colleague Jack Behrens had "one of the best-equipped electronic sound studios on the continent" (Adams 1983, 25). Schafer had coined the word "soundscape" (referring to all the surrounding sound) in his writing on music education, and he developed courses focused on an exploration of sound and its impacts. In 1972 he founded the World Soundscape Project. Studies and publications include *The Vancouver Soundscape* (1978) and *Soundscapes of Canada*, a CBC *Ideas* series based on a cross-Canada recording tour by Bruce Davis and Peter Huse. Schafer's *Creative Music Education* (1976) is a guide for helping children think about sound. Investigations led by Schafer in five different countries (Sweden, Germany, Italy, France, and Scotland), produced *European Sound Diary* (1977) and *Five Village Soundscapes* (1977), and his influential soundscape text *The Tuning of the World* (1977), assesses the ever-enlarging data on the impact of sound. Barry Truax's *Handbook for Acoustic Ecology* (1978) is a valuable reference work on acoustic and soundscape terminology. The influence of these publications has extended far beyond Canada. Many municipal noise pollution laws are based on this research, and educational systems in Brazil and Japan were modelled largely on Schafer's ideas. Although Schafer left Simon Fraser in 1975, the World Soundscape Project has continued to produce recordings and a *Soundscape Newsletter*. Hildegard Westerkamp was largely responsible for founding the World Forum for Acoustic Ecology (1993).

An awareness of space and sound can be found in a number of musical activities through this period. When Glenn Gould left the public concert stage to devote his musical performance to recordings, he became increasingly involved with radio. The three sound documentaries that make up his *Solitude Trilogy* explore the impact of Canadian spaces on the people who inhabit them. For *The Idea of North* (1967) he invented "contrapuntal radio" to overcome linearity, using technology to subvert the product of technological discourse (Dickinson 1996, 114). This documentary is built around a train trip to Churchill, Manitoba, and the sound of the train provides a foundation for the overlapping voices. The concept was to interview an eclectic group of people "who could represent [the North's] limitless expectation and limitless capacity for disillusionment which inevitably affects the questing spirit of those who go north seeking their future" (Dickinson 1996, 113).[3] *The Latecomers* (1968) and *The Quiet in the Land* (1977) also explore people's response to the space in which they live, and involve musical expressions of Newfoundlanders and Mennonites respectively.[4]

One of the most ambitious international projects of the late twentieth century was the International Year of Canadian Music – 1986. Throughout the year a wide variety of performances, including many newly commissioned Canadian works, took place across Canada and throughout the world. This ambitious year-long extravaganza did much indeed to put Canadian music and musicians on the map.[5]

Performers on the International Stage

The Tafelmusik Baroque Orchestra and Chamber Choir of Toronto has become widely known through tours and recordings; their collaborations with Opera Atelier to produce highly praised productions of Baroque and early Classical operas using acting, dance, and music conventions of the period, have been performed in France and the United States as well as in Toronto. A number of smaller ensembles, including Les violons du roy and Les boréades de Montréal, also specialize in repertoire and performance practises of pre-Classical music. Early Music Vancouver (founded 1970) is well-known in North America for its innovative programming and performances. La Nef (founded 1991)[6] assembles performers from both early Western and world music backgrounds and incorporates practises from the Middle East in interpretations of Medieval and Renaissance repertoire, frequently researched directly from European manuscripts.

Successful summer festivals include the Festival of the Sound (in Parry Sound, Ontario), and the Ottawa International Chamber Music Festival. The Winnipeg New Music Festival[7] now attracts critics and audience from around the world for two weeks of mid-winter concerts and a competition for Canadian symphonic works, with the winning works performed and broadcast across Canada on the CBC. MusicCanadaMusique 2000, a festival organized by Nicholas Goldschmidt (1908–2004)[8] to celebrate the millenium involved events across Canada, with sixty new works commissioned. The first of these, *Sound Solstice* by Daniel Janke, was presented in Whitehorse on 21 December 1999. Other commissioned works include Barbara Croall's *Caribou Song,* based on a story by Native writer Tomson Highway, *And Still We Sing* by Joe Sealy, performed by the

Nathaniel Dett Chorale, and R. Murray Schafer's *Four-Forty*, scored for string quartet and orchestra. The *Symphonie du millénaire*, presented in Montreal in June 2000 involved 320 musicians, nineteen Quebec composers, and peals of bells from many of the city's churches. "Audiences will hear performances sung by Jewish folk choirs and played on traditional Chinese instruments. ... 'I love this country,' [Goldschmidt] proclaims. 'I love it because from the first day I came to Canada, I sensed the spirit of adventure in every walk of life. I loved, still love, the diversity of our landscape and our people.'" (Alexander 2000, 135). MusicCanadaMusique 2000 was intended not only to showcase the range of musical expressions found in Canada but also to change Canadians' view of their composers. Snider comments: "It's more difficult than ever to make people aware that the composer – not the performer – is the key. How many composers are as well known as Ben Heppner? ... What I want to see is that the Canadian composer is programmed because the organizations want to program him or her, not because they make money by doing so" (Snider 1999, 15).[9] Composer Christos Hàtzis elaborates on the "cod liver oil" approach and associated problems with orchestral programming in his essay "The Orchestra as Metaphor" (2000). Composer Patrick Cardy (1953–2005) comments: "For me, the essentials of music are direction and emotion – and it's a fine balancing act to keep the direction clear and the emotion fresh ... The issue isn't what musical language is used, but whether that language allows the music to evolve in a satisfying and predictable way, while still retaining the power to surprise and astonish the listener" (Maloney 2001, 75).

Canadian Music as Distinct

In 1991 Kyle Gann of *The Village Voice* wrote: "I have heard the future of Western music and it is Canada" (Brady 1998, 29). Listeners around the world are intrigued with how Canadian musicians approach the varied intermingling strains that make up our cultural mosaic. When Canadian music is performed abroad, audiences recognize a quality that differs from the structure and logic of German music, the colour and sensuality of French, or the rhythm and conceptualism of American. Because Canada is so large and diverse, composers produce an art that is personal rather than a national art modeled on schools or great masters. Composer Tim Brady has described this phenomenon: "My own experience as a composer leads me to believe that Canada has created the ideal cultural environment for artists to explore the depth and width of their own unique cultural experiences and to synthesize a distinctly personal approach to creation ... Canada is a relatively new country with a wide variety of specific musical traditions: what links us together is more our *process* than the *sound* of the music. This is what makes us a truly forward-looking community, having created a place where many cultures can coexist but are nonetheless connected via a common approach, not a common material" (Brady 1998, 30–1). In another article Brady underlines the fact that the founders of the Canadian League of Composers – what he calls "Generation Zero" – adopted this basic principle when they determined that membership in the League should be open to professional composers regardless of their aesthetic approach: "Their goals were not the imposition of a national music curriculum, nor the creation of a national music committee to supervise and impose standards. They did not seek to create common technical devices and emotional responses that would be clearly defined as Canadian musical language. Their goals were to create their own music, their own way – and to create institutions that helped other composers do the same. By responding to the regional nature of the country and its history of cultural diversity, and to the world-wide collapse of nationalist, hegemonic forces, they created a strong and vibrant musical environment, where artists are not only allowed to, but are expected to explore at times the extreme edges of their own personal artistic vision" (Brady 2000, 6).

REPRESENTATIVE COMPOSERS OF THE 1970S[10]

Malcolm Forsyth (b. 1938 in South Africa) came to Canada in 1968 and was soon teaching at the University of Alberta. As a trombonist he has played both classical and jazz traditions, and his compositions bear testimony not only to this but to sounds of his early African experience, including Zulu music. *Sketches from Natal* (1970), scored for two oboes, two horns, and strings, evoke the Drakensberg mountains of Natal.[11] One of his major concerns is to write "player-friendly" suitable for the medium and yet challenging. "Rhythm involves the interflow of all the parameters of music but ... the durational aspects of Forsyth's faster movements emerge as the most immediately foregrounded facet for the listener. These durational patterns mirror the breadth of his practical experience covering different performance practises, as they embody African, jazz, and big band rhythmic attributes, together with polyrhythms and polymetric groupings characteristic of many 20th-century composers. Out of this mix Forsyth fashions a very personal rhythmic idiom" (Primos 1994, 17).

Michael Conway Baker (b. 1937 in Florida) settled in Vancouver in 1958, where he attended the University of British Columbia and studied with Jean Coulthard. His works include more than 150 scores for film, television, video, and ice ballet,[12] as well as some 120 concert works. In discussing his Symphony no. 1 (1977), he states: "As to the 'style' of the symphony I can only say it is my own. I follow no 'ism' and write what convinces me. No doubt there will be those who will find it – along with my other compositions – hopelessly traditional. But there are clearly delineated themes and although I don't use key signatures any more, the music is tonal, even when the tonal centres shift, as they often do. I rarely use 'effects,' but when I do, it is because I feel a specific musical need" (Stybr 1997, 16). The first movement of his *Concerto for Piano and Chamber Orchestra* (1975), op. 38, is based on traditional tonal principles, but the second movement uses an eleven-tone row. This work reflects in part Baker's great love for and inspiration from the natural beauty around Vancouver: "Within the particular frame of reference and aesthetic, artists create their own world. Success or failure, it seems to me, depends on how convincing that world is to the listener or viewer" (Stybr 1997, 19). Outstanding choral compositions of the 1970s include works by Derek Holman (b. 1931) and Imant Raminsch (b. 1943). The work of Raminsch reflects his Latvian heritage, his experience as a naturalist in Canada's National Parks, and his role as a conductor and performer; the influence of speech rhythms of the Orthodox church are evident in his *Ave, verum corpus* (1972) for unaccompanied S A T B choir.

Jacques Hétu (b. 1938) studied with Clermont Pépin in Montreal, and analysis with Olivier Messiaen in Paris. His four symphonies use traditional structures, but the musical language is contemporary. About *Symphonie no 3* (1971) he states: "[t]he main thing is not to search for an outlandish way of arranging sounds, but to identify one's own way of imagining music." Hétu delights in the timbre of each instrument, aiming to show individual colours and demonstrate how each one can be modified in time, as in a film. The third movement (marked allegro–vivace–lento) uses elements from the central adagio movement and ends with a tranquil coda that reveals the interrelationship of all contrasting elements.

"When [Jean Coulthard's] compositions ... were heard, on both sides of the Atlantic and the Pacific, it became widely accepted that she was a composer whose citizenship was Canadian, but whose music had a cosmopolitan accent" (Bruneau 2000, 25). Coulthard's *Octet: Twelve Essays on a Cantabile Theme* (1972) for strings is a re-thinking of the idea of variation in which she challenged herself to write lyrically and yet independently for all eight instruments.[13] *Canada Mosaic* (1974) is a seven-part suite.[14]

The quality of her music, whether extraordinary ... or just solidly competent and important is an example of a good composer's response to a physically beautiful place ... Coulthard's life cannot be separated from her art. Her remarkable artistic relationship with her own mother; her complex and revealing relations with her husband, daughter, grand-daughter and son-in-law; her links to the network of her former students; her vigorous and endlessly disciplined writing life; her struggles with alternately friendly and indifferent people in her home city; the ups and downs of her finances; the highs and lows of her life in the university; and her proclivity to keep moving, traveling, changing; these things cannot and must not be separated from the form, content and suspense of Coulthard's creative works. (Bruneau 2000, 26)

POSTMODERNISM AND MINIMALISM

During the 1970s and 1980s postmodernist ideas, characterized in music by the combination of elements of modernism with older traditions became more prevalent. As a review of the creative process, seeking simultaneously to understand the past and speculate about the future, postmodernism incorporates both tonality and atonality; it considers harmony, melody, rhythm, and form in various stages of Western music and draws connections with non-Western musics. It might be seen as a final stage in the continuous emancipation of Western music conceived by Schoenberg and Cage, and a reassessement of new sound resources explored during the 1960s. Postmodern elements are found in the works of many Canadian composers. One particularly interesting work is Patrick Cardy's *Virelai* (1985), a set of variations based on Guillaume de Machaut's *chanson balladée, Quant je sui mis au retour.* Elma Miller's *Margarita Anguisque* (1979) (see figure 12.1) was inspired by the life of the eighteenth-century Italian mathematician, philosopher, and scientist, Maria-Gaetana Agnesi (1718–1799).

As composers began to work with tonal centres in new ways, several developed a technique based on gradually changing ostinatos influenced by the minimalist format used by a number of American composers. From the outset, minimalism had two basic manifestations: one was largely based on non-Western practises (particularly as applied by Colin McPhee in his adaptations of Balinese and Javanese practises, and by Terry Riley, Steve Reich, and Philip Glass in their explorations of African and Indian practises); the other was based on an academic extension of the ostinato practise in the Western Baroque. Whether minimalism is seen as a grass-roots or intellectual movement, minimalist compositions are individual

Figure 12.1   Page from the score of Elma Miller's *Margarita Anguisque* (1979).

in content with an emphasis on process rather than product. In a New Age format, this emphasis was expanded into a transformative process. Some composers draw on minimalist techniques for brief passages. Others, such as Ann Southam (b. 1937) and Marjan Mozetich (b. 1948), have applied a minimalist approach to complete works. Southam combines minimalism with serialism, while Mozetich works with a layering of melodic gestures. Both composers use a more rapid rate of change than most American minimalist composers, and often more layers. Southam describes *Webster's Spin* (1993), an orchestral work, as a "process piece" that explores the melodic possibilities of a twelve-tone row. Drawing on the root form of "webster" (a female weaver), she weaves a sound fabric of ostinato figures created from the pitches of the row. In the early 1970s Mozetich was fully involved in the avant-garde of composition, but he became increasingly troubled by the fact that most contemporary music did not reach its listeners, and that he was not expected to express his own emotions in his music. He became interested in aspects of the minimalist techniques of Glass and Reich, and while he never accepted the main feature of phase-shifting, he began working with simple, direct harmonies in repetitive patterns. His *Dance of the Blind* (1980) for violin, viola, cello, and free-bass accordion was an immediate audience favorite, and other successful works include *Lament in the Trampled Garden* (1992), *Affairs of the Heart: A Concerto for Violin and String Orchestra* (1997) and *Postcards from the Sky*, an ongoing series of short pieces for string orchestra.

Directions in the Final Two Decades and the Millenium

John Weinzweig had been using ostinatos since the 1930s, but these gestures increasingly reflected melodic elements from jazz combined with rhythmic drive. Weinzweig is also one of a number of Canadian composers who have contributed contemporary repertoire for largely neglected instruments. His works include a harp concerto (1966) and *Fifteen Pieces for Harp* (1983) – one of which, ("Quarks"), is named for a sub-atomic particle. Schafer's *Concerto for flute and orchestra* (1984) was written for Canadian flutist and composer Robert Aitken. In the virtuosic first movement, marked "fast and frenzied," the solo flute instrument skitters over a cushion of orchestral sound. Schafer's interest and skill in visual arts are evident in both his musical scores, where he combines various types of notation and elaborate pictographic elements,[15] and his theatrical works. Schafer's *Patria* may be seen as part of his program of socio-political action enunciated in his essay *Music in the Cold* (1977). The non-linear

Figure 12.2
Rohahes (Iain Phillips), a
Mohawk from Kahnawake,
created the role of the
Shaman in Schafer's *Patria
X: The Spirit Garden*. He also
performs on Aboriginal flute
and drum, Baroque oboe,
Celtic harp, and bohran.

cycle consists of twelve works[16] beginning in a mythical time, shifting
to the twentieth century, then moving to the Middle Ages and to several
ancient cultures. Schafer describes these works as a hybrid of music and
theatre, rather than opera, because there are often more speaking than
singing roles. They are designed to be produced in non-traditional settings (such as a lake, a village fair, or a week in the forest), and the combined librettos employ not only various styles of language but numerous
foreign tongues, including invented or dead languages (MacKenzie 1991,
32). References to the tale "Beauty and the Beast," to the myths of Theseus
and Ariadne, and to Schafer's own "Princess of the Stars" – which is reminiscent of First Nations legends – appear throughout *Patria* as recurring dramatic motives, unifying a work set in diverse locations including
the Canadian wilderness, twentieth-century North America, and ancient
Crete and Egypt, involving medieval alchemists and a personal interior
journey in Asterion. *Epilogue* is performed each year as a week-long music
drama by sixty-four adults plus children as musicians, dancers, artists,
thespians, and wood-crafters under Schafer's direction.[17]

Schafer's String Quartets

The presence of fine string quartets and the internationally recognized Banff String Quartet Competition has stimulated much string quartet literature. John Beckwith's *Quartet* (1977) includes references to string instruments of Canada's past, such as the banjo and the mandolin. Few composers since Dimitri Shostakovich, however, have done as much for the quartet as R. Murray Schafer; in 2002 he completed his eighth string quartet. Schafer has linked a universal fascination with the concept of four to possibilities for the four string instruments in a quartet, particularly as viewed by the Iroquois: *O-yan-do-neh* representing the east, spring, childhood, and morning; *Neh-o-gah* representing the south, summer, adolescence, and afternoon; *Da-jo-ji* representing the west, autumn, adulthood, and the evening; and lastly *Ya-o-ga* representing the north, winter, old age, and the night (Schafer 2000, 11-2). His first quartet (1970), opens with a sound portrayal of four musicians trying to escape a tense relationship, and finding a voice in their situation, all expressed with extended playing techniques and microtonal pitches, with calm, static passages representing nocturnal, dream-like and other-worldly ways of being.

His second quartet (1977) was influenced by the research on ocean wave timing that determined a range of wave cycles between six and eleven seconds. Melodic cells are organized into gestures in an arched duration cycle (11, 10, 9, 8, 7, 6, 6, 7, 8, 9, 10, 11). The song of the thrush is presented by harmonics on the cello, and also whistled by the cellist. There is a reference to a fog horn, and a theatrical aspect is introduced at the end when the cellist looks at the other players through a spy glass. The third string quartet (1981) opens in an opposite manner to String Quartet no. 1, and an ensuing drama bring the players to unity; during martial fights the players use laboured breathing and cry out "om ba, ba chi, pow! shu!" A dream-like waltz, a sarcastic comment on their union, is followed by a meditation with quarter tones that provide an Oriental dream effect.

Schafer's eight quartets are interrelated through common materials and gestures. For example, the fourth quartet (1989) opens with an important cell from the second quartet, and the mood of departure and return grew out of events in Schafer's personal life (the return of his wife and the death of bp Nichol, who had performed in several works by Schafer) (Portugais and Ranzenhofer 2000, 27). The fifth quartet (1989) begins with a solo violin playing a cell (E flat–B flat–F) that Schafer was using in works associated with *Ariadne*. This work marks a return to sounds from nature: the cellist presents a wolf call and toward the end the violist and cellist use crotales. The next two quartets also begin with a solo instrument. The sixth quartet has 108 sections, each corresponding to a movement of Tai Chi. The work can be performed with a Tai Chi'iste and represents an exploration of active (*yang*) and the passive (*yin*) forces. The seventh quartet is actually a chamber opera with a soprano soloist who portrays a schizophrenic, singing texts from the files of Marion Kalkmann, director of nursing at the University of Illinois. The eighth quartet is infused with sounds of nature, beginning with elements of bird calls. The first movement is full of youthful energy, while the second is nostalgic.

Peter Paul Koprowski (b. 1947 in Poland), who came to Canada in 1971, blends old and new in his composition; strong influences include works by Ockeghem and Josquin des Près, in which long melodic lines are propelled forward by non-metrical rhythms. *Souvenirs de Pologne* (1983) for piano and orchestra is a musical comment on his first visit to Poland since his departure; in the fourth movement – "Giocoso (With a Touch of the Absurd)" – a recurring passacaglia based on a theme remembered from early counterpoint studies is used in a reflection on seeing a drunken soldier aboard a crowded train. "The listener is evermost in my mind. I write out of my own experience, yes, but I want people to find meaning for themselves. It is not a question of old and new. I write in the hope and belief that music is still to be enjoyed" (Beaubien 1993, 12).

Canadian works for wind ensembles, particularly during the 1980s and 1990s is in part due to fine wind groups, such as the York Winds (1972–1988) and the Canadian Brass (formed in 1970), and to the proliferation of contemporary music concert series with core performing groups that often include several wind players. Gary Kulesha (b. 1954) arranged his *Serenade for String Orchestra* (1985) as *Romance for Brass Band* (1985). For his personal idiom Kulesha draws on a variety of influences including pop music and African drumming, and his role as composer-in-residence for several orchestras has influenced his work. In 1995 the Canadian Opera Company produced his first opera *Red Emma* and in November 2000, his second opera *The Last Duel*, based on a historical event in Perth, Ontario, was premiered at the University of Toronto. Since winning an award in the 1984 CBC Radio National Competition for Young Composers Glenn Buhr (b. 1954) has heard his music performed in many parts of the world. His commissioned works include *Cathedral Songs* (1995) for the CBC, and *Akasha (Sky)* (1989)[18] an orchestral work written in honour of the twenty-fifth anniversary of CBC's National Radio Competition for Young Performers.

Claude Vivier (1948–83) studied first with Gilles Tremblay in Montreal, and later in the Netherlands at the Institute for Sound Research and in Germany with Karlheinz Stockhausen. A cosmopolitan individual, he spoke eight languages and was influenced by travels through the Middle East and Asia, including a long stay in Bali.[19] *Pulau Dewata* (1977), a work directly inspired by Bali, is scored for percussion ensemble or a variable group of instruments; *Cinq chansons pour percussion solo* (1980) was conceived as a poetic song for the percussionist. His opera *Kopernikus* (1980) incorporates his own invented language.[20] *Lonely Child* (1980), the work that crystalized his mature style and established him as one of the most important composers of his generation, is scored for soprano and orchestra and is based on the idea that while the timbre of the gamelan is homophonic and homogenous, the chords it forms are not; thus all music is based on a bass line melody, and the varying timbres above are based on acoustical principles whose intervals are emphasized. The work is organized into eleven sections featuring five presentations of the main melody (an arrangement of the twelve pitches in the octave) separated by interludes or transitions (Tremblay 2000, 51). Although the text is in French, Vivier chose an English title that he felt better conveyed his idea of solitude and nostalgia for childhood. *Lonely Child* is seen as marking the beginnings of the postmodern period in Quebec, where music in this paradigm is seen "as a generational conflict between the proponents of modernity who have become a 'school' in the eyes of many and those who claim the right to a more individualist, more subjective way of thinking" (Lefebvre 2001, 1151).

Denys Bouliane (b. 1955) creates works that often display the dry wit found in *Jeux de société* (1981) for wind quintet and piano; the second movement "Le jeu de téléphone" is a pseudo-pointillistic portrayal of a children's party game in which a story travels around a circle, at the end, blurring into Chopin's Étude, op. 10, no. 8. Quotations of or references to previously existing compositions became more common toward the end of the twentieth century, perhaps in part a recognition of the heritage from which a composer has emerged, or a composer's request for listeners to ponder the significance of their heritage in a new way.

Alexina Louie (b. 1949 in Vancouver)[21] studied at the University of British Columbia, earning her way as a cocktail pianist, and was particularly influenced by the sonic meditation classes of Pauline Oliveros in California. Her *Music for Heaven and Earth* (1990) is a single-movement work in five sections commissioned by the Toronto Symphony for their 1990 Pacific Rim tour. While she admits to fusing elements of Eastern heritage and Western training throughout her compositional career, this work specifically reflects Asian influences; in China, melodic and rhythmic gestures were recognized even by young audience members. This piece uses Asian instruments, such as Chinese opera gongs, hand cymbals,

Japanese temple bowls, a waterphone, and a lion's roar; the second section ("Thunder Dragon") incorporates elements of Beijing opera.[22] *Love Songs for the Planet* (1995) is one of several works that reflect her concern for environmental issues and our relationship with nature.

Denis Gougeon (b. 1951) studied electroacoustic music at the University of British Columbia with John Celona. *Piano-Soleil* (1990) – one of a series of works on the planets – symbolizes raw energy, intense heat, radiance, and diffusion that in turn generates material on which the following nine parts are built; Gougeon uses varied gestures covering the full range of the piano keyboard fully exploiting the expressive range of the instrument. Linda Bouchard (b. 1957) spent three years as composer-in-residence for the NACO. Her orchestral work *Élan* (1990), meaning "impetuous," is scored for strings, woodwinds and brass, percussion, harp, and piano. She describes the structure as a "broken form" in which the discourse is constantly interrupted. An almost constant low D provides a grounding for rapid musical gestures that never recur in the same order or juxtaposition; Bouchard's main concern is an exploration of orchestral colours, with strings and harp used pointillistically. *Ocamow* (1993), scored for baritone, guitar, percussion and cello, has a text in Cree, and her more recent works explore elements of Chinese traditions. Kelly-Marie Murphy (b. 1964) has a clearly directed but emotional style with a keen sense of colour. *This Is the Colour of My Dreams*, scored for cello and orchestra, is influenced by Celtic fiddling. In other works Murphy draws inspiration from Native legends and Leonard Cohen.

Several major First Nations composers have emerged in the last quarter of the century.[23] John Kim Bell (b. 1952 on Kahnawake Mohawk Reserve) trained as a conductor and was appointed assistant conductor of the Toronto Symphony in 1980. He also conducted several musicals on Broadway, and in 1988 he co-wrote and produced *In the Land of Spirits*. Bell subsequently wrote two television film scores – *The Trial of Standing Bear* and *Divided Loyalties*. Through the Canadian Native Arts Foundation, which he founded in 1985, Bell has helped many First Peoples artists to obtain training in the arts, and the organization recognizes major achievers in music, theatre, dance, and film each year. Barbara Croall (b. 1966 of Odawa descent) studied with Sam Dolin and later at University of Toronto and the Musikhochschule in Munich.[24] From 1998 to 2000 she was a composer affiliate of the Toronto Symphony. Many of her works draw on her First Peoples heritage: *Manitou* (1993), *Six Nations* (1996), *Revision* (1999), *The Four Directions* (1996), *Noodin* (1999), *Naawashkosiw* (2000), *Stories from Coyote* (2000).

New Directions in Opera

Chan Ka Nin (b. 1949 in Hong Kong) came to Canada with his family in 1965. He studied first with Jean Coulthard, later in the United States, and has won numerous international awards for his compositions. His chamber opera *Iron Road* was first produced by Tapestry New Opera Works in 2001 in Toronto. Mark Brownell's libretto tells a love story set in British Columbia in the 1880s against the building of the CPR and the treatment of Chinese migrant workers. The twelve-piece orchestra includes four traditional Chinese instruments, and the work is scored for four vocal soloists and two choruses, one singing in Cantonese and one in English. Chan formed his concept of the opera from two elements: the "last spike" photograph, taken at Craigellachie in 1888 that does not show any Chinese labourers; and a Victoria newspaper story from the 1860s about the arrival in BC of 265 Chinese, one of whom was a woman. (For a synopsis of the plot, see http://www.ironroadopera.ca/ story.html.) Just as the text draws on two languages – English and Cantonese Chinese – the musical score draws on Western European and Chinese musical idioms. Parodies of patriotic hymns and band music are combined with Buddhist chants, a Chinese folk lullaby and other folk-like Chinese songs. Orchestra members for the premier performance of the work included several well-known Chinese musicians, such as George Gao on the *erhu*.

Bones, a First Nations dance opera, was created by composer and director Sadie Buck of the Six Nations Reserve. The work is a product of the Aboriginal Arts Program at the Banff Centre, and was first staged at Banff in 2001 in a production that brought together performers and artists from seventeen indigenous nations. Choreographer and co-director Alejandro Ronceria combined contemporary and traditional song and dance. Buck has stated: "The story of *Bones* follows our journey on the Earth, the return of our bones to the Earth, and the return of our spirits to the Stars." The opera consists of three acts with seventeen scenes. The musical accompaniment was provided by electronic resources and three live musicians: David Deleary (bass guitar, percussion), Marc Duggan (percussion), and Mike Olsen (cello). Buck developed a new language – the "Language of the World" – from South and North American elements. The first act concerns the Earth that sustains us and our need to learn her cycles in order to live in harmony. The second act centres around our bodies that come from and go back to the earth. "The earth sustains our bodies... and like the earth our bones sustain us. Without our bones we cannot exist … We have to pick it up again … Some of the people have lost their voice and are looking for those who kept their voice ... knowledge ... intact." In the last two scenes of Act Two, the English language is used. The third act, "Spirit," opens with the story of Seven Brothers who become the seven stars of Pleiades. "We will give the gift of our knowledge from the heavens, back to the people. We will become the stars." Dance is an integral part of the work and accompanies all music. Many musical numbers are strophic, but some reflect powwow song structure with incomplete repetition forms. Some songs have a single melody line with accompaniment, while others have a form of harmony and a homorhythmic texture. Occasional Latin rhythms and textures also emerge in this fascinating eclectic score.

Information on *Iron Road* was been gathered from the web-sites www.ironroadopera.ca and www.ricepaperonline.com, www.nowtoronto.com, and the CBC broadcast of the opera. The information on *Bones* was been compiled from a presentation of excerpts and a delegates' folder for Expressions: National Gathering on Aboriginal Artistic Expression, 17–19 June 2002, in Ottawa. John Estacio's *Filumena* (2003) was also developed through the opera program at Banff, and was broadcast and toured across Canada; John Murrell's libretto for the work is based on Filumena Lassandro, the only woman executed in Alberta (see www.filumena.com).

Electroacoustic Music

Although Bouchard writes primarily for acoustic instruments, like many other composers of this period, she has been influenced by sounds from electronic sources. The difficulties of presenting electronic compositions in a concert hall with an empty stage persuaded some electronic composers, including Ann Southam and István Anhalt, to return to acoustic composition. Believing that his multi-level voyages of discovery could be best carried out in acoustic sounds, Anhalt created a series of four musical/theatrical works: *La Tourangelle* (1975), *Winthrop* (1986) *Traces (Tikkun)* (1996) and *Millenial Mall (Lady Diotima's Walk)* (2000).[25] The belief that we must learn from the past in order to understand our place and time is a continuing thread through Anhalt's work.

Other Canadian composers have continued to develop important tools for electronic composition. In 1972, in his home studio in Vancouver, Ralph Dyck built the first sequencer to which numerous synthesizers with monophonic capabilities could be attached and their effects monitored through digital interfacing. Five years later, his idea was purchased by Roland and developed into Musical Instrument Digital Interface (MIDI). In 1973 Barry Truax (b. 1947) developed the first version of what has become known as the POD (Poisson Ordered Distribution) system, a program that permits polyphonic, timbral construction of electronic sounds, creating an effect of sound moving around in space. This program and its subsequent forms[26] allow the efficient generation of complex musical structures, providing a new approach to composition based on the qualities of timbre rather than pitch. During the 1970s, Bill Buxton's

Structural Sound Synthesis Project pioneered the use of computer graphics and, in its portable version, permitted live improvisation of electroacoustic music. The Canadian Electronic Ensemble (formed 1973) was the first group in the world to create live electronic music in concert.

Using methods developed by Canadians and available commercial equipment, electroacoustic composers have continued to produce an impressive number of successful works in this demanding medium, often incorporating acoustical instruments or other media to provide additional interest in concert settings. In 1968 Marcelle Deschênes (b. 1939) went to Paris to join the Groupe de recherche musical and work with Pierre Schaeffer. Since her return to Canada she has explored her interest in combining different media and working with innovative technology. *MOLL, opéra Lilliput pour six roches molles* (1976) won the mixed-music prize at the Sixth International Festival at Bourges. Deschênes collaborated with Alain Martel in the development of the sonorous spatializer SS-1. Her primary aim is to keep sounds relevant to human lives (Gagné 1990, 21). *Big Bang II* – composed for a walk through a multi-media installation by George Dyens at the 1987 International Exposition Images du futur – takes the listener on an imaginary voyage through time and space.[27]

Barry Truax's approach is undoubtedly influenced by explorations of and reactions to sound. Later versions of POD produced increasingly higher densities of sound-events that could be generated and manipulated, but Truax was concerned with both the dissolution of the microstructure (the internal structure of sounds) and the macrostructure (the organization and distribution of sounds). In 1986 he developed GRANX, "the first program for real-time granular sound synthesis ... In granular synthesis the sound-events can be made extremely small and copied in large quantities to create very dense, flexible masses of grains. Sound, then, is conceived as consisting of particles, whereas before sound was usually conceived in a linear way, as bands of waves" (Voorvelt 1997, 51). With the GRANX system Truax has been able to apply granular synthesis to digitally recorded environmental sounds, (see Voorvelt 1997, 51–3) and this technology allows composers to explore a particular environmental sound, amplify and emphasize certain symbolic meanings, and prolong certain factors without changing the pitch. Not surprisingly Truax's compositions reflect his concerns with the development of computerized manipulation of sound and his growing understanding of the nature and impact of environmental sounds.[28] In *Riverrun* (1986), his first piece created with GRANX, granular synthesis is applied to electronically generated sound. *Song of Songs* (1992) uses recorded voices reciting fragments from the Song of Solomon while environmental sounds are combined with the live instrumental sounds of an oboe d'amore and an English horn with computer images by composer and video artist Theo Goldberg (Voorvelt 1997, 61).

Christos Hatzis (b. 1953 in Greece) studied at the Eastman School of Music with Morton Feldman before settling in Canada in 1985.[29] He has written a variety of works for acoustic instruments, but is widely known for his collages combining live music with tape tracks or electronic sounds. *Nadir*[30] was written for Canadian recorder virtuoso Peter Hannan and includes a viola and a tape track; Gypsy melodies, Orthodox chant, Brazilian tango, Middle Eastern folk music co-exist, each highlighting the beauty of the others, in a statement that the impact of violence "is best measured by the preciousness of what's around it." Hatzis has incorporated Inuit music in several recent works: *The Idea of Canada* (1992), *Footprints in New Snow* (1998), *Nunavut* (for string quartet and tape), and *Fertility Rites* (1997), which includes throat singing. One of his most interesting works combines a performance of the medieval organum *Viderunt Omnes* by Perotin with Inuit throat singing by the Ottawa-based group Aqsarniit.[31] *Constantinople*, a multimedia work for mezzo-soprano, Middle Eastern singer, violin, violoncello, piano, electronic audio and visual media was commissioned by the Gryphon Trio for MusicCanadaMusique 2000; and includes elements of Greek orthodox chant, Sufi melodies, jazz, North American pop songs, Argentinian tango, and classical chamber music

An Outburst of Operatic Production

Between 1980 and 2001 at least fifty-seven new Canadian operas were produced. Some were chamber operas with small orchestras that used multimedia approaches to reduce the cost of sets and props. This interest in opera reflects an overall increase in operatic audiences within North America since 1980. Events such as the Three Tenors concerts have helped to popularize operatic repertoire, and "surtitles" – a Canadian invention – have also played a major role in building opera audiences.[32] A significant number of the top operatic stars in the world are Canadian.[33] An infrastructure that includes opportunities for training and music and theatre productions including opera and operetta as well as musicals has given these singers the experience necessary to succeed on the international stage. Parsons points to other factors: "The advent of exciting, even controversial, new stage directors and designers into the operatic world, employing increased theatricality and techniques from film and performance art ... have revitalised traditional operatic repertoire. This has had an impact on composers, many of whom previously saw opera as too conservative. Finally, there is the matter of changing musical language: the rise of postmodernism, neoromanticism, minimalism, 'world music,' and various 'cross-over' styles, plus the decline of the modernist aesthetic that dominated the mid-20th century, have all contributed to the return of composers to the operatic medium" (Maloney 2001, 154). The year 2000 saw 900 opera performances across Canada, produced by sixteen professional companies in five provinces. By the 1990s the Canadian Opera Company (COC) had become the sixth largest opera company in North America, with highly acclaimed productions seen throughout, Canada and much of the United States.[34] While the Vancouver Opera dates back to the late 1950s, considerable growth in the west can be seen with the Edmonton Opera (founded 1963) and Manitoba Opera (founded 1973); much of the vibrancy in these three western companies is due to director Irving Guttman (b. Chatham, Ontario, 1928) (Watmough 1985, 12). Newer companies include Calgary Opera (1972), Opera in Concert[35] (1974), Pacific Opera Victoria (1979), l'Opéra de Montréal (1980), l'Opéra de Québec (1984), Opera Lyra (Ottawa 1984), Opera Atelier (1985), and Opera Ontario (formed in 1995 by a merger of the Opera Hamilton and Kitchener-Waterloo Opera), Toronto's Autumn Leaf Performance, and Montreal's Chants libres. While Canadian opera companies largely present standard repertoire, there have been exciting productions of Canadian works, particularly by smaller companies.[36] In 2001 Toronto's Opera Anonymous staged an English version of Quesnel's *Lucas et Cécile* in 2001. In 1998, the Queen of Puddings Music Theatre produced *Beatrice Chancy*, a chamber opera by James Rolfe to a libretto by Canadian poet George Elliott Clarke.[37]

Composers Choosing Canada for Its Eclecticism

During the last decades of the twentieth century a number of composers chose Canada as the place where they could best contribute to musical life. Bengt Hambraeus (1928–2000, born in Stockholm) became a professor at McGill University in 1972 and was highly regarded for his research in music history and electronic music and his compositions. He was particularly concerned with exploring timbre and collage, and his organ works have opened new avenues in the use of that instrument (Jacob 1978). Writing on Canadian music shortly after his arrival in Canada, Hambraeus commented on the possibilities of drawing from many sources and stressed three important influences: nature, the multiethnic population, and the bi-cultural basis of English and French. In

Poster for "Then, Now & Beyond ... A Festival of Music by Women," Ottawa, 24–27 January 2002.

later years he also stressed the importance of First Nations heritages (Broman 2000). Maya Badian (b. 1945 in Roumania) came to Canada in 1987 and completed a doctorate at the Université de Montréal. Her contributions to Canadian music include publications, workshops, and lectures on contemporary composers. Her *MultiMusic Canada, A Legacy for the New Millenium* (2000) grew out of her first strong impressions of Canada, with the co-existence of many cultures, dialects, and languages. Nikolai Korndorf (1947–2001, b. Moscow) described the day he arrived in Canada (23 May 1991) as "the happiest day of his life" (Miles 2001). Korndorf, well known as a conductor in Russia, has had his compositions played throughout the world, but he commented that his eclecticism was really able to blossom in his new country.

Whatever the land of their birth, composers in Canada continue to explore their musical relationship to the Canadian landscape. "Like musical compositions, landscapes are never apprehended all at once but via a compilation, aggregation and assimilation of multiple moments and details. Duration and flux are part of the experience of landscapes. The centre of interest is mobile and dispersed. The gaze does not meet with another gaze but is constantly deflected and distributed. This fact underlies landscape's democratic ethos" (Salzman 2000, 62). Regardless of approach, composers need a sense of community in order to express their reactions to place, space, and time. Some of this community comes from organizations such as the Canadian League of Composers, the Canadian Music Centre,[38] the Guild of Canadian Film Composers (founded in 1980), the Canadian Electroacoustic Community, and the Association of Canadian Women Composers.[39]

Only a small proportion of Canadian concert music composers have been named in the preceding paragraphs, but Canada indeed has a wealth of interesting young composers. Other examples include Ana Sokolovic and Brian Current (grand winners of the 1999 and 2001 CBC National Competition for Young Composers). Commissions and performances of Canadian music by musicians with international careers do much to increase the performances and reputations of these composers. For example, Piano Six[40] regularly included Canadian works in recitals in small or remote centres. Similarly string players such as Angèle Dubeau, James Ehnes, Amanda Forsyth, Ofra Harnoy, Chantal Juillet, Juliette Kang, guitarists Liona Boyd, David Essig, and Norbert Kraft, and conductors Paolo Bellomia and Kari-Lynn Wilson promote Canadian repertoire. Today the sounds of Canadian music are heard through web-sites and recordings as well as performances, and in 2003 the Canadian Music Centre launched round-the-clock broadcasting of Canadian works.[41]

New Jazz Developments

The last quarter of the twentieth century saw a wide variety of directions in jazz. The establishment of jazz studies at the university level and stage bands in high schools increased jazz opportunities for young people, and CBC jazz broadcasts have played a crucial role in promoting the careers of Canadian musicians. With the establishment of the jazz label Sackville in Toronto in 1968, the approaches of Swing, traditional and avant-garde jazz became more well-known. By 2000, the Justin Time jazz label, founded in 1983, had released more than 200 albums.

Composers who continued the easy-listening traditions of Lombardo, Farnon, and Faith include Hagood Hardy (1937–97); his major hit *The Homecoming* (1974) began as a Salada Tea commercial. Frank Mills (b. Montreal, 1942) is active as a composer, arranger, pianist, and singer; his sprightly *Music Box Dancer* became an international hit. Phil Nimmons (b. Vancouver, 1923) began as a clarinetist but was encouraged to write arrangements by Ray Norris. After studies at Juilliard in New York, he moved to Toronto where he formed his Nimmons 'N Nine in 1953. His *Atlantic Suite* won the inaugural Juno for Best Jazz Album in 1976 and he has written more than 400 original compositions for stage, television, radio, musicals, and film. He also taught at Peterson's school, the University of New Brunswick, the Banff School of Fine Arts, and the University of Toronto. Classic traditional jazz groups only appeared in Canada in the late 1940s, and a second wave of activity began in the late 1960s when a number of well-known musicians settled in Canada.[1] Saxophonist, flutist, and composer Jane Bunnett (b. Toronto 1956) began working with and supporting Cuban jazz musicians in the mid-1980s, and her Latin-tinged

The Blues in Canada

Black musicians intimately involved with the blues include Big Miller (1922–92), who came to Edmonton in 1970, and Salome Bey who moved to Toronto in 1963. Bey's highly praised show *Indigo: A History of the Blues* was presented in Toronto in 1982, toured across Canada, and two years later broadcast on CBC television. The establishment of true blues ensembles in Canada came after 1970 in response to the rise of British groups who emulated classic American blues; one of the earliest Canadian groups was the Ugly Ducklings. During the 1980s, blues societies were formed and radio programs devoted to blues were broadcast in various centres; Holger Petersen, who set up Stony Plain Records, hosts a CBC's *Saturday Night Blues*. First Peoples are also strongly drawn to this music, possibly because of the emotional content of blues texts; in 1989 Amos Key began a weekly three-hour program of blues at the Six Nations station CKRZ.

The Toronto-based Downchild Blues Band dates back to 1969, and they had a major hit with *Flip, Flop and Fly* (1973). Their shows combine old hits, new material with a good-times aura that underlines powerful guitar playing and virtuosic harmonica sparkle. Colin James (b. Regina 1964) grew up with folk music and played penny whistle and mandolin, but in 1983 he moved to Vancouver in 1983 and joined the Night Shades. Since 1988 he has had with his own band a string of hit singles beginning with *Voodoo Thing*. Colin Linden, a masterful guitarist, per-

formed and recorded with James in the 1990s; he has played on more than 150 albums and produced more than thirty CDs, working with such artists as Bruce Cockburn, T-Bone Burnett, and The Band. His album *Big Mouth* (2001) presents an old raw style of blues.

Proponents of the blues in Quebec include J.D. Slim, who combines British and American influences with the textual expertise of Jean-Pierre Ferland and Claude Dubois; his aim is to state things simply but not simplistically, and uses silence and spaces to great effect. Bob Harrison, an important blues musician in Montreal, points out a strong Latin influence in Quebec blues musicians that is not found elsewhere. Outstanding blues singers in the Maritimes include Theresa Malenfant and Dutch Mason. Mason moved to the Annapolis Valley where he played with Black musicians from Gibson Woods, and claims that Maritime blues have developed a unique character and edge (Fleming 1997, 147).

The vibrancy of the Canadian blues scene is reflected in the number of festivals: the Harbourfront Soul 'n' Blues Festival was established in Toronto in 1986; Ottawa's Bluesfest began in 1994; Saint John's Jazz and Blues Festival began in 1995. Others include Fredericton's Harvest Jazz and Blues Festival, Rivière-du-loup en Blues in Quebec, Limestone City Blues Festival in Kingston, Bluesfest International Windsor/Detroit, and Salmon Arm Roots and Blues Festival in British Columbia. For an extensive list of Canadian blues artists, see www.torontobluessociety.com.

jazz has considerably enriched the Canadian scene. This Latin influence may have inspired drummer Barry Elmes (b. Galt 1952) who wrote the chart *Tofino in May*; Elmes played in Rod McConnell's Tenor Madness and the influential Time Warp, and around 1997 formed the D.E.W. East trio with Nick Brignola and Steve Wallace.

Montreal remained a major centre for jazz, particularly with the establishment of the Montreal Jazz Festival in 1980. Newly created improvisations with Latin tinges became a prominent feature, as reflected in groups such as Ensemble de musique improvisée de Montréal. Fusion bands include UZEB,[2] who incorporated synthesizers and lighting effects and toured Europe and the Far East. Ottawa-born D.D. (Robert) Jackson (b. 1967) has become well-known for his avant-garde percussive keyboard playing and dense clusters of chords.[3] Dixieland flourished on the West Coast but swing, bebop, and more adventurous jazz forms could also be heard in Vancouver nightclubs.[4] Fraser MacPherson (b. Winnipeg, 1928–93) played saxophone, flute, and clarinet in various West Coast groups, particularly for CBC radio and television, toured with Canadian jazz musicians in Europe, and appeared at Canadian festivals. The du Maurier Vancouver International Jazz Festival, established in 1985 and sponsored by the Coastal Jazz and Blues Society, has become a showcase for musicians from Canada, the United States, Europe, Latin America, and Africa.

Women gaining international recognition include vocalist Holly Cole (b. 1963), and Montreal pianist Renée Rosnes (b. 1962) who has explored a variety of styles; in 1994 she formed the quintet Free Trade with Ralph Bowen, Terry Clarke, Peter Leitch, and Neil Swainson. Diana Krall (b. 1964) has topped jazz and pop charts with piano-accompanied renditions of standards such as *Peel Me a Grape*,[5] presented with a refreshing new look. Her shift to a cool but sultry sensuality has created some controversy, but through her career she has introduced many listeners to jazz.

The Second Wave of Singer-Songwriters

The deep tradition of folk music in Canada contributed much to a second wave singer-songwriter tradition that is reflected in the work of Stan Rogers (1949–83). After RCA records refused to take him seriously, presenting him as Canada's answer to Burl Ives (Baxter-Moore 1995, 307), he began to explore his Maritime roots. Subsequent albums popularized traditional styles of music from Atlantic Canada, paving the way for artists such as Rita MacNeil and The Rankin Family, and his last two – *Northwest Passage* and *From Fresh Water* are regional concept albums on Western Canada and the Great Lakes.[6] His music demonstrates the breadth of Canadian material. In his travels across Canada Rogers saw what Canadians had in common and tried to reveal this in his songs. His songs and his message are relevant to Canadians but have also become favourites of international singers. Bob Bossin of Stringband has commented: "A Canadian sound has emerged in folk music, and it is Stan Rogers' voice" (Baxter-Moore 1995, 309). Stringband's[7] wide range of material includes French and English traditional songs plus their own creations – including *Did You Hear They Busted the Fiddle Player?, Maple Leaf Dog,* and *Mail-Sortin' Man* – and their independent approach to recording and touring revolutionized the Canadian music scene.

New Technologies and Electronica

New technologies, including the Walkman and the CD (compact disc), have played a vital role in the decades since 1970. A number of new streams emerged as a result of developments in the electronic production of sound. Amplified acoustic instruments and electric guitars became the norm, and around 1980 synthesizers began to displace even the guitar. Beat boxes were used for dance music, and around 1985 Chicago disc jockeys combined them with funk rock elements to create house music. This sound was commercialized with the bass line machine (Roland TB 303) that could produce strong bass and effects, an important element of acid house music (Compulseve 2002, 35). In Detroit techno, more minimalist than house music (and related to breakbeat), copies of the same record are placed on each of two turntables.[8] In the early 1990s an English style of sampling used different drum rhythms, accelerated to about 130 beats per minute for raves. A jungle type of breakbeat that took over more aspects of techno emerged in the multi-ethnic London suburbs: "Accelerated and ultra-syncopated breakbeats as well as seismic bass lines" dominated a sound to which ragga was added to make happy hardcore (Compulseve 2002, 42). By the late 1990s jungle/drum'n'bass was often used for advertising jingles. Tempos were increased to 180 beats per minute and lyrical melodies added; rough and lo-fi sounds were mixed in with futuristic sounds of harps. By 2002, there were several variants of jungle, but the jump-up and hardstep (rigid and aggressive) styles remain the most popular (Compulseve 2002, 42). While electronica is not reflected on North American mainstream radio, it is the dance music of the twenty-first century and Canadians are involved in its creation.

Synthesizers such as the Emulator and the Yamaha DX-7 largely pushed aside the electric guitars that predominated popular music groups, and with the influence of disco, remixes become more important, particularly with the use of the 12-inch remix or EP. Instrument samples had been common in studio technology but after 1986, sample sounds of all types, including dialogue, were used, and the combination of rock bass lines with synthesizer dance beats changed the very nature of dance music. Canadians Richie Hawtin and John Acquaviva became involved in the techno scene in Detroit; their label +8 is named for the pitch-adjust function DJs use to play tracks as fast as possible.[9] Acquaviva formed a sublabel that introduced more funk and soul into electronic music, while Hawtin aimed to fuse elements of Detroit techno and Chicago acid into what he called "complex minimalism" under his new name Plastikman (Reynolds 1999, 228).[10]

Nature and environmental recordings represent another important development in the use of recorded sound. Dan Gibson, a leader in this field, a lover of the wilderness from his youth, prepared scores for nature films and later television. His company Solitudes, formed in 1981 released twelve albums using only sounds of nature;[11] in 1986, at the suggestion of his son Gordon Gibson he created a new Solitudes album that used music to enhance and complement the natural sounds, a concept that has met with wide-spread success and approval (see www.solitudes.com/about.html).

Reggae and Hip Hop

With the large Carribean communities in cities such as Montreal, Toronto, and Vancouver, there has been a steady influence of Jamaican-based reggae, a folk-song based, political protest expression that grew out of Rastafarianism, nyahbingi, mento, deejay style, ska, and rocksteady; dub also developed in the 1970s, and led to dancehall in the 1980s. Reggae remains a favoured form of many young Canadians and is found in three basic categories: roots reggae, dancehall reggae, and ragga. Dancehall reggae is based on "beat dub plates" produced by major record labels in Jamaica. Each plate contains a sample of 100 plus reggae beats produced by their in-house DJ. These "riddims" are sold and each DJ hopes that his riddim will be the one chosen for songs produced during the coming year. The preferred dancehall songs, in patois, exploit violent and discriminatory messages; songs mostly in English with sentiments deemed to be suitable for broadcast are called "soft" or "radio played" dancehall. In addition to money, women, and jewels, many of the texts deal with dance moves, in colourful terms such as "signal di plane," "row di boat," "pon di river."

With the growing presence and solidarity of the West Indian community in Canada, reggae became an important rubbaboo ingredient; David Campbell, who spent time in the West Indies, developed political comments stated in music relevant for Canada's First Peoples, and new forms of Black-based music appeared in specific Canadian manifestations. In the late 1960s Mojah, a vocalist and guitarist, discovered reggae in Trinidad where he grew up. In Toronto he established Truths and Rights, the seminal Canadian reggae band.[12] Funk, closely related to reggae, has been described as stripping music down to the rhythm, played by bass and drums; each instrument becomes a drum to make the "groove." Because the funk sound creates an urge to move, funk elements became the basis for dance music with technologies such as MIDI used to produce ever-expanding percussive effects. The streams of punk and disco were important streams that might be viewed as reactions to a predominant main stream of soft-rock styles. Robbie Robertson had described three types of rock in the late 1960s; "rhythm and blues, corny white rock, and rockabilly" (Stambler 1977, 37).

The aim of punk was to deconstruct rock 'n' roll, specifically removing influences of Black rhythm and concentrating on elements of noise and texture (see Christagau 1977, 57). Canadian punk drew on streams from the United States, and particularly from Britain, with lyrics longer than the eight-line American model and a less minimalist or self-conscious presentation. The essence of punk was an effort to do the opposite of whatever was seen as mainstream. By around 1977 it was being called "new wave." Punk opened up the world of contemporary popular music for women unable to break into the rock scene, and many Canadian groups with women members were punk or had strong punk influences. Because punk gets little mainstream radio and recording support, college radio programs and independent recording labels for punk emerged across Canada. D.O.A., a Canadian punk band in British Columbia has lasted for more than twenty years; Joe Keithly coined the term "hardcore" in 1981 to refer to a loud and fast sound with a defiant attitude for their second album, and he also formed Sudden Death Records to promote Canadian punk bands. Other punk bands include Cub, Von Zipper, Stand GT, and Teenage Hicks. Punkfest, an annual festival began in the 1990s; the eighth one held north of Napanee, Ontario, featured thirty bands over three days, including Day Glo Abortions, Phobia, Spotty Botty, Dirty Bird, and Goofs.

A demand for dance music from Blacks, Latinos, and members of the gay/lesbian community was filled by lounges featuring light shows and hired live musicians or DJs. These clubs became known as "discotheques" (see Graustark 1979, 59). Disco uses the same basic rhythm and harmonic structure as rock 'n' roll but the backbeat is more consistent and the harmonic rhythm slower, with an emphasis on instrumental texture rather than vocal personality. DJs work in a dance booth above the dance floor so that they can adjust the music to the activity below, juggling from one part of a song to another and adding material in the break to maintain the dance rhythms. Disco first became popular in Montreal with the French Canadian affinity for Latin music, and Montreal became a major production centre for disco records. Many Montreal performers recorded disco songs in English for the wider North American market; Patsy Gallant's *From New York to LA* became an international hit. A number of disco DJs who set themselves apart by their choice of music and presentation became culture heros in their own right.

As disco took on elements from other musics, a new direction of Black musicians took shape as rap, an initially text-based expression using the street poetry of ghetto districts in New York. Rap combined with break-dancing was eventually known as hip hop, a stream dependent on DJs who combined many different types of music with no concern for smooth segues. Instead hip hop music often consists of the most percussive sections of pieces, called the "break." By 1976 hip hop DJs were using "scratching," a technical innovation of scratching that made turntables into full-fledged rhythm instruments.[13] Because there are few mainstream outlets for hip hop, this music is heard largely on college radio stations and traded recordings. The Juno awards have gradually come to acknowledge new music categories such as reggae, calypso, rhythm and blues; a soul section and a category for rap finally appeared in 1991; *Let Your Backbone Slide* by Maestro Fresh-Wes took over the dance floors and shot to number one, becoming the first platinum album for a Black artist in Canada (Davis 1994, 48).

Rap and Related Styles

Through the 1990s the Junos took note of expanding streams of urban music by splitting existing categories and creating new ones: dance (1990), rap/hip hop (1991), and blues/gospel (1994), which was further split in 1998. Adam Krims has identified four distinctive genres of rap on the basis of the style of the musical tracks, the flow of the rapping, and the topics: Party, Mack, Jazz/Bohemian, and Reality (Krims 2000, 54–78). Maestro Fresh Wes would fall into the Party category with his prominent rhythm section, minimally layered textures, fast beat, and topics focusing on celebration, pleasure, and humour, but he adds complexity by using interior and end rhymes and couplet groupings; *Let Your Backbone Slide* includes terms such as forte, fortissimo, and crescendo and references to Beethoven symphonies. In contrast to the "sung" style of earlier Party rap singles Maestro's delivery is more aggressive and angry, and his music is funky, danceable, and interestingly layered. In later pieces, he often sampled earlier songs of Canada by Haywire and the Guess Who. Toronto rapper Snow was the first Canadian artist to win international success in this genre.

In Canada, for most of the 1990s neither record company executives nor radio and television stations understood the hip hop scene or its audience; they did not know what to look for or where to find it. Canadian hip hop has been described as full of energy, without the violent or hostile overtones largely predominant elsewhere. A vital hip hop scene blossomed mainly underground, usually based strongly in a regional or local urban scene. For example, rappers in Halifax have drawn on the historical roots of the Black community and the influence of the Nova Scotia College of Art and Design.[14] The Halifax sound is varied and eclectic and none of it is close to commercial hip-hop; often there are references to sea chanteys. In Toronto the Dream Warriors and UBAD presented a strong Caribbean identity through lyrics and visual images. Michie Mee, the best-known woman artist in Canada, laid the groundwork for further developments by women in rap and bhangra. Rascalz of Vancouver attracted national attention with their album *Cash Crop* (1994), which was re-released in 1997 with *Northern Touch* as a bonus track; this song, performed by the Rascalz with other artists including Choclair, Thrust, Kardinal Offishal, and Checkmate[15] became a hit, helping to establish Canadian hip hop artists on the international scene. Toronto rappers refer to their sound as the "T-dot sound." In Quebec hip hop first made a strong showing with the group Dubmatique; their rap of long texts is mostly recited over various genres of music including jazz, reggae, funk, and soul. In *Un été à Montréal* Dubmatique refers to the jazz festival in Montreal and includes a portion of Quincy Jones's recording of *I'm Going to Miss You in the Morning*.

Bhangra, closely related to rap, comes from a form of traditional Punjabi music consisting of songs and dances performed by men to the accompaniment of *dholak* or *dholki* drums.[16] By the late 1970s bhangra combined synthesizers and other non-folk instruments with the traditional songs and instruments. Jiten Khatri, considered the first club bhangra DJ in Toronto, began his career in the mid-1980s, working with recordings of Hindi songs and mainstream dance tracks (Warwick 1996, 32). Live performances by groups such as Dhamak and United Kulture, whose members played the *dhol* and *thumbi*,[17] led to recordings. Bhangra songs usually have a call-and-response structure; the four main styles identified by Warwick (1996, 83) are all strophic songs with short instrumental breaks punctuated by periodic shouts of "hoi" on or off a four-beat pattern with a stress on one. The songs on Nadeem Mughal's album *The Shocker* (1996) used various languages and are labelled "hip hop," "slow song," or "lounge mix." Some musicians have tried to bridge differences among Canada's large and diverse population of Indian heritage. A main aim of United Kulture is to create a musical expression that can bring together communities of Hindus, Muslims, Sikhs, and Christians, and the popular group Punjabi by Nature blends bhangra and rock with elements of Caribbean dance hall, reggae, and rap.[18] By 2001 Canadian hip-hop artists were receiving deservedly more recognition. Nelly Furtado of Portuguese heritage has been praised by rappers for her use of a live DJ in performances; her album *Whoa, Nelly!* (2000) combines Portuguese fado with a blend of pop, hip hop, and bossa nova. Toronto rapper k-os (Kheaven Brereton), who opened her 2002 tour shows, has commented that it took him six years to learn how to balance the elements "the fat beats, the acoustic melodies, the Caribbean swagger – to create the perfect 'concoction' that will appeal to a broad range of listeners, from music critics, to radio programmers, to kids gathered in a crowded dance club" (Smiderle 2002, J10).[19]

Rock and Beyond

Carole Pope paved the way for women as rock musicians. She began her career singing folk with Kevan and by 1974 had formed Rough Trade.[20] Dressed in black leather, Pope's female sexuality, daring lyrics, and lesbian orientation influenced a number of women performers through the 1980s. Parachute Club was formed in 1981 by musicians who had played together in various configurations.[21] Notable hits, strongly influenced by reggae, include *Take Me* (1977) and *High School Confidential* (1980). In 1981 they began working with producer Daniel Lanois.[22] *Rise Up* (1983) blends strong Carribean rhythms with a "tobacco-belt sound" that emerged in Toronto and south-western Ontario (Barclay, Jack and Schneider 2001, 313). Klaatu[23] created other-worldly electronic sounds; they retained their anonymity, suggesting they were the Beatles.

Bruce Cockburn began as a rock musician in the mid-1960s, joined a folk group, and in 1970 made an impact with his score for Don Shebib's quintessential Canadian film *Goin' Down the Road* (1970). Cockburn is noted for songs – such as *If I Had a Rocket Launcher* (1985), which expressed outrage at conditions he saw in Nicaragua – that address social causes, a trend that has spread through much of the global pop world. He writes in both French and English and has recorded in Spanish and Wendat. Bryan Adams formed a songwriting partnership with Jim Vallance in Vancouver and released a self-titled debut album in 1980; his second album included six hits, one of which is *Heaven*, and his album *Waking Up the Neighbors* (1991) reached record sales of more than seven million. His *Tears Are Not Enough*, the Ethiopian famine relief anthem, was written with Vallance and David Foster. Canadian rock groups include April Wine (formed in Halifax in 1969), who had their first major hit with *You Could Have Been A Lady* (1972), and Loverboy, which was formed in Calgary by Paul Dean and Mike Reno later relocated to Vancouver.

Jeff Healey played lap top guitar as a child, developing a unique approach and technique. He recorded an independent video in 1982 and in 1985 formed the Jeff Healey Band;[24] their album *See the Light* (1988) won international acclaim. For their third album, *Feel This* (1992) they added keyboard and vocalists. Healey's strong interest in jazz comes across in his own compositions and his radio programs (see King 2002, 13). The West Coast group, 54–40[25] came to prominence with *The Sound of Truth* (1984); their mixing of different styles and genres of music is a deliberate attempt to avoid being pigeonholed. The eclectic Blue Rodeo[26] (see Miller 1992, 134) draws on a variety of roots music styles of American pop; they won country music awards and have also been invited to perform at jazz festivals. The Rheostatics (formed around 1980 in Toronto) have been called the most Canadian of Canadian bands. Their album *Whale Music* (1992) came out as a mythical soundtrack for Paul Quarrington's book and was later used for the film; the lyrics of Dave Bidini's song *Rock Death America* comment on evaluations of Canadian bands against foreign groups rather than on their own merits. Elements of their quirky sound include extensive use of bowed string (as in the multi-tracked *Self-Serve Gas Station*). In 1995 they were contracted to provide music inspired by Group of Seven art at the National Gallery of Canada, and more recently they have presented stories and music for children. While many bands were expanding the borders of rock, the Nylons, a male vocal group organized in 1979, work largely with old rock classics; their cover of the Supremes' song *Na Na Hey Kiss Him Goodbye* (1986) was an international hit.

Music Videos

The Juno category for music videos first appeared in 1986, but as early as 1979 (two years before MTV) CBC was broadcasting *The New Music*.

Rush

"It's funny. When you talk to metal people about Rush, eight out of ten will tell you that we're not a metal band. But if you talk to anyone outside of metal, eight out of ten will tell you we *are* a metal band" (Walser 1993, 7). Rush, "the world's most progressive band," was formed in Toronto in 1968 by Geddy Lee, Alex Lifeson, and Neil Peart. Canada was known for hard rock, or "heavy metal," driven by a continuous one-beat bass drum (a rhythm also characteristic of traditional Indigenous music, indicating possible influences in both directions.) The lyric content of hard rock is often rebellious (as in songs of Trooper, Chilliwack, and Triumph) but rarely political. Rush took hard rock in a unique direction, developing a distinctive interplay between guitar and bass. By the mid-1970s they were working with synthesizers and leading the way for keyboard oriented rock. Bowman (2002) analyses their late 1970s songs *2112, Xanadu,* and *Cygnus X-1* to demonstrate the individualist-libertarian ideology of their progressive rock stance. *2112,* an extended work, is modelled on large-scale structures found in refined music with recurring thematic material and harmonically connected tonal areas; it also incorporates a quota-tion from Tchaikovsky's *1812 Overture.* Their album *Permanent Waves* (1980) set a new standard, fusing elements of refined music, jazz-rock, heavy metal, progressive rock, and reggae with a new emphasis on rhythm. *The Spirit of Radio* opens with heavy metal elements and a middle register electronic keyboard figure, but then introduces a bass eight-note scale ostinato gesture. These elements periodically re-enter between bursts of other material plus intricate changing drumming patterns. After a familiar I–IV–V–I progression, the eight-note ostinato returns underneath a wailing electric guitar solo. The album *Moving Pictures* (1981), digitally mixed and mastered, exploits new computer technologies and features increased keyboard along the lines of the earlier Canadian band Lighthouse. As Rush became more familiar with developments in European rock in the 1980s, they experimented with irregular metres such as 7/8 and often began creation of a piece with rhythm rather than melody. Peart began to introduce drums of other cultures such as India, and the album *Power Windows* (1985) includes Oriental melodic patterns and African rhythms. Rush lyrics often reflect environmental issues, as in *Natural Science,* and Geddy's high falsetto style singing gives Rush an identifiable sound.

In the early 1980s CBC television had a daily music video program, and in 1984 the Toronto-based MuchMusic became Canada's first Canadian music video station; by 1989 it was part of the basic cable service.[27] In a comparative analysis of a week of televised events broadcast on Much-Music and its American equivalent MTV, Karen Pegley (2002) detected major differences. MuchMusic aired more different videos with a greater variety in artists, and their content featured earlier videos from the early 1980s (3). Pegley also notes differences in the musical context; Much-Music often celebrates regions of Canada and identifies where artists are, creating a pronounced contrast with the homogenized presentations of MTV.

New Francophone Pop

Changes in Quebec during the late 1970s included Parti Québécois legislation to strengthen the French language and to protect cultural identity. One result was a number of Quebec songwriters changing their focus from popular political music to the disco movement, creating songs that were relevant elsewhere as well. In the early 1970s the Montreal *Petit Journal* established music awards (much like the *RPM* Gold Leafs), and in 1979 the Association de disque, de l'industrie du spectacle québécois et de la video founded the Félix awards (named for Félix Leclerc). Félix winners, who are chosen by juries composed of members of ADISQ, include Claude Dubois, Serge Fiori, and Richard Séguin. MusiquePlus (a French equivalent of MuchMusic), first telecast in 1986 has provided important exposure for Francophone artists, and Montreal's vibrant film industry has contributed high production standards and innovative ideas for francophone music videos. Unfortunately little attention is paid to francophone popular artists outside of Quebec, and even beyond Montreal, and the Juno francophone best album category only appeared in 1992.

René Simard was particularly successful and had a following in France and Japan. Ginette Reno (b. 1946 in Montreal), who sings in both French and English, began her career in the St Laurent Market area, and she writes much of her own material; her greatest success was with Diane Juster's *Je ne suis qu'une chanson* (1980), partially due to its connection with Vigneault's *Mon Pays*. Charlebois's hymn to a multicultural Quebec, *La bossa-nova des Esquimaux*, blends joual and academic French, folk elements, French chanson, and Latin rhythm, and *Lindberg* shows a possible shape for a *québécois* musical expression. The 1970s saw further fragmentation among a variety of streams: American-influenced popular forms (such as *western canadien*), progressive or classic rock, disco, and the new *chansonniers. Québéçois*, by La révolution française[28] was taken up by young sovereigntist Quebecers. While Charlebois influenced this group, he remained somewhat aloof from nationalistic themes; his album *Swing Charlebois Swing* (1977) celebrates happiness and a peaceful rapport with the landscape, renouncing the world of drugs and rock angst (Germain 1978, 58). Beau Dommage (formed in 1970) had the most success in blending the elements of the time (space age sounds, hard rock, country, Latin rhythms, and the Beatles). The album *L'heptade* (1976) by the rock group Harmonium used subtle lyrics, folk-like melodies and incorporated refined orchestral music. Other groups include Aut' Chose, who were more concerned with hippie movements and alliances with French or US culture "as a means of undermining the hegemony of English-speaking Canada" (Lipsitz 1994, 149).

Acadian groups include 1755 (named for the year of the expulsion) who mixed pop, country, traditional music, and rock to express their Acadian identity; their later efforts include elements of rock and zydeco, a trend continued by Zachary Richard. Partially reformed as Expresso S.V.P., they influenced the next generation of Quebec groups. With *Hélène*, Roch Voisine (b. 1963) and his friend Stephan Lessard had a huge success in Quebec and France; Voisine writes in both English and French and his songs, such as *La legende de oochigeas*, are influenced by First Nations traditions. Acadian musicians such as Edith Butler, Calixte Duguay, Angele Arsenault, and the groups, Suroît, Maniak, and Les Habitants, played a major role in the folk revival of the 1970s (Diamond 2001a, 1137). Francophone music in Ontario includes Sudbury's *La Nuit sur l'étang* (established in 1973), and the Franco-Ontarian Festival begun in Ottawa (founded 1975). Both these venues have encouraged artists such as Robert Paquette, who sometimes produces English and French versions of a song (for example *Jean Bérubé / Black Born George*). Garolou combines progressive rock with traditional music; his recording of Paul Demers' *Notre place,* which describes French-speaking Canadians outside of Quebec, was particularly popular. La Cooperative des artistes du Nouvel-Ontario,[29] an important musical and theatrical development, produced songs such as *Moi, j'viens du Nord* that spoke to francophone Ontarians but also used English (see Lamothe 1994, 131). Manitoba artists such as Daniel Lavoie received support from this Francophone community. A second wave of artists includes Joëlle Lanoix, Donald Poliquin, Micheline Scott, Janie Myner, Michel Paiement, and André Lanthier. "A younger generation includes Prince Edward Islanders La Sagouine, Nova

Scotians Les Tymeux de la Baie, and New Brunswickers Les Mechants Maquereaux" (Diamond 2001a, 1137).

André Gagnon (b. 1942) has had a varied, illustrious career as pianist, composer, conductor and arranger. As a pianist he accompanied popular Quebec singers such as Claude Léveillée in the 1960s, and he appears as a concerto soloist with orchestras. From the 1970s on he devoted more time to composition and arranging for radio, television, and films. His compositions often combine refined and popular elements, as in *Petit Concerto pour Carignan et orchestre* (1976), but pieces such as *Neiges, Smash, Chevauchée, Surprise, Donna* and *Mouvements* have established him in the disco and pop fields (L'Herbier 1992, 510).

The 1990s saw further developments. In Quebec Marjo made a major impact by showing that a woman could write her own songs, inspired by her own experiences. Her success with rock and film scores inspired other women musicians; one of these was the Belgian-born Lara Fabian, who built her career in Montreal after finding that the concept of a woman singer-songwriter was still not accepted in Europe (see Christie 2000, 40). Successful interpretative singers include Isabelle Boulay. Paul Piché's *Voila c'que nous voulons* (1993) became a theme song of the Quebec sovereignty movement. Other successful singer-songwriters include Kevin Parent, and Jim Corcoran. The melodic rock band Kermess's recording of Piché's *Y'a pas grand chose dans l'ciel à soir* shows their poetic and ironical view of the human condition. Other groups of the late 1990s include Noir silence (from Beauce) and the alternative band Groovy Aardvark who had success with Vincent Peakes's *Dérangeant* (1996). The rich Quebec scene includes Anglophone bands (such as Bran Van 3000 and Sky) and Muzion (a hip-hop group that uses French, English, and Haitian Creole) as well as upcoming artists Jean Leloup, Nicholas Ciccone, Catherine Durand, and cellist/vocalist Jorane (Young 2001, 45). Luc Plamondon (b. 1942) has been a force in the Quebec scene and the French world since the 1970s, when Diane Dufresne recorded his songs. His hit show *Starmania* (1978), created with Michel Berger, played in Quebec, France, Germany and Russia and was translated into English as *Tycoon*. His rock opera *La légende de Jimmy* (also written with Berger) is based on the story of Jimmy Dean. After Berger's death in 1992, Plamondon collaborated with Richard Cocciante on the successful stage musical *Notre Dame de Paris* (1998), premiered in France by a mainly Quebec cast.

One important outcome of the vitality of Quebec's music scene is Les disques audiogram, the largest French independent label in North America; many of the firm's executives are also involved with L'equipe spectra, a management company that controls most of the regional music scene and organizes the annual Francofolies to showcase Quebec talent. One of the success stories of that scene is Cirque du soleil; musical selections from spectacles such as *Alegria*[30] have kept Canadian musicians on the World Music charts.

Country-Infused Music

Country music may be the most frequently heard popular music stream in Canada. Successful musicians with careers dating back to the 1950s and 1960s include Lucille Starr, fiddler Eleanor Townsend, and accordionist Walter Ostanek.[31] The Good Brothers (Brian, Larry, Bruce, later the Goods) sang folk and bluegrass in the 1960s; with the rise of country rock, their combination of guitar, banjo, autoharp, dobro, and vocals, became popular. Prairie Oyster[32] is a country rock band formed in 1974; major hits include *Did You Fall in Love With Me?*, *One Precious Love*, and *Lonely You, Lonely Me.* Valdy has had extremely successful record sales and his *Rock and Roll Song* (1972) was a national favourite. Some of his albums are specifically geared to children. Both Valdy and Gary Fjellgaard have been honoured for bringing environmental issues to the fore in their songs. Other successful singers include Charlie Major (*I'm Gonna Drive You Out of My Mind*), Paul Brandt (*My Heart Has a History,* and *Calm Before the Storm*), Michelle Wright (*Take It Like a Man*), Terri Clark, Carolyn Dawn Johnston, and the Wilkinsons. Chantal Kreviazuk[33] performs at the piano and speaks directly to the audience (Burton 2000, 19); her *Leaving on a Jet Plane* was used on the 1998 soundtrack *Armageddon.* True western music that glorified the cowboy life[34] achieved a rebirth in songs of Ian Tyson, who captured this experience in the first genuine western songs written since the 1930s; his albums include *Old Corrals and Sagebrush* (1982), *Ian Tyson* (1984), and *Cowboyography* (1985).

East Coast Fluorescence

The vital Maritime musical scene is rooted in folk traditions that have nurtured the region for hundreds of years. Since 1985 Maritime music has became recognized within Canada and internationally, particularly in its Celtic forms.[35] East Coast Music Awards were established in 1988. Figgy Duff, organized by Noel Dinn in Newfoundland, performed arrangements of folk songs with amplified instruments; while frowned on by folklore purists, performances including the *bodhran* (an Irish drum) were hailed in Europe. Dinn and others wrote original songs for the group. John Allan Cameron played Scottish pipe tunes on a twelve-string guitar, toured with Anne Murray, and hosted several television shows featuring Celtic music. J.P. Cormier's *Fiddle Album* (1990) takes fiddling beyond piano or guitar accompaniment with arrangements that include drums, banjo, and mandolin (see Fleming 1997, 50). The Barra MacNeils (siblings Sheumas, Kyle, Stewart, and Lucy) expanded their instrumentation from a solid Celtic core of harp, whistle, flute, fiddle, and bodhran, to include accordion, viola, mandolin, electric guitar, and keyboards. The Rankin Family (Raylene, Jimmy, Heather, Cookie, John Morris) played a wide range of musics including country, Gaelic songs, classic rock, fiddle music for weddings, and other gatherings. Fiddler John Morris (d. 2000) is considered the first Maritimer to "electrify" the instrument, and their evolving hybrid presentation expanded to include their own original songs.

Musicians who use Gaelic materials include Mary Jane Lamond, who has studied the language from Cape Breton speakers. Ashley MacIsaac holds his fiddle with his right arm and draws on his family's heritage of fiddling and step-dancing; with his band the Kitchen Devils he brought electrification and rock to the traditional repertoire. Natalie MacMaster, a student of Stan Chapman, has been acclaimed as one of the greatest Maritime fiddlers; she combined step-dancing with fiddling, and has incorporated other traditions, such as Irish and Appalachian clogging. Lennie Gallant, of PEI, learned Acadian fiddle music, and began playing guitar, bodhran, harmonica, and mandolin with Celtic bands, and he wrote songs in both French and English. His album *Lifeline* opens with a Middle Eastern melody. Barachois (Albert Arsenault, Chuck Arsenault, Louise Arsenault, Hélène Bergeron), also based in PEI, began as a dinner theatre group in 1993, using mostly traditional instruments of the Acadian culture. Their first self-titled album consists largely of traditional Acadian songs in arrangements tinged with country, and rock. Black musicians in the Maritimes include the legendary jazz saxophonist "Bucky" Adams, a number of women's vocal groups, such as Four the Moment, Gospel Heirs, and Urban Renewal. The East Coast Music Awards category for Afro-Canadian musicians honours their contributions.

Newfoundland has its own unique musical heritage. Great Big Sea,[36] formed at a kitchen party in Petty Harbour, performs traditional songs in an updated fashion and original compositions, using an Irish drum and a snare drum; their rendition of *Lukey's Boat* was a hit, and in live concerts they promote Newfoundland in a realistic manner, refusing to be type-cast as "fisherfolk" (see Moore 2002). Spirit of the West,[37] a folk-based band added rock drums to their traditional instrumentation. Outside of the Maritimes, Celtic influences are found as with the Leahy family, who present lively shows; each member is an expert musician and dancer. In Vancouver the Celtic punk band The Real McKenzies perform in kilts and sporrans with one or two bagpipers added to a rock complement.

First Peoples: Expanding Traditional Sounds

The continuing success of Buffy Sainte-Marie encouraged other First Nations musicians to create their own expressions. Festivals that emerged during the 1980s provided performing outlets. The Stein Valley Festival in British Columbia, organized by the Lytton and Lilloet bands, and the Innu Nikamu, near Sept-Îles, Quebec were both established in 1985. Other important festivals include Jammin' on the Bay in Northern Ontario. Successful record sales plus pressure from First Nations radio and record producers resulted in a Juno category for Aboriginal music, first awarded in 1994 to Lawrence Martin.[38]

Mi'kmaqs Don Ross and Willie Dunn cite blues and hip hop among their influences; Ross is admired as a guitarist and Dunn wrote much of the music for George Ryga's *The Ecstasy of Rita Joe*. Lee Cremo, of Mi'kmaq heritage, recorded Scottish, Irish, French, and Mi'kmaq repertoire and made it to international fiddling competitions, but was unable to make a living as a musician.[39] In the 1970s Inuit singer-guitarist Charlie Panigoniak merged elements of traditional song with country music; his songs have a one-beat pulse, a melodic contour with some repeated pitches and undulations predominantly downward within a fairly narrow compass (Whidden 1981, 40). *Hinena Hoho Hine*, written by Slavey Dene musician Johnny Landry in the early 1980s, has become the unofficial anthem of the North; the most popular recording is by Susan Aglukark with a group of Dene drummers on her album *This Child* (1995). Although Aglukark has been criticized for her main-stream sound and English texts, her albums *Arctic Rose* (1992) and *Unsung Heroes* (1999) include subtle commentary about her people and their treatment by the Canadian government.[40] With electricity in most Aboriginal communities by the early 1970s, rock bands sprang up. Errol Ranville's C-Weed Band recorded several albums for the Sunshine and Hawks labels, and bands such as the Harrapashires, the Tymes, and Kinroq played a range from dance tunes to ballads in a hard-edged sound with minimal sound processing.

In the early 1970s Philippe Mackenzie was writing country-influenced songs that incorporated elements of traditional material; since the *teuei-kan* drum (with snares over and under the skin) was sacred, he decided to remove the snares and added maracas to approximate the sound. Mackenzie's example was followed by Kashtin, an Innu duo (Claude McKenzie and Florent Vollant), who had a major success with *Akua Tuta*[41] (1989) sung in their traditional language. Mohawk Murray Porter's song *Who Found Who in 1492* incorporates a blues idiom in its Native view of Columbus. The Ottawa-based group 7th Fire (named for the Anishnabe explanation of the stages of world history), led by the Deleary brothers, blended jazz and rock idioms with traditional round dances on their album *The Cheque Is In The Mail* (Patterson 1996). Jerry Alfred and the Medicine Beat, and Art Napoleon incorporate traditional sounds extensively. Alfred, a Tutchone song keeper in the Yukon, intersperses contemporary and traditional songs; his albums *Etsi Shon, Nendaä* and *Kehlonn* include traditional gambling songs, often accompanied by a frame drum. "[H]e writes contemporary songs mostly on primary chords ... He favors heavy reverberation, relating the echo to the sense of space that is rooted in his experience growing up in a remote community in the northern Yukon. His band draws on jazz stylings ... and country guitar influences ... in the (often extended) instrumental solos" (Diamond 2001f, 1280). The Southern Tutchone Daniel Tlen and Dene artists Leela Gilday and David Gon have built significant careers, frequently using their traditional language. Art Napoleon uses more English but includes traditional Dunneza (Beaver) material as well. No Reservations, a band of six members (some with university degrees in music) create songs that address contemporary social issues and fuse their presentation with a highly theatrical performance style. Tzo'kam ("chickadee" in Lil'wat [Stla'limx]) performs traditional songs with drums, sticks, and occasionally flute.

Women performers include Elizabeth Hill, a storyteller form the Six Nations Grand River Territory leads a quartet of guitars, mandolin, and cello. Jani Lauzon has expanded the use of the Native flute (see figure 13.1); her song texts deal with issues of her people and she combines traditional and contemporary elements. Nathalie Picard, a Wendat, also plays various types of flutes, and with Julien Rock of the Montagnais-Innu nation performs her own compositions and traditional materials on Iroquois bone flute, water drum, and Montagnais caribou-skin drum. Significant songs by Laura Vinson include *Sing the Violin* and *Daughters of the Dawn*; with her group Free Spirit she presents a blend of country and traditional Plains Native dancers and drummers. Asani ("rock" in Cree), a group of four women of Cree heritage, performs traditional music and contemporary indigenous songs accompanied by percussion. Performers of Inuit throat games include Laina Tulluga and Martha Sivuarapik, who appeared at the 1986 Innu Kiakamu festival. Madeleine Allakariallak and

Figure 13.1.
Jani Lauzon plays a First Nations flute with a "saddle" carved as a loon. Photograph by Claudia V. Dauria.

Phoebe Atagoyuk,[42] formed Tudjaat to perform songs (such as *When the Elders Sing to Me*) in English over a country-rock accompaniment with throat game material. Etulu Etidloiee often uses material from juggling games and uses the guitar as if it were a traditional drum. Lucie Idlout of Iqaluit has written powerful songs on the troubling issue of suicide.

A strengthening of Amerindian and Inuit fiddle traditions across the north during the 1990s is partly due to Andrea Hansen's Strings Across the Sky, a foundation set up to provide instruments and teaching in response to her discovery that there were few fiddlers due to a lack of violins and school music programs during her visit to the North on tour as a member of the TSO (see Pfeiff 2000). Encouraged by this support Charlie Tumik, Frank Cockney, and Eddie Kikoak have become prominent professional Inuit fiddlers. Excellent First Nations fiddlers include Lee Mandeville, Joe Loutchan, Colin Adjun, Thomas Manuel, Everett Kakfwi, Sinclair

Cheechoo, and Clarence Louttit. With the emphasis on oratory in First Nations societies, it is not surprising that rap has become an influential musical genre. Prominent performers include TKO of Winnipeg, whose *Sing* incorporates powwow sounds; TKO calls himself a spokesperson for CHIP (Cool Hip Indigenous People). Daybi, another Winnipeger, combines live instruments with digital sounds. Adam Krims (2000) discusses Darren Tootoosis of Hobbema (who uses Bannock as his stage name), pointing out that Tootoosis is one of many Cree rappers (2000, 187).

Alternative and World Music

The alternative category of music became common in the 1990s, as record companies realized that consumers were tired of riff-heavy melodic metal. Many Canadian bands continue to fit loosely into this category, with an emphasis on guitar sound and an authenticity in their presentations. In 1987 guitarist Michael Timmins, bassist Alan Anton, and drummer Pete Timmins merged blues and country to provide a hypnotic mellow backing for Margo Timmins's alto voice; their first album, *The Trinity Sessions*,[43] made with rudimentary equipment stayed on the charts and the single *Sweet Jane* launched them on a world tour. Their success has continued with subsequent albums and songs such as *Angel Mine*. The Tragically Hip,[44] considered the definitive Canadian alternative band, combines a hard-edged R&B sound with lyrics that specify Canadian topics including the Mounties, Millhaven penitentiary, artist Tom Thomson, bilingualism, and hockey rinks (Ivison 1997, 54). Hit songs include *New Orleans Is Sinking* (1989) and *Evelyn* (1997); the album *In Violet Light* (2002) "is an affirmation of the group's egalitarian spirit, the strength of Downie's lyrics bolstered by twined guitars and dynamic grooves – a hallmark of the band" (Christie 2002, 35). Outside of Canada, Tragically Hip is particularly popular in Australia, Belgium, and the Netherlands.

The quirky sound of the Barenaked Ladies (formed 1988)[45] blends the jazz background of the Creegan brothers, the pop of Page, with the hard rock of Stewart; they had a major hit with *If I Had a Million Dollars*, and by their third album, *Stunt*, they had become stars. *Maroon* (2000) marks a move beyond earlier material with more thoughtful songs. Page has commented that "[s]ome of it is born out of frustration with the glibness of modern culture and knowing how much we participated in that ... One of the themes of the album is about taking action – going out and doing something, instead of sitting and talking about it'" (Jennings 2000, 68). This album continued to feature unusual rhymes and a crisp, uncluttered sound with musical idioms from lounge music, country twang, Gilbert and Sullivan operetta, and rap; the lyrics are integral parts of such songs as *Helicopters* and *Tonight Is the Night I Fell Asleep at the Wheel*.

Songwriting workshops at folk festivals played a role in the development of Canadian artists; successes include Brad Roberts, who began writing songs for his Winnipeg group, the Crash Test Dummies;[46] by 1989 the material produced by this band could only have come out of Winnipeg. Their sound was characterized by a Celtic core, country and blues riffs, and the unique vocals of Ellen Reid. Hits include *Superman's Song* and *Mmm Mmm Mmm Mmm*, the first pop hit to have a vowel-free chorus (Ostick 1995, 15). The success of the Crash Test Dummies and the Cowboy Junkies made it possible for bands such as the Barenaked Ladies and individual musicians such as Rita MacNeil to be recognized by major labels. From its beginnings in 1990 the Tea Party[47] incorporated non-Western sounds and instruments (oud, tar, tamboura, dumbek, darabouka, djembe) along with dance and industrial sounds; for example, the genesis of their song *Transmission* (1997) was a loop from a Lebanese funeral march. Jeff Martin adopted the word "chemurgy" (a chemical term referring to the use of organic materials in industrial processes), to describe the band's hybrid of rock, electronica, and Middle Eastern melodies (Bliss 1997, 34; see also Lamb 2001). Sloan, a power pop grunge band from Halifax, is based on egalitarianism; *Underwhelmed* (1992) has become a Canadian classic, demonstrating bands do not have to conform to Toronto or US-based recording companies. Folk music elements play a major role in their sound along with clever lyrics and a blend of pop sounds drawn from many quarters. Wide Mouth Mason combines world music from their diverse heritages, along with elements of reggae, blues, jazz, roots, funk and pop (Kelly 2000, 37). Other notable bands include the female heavy metal Kittie based in London, Ontario (Kelly 2000b, 45). The Moffatts, a true family group, had released five albums by 2001 and have a huge fan base in the Far East (Kelly 2000c, 37).

The rich musical scene of Eastern Canada and international interest in Celtic music is linked to what has been termed "world music," a category coined by British music marketers in 1986. The first Canadians appearing on world music charts include Loreena McKennitt (b. 1957) who discovered Celtic music, bought a harp, and extended her instrumentation to fiddle, tin whistle, balalaika, and the Indian sitar and tambura. By 1981 she was performing at the Stratford Festival in Ontario and had established her own record label Quinlan Road. Her *Full Circle* (1994) was influenced by Moroccan musics and chanting heard at Saint-Benoît-du-lac, a monastery in Quebec. By 1996 she topped the world beat charts.

In spite of McKennitt's success international awareness of the wealth of world music elements in Canada has been limited. The first edition of *World Music: The Rough Guide* has no entry on Canada and the 2000 edition concentrates on Inuit, Quebec, and East Coast artists;[48] missing are René Dupéré's music for Cirque du Soleil shows that often involve non-Western instruments and influences, klezmer groups (such as Flying Bulgar Klezmer Band and Tzimmes), and the many ensembles blending elements of Asian musics. There are gamelans in Montreal, Ottawa, Toronto, and Vancouver. Performers on Indian tabla, sitar, and vina as well as Japanese and Chinese instruments are members of a number of alternative groups.

If world music refers to forms of non-Western musics, Canada has a bountiful supply.[49] The presence of these traditions and fine musicians to play them has opened up many possibilities for collaborations. Arts council programs have provided financial support and in 1998 the Canada Council sponsored a showcase of diverse artists, including First Peoples musicians, featuring not only traditional presentations but also collaborative groups that combined instruments and expressions from diverse background. For example, Asza of Vancouver combines American folk, Chinese, and Middle Eastern instruments and musicians; Montreal's Takadja combines Quebec and African musicians.[50] Musicians from very different backgrounds and fields have been using a culturally diverse palette of sounds. Mychael Danna's works have a strong Celtic influence, even in his environmental electronic collaborations with Tim Clement, and he has a special interest in the music of Southeast Asia and more recently Sri Lanka; these influences can be heard in his film scores for Atom Egoyan's *The Adjuster,* and *Exotica*. In his guitar work and electronica Michael Brook blends rock and blues with Indian mandolinist U. Srinivas, Brazilian percussionist Nana Vasconcelas, and Albanian *duduk* player Djivan Gasparyan, and his productions with Pakistani *qawwali* (devotional song) master Nusrat Fateh Ali Khan are highly acclaimed.

Canadian Divas

A number of Canadian women combined elements of the music around them, including folk and country, to create songs relating to their own experiences. Margaret O'Hara produced only one album, but her unique songs and stage presentations influenced many Canadian artists (see Wildermuth 2002). With her interest in visual media and evocative poetry, Jane Siberry (b. 1955), described as "quirky, artsy, and ethereal," produced eight albums between 1981 and 1995, "brimming with cinematic images, rhythmic adventures, and lyrical inventiveness" (Chodan 2000, 45). In *Mimi on the Beach* she takes the necessary time to create musical and literary images of a woman floating on a surfboard. Her sensuous, suggestive creations drawing on a wide range of sounds and sources –including a subversion of funk in *Flirtin' Is a Flo-Thing* (1999) – have won her an international following (Fledderus 2003, 36). Performers on her album *When I Was a Boy* (1993) include Brian Eno and k.d. lang. Jann Arden (b. Calgary 1962) is a multi-dimensional entertainer with a propensity for writing songs that reflect deep emotions with elements of sass and humour; her albums include *Time for Mercy* (1993), *Living under June* (1994), and *Blood Red Cherry* (2001), which contains the award-winning *Thing For You*.

Sarah Harmer (b. 1978) is earning praise for the erudite but colloquial lyrics of her folk-pop ballads and expressive voice. Her album *You were Here* (2000) features a deliberate "vintage sound" created with tube-amplifiers and an old type of microphone; *Basement Apt* has been called one of the most poignant ballads to come out of Canada. She also recorded the soundtrack for the Canadian curling film *Men With Brooms* with The Tragically Hip. R & B star Deborah Cox (b. 1973) has built her success on an ability to straddle the pop and dance markets. Her music comes from the Guyanese heritage of her parents who listened to calypso, jazz and blues, combined with a wide range of ethnicities in Toronto (Oh 1999, 40). The 1990s saw the makeover of child star Celine Dion (b. 1968) into a superstar interpreter of English and French pop songs. Some commentators interpret her success as a formulaic Americanization of Quebec music (Côté 2000, 45), but nevertheless she has had greater international success than any previous Quebec musician, recording more than thirty award-winning albums. Her single *My Heart Will Go On* was used in the film *Titanic*. Like Murray she selects songs carefully, choosing many composed by Canadians, including David Foster (*The Colour of My Love*).

Alanis Morissette (b. 1974) was determined to become a star from an early age. The songs from her first album (1991) are dance-oriented, with melodies presented over a bed of keyboard sound and computer-sequenced rhythms. Her second album includes lyrics with greater depth that are more aggressive and more personal. One of her principal aims is to break down the stereotypes (tramp, high-minded singer-songwriter, dance-pop diva) of female artists in the larger pop world (Grills 1997, 40). Her album *Jagged Little Pill* (1995) presents a major change of direction (see Grills 1997, 59), and a shift toward a raw and more vital rock. Morissette has admitted an interest in self-help psychological studies, and she uses this "psychobabble," speaking frankly and candidly to an audience

Constant Craving with k.d. lang

Kathryn Dawn Lang (b. 1961 in Edmonton) joined the Texas swing band in 1983 and the same year, recorded her first single under the name "k.d. lang." (For a description of a performance in Saskatoon in 1985 with her backup band, the Reclines, see Robertson 1992, 16–19.) Lang also met Ben Mink, which whom she was to write many of her songs, at this time. In 1987 she sang at the Grand Old Opry, and her album *Angel with a Lariat* went gold in Canada. Owen Bradley came out of retirement to produce her album *Shadowland*, and his choice of country, western swing, torch, and blues standards backed by top Nashville musicians opened up her artistry. Although she has toned down her dress somewhat, she still refuses to take on the expected image of a female country artist. In an interview she explains: "Androgyny is important in my life because I can deal with people on a human, not a sexual level; it's important on stage, because both men and women are attracted to me" (Scott 1988, 132). Her 1989 album *Absolute Torch and Twang* is an eclectic mix of styles (with eight songs by lang and Ming, another by lang, and three country standards) and includes explicit reference to Alberta; her sound blends the smoothness of Anne Murray, the grittiness of Patsy Cline, and the rockabilly of Presley: "The songs are about Alberta, and the video and the album cover are shot in Alberta because that's what I like. I like the Prairies. I like grain elevators ... this is where I'm from and this is where most of the imagery in my music and performance come from. And most of my humor is Canadian" (Stanley and Nicholson 1989, 38). Lang has moved on to other genres, but emerging country musicians such as Michelle Wright and Cassandra Vasik "credit her with clearing the way for them. While working with country music she refused to be marketed as a 'girl singer' sticking instead to her androgynous appearance and rankling on narrow minds everywhere" (Robertson 1992, 104). Her album *Ingénue* (1992) uses vibraphone, marimba, cello, and clarinet, and the violin in *The Mind of Love* and *So It Shall Be* has an Oriental sound. The introspective *Miss Chatelaine* has a Parisian feel, and Latin rhythms infect *Still Thrives This Love*. With its harmonized chorus *Constant Craving* has been called one of the great pop songs of all time. In an analysis of lang's songs, Sherinian wrote: "Through intentional ambiguity and gender fusion, lang claims a space in which she creates her lesbian butch subjectivity" (Sherinian 2001, 111).

that was involved in its own self-analysis (see Grills 1997, 98). By drawing on personal experiences, Morissette created lyrics that resonated around the world, and she has made the music industry realize that women should have the opportunity to speak and sing of their own experiences and be treated as people, not sex objects. Shania Twain from Timmins, Ontario, has shaken up the country music scene. Following somewhat in the footsteps of Anne Murray and Michelle Wright, Twain's songs, often co-written with Mutt Lange, expresses authenticity with a woman's view both feminine and independent; her sound retains the twang, guitars and fiddle, but not the crying. She can sing of heartbreak and also bring humour to a situation. Twain has commented on the strong influence of her step-father's Ojibwe parents about life and living. As an Ojibwe, Shania chose her name, which means "I'm on my way." The songs *Any Man of Mine* and *Whose Bed Have Your Boots Been Under?* are assertive declarations of a woman's needs, and her pop-tinged presentations have put her on both pop and country charts.

Sarah McLachlan (b. 1968) is one of the greatest songwriters to emerge in Canada since Joni Mitchell. Her first two albums reveal a beautiful voice and a potential for inner probing heard in *Out of the Shadows*. The title of her album *Fumbling towards Ecstasy* (1995) comes from a poem by Wilfred Owen, and the songs reveal a mature woman dealing with the complexities of life and the responsibilities of adulthood, a persona continued in her next album *Surfacing*. "Fans and musicians alike will say that McLachlan's music succeeds because on every level, she communicates experiences with intense personal empathy. And nothing has increased global communication like the Internet ... 'The world is sort of pulling us apart in this technological age,' she asserts, adding that she sees her role as creating 'a sense of connection, [reinforcing] the notion that we're not alone'" (Chauncey 1997, 6). Concern for women musicians became her issue when she saw the list of main acts at Lollapalooza.[51] Because no women were listed and her management would not allow her to include a woman artist on her show "because the audience would not accept two women artists in succession," she organized Lilith Fair (named for the Biblical Adam's first wife) a feminist version of Lollapalooza. From 1997 to 1999 Lilith Fair played thirty-five to forty dates each summer, showcasing women musicians; local women musicians could audition for a spot on a secondary stage. Through McLachlan's initiative many women launched viable careers, while enthusiastic audiences and sold-out houses refuted the music industry's assumptions.

Dion, Morisette, Twain, and McLachan radically changed aspects of the mega music business. All four came out of a mature and vital Canadian popular music industry. Musicians were aware of models, both Canadian and non-Canadian, that formed their own sounds, and were aware that that they were creating a rubbaboo of sounds only possible within the particular geographical landscape of Canada. This fact is epitomized in the Rush song *Closer to the Heart*. The strength and independence of Canadian pop music came about largely because of the CanCon requirements. Richard Sutherland has commented that with reforms to the copyright act, broadcasters pay not only publishers and songwriters but also performers and recording companies for the music they broadcast. "Given the fact that copyright is the fastest growing part of the music industry's revenues and may eventually outpace record sales as the largest source of its revenues, CanCon may well become a way of ensuring that the industry will receive revenues from airplay ... In exchange for this we make demands on them to reinforce and strengthen our national identity, an identity in which cultural expression such as music forms an important if unquantifiable part" (Sutherland 2002, 17).

John Beckwith's is the most obviously Canadian music, not just in its folk material, but also in its roughness. Abrupt transitions, tedious ostinati, broken by sudden shocks. It is like Canadian history and geography. Look at the museums. First one sees a picture of an Indian and his family, then a picture of a logging camp in the bush, then a picture of a Canadian Pacific Railway engine, then a photograph of modern Montreal. There is no connection between these things, or rather, the connections are missing except in your imagination, events seem to pop up abruptly out of nothing. It is the same with the space of the country. When I arrived in Halifax as an immigrant, I took the train at night and we began to make our way west. When I awoke in the morning I expected to see towns and villages. Instead I saw miles and miles, hours and hours, of trees, occasionally interrupted by sudden little clearings with a few houses clustered around a church or gas station, then more forest. The roughness of Canadian music comes from that, and when you feel that roughness you sense that the reflection is authentic. (István Anhalt, quoted in Schafer 1993, 95–6)

Anhalt articulates a unique sound of Canadian music in terms of Canada's landscape and history, arguing that the vast range of space with contrasting elements can be heard in the works of John Beckwith and other Canadian composers. For Anhalt, the identity of Canadian music is based on the experience of physical space through time. It has long been recognized that music articulates time, but Berland argues that music has even more power as an articulation of space: "If the hit parade had emerged by the time Harold Innis wrote *Empire and Communications* (1950), perhaps he would have offered some specific hypotheses about its spatial-temporal impact" (Berland 1994, 180). We experience the space around us through all our senses, and articulated sounds that involve language are often important for our survival and for bonding with other human beings. Thus creators of organized sound structures in many societies draw on sounds of their landscape. Local flavour is imparted in song lyrics, album art, a public persona, poetics of locality, or familiar local sounds; these, combined with elements from a global system of representation, create a complex field of signification. "Music and song spatially cover all parts of the earth where humans live but music is not identical everywhere nor does it remain the same, over time, in any one location. A variety of musics can coexist in any one region at the same time. It is highly divided spatially and temporally by different musical styles (or forms) or sub-styles (genres)" (Thirlwall 1992, 159). To understand how Canadians interact with their space, we must examine the effects of geography and history on musical expressions originating within the area known as Canada and the context in which those expressions have emerged. As Gordon Smith comments: "Technological factors (with their urban focus), demographic patterns (rural to urban migration and the abundance of immigrant communities in urban settings), and the emergence of strong regional musical voices are formative influences on musical production today. However, in addition to and concomitant with these emergent influences, music continues to be used by musicians as social actors in specific situations to erect boundaries, to maintain distinctions between us and them, and to confirm a sense of place. Indeed, questions of identity and authenticity are still present, if now in ever more complex cultural and ethnic configurations" (Smith 2001a, 151).

Landscape and Nature in Musical Expression

TRADITIONS OF THE FIRST PEOPLES

The First Peoples learned to survive by listening to sounds produced by birds, animals, and nature itself. Their sense of direction and intimate knowledge of the land were legendary and their awe of natural forces continues to resonate today. Documentation from the early contact period attests to their pre-occupation with tradition and ritual to maintain a balance with all creatures in their geographical space and to influence the forces of weather. This response to terrain coincides with Gaile McGregor's theory of our response to nature. McGregor argues that the dominant Canadian response to nature is one of fear and terror that ultimately leads to denial and avoidance as a means of coping with the threat.

Drawing on examples of literature and painting from the early settlement period to contemporary expressions, she traces the presence of a "siege mentality" that underlies an ambivalence in the mediation between "self" and "other" found in artworks of Christopher Pratt, Christiane Pflug, Alex Colville, and Paul-Émile Borduas among others (McGregor 1985, 56, 102–5). The First Peoples accomplished this mediation through careful observation and imitation of creatures in their natural habitat in order to obtain sustenance and maintain a balance with nature. Kohl describes Menaboju, an Ojibwe, "fishing and singing a beautiful magic song to lure the fish he wanted to catch" (Kohl 1860, 452). In the Plains region ceremonial bundles containing parts of an animal or a bird were connected to songs or dances that often imitated the call or movement of the creature. Wissler notes that Wolf Songs of the Siksika (Blackfoot) "end with a howl, or wolf call, which expresses or symbolizes whatever the singer wishes to obtain, because the wolf howls when he is out on a quest" (Wissler 1912, 267).[1] First Nations musicians also imitated bird calls on flutes or whistles.[2] Documentation includes references to songs deemed to control natural forces. Copway describes a song given in a dream to an Ojibwe: "'Look on it while I sing, yes gaze upon the tree.' He sang, and pointed at the tree [which began to sway] ... As soon as he stopped singing and let fall his hands, everything became perfectly still and quiet. 'Now', he said, 'sing the words which I have sung.' I commenced as follows: 'It is I who travel in the winds; It is I who whisper in the breeze; I shake the trees, I shake the earth, I trouble the waters on every land.' While singing, I heard the winds whistle, saw the tree waving its top, the earth heaving" (Copway 1851, 39). In the 1640s the Jesuits in the Gaspé area reported an offer from shamans to use their songs to break an ice-jam in the St. Lawrence,[3] and some Inuit cultures used Weather Songs to influence the forces of nature.

EARLY EUROPEAN SETTLERS

European settlers in the late sixteenth century heard the musical expressions of the First Peoples as demoniacal noise. This reaction may well have been due in part to the contrast in terrain and wild life between Europe and their new surroundings; they did not recognize the First Peoples' imitations of environmental sounds. To comfort themselves, they sang songs of their own heritage.[4] European melodic contours and rhythmic patterns differ significantly from those of the First Peoples. French and English melodies usually begin at a mid point, rise through undulations to a high point, then return to the starting pitch, which is also the tonal centre; there are often two to four phrases, some of which may be repeated. Melodies of First Peoples begin with or leap up to a high point, then fall in undulating stages to a final low pitch or resting tone; the final note is sometimes followed by a high pitchless "whoop." Phrases are short and may consist of a single basic gesture slightly varied in repetition. Can these two contrasting shapes be loosely connected to the terrains of their creators? A reaction to the Prairie expanse might be reflected in the wide range of traditional Plains melodies. Similarly, the moderate range and gently moulded contours of Western European melodies could express a terrain lacking Canada's striking contrasts of high mountains, wide open spaces, and endless lake-studded forests. Melodies created in Canadian space after 1600 may be influenced by Western-based emotional reactions to the character of these new landscapes. In Western-based music, a melody with a narrow range and small intervals indicates extreme tension, while larger intervals and a wider range convey a more relaxed, confident, and open atmosphere. In First Peoples' songs, the rhythms of the voices and the accompaniment cannot be readily slotted into specific metrical patterns; the percussive beats often seem to follow a completely separate pulse from that of the voice, like a second independent layer of the texture. Could this lack of regularity reflect an aspect of roughness that Anhalt notes in the Canadian landscape? Over the centuries Western Europeans regularized the surrounding terrain, and by the mid-seventeenth century had organized most of their musical expressions into specific metrical patterns; this rhythmic regularization was likely hastened by performances of polyphonic music involving large groups of singers and instrumentalists. Notably, only two First Peoples' pre-contact traditions involve even limited polyphony (Pelinski 1981, 61).[5]

As European settlers penetrated further into the land and were initially welcomed by First Peoples, these two very different musical traditions were juxtaposed. In carrying out their dual aims – procuring furs and spreading Christianity – Europeans quickly discovered that music was an effective means of communication. First Nations melodies were adapted to Christian texts and European melodies to First Peoples' languages (Keillor 1995, 109–10). Variations of European language and music emerged in particular geographical spaces; for example, Acadian singing is generally less accented than québécois (Diamond 2001a, 1136), and Franco-Ontarian songs reveal strong influence of Ojibwe culture (Lederman 2001d, 1193).[6] First Peoples picked up or imitated European secular songs and dance tunes As early as 1749 Hudson's Bay Company reports refer to fiddlers playing for dances in which First Peoples took part (Mishler 1993, 18–9); these mainly Scottish-style dances have remained a vital part of First Nations musical expressions into the twenty-first century. The Native fiddlers who adopted these tunes did not copy the exact manner of Scottish or *canadien* presentation; instead their renditions include melodic and rhythmic elements of their pre-contact musical tradition (Keillor 1995, 111–2). This adaptation process was recognized in the nineteenth century and works both ways. Robert Kennicott noted in 1862 that voyageurs and First Peoples' singers used the term *rubbaboo* for this phenomenon: "When I try to speak French, and mix English, Slavy, Loucheux words with it, they tell me, 'that's a rubbaboo.' And when the Indians attempt to sing a voyaging song, the different keys and tunes make a rubbaboo" (Kennicott 1942, 86). At a gathering in a parlour, J.J. Bigsby heard French folk songs ending with a whoop or "piercing Indian shriek" (Bigsby 1850, 119). This rubbaboo of sounds has continued. The Calgary-based fiddling group Barrage[7] (1996) promotes fiddle styles of Alberta including French Canadian, Scottish, Irish, Métis, Ukrainian, Scandinavian heritages, and explores differences between orally transmitted fiddle traditions and notated violin music.

NOTATED CANADIAN MUSIC

European cultures included traditions of both notated music and orally transmitted repertoire. Since titles and texts in both traditions reflect specific locales and people, it is not surprising that settlers followed the same practise in their new surroundings, hanging new texts about their present situations on older European tunes; this happened with both notated and orally transmitted music.[8] In the nineteenth century patriotic songs contained direct references to Canadian political and institutional concerns and composers also used texts by Canadians that reflected Canadian experiences of nature (CMH7 1987, xi; CMH3 1984, vii; CMH17 1996, vi). With a growing interest in indigenous folk music in Scandinavia, Bohemia, and Britain during the second half of the nineteenth century, composers began to use folk tunes as a melodic or rhythmic basis in their compositions. A parallel movement in Canada is perhaps due to the fact that orally-transmitted song and dance was such a prevalent part of everyday life in the still primarily rural society. Ernest Gagnon's *Le carnaval de Québec* (1862?) contains both English and French tunes (CMH 1 1983, 99). Although major composers such as Haydn and Beethoven drew on folksongs for some compositions, in nineteenth-century Europe composers were viewed as individuals of supreme genius whose insights came only from within. By the early twentieth century that opinion had changed, and composers were seen as musicians influenced by their surroundings; accordingly the compositions they produced should reflect their spatial and physical location in specific ways (Boros and Toop 1995, 219).

It was not until the late nineteenth century that commentators began to consider musical happenings in Canada beyond short notices on individual composers or musicians or a particular centre such as Toronto (Morey 1997). In Hopkins's *Canada: An Encyclopedia of the Country* (1898), Torrington covers musical activities in Toronto, Montreal, and Hamilton but does not mention any original Canadian music; in the same publication S. Frances Harrison writes: "Canada's chief musical history is concerned with choir and choral societies, teaching institutions, and vocal and piano recitals. The development of the Orchestra and the study of symphonic music have necessarily been somewhat slow, while in the highest branch of the art, namely original composition, little has been accomplished" (Harrison 1898, 389–90). Harrison lists piano compositions by Gustave Gagnon and Georges Hébert and also mentions Frances J. Hatton-Moore. An editor's note appended to this article (presumably by Hopkins) points out that Harrison, under the pseudonym of Seranus, had written several piano pieces including *Chant du voyageur,* and *The Dialogue,* and that the best original composition of Lower Canada was George E. Carter's *Canada, mon pays* (Harrison 1898, 394). Hopkins fails to note, however, that Seranus's compositions were strongly influenced by French Canadian folk song and that many of her titles were directly connected to Canada. In "Canadian Creative Composers" (1913), J.D. Logan singles out Calixa Lavallée, Clarence Lucas, W.O. Forsyth, and Gena Branscombe as the first "native-born Canadian composers to undertake the systematic creation of fine music" (Logan 1913, 486). He discusses works by each composer, but does not specifically relate their works to Canada; he does, however, criticize universities and conservatories for concentrating on literature and music created abroad and neglecting Canadian creations. This sentiment was echoed in 1917 by Frederic Pelletier, who insisted that performers should present Canadian music: "In music it is another matter since composition cannot, for obvious reasons, put the national soul on display. But nationalism can be practised in other ways; that is, in the preference given to works by our own composers whenever possible" (Poirier 1994, 245). Pelletier's statement reflects a growing internationalization of influences in the early twentieth century and a resultant conclusion that it was impossible to express nationalism in music. In 1918 Léo-Pol Morin wrote: "These works do not represent Canadian art. Rather, if this is the expression of the Canadian race, then it is insignificant, it is nothing to be proud of, it is as lacking in originality and life as could be imagined ... How remote it all is, how lacking in meaning! One could confuse all these works, mix the titles and signatures, and no personality would be affected by it, if I exclude Couture, Fortier, and M. Tanguay. There is no doubt what they want to call Canadian music ... is scarcely the threat of a movement" (Poirier 1994, 246). This stance was disputed by Arthur Letondal among others, and by 1930 Morin had changed his opinion: "The means by which a thought or a musical idea is expressed is, no doubt, universal, understood in all the countries of the world in which the same system of sounds is used, but the soul of the music, its meaning, its spirit, remain national. National music must be that. Despite current trends it still remains national, maybe more so than the various forms of modern literature ... Let there be no mistake about this expression: national music. Being national in no way diminishes music's value" (Poirier 1994, 252).

The ambiguity about how music can express a national space stems in part from a changing view of influences on the composer. In many European countries nationalism was crystallized through the works of a major composer (Sibelius in Finland, Dvořák in the Czech State), but in Canada no single significant composer had emerged; indeed musicians were generally not cognizant of music produced elsewhere throughout the country due to a lack of published music and national organizations to facilitate the exchange of information. Through the first half of the twentieth century, composers, like their fellow Canadians, tended to have a colonial mentality, and were more concerned with keeping up to date on compositional developments in Europe; as a result their compositions could sound derivative. An explosion of modern media – telephone, radio, film, recording technologies – facilitated an awareness of new trends to some degree, and a number of composers endeavoured to pursue these avenues. However, with the rapid urbanization that accompanied these innovations composers in cities were cut off from venues that had encouraged the use of folk songs and dance tunes – the rubbaboos that emerged across the country through the nineteenth century as different cultures came into contact with each other in the context of specific Canadian landscapes.

The only region where knowledge and performance of folk song and dance heritage remained prominent in urban settings and on radio broadcasts was Quebec. Writing to Marius Barbeau in 1911 Ernest Gagnon commented: "It has always been my belief that the 'discovery' of our roots would help establish a sense of national identity. With particular reference to music, I intended my work on our folksongs and the music of our native Indians to lay a foundation for a musical language based on these repertoires. Perhaps you will continue to encourage Canadian composers to seek out these sources in their musical works" (quoted in Smith

1989, 32).[9] The use of orally-transmitted material from First Peoples, anglophone, and francophone cultures remains a significant element in works produced in non-francophone parts of the country (Keillor 1995a). The prominence of anglophone elements has varied according to location and period; composers from Britain were establishing themselves across the nation, particularly in anglophone centres, and they came to exert a strong influence on musical developments. Leo Smith, one of these composers, said that "he wished 'to pipe Canadian tunes' but feared they would always be 'sung to an English ground bass'" (Kallmann 1992, 1228).

Landscape Studies

The musicological field of landscape studies was launched by the publication of John Burke's *Musical Landscapes* (1983) and a series of BBC programs with Richard Baker in 1988 (Peter Howard, in Thirlwall 1992). A subfield of music in cultural geography was created with an article by Peter Hugh Nash (1968), and subsequent work has established this area as a study of sound – of the overall impression on the listener rather than a detailed analysis of the manipulation of elements that make up what Morin called "the system of sounds" (Thirlwall 1992, 5). The use of orally-transmitted rhythms, melodies, and texts with Canadian references can clearly mark the origin of a piece of music. Rodolphe Mathieu, writing in 1932, was the first to articulate the development of a unique sound: "For Canada, it is possible ... to conceive of a music completely different [from folklore], far more Canadian perhaps; an immense music with expansive melodic lines, with buoyant rhythms, with rich and varied harmonies, with the sonorities of the forest, giving a feeling of grandiose immensity, in quiet as in powerful moments. There would be, lastly, a special technical principle in the melody, harmony, rhythm and form; it would be an essentially musical creation, with a purely musical, and not literary, character" (quoted in Poirier 1994, 264).

PARSONS' STUDY OF LANDSCAPE IMAGERY IN CANADIAN MUSIC

David Parsons begins his study, "Landscape Imagery in Canadian Music: A Survey of Composition Influenced by The Natural Environment" (1987), with an anecdote from Harry Freedman about nationalism in music; Freedman relates an encounter with Darius Milhaud who was able to identify music written by Canadians without knowing the identity of the composer, quoting Milhaud as saying, "Your music has the same gaunt, lonely quality that I have heard in a good deal of Canadian music."

Milhaud's limited exposure to Canadian works included the music of Harry Somers (Parsons 1982, 22). Freedman comments: "Gauntness and loneliness may not be particularly attractive to audiences reared on the lush romanticism of 19th-century European music. But this is not the 19th-century and this is not Europe. And I find 'gaunt' and 'lonely' two very fitting adjectives to describe the particular beauty of a great deal of Canada's varied landscape (Freedman 1958). Freedman also pointed out the music of Sibelius, whose Finnish landscape is somewhat gaunt and lonely, but Parsons argues that Canadian composers go "much farther in their realizations of a bleak, alien landscape than Sibelius ever did" (Parsons 1987, 22), because of Canada's larger natural space with more threatening extremes in the wilderness environment, and the expansion of sound resources such as dissonance that allow greater tension and a more graphic representation of harshness and violence. Parsons examines Canadian concert works in relation to specific concepts: soundscapes, the land, visual art, mountains, the North, and cityscapes (see appendix 14.A).

Shafer's term "soundscape," referring to all that is audible in a given landscape, is similar to the principle of First Peoples' traditional music, which incorporates a wide variety of natural sounds. Parsons identifies two prominent bird songs – the white-throated sparrow and the loon[10] – that have appeared in Canadian works. Louise Murphy used the sparrow's call in *Sweet Canada* (1923), and composers including Murray Adaskin, John Beckwith, John Weinzweig, John Hawkins, Murray Schafer, and Norman Symonds have also deliberately copied it (Keillor 1994, 278). Norman Symonds has named a number of works for the landscape; his *Travelling Big Lonely*, a CBC series based on a trip across Canada, is named for a phrase used by Canadian hoboes to describe the country through which they moved. In his writing about his fascination with and inspiration from the land, Symonds comments that "space and distance have become what one might call the Canadian platitude" but that another image in this phrase suggests "the deep-rooted feeling of the people who live in this country and who are forever conscious of their smallness – as a population in a large and intimidating land ... I started thinking of the sides of mountains, of the hills in the Yukon, in the late summer, which is their fall, they have these strokes of dark blue and green, and here and there a touch of orange or gold ... Could I mirror that in sound? And could I write music to express those distances?" (quoted in Parsons 1987, 26, 29–30). Parsons also examines compositions referring to trains passing through the landscape. The railroad, a component of Canada's original constitution, is an important Canadian symbol. Schafer has commented on the distinctive rhythm of the short-section unwelded tracks used in North America (Schafer 1993, 123), and his *Train* (1976) translates the distance between Vancouver and Montreal (4633 km) into time and the altitudes of stations along the route into pitch.[11]

Paintings by the Group of Seven and other artists such as Emily Carr, Jean-Paul Riopelle, Christopher Pratt, and Paul-Émile Borduas represent an important way in which Canadians see their country, and a number of Canadian composers have conceived musical works inspired by landscape art that is "one step further back from the natural environment" (Parsons 1987, 38).[12] Parsons notes regional differences in works inspired by paintings, and points out that Jean Coulthard's *The Pines of Emily Carr* is one of the few landscape works that does not portray Canada as a cold, inhospitable place; he describes this work as "a jubilant celebration of the splendour of a particular locale ... [with] a sense of something mysterious, brooding, and lying just out of reach" (Parsons 1987, 44). Overall Parsons concludes that there are similarities in the approach of Canadian painters and composers to landscape subject matter; there is an ambivalent response to the wilderness and extensive use of abstraction to cope with its overwhelming presence (Parsons 1987, 45). Under the heading of "mountain music" Parsons discusses Claude Champagne, whose *Altitude* (1959) was inspired by his first encounter with the Canadian Rockies in the 1950s. Champagne uses the *ondes martenot* to provide a soaring, eerie melodic line and the score includes a "schema topographique," outlining a mountain range (Parsons 1987, 48). Parsons comments that Canadian composers seem to turn the reality and permanent nature of mountains into a "threat against self" (Parsons 1987, 54), but that compositions dealing to a greater extent with valleys have a measure of contentment, none arising from a desire to attain the heights (Parsons 1987, 54).

Pierre Berton has commented: "Few have seen the cliffs of Baffin or the eskers of the tundra but we all live cheek by jowl with the wilderness; and all of us, I think, *feel* the empty and awesome presence of the North" (Berton 1982, 109). For Canadians the simple fact of winter is a powerful binding experience. One of the "Arctic-cold" works discussed by Parsons is François Morel's *Iikkii* (1972) – named for the Inuktitut word meaning "coldness" – a work characterized by crisp sonorities and rigorous formal structure.[13] Parsons found a varying rate of success in works that evoke the Northern atmosphere. Those that worked best involved glittering open sonorities to characterize the whiteness and purity, but destructive actions of mankind have also left their mark; compositions dealing with environmental issues include Schafer's *North/White* (1973).[14] Parsons concludes that musicians working in popular idioms – such as Joni Mitchell with *Big Yellow Taxi* – manage to express environmental concerns more effectively. Parsons notes a paucity of cityscape works – George Fiala's *Montreal* (1967) is an exception – and suggests this may be due to the lack of a distinctive Canadian urban environment (Parsons 1987, 74). Canadian composers raised and bred in cities still look to the rural, natural landscape for inspiration (Keillor 1994, 108–9).[15] Schafer maintains that composers wishing to be distinctly Canadian return to the land for their inspiration: "If you are looking for a Canadian identity in music you have to ask yourself what we have in our total acoustic environment that makes us different from people in other parts of the world. Not only do we have forests, but in our soundscape we have a very spaced out, very quiet acoustic environment. We don't experience that here in Toronto, but this is not really typical Canada. Typical Canada is a Canada of wilderness; it's a Canada that exists not necessarily as a physical reality for most people but as a mental reality. The average Canadian carries around with him in his head a vision of spaciousness" (MacMillan 1978, 6).

FURTHER EXPLORATIONS
Sherrill Grace and Stefan Haag use much of the material gathered by David Parsons to situate Canadian refined music in a context of northern imagery and nationalist rhetoric by examining links between music and painting, poetry and installation art; their discussion highlights *Kiviuq, an Inuit Legend* (1985) by Diana McIntosh,[16] *Northern Landscape* (1978) Violet Archer,[17] and *Winter Music* (1989) by Alexina Louie.[18] After examining a variety of contemporary Canadian creations in paint, performance art, and sound, the authors conclude: "When viewed in an inter-artistic context and with a northern topos as the unifying element, such compositions suggest not only that music is representational but that it can and does participate fully with the other arts in the cultural discourse of a nation" (Grace and Haag 1998, 118). David Parsons points out that works by Canadian composers who were concerned with a specific region or locale could have different overall sound effects. The first major cultural geographical consideration of music in Canada – Stephen Thirlwall's *Musical Landsape* (1992), is limited to Quebec. In a discussion of legitimate music by Quebec composers, Thirlwall reviews developments leading to the important contributions of Claude Champagne, characterizing *québécois* compositions of the 1970s and 1980s as "primarily focused on '*faire beau et simple*' ... pure, direct, clear, concise, and containing

silence." Even an exploration of urban life – Claude Vivier's *Et je reverrai cette ville étrange* (1981) – "projects the feel of being alone yet surrounded by strange sounds, especially mechanical-electronic sounds" (Thirlwall 1992, 348).[19] In these two decades, Thirlwall argues, Quebec composers were much more cosmopolitan in their education and influences and were no longer almost dependent solely on France. In some circles, he recognizes sharp divisions between "classical" and traditional folk musicians and musicians involved in various genres of popular musics, but he also notes important cross-over musicians such as André Gagnon, Raoul Duguay, and François Dompierre (351).[20] Thirlwall discusses two compositions by André Gagnon: *Le Saint-Laurent* and *Neiges*: In Gagnon's *Le Saint-Laurent*: "[t]he river is portrayed in its vast majesty as it slowly but steadily surges towards its purpose. Regionally, the St. Lawrence River is central to the life experience and often livelihood of the people who live on or nearby its shores ... The lowlands around it are the cradle and home of Quebec culture ... *Neiges* [is] a reminder of the ever-present themes and reality of Quebec life: winter and isolation, yet this time with a certain beauty" (351–2).

Not all refined composers acknowledge the impact of their locale on their music. Even Schafer initially had doubts about the influence of physical space and the viable use of sonic materials created in that locality (Harley 1998, 120); his soundscape exploration and his increasing interest in deep ecology likely contributed to a radical change of opinion (Harley 1998, 137). Other composers to articulate a resonance of specific sounds in their works include Jean Coulthard and Gilles Tremblay, both of whom note waterways. If landscape sounds are present in refined compositions, can the same be true, at least in part, for genres more driven by commercial needs?

Thirlwall argues that the clearest musical representation of Quebec is found in popular musics based on the singer-songwriters who often draw on personal experiences, interpreting them in an intimate and personal way (Thirlwall 1992, 358), and using texts to underline a particular space. Madame La Bolduc and Felix Leclerc broke from traditional folk materials to create new songs based on the realities of the day but still strongly rooted in the rural countryside (Morrison 2001, 1157). With radio broadcasts and vinyl 45 singles, song became "a medium to reach a lot of people" (Thirlwall 1992, 370). The first Radio-Canada awards for québécois music were presented in 1957, and soon *boites à chansons* sprang up to nurture these musicians. Anglophone singer-songwriters flourished, using material from folklore collections for performances on radio broadcasts

Gilles Vigneault

Stephen Thirlwall comments that Gilles Vigneault had the ability to articulate new sentiments that, once expressed, listeners could identify with. One of his strongest themes was nature used as metaphor for human situations. His view of nature is within the context of two seasons – a long winter and a short summer in "a land of snow, cloud, rocky coast, sandy shore, thick forest, mountains, ice, rivers, birds, wild animals, and the marine environment of the North shore ... only broken by the small villages, the activities of the fishermen in their boats, and the characters which filled village life" (Thirlwall 1992, 407–9). In *Pendant que* Vigneault describes cycles of harmony and conflict between the boats and the sea, the movement and connection of the river, sun, and clouds. He also evokes the cities but his root images come from nature and rural life. "Though a degree of quebecoisness had come, a unified *pays* had not yet come. In his song *Tout le monde est malheureux* he draws from this internal contradiction the humour of how life works, and does this in the form of a traditional dance tune. This harmony of words and music was Vigneault's specialty (Thirlwall 1992, 409). Vigneault's *Mon Pays* became an Quebec anthem and the chorus of *Gens du pays* is used as the equivalent of the English rhyme *Happy Birthday*. In *Mon Pays II* Vigneault looks at the world "as many scales of *pays*, as a child from a window, *mon pays* as a town, *mon pays* as a province, and *mon pays* as the planet Earth" (Thirlwall 1992, 411). *Il me reste un pays* "is a sort of manifesto from a personal perspective."

It suggests that the idea of *pays* ... starts with the individual initiative through the process of naming and in finding a vision of place in the individual's heart. *Voilà le pays que j'aime*. This idea starts a quest to discover the realities of this place, to 'know' it. One knows it through (re)making it firstly by building bridges over the river beyond *l'Ennui*, those things which tie us down ... One day bells will ring with the first signs of life in this place. At this point the individual becomes a collective force of individuals with a shared *vision of pays* in which they need to partake and develop ... making it a *pays du monde*. The song ends: now there waits for us *un pays* to understand and to then to change, once the first dream has been attained, presumably in an ever advancing creative growth and with a shared collective vision ... Vigneault comments that this song talks of both an inner spiritual country and a physical country, Quebec – "both of them; they can agree to get along together. One is dependent on the other, that is, the physical country – with or without frontiers ... – the topographical, geographical country, is perfectly tributary and dependent upon the spiritual, interior country, the inner life of every Quebecker." (Thirlwall 1992, 414–5) and the coffee houses; Stringband is a good example of this florescence, since their repertoire includes French Canadian folk songs, newer English-language folk songs, fiddle music, and new songs based in Canadian experience. Texts were primary, and melody or accompaniment secondary. Gradually the music too came to reflect more of the Canadian reality. The most successful of the francophone artists captured the concerns and life experiences of the average Quebecer.

Quebec musicians were involved in other popular musical streams. Willie Lamothe and Patrick Normand, singing the French texts with anglophone country music themes, were in the forefront of "cowboy" music in Quebec.[21] Michel Louvain played an important role in the development of *yé-yé*, a francophone rock 'n' roll aimed at an adolescent audience: the formula included solo singers/charmers and groups consisting of a lead singer, guitarist, bass, and drummer (Thirlwall 1992, 427). Thirlwall comments that bands had a distinct visual as well as sound image, and that the *yé-yé* song texts were superficial and materialistic, dealing with daily preoccupations of teenagers, but he points out that this music had a wider audience that was less politically or socially conscious than that of the chansonniers. Thirlwall concludes that the chansonnier redefined the character of *le pays* and that *yé-yé* integrated Quebec into the broader Canadian and world systems (Thirlwall 1992, 428–9). Thirlwall notes that most of the music of Quebec contains reminders of past tradition but that each generation incorporates new influences of their contact with other cultural groups (Thirlwall 1992, 506). In popular musics Baillargeon and Côté identify six major influences: traditional folk songs from France; traditional Celtic (Irish and Scottish) and European dance music of the 1700s and 1800s; popular music from France (particularly cabaret); Afro-Latin music; American country and western music; American pop (especially rock).

Even in copying the dominant American or British sounds, Thirlwall argues quebecois music is distinctive. An obvious distinction is the use of French, but when quebecois use English their approach to themes and the general flavour of the sound still stands out from anglophone singers. Quebecois music remains very much an oral tradition that differs from all its influences. "It has become its own sound, which incorporates a certain intimacy, integrity, purity of vision, sincerity, and gentleness. It also encompasses a sense of vast space and silence, the confinement of snow, the ethereal atmosphere of the St. Lawrence River's coast ... small sounds of life in the village or the city, and the deep feelings of joy and sorrow. The present quebecois pop music industry operates almost totally independently of the English Canadian and American music industries.

What marks quebecois music as distinct is its sensitivity to landscape: place, region, and people and passion for life and love in terms of daily life (Thirlwall 1992, 506–7).

As of 2003 no other detailed landscape or cultural geographic studies of the musics produced in a Canadian locale had been done, and comprehensive studies of a particular genre on a national or local level are also lacking. A sense of distinctiveness can never be found solely in the continuity of a culture or tradition; "authenticity is relational, there can be no essence except as a political, cultural invention, a local tactic" (Stokes 1994, 12). In Canada, political interventions and governmental policies have fostered music of a more regional and local character (Shepherd 2001, 315). In a study of important ramifications of the CRTC broadcast regulations for anglophone country music, John Lehr documents the popularity of country music (147 radio stations, 41 of them full time) (Lehr 1985/1994, 362) and notes lyrics and images of place, which, because most country music originates in the American South, predominantly reflect that area. "The CRTC can encourage Canadian composers and lyricists, but it cannot ensure that they will celebrate Canadian places in their music. The chance of commercial success in the North American market is improved if the lyrics can deal in familiar images ... Canadian country music labours under a further disadvantage in that it has yet to develop distinctive regional substyles that are readily recognizable to the average listener (Lehr 1985/1994, 365).[22] Lehr argues that as of 1985 Canadian country musicians faced other difficulties: "Since the late 1960s Canadian songwriters have begun to employ the prairies and Alberta as an image with complex structures similar in some ways to that of Texas or Tennessee in the United States. At the most basic level the West is used as a surrogate for the ideal ... But the image of the Canadian West is more complicated, since it has been used as a place-specific metaphor of the rural-urban dichotomy basic to country music. In part, the image of the West has been moulded by the demographic shifts which took place in Canada after the revitalization of the hydrocarbon resource industries in Alberta and Saskatchewan and some erosion of the dominance in the national economy by the metropolitan heartland of Ontario" (Lehr 1985/1994, 367). In his interviews with Manitoba disc-jockeys, Lehr discovered a demand for Canadian-specific country songs, and comments that musicians such as Ian Tyson are conveying "major socio-geographical regional differences with precision and feeling through the use of simple spatial imagery (Lehr 1985/1994, 368). Lehr argues that "a measure of Canada's maturity and self-confidence" will emerge when radio stations draw "with equal facility from throughout Canada and the United States for evocative images of space and sound" (Lehr 1985/1994, 368). Indeed, in the late 1990s that seemed to be happening, but many Canadians were still ambivalent about describing the sound identity of their space.

Defining a Canadian Sound in Space

CANADIAN INNOVATORS

Rice and Gutnik state that with his eclectic style Bruce Cockburn "endeared himself to a Canadian public in need of self-definition, and the articulation of Canadian perspectives" (1995, 251). In 1984 Poirier argued that a major difference between the United States and Canada was that American composers felt able to define their own music aided by Hollywood and the mega-industries of music publishing and recording while in Canada, this definition was left to society (Poirier 1994, 256). If society must define its music, then its people need the opportunity to know what has been produced within its borders, to listen to and identify that rubbaboo as being Canadian. Unfortunately, prior to the 1970s this was rarely the case.

Canadians have been at the forefront of major changes that have subsequently become part of mainstream sound in a number of genres. In 1924, when the Lombardo brothers left London, Ontario, to play US gigs, they continued to evolve their style based on the Scottish roots of their Canadian locale. They slowed down the dance beat of the day, introduced medleys of tunes, used a sax sound with a flute-like vibrato, toned down a heavy drum beat, and where possible favoured a group with two pianos to provide rippling watery background. They were soon established in the United States with regular radio broadcasts and live dates and their sound influenced much of American band music of the era.[23] Lehr bemoans the lack of widespread Canadian spatial imagery in country songs, but Canadian-born composers Bob Nolan, Wilf Carter, and Hank Snow[24] had considerable influence on the emergence of the "classic" country songs adapted for urban life in the United States. Colin McPhee's *Tabuh Tabuhan* (1934) blends elements of Balinese music with sound structures honed in Toronto to create a texture that has since been labelled "minimalism."[25] Writing for bands of CBC's *The Happy Gang* Show and the Canadian Expeditionary Forces, Robert Farnon developed with the lush sound of strings available in Toronto at that time. His knack for highlighting the main melody above a colourful tapestry of lines influenced composers such as Rob McConnell and Johnny Mandel, and he wrote arrangements for top international singers of his day.

The omnipresence of the US media and its control of much that is heard and seen in Canada has given Canadians an opportunity to assess various currents from the outside, and to create new rubbaboos that are often refreshing and more palatable for the US music megabusiness. The Crew Cuts managed to cover black R&B hits with a more prominent tenor lead and a vocal style similar to barber shop quartets; their version of *Sh-boom* was an important soundmark in the mixing of Black and white American music genres in the 1950s. The Band has been described as the most important and innovative rock 'n' roll group;[26] with their process of listening to each other to achieve a balance "singers began unconsciously developing complex triple leads, rotating leads, and using the novelistic approach of shifting points of view" (Flippo 1994, 28). Many successful rock and alternative bands have since based their co-operation on this principle of egalitarianism.

The above examples are a few of many Canadian musicians and groups that made major musical contributions. Is the difficulty of finding a Canadian identity due in part to the fact that we do not recognize our sound when non-Canadians use it? Another possibility is that as Canadian musicians become more successful in the international music industry, they may be influenced by demands of their non-Canadian record managers. The successful alternative band Our Lady Peace sold millions of records worldwide but faced a crisis with their fifth album, *Gravity* (2002); after two trips abroad their sound did not seem to reflect what they wanted. Raine Maida found he had to simplify the lyrics (Deziel 2002, 35) and strip away many of the complex layers to allow melodies to soar as they did in live performances. The end result was a more spaced-out sound with prominent silences. Our Lady Peace was able to insist on their conception for the final recorded product, but other Canadian musicians seem to have lost some of their individual sound when directed by major recording labels. For example, Calgary-based guitarist Oscar Lopez displayed a range of styles with his Chilean Latin heritage, but recent CDs produced by Narada have a more homogeneous sound with a backing of electronic instruments and samples.

Another reason for the difficulty in pinpointing the Canadian soundmark is likely the extreme diversity of musical experiences that a composer unhampered by corporate conceptions can draw on in the creation of a musical work. Diverse cultures are celebrated in community festivals, and the first multiculturalism act (1988) gave official sanction to a "mosaic" that has joined other persistent Canadian myths (the Wilderness, the North, the railway, the Royal Canadian Mounted Police, the snowshoe, hockey, and the canoe; Diamond 2001b, 1059).[27] Ethnomusicologist James Robbins has argued that our distinctiveness might be in our Canadian plurality (1990, 48), and other scholars have pointed out particular Canadian ways of syncretization (Taft 1993) and parody (Flaherty and Manning 1993).

MUSIC OF CULTURAL COMMUNITIES

By 1861 there were German musical societies in Berlin (now Kitchener, Ontario) and Victoria, and *Sängerfests* remained a vibrant part of German communities into the early twentieth century. A revival of these came with renewed German immigration after 1945 and *Oktoberfest* is an annual event in Kitchener. The Islendinga Dagurinn (Icelandic festival of Manitoba), begun in 1890, continues today in Gimli (Diamond 2001d, 1251). The Krivan Slovak group of Sudbury dates back to the early 1920s, a decade that also saw some recognition of diverse cultures through the CPR folklore festivals (Kallmann/Potvin 1992, 327). Many European cultures –including Norwegian, Swedish, Finnish, Estonian, Latvian, Lithuanian, Italian, Spanish, Portuguese, Hungarian, Polish, Czech, Slovak, Slovenian, Croatian, Serbian, Macedonian, and Bulgarian – have community choral and folk ensembles that perform for important events. Traditional instruments were increasingly combined with electric instruments (guitars and keyboards) through the second half of the twentieth century, and Canada has produced fine builders of these instruments.[28]

The first Syrian and Lebanese immigrants arrived in Canada around 1882, and through the twentieth century Palestinian, Egyptian, and other Middle Eastern communities have become established. The folk, dance, and classical traditions of these cultures continue to be supported through associations.[29] Caribbeans brought calypso, steel band, *soca*, reggae, ska, dub poetry, rap and hip hop, all of which have fed into various forms of commodified popular music in a more direct manner than that found in the United States. Immigrants from Africa, including countries such as Somalia, Ghana, Nigeria, Central Africa, Ethiopia, Eritrea, Mali, Senegal, Zaire, Cameroon, Guinea-Bissau, and South Africa, have included many gifted musicians who continue to perform both traditional and more contemporary musics (such as Ghanaian "high-life," *soukous*, or *mbaquanga*) and have also joined fusion ensembles (Lederman 2001f, 1213).[30] Montreal is a particularly vital centre for new Afrocentric musical creations with its large African and Caribbean communities and festivals such as Nuits d'Afrique, and Rythme du monde. African-derived and Latino dance musics from the Caribbean are heard at clubs throughout

Figure 14.1
Chinese opera
performed by the
Chinese Dramatic Club
in Edmonton during
the Chinese Folk
Festival organized by
the Chinese Students
Association of the
University of Alberta,
1974. Photograph by
Fred Fagan. Canadian
Museum of Civilization
K74-995.

the country. The Toronto band Syncona (1972–86) played *cadence* and *zouk,* as well as salsa, which has become a favourite Latino dance music since 1980 (Diamond 2001g, 1085).

Asian communities have become more diversified and vibrant through the twentieth century. Chinese traditional music and opera flourished in British Columbia as early as the 1890s and Cantonese music societies first appeared in the 1930s.[31] Many societies specialize in Mandarin traditions such as Beijing opera, and sponsor Mandarin-language choirs. Fine performers on traditional instruments such as Lan Tung and George Gao on the *erhu*, Fan Sheng-E and Mei Han on the *zheng*, Liu Fang on the *pipa* are adding their talents to the Canadian soundscape, and have become involved with fusion endeavours such as the Orchid Ensemble in Vancouver and Le trio parfum d'orient in Montreal. Japanese taiko drum ensembles have been formed in several Canadian cities, as have Utai societies to promote *noh* drama, folk and classical dance, and instruction on the *koto, shakuhachi*, and *shamisen*. Other Asian musics are heard and encouraged as new Canadians make use of the Internet to keep in touch with their roots. The South Asian musical scene is particularly vibrant. Almost every city with a sizable population of Indian or Pakistani heritage has one or more societies to encourage the performance of the Hindustani and Karnatic classical traditions, provide religious, dance, vocal and instrumental instruction, and sponsor touring artists. By the 1920s the Punjabi (Sikhs) had established temples in Vancouver, and as many as ten *gurdwaras* were in existence by 1970 (Qureshi 1972, 396).[32] During the last quarter of the twentieth century many professional musicians of classical traditions have come to Canada.[33] In 1994 Rashtravani was formed in Toronto to encourage and teach the performance of *ghazals*, folksongs, *Bhajans*, Bharatanatyem, Khatak dance music, and to explore various fusion musics. Drummers playing tabla and other Eastern and South Asian percussion instruments are often heard in ensembles of various genres.[34] Tibetan ensembles appeared in communities including Bancroft, Ontario, and the North American premiere of *Sukyi Nyima*, a fully staged Tibetan opera, was presented in 1999 by the St Norbert Arts and Cultural Centre in Winnipeg, which hosted artists from the Tibetan Institute of Performing Arts and the Chaksampa Tibetan Dance and Opera Company (Oesterle 2000, 54). The Aboriginal *dijeridu* is heard frequently in fusion ensembles including Celtic groups, and particularly in the band Brothers in the Sun.[35] It is not uncommon to see buskers on Canadian city streets playing instruments from South America including the panpipes, flutes, and the armadillo-bodied *charango*. This plurality of sounds from around the world undoubtedly continues to have an impact on sounds created in the Canadian space, as is evident in the many Canadian musicians recognized as leaders in world music.[36]

An Elusive Identity

In the introduction to this book I described music as multi-dimensional in form and impact. Because of its nature the decoding of music as a cultural process requires approaches from several different angles including multi-disciplinary, co-operative, and international approaches. Only in the 1980s and 1990s have efforts along these lines gradually begun. A basic premise for success in these endeavours is a consideration of music as sound, rather than object, and to discover how individuals receive a sound that must land somewhere, whether created abroad or locally. When Jennifer Giles made a study of the music consumption of anglophone female teenagers in Montreal in the mid-1980s, one of her main findings was that these women did not relish Canadian popular music as much as that of the United States or Britain, the main reason being that it was not good enough or authentic.[37] They seemed bewildered that Canadian musicians could be so well received abroad. In part the young women's reaction is linked to Canada's geographical size, where problems are seen on a local rather than a national level. Giles comments:

The establishment of identity is a process which takes place internally, externally, voluntarily and involuntarily. The identity of the girls is that they are English Montrealers. Certainly they adopt styles presented to them from other cultures, but they recognize that they are imitating and in doing so mostly for show and not because they are trying to "say" anything ... As Cathy says, "I can *dress* Punk and not *be* Punk as a person." This same process of meaning negation occurs in popular music, and the resulting interpretation of the Canadian material is that it is "bland," "boring," and "a plaster cast of rock 'n roll." But this is only the response to Canadian musicians of international stature. (Giles 1987, 84)

The whole-hearted support from local fans that played an important role in the development of groups in the Winnipeg scene has been noted earlier. Giles found that the young Montrealers were enthusiastic about local performers and groups. These musicians spoke in language that dealt with their concerns and presumably the sounds were recognized as local. This for them was authentic music. But because the sound of successful Canadian musicians conformed more closely to the international norm – even though the substantive motivation was not grounded in the British or American authenticity – their music was not seen as Canadian culture and the young women unconsciously responded to that. "Basically the girls just want to have fun with the music ... They want it to really move them, but they don't want to have to take it seriously. Yet if it does not come from a serious base it doesn't move them" (Giles 1987, 87).

This dilemma fades somewhat in an examination of the highlights of popular music in 1998. According to Bruce Pollock, this was a watershed year in which the popular music industry finally began to recognize that the music they were delivering was not what the masses wanted to hear. In the early 1990s the range of music had narrowed considerably; this meant that Canadian musicians wanting success abroad were confined more closely within the rigid borders of the industry's norm – that is, the music monopolies in the United States. Pollock coined the phrase "Middle of the Dirt Road" to describe a type of music that appealed to the masses and he notes that this folk-based sound was released much more generously in 1998; Canadian examples include Rufus Wainwright, *The McGarrigle Hour*, Robbie Robertson's *Unbound*, and Loreena McKennitt's *Mummer's Dance*. On the other hand, film songs were still influential; Canadian successes in 1998 include Dion's *My Heart Will Go On* (for *Titanic*) and *Touched By an Angel* (for the television program *Love Can Move Mountains*) and Chantal Kreviazuk's *The Prayer* (for the film *Quest for Camelot*) and her revival of John Denver's *Leaving on a Jet Plane*. *Billboard* did not introduce new top 40 charts until 5 December 1998, but Canadians had many top hits that year.[38] Pollock is of the opinion that the charts, even with the recent changes in construction, were still largely ruled by teenage tastes, and bemoans the fact that songs with the "charming psychobabble" in the Barenaked Ladies' *One Week* "hardly stand a chance on a regular basis" (Pollock 1998, xxiv).

The arrival of MP-3 allowing free downloads of songs on the Internet was a promising development, and this technology has made it possible for many musicians to reach a wider audience, especially as other media become more restrictive in scope. In spite of the subsequent legal orders, many musicians particularly in Canada have chosen to place sound clips on the Internet. Diamond points out for performers in the Yukon, Nunavut, and Northwest Territories, the Internet is a vital marketplace that is used extensively now that there are first-rate recording studios available in the North (Diamond 2001f, 1279).[39] Northern non-Aboriginal musicians have found the Internet an important tool.[40] This burgeoning musical activity in the North since 1980 to some degree reflects similar earlier events in southern Canada.[41] Because of sparse population in the North, most musicians become involved in a variety of genres, leading to unique combinations and often successful fusions. With the Internet there has been a growing awareness of the vitality of the Canadian musical scene in a seemingly unlimited range of genres and streams. These developments may destroy, once and for all, the wide-spread conception that Canadian musics are "imported commodities" and that "the best Canadian musicians can do is modify these forms" (Eagles 1995, 57). A certain portion of that imported sound has already been transformed by Canadians and should be recognized as such. Canadian musicians have used textures, licks, and riffs often not realizing that these stylings had originally been introduced into the popular mainstream by Canadian-born musicians. By the 1990s those musicians could identify the Canadian song from which a specific lick had come. Tribute bands were formed to deliberately imitate successful Canadian groups, and this became a viable career choice. This process of imitation revealed that musical textures required openness and silences to authentically reflect the Canadian space. Even

Accordions in the North

Until more detailed studies of these musical expressions have been made it will be difficult to assess, for example, the intermingling that has gone on in Canadian accordion music, an area where Canadians have become very prominent in both popular and refined genres. Norwegian-Canadian Olaf Sveen has written more than 180 original compositions for accordion; Philippe Bruneau's québécois style has been studied by Bégin; accordionist Walter Ostanek has won numerous awards; and performers Joseph Macerollo and Joseph Petric have inspired numerous new compositions. The button accordion became very popular with the Inuit and in 1996 the CBC sponsored a festival at Iqaluit devoted to Inuit accordion music (Hiscott 2000, 16).

"Accordion music was brought to the north of Canada by European and American whaling crews, who were active from the 1600s through the end of the 19th century. ...There would often be musicians on board the whaling vessels: fiddlers and, later, accordion players ... Andrew Atagotaaluuk ... from Inukjuak remembered how his mother spoke fondly of the dances held at the old Hudson's Bay post when the whaling ships were in" (Hiscott 2000, 17). The Inuit left their accordions in an abandoned whaling station when they went out hunting or whaling, "in order to keep them safe from accidents. There would be over 30 accordions of different shapes and sizes at any one time." Hiscott makes an initial assessment of the Inuit style of accordion playing as follows: "The accordion style is reminiscent of Newfoundland, and possibly, Quebec, styles. The dance steps are variants of the square dances that you find in various forms across Canada. Tunes are reels, polkas, jigs. There's a short list of old tunes which are very popular throughout the north. Many players now learn tunes from records and the radio, played by southern musicians such as Harry Hibbs. It's interesting that Irish polka and slide rhythms are so strongly represented in the older Inuit tunes, as they are in Newfoundland music" (Hiscott 2000, 17). He concludes his overview essay by stating: "Inuit button accordion music is a unique Canadian culture. Like other original traditional musics in this country, it helps us to see ourselves as creators rather than merely consumers of the music from other places. Hopefully we will get to know this tradition better in the future, so we can enjoy it, and share it with others around the world" (Hiscott 2000, 19). His conclusion could be said about many other musical cultures in Canada.

where these are commonly found elements of Canada's musical expressions, local and regional influences will cause them to be heard in different ways; Prairie musicians often refer to how their music reflects the sound of the wind in their particular locale.

For the fiftieth anniversary of the United Nations the Canada Council produced *Here and Now: A Celebration of Canadian Music*, a four-CD set ranging from folk and Native traditional through jazz, classical and world music. This venture could be seen as a method of allowing "society to define" since the set was selected though a competitive process. Only a limited number were made and the Council seemed dumbfounded that there would be such demand for the collection. Even though the two-CD Naxos set *Introduction to Canadian Music* is not widely distributed, more than 4,000 copies were sold in less than ten months. In other words, given the opportunity, Canadians do want to listen to the sounds of their space. As yet there is little recorded documentation of earlier forms of music heard in Canadian space, but some musicians realize that their music is strongly influenced by earlier traditions. Charlebois considers his experience of Gregorian chant as a choir boy to be one of the major formative influences on his melodies (Pantchenko 1997). Church music heard in nineteenth-century Canada has ramifications far beyond religious denominations of the day; *Palace of Shushan*, one of Jane Siberry's recent albums, consists of religious music and hymns.

In jazz, an urban genre, the accepted wisdom is only the Canadian musicians are unique, but Canadian jazz seems to be greatly influenced by Cool and West Coast jazz. Perhaps this is not so surprising since Canadian-born Gil Evans initiated this sound. Canadian jazz history is only now coming to light with the work of Mark Miller and John Gilmore. As yet, we know little of what earlier jazz sounded like; few recordings were made in the 1920s and sources are limited even into the 1940s. When oral documentation is done and charts possibly located, more precise identification of a Canadian approach to jazz will be discovered. Some original jazz compositions – such as Oscar Peterson's *Canadiana Suite* – have direct references to Canadian space but the overall sound of Canadian jazz groups often incorporate identifiable textures and effects similar to those found in other genres.

These musicians too find a resonance with the landscape that expresses itself in the contrasting bursts of energy noted by Anhalt. For Canadians nature is not idealized in a nineteenth-century European or American sense. Our space is perceived as immense, empty, mysterious, harsh, indifferent, producing a response of awe mingled with terror and an intense sense of spiritual loneliness. To identify Canadian soundmarks in the musickings of Canada's peoples, we must listen carefully to the sounds around us and to hear what musicians say about their reaction to these sounds. As the Alberta composer Allan Bell has written: "I still imagine a music that recreates the long horizontal and the dome of the sky; that is polychronic; that contains the polyphony of coyotes and grasswaves; that reconciles an urban sophistication with an irrational wilderness. Sometimes I even write it down" (Bell 1991, 20).[42]

Appendices

Appendix A

Representative melodic contours from the eight geographical regions of First Peoples Cultures

Northwest Coast – Little Woman Doctor Song, sung by Mary Wamiss (Kwakwa̱ka'wakw), recorded by Ida Halpern: *A Folksong Portrait of Canada* (Mercury 769748000-2: CD3-28 from Folkways FE 4523)1.

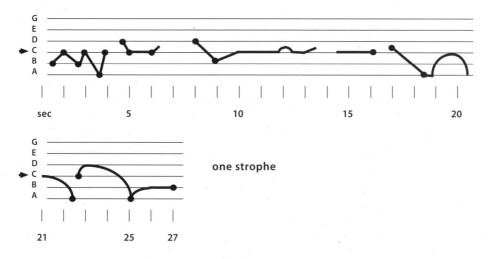

Western Subarctic – Tłicho (Dogrib) Tea Dance Song, sung by Chief Jimmy Bruneau School Drummers: *Drum Dance Music of the Dogrib* (Canyon CR-6260, track 14).

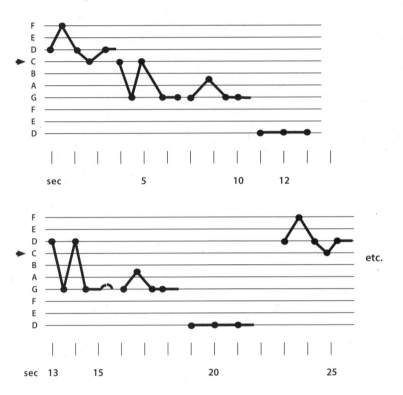

Plateau – Tiumtan, a song sung while riding a horse by _oipêtist of the Secwepemc (Shuswap) culture, recorded by James A. Teit, Canadian Museum of Civilization, Teit Fonds, 147 VI M 181.

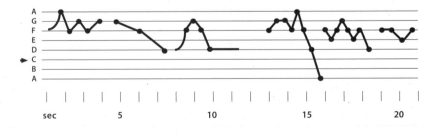

Plains – Cree Victory Song, sung by Mrs. Ropderick Thomas, recorded by Barbara Cass-Beggs: *A Folksong Portrait of Canada* (Mercury 769748000-2: CD3-5 from Folkways FE 4312).

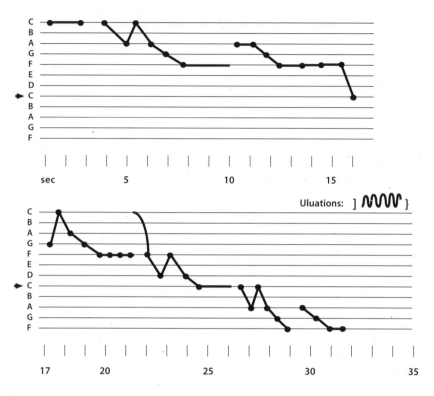

Eastern Nomadic – Dream Song, sung by Awûn'akûm'ïgïckûň and used in the Woman's Dance, recorded by Frances Densmore: *Songs of the Chippewa* (Library of Congress A A FS-L22). [In performance there is an incomplete repetition structure: A B C D-B C D]

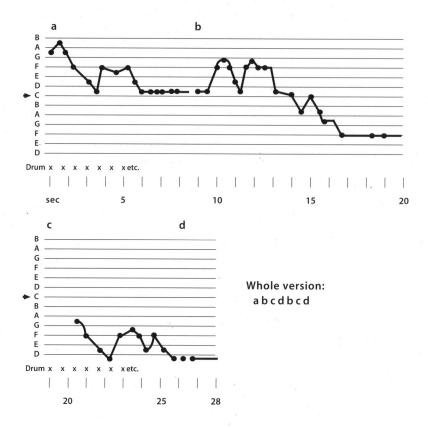

Whole version:
a b c d b c d

Eastern Sedentary – Inoria Kwénotani (Songs of Welcome), sung by François Vincent Kiowarini, Claude Vincent Sawatanin with drum and rattle. When strangers arrive, a circle is formed with four men, one of whom had a drum, in the centre. The dancers move around the circle, using different steps and singing. *Wendate asta: Huron Ritual Songs* (CBC/Boot Records SQN-102).

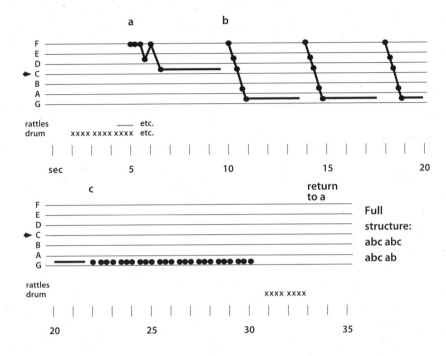

Maritime – Mi'kmaq (Micmac) War Dance, sung by William Paul, Marin Sack, John Knockwood, recorded by Helen Creighton: *A Folksong Portrait of Canada* (Mercury 769748000-2: CD3-1 from Folkways FM 4006).

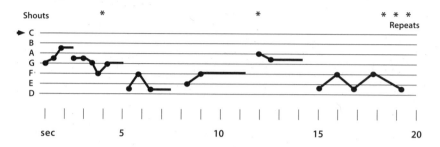

Arctic – Iglulik Song about waiting for the seal by a breathing-hole, sung by Awa of Naajanruluk, recorded by Jean Malaurie: *Jean Malaurie: Chants et tambours Inuit de Thule au Detroit de Bering* (Ocora C 559021: CD, track 12).

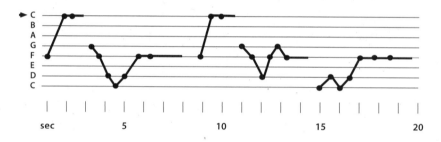

Appendix B
Conrad Laforte's classification system for French folk songs

A standardized form of documentation was needed to facilitate reference and research on the thousands of known French folk songs. To meet this need, Conrad Laforte of Laval University compiled *Le catalogue de la chanson folklorique française* (6 vols, 1977–1987).

1 Chansons en laisse – 353 songs, of which 34 are unique to Canada

Each song is listed under a standardized title, syllabic count per line, publications, and recordings. Most of these *laisses*[1] have more versions recorded or published in Canada than in any other French-speaking area. Laforte has subdivided them by motif: each motif is assigned a letter so that the *laisses* are identified and grouped by letter and number. Many *laisses* occur in versions with refrains modelled on the *rondeau*, an old poetic form: some refrains are related textually to the *laisse*, some are independent, and some have an onomatopoetic nature.

---

1 *The New Grove Dictionary of Music and Musicians* (2001), vol. 14: 118–32. I use the term "lay" in English in the sense of an extended song form. It is not the equivalent of the cultivated *lai* which in France may have been originally inspired by the Irish *loid* (meaning blackbird's song) documented in the mid-ninth century. See the discussion by David Fallows under "Lai" in the *New Grove Dictionary of Music and Musicians*, 2nd ed. A *laisse* or lay is a structure that uses the old French epic strophe with lines of six to sixteen syllables with assonance (the resemblance of a syllabic sound that occurs at the inner break or the end of a line). When there are ten or more syllables (according to prosodic counting rather than the spoken version) in a line, the line is split by mean of a caesura which has a feminine or masculine ending while the end of the line will have the opposite. By examining many versions of the same *laisse* Laforte established an ideal formula for each song, stating the number of syllables per line, the placement of the masculine or feminine ending and the specific assonant masculine ending used throughout the lay. For example, 12 (6f – 6m *ou*) indicates that the *laisse* line has twelve syllables with a caesura after the sixth syllable which is feminine in character, while the masculine assonant ending occurs throughout as "ou."

2   Chansons strophiques – strophic chansons

Laforte subdivides strophic chansons into categories (or *poétiques*): chansons in dialogue, enumerative chansons, chansons with less than four strophes, chansons written to a pre-existing tune (*timbre*), and literary composed songs that have passed into the oral domain. The chansons are also analyzed as isometric (lines of the same length with strophes of two, three, or four lines) or heterometric (strophes of three, four, five, six, eight, or nine lines), and further subdivided into narrative (telling an epic, religious, or comic story or a melodramatic adventure) and non-narrative or theme (describing idyllic or bucolic love; a season, day, voyage, departure, or return; a social condition such as a hermit, a husband, a servant, a happy marriage; a life event; a celebration of wine).

3   Chansons en form de dialogue

This volume contains chansons with dialogue text throughout: for example, between a girl and her lover, a shepherdess and a cavalier, a girl and her mother, a girl and her father or priest, a woman and her husband, a person and a group, or characters from legend or history.

4   Chansons énumératives

French repertoire is particularly rich in this form. Laforte subdivides these chansons into (a) those with simple enumeration and (b) those with cumulative lists. The chansons are further grouped according to type of element: simple numbers to 9 or 10 (A); numbers crossing (B); days, months, years, seasons, ages (C); letters, vowels, alphabet (D); clothing (E); parts of human body (F); body parts of animals, birds, fish (G); jobs or professions (H); qualities of men, women (I); animals, birds (J); contents (K); enumeration based on a verb (L); miscellaneous (fibs, proper names, places, colours, trees, musical instruments, etc. – M); equivocal texts (N).[2]

5   Chansons brèves (les enfantines)

This volume contains lullabies, childrens' game songs, prayers, alphabet rhymes, and action songs. The subdivisions include songs sung by adults to children, songs sung by children, and songs sung by either children or adults.

6   Chansons sur des timbres

This large volume contains orally transmitted chansons based on tunes that can be clearly identified as existing prior to the text; many of these chansons

---

2 *Alouette* (Gb-1), a well-known chanson strongly associated with Canada, is a cumulative enumeration of body parts of a skylark. *Chanson de mensonges* (*Les menteries*) (Ma-26) is a recitation of lies (I took two bulls on my back / My plow in my belt / I plowed where there was no earth / A dead man was eating all my grass)

were created in Canada.[3] Examples include new texts for tunes associated with a *laisse* (such as *Trois cavaliers fort bien montés*) or a religious melody (such as the *Pater noster*). The chansons are subdivided into parodies (A), historical texts (B), local texts (C), political texts (D), and *cantiques* or carols (E). Laforte also proposed a category for folk songs originally published in notated form that have since passed into oral transmission.

Laforte's catalogue is an excellent tool for tracing information about a particular folk song, but his approach, although very much in the French tradition of classification, has not been universally accepted. While he uses poetic structures as his main criterion, his thematic subdivisions can be idiosyncratic. Some scholars, including Paquin, have also pointed out that categories 3, 4, 5, and 6 all deal with strophic chansons that should properly be subdivisions of category 2. Paquin argues that it might be more helpful to organize French folk songs along the loose lines used for English folk songs, with particular emphasis on the ballad, and suggests that French folk songs corresponding to the English "ballad" (a narrative folk song with little commentary) should be classified as *ballades folkloriques*. These narrative songs might have a refrain and they could be in *laisse* structure or strophic or dialogue form. They could be clearly distinguished from enumerative songs, lyrical songs (which are often in the first person), carols, and other non-narrative songs (Paquin 1980). Such a system could encourage interesting comparative thematic studies involving the French and English folk song heritages of Canada.

3 See Carrier and Vachon 1977 and 1979 for numerous examples; vol. 2 of their collection includes "C'est la faute à Papineau," to the tune of *Turkey in the Straw* or *Old Zip Coon* (1834), which was previously used for the French song *Voilà l'effet de l'argent* (1979, 31)

A list of nineteenth-century Canadian tunebooks and hymnals, compiled by John Beckwith

Publication	Title	Compiler	Later editions
1801 Saint John	*Union Harmony*	Stephen Humbert	1816, 1831, 1840
1819 Quebec	*Nouveau recueil de cantiques*	Jean-Denis Daulé	
1821 Montreal	*A Selection from the Psalms of David*	George Jenkins	
1832 Port Hope	*Colonial Harmonist*	Mark Burnham	
1835 Saint John	*New Brunswick Church Harmony*	Zebulon Estey	
1835 Toronto	*A Selection of Psalms and Hymns*	William H. Warren	1857, 1861
1836 Pictou, Nova Scotia	*The Harmonicon*		1841, 1855
1838 Toronto	*Sacred Harmony*	Alexander Davidson	1843, 1845, 1847, 1848, 1851, 1855, 1856, 1858, 1860, 1861
1844 Quebec	*Lyre sainte, I*	T.F. Molt	
1845 Toronto	*The Canadian Church Psalmody*	James Paton Clarke	

1845 Quebec	*Lyre sainte, II*	T.F. Molt	
1848 Montreal	*A Collection of Original Sacred Music*	F.H. Andrews	
1848 Montreal	*A Selection from the Psalms of David*	George Talbot	
1851 Montreal	*The Presbyterian Psalmody*		
1854 Montreal	*The Psalmist*	George Anderson	
1858 Halifax	*The Psalmody Reformer*	Gideon Wolaver and John B. Wallace	
1861 Toronto	*A Selection of Chants and Tunes*		1867
1861 Toronto	*Church Hymn Tunes, Chants and Responses*	H.R. Fripp	
1862 Montreal	*Chants évangéliques*	L.E. Rivard	1875, 1888, 1891, 1895, 1910, 1914
1863 Toronto/ Montreal	*The Canadian Warbler*	L.C. Everett	
1864 Toronto	*The Canadian Church Harmonist*		1865, 1866
1865 Toronto	*The Vocalist*	George W. Linton	1867
1865 Montreal	*Livre des sept nations*		
1866 Toronto	*The Canadian Sunday School Harp*		1867
1867 Toronto	*The Gem*	Henry J. Clark	1868
1868 Toronto	*The Union Chimes*	George W. Linton	
1870 Montreal	*The Canadian Musical Fountain and Revival Singer*	C.W. Coates & Brothers	
1871 Toronto	*The Canadian Sunday School Organ*		
1873 Toronto	*The Jewel*		

1874 Toronto	*Cantate Domino*	John Black	
1874 Toronto	*A Collection of Hymns*	F.H. Torrington and Thomas Turvey	
1875 Toronto	*The Lesser Hymn and Tune Book*		
1876 Toronto	*The Canadian Sunday School Harmonium*		
1877 Toronto	*Songs of Christian Life and Work*	T. Bowman Stephenson	
1879 Halifax	*The Choir*		1885, 1887
1880 Toronto	*The Wave of Sunday School Song*		
1881 Toronto	*Hymnal of the Presbyterian Church in Canada*	D.J. MacDonnell	1884, 1896
1881 Toronto	*Methodist Tune Book*		
1883 Toronto	*The Dominion Hymnal*		
1884 Toronto/ Montreal	*Children's Hymnal of the Presbyterian Church in Canada*		
1885 Toronto	*Sing Out the Glad News*	J.M. and D.A. Whyte	
1886 Toronto	*Band Music*	D. Savage and J.H. Hathaway	
1886 Montreal/ Rouses Point	*Church Hymnal*		
1887 Toronto	*Songs of Salvation*	H.D. Crossley	
1889 Toronto	*The Canadian Hymnal*		1892, 1894, 1895, 1900, 1904, 1906, 1915
1889 Toronto	*Songs of Calvary*	J.M. and D.A. Whyte	
1889 Toronto/ Medina	*St. Basil's Hymnal*		

1889 Toronto	*Revival Hymns*	J. McD. Kerr	
1890 Ottawa	*Hymns of the Holiness Movement*	R.C. Horner	1899
1891 Toronto	*The Evangel of Song*	J.H. Hathaway	
1894 Toronto	*The Methodist Hymn and Tune Book*	T.C. Jeffers and F.H. Torrington	1918, 1925
1894 Toronto	*The Great Redemption*	J.M. Whyte	
1897 Oxford/ Toronto	*The Presbyterian Book of Praise*	Alexander MacMillan	1901, 1904, 1909, 1912, 1918
1897 Toronto	*Nuggets of Gold for Temperance Campaigns*	J.M. Whyte	

The first barrel organ built by Richard Coates for the Children of Peace had 133 pipes and four stops, covering a compass of 37 notes. Two barrels pinned by Coates are still exant, each containing ten tunes: *Wells, In the Cottage* (La bonne aventure), *Angel's Song, University, Sheffield, Old Hundred, St Mirren's, Lincoln, Egypt, Hanover, St Ann's, Abridge, Shirland, Armley, Bedford, Peckham, China, St Martin's, Seaman's Song, Mount Pleasant* (Schau 1983, 35; 1985, 19). All the tunes are of European origin except for *China*, written by the American Timothy Swan and published in Boston in 1793. *In the Cottage* (see figure 5.1) is often listed as an English folk song (for example, in *Riley's Flute Melodies* (Edward Riley, 1816/1973) but it has also been found in French sources such as Ségur 1866. It was likely included at Willson's request and based on a printed source from the United States. *Angel's Song/Hymn* (see figure 5.2) was written by Orlando Gibbons. Ann Schau (1985, 20) has identified the models for *Old Hundred* and *Hanover* as printed music sheets in Hester Hannah's Book (one of nine volumes of music now known as the Coates Collection of the York Pioneer and Historical Society). For tunes that did not fill a complete revolution of the barrel, Coates composed interludes to fill the gap.

Appendix E

Dances current in Quebec, ca. 1800–1850

The following information, extracted from newspaper accounts, is from Voyer and Tremblay 2001, 78.

1806	minuets, English country dances, reels, jigs, and cotillions
1820	quadrilles and waltzes
1821	Scottish, Irish and waltz steps, strathspeys, reel of three or four, new quadrilles
1822	double long figures and new quadrilles, gavottes, Scottish and Irish reels
1823	new Spanish dances and different German waltzes
1825	Shawl hornpipe, Scottish high dances
1829	Spanish dances, new gavotte and gallopade, Scottish and Irish reels and jigs
1831	national dances including mazurkas
1833	Spanish dances, caledonians, hibernians, new quadrilles
1833	the oriental mazurka
1835	royal Spanish quadrilles
1839	Swedish dances, Bohemian waltzes, Royal Victoria, gallopades, new French style of waltzing
1841	gavotte
1843	polka

St John's Choral Society, Newfoundland, founded 1878

Institute Musical Association, St John's, Newfoundland, founded 1890

Orpheus Club, Halifax, founded 1882, as Philharmonic Society active until 1954

Union Musicale de Québec, Quebec City, founded 1866, active into 1920s

Mendelssohn Choir, Montreal, 1864–94

Philharmonic Society, Montreal, 1880, 1877–99

Schubert Club, Ottawa, founded 1894; later Ottawa Choral Society active
    1895–1914

Orpheus Glee Club, Ottawa, 1906–16, later Orpheus Amateur Operatic Society,
    as Orpheus Operatic Society of Ottawa, 1949–present

Philharmonic Society, Toronto, revived 1872, active 1873–94

St. Andrew's Choral Society, later Toronto Choral Society, 1879–91

Mendelssohn Choir, Toronto, 1894–present

National Chorus, Toronto, 1903–28

Toronto Oratorio Society, 1910–ca 1926

Hamilton Choral Society, founded 1883; later Hamilton Philharmonic Society
    to 1891

Elgar Choir, Hamilton, 1905–ca 1940; 1946 amalgamated with Bach Choir to
    form Bach-Elgar Choir – present

Liedertafel, male choir, Waterloo, 1865–1914?

Orpheus Singing Society, Waterloo, formed 1866, and Sängerbund of Berlin
    [Kitchener], formed 1883, amalgamated into Harmony, active to 1914

Berlin Philharmonic Society, established 1883, active until 1914

Orpheus Male Choir, Kitchener, founded 1917, merged into the Kitchener-
    Waterloo Philharmonic Choir, 1922–present

Windsor and Walkerville Choral Society, 1905–19

Thunder Bay Philharmonic Society (Fort William / Prince Arthur), founded
    1910, active to ca. 1930

Winnipeg Operatic Society, 1883–ca. 1899

Men's Musical [later Music] Club, Winnipeg, 1915, organized Winnipeg Male Voice Choir, 1916; assisted formation of Winnipeg Philharmonic Society, 1922–present

Winnipeg Oratorio Society, 1908–24

Regina Philharmonic Society, founded 1904, became Regina Choral and Orchestral Society, in 1919, then Regina Choral Society in 1922

Saskatoon Philharmonic Society, founded 1908, later Orpheus Society, to late 1920s?

Calgary Philharmonic Society, 1904–08

Apollo Choir, Calgary, 1908–1918

Victoria Operatic Society, Victoria, 1886–1908.

Repertoire and choral groups for the 1903 Cycle of Music Festivals organized by Charles A.E. Harriss

Orchestral works

F. Cliffe: "Ballade" (from Symphony in C minor)
F.H. Cowen: *Scandinavian Symphony*
F. Corder: *Overture "Prospero"*
Edward Elgar: "Prelude" and "Angel's Farewell" from *Gerontius*
Edward German: *Gipsy Suite*
H. MacCunn: *Overture "Ship o' the Fiend"*
H. MacCunn: *Overture Land of the Mountain and the Flood*
A.C. Mackenzie: Suite *"London Day by Day"*
A.C. Mackenzie: Ballade *"La belle dame sans merci"*
A.C. Mackenzie: *Two Scottish Rhapsodies*
A.C. Mackenzie: *Overture "Cricket on the Hearth"*
A.C. Mackenzie: *Overture "Britannia"*
A.C. Mackenzie: *Coronation March*
C.V. Stanford: *Irish Rhapsody no. 1*
C.V. Stanford: *Irish Symphony*
Arthur Sullivan: *Overture "Di Ballo"*

Choral works

F.H. Cowen: *Coronation Ode*
Edward Elgar: *Coronation Ode*
Edward Elgar: *The Banner of St George*
C.A.E. Harriss: *Choruses from Torquil*
C.A.E. Harriss: *Coronation Mass Edward VII* (composed for these festivals)
A.C. Mackenzie: *The Cotter's Saturday Night*
A.C. Mackenzie: *The Dream of Jubal*
H. Parry: *St. Cecilia's Day*
H. Parry: *Blest Pair of Sirens*
C.V. Stanford: *The Revenge*

C.V. Stanford: *The Battle of the Baltic*
Arthur Sullivan: *The Golden Legend*
Coleridge Taylor: *"The Death of Minnehaha" (Hiawatha, part 2)*

Schedule for the Cycle of Music Festivals

City	Choir and number of voices	Date	Associate conductor	Orchestra
Halifax	Orpheus Society (150)	March 3	C.H. Porter	Montreal Symphony Orchestra
Halifax	Orpheus Society (150)	April 1	C.H. Porter	Montreal Symphony Orchestra
Moncton	Festival Chorus (100)	April 2	G.H Brown	Montreal Symphony Orchestra
Saint John	Festival Chorus (150)	April 3	J.S. Ford	Montreal Symphony Orchestra
Saint John	Festival Chorus (150)	April 4	J.S. Ford	Montreal Symphony Orchestra
Hamilton	Festival Chorus (200)	April 13	C.L.M. Harriss	Chicago Symphony Orchestra
Brantford	Festival Chorus (200)	April 15	H.K. Jordan	Chicago Symphony Orchestra
Woodstock	Festival Chorus (150)	April 15	J.H. Chadfield	Chicago Symphony Orchestra
London	Festival Chorus (300)	April 15	R. Pococke	Chicago Symphony Orchestra
Toronto	Toronto Festival Chorus (350)	April 16	F.H. Torrington	Chicago Symphony Orchestra
Toronto	Toronto Festival Chorus (300)	April 17	F.H. Torrington	Chicago Symphony Orchestra
Toronto	National Festival Chorus (300)	April 18	A. Ham	Chicago Symphony Orchestra
Ottawa	Choral Society (200)	April 20	J.E. Birch	Chicago Symphony Orchestra

Ottawa	Choral Society (200)	April 21	J.E. Birch	Chicago Symphony Orchestra
Montreal	Festival Chorus (300)	April 22	C.A.E. Harris	Chicago Symphony Orchestra
Montreal	Festival Chorus (300)	April 23	G. Couture	Chicago Symphony Orchestra
Montreal	Oratorio Society (200)	April 24	H. Reyner	Chicago Symphony Orchestra
Winnipeg	Festival Chorus (250)	April 29	Rhys Thomas	Minneapolis Orchestra
Winnipeg	Festival Chorus (250)	April 30	Rhys Thomas	Minneapolis Orchestra
Brandon	Festival Chorus (150)	May 1	F.B. Fenwick	Minneapolis Orchestra
Vancouver	Festival Chorus (250)	May 4	F. Dykes, H. Smith	Portland and Seattle Orchestras
Vancouver	Festival Chorus (250)	May 5	F. Dykes, H. Smith	Portland and Seattle Orchestras
New West-minster	Festival Chorus (150)	May 6	A.E. White	Portland and Seattle Orchestras
Victoria	Festival Chorus (250)	May 7	G. Taylor, H. Russell	Portland and Seattle Orchestras
Victoria	Festival Chorus (250)	May 8	G. Taylor, H. Russell	Portland and Seattle Orchestras
Victoria	Festival Chorus (250)	May 9	G. Taylor, H. Russell	Portland and Seattle Orchestras

Appendix H
Recordings of Canadian music released on Folkways Records to 1962

Historical

FA2312 *Songs of the Sea* (Alan Mills)

FW3001 *O Canada: A History in Song* (Alan Mills)

FG3502 *My Life in Recording Canadian-Indian Folklore* (Marius Barbeau)

FG3505 *Songs and Ballads of Newfoundland* (Kenneth Peacock)

FO3531 *Old Time Fiddle Tunes* (Jean Carignan)

FO3532 *Songs and Fiddle Tunes and A Folk Tale from Canada* (Alan Mills, Jean Carignan)

FG3560 *Songs of French Canada* (Jacques Labrecque)

Radio Programs

FS3862, FS3872, FS3873, vols. 1–3 *Rawhide* (Max Ferguson)

Ethnic Folkways Library

FM4005 *Folk Songs of Ontario* (collected by Edith Fowke)

FM4006 *Folk Music from Nova Scotia* (collected by Helen Creighton)

FM4051 *Songs of the Ottawa Valley* (O.J. Abbott)

FE4444 *The Eskimos of Hudson Bay and Alaska* (collected by Laura Boulton)

FE4450 *Songs from Cape Breton* (various artists)

FE4464 *Indian Music of the Canadian Plains* (collected by Kenneth Peacock)

FE4482 *Songs of French Canada* (various artists).

Children Series

FC7676 *More Songs to Grow On* (Alan Mills)

FC7018 *French Folk Songs for Children in English* (Alan Mills)

FC7021 *Animals*, vol. 1 (Alan Mills)

FC7022 *More Animals*, vol. 1 (Alan Mills)

FC7108 *The Story of the Klondike* (Pierre Berton)

FC7208 *French Folk Songs for Children* (Alan Mills)

FC7214 *Game Songs of French Canada*

FC7229 *French Christmas Songs: Chants de Noël* (Hélène Baillargeon)

FC7719/7720/7721/7722 *Chantons en français: French Songs for Learning French*, parts 1–4 (Hélène Baillargeon)

FC7750 *Christmas Songs from Many Lands* (Alan Mills).

International Series

FW6821 *Folk Songs of the Canadian North Woods* (Wade Hemsworth)

FW6831 *Folk Songs of Newfoundland* (Alan Mills)

FW6880 *Man of the Whole Wide World* (Art Samuels, Montreal Youth Choir).

FW6918 *Duet Songs of French Canada* (Alan Mills, Hélène Baillargeon)

FW6923 *Chansons d'Acadie / Songs of Acadia* (Hélène Baillargeon)

FW6929 *Folk Songs of French Canada* (Alan Mills)

FW6951 *Songs and Dances of Quebec* (collected by Sam Gesser)

FW8744 *Songs of the Maritimes: Lumberman Songs and Songs of the Sea* (Alan Mills)

FW8764 *Songs and Ballads of Northern Saskatchewan and Manitoba* (various artists)

FW8771 *We'll Rant and We'll Roar: Songs of Newfoundland* (Alan Mills)

FW8810 *The Black Watch and other Pipe and Drum Tunes* (Royal Highland Regiment)

FW8825 *Honor your Partner: Square Dances with Calls* (N. Roy Clifton)

FW8826 *Jigs and Reels*, vol. 2 (Per Nørgård).

Literature Series

FL9805 *Six Montreal Poets*

FL9806 *Six Toronto Poets*

FL9905 *Voix du 8 Poetes du Canada*

New Releases

FG3522 *An Irishman in North Americay* (Tom Kines)

FG3547 *Through Streets Broad and Narrow: Karen James*, vol. 2

FG3549 *Karen James*

FG3569 *Bunkhouse and Forecastle Songs of the Northwest* (Stanley G. Triggs)

FM4051 *Irish and British Songs from the Ottawa Valley* (O.J. Abbott)

FM4052 *Lumbering Songs from the Ontario Shanties* (collected by Edith Fowke)

FM4053 *Folk Songs of the Miramichi: Lumber and River Songs from the Miramichi Folk Fest, Newcastle, New Brunswick* (various artists)

FM8767 *Songs from Shakespeare's Plays and Songs of His Time* (Tom Kines).

Appendix I
Works discussed by David Parsons in "Landscape Imagery in Canadian Music" (1987)

Soundscape

Murray Adaskin: *Algonquin Symphony* (1958)

John Beckwith: *Canada Dash: Canada Dot* (1967), *The Great Lakes Suite* (1949)

Keith Bissell: *How the Loon Got Its Necklace* (1971)

Claude Champagne: *Symphonie Gaspesienne* (1945)

Jean Coulthard: *The Birds of Landsdown* (1972)

Robert Fleming: *Shadow on the Prairie* (1951), *Of a Timeless Land* (1975)

James Gayfer: *Canadian Landscape* (1974)

Alexina Louie: *The Eternal Earth* (1986)

Quentin Maclean: *Algonquin Legend* (1939)

Pierre Mercure: *Tetrachromie* (1963)

John Hawkins: *Remembrances* (1969)

Eldon Rathburn: *Aspects of Railroads* (1969)

R. Murray Schafer: *Music for Wilderness Lake* (1979), *The Princess of the Stars* (1981), *Miniwanka or the Moments of Water* (1971), *Epitaph for Moonlight* (1968), *String Quartet No. 2: Waves* (1976), *Train* (1976)

Harry Somers: *North Country* (1948) and *Evocations* (1966)

Norman Symonds: *Three Atmospheres* (1971), *Deep Ground: Long Waters* (1968), *Big Lonely* (1975), *On an Emerald Sea* (1983), *Pastel Blue* (1963), *The Gift of Thanksgiving* (1980), and *Forest and Sky* (1977)

Gilles Tremblay: *Fleuves* (1976).

Andrew Twa: *Prairies* (1947)

John Weinzweig: *Our Canada* (1944).

Charles M. Wilson: *Symphonic Perspectives: Kingsmere* (1974)

Visual Art

Murray Adaskin: *In Praise of Canadian Painting in the Thirties* (1975)

Jean Coulthard: *The Pines of Emily Carr* (1969)

Harry Freedman: *Images* (1958), *Tableau* (1952), *Klee Wyck* (1970), *Graphic I*
   "Out of silence..." (1971)
Diana McIntosh: *Greening* (1979)

Mountains

Michael Conway Baker: *Okanagan Landscapes* (1971)
Allan Bell: *Monashee Sketches* (1982)
Alexander Brott: *From Sea to Sea* (1947)
Neil Chotem: *Camera on Camera* (1963)
Jean Coulthard: *Kalamalka* (1974)
Robert Farnon: *Mountain Grandeur, Gateway to the West, Cascades to the Sea,*
   Springtime in the Rockies
James Gayfer: *The Lake in the Mountains* (1981)
Diana McIntosh: *Paraphrase No. 1*
Robert McMullen: *Sketches from the Rocky Mountains*
Barbara Pentland: *Song Cycle* (1945), *Suite Borealis* (1966)
Ann Southam: *Altitude Lake* (1963)

Arctic and Cold

Murray Adaskin: *Qalala and Nilaula of the North* (1969)
Robert Aitken: *Icicle* (1977)
Louis Applebaum: *Inuit* (1977), *Legend of the North* (1957)
Violet Archer: *Northern Landscape* (1980)
Milton Barnes: *Anerca I* (1979), *Anerca II* (1980), *Anerca III* (1981)
Robert Bauer: *Aurora* (1981)
Neil Chotem: *Glaçons, North Country* (1967), and *Aurores Boréalis*
Victor Davies: *Anerca* (1969)
Harry Freedman: *Anerca* (1966)
Serge Garant: *Anerca* (1961)
Glenn Gould: *The Idea of North*
Derek Healey: *Arctic Images* (1971), *Desert Landscapes with Figures* (1978)
Jan Jarvlepp: *Ice* (1976), and *Aurora Borealis* (1976)
Talivaldis Kenins: *Naacnaaca* (1975)
Michel Longtin: *Latitude 60° Nord* (1969), *Au nord du Lac Superieur* (1972), *Un*
   Croix de Bouleau au nord (1972), *Le Reveil de Fedhibo* (1972), and *Pohjatuuli*
   (1982)
François Morel: *Nuvattuq* (1967–75) and *Iikkii* (1971–74)
Marjan Mozetich: *Ice* (1980)
Barbara Pentland: *Arctica* (1973)
Wendy Prezament: *Glacial Fragments* (1984)
Murray Schafer: *North/White* (1973)
Harry Somers: *Those Silent, Awe-filled Spaces* (1977).
John Weinzweig: *Edge of the World* (1946)
Leon Zuchert: *In the Gleam of Northern Lights* (1974)

Appendix J
Selected Noteworthy Canadian Compositions

Names of composers are given in parentheses after the title. Popular musics include traditional music, rock, and jazz; titles of albums appear in capital letters. Some earlier dates for folk and traditional music are approximate.

DATE	REFINED MUSIC	POPULAR MUSICS
1600s		
1606	Réception: *Théâtre de Neptune* (Lescarbot)	folk: *À la claire fontaine* (sung)
1640s	carol: *Jesous Ahatonia* (Brébeuf)	
1684	prose: *Sacrae familiae*	
1700s		
[n.d.]	newly composed motets	broadside: *Taken of Louisbourg*
1789	opera: *Colas et Colinette* (J. Quesnel)	
1791	band: *Royal Fusiliers' Arrival* (Argenson)	folk: *Faux plaisir, vains honneurs* (sung)
1800s		
1800s		[n.d.] fiddle: *The Red River Jig* (fiddle tune)
1807	organ: *Marche* (F. Glackemeyer)	
1809	opera: *Lucas et Cécile* (Quesnel)	

1827	song: *The Fairy Song* (S. Codman)	
1816	choral: *Singing School* (S. Humbert)	
1841	piano: *The Canada Union Waltz* (anon.)	*The Merry Bells of England* (Lehmann)
1845	Mélodie: *Le Grillon* (A. Dessane) Choral: *Trisagion* (J.P. Clarke)	
1848	*Marche de la St-Jean-Baptiste* (J.C. Brauneis)	
1849	*Centenary* (A.H. Lockett)	
1852	*Magic Bell Polka* (G. Strathy)	
1853	collection: *Lays of the Maple Leaf* (J.P. Clarke)	
1855	*Quadrille canadien* (A. Dessane)	[n.d.] folk: *Les raftsmen*
1858	*Stadaconé* (E. Gagnon)	*Le drapeau de Carillon* (C.W. Sabatier)
1860	*Messe de Noël* (J.J. Perrault)	
1866	operetta: *TIQ – The Indian Question* (C. Lavallée)	*When You and I Were Young, Maggie*
1867	*I am waiting for thee* (E. Gledhill)	*The Maple Leaf For Ever* (A. Muir)
1870		glee: *The Social Glass* (C.W. Coates)
1872		*Lacrosse* (H.F. Sefton)
1874	piano: *Le Papillon* (C. Lavallée) orchestra: *Ouverture Patrie* (C. Lavallée)	
1876		*One Sweetly Solemn Thought* (P. Ambrose)
1879	pageant: *Canada's Welcome* (A. Clappé)	
1880	operetta: *The Widow* (Lavallée)	*O Canada* (C. Lavallée)
1882	*Novembre* (E. Lavigne) *Souffle parfumé* (J. Vézina)	*Vir'de bord mon ami Pierre* (Blain de St Aubin)

1885	*No! A Temperance Song* (J.J. Roberts)	
1886	*Clos ta paupière* (A. Contant) Lied: *Frühlingsabend* (W.O. Forsyth)	[n.d.] folk: *Chanson de Louis Riel*
1887	Oratorio: *David and Jonathan* (Eva York)	
1889	Operetta: *Leo, the Royal Cadet* (O. Telgmann)	
1890	Cantata: *Daniel Before the King* (C. Harriss)	
1891	*When Comes the Spring* (C. Lucas) Cantata: *Gulnare* (F. d'Auria)	
1892	*Mon bouquet* (A. Fortier)	
1896	Opera/oratorio: *Torquil* (C. Harriss)	[n.d.] minstrel show: *The Little Whytes*
1898	*The British African Gavotte* (G. J. Burnett)	
1899		*A Rag Time Spasm; The Cake Winner*

1900–1920

1900	*Cavalcade* (G. Branscombe) *Fugue* (C. Lucas) organ: *Prelude and* Fugue (S. Warren) *The Birth of Christ* (C. Lucas)	
1902	*Indian Maid's Lament* (E. Manning) *The End of the Day* (E. Whyte)	*Cave of the Winds* (Nathaniel Dett)
1904	anthem: *Thou, O God, Art Praised in Zion* (C. Ford)	
1905	oratorio: *Caïn* (A. Contant)	musical: *Peggy Machree* (C. Lucas)
1907	*Musique* (A. Contant) *Le Souvenir* (G. Couture) *Piano Trio* (A. Contant)	*Raggity-Rag* (Lafrenière)
1910	*Some of These Days* (S. Brooks)	*Come Josephine in My Flying Machine*

1911	*Happiness* (G. Branscombe) *Tintamarre* (H. Anger) *Gisèle* (A. Lavallée-Smith)	
1912	operetta: *Le Fétiche* (J. Vézina)	
1914	oratorio: *Jean le précurseur* (G. Couture)	
1915	*Trois Prèludes* (R. Mathieu)	
1916	*Rondel de Thibault* (H. Gagnon) *Introduction, Passacaglia & Fugue* (H. Willan) *Four Piano Sketches* (C. McPhee)	
1917		*Darktown Strutters' Ball* (Brooks)
1918	*Sweet Memories Waltz* (H. Clarke) *England, an Ode* (E. MacMillan)	*K-K-K-Katy* (G. O'Hara)
1919	*Listen to the Lambs* (N. Dett) *Pilgrims of Destiny* (G. Branscombe)	revue: *Biff, Bing, Bang* (Dumbells) *The World Is Waiting For* *the Sunrise* (E. Seitz)

1920–1949

1921	Violin/piano: *Lied* (R. Mathieu) *Prière* (G.-E. Tanguay)	
1923	Opera: *Gisèle* (A. Lavallée-Smith)	
1924	*Messe* (G. Cusson)	
1927	*Sketches for String Quartet* (E. MacMillan)	
1928	*Rise Up, O My Love; Fair in* *Face* (H. Willan) *Bell Carol* (A. Whitehead)	*Sweethearts on Parade* (C. Lombardo/Loeb)
1929	*Danse villageoise* (C. Champagne) *Suite canadienne* (L.-P. Morin)	
1930		*Ça va venir découragez-vous* *pas* (Bolduc)
1931	*May Day Dancing* (G. Branscombe)	
1932	*Ruins (Ypres, 1917)* (B. Pentland)	

1933		country: *My Swiss Moonlight Lullaby* (W. Carter)
1934	*Tabuh Tabuhan* (C. McPhee)	*Tumbling Tumbleweeds* (B. Nolan)
1936	*The Christmas Rose* (Anderson) *A Lavender Lady* (B. Pentland)	
1937	*Serenade* (G. Cusson)	*Boo-Hoo* (C. Lombardo/Loeb)
1938	*Symphony No. 1* (R. Farnon) *Ballade for Viola and String Orchestra* (G. Ridout)	
1939	*Dirgeling* (J. Weinzweig)	*Cheerio* (P. Faith) *I'll Never Smile Again* (R. Lowe)
1941	*Studies in Line* (B. Pentland)	
1942	*Symphony No. 2 "Ottawa"* (R. Farnon)	*L'adieu de soldat* (R. Lebrun)
1944	*Piano Concerto* (H. Willan)	
1945	*Symphonie gaspesienne* (C. Champagne)	*Just a Moment More With You* (A. Hallman)
1946	*Divertimento no. 1* (J. Weinzweig) *Carnival Overture* (O. Morawetz) opera: *Deirdre* (H. Willan)	
1947	*Quatrains* (J. Papineau-Couture)	*Jumping Bean* (R. Farnon)
1948	*North Country* (H. Somers) *Quebec May* (J. Coulthard)	*There's a Bluebird on Your Windowsill* (Clarke/ Rhythm Pals)
1949	ballet: *Red Ear of Corn* (J. Weinzweig) *The Great Lakes Suite* (J. Beckwith)	*The Blackfly Song* (W. Hemsworth)

1950–1959

1950	*Piano Sonata no. 4* (H. Somers)	*I'm Moving On* (H. Snow) *Cool Water* (B. Nolan)
1951	*String Quartet* (C. Champagne)	
1952	*Neighbours* (N. McLaren) *Guernica* (C. Pépin)	

1953	*Antiphonie* (F. Morel)	
	Fanfares for Stratford (L. Applebaum)	
1954	*Passacaglia & Fugue for Orchestra* (H. Somers)	*ShBoom* (Crew Cuts)
1955	*Dripsody* (H. LeCaine) *Opening Night: A Theatre Overture* (R. Turner)	*Moments to Remember* (The Four Lads) *Hard To Get* (Gisèle MacKenzie)
1956		*Walk Hand in Hand* (Johnny Cowell)
1957	*Pièce concertante no. 1* (J. Papineau-Couture)	*Diana* (P. Anka) *Little Darlin'* (The Diamonds) *FELIX LECLERC ET SA GUITARE*
1958		*MARCEL MARTEL ET SES CHANSONS* *Swinging Shepherd Blues* (M. Koffman) *ACROSS CANADA WITH THE TRAVELLERS*
1959	*Triptyque* (P. Mercure)	

1960–1969

1960	*Electronic Composition No. 3* (I. Anhalt)	*Travellin' Man* (T. Hunter/ Rain)
1961	*Improvvisazioni Concertanti* (N. Beecroft) *Fall Fair* (G. Ridout) *Suite for the Monteregian Hills* (M. Calvert)	
1963	*Stereophony* (H. Somers) *Suite Hebraique* (S.I. Glick)	*Themes for Young Lovers* (P. Faith) *Mer Morte* (Les Jaguars) *Bo Diddley* (R. Hawkins) *FOUR STRONG WINDS* (Ian & Sylvia) *JACK KANE BAND CONDUCTED BY BERT NIOSI*

1964	Deuxième Suite pour piano (R. Jaque)	Fortune Teller (B. Curtola)
	Lignes et points (P. Mercure)	THAT GIRL
	Picasso Suite (H. Somers)	(Phyllis Marshall)
		VOICE OF AN ANGEL I
		(C. McKinnon)
		It's My Way (B. Sainte-Marie)
		CLAUDE LÉVEILLÉE À
		PARIS
		Canadiana Suite (O. Peterson)
1965	Loving/Toi (R.M. Schafer)	Mon pays (G. Vigneault)
1966	Evocations (H. Somers)	Suzanne (Leonard Cohen)
		The Canadian Railroad
		Trilogy (G. Lightfoot)
1967	opera: Louis Riel (H. Somers)	Ca-na-da (B. Gimby)
	Quasars (Symphonie No. 3)	WE'RE OFF TO DUBLIN
	(C. Pépin)	IN THE GREEN (Carlton
	The Confession Stone (R. Fleming)	Showband)
	electronic: Katimavik (O. Joachim)	
1968	Memorial to Martin Luther King	Lindberg (Charlebois)
	(O. Morawetz)	
	I never saw another butterfly	THE FIRST OF THE IRISH
	(S.I. Glick)	ROVERS
		Born to be Wild (Steppenwolf)
1969	Dummiyah (J. Weinzweig)	BLOOD SWEAT AND TEARS
	Music for Vancouver (B. Mather)	BUD THE SPUD (T. Connors)
	Diversion for Orchestra	STINK
	(M. Adaskin)	(McKenna Mendelson Blues)
	Offrande I (S. Garant)	You, Me and Mexico
	Illumination II (Otto Joachim)	(Edward Bear)
		Sugar, Sugar (Andy Kim
		[Baron Longfellow])
		musical: Hair (G. MacDermot)
		Snowbird (MacLellan /
		A. Murray)
		Which Way You Goin' Billy?
		(Poppy Family)
		THE BAND

1970–1979

| 1970 | Threnody (R.M. Schafer) | American Woman |
| | | (Guess Who) |

From the diary of Anne Frank (O. Morawetz)	*Big Yellow Taxi* (Joni Mitchell)
Geste (M.-G. Brégent)	*JAUNE* (Jean Pierre Ferland)

1971	*Arctic Images* (D. Healey)	*Sweet City Woman* (The Stampeders)
	Symphonie no 3 (J. Hétu)	*DR MUSIC* (Doug Riley)
	How the Loon Got Its Necklace (K. Bissell)	*ONE FINE MORNING* (Lighthouse)
	Miniwanka (R.M. Schafer)	*Black Hallelujah* (R. Little/ N. Symonds)
	Musique pour Rouen (Bruce Mather)	

1972	*Interplay* (B. Pentland)	*What a Feeling* (Crowbar)
	Graphic II (H Freedman)	*I'M A WOMAN* (J. Drake)
	12 Essays on a Cantabile Theme (J. Coulthard)	*HARVEST* (Neil Young)
		The Homecoming (Hagood Hardy)
		OFFENBACH SOAP OPERA (Offenbach)

1973	*Shadows II, 'Lalita'* (R. Aitken)	*LANDSCAPES* (Valdy)
		STRAIGHT UP (Downchild Blues Band)
		COAST TO COAST FEVER (David Wiffen)

1974	*Canada Mosaic* (J. Coulthard)	*BORN A WOMAN* (Rita MacNeil)
		J'AI VU LE LOUP ... (Charlesbois, Leclerc, Vigneault)

1975	*...chants d'amours* (S. Garant)	*NEIGES* (André Gagnon)
		Le blues de la métropole (Beau Dommage)
		From New York to L.A. (P. Gallant)

1976	*Disasters in the Sun* (B. Pentland)	*THE WHOLE WORLD'S GOING CRAZY* (April Wine)
	Concerto for Piano and Orchestra (M. Baker)	*DANCER WITH BRUISED KNEES* (McGarrigles)
	Fleuves (G. Tremblay)	*ATLANTIC SUITE* (P. Nimmons)
	Siddartha (C. Vivier)	*BEGINNING TO FEEL LIKE HOME* (C. Peterson)

		SINGABLE SONGS FOR THE VERY YOUNG (Raffi)
		2112 (Rush)
		L'HEPTADE (Harmonium)
1977	Sonic Landscapes no. 3 (B. Truax)	PRETTY AIN'T GOOD ENOUGH (Good Brothers)
	Quartet (J. Beckwith)	Sometimes When We Touch (D. Hill)
		Fogarty's Cove (S. Rogers)
		UNE FOIS CINQ (Charlesbois, Vigneault, Léveillée, etc.)
		rock opera: Starmania (L. Plamondon)
1978	The Shivaree (J. Beckwith)	Music Box Dancer (F. Mills)
	Déja vu (Michael Colgrass) [Pulitzer Prize]	BROTHER TO BROTHER (G. Vannelli)
		GAROLOU
1979	Minuet for the RCMP (Ian McDougall)	JE NE SUIS QU'UNE CHANSON (G. Reno)
		NIRVANA BLEU (D. Lavoie)
		BALDRY'S OUT (J. Baldry)
		DANCING IN THE DRAGON'S JAWS (B. Cockburn)
		ONE ELEPHANT, DEUX ÉLÉPHANTS (Sharon, Lois & Bram)
		LIBRE (A. Arsenault)

1980–1989

1980	Lonely Child (C. Vivier)	AVOID FREUD (Rough Trade)
		MUSIC OF CANADA (Tamarack)
1981		GET LUCKY (Loverboy)
		My Girl (Gone, Gone, Gone) (Chilliwack)
1982	Spirit Reel (James Hiscott)	ONE SIZE FITS ALL (Nylons)
	In the stillness between... (B. Cherney)	SWING IS IN — LET'S DANCE (Dal Richards)

1983	*Jeux de société* (Denis Bouliane)	*Sunglasses at Night* (Corey Hart)
1984		*MOONLIGHT GROCERY* (Connie Kaldor)
		NO BORDERS HERE (Jane Siberry)
		AKIMBO ALOGO (Kim Mitchell)
		JE M'APPELLE ÉDITH (É. Butler)
1985	*Virelai* (Patrick Cardy)	*RECKLESS* (Bryan Adams)
	Missa Brevis (Nancy Telfer)	*LIGHTS OF BURGUNDY* (Oliver Jones)
		BEST OF DAVID WILCOX
1986	*Autour d'Ainola* (M. Longtin)	*Try* (Blue Rodeo)
	Due North (S. Chatman)	*OYSTER TRACKS* (Prairie Oyster)
1987	*The August Collection* (Walter Buczynski)	*HONEY AND SPICE* (Fraser MacPherson)
	Cantate pour cordes (André Prévost)	*Douze grands succès* (P. Norman)
1988	*The Mechanical Advantage* (Omar Daniel)	*SEE THE LIGHT* (Jeff Healey Band)
	Berliner Momente (Walter Boudreau)	*Swinging on a Star* (M. McLauchlan)
		Voodoo Thing (Colin James)
		Humout Me (Jesse Winchester)
		EL MUNDO (Mitsou)
1989	*Akasha* (Glenn Buhr)	*MARDI GRAS MUNDO* (Z. Richard)
	Pieces of Eight (Clifford Crawley)	*GIRL TALK* (Holly Cole)
	BEYOND THE SOUND BARRIER (A. Lauber)	*UP TO HERE* (Tragically Hip)
	Yo soy la desintegración (J. Piché)	*SYMPHONY IN EFFECT* (Maestro Fresh Wes)

1990–1999

1990	*Changes* (Melissa Hui)	*SUDDEN STOP* (Colin James)
	Jappements à la lune (C. Butterfield)	*WORLD TOUR 1990 – UZEB* (Eusèbe jazz)
	LIGNE DE VIE (Christian Colon)	
	Celestial Machine (O. Underhill)	

1991	*À l'aventure* (Denis Gougeon)	*(Everything I Do) I Do It for You* (Adams)
	Sonata: für Elaine (Deirdre Piper)	*Something to Talk About* (Shirley Eikhard)
	Violin Concerto (Andrew MacDonald)	*Life Is a Highway* (Tom Cochrane)
	Charnière (Michelle Boudreau)	show: *The Evolution of Jazz* (Alleyne)
	The Celtic Mass for the Sea (Scott MacMillan)	*THE YELLOW TAPE* (Barenaked Ladies)
	Riverrun (Barry Truax)	*Jusqu'aux p'tites heures* (Bottine Souriante)
1992	*Trilogy* (Alcides Lanza)	*SPIRITS OF HAVANA* (Jane Bunnett)
		Whale Music (Rheostatics)
		INGENUE (k.d.lang)
		DANNY BOY (John McDermott)
1993	*Webster's Spin* (Ann Southam)	*Mmm Mmm Mmm* (Crash Test Dummies)
	DIALOGICS (David Keane)	*FUMBLING TOWARDS ECSTASY* (Sarah McLachlan)
		NORTH COUNTRY (Rankin Family)
		THE COLOUR OF MY LOVE (Celine Dion)
		Julie (Les Colocs)
1994	*Spirit Trail* (Allan Gordon Bell)	*LIVING UNDER JUNE* (Jann Arden)
	TIME TRIP TO BIG BANG (U. Kasemets)	*The Mask and the Mirror* (L. McKennitt)
	Another Byte of McIntosh (McIntosh)	*COUP DE TÊTE* (Roch Voisine)
	Ophélie (Jeffrey Ryan)	*AKUA TUTA* (Kashtin)
1995	*Forgotten Dreams* (John Burge)	*THIS CHILD* (Susan Aglukark)
	String Quartet (John Burke)	*THE WOMAN IN ME* (Shania Twain)
	TERRA NOVA (John Winarz)	*HI HOW ARE YOU?* (Ashley MacIsaac)
		JAGGED LITTLE PILL (Alanis Morissette)
		Pigeon d'argile (Kevin Parent)

1996	*Piano Concerto* (Larysa Kuzmenko)	GLENCOE STATION
	... I, Laika... (Hope Lee)	(John Allan Cameron)
	Solus (Heather Schmidt)	OH, WHAT A FEELING
	DAUGHTER OF OLAPA	(4-CD set)
	(Carol Ann Weaver)	AFRICVILLE SUITE
		(Joe Sealy)
		OFF THE FLOOR LIVE
		(Amos Garrett)
		Pure (Lara Fabian)
		Portraits (Jim Corcoran)
		La force de comprendre
		(Dubmatique)
1997	*Corals of Valais* (Alison Cameron)	
	Bird in the Tangled Sky (Jocelyn Morlock)	
	Intermezzo (Anthony Genge)	
	NORTHERN LANDSCAPES (V. Archer)	
	LYRE (Michael Parker)	
1998	*The Lyre of Orpheus*	ÉTATS D'AMOUR
	(Raymond Luedeke)	(Isabelle Boulay)
	Procession Burlesque	LENNY BREAU, BOY
	(Chris Harman)	WONDER
	This Is The Colour of My	BIG BAND CHRISTMAS
	Dreams (Kelly)	(R. McConnell, M. Murphy,
	AEROSOL (Ned Bouhalassa	Boss Brass)
	Ambient V (Ana Sokolovic)	
	opera: *Elsewhereless* (Rodney Sharman)	
	ICICLE BLUE AVALANCHE (J. Oliver)	
1999	SHATTERED NIGHT,	P.J. PERRY AND THE ESO
	SHIVERING STARS (A. Louie)	NEW HORIZONS
	PLUNDERPHONICS	(Bernie Senensky)
	(John Oswald)	WHEN I LOOK IN YOUR
		EYES (D. Krall)

2000–2005

2000	*Canadian Mosaic* (D. Patriquin)	*Blood Red Cherry* (Jann Arden)
	The Book of Mirrors (Gary Kulesha)	WELCOME TO MY DREAMS
	FLIGHTS OF FANCY (Jan Jarvlepp)	(Ralph Fraser)
	Lo que vendra (Inouk Demers)	TURN (Great Big Sea)
	AFFAIRS OF THE HEART	RUNNING BACK THRU
	(Marjan Mozetich)	CANADA (Guess Who)
		SWINGIN' (Mart Kenney)
		Whoa, Nelly (Nelly Furtado)

RISING SUN (Gilles Sioui)
YEARNING FOR POLKAS AND WALTZES (W. Ostanek)
TALE OF THE FINGERS (Dave Young)

2001	*GOLDEN FIRE* (Timothy Sullivan)	*SILVER SIDE UP* (Nickelback)
	IMPULSION (M. Coulombe St-Marcoux)	*How You Remind Me* (Nickelback)
	La Pietra Che Canta (Serge Prévost)	*BIG MOUTH* (Colin Linden)
	REDEMPTION (P.P. Koprowski)	*BAD DREAMS* (Swollen Members)
	Legend of Heimdall (E. Raum)	*NIPAIAMIANAN* (F. Vollant)
	Lyra (S. Wilkinson)	
2002	*Fondly, through the madness breathing* (M. Roi)	*ATTACHE TA TUQUE* (Cowboys Fringants)
	For the Time Being (Brian Current)	*FAILER* (Kathleen Edwards)
	Playing Guitar: Symphony No. 1 (T. Brady)	*Let Go* (Avril Lavigne)
	Partly True, Mostly Fiction (A. Carastathis)	
	Par-çi, par-là (Chan Ka Nin)	
	Autoportrait sur Times Square (Y. Plamondon)	
	EARTH CHANTS (Imant Raminsh)	
	KLEZMER SUITE (Sid Robinovitch)	
	INTO INDIA (Hildegard Westerkamp)	
2003	*PHILOSOPHER IN THE KITCHEN* (Lothar Klein)	*I Just Wanna Be Mad* (Terri Clark)
	Seriosity (Rose Bolton)	*TALKIN' HONKY BLUES* (Buck 65)
	opera: *Filumena* (John Estacio)	*LUMIÈRES* (Louise Forestier)
	Touch Piece (Alex Pauk)	*L'INSTANT D'APRÈS* (Natasha St-Pier)
	Volando (Isabelle Panneton)	
2004	*Sing All Ye Joyful* (Ruth Watson Henderson)	*AMOUR ORAL* (Loco Locass)
		TAIMA
		LET IT DIE (Leslie Feist)
		FUNERAL (Arcade Fire)
		JOYFUL REBELLION (k-os)
2005	*AWAKENING* (Christos Hatzis)	*SÉRVICES RENDUS* (Groovy Aardvark)
		IT'S TIME (Michael Bublé)

Notes

1 Many researchers and young scholars from coast to coast were involved in the first edition of EMC, which was published in both English (1981) and French (1983) versions. This treasure-house of information stimulated so much new research that a 2nd edition appeared in 1992. The online-version (available at www.histori.ca) is continually updated.

2 In some cases only a title or a single copy was found. By 1999, however, the CMHS had published a series of twenty-five volumes, each presenting a single genre, with an extensive introduction placing the music in historical and musical context. Throughout this book, these volumes are referred to as CMH plus the volume number (for example, CMH6); see References for complete titles of these volumes. *The Historical Anthology of Canadian Music (HACM)* is an anthology of 152 compositions from the CMHS volumes. The CMHS also developed an on-line inventory of Canadian compositions prior to 1950. This inventory, containing some 30,500 works, can be searched under various categories including place, date, genre, title, and composer; it is now available at www.cliffordfordpublications.ca.

3 The growing number of books on Canadian music include: George Proctor 1980; Jackson 1994 and 1996; Martin Melhuish 1996; Morey 1997; and Miller 2001.

4 Nägeli's advertisement in the *Allgemeine musikalische Zeitung* for 25 May 1803 read: "I am interested mainly in piano solos in the grand style, large in size, and with many departures from the usual form of the sonata ... distinguished by their wealth of detail and full sonorities. Artistic piano figuration must be interwoven with contrapuntal phrases" (Jones 1999, 9).

5 'Highbrow,' first used in the 1880s to describe intellectual or aesthetic superiority, and 'lowbrow,' first used shortly after 1900 to mean someone or something neither 'highly intellectual' or 'aesthetically refined,' were derived from the phrenological terms 'highbrowed' and 'lowbrowed,' which were prominently featured

in the nineteenth-century practice of determining racial types and intelligence by measuring cranial shapes and capacities" (Levine 1988, 221–2). In the latter half of the nineteenth century, "cultural" values were distinguished vertically; the fine, the worthy, and the beautiful were viewed as existing apart from ordinary society. "In 1894 Hiram M. Stanley defined the 'masses' as those whose sole delight rested in 'eating, drinking, smoking, society of the other sex, with dancing, music of a noisy and lively character, spectacular shows, and athletic exhibitions' ... This practice of distinguishing 'culture' from lesser forms of expression became so common that by 1915 Van Wyck Brooks concluded that between the highbrow and the lowbrow 'There is no community, no genial middle ground'" (Levine 1988, 225).

6 "As the traditional spatial distinctions among pit, gallery, and boxes within the theatre were undermined by the aggressive behavior of audiences caught up in the egalitarian exuberance of the period and freed in the atmosphere of the theatre from many of the demands of normative behavior, this urge gradually led to the creation of separate theatres catering to distinct audiences and shattered for good the phenomenon of theater as a social microcosm of the entire society" (Levine 1988, 60).

7 "Matilda Despard congratulated New York operagoers and urged them to keep progressing along the neat evolutionary path she laid out, which had thus far taken them 'through quaint old English operettas, English versions of Italian and German operas, pure Italian and German compositions of Rossini, Bellini, Verdi, Spohr, Weber, and Mendelssohn, up to the present high development of taste for and appreciation of Meyerbeer, Gounod, Schumann, and colossal Richard Wagner'" (Levine 1988, 102).

8 "In 1877 the *Atlantic Monthly* distinguished between 'false culture' and 'real culture' and reminded its readers that not everyone had the capacity to acquire culture ... John Sullivan Dwight labored to teach his readers to distinguish between 'pure art' and 'skill,' between 'mere music and the art of music'" (Levine 1988, 218).

9 Smith 1995, 39. Smith continues "The first to describe the virtues of folk music in France, and to champion its cause, were Romantic writers such as Chateaubriand, Champfleury, Gérard de Nerval, and George Sand. Believing in the intrinsic value of oral tradition, and an exalted notion of the 'folk,' these writers employed the technique of incorporating folksong texts into their literary works in order to provide local colour, and to illustrate more vividly the qualities of peasant life."

10 I can recall in 1970 Dr. Arnold Walter railing against the *Globe & Mail* for placing coverage of symphony concerts and operas in the "Entertainment" section. He, of course, was taking a European and American "high culture" point of view. Today the "Arts" section of most Canadian newspapers covers everything from symphony concerts, to jazz, folk music, rock, movies, literature, painting, sculpture, and performance art.

11 There is no commonly accepted label (except, perhaps, the term "legit," used by musicians such as Tommy Banks to distinguish the repertoire of symphonies, opera, etc. from jazz or "popular musical idioms.") The term "legitimate" is derived from theatre where it designates drama acted on stage, as opposed to motion pictures and other stage entertainment such as vaudeville or burlesque. I think "legitimate" can also account for differences in non-Western musics where religious institutions and/or the nobility encouraged the rise of highly-developed musical expression based on, but different from, oral folk or modern media-influenced musics found in the same country or area. Various other terms – such as "vernacular" instead of "popular" and "art music" to replace "classical music" – have been propounded. Bonds illustrates how these alternatives break down on close inspection and states that the two categories are "not mutually exclusive" and that their contents do not remain static at any one period. Any distinction attempted "is conceptually fuzzy and impossible to define in any consistent way" (2003, 610). Accordingly he concludes: "Music of all kinds can be fruitfully studied and performed from both an art and popular point of view. Neither is superior to the other. Both are legitimate, and both represent valid ways of making – and listening to – music" (611). Most commonly, legitimate musical expressions are lumped under "classical," but this term is also used to refer to European- and European-derived works written ca. 1740–1825. Even if a wider historical designation is alluded to, it rarely encompasses pre-1700 notated European chants and dances or post-1900 compositions involving organized electroacoustic sound. "Refined" can suggest that at the end of the spectrum composers of this type of music normally aim to produce something different by giving themselves a challenge to try to solve. Whereas at the other end of the spectrum for so-called popular commercial music, the practitioner, for example, Chad Kroeger of Nickelback, studies carefully previous commercial successes to derive an effective model.

12 For example, the practice of performing Handel's *Messiah* during the Christmas season began in the early 1800s in centres such as Halifax and Quebec City, but was not done until the early 1980s in Yellowknife, Northwest Territories.

13 For example, many important Canadian works (such as, Calixa Lavallée's *Patrie*, the first Canadian orchestral work to be performed in Europe), have never been recorded. Unfortunately, none of the Canada Music Fund programs of Canadian Heritage address the lack of recordings of earlier Canadian compositions. The "Canadian Music Memories Program" is concerned only with making existing recordings available in modern format. Mark Miller points out that before 1980 Canadian jazz musicians were largely unrecorded (Miller 2001, v). It will take much sleuthing through extant self-recorded gigs and radio broadcasts to put together a full history of Canadian jazz.

14 One of these is *Oh! What a Feeling 2*. Unfortunately even the excellent set of Mercury recordings, *A Folksong Portrait of Canada* and *Singers and Songs of Canada*, are no longer available. Instead readers are directed to reissues of the

Folkways recordings from which much of the Mercury material was drawn (see www.folkways.si.edu).

15 CBC Radio Two "In Performance" 8 May 2002.

16 Ghaznavi 2002, 86; she continues, "It is therefore apt when one walks into the exhibition 'Landmark,' featuring the work of Robert Houle and John Abrams, that one passes through a room filled with Tom Thomson's work in a gallery named for him. The exhibition ... is a thought-provoking juxtaposition of paintings that brings issues of land, history and memory to the foreground"

17 The term *rubbaboo* has a number of different spellings. It was borrowed from a soup made from pemmican, water, and a flavouring (such as Saskatoon berries) in the Northern Plains area.

18 Duke Redbird was born in 1939 on the Saugeen Reserve, Bruce Peninsula, near Owen Sound, Ontario. He is a writer, former president of the Ontario Métis Association, and a reporter. He wrote "I Am a Canadian" for presentation to Queen Elizabeth II in Ottawa on 17 October 1977. This text is reproduced here with kind permission of the author.

CHAPTER TWO

1 Amerindian is a term coined by the Indigenous historian Olive Dickason. Designations used in Canada include First Peoples, First Nations; Aboriginal is used by the Canadian government for Aboriginal Day (21 June) and the Aboriginal Portal website. In the United States the terms, Indian and Native American are more common. George Herzog (1923) and Helen Roberts (1930) devised the first mappings of regional stylistic areas and Bruno Nettl (1954) delineated six musical areas in North America, but numerous cultures (including a large number in Canada) had not been studied at all; Marcia Herndon (1980) refers to these attempts at classification without adequate research as "fossils."

2 In some cases, however, there is no agreement among branches considered to be the given culture; in such cases, I have tried to use designations most commonly found today. It is unfortunate that publications such as the multi-volume *Handbook of North American Indians* (1978–) and *The Gale Encyclopedia of Native American Tribes* (1998) have in many cases used misattributions.

3 There is no agreed definition of what constitutes a living language, but since 1995, languages have been resurrected through older recordings or the knowledge of a single elder. Ida Halpern, a comparative musicologist, came to Vancouver in 1939 and over the next four decades worked with informants of several major cultures, including the Kwakiutl, recording traditional materials and ethnographic information. She recorded more than 500 songs, many of which were released on Folkways recordings along with detailed liner notes and analysis. Halpern was the first to argue the importance of vocables as a structural feature. As of 2002, extensive studies of musical expressions had been done for only nine of the twenty major Northwest Coast linguistic groups: these studies include

Barbeau (1951) for Nisga and Gitksan Tsimshian; Densmore (1939) for Makah; Kolstee (1982) for Bella Coola; Roberts and Swadesh (1955) for Tseshaht and Opetchesaht Nootka; Stuart (1972) for Central Coast Salish; de Laguna (1972) for Yakutat Tlingit; Halpern for Kwakiutl (Folkways 4122, released 1981) and for Haida (Folkways 4119, released 1986); Enrico and Stuart (1996) for Masset Haida.

4 Chief Don Assu of the Kwagiulth considers all traditional songs, except those used in the gambling game of lahal, to be owned and thus not appropriate to be heard outside Kwagiulth territory (personal communication 2002).

5 "Potlach" is a Chinook jargon word meaning "to give" (Coull 1996, 10). Residents of the Northwest Coast area often spoke three or four languages for trade purposes. Chinook is a newer language developed to facilitate trade. Initially Chinook used only Salishan and Wakashan words, but later French and English terms were added; it was used into the early twentieth century (12).

6 "During the singing of each person's songs, members of his family lineage wore mourning masks" (Hawthorn 1979, 36). The Mourning Song of Ha'etla'las, Mamalilikala, begins with a five-pulse pattern with percussive beats on one, three, and five. The solo voice enters with short undulating phrases (about a 6th in range), followed by a male unison chorus singing similar phrases; then the soloist sings a syncopated chant about an octave higher than the lowest pitch (the tonal centre) of the melody. For recordings of some of these songs, see the CD *Rising from the ashes* UCCCD-9901 (U'mista Cultural Society). I am grateful to Andrea Sanborn of the U'mista Cultural Society for reviewing this material and providing current spellings.

7 The terms for love and mourning are identical in Kwakwaka'wakw. A phrase in English translation – "Whenever I eat, I eat the pain of your love, mistress" (Boas 1921, 348) – indicates the sombre nature of love songs.

8 The U'mista Cultural Society website and www.nativedrums.ca have illustrations of items that have been returned.

9 "The chief, while he was making a speech, shook the rattle to emphasize what he was saying. The chief's rattle was held always pointed downward ... the general form ... was that of a bird, the handle being the tail, the back of the bird a platform on which assorted small figures were carved, and the belly emphasized by a bird's face and beak" (Hawthorn 1976, 95).

10 "The women moved their feet only, but the men carried a stick or bone 'dagger' in their right hand, 'which they keep extended above the head, in continual motion.' Their left arm was extended horizontally and moved back and forth, 'while they leap about ... to the measure of the music, always bringing their heels close to each other at every pause" (Abel 1993, 39).

11 Athapaskan drums have one to three snares fastened either above or below the skin; Dogrib drums normally have two snares above the skin. An example can be viewed at www.nativedrums.ca.

12 In Dogrib territory, *Lila nats 'I to t'a dagowo* was probably influenced by settler contact and may date from the mid-twentieth century.

13 Singing Love Songs reconfirms the social values of the Dene, a society based on respect for the elders; the ideal was to develop friendship with all peoples, and the worst crime was to deny food to another person. Listening to and learning Songs of the Land inculcates enjoyment of the Land and knowledge about how the Dene have survived in their terrain since time immemorial.

14 These vocal pulsations, usually coinciding with the pulse of the song, are created with the diaphragm.

15 Samuel Hearn, writing between 1769 and 1772, documented a dance song performed at night using the vocables "hee, hee, ho, ho" and accompanied by a drum and sometimes a rattle "made with a piece of dried buffalo hide skin" (Hearne 1911, 318).

16 In his fieldnotes, James Teit gives the following account of the reception of a protective song: "He [a Nlaka'pamux] had a dream and believed he was travelling east over a mountainous semi-open country. Coming to the foot of a long grassy slope he heard singing and looked up, saw a grizzly bear coming down the slope from the east and the sun was just rising over him. The grizzly was singing this song as he traveled along. When he came to the middle of the slope [he] thought: 'The bear must come no further, if he comes to me he may harm me. He must go back.' The grizzly at once knew or heard his thoughts and turning around went back up the slope singing until he was out of sight. [He] woke up and immediately sang this song he had heard the grizzly singing. The grizzly bears were friendly with him and there was a bond between him and them. He obtained certain powers and knowledge from them and they were his protectors" (Teit 1915–21, VI.M.93).

17 Soon after the kill the hunter would address the bear with deep respect, often weeping, and asking for pity for having killed him, but also gratefulness for the bear's generosity (Teit 1915–21, VI.M.79)

18 Among the Nlaka'pamux, the father of twins, immediately after their birth, put on a headband and went outside and walked around the house in a circle hitting the ground with a fir-bough and singing the song. A young man was engaged by the parents to sing the song whenever the babies cried walking around them four times, and during the first month at least four times a day (Teit 1915–21, VI.M.122).

19 Teit's informants indicate that words and vocables were placed with these pitches as follows: "(1) words used by the Manitou when the protégé obtained the song; (2) words used by the singer descriptive of the incident of obtaining the song; (3) words descriptive of the appearance and peculiarities of the Manitou; (4) words descriptive of the Manitou's powers; 5) words describing the powers of the protégé's power; (6) words spoken by the protégé to the Manitou; (7) words in praise of the latter; (8) supplication of the Manitou; (9) words spoken familiarly or jokingly to the Manitou" (Teit 1915–21, VI.M.96).

20 The three major dialect divisions of the Cree dialect are the Plains Cree Hakawiyiniwak (Alberta and Saskatchewan), Woods Cree Paskwyn-wiyiwak (Saskatchewan and Manitoba), and Swampy Cree Naskakowak (Manitoba, Ontario,

Quebec); the following discussion is limited to Cree dependent on the bison. The first European description of the Cree is by Father Pierre-Gabriel Marest, who travelled among the Cree with Le Moyne d'Iberville in 1694–95: "The Crees are numerous and their country is much the larger ... [The Assiniboin] are sedate and seem to be phlegmatic. The Crees are more sprightly, always in motion, always dancing or singing. Both are brave and love war" (Marest 1968, 123–4).

21 During the ritual voices and rattle sounds were heard wildly beating against the sides of a tent one metre square and two metres high made of four strong posts and rawhide (Dion 1979, 56). Eastern Cree songs and stories can be heard on www.carleton.ca/ecree/en/index.html.

22 Buffy Sainte-Marie plays a mouth bow on the video *Buffy Sainte-Marie: Up Where We Belong*, CBC/Astral A1107.

23 Anishinaabeg is the plural form; the singular is Anishinaabe.

24 Wild rice was a staple of the Great Lakes or "three fires" cultures: the Potawatomi, who safeguarded fire on the ancient migratory path, the Odawa (Ottawa) who looked after trading, and the Ojibwe who protected spiritual beliefs.

25 Manidog is the plural of manitou.

26 Frances Densmore did most of her fieldwork among Ojibwe in the United States. However, she recorded eleven dream songs sung by Awûn'akûm'ïgĭckûṅ, who came from the Canadian side. These songs could be used for various dances and other purposes, even though they were considered personal in nature and came from supernatural sources. Other classifications used by Densmore include war songs (war medicine, war charms, war expedition, and war success), love songs, moccasin game songs, a Begging Dance (acquired from the Sioux), gift songs, Pipe Dance songs, songs for children, and Woman's Dance songs (acquired from the Sioux). Songs connected with the *Midé*, include those for ceremonies, initiation, dying chief, success, curing, medicine, and love-charms. Older songs in the Densmore collection have a descending contour ending on the tonal centre and using three to five pitches; each song is normally performed four times.

27 The keeper of the pipe removed it from the case, performed prayers and chants, offered it skyward, earthward, and to the four cardinal points, then danced it around the central fire. The pipe was then passed to each celebrant in turn to dance with it (Johnson 1976, 140–41).

28 A moccasin game is a gambling game in which two pairs of moccasins are used to conceal four objects, one of which is specially marked.

29 The Seventh Fire prophecy of the Anishinabe (the Northern Algonkian-speaking cultures) refers to seven eras of human history. There are various versions, all of which foretell an Eighth Fire or golden age when all peoples, red, yellow, black, and white, will choose to cooperate together. Algonquin Elder William Commanda of Kitigan Zibi near Maniwaki, Quebec – the keeper of three wampum belts, one of which is the Seventh Fire Prophecy belt made in the 1400s – teaches that people of the world have to choose the red road of spirituality and respect for the earth rather than the black road of technology and over-development. Otherwise the earth cannot survive.

30 For fine examples from the Innuat culture see Diamond, Cronk, and von Rosen 1994, 125.

31 In 1634, Jesuits estimated their population to be at least 40,000.

32 Archeological evidence dates back to the Norse settlement at L'anse aux meadows in northern Newfoundland, ca. 1000. Interchange with the Norse is suggested by the range of hair colour indicated in an early seventeenth-century description of the Beothuks; see Howley 1974, 17.

33 John Cabot claimed to have visited Nova Scotia and Labrador in 1498 and in 1501 the Portuguese Gaspar Corte-Real captured fifty-seven Amerindians – possibly Beothuks. In 1534 Cartier forced the sons of Donnacona, Taioagny and Domagaya to go to France with him in 1534 (Sioui 1992, 42); after returning them home in 1535 Cartier abducted ten more Amerindians, including a young girl. Another epidemic occurred in 1535–36 just after Cartier's trip, and these scourges became ever more virulent and devastating in the early 1600s.

34 The Mi'kmaq sea-going canoes were originally made of dehaired oil-soaked moose skins stretched over a frame, with upright leafy branches to deter whales and other large sea mammals (Whitehead 1991, 20–1). During winter they travelled by toboggan (a Mi'kmaq word) with dogs.

35 In 1616 Father Biard at Port-Royal described the yearly hunting and fishing cycle of the Mi'kmaq: see Thwaites 1959, 3: 79–83.

36 "During the first era, animals, including terrifying monsters, dominated the earth. People were insignificant. The beginning of the second era was heralded by the arrival of a transformer, Glooscap, who banished the monsters and readied the earth for people. People and animals spoke the same language. Glooscap lived among people, and taught them how to live. When Glooscap departed [singing a song] the third era began. People and animals could no longer communicate easily with each other. Only men and women gifted with extraordinary powers could keep up the ancient connection. Glooscap lives with his friends and is master of the weather and sea. In the fourth era to come Glooscap will return to the people" (Leavitt 1995, 92).

37 *Inuksuit* is the plural form; the singular form is *inukshuk*.

38 *The Central Eskimo*, the first major monograph on the Inupiat-speaking peoples within Canada, is a product of the time Boas spent on Baffin Island between 1883 and 1888 for cartographic work on Baffin Island. Four of the transcriptions in this publication come from other sources; the rest are drawn from his own experience.

39 This distinction of *pisik* and *aton* is based on the fieldwork of Richard Leveillé, Montréal. The terms are referred to in *Songs of the Copper Eskimos* (Roberts and Jenness 1925), but distinctions are based on the drum used by the performer in the *pisik*, and possibly no drum at all in the *aton*.

40 This information was kindly provided by Debbie Gordon-Ruben of the Inuvialuit Drumming/Dancing group. The group was formed in 1989 to learn old songs from the elders. Currently groups in Aklavik, Inuvik, Tutoyaktuk, Paulatuq, and

Holman (Ulukhaqtuuq) meet weekly to practise, and also perform at community functions. The Inuvialuit use a squeaker – a form of wooden whistle – to attract muskrats within shooting range.

CHAPTER THREE

1 "And ... more than a thousand people came out to greet us ... making great signs of joy, for the men danced in one band, the women in another, and the children also, after which they brought stores of fish and of bread made from Indian corn" (Cartier 1865, 9).

2 The most important musical components of the mass are the five sections that make up the Ordinary: Kyrie, Gloria, Credo, Sanctus, and Agnus Dei. The sections that make up the Proper vary according to liturgical function and date in the church year. These sections come in the following order, with intervening spoken prayers and lessons in parentheses: Introit, Kyrie, Gloria, (Collect; Epistle), Gradual, Alleluia/Tract, Sequence/Prose, (Gospel), (Homily), Credo, (General Intercession), Offertory, (Preface), Sanctus, Benedictus, (Eucharistic prayers, Pater noster), Agnus Dei, Communion, (Post-Communion prayer). Mass often ends with a sung *Ite missa est*, and the order of the individual items may vary to a degree. Other musical insertions include hymns (sometimes with vernacular texts) and motets (usually with Latin texts). Motets were often performed during the Eucharistic ritual either by solo singers or a small choir, often with instrumental accompaniment. They were usually set in a polyphonic style, but monophonic settings were used if musical resources were limited. The Offices (eight worship services performed at intervals through the day and night) are also a combination of constant and variable elements that vary through the year. One of the most frequently set Office texts is the *Magnificat*, which comes near the end of Vespers.

3 A soldier, Sieur de Champigny, was able to sing the treble part (Thwaites 1959, 28:249). The account of Christmas observances for the same year gives us some idea of how frequently high mass was heard with singing: "We rang [a bell] on Christmas eve, at 11 o'clock; ... at midnight ... we began the *Te Deum*, and then mass. I [Jerome Lalemont] said two masses ... one high, and one low; Father Vimont afterward said two ... Father Gabriel Lalement said two, and the 3rd at the Ursulines.' I said high mass at 8 o'clock, and Father Defretat, afterward, his 3 masses" (Thwaites 1959, 28: 249, 251).

4 While there were a few Calvinist ministers and settlers in Acadia and New France, the growing strength of the counter-Reformation had made it possible for Roman Catholic authorities to ban Huguenot missionaries and, with the repeal of the Edict of Nantes in 1685, to outlaw the Reformed Church. Most Huguenots either became Roman Catholics or practised their Protestant faith in secret, but extant books from New France in this period include a French Bible published in Geneva in 1642 and music for the Psalms sung by Huguenot Calvinists.

5 Although the various orders followed different rules, the Roman style of liturgical practise prevailed with some local variation in the parishes, missions, and religious communities. This meant that ritual was more important than in most Parisian parishes. Noting the variation in rules used in New France, Mgr de Saint-Vallier, the second bishop of Quebec, published the *Rituel du diocèse de Québec* (Paris: Simon Langlois, 1703), a document that laid down rules for the rites, and sacraments, the calendar of feast days (including Saint Joseph, Saint Francis-Xavier, and *La sainte famille*, which were specific to New France) and also contained some plainchant (Dubois and Gallat-Morin 1995, 71).

6 This treaty, recorded on a great wampum belt, was made on the urging of Pesamoet, the Grand Captain of the Mi'kmaqs, who had spent a year in Paris and recognized the need for establishing good relations. Under the terms of the *Concordat* the Mi'kmaqs agreed to protect priests and French Catholic settlers.

7 When Antoine Gaulin arrived in 1713 he found the Mi'kmaqs carefully using hieroglyphic leaflets for morning, noon, and evening prayers (Schmidt and Marshall 1995, 8). After the death of Pierre Maillard in 1762 the Mi'kmaqs had no ministering priest until the mid-nineteenth century, but the *Concordat* gave leaders of their own community the right to perform the church rituals of baptism, marriage, and funerals.

8 Laval was accustomed to the Ursuline practise in Paris where only psalms and hymns were sung in the simple recitation style of plain chant. Marie de l'Incarnation came from Tours where Ursuline musical practises included ornamentation of plain chant and polyphonic renditions. In a letter of 1661 she wrote: "Our singing has almost been all cut out. He is leaving us only our Vespers and our Tenebrae, which we sing as you did when I was at Tours. He wants High Mass to be chanted in *recto tono* [monotone], with no regard for what is done either at Paris or at Tours but only for what his spirit suggests to him is for the best. He fears that singing encourages vanity in ourselves and complacency in outsiders. We no longer sing at Mass, because, he says, this is distracting to the celebrant and he has never seen it elsewhere" (Marshall 1967, 259).

9 Martin, the second Canadian to be ordained priest, was subsequently assigned to Ste-Foy and was canon at the Cathedral in Quebec City. The Prose was later translated into Abenaki. A copy of Nivers' *Graduale romanum* (Paris, 1697) belonging to the Quebec Seminary has an Abenaki translation written into it. Other manuscripts consist of works with French, Latin, and various First Nations languages for plainchant, canticles, faux-bourdon, polyphonic motets, hymns such as *Veni Creator, Pange Lingua, Te Deum, and Salve Regina*, Litanies, psalm tones, and various masses.

10 Documentation indicates that there were at least two published copies of *Cantates françoises* by Elisabeth Jacquet de La Guerre (1665–1729) in New France; one of these was sent to Marie de l'Incarnation. La Guerre's stature as a distinguished composer at the French court would have been an inspiration for the compositional efforts of women in New France.

11 Translation of the text for figure 3.2: Sing ye to the Lord a new canticle. Let his praise be in the church of the saints. For the Lord is well pleased with his people, and he will exalt the meek unto salvation. This motet has been recorded on *L'Épopée mystique: Marie Guyart de l'Incarnation, Les Ursulines et Augustines Te Deum*, Anthologie de musique historique du Québec, vol. 4, S-190906.

12 For example, the organ should not overshadow the choir or play too long or elaborately. The organist should alternate with the choir in the Kyrie, Gloria, Sanctus, Magnificat, and other canticles. In a Kyrie the organ played the odd presentations through nine while the choir sang the second, fourth, sixth, and eighth renditions.

13 "*Récits* are played on the *Cornet*, the *Tierce*, the *Cromhorne*, the *Trompette* or the *Voix humaine*, sometimes in a dialogue between two organ colours" (Gallat-Morin and Gilbert 1988, xiii).

14 Barbeau points out that although the texts of these songs show ingenious structures, they are not the product of the troubadour/ trouvère lineage that descended from medieval Latin prosody. Although they were mocked by troubadours and minstrels for their lack of writing skill, *jongleurs* travelled from place to place so many people heard and remembered their renditions of events and feelings. The *jongleurs* had disappeared from France by the end of the sixteenth century (two hundred years after the troubadours died out), just as printing and broadsides became more prevalent. Some monophonic songs that may have been perpetuated or even created by the *jongleurs* were written down; indeed more than 250 monophonic secular songs with French texts have been found in manuscripts dating from 1490 to 1520 (Rahn 1988, 16). These song texts differ substantially from the courtly chansons ca. 1500, but they have similar characteristics to those found in French-Canadian folk songs. The use of assonance, half-rhyme, and non-rhyme; erratic use of the unaccented e; syllable counts varying from line to line; ten-syllable lines divided into five-plus-five, not the courtly four-plus-six; the non-courtly laisse form of approximately isosyllabic lines all ending in the same syllable; the non-elite imbricative usage in which the last half of one verse becomes the first half of the next; refrains constructed in a parallel manner so that the second half is a modified form of the first, again a practise that would not be favoured at court (Rahn 1988, 17–18).

15 Apart from love songs, these themes include: *chansons narratives* (ballads, *complaintes*), *de mal mariés et malmariées* (unhappy marriages), *d'aventuriers* (adventurers), *politiques* (political), *historiques* (historical), *pastourelles* (shepherds or shepherdesses), *rustiques* (country life), *satiriques* (satirical), *grivoises* (licentious), *sottes* (silly), and *bachiques* (drinking) (Rahn 1988, 20).

16 In Laforte's *laisse* catalogue, *À la claire fontaine* is G-10, with a line structure of 12: 6f – 6m(*é*); see appendix B.

17 For example, if there are the seven pitches (as in a major scale), the seventh note does not usually rise to the tonic or tonal centre. Instead, the tonal centre is approached from above as in the older Ionian mode. Dorian and Aeolian modes also appear frequently (Laforte and Kelher 1997, 1: 54).

18 The Poitou *cornemuse* is a bagpipe with one drone. The Scots two-drone and three-drone (Highland) versions of bagpipes likely arrived with the early Scottish settlers (Gibson 1998, 157).

19 The fife is a small transverse flute with six holes.

20 *Vaudevilles* (or *voix de villes*) are short, folk-like melodies with a narrow range, a persistent rhythmic pattern, and occasional irregular phrase structures. Many tunes are of dance origin.

21 Lists of items in Dupuy's library include the following musical items: operas and ballets by Lully (*Acis et Galathée, Achille et Polixène, Alceste, Amadis, Armide, Atys, Bellérophon, Cadmus et Hermione, Persée, Phaëton, Prosperine, Roland, Le temple de la paix, Le triomphe de l'amour, Idylle sur la paix*); *De profundis* by Lully; *Enée et Lavinie*; *Brunettes ou petits airs tendres* (3 vols); *Vaudevilles*; motets by Paolo Lorenzani (in parts, 12 vols); motets by André Campra (2 vols); motets by Nicolas Bernier (2 vols); sonatas by Michel Mascitti (2 vols); sonatas by Arcangelo Corelli (3 vol); cantatas by Nicolas Clérambault (2 vols); works for viol by Marin Marais (2 vols); a treatise on the musette [a French bagpipe]; music books with Italian, French, and Latin texts, both published and manuscript.

22 The serpent was a low-pitched wind instrument often used to support singers in both sacred and secular music.

23 The *bombarde* is commonly known in English as a jaw's harp (Gallat-Morin and Pinson 2003, 376). Most ethnomusicologists avoid the term "Jew's harp" as there is no basis to attach this lamella instrument to the Jewish culture more than any other.

24 Around 1860 a collection of twelve viols was found in a sealed off basement area in Quebec City. They were likely placed there for safety during a bombardment and then forgotten (Emond 1986). Five of these viols can be traced to the present day. One was sold in 1913 to R.S. Williams & Sons and is now at the Royal Ontario Museum (Catalogue 913.1.6; see Cselenyi 1971). Three more – a bass viol made by Nicolas Bertrand in Paris (1720), a dessus by Cabroly of Toulouse (1730), and a dessus by Jean Vuillaume (1743) – are at the Metropolitan Museum in New York (Metropolitan Museum or Art, 1979: see Bertrand 89.4.1343, Cabroly 89.4.1345, Vuillaume 89.4.1344). A letter of 1898 from Mr Smith, who acquired the instruments from the Convent of the Hôpital général in 1861, states that they were played at the convent prior to 1759. Another viol, reconstructed from parts, is at l'Université de Montréal.

25 Madame Elisabeth Bégon (1696–1755) was the widow of the governor of Trois-Rivières. Between November 1748 and April 1753 she wrote numerous letters to her son-in-law in Louisiana describing affairs in Montreal.

26 The letters of the Marquis de Montcalm, 1756–59 contain numerous references to balls and the need to hire musicians (Chapais 1911, 201): "High life in spite of the miseries and impending loss of the colony has been most active in Quebec ... There have never been so many balls and so much gambling" (Chapais 1911, 496, 498; my translation).

CHAPTER FOUR

1 During the winter of 1755, British troops from Halifax were burning the fertile Acadian farms built on reclaimed salt marshes and expelling their owners. Soon they were rounding up any Acadians who had not managed to find refuge with the Mi'kmaqs and placing them on ships bound for France or French territories, using the oath of allegiance issue as an excuse (although most French settlers had become British subjects when the area was ceded to Britain in 1713 under the Treaty of Utrecht). A total of about 6,000 Acadians were expelled, some of whom formed the Cajun communities in Louisiana.

2 The name Canada derives from a Wendat-Iroquois word *kanata*, meaning "settlement." Cartier heard the term in 1534, in reference to Stadacona (the site of Quebec City). In 1603 Champlain referred to the river of Canada, but by 1613 he spoke of the gulf as the St Laurens. Thereafter, "Canada" was used loosely as a synonym for New France. In the *Jesuit Relations* of 1616 and *Historia Canadensis* of 1664, "Canada" is defined as the part of New France extending along the banks of the great River Canada, and the gulf of St Lawrence.

3 Bourassa-Trépanier and Poirier 1990, 19. The complement of paired winds was modelled on the *harmonie*, ensembles of two to twelve instrumentalists employed by the European aristocracy to provide background music at dinners and for social events and to participate in private and public concerts. In France they played *pièces d'harmonie* (short pieces often arranged from operas); in England they played groups of short movements consisting of original music, dances, and military pieces.

4 Dancing assemblies were organized by a group of directors, usually prosperous merchants and military personnel, who booked a location (a café, tavern, private home, hotel, or Mason hall), obtained subscribers and notified them of each event, advertised in newspapers, found partners for new subscribers, hired musicians, and administered the finances (Bourassa-Trépanier and Poirier 1990, 8).

5 Because complex figures were completed by each couple, it could take at least an hour for a set of twenty-five couples to complete a dance. For more details on country dances, see p. 71.

6 Hannah Jarvis, a resident of Newark (Niagara-on-the-Lake) in 1792 described one of the fortnightly balls she attended: "At six o'clock we assembled at the Place appointed – when I was called to open the Ball – Mrs. Hamilton not choosing to dance a minuet – this is the first assembly that I have been at in this country that was opened with a Minuet – not one in the room followed my example – of course Country Dances commenced – and continued until Eleven when supper was announced ... supper being ended the company returned to the Ball room when two Dances finished the night's entertainment with the sober Part of the company. The rest stayed until Daylight and w'd have stay'd longer if their servants had not drank less than their Masters" (Innis 1965, 10). The music for this event was provided by the regimental band of the 5th Fusiliers.

7   This may explain why Hannah Jarvis only danced the minuet once in Canada (see note 6 above).

8   "[The *Dancing Master*] contained the music and directions of dances which were performed by the people now ruling the country. Some of these were derived from folk origins, as were some of the tunes, but the largest proportion were specially arranged by dancing masters, so that they would appear decorous in the new society. Such elements as the high jumping of the Morris, the fertility leaps of La Volta, gay jigging, and couple dances were eschewed. All permitted dances were longways or circular sets, in which many took part and continually changed partners so that there could be no accusation of flirtatious behaviour" (Gravier 1904, 57).

9   There were three basic formations for these dances: circular, longways (*en colonne*) with men on one side and women on the other, and square. Longways dances with couples organized into "sets" were progressive: the "head" couple danced a figure with the second (and sometimes the third) couple. Once they had completed all the figures of the dance, the head couple repeated the process with the next couple(s) down the set, eventually dancing with every couple. At balls or assemblies each couple might have a chance to "call" a dance – i.e. to choose and possibly explain their favourite dance before it began (Feyock 1995, 212).

10 Changes – customary introductions to the dance – included *Le grand rond* (a circle to the left and then back), *Le grand chaine* (grand chain), *moulinet* (mill or star), *Le petit quarre* (small square), and *La queue du chat* (cat's tail) (Feyock 1995, 213).

11 *Le pantalon* was adapted from the French air *Le pantalon / De Madelon / N'a pas de fond*. *L'été* was a complicated country dance popular in 1800. *La poule* was a country dance popular in 1802 that imitated the fowl. *La pastourelle* was a ballad tune played by the cornetist Collinet; it was often replaced by *Trénis*, a dance developed by a famous dance master of the same name. The *Finale* was usually a fast dance, also called the *Galop* (Buckman 1978, 135).

12 In England and northern continental Europe a theatrical jig included a comedic song and dance routine for two to five characters using well-known tunes of the day. By 1674 the dance jig had reached Ireland and the dance has remained closely connected to that country. Meanwhile European dancing masters were also choreographing specific steps.

13 For renditions of some of these dances see the video, *Metis Dance*, by the Edmonton Metis Cultural Dancers. For detailed descriptions of this type of dancing as done by the Gwich'in Athapaskan, see Mishler 1993.

14 This guide states that the polka is danced in 2/4 time with four beats to the bar, three steps on the first three beats, and a rest on the fourth, and that the galop, also in 2/4, is faster with only two steps to the bar (*Canadian Ten-Cent*, 1871, 29–31).

15 Macmillan 1983, 71. A traveller staying in an inn near present-day London, *ca.* 1820 overheard a discussion of this matter: "It appeared from what they said,

that balls had formerly been of frequent occurrence in the settlement; but that the priest, anxious about the spiritual welfare of his parishioners, had issued an order prohibiting the amusement altogether. However, notwithstanding this, dances occasionally took place at private houses in a quiet way. The holy father, when informed that such was the case, determined to put down the evil in an effectual manner, and accordingly sent for the musicians, and told them, that if they continued to exercise their art at balls, they would forfeit every chance of happiness in the next world, and be the means of drawing many souls into the vortex of destruction" (Howison 1821, 214–5).

16 Down East fiddling is a mixture of Scottish, Irish, English, German and American traditions.

17 Much more attention has been paid to the tunes themselves, and the positioning and fingering of the left hand, but a thorough analysis of bowing techniques would include numerous details: the grip on the bow, elbow position, wrist movement, how the bow is pulled, the length used for specific effects, the slant of the bow (and amount of horse hair contacting the strings), as well as types of articulations, ornamentation, bowing changes on repeats.

18 In Prince Edward Island Acadians (who the British allowed to stay after 1763) were joined by Scottish settlers in the late 1700s, and Irish groups began to arrive around 1810.

19 Prior to the eighteenth century the word "ballad" referred to a variety of popular and semi-popular lyric or narrative songs, but with the rise of printed broadsides the term was restricted to popular narrative poetry. Verse forms of ballads date back to the twelfth century, and it is possible that they derive from Latin hymn style: stanzas of rhyming lines with a regular pattern of syllables or accents. Ballad tales are related to medieval romances, particularly lays (narrative poems about a single incident).

20 The 305 ballads in Child's collection are numbered and divided into five categories: (1) ballads from the common stock of international folk-song (magic, romantic and tragic, or chivalry ballads); (2) ballads from late medieval minstrels; (3) ballads of yeoman minstrelsy (including the Robin Hood) ballads; (4) historical ballads (dealing with real, semi-historical, or minor local events); (5) comic songs. These ballads are anonymous, narrative poems, mostly in stanzas of two or four lines, dealing with a single situation, presented dramatically in a series of rapid flashes known as montage. There is much use of dialogue, but the narrator does not intrude or impose a moralistic or didactic tone. Standard descriptive phrases (for example, "twinning branches" or "rose and brier" themes) appear in many ballads.

21 For a discussion of how the basic framework of a dying man who has sent a message to his beloved has been modified with references to Canadian place names and objects, see (Williamson 1991, 10).

22 The narrator is clearly present and the ballad often opens with a phrase such as "Come and hear my song," or "As I went out one day." The last strophe is a moralistic comment on the story. Since many Irish tunes were known in England

at the time and many of the poets were Irish, a high number of broadside tunes have an ABBA structure with the final pitch repeated three times. This description of an Irish song comes from an 1816 issue of the *Dublin Examiner*: "They are for the most part formed of four strains of equal length – the first soft, pathetic and subdued, the second ascends the scale and becomes bold and energetic and impassioned – the third, as the repetition of the second, is sometimes a little varied and more florid, or leads often by a graceful or melancholic cadence to the fourth, which is always a repetition of the first" (O'Neill 1913, 113).

23 For a recording, see *N uair nighidh tu* Folkways FM 4450 (reissued on *A Folksong Portrait of Canada*, CD 1, track 6). The English translation of the text is: "When you wash, splash, dry, the soap will make the clothes neat." For a discussion relating Gaelic text and musical settings, see Sparling 2003.

24 Calvinist tradition initially excluded all musical presentation (including instruments) from church except for metrical psalms sung in the vernacular. Because few tunes fit the psalm texts translated from French into English, the range of music was limited. During the eighteenth century, non-scriptural hymns were gradually introduced into Protestant traditions under the influence of Lutheran thought; Luther had argued that congregations should praise God in song in their own languages.

25 Since the thirteenth century, song schools in Scotland had provided elementary education and music instruction. In England, itinerant singing masters used publications that included instructions for reading music (such as the 1651 edition of the well-known Sternhold and Hopkins English psalms). This tradition of singing-master instruction spread to North America as early as 1710, when a singing school was reported in Virginia (Britton 1950, 61). In 1721, two important instruction books (*A Very Plain and Easy Introduction to the Singing of Psalm Tunes* by John Tufts and *The Grounds and Rules of Music Explained, or An Introduction to the Art of Singing by Note*, by Thomas Walters) were published to fill a demand for instruction in the Boston area. Soon most compilations of hymn tunes included a simplified explanation of musical notation. In the Thirteen Colonies there were about 160 tune books published before 1801 in either oblong (longboy) or normal format; eighty-eight of these contained music instruction (Britton 1950, 6, 129)

26 These anthems were more demanding compositions, similar to motets, with solo sections, choruses, and instrumental sections.

27 This collection, published in 1761, is the first American collection with original compositions and settings in four parts (as well as two and three). Except for the six original compositions and the anthems, only the music is given but the tunes are organized according to metrical count. For example, a tune labelled 8686 could be used for any text that had four-line strophes with alternating eight- and six-syllable lines. The 8686 syllabic formation also occurs frequently in broadside songs.

28 The catholic tastes of the British are reflected in the wide range of current and historical European and English works heard in London at the Hanover Square

Series, the Vauxhall Gardens, and the Ancient Concerts, and the first histories of music were published by Englishmen. In *A General History of the Science and Practice of Music*, John Hawkins argues that music must be understood in terms of what was actually being performed now and what was still valuable from the past to be heard (Weber 1994, 515). Throughout his extensive travels in Europe, Charles Burney wrote about current musical practises, alerting the British to significant developments abroad. This broad canon of musical works was transplanted to the Canadian scene.

29 In eighteenth-century England the word "opera" was used loosely to refer to any stage production that included music, but other terms were also used. Masques were short dramas with recitatives, solos, and ensembles, frequently interpolated into larger spectacles. Pantomimes (often used as afterpieces) had continuous music but the subject material was lighter; a mime character was accompanied by instrumental numbers based on popular folk melodies, and the other characters sang in aria and recitative style. In a pastorale, spoken dialogue in rhyming verse was interspersed with songs (usually of folk or popular origin). Ballad operas had simple, strophic songs (often adapted from folk songs) with tunes composed by the compiler or adapted from other composers; the first well-known English example is *The Beggar's Opera*, produced in 1728. Burlesques had spoken dialogue interspersed with songs or with newly composed continuous music in the style of folk tunes, and they often satirized other stage works. Comic operas had spoken dialogue along with newly-composed music in a variety of styles from simple airs to complex arias and ensembles; after the success of *Love in a Village* in 1762 at Covent Garden, they became the vogue on the London stage.

30 M. Dolmont has raised his foster-daughter, Colinette, and now wants her to marry the man of her choice. However, the Bailiff is enamoured with Colinette and would like to make her his wife. Toward this end he does not hesitate to dupe Colas who is Colinette's beloved when Colas asks the Bailiff for assistance in asking for Colinette's hand from M. Dolmont. Colinette sees through the Bailiff's deceit and is not impressed with his wealth. She prefers the honest peasant Colas so the opera ends on a happy note.

CHAPTER FIVE

1 Southesk (1969) speaks of a food "rubaboo" (fried pemmican flavoured with Saskatoon berries), but does not use the term to refer to the songs he heard. Toma, his Iroquois cook, and Baptiste, his wagon driver, sang canoe songs, probably of French origin, while Matheson, a Scotsman, sang "snatches of gay songs all the day" (302, 47).

2 Stephen Humbert (1766/7–1849), a Loyalist who came to New Brunswick in 1783, organized Saint John's first Methodist congregation in 1791 and in 1796 opened a sacred vocal music school. No copy of the first edition *Union Harmony* (1801) has been located. The second edition (1816) was advertised as "three hundred pages of Select English, American and Original Music, adapted to Devotional

and Scholastic Exercises ... this Edition will be sold much cheaper than music Books introduced from the United States" (Farquharson 1983, 19). Later editions appeared in 1831, and 1840.

3 The fa-sol-la system current in seventeenth-century Europe used the syllables *fa–sol–la–fa–so–la–mi–fa*. In the eighteenth century, "to sing by note" meant to sing with the fa-sol-la syllables. A French seven-syllable system (*ut–re–mi–fa–sol–la–si*) was advocated in some American tunebooks beginning in the 1760s (Britton 1950, 199), and the Italians adopted the syllables *pa–sol–la–se–do–re–me*. During the nineteenth century solmization was connected with the concepts of major and minor keys (Taddie 1991, 47).

4 Mason's preferences can be seen in the title of his *Collection of Church Music as used by the Boston Handel and Haydn Society* (1822), and his efforts led to the inclusion of vocal music as a required subject in the public schools of Boston in 1837. The archives at Sharon include copies of two publications by Mason: *The Odeon* (ca. 1837), a collection of secular tunes, and *The Boston Anthem Book* (1839) (Schau 1985, 84–5).

5 Benoit was inspired by the *Montagnards basques*, a French touring company directed by Alfred Rolland. The choir was later known as Les Orphéonistes de Montréal (1864).

6 "Jacob, the Mohawk ... danced Scotch reels with more ease and grace than any person I ever saw ... A large party from the garrison to dinner. A boat with music accompanied them; we heard it in the evening until they had passed the town." (Simcoe 1965, 174).

7 There is no record of which Beethoven and Mozart symphonies were performed. Since the program for a concert given by 100–150 amateur and professional instrumentalists at St George's Church on 25 June 1845 included Beethoven's Symphony no. 1 and a "Sinfonia" by Mozart, it is likely that these works were repeated for the Philharmonic concert (Keillor 1997, 55). A concert on 23 March 1846 included Mozart's *Linz* symphony, K 425. Because of the difficulties of obtaining scores and instrumental parts for larger works in Canada (a situation that lasted well into the twentieth century), the same works may have been repeated at a number of concerts.

8 David Sale (1868, 43) made a systematic analysis of the repertoire presented by three organizations operating in Toronto and worked out percentages for eight European composers

	Metropolitan Choral Society 1856–66	Toronto Musical Union 1862	John Carter's Concerts 1864–67
Bellini	—	—	6.3%
Beethoven	—	6.0%	—
Handel	35.4%	29.3%	29.9%
Haydn	36.4%	7.5%	9.2%
Mendelssohn	—	14.9%	3.4%
Mozart	2.6%	—	—
Rossini	—	—	2.9%
Verdi	—	—	28.2%

9 The musical urban-rural division that had emerged in the United States by the mid-nineteenth century was largely due to the activities of Lowell Mason (Kingman 1990, 145f.).

10 Ash, a farmer, made at least seven violins and a dulcimer. "Mozart's Waltz" seems to have been widely known; the same two dance tunes appear in a piano version in the key of C in *The Home Circle* (Boston: Oliver Ditson, 1859), p 55. Another keyboard version (in B flat), published in New York and purchased in 1844 at Nordheimer's in Toronto, was later bound into a volume now held by Library and Archives Canada in Ottawa.

11 The Mechanics' Institute played an important role in the establishment of public halls in Canada. The first Mechanics' Institutes in Canada were in Montreal (1828), York (1830), and Saint John (1840); by 1895, there were 311 in Ontario. No records indicate the presence of music books in the Mechanics' Institute lending libraries but some music magazines were available in the reading rooms. Music periodicals were an important source for notated music, and they also provided a publishing outlet for Canadian composers.

12 Charles Hamm underlines Russell's multicultural role in establishing a new type of popular song for North America: "an English-born Jew who studied in Italy, first came to Canada, and then furnished Americans with songs in an Italian musical style, mostly to texts reflecting an Irish type of nostalgia" (1979, 184).

13 Tickets for this event cost a minimum of three dollars. Members of Lind's company for the two Toronto concerts were clarinetist Signor E. Belletti, singer Signor Salvi, pianist Otto Goldschmidt, and violinist Joseph Burke. Lind sang the Prayer "Und ob die Wolke" from Weber's *Der Freischütz*; the recitative "Ah mie fedeli" and aria "Ma la sola" from Bellini's *Beatrice di Tenda*; the cavatina "Raimbaut" from Meyerbeer's *Robert le diable*; "Bird Song" by Taubert; a Scotch ballad "John Anderson My Jo"; and The Echo Song, a Norwegian melody. Belletti played his own Fantasia on themes from Bellini's *La Sonnambula*; Salvi sang "Una furtiva lagrima" from Donizetti's *L'Elisir d'amore* and the cavatina "In terra di divisera" from Mercadante's *Illustri Rivali*; Goldschmidt played Thalberg's Fantasia on themes from Auber's *Masaniello* and his own "Reverie"; Burke played a Fantasia "Le Tremolo" by De Bériot, on a theme by Beethoven.

14 In February 1848 the twenty-five young men of The Germania Musical Society in Berlin signed an agreement that included the following statement of purpose: "[T]o further in the hearts of this politically free people [USA] the love of the fine art of music through performance of masterpieces of the greatest German composers of Bach, Haydn, Mozart, Beethoven, Spohr, Schubert, Mendelssohn, Schumann; also Liszt, Berlioz, and Wagner" (Johnson 1953, 75).

15 Gottschalk's observations and comments reveal some of his own prejudices, such as his contempt for the French spoken in Canada and his cynicism regarding the Roman Catholic church, but his remarks vividly confirm the performance of shortened versions of grand operas.

16 For a thorough analysis of women's participation and the connotations of class and society at the time in a *soirée musicale* given in Toronto in 1844, see Guiguet 2004.

17 Many community bands reflected the situation in the US, where by the mid-nineteenth century there were three types of bands: woodwind and brass; brass bands; and "cornet" bands (Shive 1997, 449).

18 The Longueil manuscript contains French, English, and Irish folk songs, some American tunes (including Negro sand jigs, plantation dances and walk rounds), plus a few current dances and marches. Titles include: *God Save the Queen*, *À la claire fontaine*, *À St-Malo*, *Margot*, *Buy a Broom*, *Marche russe*, *Le petit tambour*, *Cracovienne*, *En roulant*, *Marche de l'echo*, *Canadienne*, *Rory O'Moore*, *Dandy Sims*, *Miss Lucy Song*, *Hungarian Waltz*, *Old Dan Tucker*, *Nelson's March*, *Cotillion*, *Jim Crow March*, *Marche des gardes du pape*, and *Marche du sultan*. A private donor gave this manuscript to the Canadian Musical Heritage Society; it is now part of that Fonds at Library and Archives Canada.

19 Three clarinets, three cornets, alto and bass saxo-tromba plus percussion.

20 John F. Lehmann (*ca.* 1795–1850) was choirmaster of Christ Church in Bytown (later Ottawa) after 1839; he also taught piano, violin, guitar, and voice.

21 James Paton Clarke (*ca.* 1807–77) emigrated from Scotland in 1835; in 1846 he received the first bachelor of music degree awarded in Canada.

22 Mark Burnham (1791–1864) was a Loyalist who settled in the Cobourg area. *Colonial Harmonist* was the first tunebook published in Upper Canada. For publication information on *Colonial Harmonist* and the other tunebooks referred to in the following paragraphs, see Appendix 5.A.

23 Alexander Davidson (1794–1856), an Irish immigrant, also compiled the first speller in Upper Canada.

24 Jean-Chrysostome Brauneis II (1814–1871) is probably the first Canadian-born professional musician to study in Europe. On his return to Montreal in 1833 he brought with him the latest approaches in piano pedagogy.

25 The *Canada Union Waltz* was first published in England in 1841 and subsequently reprinted in the periodical *The Albion: or, British, Colonial, and Foreign Weekly Gazette* [New York] 20 (1 January 1842).

26 A.H. Lockett probably lived in the Halifax area, but no biographical information has been discovered to date. The polka has a 2/4 metre with three steps on the first three eighth notes of the bar and a rest on the fourth. The galop, also in 2/4, has a faster tempo with two steps to the bar.

27 George Strathy (1818–1890) was a music teacher who claimed to have studied with Mendelssohn. He was the first Canadian to hold the academic title, "Professor of Music," with an actual attachment to a university. His appointment to the University of Trinity College in 1853 appears to have been incidental, based on students' interest. His doctor of music degree from that institution, received in 1858, is the first known doctorate awarded in Canada.

28 Antoine Dessane heard some of these folk songs shortly after his arrival in Canada in 1849 while on a fishing trip up the St-Charles River, sung by people as they went about their daily work. His *Quadrille canadienne* has five sections, each of which is based on a French Canadian folk tune: no. 1 *Pantalon: La claire fontaine*; no. 2 *Été: Dans les prisons de Nantes*; no. 3 *Poule: C'est la belle cana-*

dienne; no. 4 *Pastourelle: Vive la canadienne*; no. 5 *Galop: Roule ma boule.* The tune is usually heard in the second part of the section, after the first double bar, but in nos. 3 and 5, the tune comes in the chorus section.

29 Ernest Gagnon (1834–1915) originally published *Chansons populaires du Canada,* in six issues of *Le foyer canadien* (1865–67). This collection includes the five tunes Dessane used in his *Quadrille.*

30 Stadacona is the village to which Jacques Cartier was led on his second voyage in 1535 (Keillor 1995b, 191).

31 For example, according to his granddaughter, Antoine Dessane wrote a string quintet with flutes that he orchestrated in 1863.

CHAPTER SIX

1 The program included two works played by the orchestra, three choruses, six songs, a vocal duet and double quartet, a piano quartet (presumably four pianists at two or four pianos), two violin numbers, and concluded with *The Maple Leaf, God Save the King.* Of the composers represented, only Tosti, Mascagni, and Schumann are recognized today.

2 A photograph of a concert given by Galli Curci on 16 October 1926, sponsored by the Calgary Women's Musical Association, shows an absolutely packed arena for the occasion (Lyons 1999, 30).

3 Her program consisted of works by Donizetti, Verdi, Liszt, Meyerbeer, Handel, Mendelssohn, Widor, and Sullivan.

4 Curwen's method dispensed with the staff entirely and used the abbreviations d-r-m-f-s-l-t-d. The Ontario Department of Education public school music syllabus for 1895 outlined two courses: one using Tonic Sol-fa, and one using staff notation (Green and Vogan 1991, 62).

5 Writing in 1898, Susie Frances Harrison described the latter as found "in the small private dwelling in a back street, boasting a large gold sign, and [music] evidently the pet hobby of some enthusiastic but untrained amateur" (Harrison 1898, 4:390).

6 The Paris Conservatoire was a state institution founded in 1795. Teachers were paid a salary and students were admitted on scholarship by audition. A three-year program provided private instruction in a range of disciplines, with compulsory solfège and music theory, students had to pass regular competitions where their accomplishments were judged against a set of standards.

7 The Leipzig Conservatory (founded in 1843) was a small, selective school run according to the "conservatory method" (a classroom teaching method developed by Johann Bernhard Logier). In addition to performance disciplines, students studied harmony, counterpoint, and fugue; other subjects included score-reading, conducting, form and composition, history, aesthetics, and acoustics.

8 These three institutions were founded between 1865 and 1868. The American conservatories offered three- to five-year programs leading to a diploma, but few students managed to complete a full program of practical and theoretical

requirements. The fees were charged by the term and the "conservatory" method was encouraged.

9 For example, in Ottawa around 1879 the Congrégation de Notre Dame offered private piano lessons at $30 per annum, harp at $50, guitar at $20, and organ at $40. The number of students taking music at the Ottawa Ladies' College increased from 55 in 1873 to 122 in 1874. This prompted a decision to establish a conservatory affiliated with the College. By 1876 graduation requirements for College piano students included the following repertoire: Bach's Prelude and Fugue no. 17 in A flat major; Handel's *Harmonious Blacksmith*, Haydn's Sonata in E flat major; Mozart's Fantasia and Sonata in C minor; Beethoven's Sonata in A flat major, op. 26; Weber's *Polacca brillante*, op. 78; Schumann's *Kreisleriana*; Mendelssohn's *Capriccio*, op. 33, no. 3; Thalberg's Variations on *Home Sweet Home*, Chopin's Ballade in F minor; and Liszt's Hungarian Rhapsody no. 1 (Keillor 1988, 30).

10 From 1892 to 1901, there were two examination divisions for the three-year course of study: an academic division for young students and amateurs, and a collegiate division that granted certificates and diplomas for artists and teachers. After 1901, the TCM adopted some aspects of the systems that had been developed in Britain, and laid a greater emphasis on an examination system for all situations.

11 The introduction to the Toronto Conservatory of Music *Selected Etudes for the Intermediate Pianoforte Examination* (Toronto: Anglo-Canadian Music, n.d.) states that this collection contains "a number of carefully selected chosen and well contrasted studies taken from such valuable material as the Cramer-Bülow 'Fifty Selected Pianoforte Studies' and Czerny's indispensable 'The Art of Finger Dexterity,' op. 740 ... In arranging for the publication of special editions of etudes ... the Board of Governors have been actuated by a desire to provide candidates and students of music generally with the most highly approved and thoroughly tested technical material, attractively issued, uniformly edited, and procurable at less cost than would otherwise be the case."

12 The Hambourg Conservatory was operated by various members of the Hambourg family (Michael, Jan, and Boris). In 1914 it had thirty piano teachers, eleven voice teachers, eight violin teachers, four theory teachers, two each of cello, organ, flute, mandolin/banjo, and composition, and one each for drama, French, German, and dancing (Kallmann 1992, 573).

13 In 1912 the Toronto String Quartette gave its first of a number of performances of Debussy's String Quartet (1893).

14 "The correspondence on the examinations had sparked off a controversy across the Atlantic, not so much because of its content but more because of its tone. Aitken [Samuel, secretary] and other Associated Board members were arrogant and patronizing. They were bringing culture to the masses with the intent of filling their own coffers with gold. Fisher, Torrington, Anger and the like resented being treated like colonial upstarts ... The examination system of the TCM, and

other Canadian schools, were far from perfect. But their teachers did not need to have the Associated Board sweep its tentacles over Canada and assume a monopoly. Furthermore, all these men had invested their career energies in a Canadian situation. Their united outlook was just unfathomable to a bigoted Britisher like Aitken" (Jones 1989, 129).

15 Even though Canadian universities that offered examinations in music in the nineteenth century did not have a full-time professor in music, many students applied to write the series of examinations in order to obtain a Bachelor of Music degree. Most students found private tutors or studied on their own and paid fees for each examination and for the degree of musical bachelor. In 1884 Trinity College (later part of the University of Toronto) stated in its Calendar that five years of study or practise were required plus being a graduate of the university in law or theology to obtain a bachelor of music degree. The candidate had to pass the first, second, and final exams with a year between each part. The first year examination concentrated on harmony; the second year on counterpoint, canon, and fugue; the final year on history, form, and orchestration. Also the candidate must prepare a four-part composition with accompaniment of organ, piano, or string band. Of the students that were successful in 1884, two women, Helen Emma Gregory and Lillius Matilda Howland, graduated. In 1885 four of the successful 39 graduates were women. Bishop's University passed a statute to allow women to join the music program in 1894 (Keillor 1995, 105-6).

16 As of 2005, there are ten examination systems in Canada operated by Canadian institutions. A few are limited to students of teachers at a particular institution, while others are regional. Conservatory Canada is a national organization, and the RCM is international. See Babin 2005.

17 Warren is known to have built more than 350 pipe organs, and his firm also made melodeons; one of these, dating from 1865, is now at the Sharon Temple (Raudsepp 1999, 15).

18 Among the most important Ontario companies were the Andrus Brothers Organ, London, 1847–74; Bell Piano and Organ, Guelph, 1869–1934; R.H. Dalton, Toronto, 1869–82; W. Doherty, Clinton, 1875–1924; Dominion Organ and Piano, Oshawa, 1875–1936; Goderich Organ, Goderich, 1890–1910; John Jackson Organ, Guelph, 1872–83; Lye Organ, Toronto 1873–1934; Rappe, Kingston, 1871–87; James Thornton, Hamilton, 1871–89 (Kelly 1991, 131–2).

19 Export figures for Canadian organs and pianos show that in 1900 fewer than 500 pianos were exported in comparison to 5,000 organs. From that point on, numbers for organs fell sharply to around 200 in 1930, while piano exports began to rise in 1915 reaching about 1,000 by 1920 (Kelly 1991, 35).

20 "By 1905 at least five Ontario companies presented advertising claims that their factory size, sales records, export trade, quality products, or some other attribute made them 'Number One.' Bell boasted being 'the largest maker of pianos in Canada;' so did Karn in Woodstock and Dominion in Bowmanville. Whaley-Royce said that its product was 'unexcelled in tone, faultless in construction.'

Gourlay pianos were 'not merely first class, they are something better.' And Morris, with its 'most modern and finest equipped piano factory in Canada,' claimed that it had 'the highest grade pianos' possible" (Kelly 1991, 31).

21 Theodor Heintzman apprenticed to a piano maker in Berlin, Prussia, then worked with Steinweg, later known as Steinway in New York. He moved to Canada in the late 1850s to work for various piano manufacturers, and in 1866 he opened his own business in Toronto.

22 Production of upright and grand pianos dropped from a peak of 3,000 instruments in 1922 to less than 200 during the Depression, and the last Heintzman piano was manufactured in the 1980s. Canadian pianist Anton Kuerti has said: "Heintzman was a product that Canada can be justly proud of; the best Heintzmans are exquisite instruments indeed, with a very individual, characteristic tone that is bright without becoming metallic or distorted ... I think it is not unfair to contend that Heintzman ranks among the top ten pianos built in ... [the twentieth] century" (Kelly 1991, 145).

23 By 1950, Lesage had made 30,000 instruments. With growing competition from Japanese and Korean imports, Lesage tried to survive by turning to the production of electronic keyboards in the late 1970s, and reintroducing the manufacture of grand pianos in 1981.

24 The Royal Ontario Museum in Toronto has a fine collection of musical instruments that were originally assembled by Williams.

25 The first phonograph recording made in Canada was at the Governor-General's residence on 17 May 1878. Lady Dufferin wrote: "It is quite a small thing, a cylinder which you turn with a handle, and which you place on a common table. We were so amazed when we first heard this bit of iron speak that it was hard to believe there was no trick! But we all tried it. Fred sang 'Old Obadiah' ... the Colonel sang a French song, and all our vocal efforts were repeated. As long as the same piece of tinfoil is kept on the instrument you can hear all you have said over and over again" (Dufferin 1969, 292).

26 A mechanical piano player, a device placed in front of the keyboard of a regular piano "played" by means of cues from a rotating paper roll operated by a foot pedal, was patented in Germany in 1890. However, around 1901 the player piano, a much more compact device built into a regular piano, became more popular. Various improvements were made to player pianos including the addition of an electric motor to drive the sensitive paper rolls. When Robert J. Flaherty was searching for iron-ore deposits in the Northwest Territories during the First World War, he took his player piano with him. The Inuit called it a "singing box." When Flaherty left the Belcher Islands he presented the piano to Wetallock, who was unable to get it into his igloo. In the end, Wetallock put the piano on a sled and transported it 280 miles south to Fort George where he returned it to an astonished Flaherty (Kelly 1991, 38).

27 Even with the combination of visiting orchestras and local orchestral efforts, it was not until 1914 that all of the Beethoven symphonies had been performed in Toronto. Gradually other works that have since become standard fare were

introduced, including Tchaikovsky's *Romeo and Juliet*, Berlioz's *Symphonie fantastique* (New York Symphony with Damrosch, 1907), Franck's Symphony in D minor (Chicago Orchestra with Stock, 1908), and Schumann's Symphony no. 4 (Cincinnati Orchestra with Van der Stucken 1903) (Morey 1988, 106).

28 The illustrations in George Lyon's *Community Music in Alberta* document various ensembles in Alberta from the earliest days of photography through to the mid-twentieth century. In addition to the more varied musical traditions (such as the Norwegian *hoppwaltz*, the Ukrainian *kolomayka*, and *polkas* of many kinds) this book traces the transition from small ad hoc groups of singers or instrumentalists to more formal organizations including a small orchestra of Calgary formed in 1891, the Hillcrest Orchestra of Pincher Creek Shield (1926), and the Crowsnest area orchestra in Blairmore (1942).

29 The concept of a competitive music festival came from Great Britain. Prior to Earl Grey's efforts there had been several band competitions (beginning with one in Toronto in 1858), and a fiddlers' competition in Montreal in 1867. In 1886 the Ontario Music Teachers' Association (founded in 1885; later the Canadian Society of Musicians) held a composition competition for which works were submitted under *noms de plume*. The four composers who obtained "the marks necessary to pass" were A.E. Fisher, Frances Hatton-Moore, Davenport Kerrison, and G.W. Strathy. At their second annual convention, 28–30 December 1886, Angelo Reed gave a paper entitled "Encouragement of Canadian Composition" and programs included piano pieces by Susie F. Harrison, G. W. Strathy, Frances Hatton-Moore, a part song, and *Gavotte* for string quartet by Kerrison.

30 The Halifax Symphony Orchestra was initially sponsored by the Local Council of Women and eleven of the eighteen string players were women.

31 Symphonies by Schubert (*Unfinished*), Dvořák (*New World*), Haydn, Mozart, Beethoven, Mendelssohn (no. 3 and no 4), and Tchaikovsky (no. 4, no. 5, and no. 6) – but none by Brahms – along with several tone poems including Richard Strauss's *Death and Transfiguration*.

32 In June 1888, the Leipzig correspondent to the *Toronto Musical Journal* commented: "The most advanced students, who are from Toronto, are Miss Lampman, Miss Higgins and Mr. W.O. Forsyth ... Mr Forsyth has undertaken to do more than either of the foregoing, being one of Jadassohn's very foremost pupils in composition, harmony, counterpoint, canon, and fugue" (Keillor 1973, 101)

33 The score of Lavallée's *Ouverture: Patrie* was only located in the 1990s. The form of this work conforms to the outline for a concert-overture in Czerny's *School of Practical Composition* (1839). The principal sections are *Allegro* (1A), *Brillante* (2A), *Andante maestoso* (B), and *Moderato e cantabile* (C), which has rhythmic links to the *Andante*. The overall form can be summarized as follows: introduction (F major), 1A (D minor), 2A (D major), 1A (D minor), 2A (E flat major), B (F major), C (G major), 1A (D minor), B (D major), 2A (D major), bridge (related to C), 2A (D major). Lavallée uses brass instruments to reinforce the woodwinds. There are some interesting combinations of lower strings and winds as well as a melodic dialogue played by solo woodwinds.

34 The score illustrates Couture's skill in orchestration. Obviously he had been studying Wagner's music as the work begins with the famous "Tristan" chord, a half-diminished seventh.

35 Although the writing shows a strong debt to Handel, Harriss was obviously aware of harmonic developments in the late nineteenth century. The King's Air (no. 17) following Daniel's imprisonment in the lions' den is based on two widely separated keys, F minor and A major.

36 The story of *Gulnare* is based on the First Crusade (1096–9), and the libretto was prepared by Torontonian Mrs. Edgar Jarvis.

37 *The Birth of Christ* was praised as being "daringly original" (Logan 1913a, 491). Lucas taught and performed extensively in Hamilton, Toronto, and New York up to the mid-1890s after which he based the remainder of his career in New York, England, and France where he was active as a composer, arranger, conductor, editor, photographer, and music journalist.

38 The chorus plays an unusually large role in *Caïn*; in fact, Contant commented: "You might say that ... the chorus accompanies the orchestra, rather than the orchestra accompanying the chorus" (*CMH18*, x).

39 A review of this performance in the Montreal *Standard* began: "As I listened to the recitatives, the arias, the choruses, the orchestration, and to the glorious harmonies which ever and anon thrilled and held one spellbound, it was hard to believe that the musician to whose brain they were born and developed was none other than the lovable, little, black whiskered man who went in and out among the people of Montreal for so many years with a folio of music held snuggled under his arm and a cane in his right hand" (*CMH15* 1994, x).

40 *TIQ* consists of twenty-six musical numbers; selections are published in *CMH-10*, 27–54. *Marche Indienne*, dealing with negotiations between the Sioux chief Sitting Bull and Colonel Carter of the US Army, has been arranged for band by John Beckwith.

41 *The Widow*, a three-act opera with an overture and thirty vocal numbers, received several performances in the following two years. Lavallée likely created his music for a French libretto (Barrière 1999, 40), but the rights for the opera were bought by the C.D. Hess Acme Opera Company who performed it in English. Although the musical writing is excellent, the vocal lines do not always fit the English accentuation.

42 Harrison's *Pipandor* (which has not been located) is said to be based on French Canadian folk songs, a special interest of Harrison. *Canada's Welcome*, was scored for thirteen soloists (representing Canada, Ontario, Quebec, New Brunswick, Nova Scotia, Prince Edward Island, Manitoba, British Columbia, an Indian chief, and the four Seasons), a chorus of one hundred voices, and orchestra.

43 Fuller emigrated to Canada around 1870. His second Canadian libretto was a musical burlesque and comical satire on Canadian politics. "The play is a satirical attack on the conservative government's protectionist economic 'National Policy' of high tariffs, on government bureaucracy, political opportunism, patronage, nepotism, and the personal foibles of political leaders of the time"

(Wagner and Plant 1978, 12). The director of the McDowell Comedy Company increased the burlesque side of the production by casting Mrs. Butterbun, an advocate of the National Policy, as a man and dressing the bearded old Senators as women.

44 *Leo* is a four-act operetta with thirty-five numbers involving sixteen soloists, chorus, and orchestra. First staged at Martin's Opera House in Kingston in July 1889 with an all-Kingston cast, the work went on the road with several troupes. By 1925 it had had an estimated 150 performances.

45 Torontonians saw *The Flying Dutchman* in 1887, *Lohengrin* in 1888, *Tannhäuser* in 1891 (and subsequently in 1904 and 1905), and both *Die Walküre* and *Parsifal* in 1905. Also in 1905, the Quinlan Opera Company performed Wagner's complete Ring Cycle in Montreal, a feat that was not to be repeated in Canada during the twentieth century. Two Canadian touring companies, both located in Montreal, presented full performances of grand opera: the Société d'opéra français flourished from 1893 to 1896; and the Montreal Opera Company was active from 1910 to 1913. During the Montreal Opera Company's first season, clerical opposition forced a cancellation of Massenet's *Manon* and Puccini's *Tosca* in Québec City. In the second season the Company presented twelve different operas in 97 performances. With the outbreak of war in 1914 and unsettled economic conditions in the years between 1918 to 1939, the era of the big touring companies came to an end.

46 Unfortunately, scores for many earlier works apparently written have not been located: for example "Lavallée is said to have written [a magnificent suite for cello and piano], two string quartets and a piano trio, George Graham (fl. 1854–66) a piano quintet, and A.E. Fisher (1848–ca 1912) a string trio" (*CMH11* 1989, v).

47 In the 1890s, Manning studied with Edward MacDowell in New York, and then taught at the Oberlin Conservatory. After a year's study with Engelbert Humperdinck in Berlin, he taught at Columbia University, and later became music supervisor for the New York City public schools.

48 Robin Elliott has pointed out that the second movement of the *Piano Trio* opens with the theme in the cello, in the same tempo and key as Brahms selected in the third movement of his Piano Concerto no. 2 (*CMH9* 1989, vi).

49 According to F.R.C. Clarke, Willan liked to tell two stories about the genesis of this work. One was that after hearing Reger's *Passacaglia in D minor* at an organ recital, his friend Dalton Baker said that only a German philosophical mind could compose such a work, and Willan set out to prove him wrong. The other was "that he wrote the variations for the passacaglia while riding on the radial (inter-urban tram) between Toronto and his summer cottage on Lake Simcoe – one variation each trip" (Clarke 1983, 180). French organist Joseph Bonnet spoke of Willan's passacaglia as "one of the most significant since Bach's and called it 'a rare and admirable composition, conceived in an extraordinarily pure and lofty spirit, built up on solid architectural lines, illuminated by the light of harmonies by turns sumptuous and delicate'" (Clarke 1983, 182–3).

50 Anger may have been aware of the Acadian celebration of *tintamarre* on 12 August, in which celebrants use spoons, whistles, and musical instruments to make as much sound as possible. The works usually identified for the first use of tone clusters are by two American composers: Henry Cowell's *The Tides of Maunaunaun* (published 1913) and Charles Ives's *Majority (The Masses)* (1914).

CHAPTER SEVEN

1 Professional entertainers included singers who performed ballads and broadsides, newly composed songs, and operatic selections as well as comic acts, monologues, stereotyped presentations (such as a Black person or a Jew), and perhaps acrobats or magicians.

2 A similar activity in the United States soon developed a distinctive profile for composers such as Stephen Foster; the following description from the *Albany State Register* (quoted in Hamm 1983, 230–1) indicates that Foster's *Old Folks at Home* was widely known only a year after its publication in 1851, illustrating the influence of a "popular" song: "Pianos and guitars groan with it, night and day: sentimental young ladies sing it; sentimental young gentlemen warble it in midnight serenades; volatile young 'bucks' hum it in the midst of their business and their pleasures; boatmen roar it out stentorianally (sic) at all times; all the bands play it; amateur flute players agonize over it at every spare moment; the street organs grind it out at every hour; the 'singing stars' carol it on the theatrical boards, and at concerts; the chamber maid sweeps and dusts to its measured cadence; the butcher's boy treats you to a strain or two of it as he hands in the steaks for dinner; the milk-man mixes it up strangely with the harsh ding-dong accompaniment of his tireless bell; there is not a 'live darkey,' young or old, but can whistle, sing, dance, and play it ... Indeed at every hour, at every turn, we are forcibly impressed with the interesting fact, that – 'Way down upon de Swanee Ribber, Far, far away, Dere's whar my heart is turnin' ebber, Dere's whar de old folks stay.'"

3 Even before 1760 French-speaking settlers of New France were commonly called *canadiens*, and up to about 1860 "Canadians" referred to francophone residents of Canada; other residents were identified by their country of origin (Irish, Scottish, English, Dutch, German, or Loyalists). The new text has a lay structure: the full *laisse* line is "Vive la canadienne et ses jolis yeux doux." Each line ends with the masculine sound "ou" and there is a feminine "e" on the sixth syllable of the twelve-syllable line. The full strophe is organized with a burden "Vole, mon coeur, vole!" inserted between two presentations of the first half of the line; the second half of the line is presented three times. (*Vive la canadienne! Vole, mon coeur, vole! Vive la canadienne et ses jolies yeux doux, / Et ses jolis yeux doux, doux, doux, et ses jolis yeux doux.*)

4 Bytown was the lumbering centre selected by Queen Victoria as the capital of Canada in 1867.

5　These three songs are included in Fowke 1973, 75–81, with commentary by Germain Lemieux. *Vie penible des cageux* describes a raftsman in the lumber industry.

6　Since the lay line is only eight syllables there is no inner caesura, but the final syllable is almost always the masculine "é," as in "Et par Bytown y sont passés." English translation: Where are all the raftsmen? / They've gone up to the logging camps. Chorus: Bing on the ring! Bang on the rang! / Let the raftsmen go by, / Bing on the ring! Bing bang! / They went via Bytown / With the provisions they bought. / They went up in bark canoes / With great pleasure. / They ate pork and beans / To ease the hunger in their stomachs. / When they arrived in the logging camps / They made handles for their axes. / How the Ottawa (River) is astonished / At the noise of their felling-axes. / When work in the camps was finished / They went home. / They kissed their wives and sweethearts, / Very happy to be home again.

7　In fact O. J. Abbott's version of *Hogan's Lake* refers to a well-known music hall song, *The Girl that Wore the Waterfall* (a hair style of the day), in the final line.

8　In Eastern Canada English-language folk songs usually have a double-stanza pattern with four strong stresses in each line of a four-line strophe. The rhyming pattern is often *aabb*. Tunes for such texts are usually "long tune" (sixteen measures in Western notation), rather than "short tune" (eight measures). Broadsides, lumbering songs, and local songs are frequently found in long tune form. Some published popular songs are doubled to provide a sixteen-measure strophe plus a sixteen-measure chorus.

9　For a recording of *The Wreck of the Asia* from Edith Fowke's collection see *Songs of the Great Lakes* (Folkways FM 4018).

10　In the Guelph area, *Poor Little Girls* was commonly sung to the tune of *The Little Brown Jug* (a song by Jos. E. Winner first published in Philadelphia and New York in 1869). Around Belleville they used *Yankee Doodle*; for a discussion of versions and appearances of *Yankee Doodle,* see Virga 1982.

11　The details given in the ballad are quite accurate. Both the tune and the text of the ballad are modelled on the well-known American murder ballad of the day *Charles Guiteau*; Guiteau was executed in 1882 for killing President Garfield.

12　The introduction to this collection states: "In selecting our Newfoundland songs we have made a special effort to give precedence to those only that are racy of the soil and illustrate the homely joys and sorrows of our people. Most of our local poets and song writers have been true to nature in their compositions and therein lies the charm and merit of their songs. We wish to make it clear to our readers that there is no ridicule or disparagement intended in any of the local allusions in the songs we have selected. We appreciate them too highly for that, as all these songs are of the people and from the people of our Island Home, and are redolent of a happy past, and breathe a spirit of co-mingled freedom, independence, and human sympathy that characterized the good old days of our forefathers ... It is a well known fact that there is often more interesting history in the Songs of a country than in its formal political records and State documents. Actuated by those thoughts we came to the conclusion that these old songs should not be lost to coming generations and have made this attempt to preserve and perpetuate them. Where the names of the authors could be ascertained due credit is given. In the case of writers whose identity we have been unable to discover we regret that it is not possible to give credit. However, we deem their poetical effusions too meritorious to go unrecorded, anonymous though they be."

13 In Irish traditions a single jig has a quarter/eighth rhythm, a double jig has a sub-division of three eighth notes; simple tunes in duple (2/4) time with an emphasis on the off-beat are referred to as polka.

14 Del Giudice has theorized that the reasons for this late start can be attributed to the district-specific repertoire involved and a general assumption that Italian song consisted only of operatic arias and *O sole mio*. Also, many immigrants who came from very poor areas such as Calabria did not want to revive memo-ries of difficult times.

15 Because the Doukhobors reject the orthodox church liturgy, believing that God dwells in each person rather than in a church, these religious songs are sung at *sobranya* – gatherings that serve both as religious services and community meetings.

16 Mai-yu Chan 1981, personal communication. Research in this area, so far, has been limited. For a recent overview see Qiu 2005.

17 A stereotyped genre of minstrel songs sung by white performers in black face were popular in the United States; examples include *Zip Coon* and *Jim Crow*, written in 1832 by Thomas Rice (1808–60), a New Yorker. Unlike his earlier minstrel or "Ethiopian" songs, Foster's plantation songs used little dialect; they portrayed Black people as human beings experiencing pain, sorrow, love, joy, and nostalgia. Examples frequently heard in Canada include *Old Folks at Home*, *Massa's in de Cold Ground*, *My Old Kentucky Home, Good Night,* and *Old Black Joe.*

18 The first verse begins: "I'm on my way to Canada, that cold and dreary land. The dire effects of slavery I can no longer stand." The complete text was published in *The Voice of the Fugitive*, Sandwich, Ontario, in 1851. For this song and *Follow the Drinkin' Gourd,* another song for slaves escaping to Canada, see Hehner 1999.

19 Alexander Muir (1830–1906) was apparently inspired by a maple leaf that settled on his coat as he walked along Queen Street East in Toronto. Unable to find a suitable tune, he composed his own. This song was a patriotic mainstay of anglophone Canada for almost a century, but the obvious British emphasis on "Wolfe, the conquering hero" and "thistle, shamrock, rose" never appealed to francophones. Attempts to create new or revised words include the one used at the 1999 Pan-American Games in Winnipeg.

20 Henry Sefton (ca. 1808–1882) was a music teacher in the Toronto schools from 1858 to 1882.

21 Laws passed as early as the 1780s prohibited Blacks from presenting frolics in predominantly white areas of Nova Scotia (Johnston 1980, 19).

22 For example, the Fisk University Jubilee Singers, a group of students from Nashville, embarked on a national tour. On 28 May 1885 the *New Glasgow Eastern Chronicle* reported: "The Fisk Jubilee Singers performed in the United Church to a large audience last Thursday evening ... The audience was charmed and delighted, and the singers were called back at the end of almost every piece" (Croft 2000, 31).

23 The script of *The Lillie Whytes* is held by the Library of Congress, and there is a microfilm copy at St Mary's University, mf. C.D. Coll 10.03. The suggested minstrel melodies include *Darling Nellie Gray, Old Black Joe, My Old Kentucky Home, Carry Me Back to Old Virginny, Shoo Fly, Don't Bother Me, A Little More Cider, So Early in the Morning, Such a Getting Up-Stairs, I'm Off to Charlestown, The Old Folks at Home, Stop that Knocking, Down in Dixie, Hear dem Bells.*

24 At The Society for Ethnomusicology conference, 5 October 2003, Susan Hurley-Glowa underlined this shift from professional to amateur production through the publication of numerous "how-to" manuals for putting on a minstrel show. She has identified the production of 228 manuals between 1901 and 1970.

25 After the Civil War, an increasing demand for beef was filled by the Texas trail herd and open range industry. Companies bought huge blocks of grasslands in Colorado, New Mexico, and Texas to graze thousands of cattle, which cowboys rounded up for the long trek north to slaughter houses at a railway centre; by 1883 an estimated 10,000 cowboys were employed in this business. On the drive north, while the herd was feeding on pasture land, the cowboys used their spare time to practice their skills at roping and compete with each another. This event became known as a rodeo from the Spanish word *rodea*. In 1883 Buffalo Bill Cody hired cowboys for a Wild West show to give demonstrations of trick roping, and fancy riding, and he included mock battles with First Nations on one side and cowboys and the US Army on the other (Farnum 1992, 11).

CHAPTER EIGHT

1 In 1929 Ralph Vaughan Williams complimented Jean Coulthard on her pretty dress but failed to provide worthwhile guidance for the compositions she produced (Cornfield 2002).

2 "With the arrival of talking films, the large movie-houses on St Catherine Street dismissed their orchestras ... Douglas Clarke gathered men together for rehearsals, taught some of them (those who had never heard of Wagner or Brahms), produced food, transportation on occasion, and rent out of his own pocket" (Prower 1964).

3 Morin played Mendelssohn's *Caprice brillant*; the other works were Beethoven's Leonore Overture no. 3, Tchaikovsky's Symphony no. 6, Debussy's *Prélude à l'après-midi d'une faune*, and Karl Goldmark's *Sakuntala Overture*.

4 Wilfred Pelletier (1896–1982) was born in Quebec but his musical career had taken him to both Europe and the United States. In 1929, he became one of the regular conductors of the Metropolitan Opera in New York,

5 These concerts were presented at 5:00 p.m. in the free time between the matinée and evening shows (Schabas 1994, 101). Sunday was also free as the theatres were closed.

6 The name "Toronto Symphony Orchestra" formerly belonged to the orchestra organized by Frank Welsman, which was active between 1908 and 1918 (Warren 2002, 5, 7).

7 This position was established through a grant from the Carnegie Institute.

8 "The professionals agreed to play without remuneration. The members are 45 in number, the instrumentation being divided into 24 violins, 3 violas, 5 cellos, 2 string basses, 2 flutes, 2 clarinets, 1 oboe, 1 bassoon, 2 trumpets, 1 horn, 2 trombones, and tympani" (Fricker 1933, 43).

9 Examples of educational programming include Emiliano Renaud's piano lessons broadcast from Montreal in 1925 and the Vancouver School Board broadcasts on CNRV in 1927.

10 At this time Hector Charlesworth (1878–1945), an influential music critic, was editor of *Saturday Night* magazine; he describes his term as chair of the CRBC in *I'm Telling You* (Toronto 1937).

11 The program included *Symphonette* by Robert Farnon, *Rondo* by Barbara Pentland, *Berceuse* by Claude Champagne, *Island of the Fay* by Walter MacNutt, *The Whirling Dwarf* by John Weinzweig, *Nocturne* by Gerald Bales, and *A Comedy Overture* by Godfrey Ridout.

12 These hotels, all in a distinctive architectural style, include the Chateau Frontenac in Quebec City, the Royal York in Toronto, the Royal Alexandra in Winnipeg, the Hotel Saskatchewan in Regina, the Palliser in Calgary, Chateau Lake Louise and the Banff Springs Hotel in the Rockies, and the Empress Hotel in Victoria.

13 For more details on these concerts, see Keillor forthcoming.

14 Gascgoine's *Chansons of Old French Canada*, with a preface by Marius Barbeau, was published in 1920 by the CPR; a French version appeared in 1923. This collection of eleven songs was "highly popular with American tourists because the *chansons* were so unlike their own folk music" (Kines 1988, 100), and the piano accompaniments "were graceful but simple in their technical demands and hence accessible to most amateur pianists" (Morey 1998, 36).

15 Charles Marchand (1890–1930) left the civil service in 1919 after attending one of Barbeau's *Soirées du bon vieux temps* to devote himself to promoting Canadian folk music. His vocal quartet *Le carillon canadien* sang folk song arrangements and original material by Oscar O'Brien. Marchand initially rejected Gibbon's offer because he felt that French Canadian folk songs were being patronized as "habitant stuff, peasant stuff" (Kines 1988, 106).

16 *Canadian Folk Songs* (Toronto: Dent, 1927) is a collection of thirty of Marchand's most successful songs. The tunes were collected by Barbeau, Massicotte,

O'Brien, Marchand, and Joseph Levac; arrangements are by O'Brien and Geoffrey O'Hara; translations are by Gibbon.

17 Julliet Gaulthier was born in Ottawa. After operatic studies in Europe she turned her interests to folklore, learning several Inuit and Amerindian dialects. Gaulthier advised Gibbon to use entirely Canadian talent and suggested Ernest MacMillan as a good arranger (Kines 1988, 112). In *The Phonograph Monthly Review* 4, no. 11 (August 1930, 365–6), her Victor recordings and her presentations of songs in "costume recitals" are described as "free from false harmonizations, and accompanied only by such instruments as the native musicians themselves use."

18 In his review of *Folk Songs of French Canada* (1925) by Marius Barbeau and Edward Sapir, MacMillan commented that two songs – *Notre Seigneur en pauvre* and *À Saint-Malo* – appealed to him; Gibbon asked MacMillan to arrange them for the 1927 festival. *Two Sketches for Strings* has since become a Canadian classic. In *Notre Seigneur en pauvre* (HACM–93; CMH13,83–6) the modal tune is complemented by appropriate cadences and contrapuntal textures. Although he uses the tune as a source for short melodic cells in contrapuntal lines, complete A and B phrases of the tune appear in the first violin after the introductory fourteen bars, and again near the conclusion.

19 The prize for the first category, a orchestral suite or tone poem, was $1,000. The five judges were Achille Fortier, Paul Vidal, Eric De Lamarter, Ralph Vaughan Williams, and Sir Hugh Allan. The orchestral, string quartet and cantata categories were open to international competition.

20 The six concert groups were: Marjory Kennedy-Fraser and Margaret Kennedy; Stanley Maxted and Frances James; Florence Hood, Jean Rowe, and Winifred MacMillan; John Goss; the Hart House String Quartet; Rodolphe and Lucien Plamondon.

21 The term "mosaic" was used by American writer Victoria Hayward in *Romantic Canada* (1922) in reference to the variety of architectural styles created by the different cultures in the Prairies. Kate A. Foster's extensive survey written for the YWCA as a social worker's manual was published under the title *Our Canadian Mosaic* (1926); Foster ceded her rights to the term to Gibbon who popularized it as a Canadian descriptor.

22 The salaries of the Hart House Quartet were guaranteed by the Massey Foundation, making them the first fully subsidized quartet in Canada. They gave their first concert in Hart House in 1924.

23 In May 1916 he wrote home to say he "was completing the first version of his String Quartet in C minor" (MacMillan 1988, 176). Other compositions completed in the camp include the song *Were I But Crazy for Love's Sake* (CMH14, 122); the text is from *The Countess Cathleen* by W.B. Yeats, a play produced at Ruhleben. Hall points out that MacMillan captures the nuances of the text: "The dramatic broken chords, forzato introduction to the insertion of the spoken text, chromatic passages ... and wide voice range all add to the expressiveness of the setting" (CMH14, ix). MacMillan's awareness of contemporary trends is evident

in the whole tone passage in the piano at m. 31, the changing metres, and the final haunting minor seventh chord under the long E in the voice.

24 In England, Willan was strongly influenced by the Oxford Movement, which in musical terms meant Anglican church music of the Renaissance and Gregorian chant as sung in Anglo-Catholic churches. At St Mary Magdalene Willan was given sole charge of all music and considerable control over its use in services.

25 For a recording, see *An Introduction to Canadian Music*, Naxos 8.5501711-2.

26 Champagne received his early music training through the Dominion College of Music, the Conservatoire national de Montréal, and the Canadian Grenadier Guards Band, which was conducted by J.-J. Gagnier. Champagne's compositions for the band include *Ballade des lutins* (1914) (*CMH21*, 247–52),

27 Students of Champagne include Violet Archer, Jocelyne Binet, Maurice Dela, Marvin Duchow, Serge Garant, Rhené Jaque, Roger Matton, Pierre Mercure, François Morel, Clermont Pépin, Gilles Tremblay, Robert Turner, and Jean Vallerand.

28 *Danse villageoise* was written at the request of Léo-Pol Morin who wanted a "typically Canadian" piece. It was perhaps inspired by the memory of Champagne's paternal grandfather, who was a *violoneux*; the form – a combination of rondo and double variation – is derived from a fiddle tune structure with two eight-bar strains: A B A^1 B^1 A^2 B^2 A^3 C A.

29 For a recording, see *Introduction to Canadian Music*, Naxos 8.550171-2.

30 According to McPhee the title of *Tabuh-Tabuhan* (*CMH16*, 6–62) "derives from the Balinese word *tabuh*, originally meaning the mallet used for striking a percussion instrument, but extended to mean strike or beat (the drum, a gong, xylophone or metallophone). *Tabuh-Tabuhan* is thus a Balinese collective noun, meaning different drum rhythms, metric forms, gong punctuations, gamelans, and music essentially percussive."

31 In the first movement five ostinatos, each with its own shifting pitches and accents, register, and instrumental "sound" create a pattern of intervallic and motivic relationships. "Nocturne," uses modified forms of McPhee's transcriptions of *Lagu ardja, Keyyar ding* and an original creation of the *anklung* idea: "The constant interlocking of ... parts, and the sudden rhythmic breaks that occur from time to time, maintain a steady tension throughout the music" (McPhee 1966, 254). The finale "moves continually forward with no final reprise [but] ... has four principal sections and quotes from several gamelan compositions" (Oja 1990, 104).

32 The next performance was a radio broadcast of two movements in New York in 1947. On 16 October 1953 Leopold Stokowski included it in a concert of Canadian works in New York sponsored by BMI. There were subsequent performances in 1955 and at the United Nations in 1956, when it was recorded by the Eastman Rochester Symphony Orchestra under Howard Hanson. Interest in and performances of the work of McPhee in recent years is largely the result of Oja's research on the music of McPhee and a film of McPhee's work in Bali.

33 Other scholars attribute minimalist composition to La Monte Young, a student at UCLA who was possibly influenced by McPhee.

CHAPTER NINE

1 Composer Charles K. Harris listed the main types of popular vocal music in 1906: the home or mother song, the descriptive, or sensational story ballad, the popular waltz song, the coon song, the march song, the comic song, the production song (used in musicals), the popular love ballad, high class ballads, and sacred songs.

2 See the sound recording chronology on the Library and Archives Canada website: www.collectionscanada.ca/gramophone/m2-3000-3.html; see also www.capsnews.org/barrrca.htm.

3 Burr (1885–1941, born Harry McClaskey in New Brunswick) recorded some 12,000 titles for seventy-six labels under at least eleven pseudonyms. For a few years he operated a New York publishing firm, and he was a lead soloist on the popular Chicago radio program *National Barn Dance*.

4 Canadians involved in early radio technology include Guglielmo Marconi, an Italian immigrant who developed a "wireless" and eventually succeeded in transmitting from Cornwall, England to Signal Hill, Newfoundland, and Reginald Aubrey Fessenden who, in 1901 transmitted human voices from Brant Rock near Boston to several ships at sea and in the process discovered AM radio. Under the Radio-Telegraph Act of 1913, a government minister had the power to license radio broadcasting stations and to charge a license fee of one dollar on each receiving set. The first scheduled radio broadcast in the world was from Montreal's XWA (now CFCF) on 20 May 1920.

5 Graves wrote several more songs during this period, but the hydro song was his greatest success. The song has a strophe and chorus, each sixteen bars long. The four-bar introduction has a music-hall phrase structure (ABAC); the solo chorus has contrasting strains (DEDF).

6 In Canada the Chautauqua movement was closely linked to Methodist Temperance. The Dominion (after 1926 Canadian) Chautauqua formed by John M. Erickson operated a successful circuit from Quebec to the Pacific until 1935, offering a range of musical and dramatic entertainment.

7 This song has a three-bar introduction and an unusual phrase structure: A B C(A) D A B C(A) C F. The descending tendency in some phrases might indicate an Amerindian influence.

8 The four-bar introduction is followed by a two-bar vamp that is repeated until the soloist begins. The strophe and chorus, both 16 bars, have four phrases each: A B A B and C D C D. The technique of writing a catchy easily-remembered chorus is referred to as a "hook."

9 Ernest Seitz (1892–1978) studied with Josef Lhevinne and became a pianist and teacher based in Toronto. Eugene Lockhart became a Hollywood character actor, appearing in more than 300 movies including *Casablanca* (1942) and *Going My Way* (1944).

10 Benny Goodman's orchestra recorded a famous version in 1943 and Goodman also recorded it with his sextet in 1948. In the Laurel and Hardy film *Sons of*

the Desert Laurel plays it on a bed spring! A 1951 country-styled recording by Mary Ford with Les Paul uses multi-track recording techniques. Recent Canadian recordings were made by Mary Lou Fallis in 1997 and Ben Heppner in 1999. Augustus Bridle explained the popularity of *Waiting for the Sunrise* in the *Toronto Star* on 13 August 1939: "It's always a problem, whether text or tune is the thing that most sells a song. Memory is the best. If all the millions who know this song ... could be asked what "sold" the song to them, 999 in every 1,000 would say "the tune" because not one in 1,000 can even remember the words. Personally, I belong to the 999. I've known the tune for years, and I don't yet know the words past the first line ... The words are good, or the song as such never would have been such an epidemic ... But the tune written by Ernest Seitz has been danced to by millions in many countries who never knew more than one line of the words."

11 William Eckstein (1888–1963) was renowned in Montreal as a child pianist and also played violin, cornet, flute, xylophone, ocarina, and tin whistle. Billed as "The Boy Paderewski," he began working in vaudeville at age twelve, and toured North America and Europe on the Keith and Proctor circuits.

12 Sergei Rachmaninoff heard Eckstein in Montreal and reportedly left the theatre muttering, "I don't believe it" ("The Memory Lingers," *Montreal Star*, 31 January 1970, 45).

13 The song, inspired by a Toronto restaurant, opens with a 9-bar introduction followed by a 2-bar vamp. The 16-bar strophe has four phrases (A B C D), and the chorus is almost twice as long (E F G H E I[F] J K).

14 Sam Howard's text reflects social changes of the Roaring Twenties: "'S'nice when he put's his arms around me/'S'nice when he's glad he found me/ev'rytime that boy starts to kiss/ Oh lordy it's heavenly bliss" The 16-bar strophe has four phrases (A B[A] C D); the 40-bar chorus with irregular phrasing can be analysed as E F G H.

15 The Maple Leaf Club, a gambling house and bordello in Sedalia, Missouri, had apparently been a "safe house" in the days of the Underground Railway; the two operators, Will and Walter Williams, were said to be from either London or Windsor in Ontario. The *Maple Leaf Rag* became a local favourite and was published in St Louis.

16 *Delirious Rag* has four sections (A A B B C C D D C); arpeggio figures in both hands indicate a classical influence. Eckstein's *Some Rag* (C M H 22, 198) is A A B B A vamp C D (or 12-bar bridge).

17 Shelton Brooks was born in Amherstburg, Ontario in 1886 or 1896, and died in Los Angeles in 1975.

18 The four-phrase strophe (A B C D) was favoured by post-1910 Tin Pan Alley composers. Sophie Tucker, "the last of the red-hot mamas," had a wide range and a forceful voice and her 1911 recording with an unknown New York dance band reveals that she must have been listening to Black singers of the blues. The vocal accents before and after the beat contrast with the steady tempo of the band, and some phrases are almost spoken.

19 The following numbers from a 1919 dance program in Victoria include tunes from the First World War and Shelton Brooks *Darktown Strutters*: waltz (*Forget-me-not*); medley one-step (*Oui Oui Marie*); foxtrot (*Everything*); one step (*When You Come Back*); waltz (*Kisses*); one step (*Me-ow*); foxtrot (*Smiles*); waltz (*Roses of Picardy*), foxtrot (*Darktown Strutters*); one step (*On Frenchy*); one step (*You're in Style*); foxtrot (*Jealous Moon*); waltz (*My Paradise*); medley one step (*Howdy*); foxtrot (*Tickle Toe*); one step (*Katy*); waltz (*Blue Rose*); foxtrot (*Mother, Dixie and You*); one step (*There's a Ship Bound for Blighty*); waltz (*Perfect Day*)

20 In May 1921 *Biff Bing Bang*, the first Canadian musical revue to appear on Broadway, opened for a twelve-week run at the Ambassador Theatre in New York. The Dumbells made eleven more cross-country tours before 1932.

21 Up to 1958, recordings were banned during the evening CBC programs to encourage the use of live talent.

22 A song folio published in Toronto by Canadian Music Sales Corporation, n.d. includes: *Take Me Back to My Boots and Saddle, Brazil, Can't Get Out of the Mood, Home on the Range, Rockin' Chair, Lazybones, I'll Keep on Loving You, Der Fuehrer's Face, Do I Worry, Till Reveille, Ship A Hoy, Sailor Boy, Georgia on My Mind, My Juanita*. The Mart Kenney band remained active into the 1970s.

23 Farnon's Symphony no. 1 (1938) was performed in Toronto and Philadelphia; his Symphony no. 2 ("Ottawa") was premiered in 1942.

24 Of the three bands formed to entertain allied troops (American, British, and Canadian), the Canadian band was commonly accepted as the finest.

25 Sohner Park, an amusement park in Montreal's east end founded by Ernest Lavigne (1851–1919) included gardens, a pavilion, a restaurant, kiosques, and a zoo, and in 1896, the first Canadian projection of motion pictures. The park was destroyed by fire in 1919. The popularity of amusement parks increased after free admission was introduced in 1909. Joseph-Ernest Ouimet (1877–1972) had been the lighting technician at the Sohner Park.

26 *Les veillées* (1921–41) was a popular concert series featuring folk music at the Monument national in Montreal. Singers included Charles Marchand, (1891–1930), who was advertised on Buckingham Cigarettes as "le plus grand chanteur folkloriste du Canada."

27 *Chez ma tante Gervais* is based on *Menteries*, a song in the *Formulaire fort récréatif* (1554) of Bredin le Cocu (Tétu de Labsade 2001, 400); *Ca va venir découragez-vous pas* (HACM–109; CMH12, 34) a song about unemployment, is brightened with the fiddle tune *Reel de Tadoussac*. Most of Bolduc's songs have a strophe and refrain of equal length. *Turluter* is a vocal imitation of a fiddle tune, as in the *Reel turlute*.

28 He created his first song, *L'adieu du soldat*, while playing his guitar at Valcartier, Quebec, and according to his autobiography, a publisher heard him perform at a soldiers' entertainment (CMH12, ix).

29 Gadbois was disturbed by what he viewed as immoral American influences in language and text in the songs of performers such as Madame Bolduc. Accordingly some texts in *La bonne chanson* were modified to better reflect Roman

Catholic teachings and Gadbois's moral views. From 1939 to 1952, he had fifteen-minute broadcasts of songs, on Radio-Canada, and CKAC, and after 1954 on CJMS.

30 *Le violon accordé comme une viole*, a tune Carignan learned from his father, is probably influenced by Scottish traditions, since it uses scordatura tuning.

31 *Blackfly* (NFB 1991) is sung by Hemsworth; *The Log Driver's Waltz* (NFB 1979) is sung by the McGarrigle Sisters.

32 See www.members.tripod.com/fiddlemusic/andy-text.htm for details of his career.

33 *Tumbling Tumbleweeds*, a classic cowboy song was originally written as *Tumbling Leaves*, revised in 1934, and sung by Gene Autry in the movie *Tumbling Tumbleweeds* (1935); it was also used in *Silver Spurs* (1943), *Hollywood Canteen* (1944), and *Don't Fence Me In* (1945); Bing Crosby's version topped the hit parade in 1940. The song has a four-bar introduction, a twelve-bar strophe (a–b–a–c–d–e) ending on the dominant, and a 28-bar refrain characterized by chromatic phrases (B: f f g h; B; C: i j; B).

34 An advertisement for the popular Tennessee Ten (actually seven musicians) who toured the Orpheum circuit in western Canada in 1917 and 1919, claimed that they presented "Ethiopian songs, dances and antics, introducing their famous Jazz band" (Winnipeg *Tribune*, 19 August 1919, p. 7) (See figure 9.4).

CHAPTER TEN

1 Hubert's students include Henri Brassard, Marc Durand, Janina Fialkowska, Marc-André Hamelin, Francine Kay, André Laplante, Stéphane Lemelin, Louis Lortie, William Tritt, and Ronald Turini.

2 Krauss's outstanding students and recital partners include Elizabeth Benson Guy, Andrew MacMillan, Lois Marshall, Mary Morrison, Gary Relyea, Roxolana Roslak, R. Murray Schafer, and Patrick Wedd.

3 The first music teachers registration act in Canada was passed in 1938 by the Legislative Assembly of Saskatchewan. Gustin's students include Garth Beckett, Reginald Bedford, Evelyn Eby, Neil Chotem, Robert Fleming, Thelma Johannes O'Neill, and Douglas Voice.

4 Egbert's students include Jane Coop, Marek Jablonski, Minuetta Kessler, Diana McIntosh, and Linda Lee Thomas.

5 Vinci trained many of Canada's successful singers including Robert Goulet, Elizabeth Benson Guy, Andrew MacMillan, Mary Morrison, Roxolana Roslak, Bernard Turgeon, and Portia White.

6 His father James Reilley (1886–1956) founded one of Canada's earliest jazz bands and also the Elmdale Harmonica Band (*National Post* 3 October 2000)

7 Galper's best known student is James Campbell.

8 The Conservatoire de musique du Québec was a state-supported system modeled on the Paris Conservatoire as Lavallée envisioned decades before. The seven

institutions are in Monteal, Quebec City, Trois Rivières, Gatineau, Chicoutimi, Val-d'Or, and Rimouski.

9 Arnold Walter was elected president; other prime movers of CAUSM were Harvey Olnick, Ezra Schabas, Godfrey Ridout (Toronto); Clément Morin, Jean Papineau-Couture (Montréal); Lucien Brochu (Laval); Helmut Blume, Marvin Duchow, Istvan Anhalt (McGill); Kenneth Bray (University of Western Ontario); Lorne Watson (Brandon); Howard Brown, George Proctor (Mount Allison); Violet Archer (Alberta); Welton Marquis, Cortland Hultberg (University of British Columbia) (Beckwith 1999, 2).

10 At this time Carleton University was the only school that had a Canadian music course in its calendar .

11 In 1955 the name changed to Opera Festival Company of Toronto; the name Canadian Opera Company was adopted in 1958.

12 Examples include soprano Lois Marshall, baritone Louis Quilico, violinist Steven Staryk, and tenor Jon Vickers.

13 In a moving presentation, singer Frances James said: "I have recently completed a coast-to-coast concert tour of Canada during which I gave sixteen song recitals. My income was $3200; my expenses (hotel and incidental, fees paid my manager and accompanist, and rail fares) were $2700. I therefore realized $500 from my season's concerts. Supplementing this was my income from the Canadian Broadcasting Corporation. This was practically all absorbed by expenditures for clothes, accompanist's rehearsal fees, printing, photographs, and other expenses pertaining to my year's engagements." (Lazarevich 1988, 168).

14 Jacques Singer, conductor of the 1950 Vancouver Symphony and largely responsible for organizing the Vancouver Symposium, was fired from his position in circumstances that seemed directly linked to his promotion of contemporary music.

15 For example, in the first twenty years, the number of opera companies assisted by Canada Council grants rose from two to nine, and orchestras from ten to thirty-one.

16 The program consisted of Sonata for Violin and Piano, *Israel* (Sonata for Violoncello and Piano), *Three Songs Of Time and the World,* Piano Sonata, Divertimento no. 2, *Interludes in an Artist's Life,* and Divertimento no. 1. The Performers were Murray Adaskin, Leo Barkin, Perry Bauman, George Brough, Gordon Day, Reginald Godden, Isaac Mamott, and a string orchestra conducted by Ettore Mazzolini.

17 The catalogue includes works for students by Murray Adaskin, Violet Archer, John Beckwith, Keith Bissell, Robert Fleming, Harry Freedman, Talivaldis Kenins, Clermont Pépin, Jean Papineau-Couture, R. Murray Schafer, and Harry Somers.

18 Nine were of the generation born at the close of the nineteenth century, and the rest, mainly age twenty-four to thirty-eight, represented the new generation: Violet Archer, John Beckwith (*Music for Dancing*), Alexander Brott (*From Sea to Sea*), Jean Coulthard, Robert Fleming, Harry Freedman, Oskar Morawetz, Ken-

neth Peacock, Barbara Pentland (*Sonata for Violoncello and Piano*), Clermont Pépin (*Symphonic Variations*), Godfrey Ridout, Harry Somers (*North Country, Testament of Youth*) Andy Twa, Jean Vallerand (Keillor 1994, 38)

19 Garant's *Nucléogame* was likely the first combination of acoustic and taped sounds heard after the première of Varèse's *Déserts* in Paris in 1954 (Lefebvre 1986, 52).

20 Music presented during the conference was divided between five concerts: An orchestral program with the National Festival Orchestra and Wind Ensemble conducted by Victor Feldbrill; a chamber music program; an electronic music program; an orchestral program with Roy Harris conducting the Orchestra of the International String Congress; and an orchestral program with Walter Susskind conducting the CBC Symphony Orchestra. Canadian composers represented on these programs include István Anhalt, Harry Freedman, Otto Joachim, Jean Papineau-Couture, Godfrey Ridout, and John Weinzweig; international composers include Luciano Berio, Ernst Krenek, Olivier Messiaen, Igor Stravinsky, Edgar Varèse, and Heitor Villa-Lobos. In addition to conference events the group heard a regular Festival concert: Glenn Gould, Leonard Rose, and Oscar Shumsky in a Beethoven trio program.

21 About half of the CBC Symphony personnel were also members of the TSO. Stravinsky was so impressed with the CBC orchestra and the Toronto Festival Singers that he insisted on using these ensembles in Toronto for Columbia recordings of his works. The choir and orchestra also made recordings of works by Schoenberg.

22 For Expo '67 Ten Centuries gave four concerts and commissioned works from Norma Beecroft, Ron Collier, Bruce Mather, André Prévost, and Norman Symonds.

23 Weinzweig wrote a series of divertimentos; all except nos. 5 (trumpet and trombone), 9 (orchestra), 10 (piano), 12 (woodwind quintet) feature a solo wind instrument with a string ensemble. Divertimento no. 1 received the chamber music medal at the 1948 Olympics.

24 At the end of his study year (financed with a scholarship from the Amateur Hockey Association) Somers applied serial technique in one of his assignments, just to see if Milhaud would spot it – he didn't.

25 *Kuyas* is based on motivic ideas of a lament of Skateen, the Wolfhead chief of a Nass River tribe, British Columbia – as collected and notated by Marius Barbeau and Ernest MacMillan – and the Cree words from a grammar by H.E. Hives and an English-Cree primer by F.G. Stevens; the words in the last section come from a story as told by Coming Day, a resident of the Sweetgrass Reserve. The accompanying instruments – drum and flute – would have been used by the First Peoples in the early contact period. In 1967, Somers submitted *Kuyas* as a test piece for the Montreal International Voice Competition which required vocal texts in languages not likely to be known by any of the competitors.

26 *Feller from Fortune* (which appeared in the 1955 edition of Gerald S. Doyle's *Old-Time Songs of Newfoundland*) illustrates his rhythmical and contrapuntal treat-

ment of the original tune. Peacock suggests that it is likely one of a family of songs that also includes *The Feller of Burgeo* (1965, 54).

27 The symphony manager had told him to "write something like [Johann] Strauss because the audience likes that music" Schafer turned to Richard Strauss, using quotations from *Heldenleben.*

28 Weinzweig's *Dirgeling* (1939) is an earlier example

29 This work received critical praise at a concert of Canadian works conducted by Leopold Stokowski at Carnegie Hall in New York, 16 October 1953.

30 The *automatistes* encouraged Paul-Émile Borduas to issue *Refus global* (1948), denouncing the conservatism of society and demanding freedom for artists in Quebec. "Even though no musician signed this manifesto, the formalist and abstract musical trend that emerged from it lasted until the end of the 1970s" (Lefebvre 2001, 1151).

31 "[A]ttacks of the notes ... reverberations, playing the tape backwards, combinations of different elements and textures, slowing down and speeding up the tape, etc. – all this I have transferred to the symphony orchestra" (quoted in Proctor 1980, 110)

32 McLaren made thirteen films using this process, including the renowned *Neighbours* (1952).

33 Osmond Kendall's composer-tron "derived sounds from a number of generators, and combined them using a control panel and an oscilloscope screen, so that composers could adjust the sounds" (Young 1989, 57).

34 Unfortunately Robb was unable to obtain financial backing; he produced less than 20 instruments. By 1939 the Allen organ, a US instrument, was on the market.

35 Canadian industry, however, could not see the potential of such a product; in 1964 Robert A. Moog, influenced by Harald Bode, produced the first commercial modular synthesizer.

36 "It was completely polyphonic – a new concept during the '50s, when this machine was built. All the voltage-controlled synthesizers of the '60s were still monophonic" (Lanza 2002, 46).

CHAPTER ELEVEN

1 In 1949 Capitol Records gave Regal Records of London, Ontario, a contract to press Capital releases in Canada. Capitol Records had been releasing recordings in three speeds (78, 45, and 33 1/3 rpm). The following year EMI bought Capitol, including the Canadian division.

2 Edith Fowke indexed more than 30,000 poems published in the "Old Favourites" column, and estimated that some fifteen percent were songs. See "Old Favourites": A Selective Index," *Canadian Folk Music Journal* 7 (1979), 29–56.

3 Winnipeg-born Oscar Brand had largely kept oral transmission of folk songs alive in the United States; his folk song show on WNYC (New York), broadcast

from 1947 into the 1960s, inspired the establishment of the Newport Festival (1959).

4 In January 1941, he arranged for some of his informants, along with Madame Bolduc, to perform on a CBS Columbia radio program in New York presented by Alan Lomax.

5 In a letter to Moses Asch, Barbeau proposed contents for seven recordings; Barbeau to Asch, 27 December 1955, Canadian Museum of Civilization, Archives, Barbeau fonds, B239 f. 24.

6 The 1960s saw the rise of folk festivals. Earlier attempts include the Folk Festival (Toronto), founded in 1938; on 21–22 June 1940, twenty-five musical heritages were represented under the direction of Brownlow Cord with Carroll Lucas and his orchestra. In 1957, Barbeau, Sam Gesser, and Francis Coleman proposed an annual International Folk Festival but the project was never realized.

7 Mariposa is Stephen Leacock's fictional name for Orillia. In his autobiography Murray McLauchlan comments that performers reached a certain threshold in the Canadian musical scene when they were invited to perform at the Riverboat (a coffee house in Toronto), and Mariposa (1998, 85, 146).

8 The eighth Annual Mariposa Folk Festival (9–11 August 1968) held at Toronto's Centre Island featured more than 120 performers and 25 informal workshops and seminars, always an important part of Canadian folk festivals. The Friday evening concert hosted by Oscar Brand featured the Beers Family, Mike Cooney, Henry Chowning & Son, Joni Mitchell, Tony & Irene Saletan, and Bukka White. Other performers heard in the Saturday and Sunday evening concerts were Murray McLauchlan, Steve Gillette, Bill Monroe Bluegrass Boys, Tom Kines, Judy Roderick, Howlin' Wolf Blues Band, Mary Jane & Winston Young, Sara Grey, Jim McHarg's Metro Stompers, David Rea, Mike Seeger, the Travellers, Gilles Vigneault, and the Young Tradition. Other cultural traditions were presented through folk music and dance presented by Toronto's many multicultural groups including the Know India Cultural Society. First Peoples were represented by the Saugeen Indian Dancers and Duke Redbird, who took part in the poetry seminar.

9 The Crew Cuts – originally the Canadaires – consisted of tenors Pat Barrett, Johnnis Perkins, baritone and arranger Rudy Mangeri, and bass Ray Perkins, all former students at St Michael's Choir School in Toronto.

10 The Four Lads (tenors James Arnold, Bernard Toorish, baritone Frank Busseri, and bass Connie Codarini) were also from Toronto and trained at St Michael's Choir School.

11 The Diamonds original personnel (1953), students at UofT, included lead Dave Somerville, tenor Ted Kowalski, baritone Phil Leavitt, bass Bill Reed but there were several subsequent changes. Assisted by Bill Randle, a Cleveland disc jockey who also worked with the Crew Cuts, they auditioned successfully for Mercury Records, a company that defined rock 'n' roll as mass-market imitations of Black records.

12 An exaggerated falsetto and bass is paired with cowbells, castanets, Spanish rhythm guitar, and piano glissandos. "In the obligatory talking break (... the 'rap'), the singer's conventional romantic pleas – 'To hold in mine your little hand/I know too soon that all is so grand/Please hold my hand' – are deflated by the prominent plucking of harps, which comically comment on the lowbrow sentimental *angst* of the singer. In short, it is a song which pokes fun at its own tradition: it takes an ironic distance from the genre of the sentimental romantic ballad, the genre to which it apparently belongs, by playing with its conventions ... Just as playing off American genres is integral to a good deal of interesting Canadian cinema, so playing with the conventions of rock music is an important aesthetic possibility for Canadian popular music" (Grant 1986, 118).

13 The Beau-Marks consisted of pianist Joey Frechette, lead guitar and vocals Ray Hutchinson, rhythm guitar Mike Robitaille, drummer Gilles Tailleur.

14 "Let's get three guitar players and we'll orchestrate them like horns. Instead of strumming away, let's orchestrate them around the piano. And find a jazz-oriented bass player and drummer, and still keep it a rock band" (Jennings 1997, 128).

15 "The Spoonful's 'good-time sound' – a mix of country, blues, rock and jug-band sounds – was a refreshing change from the protest music that had dominated the Greenwich Village scene" (Jennings 1997, 126).

16 Among their major hits were *Monday Monday* (1966) and *California Dreamin'*, which Doherty wrote in New York and the Virgin Islands. Their hit recordings popularized the "beach-bum vocal sound" (Jennings 1997, 126).

17 Steppenwolf, formed in Toronto in 1964, with John Kay (vocals, harmonica, guitar), Dennis Edmonton (guitar), Goldy McJohn (organ, piano), Nick St Nicholas (bass guitar), and Jerry Edmonton (drums).

18 Their *Born to be Wild* (1967) written by Mars Bonfire of the Sparrows and used in the film *Easy Rider*, includes the line "heavy metal thunder."

19 Mashmakan, named for a drug, was originally formed in 1960 as a backup group: Ray Blake, guitar, Brian Edwards, bass, vocals, Pierre Sénécal, flute, Jerry Mercer, drums.

20 Both *Diana* and *Lonely Boy* (1959) have a chorus-bridge form, derived from Broadway musicals and also used by the Beatles, that focuses interest on the beginning of the song. Other international groups, such as the Rolling Stones, use the older verse-chorus format. Anka's theme for *The Tonight Show* (1962) was used until Johnny Carson's retirement in May 1992.

21 This unique sound was the result of a blend between Ian's warm and smooth tone and Sylvia's cooler harmony line as well as their unusual harmonies and arrangements using Sylvia's autoharp. "According to Sylvia, the secret to their success was simply hard work: 'We did something that nobody else on the local folk scene did – we rehearsed ... In terms of what else was around, we were a pretty polished act'" (Jennings 1997, 23).

22 "[T]he song worked on many levels. It conveyed the vastness of Canada and the striking beauty of its landscapes. It somehow achieved what historians, journal-

ists and politicians had failed to do: bring the country together with a proud sense of its past" (Jennings 1997, 145). Lightfoot has admitted the influence of the US folk singer Bob Gibson, whose *Civil War Trilogy* has a slow middle section framed by two faster sections, but the structure of *Canadian Railroad Trilogy* is more complex: there are five separate sections, some of which are repeated, and most of which have different metres and melodic contours.

23 He hosted a radio show in the late 1940s and from 1951 to 1957 toured with his wife Noëlla Therrien and his daughter Renée; *Marcel Martel* was broadcast from CHLT Sherbrooke during the years 1962 to 1965.

24 He became a scriptwriter for CBC Montreal in 1941; his popular series include *Je me souviens,* and *Félix Leclerc et ses chansons.*

25 "Osstidcho" is a homonymous play on words: *Ostie,* 'the host' in a Catholic Mass (and the worst French language swear word), and *cho,* a vernacular word play on the English word *show.*

26 Charlebois may have known about covers made in the late 1950s by the Jérolas (*Yakety Yak, Jones s'est montré, Charlie Brown,* and *Méo Penché*) using a form of French spoken in Quebec with lots of humour.

27 MacDermot was involved in the production of *My Fur Lady,* the popular McGill University "Red and White Revue" that toured Canada in 1957–58.

28 In 1969, sixteen of the twenty-nine songs (*Aquarius* being the most notable) were released as singles; four made the top forty. *Hair* ran for 1,729 performances on Broadway before closing in 1972; In 2006, Canadian Stage in Toronto mounted a new production.

29 Bop is a shortened version of "bebop," a word commonly used in scat singing. Musicians largely associated in the development of bop are Dizzy Gillespie, Charlie Parker, Bud Powell, Thelonius Monk, Kenny Clarke, and Max Roach.

30 From 1963 to 1958 his trios consisted of piano, guitar and bass, after which he reverted to the formation with drums popularized by Nat King Cole.

31 "Place St-Henri" is the section of Montreal where he grew up; "Wheatland" is a musical soundscape of the Prairies.

32 According to his widow, he always referred to himself as Canadian even though most of his professional activity was based in New York or California.

33 From 1944 to 1947 he had been a member of an avant garde bebop band headed by singer Billy Eckstine that also included Charlie Parker, Dizzy Gillespie, Miles Davis, and Art Blakey.

34 Round dances and two-steps, often accompanied by traditional music and using partners, lines, or squares rather than Aboriginal formations, were performed when First Peoples congregated for competitive rodeos. At the first Calgary Stampede in 1912, the only Canadian to win major top awards was Tom Three Persons, a Blood Indian. Since government and tourist authorities wanted to present a history in which the West was empty prior to the arrival of settlers, cowboys, fur traders, and the North-West Mounted Police, a 1914 amendment to the Indian Act forbade participation in dances, rodeos, and public exhibitions

off reserves in the Western provinces and territories subject to the approval of local Indian agents of the Canadian government.

35 "The Hawks, he said, 'played the fastest, most violent rock and roll I'd ever heard. It was exciting and exploding with dynamics. The solos would get *really* loud. Ronnie would come in and growl, then it would get quiet, then fast and loud again. It was these cool-looking guys doing this primitive music faster and more violent than anybody, with overwhelming power'" (Jennings 1997, 24).

36 Buffalo Springfield consisted of three fellow Canadians – Stephen Stills, Richie Furay, Dewey Martin – plus two Americans.

37 Liona Boyd often performs her own works combining influences from various musical styles, including flamenco, Latin American, country with classical guitar traditions.

38 The haunting descending melodic line is used in a four-verse plus coda structure. Gene MacLellan wrote *Snowbird* four years earlier on a Prince Edward Island beach as he watched a flock of snow buntings; the Nashville Songwriters Association chose MacLellan as best composer for 1970.

39 The Hahns (or Harmony Kids) of Saskatchewan – Lloyd, Robert, Kay, and Joyce – managed a musical career in the 1930s, barnstorming through small towns in Northern Ontario, the Prairies, and the northern United States and passing the hat after each show. After a few breaks on New York radio, they survived by busking in the Big Apple of the early 1940s. The pinnacle of their success was a steady booking at the Red Robin, where a crew member of a Canadian freighter requested *The Maple Leaf Forever* (Hahn 1985, 173).

40 With a major hit royalty payments as low as six cents for sheet music or twenty-five cents per radio broadcast can amount to a sizeable income.

41 The first recipient of the new award (an eighteen-inch elongated walnut metronome designed by Stan Klees), was Diane Leigh for top female country vocalist.

42 The Anik A-1, stationed 58,000 kilometres above the equator, due south of Regina, transmitted television and radio signals and telephone calls, permitting much improved reception across Canada.

43 The government of Trinidad and Tobago sent the steel pan orchestra Esso Tripoli to Expo 67 in Montreal. Their performance in Toronto's City Hall Square introduced many Canadians to steel pan music. Peter Marcelline recalls: "They were astounded at hearing this beautiful sound coming out of the steel band" (Foster 1995, 59).

44 "All countries are simultaneously geographic places, imagined communities (nations) and scales of organisation (States) maintained despite the economic, political and cultural forces that promote other scales. Compared to other nations, Canadians frequently find such forces to be particularly significant because of their country's vast area, sparse population and pronounced regional disparities. Each province is still largely self-governing and regional differences have encouraged an ongoing dispute over the national constitution, fuelled by claims from Quebec's French Canadians and its native population ... In the face of internal disagreement the country has always maintained an 'ironic' relation

to the symbols, practises and policies of national identity that many other countries take for granted" (Duffett 2000, 4).

CHAPTER TWELVE

1 This report shifted the state's cultural role from proprietor and regulator to custodian, patron, and catalyst. They discarded schema that equated the governance of culture with Canadianization and the commercialization of culture with Americanization, as well as the use of art for a symbol of national unity (Gaskr 1997, 26).

2 For example, in 1998 federal restrictions on advertising by tobacco companies had a major effect on events such as the du Maurier New Music Festival in Winnipeg (Dick 1998, 18); Mark Duffett has pointed out the importance of such sponsorship (Duffett, 1–2).

3 The discourse explores the meanings of North for Canadians, most of whom have never experienced that space. Gould interviewed a nurse, a sociology professor, an ex-government official, a British anthropologist and geographer, and an aged surveyor; there are no voices of First Peoples.

4 For example, religious music sung by the Mennonite Children's Choir and the Kitchener-Waterloo United Mennonite Church congregation was juxtaposed with *Mercedes Benz* by Janis Joplin and *My Foolish Heart* by Ned Washington and Victor Young.

5 For more detailed information on events during 1986, see the *Encyclopedia of Music in Canada* and Keillor 1987.

6 La Nef was founded by Sylvain Bergeron, Claire Gignac, and Viviane LeBlanc.

7 The Winnipeg New Music Festival was founded in 1992 by the Winnipeg Symphony Orchestra under the direction of conductor Branwell Tovey and composer-in-residence Glenn Buhr. The eclectic programming encourages crossovers with jazz, legitimate, and pop in a relaxed ambiance with audience seated on stage, pre-concert chats by composers, and a general invitation for everyone to mingle in post-concert cafés (Dick 1998, 18).

8 Other large-scale festivals organized by Goldschmidt include the first Vancouver International Festival (1958), Festival Canada (a nation-wide series of events, 1967), the Guelph Spring Festival (launched in 1968), the Algoma Fall Festival (a choral festival in Sault Ste Marie, 1973), the International Bach Piano Competition (1985), the International Choral Festival (1989), an International Mozart Festival (1991), and a Benjamin Britten Festival (2003).

9 In 1993 SOCAN rescinded a royalty structure that calculated payments for "classical" works on a higher scale than that used for popular music (on the grounds that it takes longer to produce an extensive chamber or orchestral work than a three-minute song), with the result that royalty incomes for concert music plunged. Publishers receive half the royalty, but because most performances of and interest in Canadian concert works take place within Canada, international

publishers lost interest in publishing these works, and a number of Canadian music publishers went out of business; survivors include Archambault, Frederick Harris Music, Waterloo Music, and Doberman-Yppan. Many composers now publish their own music and can thus claim both publishing and composition royalties.

10 The selection of works discussed in this section has been largely pre-determined by available recordings, and particularly works included on *Introduction to Canadian Music*, Naxos 8.550171–2.

11 The first of the two sketches evokes the massive Mont-aux-Sources; the second, entitled "Umfaan in the Hills" includes a simulation of a Zulu boy's cheerful call and response song (Primos 1994, 15).

12 Baker's score for *The Grey Fox* (1983) won a Genie; *Cinderella: Frozen in Time* was written for Dorothy Hamill's Ice Capades

13 On one level, the twelve essays can be read as forming an arch (similar to a structure often used by Bartók) but on another level, they hark back to a sonata-allegro form with exposition, development, and recapitulation. Each essay has a programmatic title.

14 *Canada Mosaic* was commissioned by the Vancouver Symphony Orchestra for an Asian tour. Coulthard chose to base the work on Canadian folk materials in response to requirements of Chinese officials that the orchestra should perform "music of the people." The third movement, "D'Sonoqua's Song" uses formulas and rhythms from a First Nations song collected by Ida Halpern; the final movement, "New Year in Chinatown" expresses Coulthard's memories of Chinese lion dances.

15 For an overview of some of Schafer's scores, see Rumson 2000.

16 Prologue: The Princess of the Stars (1981); Patria I: Wolfman (1966–74); Patria II: Requiems for the Party Girl (1972); Patria III: The Greatest Show (1987); Patria IV: The Black Theatre of Hermes Trismegistos (1988); Patria V: The Crown of Ariadne (1991); Patria VI: Ra (1983); Patria VII: Asterion; Patria VIII: The Palace of the Cinnabar Phoenix (2000); Patria IX: The Enchanted Forest (1993); Patria X: The Spirit Garden (1995–97); Epilogue: And Wolf Shall Inherit the Moon (1988).

17 "Gathered around a campfire in the Canadian wilderness [t]hey listen to a totem-istic legend told in an archaic style by a first-generation East-Indian Canadian. They laugh at a comic poem recited in a heavy Kurosawa accent by a Japanese-Canadian counter-tenor. Together they croon the triadic harmonies of an Austrian folksong. They chant along with a masked story-teller, Wordshaker, thoroughly enjoying a poem they have often heard before and know intimately. A young Anglo-Canadian plays an Andean melody on the quena, a bamboo flute. Someone is heard to invoke "all my relations" in a translation of the Lahota-Sioux phrase, mitakuye oyasin. Serene vocal music floats far down the lake, answered by the haunting call of a loon, the soft plash of a paddle in the still water, the low chanting of heterophonous voices. The seemingly contradictory co-existence of

diverse cultural elements is made plausible by the enveloping wilderness; words and music of many cultures are harmonized in a unifying matrix of forest, rock, and lake" (Waterman 1998, 7).

18 In the midst of usually pentatonic string patterns spiralling through a wide register often in contrary motion, a group of wind instruments present a homo-rhythmic gesture built of non-third chords in the central part of the texture. At points a clear tonal centre is suggested and leads to the closing pitch.

19 Vivier said: "I wrote a piece, a tribute to Bali, yes, but all the rest of my music afterwards was more or less a tribute to Bali ... a lesson in love, in tenderness, in poetry and in respect for life" (Gasser 1996, 28).

20 *Kopernikus* is a chamber opera scored for seven voices and eight instrumentalists. The plot revolves around the transformation of a woman, Agni, and is played out in dream sequences with characters such as Lewis Caroll, Merlin, the Queen of the Night, Tristan and Isolde, and Copernicus and his mother. It was first staged in 2000 as a co-production of Opéra de Montréal and Autumn Leaf Performance in Banff, August 2000.

21 Alexina Louie is one of a number of Canadian composers – including Vivian Fung, Alice Ho, Melissa Hui, and Chan Ka Nin – with Asian roots.

22 The libretto of Louie's kabuki inspired opera *The Scarlet Princess* (2002), written by David Henry Hwang (of *M. Butterfly* fame) features a beautiful princess and a lovelorn monk who are caught up in a maelstrom of illicit passion, betrayal, and murder.

23 Members of Canada's First Nations have been performing Western concert music since the early 1600s. Some became skilled players on viols and violins and by the end of the nineteenth century on pump organs and pianos. S.K. Hutton describes a service with an Inuit organist: "Jerry, our Okak organist, plays by ear, and coaxes splendid harmony out of our aged pipe organ ... and when the hymns are announced he pulls out his stops and shuffles his feet on the pedals, and with a mighty burst of music the congregation breaks forth into singing, while Jerry, with his magic touch, leads the voices steadily on, in perfect tune and stately time" (1912, 332). E.W. Hawkes refers to an anthem composed by an Inuk at one of the Moravian missions in Labrador (1916, 123), and it is likely that a number of First Nations musicians were creating refined music.

24 See www.ergoprojects.org for more information on Croall's career.

25 *La Tourangelle,* a musical tableau, explores the life of Marie de l'Incarnation before her arrival in Canada in 1639. *Winthrop* is a historical pageant about John Winthrop (1587–1649), a Puritan who founded Boston, and whose descendants came to Canada as United Empire Loyalists; the inherent contradictions in Winthrop's theme of "liberty" present a relevant and instructive comment on important threads in Canada's social fabric. *Traces (Tikkun)* is a pluri-drama in which a displaced person escapes danger and eventually finds a place in a North American city that feels like "home." *Millenial Mall (Lady Diotima's Walk)* is set in an imaginary shopping mall.

26 The 1982 version includes a DMX-1000 signal processor. POD6 is a computer program for real-time frequency modulation (FM) synthesis: "sounds are understood as events, which are – on the macrolevel – distributed within a time/frequency field according to Poisson distributions," a probability theory (Voorvelt 1997, 50).

27 This voyage takes place on four different levels, the universal from the smallest element in nature to the largest constellation, the organic appearance of life through fusion, fission, eruption, and explosion, the human impact with the development of industry, through chaos, the holocaust, robots and general deterioration of the state of the earth, and the fourth synthetic level, beyond the twentieth century to states completely unknown and different (Gagné 1990, 23).

28 Truax's works between 1969 and 1974 are characterized by texts and theatrical elements; those written between 1975 and 1985 are almost exclusively for tape – sometimes with an acoustic instrument or voice – using FM synthesis as the main sound source.

29 An earlier visit to Canada convinced him that this country, with its openness and multicultural character, was an ideal place to pursue his endeavours.

30 *Nadir*, is a portion of Hatzis's *Earthrise Cycle* (1988). While it is a memorial to Canadian poet Gwendolyn MacEwen and to Morton Feldman, it has an air of defiance. It is a musical comment on the Iran-Iraq conflict and Hatzis comments that its heterogeneous stylistic elements serve as a "form of exorcism against the absurdity of war and senseless violence" (<http://www.chass.utoronto.ca/~chatzis/curriculumvitae/>). The 2005 recording of his two string quartets (*Christos Hatzis: Awakening*, EMI Canada 724355803825) topped the charts for chamber music in Europe and America.

31 Hatzis's *Viderunt Omnes* was commissioned by the CBC as part of an international project sponsored by the European Broadcasting Union – for which a composer from each member country contributed an electronic work that in some way incorporated Perotin's organum – broadcast around the world on 1 January 2000. The concert premiere, given by the Toronto Consort on 12–13 January 2001, included projected images of the Northern Lights and stained glass windows in Notre Dame Cathedral of Paris (where the organum *Viderunt Omnes* was first performed).

32 The COC introduced surtitles – an adaptation of the subtitles as used in films – on 21 January 1983 for a production of *Elektra* (Morey and Schabas 2000, 166). At first the surtitles were done with hundreds of slides in projectors, but a simpler process using computerized video projectors was soon adopted and picked up by opera companies around the world.

33 The success of singers such as Teresa Stratas, Maureen Forrester, Edith Wiens, Jon Vickers, Louis Quilico, Victor Braun has been followed by a steady stream of young singers from the next two generations including Isabel Bayrakdarian, Russell Braun, Donna Brown, Norine Burgess, Benjamin Butterfield, Tracey Dahl, Sally Dibble, Gerald Finley, Karina Gauvin, Diana Gilchrist, Ben Heppner, Heidi Klassen, Suzie LeBlanc, Marie-Nicole Lemieux, Richard Margison, Dion Mazerolle, Julie Nesrallah, Nathalie Paulin, Brett Polegato, and Daniel Taylor.

34 COC's 1993 production of *Bluebeard's Castle* and *Erwartung* was mounted in New York and at the Edinburgh International Festival (1993), in Australia (1994), and at the Hong Kong Arts Festival (1996).

35 In its first twenty-five years, Opera in Concert presented eighty different productions with all-Canadian casts.

36 For a list of Canadian operas, opera companies, and their performances abroad, see Maloney 2001, 153–62.

37 The plot of *Beatrice Chaney*, set in Nova Scotia in 1801, concerns the sixteen-year-old Black daughter of a wealthy white Annapolis Valley landowner and his late slave-mistress. The music includes references to Black musical traditions of the early nineteenth century within a contemporary context.

38 In 2002 The Canadian Music Centre had more than 500 associate composers, about fifteen percent of whom are women. However, since composers published by the Canadian Musical Heritage Society are treated as associate members, a significant proportion of the 500 composers are deceased.

39 This organization, was formed by a group of women professional composers for mutual support and encouragement in 1981. Guided initially by Mary Gardiner, the Association now celebrates performances of members' works at festivals such as Donne e musica and on broadcasts throughout the world.

40 Piano Six consisted of Janina Fialkowska, Angela Hewitt, Angela Cheng, Jon Kimura Parker, Marc-André Hamelin, André Laplante

41 New media – audiocasting, internet radio, digital radio, desktop broadcasting – will likely prove a valuable means for access to Canadian content.

CHAPTER THIRTEEN

1 Among these were Jim Galloway, Brian Towers, Kid Bastien, and Charlie Gall.

2 UZEB was active between 1976 and 1992; members include Alan Caron, Michel Cusson, and Paul Brochu.

3 Jackson was originally trained in legitimate music, and in 2002 was working on symphonic commissions and an opera.

4 For an account of the Vancouver jazz scene from the 1950s on, see Reid 2002, 61–9.

5 Krall's important influences include Oscar Peterson and Don Thompson, and she stresses the important role of CBC jazz broadcasts and six Canada Council grants in developing her craft and her career.

6 His death cut short plans for an album on the North and a bilingual one on Quebec.

7 The core of Stringband (formed in 1972) are Bob Bossin and Marie-Lynn Hammond.

8 "[R]ecord A is started and, a little later, record B, after which the DJ passes from one to the other for a repetitive effect" (Compulseve 2002, 36)

9 They increased the speed on each release up to 1993, when they reached a dead end; in the Netherlands their music was used to shout soccer chants (Reynolds 1999, 227).

10 Hawtin rearranged tracks and loops to play sets ranging from intense techno to lush deep house; he produced a new composition for the 2006 Winter Olympics opening ceremony. For details on his work, see www.plastikman.com/ and en.wikipedia.org/wiki/Richie_Hawtin (accessed 17 February 2006); for Acquaviva see www.john-acquaviva.com/ (accessed 17 February 2006).

11 The series is named for Duke Ellington's song, *In My Solitude*.

12 "When one picked up a Truth and Rights recording, whether it was *Acid Rain* or *Metro's No. 1 Problem*, it was clear that it was a Canadian brand of reggae" (Walker 1990, 46). Mojah's later band V, which included Lorraine Segato, Billy Bryans, and Terry Wilkins and fused Latin, calypso, and reggae styles might be considered an early "world beat" sound; some of these musical ideas also achieved fame with the Parachute Club.

13 DJs use previously recorded materials and have established their own trade ethics. A DJ sells a master to a distributor who makes copies; the master is viewed as a franchise and the DJ plays the role of an artist (Schloss 1997).

14 Buck 65, a DJ who began in 1982, comments: "we have the largest indigenous Black population in Canada. There's also a lot of jazz history, so as a beat-maker, I can tell you that the record shopping is dope here" (Arnold 2001, 109). The first wave – Speak, Buck 65 with the Sebutones, and Dabs – were followed by Cops, Lope, Chile, and Dose. In 2001 Homewreckerz, Cabin Fever, Sector, Fatso, Thesis, Seka, and the women Gillian and Christy were among the most popular.

15 Choclair's album *Ice Cold* (1999) includes the hit *Let's Ride*. Kardinal Offishal signed to Wu Records and Saukrates to the large hip hop label Def Jam.

16 After many Punjabis immigrated to Britain in the post-1945 period, bhangra was popularized by performers on the wedding circuit and through recordings.

17 The *dhol* is a wooden barrel drum held with a shoulder strap; the *thumbi* is a one-stringed gourd fiddle that plays short ostinato patterns.

18 For a discussion of forms of bhangra with techno and hip hop developed in British Columbia, see Foran 2006.

19 A performance of k-os (accompanied by a DJ, rock drummer, and tabla player) with the CBC Orchestra was broadcast on CBC television in February 2006. Other recent successes include Swollen Members and the francophone Loco Locass.

20 Original membrs were John Cessine and Mary Kanarek, percussion, Happy Roderman, bass, and Sharon Smith, piano.

21 Members include Lorraine Segato, Lauri Conger, Julie Masi, Margo Davidson, Keith Brownstone, Billy Bryans, Dave Gray, and Steve Webster.

22 Lanois, a Franco-Ontarian, has produced albums for Martha and the Muffins, Parachute Club, Luba, Ian Tyson, Willie P. Bennett, Sylvia Tyson, Bob Dylan, Peter Gabriel, Robbie Robertson, Neville Brothers, and U2. His own work includes the album *Acadie* (1989) and he worked with Brian Eno to create ambient music for club background sounds.

23 Klaatu was named for a character in *The Day the Earth Stood Still*; members were Terry Draper, Dee Long, and John Woloschuk.

24 Other members were Joe Rockman and Tom Stephens.

25 The band, formed in 1981, is named for a slogan of US president James Polk. Band members were Darryl Neudorf, Phil Comparelli, Brad Merritt, and Neil Osborne; Matt Johnson later replaced Neudorf.

26 Blue Rodeo was formed by Jim Cuddy and Greg Keelor; later members include Bobby Wiseman and Mark French.

27 One result is that MuchMusic operates under CRTC CanCon regulations. In 1999 the CRTC requirements stipulated 30 percent Canadian content for sound recordings played on AM and FM radio stations. Quebec pop-music stations must program a minimum of 65 percent in French. See "Canadian Content Rules" at www.pch.gc.ca/culture/can-con/can_con.html.

28 Members were François Guy, Richard Tate, and Angelo Finaldi.

29 La cooperative, under André Paiement, was partially inspired by La bastringue, a group from Hearst who combined theatrical rock with traditional musics prior to the multidisciplinary L'Osstidcho concert in Quebec.

30 René Dupéré's music for *Alegria* includes elements from the Middle East, Sub-Saharan Africa, and Chinese traditional music.

31 In the 1950s Starr joined Bob Regan to form the Canadian Sweethearts. Ostanek formed a polka band in 1957 and began recording in 1963.

32 Members were Russell deCarle, Keith Glass, Dennis Delorme and Alastair Dennett; Joan Besen and John Allen joined in the early 1980s, and Bruce Moffat replaced Dennett.

33 "Her forthright approach, talking directly to audience members, and her from-the-heart retelling of the stories behind the songs, wins over the audience night after night" (Burton 2000, 19).

34 In 1949 *Billboard* linked "country" and "western" (i.e. cowboy) musics together, and this combined definition was used for the next fifty years. Part of the confusion between the two strains was caused by Gene Autry who recorded both cowboy and hillbilly songs (Tyson/Escott 1994, 54).

35 The CBC radio and television shows *Country Hoedown* (1956–65), *Don Messer's Jubilee* (1959–69), *Singalong Jubilee* (1961–74), *Countrytime* (1970–74), and *Rita & Friends* (1990s), broadcast the artistry of Maritime musicians across Canada (Pevere and Dymond 1996, 140).

36 Band members include Alan Doyle, Bob Ballett, Sean McCann, and Darrell Power.

37 The band, formed in 1983, consists of Ditrich, Kelly, Mann, McMillan, and Linda McRae.

38 Subsequent winners include Robbie Robertson, Jerry Alfred, Mishi Donovan, Chester Knight, and Florent Vollant.

39 Cremo played a hand-made fiddle given to his great-grandfather by a Scottish settler. His students included both Ashely MacIsaac and Natalie MacMaster.

40 The song *E186* refers to a government practise of numbering each Inuk rather than figuring out the Inuktitut names.

41 Translation: "Take care of your homeplace, of your grandmother, of yourself."

42 These two women learned throat games from their grandmother and practised by telephone after they were moved to different settlements.

43 The album is named for Toronto's Church of the Holy Trinity where the recording was made.

44 Members were Gordon Downie, Paul Langlois, Bobby Baker, Gord Sinclair, and Johnny Fay.

45 Members in 1991 include Andy Creegan (replaced by Kevin Hearn in 1995), Jim Creegan, Steven Page, Ed Robertson, and Tyler Stewart.

46 Members include Benjamin Darvill, Dan Roberts, Michel Dorge, and Ellen Reid.

47 Members were by Jeff Martin, Stuart Chatwood, and Jeff Burrows.

48 Listings include La bottine souriante, Loreena McKennitt, Stan Rogers, four Toronto Baltic/Turkish influenced groups, and the Montreal groups, Afro Nubians and Zekuhl.

49 In 1991 the United Nations declared Toronto to be the most culturally diverse city in the world; in 2001 Vancouver had musical groups for expressions from China, Japan, Laos, Indonesia, Fiji, India, Kurdistan, several African countries, Croatia, and five different Latin American nations.

50 In *Alma Chillim*, Mark Duggan plays marimba and Bill Brennan plays mbira.

51 Lollapalooza was a travelling North American version of the annual Reading Festival in Britain held from 1991 to 1995.

CHAPTER FOURTEEN

1 The Earl of Southesk wrote: "In all Indian music that I have heard there is a remarkable likeness to the howling of wolves, mingled with the droning growl of a bear" (Southesk 1875/1969, 158).

2 A flute in my personal collection, made in Manitoba in the early 1990s, has a loon carved on the external block ("bird on a roost"). Wheeler notes that "[t]he Indian regards his loon with almost religious veneration" (Wheeler 1914, 65).

3 "If you wish, we will turn away the ice-floes. Let us invoke our demon with our chants and our drums" (Thwaites 1896–1901/1959: V32 201).

4 The first song specifically identified is *À la claire fontaine*, sung at Port Royal in the early 1600s. This song – which includes a reference to a nightingale, a bird not found in Canada – was soon spreading across the land. Robert Kennicott (1835–66), writing in the mid-nineteenth century, reports singing this song close to the Mackenzie River while driving his dog team (1942, 109).

5 Polyphonic forms are found in the Caribou Inuit region and in some Northwest Coast cultures (Pelinski 1981, 61).

6 Some response songs have a Ojibwe refrain or use single Ojibwe words and pronunciation (Lederman 2001d, 1193).

7 Members of Barrage include leader Dean Marshall and core fiddlers John Crozman, Anthony Moore, Jana Wyler, and Larry Soloff.

8 For example, *Les repas dans les chantiers* (Béland 1982, 287) a song about food in the lumber camps is sung to the tune of *Les filles de Parthenay*; *The Baskatong* (Fowke 1970, 66), a text about a shantymen in the Ottawa Valley uses an adaptation of the Irish tune *The Poor Country-man*. In notated music, while no specific tune has been identified as the model for George Pfeiffer's *Canadian Dance* (published ca. 1817), the rhythm and character of this piano piece reflects Celtic-influenced jig tunes played by Euro-Canadian and Métis fiddlers (CMH1 1983, v).

9 In 1919 Barbeau organized the first of a number of concerts of Canadian folk music drawing on the country's multicultural heritage; later concerts combined First Nations and francophone songs, and representation of anglophone songs increased as ethnologists such as W. Roy Mackenzie, Louise Manny, and Helen Creighton produced collections (Keillor 1995a, 193). Use of this folk and traditional material as a basis for notated works received a boost through the participation of a number of anglophone composers in the CPR Folk Festivals of the late 1920s (Kallmann 1992, 327).

10 The staccato-like call of the white-throated sparrow sounds like "Ca-na-da." Schafer points out the call of the loon as "a truly uncounterfeiting and uncounterfeitable soundmark of Canada" that "belongs to that select class of natural utterances that once heard will never be forgotten. The call consists of two parts: a slow, haunting yodel and a maniacal laugh that can make a listener's hair stand on end by its suddenness and its resemblance to a woman's voice" (Schafer 1993, 83).

11 The foundation of strings rises and falls with the terrain, wind instruments interject the sound of train whistles, and large complement of percussion marks the cities on the CPR line – metallic sonorities for night, wooden ones for day (Parsons 1985, 35).

12 Both Harry Freedman and R. Murray Schafer were also painters.

13 Here the "long line," a prominent concept in Canadian landscape works, is treated in an original manner: notes are "passed" from one instrument to the next, penetrating the entire ensemble. "[T]he result is like a glittering thread that weaves its way throughout the texture." At the end, a central pitch (E) in the same register moves from instrument to instrument; this timbral and dynamic shifting creates a magical effect that is suddenly "cut off with a crack from the claves like a brittle twig snapping in the cold – then there is only silence (Parsons 1987, 59–60).

14 This piece is an early musical statement of Schafer's position in *Music in the Cold* (1977).

15 A British study by John Burke divides Britain into geographical areas and examines composers who have lived in and been influenced by specific areas. He lists concert works identified with an area by title or other means, but although he repeatedly comments on a composer's need of the countryside for inspiration and renewal there is little direct reference to how a particular area "sounds" (Burke 1983, 103). In other words he claims that most British composers are rural- rather than urban-based.

16 McIntosh uses a Kiviuq rhythm and theme associated with her experience in the North.

17 Violet Archer uses text by Canadian poet A.J.M. Smith. "The music is spare with an angular melodic line, a dramatic use of dissonance, and strong harmonic progressions which capture the rhythmic qualities of alliteration and onomatopoeia in the poem" (Grace and Haag 1998, 107).

18 Louie's work creates "the sensation of eerie space familiar from Somers, Weinzweig, Morel, and Forsyth … high, thin, sustained notes on the violin followed by gentle glissandi, create a magical quality of icy, delicate beauty. Rapid bowing on the cello suggests the accumulation of snow drifts. Percussion … is used to create a tinkling, brittle sound, and the harp introduces qualities of lightness or softness … it is only the strong minor progression, which concludes the piece, that introduces a heavier, more sombre stillness" (Grace and Haag 1998, 113).

19 "[Vivier's] friend and collaborator, Michel-Georges Brégent explored the dimensions and qualities of musical space, its densities, horizontal and vertical axes, and so on, in building forms and structures within this infinite space. Antoine Padilla saw a similar silence in her music which was personally spiritual, *'une musique à l'intérieur de laquelle on sent un peu l'éternité: une musique de calme, d'isolement, de silence'"* (Thirlwall 1992, 349).

20 Thirlwall's analysis of divisions within *québécois* genres and a growing recognition of all types of music as an expression of identity in the post-1980 period is further developed by Lefebvre (2001).

21 The Quebec version of western-style cowboy life was initially based on twenty-four popular books and supposed autobiography (*Lone Cowboy: My Life Story*) by Joseph Dufault (1892–1942).

22 The Canadian success of Rick Neufeld's *Moody Manitoba Morning* was not reflected south of the border; Neufeld had refused to change "Manitoba" to "Minnesota" (Lehr 1985/1994, 366).

23 In a special issue of *Variety* (September 1949) honouring Guy Lombardo, Louis Armstrong who listened to them from the mid-1920s on and sat in as a performer on occasion, stated: "Guy Lombardo and the Royal Canadians has always been my favorite band."

24 Nolan wrote *Tumbling Tumbleweeds* and *Cool Water,* Wilf Carter wrote *Blue Canadian Rockies*, and Hank Snow wrote *I'm Moving On.*

25 The origin of minimalism is usually assigned to American composer La Monte Young, who was at the University of California Los Angeles when McPhee was teaching there in the 1950s.

26 When The Band made the cover of *Time* Magazine (12 January 1970) the headline read "The New Sound of Country Rock" (Flippo 1994, 9).

27 Each of these myths has inspired musical compositions, but hockey is likely the most influential. Practically every Canadian is familiar with the theme of CBC's *Hockey Night in Canada* composed in 1968 by Dolores Claman.

28 Instruments include the Greek lyra, *baglama, tzoura*, and bouzouki, Romanian panpipes and *tilinca*, and the Hungarian *cimbalon*. Robert Zildjian exports cymbals, hammered out by hand, around the world, and Earle Wong, a renowned

maker of steel drums, moved to Canada in 1968 (Bégin 1992). Perhaps because of this attention to unique types of instruments, traditional epic singing with the one string bowed lute is still nurtured in some instances (Markoff 2001, 1197).

29 The Classical Arabic Music Quintet (formed in 1978, now the Traditional Arabic Music Ensemble; Sawa 2001, 1219) in Toronto is directed by George Sawa who also heads the Centre for Studies in Middle Eastern Music. Beginning in 1971, Regula Qureshi has recorded Muslim chant, instrumental music, folk and popular songs, religious and folk songs of the Egyptian-Copts in Alberta's Lebanese-Syrian community (Qureshi 1972, 393).

30 Yaya Diallo, a drummer from Mali who came to Canada in 1967 and now lives in Vancouver, has taught traditional drumming for many years and formed the fusion groups Kléba and Kanza (Lederman 2001g, 1170).

31 The first Cantonese society, Jin Wah Sing, was founded in Vancouver in 1935.

32 Since 1970 field recordings of Sikh religious chant and hymns, Pakistani folk and popular songs, and North Indian classical music have been made (Qureshi 1972, 393).

33 Prominent examples include Trichy Sankaran, a world-renowned mridangam performer, sārangī player Aruna Narayan Kalle, singer Rashmi Venkateswaran and her violinist sister Meena Venkateswaran, sitarist Prem Lata Mahajan, veena player Lakshmi Ranganathan, and sarod player Aditya Verma.

34 The Canadian percussion ensemble Nexus paved the way by bringing in drummers from around the world for workshops.

35 Brothers of the Sun members are Brad Go-Sam, an Aboriginal of the Ravenshoe people in North Queensland, Australia, Keith Bolton of Australian settler heritage, and Pablo Russell of the Old Agency Clan (Aa'ḵaaksimaaks) in Alberta.

36 As of June 2000, the CBC's *Global Village* had featured more than fifty Canadian musicians or groups, including Lhasa, Oscar Lopez, Mighty Popo, Grupo Taller, Kiran Ahluwalia, Dario Dominguez, Madagascar Slim, Qiu Xia He & Silk Road Music, Uzume Taiko, Irshad Khan, Salsa Piccante, Khac Chi ensemble, Lee Pui Ming, and Alpha Yaya Diallo.

37 "The Canadian bands that make it I hate. Like Loverboy and the Heavy Metal bands, and all those horrible horrible people ... And I don't like Corey Hart and Bryan Adams very much ... It's rock 'n' roll but not even the real good old stuff. It's sort of plaster cast rock 'n' roll ... And Corey Hart is actually doing a lot better in the States than he is here" (Giles 1987, 83).

38 Twain and Lange's *You're Still the One, From This Moment On,* and *Honey I'm Home*; Morissette's *Uninvited, Thank U,* and *That I Would Be Good*; Sarah McLachlan's *Adia* and *Sweet Surrender*; Joni Mitchell's *Crazy Cries of Love* and *Stay in Touch*; Foster's *To Love You More*; Kate McGarrigle's *(Talk to Me of) Mendocino*; Rufus Wainwright's *April Fools*; Our Lady Peace's *Clumsy*; and *26 Cents* by Steve Wilkinson and William Wallace.

39 There are good recording studios in Whitehorse and Yellowknife. *Inuit Artist World Showcase*, the first CD released by Inukshuk Productions (formed 1994) in Inukjuak, includes throat singing, gospel, country and western, fiddle, accordion,

folk, and blues, and has been very successful. Jerry Alfred's albums containing both traditional and folk songs based on the Northern Tutchone tradition are supported by an extensive web site.

40 Groups include the Gumboots, Northern Skies (a Celtic folk trio), Kim Barlow (backed by plucked cello, marimba, and percussion), Inconnu (a Whitehorse band combining Cajun with jazz, punk, and rock), and rappers such as Unonymous of Yellowknife (Diamond 2001f, 1280).

41 For example, in 1984 I attended the first full performance of Handel's *Messiah* performed with orchestra in Yellowknife.

42 Inzwischen stelle ich mir weiterhin eine Musik vor, die den langen Horizont und die Kuppel des Himmels wiederschafft, eine Musik, die viele Zeiten und die Polyphonie der Koyoten und der Getreidewogen in sich enthält, die städtische Raffinesse mit irrationaler Wildheit versöhnt. Irgendwann werde ich sie einfach aufschreiben.

References

CANADIAN MUSICAL HERITAGE SOCIETY PUBLICATIONS

The Canadian Musical Heritage Society (CMHS) was founded in 1982 to locate, select, edit, and publish Canadian compositions written prior to 1950. By 1999 the CMHS had published a series of twenty-five volumes, each presenting a single genre, with an extensive introduction placing the music in historical and musical context. Throughout this book, publications of the Canadian Musical Heritage Society are referred to as *CMH* plus the volume number (for example, *CMH6*). The *Historical Anthology of Canadian Music (HACM)* is an anthology of 152 compositions from these volumes. Examples from this anthology are referred to as *HACM* plus the composition number (for example, *HACM–24*). The CMHS also developed an on-line inventory of Canadian compositions prior to 1950. This inventory, containing some 30,500 works, can be searched under various categories including place, date, genre, title, and composer; it is now available at www.cliffordfordpublications.ca.

CMH1. 1983. *Piano Music I*, ed. Elaine Keillor. Ottawa: CMHS.
CMH2. 1984. *Sacred Choral Music I*, ed. Clifford Ford. Ottawa: CMHS.
CMH3. 1984. *Songs I to English Texts*, ed. Frederick A. Hall. Ottawa: CMHS.
CMH4. 1985. *Organ Music I*, ed. Lucien Poirier. Ottawa: CMHS.
CMH5. 1985. *Hymn Tunes*, ed. John Beckwith. Ottawa: CMHS.
CMH6. 1986. *Piano Music II*, ed. Elaine Keillor. Ottawa: CMHS.
CMH7. 1987. *Songs II to French Texts*, ed. Lucien Poirier. Ottawa: CMHS.
CMH8. 1990. *Music for Orchestra I*, ed. Helmut Kallmann. Ottawa: CMHS.
CMH9. 1988. *Sacred Choral Music II*, ed. Clifford Ford. Ottawa: CMHS.
CMH10. 1991. *Opera and Operetta Excerpts I*, ed. Dorith Cooper. Ottawa: CMHS.
CMH11. 1989. *Chamber Music I: Piano Trios*, ed. Robin Elliott. Ottawa: CMHS.
CMH12. 1992. *Songs III to French Texts*, ed. Lucien Poirier. Ottawa: CMHS.

CMH13. 1992. *Chamber Music II: String Quartets,* ed. Robin Elliott. Ottawa: CMHS.

CMH14. 1993. *Songs IV to English Texts,* ed. Frederick A. Hall. Ottawa: CMHS.

CMH15. 1994. *Music for Orchestra II,* ed. Elaine Keillor. Ottawa: CMHS.

CMH16. 1995. *Music for Orchestra III,* ed. Elaine Keillor. Ottawa: CMHS.

CMH17. 1996. *Secular Choral Music,* consulting ed. Richard Johnston. Ottawa: CMHS.

CMH18. 1995. *Oratorio and Cantata Excerpts,* ed. John Beckwith. Ottawa: CMHS.

CMH19. 1997. *Organ Music II,* ed. Hugh McLean. Ottawa: CMHS.

CMH20. 1997. *Mass Excerpts,* ed. Clifford Ford. Ottawa: CMHS.

CMH21. 1998. *Music for Winds I: Bands,* ed. Timothy Maloney. Ottawa: CMHS.

CMH22. 1998. *Piano Music III: Marches and Dances,* ed. Helmut Kallmann. Ottawa: CMHS.

CMH23. 1998. *Chamber Music III,* ed. Robin Elliott. Ottawa: CMHS.

CMH24. 1999. *Music for Winds II,* ed. Timothy Maloney. Ottawa: CMHS.

CMH25. 1999. *Sacred Choral Music III,* ed. Clifford Ford. Ottawa: CMHS.

REFERENCES

Anon. 1863. *Les Ursulines de Québec.* Quebec.

Abel, Kerry. 1993. *Drum Songs: Glimpses of Dene History.* Montreal: McGill-Queen's University Press.

Acadian celebrations. http://www.teleco.org/museeacadien/francais/fetes/fetes. html (accessed 20 Jan. 2006).

Adria, Marco. 1990. *Music of Our Times: Eight Canadian Singer-Songwriters.* Toronto: Lorimer.

Alasuak, Alasi, and Nellie Nunguak. 1985. "Throatsinging." *Musicworks* 31, no.1 (1985): 6–7.

Alburger, Mark. 1997. "Spacing Out with Henry Brant." *20th-Century Music* 4, no. 11: 1–7.

Alexander, Ian. 2000. "Impresario for the 20th and 21st Centuries: Nicholas Goldschmidt." *Nuvo* 2, no. 3 (Winter 2000): 116–35.

Amato, Joe, ed. 1994. *Canadian Jazz/Jazz du Canada: The First All-Canadian Jazz Fakebook.* Toronto: Beldriana.

Amtmann, Willy. 1975. *Music in Canada 1600–1800.* Montreal: Habitex.

Anderson, Stephen D., with Ronald Cid. 2000. *Visions: A Personal Tribute to Jazz Guitarist Lenny Breau.* Montreal: Jazz Guitar.

Applebaum, Louis, and Jacques Hébert. 1982. *Report of the Federal Cultural Policy Review Committee.* Ottawa.

Arnold, Eric K. 2001. "Charting the Streets of the Hip-hop Nation: Hali Agents." *The Source* 140 (May): 109–10.

Aronchick, Amanda. 1995. *"Hors-Phase* – Detuning." *Contact!* 8, no. 2: 27–8.

Babin, Ann. 2005. "Music Conservatories in Canada and the Piano Examination System for the Preparatory Student: A Historical Survey and Comparative Analysis." MA thesis, University of Ottawa.

Baillargeon, Morgan, and Leslie Tepper. 1998. *Legends of Our Times: Native Cowboy Life*, Vancouver: UBC Press, Canadian Museum of Civilization.

Baillargeon, Richard, and Christian Côté. 1991. *Destination Ragou: une histoire de la musique populaire au Québec*. Montréal: Triptyque.

Baker, Raymond F. 1978/1995. *A Campaign of Amateurs: The Siege of Louisbourg.* Ottawa: Parks Canada.

Banasiewicz, Bill. 1988. *Rush Visions: The Official Biography.* London: Omnibus.

Barbeau, Marius. 1923. *Indian Days in the Canadian Rockies.* Toronto: Macmillan.

– 1935. *Folk-songs of Old Quebec.* Bulletin 75, Anthropological Series No. 16. Ottawa: National Museum of Canada.

– 1951. "Tsimshian Songs." In *The Tsimshian: Their Arts and Music*, ed. Marian W. Smith, 95–280. Publications of the American Ethnological Society 18. New York, J.J. Augustin.

Barclay, Michael. 1999. "Move with the Maestro," *Canoe* <http://www.canoe.ca/JamMusicArtistsM/maestrofreshwes.html> (accessed 18 June 2000)

Barclay, Michael, Ian A.D. Jack, and Jason Schneider. 2001. *Have Not Been the Same: The CanRock Renaissance, 1985–1995.* Toronto: ECW Press.

Barr, Steven C. "History of Recorded Sound in Canada: The Canadian Connection." Canadian Antique Phonograph Society <www.capsnews.org> (accessed 21 Aug. 2000).

Barrière, Mireille. 1999. *Calixa Lavallée*. Montreal: Lidec.

– 2000. "Ascension et chute de l'opéra français de Montréal (1893–1896)." *Cahiers de la Société québécoise de recherche en musique* 4, no. 1: 71–80.

Barris, Alex. 1998. "Nine to the Bar: A Profile of Phil Nimmons." *Jazz Report* 11, no. 4: 24–6.

Barris, Alex, and Ted Barris. 2001. *Making Music: Profiles from a Century of Canadian Music.* Toronto: Harper Collins.

Baxter-Moore, Nick. 1995. "Popular Music: Myth-making and Identities – The Songs of Stan Rogers." *British Journal of Canadian Studies* 10, no. 4: 306–29.

Beaubien, Andrea. 1993. "Taking Risks – The NAC Commissions a Major New Work." *Prelude: National Arts Centre* 15, no. 3 (Jan.–Feb.): 10–2.

Beaudry, Nicole. 1992. "The Language of Dreams: Songs of the Dene Indians (Canada)." *The World of Music* 34, no. 2: 72–90.

– 2001a. "Arctic Canada and Alaska." In *Garland Encyclopedia of World Music*, 3: 374–82. New York: Garland.

– 2001b. "Subarctic Canada." In *Garland Encyclopedia of World Music*, 3: 383–92. New York: Garland.

Becker, John. 1983. "The Early History of the Toronto Conservatory of Music." MA thesis, York University, Toronto.

– 1989. *Discord: The Story of the Vancouver Symphony Orchestra.* Vancouver: Brighouse Press.

Beckwith, John. 1969. "About Canadian Music: The PR Failure." *Musicanada* 21 (Jul.–Aug.): 4–7, 10–13.

– 1987. "On Compiling an Anthology of Canadian Hymn Tunes." *Sing Out the Glad News: Hymn Tunes in Canada*, 3–32. CanMus Documents 1. Toronto: Institute for Canadian Music.

– 1988. "Tunebooks and Hymnals in Canada, 1801–1939." *American Music* 4, no. 2: 193–234.

– 1991. "Le *Lucas et Cécile* de Joseph Quesnel: Quelques problèmes de restauration." *Cahiers de l'ARMUQ* 13 (mai): 10–28.

– 1995. *Music at Toronto: A Personal Account.* Toronto: Institute for Canadian Music.

– 1997. *Music Papers: Articles and Talks by a Canadian Composer 1961–1994.* Ottawa: Golden Dog.

– 1999. "CUMS Remembered." *Canadian University Music Review* 20, no. 1: 1–4.

– 2002. *Psalmody in British North America: Humbert, Daulé, Jenkins, Burnham.* Toronto: Coach House.

Beckwith, John, and Ruth Pincoe. 1979. *Canadian Music in the 1960s and 1970s.* Commemorative program prepared for the Celebration Concert honouring the twentieth anniversary of the Canadian Music Centre. Presented by New Music Concerts, 20 October 1979, Toronto.

Beckwith, John, and Udo Kasemets, eds. 1961. *The Modern Composer and His World: A Report from the International Conference of Composers, August 1960.* Toronto: University of Toronto Press.

Bégin, Carmelle. 1983. *La musique traditionelle pour accordeon diatonique Philippe Bruneau.* Mercury Series, Canadian Centre for Folk Culture Studies Paper 47. Ottawa: National Museum of Man, National Museums of Canada.

– 1992. *Opus: The Making of Musical Instruments in Canada.* Hull, QC: Canadian Museum of Civilization.

Bégon, Élizabeth. 1972. *Lettres au cher fils: Correspondance d'Élizabeth Bégon avec son gendre, 1748–1753.* Ed. Nicole Deschamps. Montréal: Hurtubise HMH.

Béland, Madeleine. 1982. *Chansons de voyageurs, coureurs de bois et forestiers.* Québec: Presses de l'université Laval.

Bell, Allan Gordon. 1991. "Neue Musik in der Prärie." *Positionen: Canadian New Music, Beiträge zur Neuen Musik* 33 (Nov. 1991): 17–20.

Berg, Wesley. 1985. *From Russia with Music: A Study of the Mennonite Choral Singing Tradition in Canada.* Winnipeg: Hyperion.

– 1986. "Music in Edmonton, 1880–1905." *Canadian University Music Review* 7: 141–70.

– 2001a. "Prairies Overview." In *Garland Encyclopedia of World Music*, 3: 1224–31. New York: Garland.

– 2001b. "Music of Christian Minorities." In *Garland Encyclopedia of World Music*, 3: 1237–40. New York: Garland.

Berg, Wesley, and Gerry Paulson. 1997. "Mrs. J.B. Carmichael and the Edmonton Civic Opera Society." *Canadian University Music Review* 17, no. 2: 30–48.

Berland, Jody. 1994. "Radio Space and Industrial Time: The Case of Music Formats." In *Canadian Music: Issues of Hegemony and Identity*, ed. B. Diamond, R. Witmer, 173–87. Toronto: Canadian Scholars' Press.

– 1998. "Locating Listening: Technological Space, Popular Music, and Canadian Mediations." In *The Place of Music*, ed. A. Leyshon, D. Matless, and G. Revill, 129–50. New York: Guilford.

Bernier, Maurice. 1977–78. "Notre Orchestre symphonique voyait le jour sous les auspices les plus favorables, il y a soixante-quinze ans." *À Québec* 1 no. 10 (oct.): 38–9; 1 no. 11 (nov.): 42–3; 1 no. 12 (déc.): 50–2; 2 no. 1 (jan.): 32–3; 2 no. 2 (févr.): 34–5; 2 no. 3 (mars): 30–2; 2 no. 4 (avril): 14–8.

Berton, Pierre. 1982. *Why We Act Like Canadians*. Toronto: McClelland & Stewart.

Bidini, Dave. 1998. *On a Cold Road: Tales of Adventure in Canadian Rock*. Toronto: McClelland & Stewart.

Bigsby, John J. 1850/1969. *The Shoe and Canoe, or Pictures of Travel in the Canadas*. 2 vols. Repr. New York: Paladin. (Orig. pub. London, 1850)

Bilodeau, Dominique. 1996. *Je vous entends chanter: recueil des textes de l'exposition*. Québec: Musée de la civilisation.

Bird, Jennifer. 2001. "Discovering the Irrepressible Barbara Pentland." *Musicworks* 80, no. 2: 18–25.

"Birth of Radio-Television in the Northwest Territories." http://quebec.ifrance.com/inuit/pages/1b.htm (accessed 21 Aug. 2000).

Bishop, A.E. 1974. "The Montreal Orchestra Retrospect 1930 to 1941." Typescript. Montreal.

Blacking, John. 1973. *How Musical Is Man?* Seattle: University of Washington Press.

Blesh, Rudi, and Janis Harriet. 1959. *They All Played Ragtime*. New York: Grove Press.

Bliss, Karen. 1997. "The Tea Party." *Canadian Musician* 19, no. 5: 34–9.

Bliss, Michael. 1994. "Northern Wealth: Economic Life in the 20th Century." *The Beaver* 74, no. 6: 4–16.

Blondin, George. 1990. *When the World Was New: Stories of the Sahtú Dene*. Yellowknife: Outcrop.

Bloom, Ken. 1982. "The Bandura in Canada." *Canadian Folk Music Bulletin* 16, no. 2: 27–8.

Boas, Franz. 1921. *Ethnology of the Kwakiutl*. Washington: Bureau of American Ethnology.

– 1964. *The Central Eskimo*. Repr. Lincoln: University of Nebraska Press. Orig. publ. 1888.

Boivin, Jean. 1995. *La classe de Messiaen*. Mesnil-sur-l'Estrée, France: Christian Bourgois.

Bonds, Mark Evan. 2003. *A History of Music in Western Culture*. Upper Saddle River, NJ: Prentice Hall.

Boros, James, and Michael Toop. 1995. *Brian Ferneyhough: Collected Writings*. Contemporary Music Studies 10. Amsterdam: Harwood, 1995.

Bouchard, Guy. 1997. *Airs tordus du Québec: Crooked Tunes*. 2nd ed. Québec: Trente Sous Zéro.

Bourassa-Trépanier, Juliette, and Lucien Poirier. 1990. *Répertoire des données musicales de la presse québécoise, tome I: 1764–1799*. Quebec: Presses de l'université Laval. [http://www.nosracines.ca//www.ourroots.ca]

– 2003. *Les Divertissements urbains: confrontation de deux cultures, tome II: 1800–1824*. Quebec: Université Laval. [http://www.nosracines.ca //www.ourroots.ca]

Bowman, Durrell S. 2002. "'Let Them All Make Their Own Music': Individualism, Rush, and the Progressive/Hard Rock Alloy 1976–77." In *Progressive Rock Reconsidered*, ed. Kevin Holm-Hudson, 183–220. New York: Routledge.

Bradley, Ian L. 1982. *Twentieth Century Canadian Composers*, vol. 2. Agincourt, ON: GLC.

Brady, Tim. 1998. "James Bond, Tan Dun, and the Canadian Future of Music." *Musicworks* 71 (Summer): 29–31.

– 2000. "Why Canadian Music Doesn't Exist – and Why I Love It: Homage to Generation Zero." *Musicworks* 77 (Summer): 5–6.

Britton, Allen Perdue. 1950. "Theoretical Introductions in American Tune-Books to 1800." PhD diss., University of Michigan.

Broman, Per F. 1999. *"Back to the Future:" Towards an Aesthetic Theory of Bengt Hambraeus*. Göteborg: University of Gothenburg.

– 2000. "Bengt Hambraeus and the Canadian Dream." Paper given 5 November 2000 at "Musical Intersections," the Canadian University Music Society meeting, Toronto.

Bronson, Bertrand Harris. 1976. *The Singing Tradition of Child's Popular Ballads*. Princeton, NJ: Princeton University Press.

Broughton, Simon, and Mark Ellingham, eds. 2000. *World Music, vol. 2: Latin and North America, Caribbean, India, Asia and Pacific*. London: Rough Guides.

Bruneau, William. 1996. "With Age the Power to do Good: Jean Coulthard's Latest Decades." *Classical Music Magazine* 19, no. 2 (June): 14–9.

– 2000. "Jean Coulthard: An Artist's Voyages, 1908–2000." *Journal of the IAWM* 6, no. 3: 23–8

Bruneau, William, and David Gordon Duke. 2005. *Jean Coulthard: A Life in Music*. Vancouver: Ronsdale.

Bruzzi, Stella. 1997. "Mannish Girl: k.d. lang – From Cowpunk to Androgyny." In *Sexing the Groove: Popular Music and Gender*, ed. Sheila Whitely, 191–206. New York: Routledge.

Buckman, Peter. 1978. *Let's Dance.* New York and London: Paddington.

Burke, John. 1983. *Musical Landscapes.* Exeter: Webb & Bower.

Burton, Susan. 2000. "Chantal Kreviazuk ... Moving and Still." *Performing Arts* 33 no. 1: 18–19.

Bush, John. n.d. "Maestro Fresh-Wes," *All Music Guide* <http://www.allmusic.com/cg/amg.dll?p=amg&sql=B84n2or8ac48b> (accessed 18 June 2000).

Canadian Dances. http://www.marianrosa.com (accessed 15 Oct. 2005).

Canadian History. http://www.allmusic.com/cg/ amg.dll?p=amg&sql=B84n2or 8ac48b> (accessed 5 July 1999).

Canadian Music Centre. <www.musiccentre.ca> (accessed 30 Dec. 2005).

Canadian Broadcasting Corporation. Global Village <http://radio.cbc.ca/programs/global/profiles.html> (accessed 15 Apr. 2002).

Canadian Ten Cent Ball-room Companion and Guide to Dancing. 1871. Toronto: Wm. Warwick. [mcf CIHM/ICMH 01094]

Candelaria, Fred, and Colin Miles. 1986. "New: West Coast Composers." *West Coast Review* 20, no. 3 (Jan.): 1–177.

Carney, G.O. 1980. "Country Music and the South: A Cultural Geography Perspective." *Journal of Cultural Geography* 1: 16–33.

Carpenter, Carole Henderson. 1979. *Many Voices: A Study of Folklore Activities in Canada and Their Role in Canadian Culture.* Canadian Centre for Folk Culture Studies Paper 26. Ottawa: National Museums of Canada.

Carrier, Maurice, and Monique Vachon. 1977. *Chansons politiques du Québec,* tome 1: *1765–1833.* Ottawa: Leméac.

– 1979. *Chansons politiques du Québec,* tome 2: *1834–1858.* Ottawa: Leméac.

Carruthers, Glen, and Gordana Lazarevich, eds. 1996. *A Celebration of Canada's Arts 1930–1970.* Toronto: Canadian Scholar's Press.

"Catholic Church in the Wilderness, The." 1868. *Irish Ecclesiastical Record* 41: 238–54.

Cavanagh, Beverley. 1982. *Music of the Netsilik Eskimo: A Study of Stability and Change.* Canadian Ethnology Service Paper 82. Ottawa: National Museums of Canada.

Chamberland, Roger. 2001. "Rap in Canada: Bilingual and Multicultural." In *Global Music: Rap and Hip-hop outside the USA,* ed. Tony Mitchell, 306–26. Middletown, CT: Wesleyan University Press.

Chandler, Ronald. 1990. *Alumni Directory: Faculty of Music, University of Toronto and Historical Introduction.* Toronto.

Chapais, Thomas. 1911. *Le Marquis de Montcalm (1712–1759).* Quebec: Garneau.

Chapeau bas: reminiscences de la vie théâtrale et musicale de Manitoba français. 1980. 2 pts. Saint-Boniface: Éditions du Blé.

Charron, Claude. 1978. "Towards Transcription and Analysis of Inuit Throatgames: Micro-structure." *Ethnomusicology* 22, no. 2: 245–51.

Chauncey, Sarah. 1997. "Sarah McLachlan." *Canadian Musician* 19, no. 5 (Oct.): 40–3.

– 1998. "Wide Mouth Mason." *Canadian Musician* 20 no. 3 (May): 40–44.

Cherwick, Brian. 2001. "Ukrainian Music." In *Garland Encyclopedia of World Music*, 3: 1241–4, New York: Garland.

Chodan, Lucinda. 2000. "Jane Siberry." *Canadian Musician* 22 no. 2 (Mar.–Apr.): 42–5.

Christgau, Robert. 1977. "A Cult Explodes – and a Movement Is Born." *Village Voice*, 24 October: 57.

Christie, Rod. 2000. "Lara Fabian." *Canadian Musician* 22, no. 5 (Sep.–Oct.): 40–3.

– 2001. "Sarah Harmer." *Canadian Musician* 23, no. 2 (Mar.–Apr.): 46–9.

– 2002. "The Tragically Hip." *Canadian Musician* 24, no. 4: 34–7.

Clarke, F.R.C. 1983. *Healey Willan: Life and Music.* Toronto: University of Toronto Press.

Clutesi, George. 1969. *Potlatch.* Sidney, BC: Gray's Publishing.

Compulseve. 2002. "Histoire de la musique jungle: A Jungle Story." *Muzik Etc / Drums Etc* 14, no. 1: 35–6, 42.

Conlon, Paula. 1983. "The Flute of the Canadian Amerindian: An Analysis of the Vertical Whistle Flute with External Block and Its Music." MA thesis, Carleton University.

Coodin, David. 2005. "Jew Funk," *The Walrus* 2, no.7 (Sep.): 68–71.

Cooper, Dorith. 1984. "Opera in Montreal and Toronto: A Study of Performance Traditions and Repertoire, 1783–1980." PhD diss., University of Toronto.

Cooper, Timothy G. 1990. "John Medley: Canadian Choral Pioneer." *The Choral Journal* 31, no. 2: 35–6.

Copway, George. 1851. *Recollections of a Forest Life or Life & Travels of Kah-Ge-Ge-Gah-bowh.* London: Gilpin.

Cornfield, Eitan, comp. and ed. 2002. *Canadian Composers Portraits: Jean Coulthard.* 2 CDs. Centrediscs CMCCD 8202.

Côté, Gérald. 2000. "Métissage à la québécoise: histoire, crises et composites." *Cahiers de la Société québécoise de recherche en musique* 4, no. 4 (déc.): 41–8.

Coull, Cheryl. 1996. *A Traveller's Guide to Aboriginal B.C.* Vancouver: Whitecap.

Courville, Louise. 1998. Notes for CD, *Victoires et Réjouissances à Québec (1690–1758),* L'ensemble Nouvelle-France, Anthologie vol. 2, ORCD 4109.

Couture, Patrick. http://www.republiquelibre.org/cousture

Creighton, Helen and Ronald Labelle. 1988. *La fleur du rosier: Acadian Folksongs.* Ottawa: University College of Cape Breton Press, Canadian Museum of Civilization.

Creighton, Helen. 1932/1966. *Songs and Ballads from Nova Scotia.* Toronto: Dent. Repr. New Dover.

Cristall, Gary. 2003. "Stringband: 'There's some played harder, and there's some played smarter, but nobody played like you.'" CD notes for *Stringband: The Indispensable 1972–2002,* NICK 10.

Croft, Clary. 2000. "African Nova Scotian Music – A Brief Overview." In *Juba'lee: A Celebration of Black Culture in Nova Scotia*, 27–33. Black Cultural Society of Nova Scotia.

Cross, Alan. 1995. *The Alternative Music Almanac*. Toronto: Collector's Guide Publishing.

Crysler, Elisabeth. 1981. "Musical Life in Present Day Niagara-on-the-Lake in the Late Eighteenth and Nineteenth Centuries." MA thesis, Carleton University.

Cselenyi, L. 1971. *Musical Instruments in the Royal Ontario Museum, Toronto*: Royal Ontario Museum.

Culin, Stewart. 1907. *Games of the North American Indians*. 24th annual report, Bureau of American Ethnology, 1902–3. Washington: Smithsonian Institute.

Davis, Geoffrey. 1994. "Maestro Fresh-Wes is drinkin' milk now, south of the 49th parallel!" *Canadian Musician* 16, no. 3: 46–8.

Dawson, Aeneas McDonell. 1881. *The North-West Territories and British Columbia*. Ottawa: Mitchell.

Daybi. 2000. Biography. <http://www.rapstation.com/artists> and <http://listeningroom.lycos.com/fan/bands/daybi/bands.html (accessed 10 June 2001).

Deaville, James, ed. 2000. "Colloquy/Débat: Violet Archer, Jean Coulthard, and Barbara Pentland Remembered." *Canadian University Music Review* 20, no. 2: 1–15.

Del Giudice, Luisa. 1994. "Italian Traditional Song in Toronto: From Autobiography to Advocacy." *Journal of Canadian Studies* 29, no. 1: 74–89.

Deleary, Nicholas. 1990. "The Midewiwin, An Aboriginal Spiritual Institution Symbols of Continuity: A Native Studies Culture-based Perspective." MA thesis, Carleton University.

De Laguna, Frederica. 1972. *Under Mount St Elias: The History and Culture of the Yakutat Tlingit*. Smithsonian Contributions to Anthropology 7. 3 vols. Washington, DC.

– 1995. *Tales from the Dena: Indian Stories from the Tanana, Koyukuk, and Yukon Rivers*. Seattle: University of Washington Press.

De Mallie, Raymond J., ed. 2001. *Handbook of North American Indians*, vol. 13: *Plains*, part 1. Washington, DC: Smithsonian.

Dempsey, Hugh A. 1994. *Calgary: Spirit of the West*. Calgary: Glenbow; Saskatoon: Fifth House.

Densmore, Frances. 1910. *Chippewa Music*. Bureau of American Ethnology Bulletin 45. Washington, DC: Government Printing Office.

– 1913. *Chippewa Music—II*. Bureau of American Ethnology Bulletin 53. Washington, DC: Government Printing Office.

– 1939/1972. *Nootka and Quileute Music*. Repr. New York: Da Capo Press.

– 1979. *Chippewa Customs*. Minneapolis: Minnesota Historical Society Press.

Dewdney, Selwyn. 1975. *The Sacred Scrolls of the Southern Ojibway*. Toronto: University of Toronto Press.

Deziel, Shanda. 2002. "Our Lady Peace's Day in the Sun." *Maclean's* 115, no. 22 (3 June): 35.

Diamond, Beverley. 2000a. "The Interpretation of Gender Issues in Musical Life Stories of Prince Edward Islanders." In *Music and Gender*, ed. P. Moisala and B. Diamond, 99–139. Urbana: University of Illinois Press.

– 2000b. "What's the Difference? Reflections on Discourses of Morality, Modernism, and Mosaics in the Study of Music in Canada." *Canadian University Music Review* 21, no. 1: 54–75.

– 2001a. "Acadian Music." In *Garland Encyclopedia of World Music*, 3: 1135–7. New York: Garland.

– 2001b. "Identity, Diversity and Interaction." In *Garland Encyclopedia of World Music*, 3: 1056–65. New York: Garland.

– 2001c. "Intercultural Traditions on the Canadian Prairies." In *Garland Encyclopedia of World Music*, 3: 342–4. New York: Garland.

– 2001d. "Northern and Central European Music [in the Prairies]." In *Garland Encyclopedia of World Music*, 3: 1249–51. New York: Garland.

– 2001e. "Northern Canada Overview." In *Garland Encyclopedia of World Music*, 3: 1274–8. New York: Garland.

– 2001f. "Northern Canada Popular Music." In *Garland Encyclopedia of World Music*, 3: 1279–81. New York: Garland.

– 2001g. "Overview of Music in Canada." In *Garland Encyclopedia of World Music*, 3: 1066–1100. New York: Garland.

– 2001h. "Overview of Northern Canada." In *Garland Encyclopedia of World Music*, 3: 1274–8. New York: Garland.

Diamond, Beverley, M. Sam Cronk, and Franziska von Rosen. 1994. *Visions of Sound: Musical Instruments of First Nations Communities in Northeastern America*. Waterloo: Wilfrid Laurier University Press.

Diamond, Beverley, and Robert Witmer, eds. 1994. *Canadian Music: Issues of Hegemony and Identity*. Toronto: Canadian Scholar's Press.

Dick, Valorie. 1998. "The Winnipeg New Music Fest." *La scena musicale* 3, no. 6 (April): 18

Dickason, Olive Patricia. 1992. *Canada's First Nations: A History of Founding Peoples from Earliest Times*. Toronto: McClelland & Stewart.

Dickinson, Peter. 1996. "Documenting North in Canadian Poetry and Music." *Essays on Canadian Writing* 59: 105–22.

Dion, Joseph F. 1979. *My Tribe: The Crees*. Calgary: Glenbow Museum.

Dixon, Gail. 1980. "Harry Freedman: A Survey." *Studies in Music from the University of Western Ontario* 5: 122–44.

Dôle, Gérard. 1995. *Histoire musicale des Acadiens de la Nouvelle-France à la Louisiane 1604–1804*. aris: Éditions l'Harmattan.

Domett. Alfred. 1955. *The Canadian Journal of Alfred Domett*. Ed. E.A. Horsman and Lillian Rea Benson. London: University of Western Ontario.

Dorion-Paquin, Leah, coordinator. 2002. *Drops of Brandy: An Anthology of Métis Music*. Saskatoon: Gabriel Dumont Institute.

Dorman, Loranne S., and Clive L. Rawlings. 1990. *Leonard Cohen: Prophet of the Heart*. London: Omnibus.

Doyle, Gerald S. 1955. *Old-Time Songs of Newfoundland*. 3rd ed. St. John's: Gerald S. Doyle.

Drucker, Philip. 1955. *Indians of the Northwest Coast*. Garden City, N Y: National History Press.

Dubé, Jean-Claude. 1969. *Claude-Thomas Dupuy, Intendant de la Nouvelle-France 1678–1738*. Montreal: Fides.

– 1975. "Les intendants de la Nouvelle-France et la République des lettres." *Revue d'histoire de l'Amérique française* 29, no. 1: 31–48.

Dubois, Paul-André, and Élisabeth Gallat-Morin. 1995. C D notes for *Le Chant de la jerusalem der terres froides*. Les chemins du Baroque en Nouvelle France. K617052.

Dueck, Jon, and Regula Burckhardt Qureshi. 2001. "Issues of Identity: Class." In *Garland Encyclopedia of World Music*, 3: 50–3. New York: Garland.

Dufferin, Lady. 1969. *My Canadian Journal 1872–1878*, ed. Gladys Chantler Walker. Don Mills: Longmans Canada.

Duffett, Mark. 1994. *Bryan Adams: A Fretted Biography*. Winslow, U K: Duff Press.

– 2000. "Going Down Like a Song: National Identity, Global Commerce and the Great Canadian Party." *Popular Music* 19, no. 1: 1–11.

Duke, David Gordon. n.d. [1993] "The Orchestral Music of Jean Coulthard: A Critical Assessment." Ph D diss., University of British Columbia; available at <http://www.edst.educ.ubc.ca/coulthard/Thesis/>

– 1998. "Notes towards a Portrait of Barbara Pentland: Issues of Gender, Class, and Colonialism in Canadian Music." *Musicworks* 70, no. 1: 16–20.

– 2000. "Barbara Pentland (1912–2000): A Forgotten Pioneer." *Journal of the IAWM* 6, no. 3: 29–31.

Dunlay, K.E., and D.L. Reich. 1986. *Traditional Celtic Fiddle Music of Cape Breton*. East Alstead, N H: Fiddlecase.

Eagles, Wayne. 1995. "Identity in Canadian Popular Music: Analysis of Empirical Research and Existing Literature." M A research essay, Carleton University.

Eastman, Sheila, and Timothy J. McGee. 1983. *Barbara Pentland*. Toronto: University of Toronto Press.

Eatock, Colin. 1993. "Early Canadian Opera Has Long-awaited Premiere." *Classical Music Magazine* 16, no. 5: 15.

– 1994. "The Next Generation: An Interview with Chris Harman, Melissa Hui and Paul Steenhuisen." *SoundNotes* 6: 4–11.

Echard, William. 1994. "Inventing to Preserve: Novelty and Traditionalism in the Work of Stompin' Tom Connors." *Canadian Folk Music Journal* 22: 8–22.

– 2002. "Expecting Surprise Again: Neil Young and the Dialogic Theory of Genre." *Canadian University Music Review* 22, no. 2: 30–47.

Einarson, John. 1995. *American Woman: The Story of The Guess Who*. Kingston: Quarry Press.

Elliott, Bruce S. 1997. "Early Music Books Offer Interpretive Possibilities at Horaceville." *Horaceville Herald* 29: 1–3.

Elliott, Robin. 1997. *Counterpoint to a City: A History of the Women's Musical Club of Toronto.* Toronto: ECW Press.

– 2001. "The Toronto Women's Musical Club." In *Garland Encyclopedia of World Music,* 3: 1209–10. New York: Garland.

– 2004. "A Canadian Music Bibliography, 1996-2004." *Institute for Canadian Music Newsletter* 2, no. 3 (Sept.); available at www.utoronto.ca/icm.

Emond, Viviane. 1986. "Musique et musiciens à Québec: souvenirs d'un amateur de Nazaire Levasseur (1848–1927): Étude critique." MA thesis, Université Laval.

Enrico, John, and Wendy Bross Stuart. 1996. *Northern Haida Songs.* Lincoln: University of Nebraska Press.

Enright, Robert. 2001. "Words and Pictures: The Arts of Joni Mitchell." *Border Crossings* 20, no. 1: 18–31.

Farmer, Henry George. 1912. *The Rise and Development of Military Music.* London: W. Reeves.

Farnum, Allen L. 1992. *Pawnee Bill's Historic Wild West: A Photo Documentary of the 1900–1905 Show Tours.* West Chester, PA: Schiffer.

Farquharson, Dorothy H. 1983. *"O, For a Thousand Tongues to Sing": A History of Singing Schools in Early Canada.* Waterdown, ON: author.

Feintuch, Burt. 2004. "The Conditions for Cape Breton Fiddle Music: The Social and Economic Setting of a Regional Soundscape." *Ethnomusicology* 48, no. 1: 73–104.

Fetherling, Douglas. 1991. *Some Day Soon: Essays on Canadian Songwriters.* Kingston: Quarry Press.

Feyock, Merry. 1995. "Dance, Our Dearest Diversion: Historical Dance Reconstruction." In *Communities in Motion: Dance, Community and Tradition in America's Southeast and Beyond,* ed. Susan Eike Spalding and Jan Harris Woodside, 203–20. Westwood, CT: Greenwood Press.

Fitzgerald, Judith. 2000. *Sarah McLachlan: Building a Mystery.* Kingston: Quarry Press.

Fledderus, France. 2003. "Funk, or 'It's a Man's Man's World': Genre Subversion in 'Flirtin' Is a Flo-Thing' by Jane Siberry." *Women & Music* 7: 53–63.

Fleming, Lee. 1997. *Rock, Rhythm and Reels: Canada's East Coast Musicians on Stage.* Charlottetown: Ragweed Press.

Flippo, Chet. 1994. *The Band Across the Great Divide.* CD notes for Capitol 89565 2.

Foran, Charles. 2006. "The Surrey Sound." *Canadian Geographic* 126, no. 1: 46–55.

Ford, Clifford. 1982. *Canada's Music: An Historical Survey.* Agincourt, ON: GLC Publishers.

Forster, Audrey. 1996. "From the CPR to the Canada Council." In *A Celebration of Canada's Arts 1930–1970,* ed. Glen Carruthers and Gordana Lazarevich, 213–26. Toronto: Canadian Scholars' Press.

Foster, Cecil. 1995. *Caribana, The Greatest Celebration*. Toronto: Ballantine.

Foster, Michael K. 1974. *From the Earth to beyond the Sky: An Ethnographic Approach to Four Longhouse Iroquois Speech Events*. Mercury Series, Canadian Ethnology Service Paper 20. Ottawa: National Museum of Man.

Fowke, Edith. 1965. *Traditional Singers and Songs from Ontario*. Hatboro, PA: Folklore Associates.

– 1970. *Lumbering Songs from the Northern Woods*. Memoir Series. Publications of the American Folklore Society 55. Austin: University of Texas Press.

Fowke, Edith, ed. 1973. *The Penguin Book of Canadian Folk Songs*. Thetford, UK: Penguin Books.

– 1976. *Folklore of Canada*. Toronto: McClelland & Stewart.

Freedman, Harry. 1958. "Comment." *CBC Times*, Nov. 1–7.

Fricker, H. Cecil. 1933. "Music in Canada: Saskatoon Symphony Orchestra." *The Twentieth Century* 1, no. 12 (July): 43–4.

Gagné, Mireille, Anne Lauber, Ginette Martin, Augustin Rioux, and Gertrude Robitaille. 1990. *Sons d'aujourd'hui: Guide pédagogique*. Montreal: Louise Courteau.

Gagnon, Ernest. 1865. *Chansons populaires du Canada*. Montreal: Beauchemin.

– 1902. *Louis Jolliet: Étude biographique et historiographique*. Quebec: n.p.

Gallat-Morin, Élisabeth. 1981. "Le livre d'orgue de Montréal aperçu d'un manuscrit inédit." *Canadian University Music Review/Revue de musique des universités canadiennes* 1: 1–38.

– 1988. *Un manuscrit de musique française classique: Le Livre d'orgue de Montréal*. Paris and Montreal: Aux Amateurs de Livres.

Gallat-Morin, Élisabeth, and Antoine Bouchard. 1981. *Témoins de la vie musicale en Nouvelle-France*. Quebec: Archives nationales du Québec.

Gallat-Morin, Élisabeth, and Kenneth Gilbert. 1985, 1987, 1988. *Livre d'orgue de Montréal: Critical Edition*. 3 vols. Saint-Hyacinthe: Éditions Jacques Ostiguy.

Gallat-Morin, Élisabeth, and Jacques Guimont. 1996. "L'archéologie au service de l'histoire de la musique en Nouvelle-France: la découverte d'un artefact musical." *Cahiers de l'ARMUQ* 17: 45–55.

Gallat-Morin, Élisabeth, and Jean-Pierre Pinson. 2003. *La vie musicale en Nouvelle-France*. Sillery, QC: Éditions du Septentrion.

Garneau, D. "New France Quebec Cultural Roots." http://www.telusplanet.net/public/dgarneau/french.htm (accessed 20 Aug. 2000).

Garofalo, Reebee. 1997. *Rockin' Out: Popular Music in the USA*. Boston: Allyn and Bacon.

Gasser, Alan. 1996. *Introduction to Canadian Music/Florilège de la musique canadienne*. CD notes for Naxos 8.550171–2.

Genovese, Vanderhoof and Associates, Centre for Cultural Management (University of Waterloo), and the Association of Canadian Orchestras. 1995. *An Economic Case for Government Support: Revenues and Performance Activity of the Not-for-profit Performing Arts Industry in Comparable Markets in the United States and Canada*.

Germain, Georges-Hébert. 1978. "Un golfeur bien ordinaire." *L'actualité* (avril): 56–63.

Ghaznavi, Corinna. 2002. "Robert Houle, John Abrams: Tom Thomson Memorial Art Gallery, Owen Sound." *Canadian Art* 19, no. 2: 86, 88.

Gibbons, Roy W. 1981. *Folk Fiddling in Canada: A Sampling*. Canadian Centre for Folk Culture Studies, Paper 35. Ottawa: National Museums of Canada.

Gibson, John G. 1998. *Traditional Gaelic Bagpiping, 1745–1945*. Montreal: McGill-Queen's University Press.

– 2002. *Old and New World Highland Bagpiping*. Montreal: McGill-Queen's University Press.

Giddins, Gary. 1998. *Visions of Jazz: The First Century*. New York and Oxford: Oxford University Press.

Giles, Jennifer. 1987. "Music Consumption among English Speaking Teenage Girls in the City of Montreal." MA Research Essay, Carleton University.

Gilmore, John. 1989. *Who's Who of Jazz in Montreal: Ragtime to 1970*. Montreal: Véhicule Press.

Ginsberg, Murray. 1998. *They Loved to Play: Memories of the Golden Age in Canadian Music*. Toronto: eastendbooks.

Goddard, Peter, and Philip Kamin, eds. 1989. *Shakin' All Over: The Rock 'n' Roll Years in Canada*. Toronto: McGraw-Hill Ryerson.

Godley, John Robert. 1844. *Letters from America*. 2 vols. London: n.p.

Gooding, Erik D. 2001. "Plains." In *Garland Encyclopedia of World Music*, 3: 440–56. New York: Garland.

Goodman, Linda J. 2001. "Northwest Coast." In *Garland Encyclopedia of World Music*, 3: 394–403. New York: Garland.

Gordon, Tom. 1991. "Music in absentia: Bishop's Faculty of Music, 1886–1947." *Canadian University Review* 11, no. 2: 33–50.

– 2003. "Seal Oil and String Quartets." *MMAP [Music, Media and Place Memorial University of Newfoundland] Newsletter* 1, no. 2: 1–3.

Gottschalk, Louis Moreau. 1964. *Notes of a Pianist*. Jeanne Behrend, ed. New York: Alfred A. Knopf.

Grabell, Robin. 1990. "The Huron Soundscape, 1623–1649: An Exploration of Cross-cultural Interaction, Conflict and Change, As Articulated Within the Domain of Ritual and Ceremony." MA thesis, Carleton University.

Grace, Sherrill, and Stefan Haag. 1998. "From Landscape to Soundscape: The Northern Arts of Canada." *Mosaic* 31, no. 2: 101–22.

Graham, Clara. 1945. *Fur and Gold in the Kootenays*. Vancouver: Wrigley.

Grant, Barry S. 1986. "'Across the Great Divide': Imitation and Inflection in Canadian Rock Music." *Journal of Canadian Studies* 21, no. 1: 116–27.

Graustark, Barbara. 1979. "Disco Takes Over." *Newsweek* 93, no. 14 (2 April): 56–64.

Gravier, Henri. 1904. *Colonisation de la Louisiane à l'époque de Law, octobre 1717–janvier 1721*. Paris: Masson.

Gray, Hugh. 1809. *Letters from Canada, Written during a Residence There in the Years 1806, 1807, and 1808*. London.

Green, J. Paul, and Nancy F. Vogan. 1991. *Music Education in Canada: A Historical Account*. Toronto: University of Toronto Press.

Green, Marvin, ed. 1983. "Music of the Inuit; Katajaiit; Inuit Throat and Harp Songs; I am from Nutak; Traditional Inuit Music; Once in a While." *Musicworks* 31, no. 1: 10–5.

Greenhill, Pauline. 2001. "Winnipeg Festivals." In *Garland Encyclopedia of World Music*, 3: 1232–6. New York: Garland.

Greenleaf, Elizabeth, and Grace Mansfield. 1933/1968 *Ballads and Sea Songs of Newfoundland*. Hatboro, PA: Folklore Associates.

Grégoire-Reid, Claire. 1988. "Les Manuels canadiens de théorie musicale publiés au Québec entre 1811 et 1911." *Cahiers de l'ARMUQ* 10: 58–73.

Greyeyes, Michael. 1997. "Powwow a Long Journey." *Aboriginal Voices* 4, no. 1: 28–33.

Grills, Barry. 1996. *Snowbird: The Story of Anne Murray*. Kingston: Quarry Press.

– 1997. *Ironic: Alanis Morissette The Story*. Kingston: Quarry Press.

Grove, Chris. 2000. "Last of Mr. B's Band: Linton Garner." *Nuvo* (Winter): 240–54.

Grover, Carrie B. 1973. *A Heritage of Songs*. Norwood, PA: Norwood Editions.

Guérard, Daniel. 1996. *La belle époque des boites à chansons*. Montréal: Stanké.

Guiguet, Kristina. 2004. *The Ideal World of Mrs. Widder's Soirée Musicale: Social Identity and Musical Life in Nineteenth Century Ontario*. Mercury Series Cultural Studies Paper 77. Gatineau: Canadian Museum of Civilization.

Gustin/Trounce Heritage Committee. n.d. *Gustin House*, pamphlet.

Hahn, Robert H. 1985. *None of the Roads Were Paved*. Markham: Fitzhenry & Whiteside.

Hall, Frederick A. 1983. "Musical Life in Eighteenth-Century Halifax." *Canadian University Music Review* 4: 278–306.

– 1989. "A Prince's Sojourn in Eighteenth-Century Canada." *Studies in Eighteenth Century Culture* 19: 247–66.

Halpern, Ida. 1981. *Kwakiutl: Indian Music of the Pacific Northwest*. Liner notes for Folkways FE 4122. New York: Folkways Records.

– 1986. *Haida: Indian Music of the Pacific Northwest*. Liner notes for FE 4199. New York: Folkways Records.

Hambraeus, Bengt. 1986. "Kanadensisk musik-finns den?" *Artes* 12, no. 3: 67–7.

– 1973/74 "Unga tonsättare i Kanada." *Nutida Musik i* 17, no. 3: 46–9.

Hamm, Charles. 1979. *Popular Song in America*. New York: Norton.

– 1983. *Music in the New World*. New York: Norton.

Hare, John E. 1983. "Joseph Quesnel." In *Dictionnaire biographique du Canada*, vol. 5: de 1801 à 1820. Quebec: Presses de l' université Laval; Toronto: University of Toronto Press.

Harley, Maria Anna. 1998. "Canadian Identity, Deep Ecology and R. Murray Schafer's 'The Princess of the Stars.'" *Yearbook of Soundscape Studies* 1998: 119–42.

Harrison, Susie Frances. 1898. "Historical Sketch of Music in Canada." In *Canada: An Encyclopedia of the Country,* ed. John Castell Hopkins, 4: 389–94. Toronto: Lincourt.

Hartman, James B. 1997. *The Organ in Manitoba: A History of the Instruments, the Builders, and the Players.* Winnipeg: University of Manitoba Press.

– 1999. "Canadian Organbuilding." *The Diapason* 90, no. 5: 16–18; no. 6: 14–15.

Hastie, Christine. Canadian History Time Line. http://www.securenet.net/members/chastie/hisintro.html (accessed 9 Oct. 2001).

Hatzis, Christos. 2000. *The Orchestra As Metaphor.* <http://www.chass.utoronto.ca/~hatzis/orchestra.htm>

Hawkes, E.W. 1916. *The Labrador Eskimo.* Ottawa: Department of Mines Geological Survey.

Hawthorn, Audrey. 1979. *Kwakiutl Art.* Vancouver: Douglas & McIntyre.

Hawtin, Richie. <www.mote.com/mute/novamute/hawtin/hawtin.htm> (accessed 10 Nov. 2001).

Hearne, Samuel. 1795. *A Journey from Prince of Wales' Fort in Hudson's Bay to the Northern Ocean in the Years, 1769, 1770, 1771, and 1772.* London: A. Strahan and T. Cadell.

Hehner, Barbara, ed. 1999. *The Spirit of Canada: Canada's Story in Legends, Fiction, Poems, and Songs.* Toronto: Malcolm Lester.

Helm, J. and N.O. Lurie. 1966. *The Dogrib Hand Game.* National Museum of Canada Bulletin 205, Anthropological Series 71. Ottawa: National Museum of Canada.

Henighan, Tom. 2000. *The Maclean's Companion to Canadian Arts and Culture.* Vancouver: Raincoast.

Herndon, Marcia. 1980. *Native American Music.* Norwood, PA: Norwood Editions.

Hiscott, Jim. 2000. "Inuit Accordion Music: A Better Kept Secret." *Canadian Folk Music Bulletin* 34, no. 1–2: 16–9.

Hockenhull, Oliver. 2001 "Banff: Utopian Memeplex Machine Making the Invisible Visible." *Fuse* 24, no. 1: 17–25.

Holm, Bill. 1983. *Smoky-Top: The Art and Times of Willie Seaweed.* Thomas Burke Memorial Washington State Museum Monograph 3. Seattle: University of Washington Press.

Howard, Peter. 1991. *Landscapes: The Artists' Vision.* New York: Routledge.

Howison, John. 1821. *Sketches of Upper Canada, Domestic, Local and Characteristic.* Edinburgh: n.p.

Howley, James P. 1974. *The Beothuks or Red Indians: The Aboriginal Inhabitants of Newfoundland.* Org. publ. 1915, Toronto: Coles.

Hutton, Charles. 1906. *Newfoundland Folio of Over Fifty Old Favorite Songs.* Springfield, IL: author.

Hutton, Jack. 2000. *The World Is Waiting for the Sunrise: How a Canadian Melody Tugged at the World's Heart Strings!* Bala: Bala's Museum.

Hutton, S.K. 1912. *Among the Eskimos of Labrador.* London: Sealey, Service & Co.

Innis, Harold. 1950. *Empire and Communications.* Oxford: Oxford University Press.

Innis, Mary Quayle, ed. 1965. *Mrs. Simcoe's Diary.* Toronto: Macmillan.

Ives, Edward D. 1999. *Drive Dull Care Away: Folksongs from Prince Edward Island.* Includes CD. Charlottetown, PEI: Institute of Island Studies.

– 1977. "Lumbercamp Singing and the Two Traditions." *Canadian Folk Music Journal* 5: 17–23.

Ivison, Douglas. 1997. "Canadian Content: Cultural Specificity in English-Canadian Popular Music." *Canadian Issues: Canadian Cultures and Globalization* 19: 47–56.

Jackson, Rick. 1994. *Encyclopedia of Canadian Rock, Pop and Folk Music.* Kingston: Quarry Press.

– 1996. *Encyclopedia of Canadian Country Music.* Kingston: Quarry Press.

Jacob, Werner. 1978. "The Contribution of Bengt Hambraeus to the Development of a New Organ Music." *Studies in Music from the University of Western Ontario* 3: 23–34.

James, Willis Laurence. 1995. *Stars in De elements: A Study of Negro Folk Music by Willis Laurence James.* Durham: Duke University Press.

Jameson, Anna. 1838/1990. *Winter Studies and Summer Rambles.* Repr. Toronto: McClelland & Stewart. Orig. publ. London: Saunders & Otley.

Jennings, Nicholas. 1997. *Before the Gold Rush: Flashbacks to the Dawn of the Canadian Sound.* Toronto: Penguin.

– 2000. "Ladies on Top." *Maclean's* 113, no. 39 (25 September): 66–70.

Johnson, H. Earle. 1953. "The Germania Musical Society." *Musical Quarterly* 39: 75–93.

Johnston, Basil. 1976. *Ojibway Heritage: The Ceremonies, Rituals, Songs, Dances, Prayers, and Legends of the Ojibway.* Toronto McClelland & Stewart.

Johnston, Thomas F. 1976. *Eskimo Music By Region: A Comparative Circumpolar Study.* Canadian Ethnology Service Paper 32. Ottawa: National Museums of Canada.

– 1980. "Music and Blacks in 18th- and 19th-century Canada." *Anthropological Journal of Canada* 18, no. 4: 19–21.

– 1981. "Blacks in Art Music in Western Canada." *Anthropological Journal of Canada* 19, no. 2: 23–9.

Jones, Gaynor. 1989. "The Fisher Years: the Toronto Conservatory of Music, 1886–1913." In *Three Studies: College Songbooks, Toronto Conservatory, Arraymusic,* 59–146. CanMus Documents 4. Toronto: Institute for Canadian Music.

Jones, Timothy. 1999. *Beethoven: The 'Moonlight' and other Sonatas Op. 27 and Op. 31.* Cambridge: Cambridge University Press.

Jury, Elsie McLeod. 1977. *The Neutral Indians of South-western Ontario*. Bulletin of the Museums – Museum of Indian Archaeology 13. London: Museum of Indian Archaeology, University of Western Ontario.

Kallmann, Helmut. 1960. *A History of Music in Canada 1534–1914*. Toronto: University of Toronto Press.

– 1996 "Taking Stock of Canada's Composers: From the 1920s to the *Catalogue of Canadian Composers* (1952)." In *A Celebration of Canada's Arts 1930–1970*, ed. G. Carruthers, and G. Lazarevich, 15–28. Toronto: Canadian Scholars' Press.

Kallmann, Helmut, and Gilles Potvin, eds. 1992. *Encyclopedia of Music in Canada*. 2nd ed. Toronto: University of Toronto Press; updated edition at www.thecanadianencyclopedia.com.

Kasemets, Udo. 1991. "A Proposal for a Study of the Genealogy of Twentieth-Century Canadian Music." *Musicworks* 51 (Autumn): 30–1.

– 1995. "A Concise Summary of I Ching Systems." *Musicworks* 62, no. 2: 7–21.

Keane, David. 1984. "Electroacoustic Music in Canada: 1950–1984." In *Celebration*, ed. G. Ridout and T. Kenins, 57–72. Toronto: Canadian Music Centre.

Keel, Beverly. 1977. "Between Riot Grrl and Quiet Girl: the New Feminist Movement in Country Music." Paper given at SEM/IASPM Conference, Pittsburgh, 1997.

Keillor, Elaine. 1973. "Wesley Octavius Forsyth 1859–1937." *Canada Music Book* 7: 101–22.

– 1985/86. "Les Tambours des Athapascans du Nord." *Recherches amerindiennes au Québec* 15, no. 4: 43–52.

– 1986. "The Role of Dogrib Youth in the Continuation of Their Musical Traditions." *Yearbook for Traditional Music* 18: 61–76.

– 1987. "1986: The International Year of Canadian Music." *Queen's Quarterly* 94, no. 1 (Spring): 173–86.

– 1988. "Musical Activity in Canada's New Capital City in the 1870s." In *Musical Canada: Words and Music Honouring Helmut Kallmann*, ed. John Beckwith and Frederick A. Hall. Toronto: University of Toronto Press.

– 1994. *John Weinzweig and His Music: The Radical Romantic of Canada*. Metuchen, NJ: Scarecrow Press.

– 1995a. "The Emergence of Postcolonial Musical Expressions of Aboriginal Peoples within Canada." *Cultural Studies* 9, no. 1: 106–24.

– 1995b. "Where Do We Go From Here?" In *With a Song in Her Heart: A Celebration of Canadian Women Composers*, ed Janice Drakich, Edward Kovarik, and Ramona Lumpkin, 95–110. Working Papers in the Humanities 3. University of Windsor.

– 1997. "Auf Kanadischer Welle: The Establishment of the Germanic Musical Canon in Canada." In *Music in Canada/La Musique au Canada*, ed. Guido Bimberg, 49–76. Bochum: Brockmeyer.

– 1998. "*Chanson de Riel*: A Musical Rubbaboo." *Cahiers de la Société québécoise de recherche en musique* 2, no. 1: 23–8.

- 2003. "The Canadian Soundscape." In *Profiles of Canada*, ed. Kenneth G. Pryke and Walter C. Soderlund, 447–86. 3rd ed. Toronto: Canadian Scholar's Press.

- 2004. "Marius Barbeau and His Performers." *Canadian Journal for Traditional Music* 31: 24–38.

Kelly, Jim. 2000a. "Cooking Up Some Jams with Wide Mouth Mason." *Canadian Musician* 22, no. 4 (July–Aug.): 34–7.

- 2000b. "Kittie." *Canadian Musician* 22, no. 6 (Nov.–Dec.): 44–8.

- 2000c. "Songwriting." *Canadian Musician* 22, no. 6 (Nov.–Dec.): 34–9.

Kelly, Wayne. 1991. *Downright Upright: A History of the Canadian Piano Industry*. Toronto: Natural Heritage/Natural History.

Kennicott, Robert. 1942. "Journal." In *The First Scientific Exploration of Russian America and the Purchase of Alaska*, ed. James A. James, 46–136. Evanston: Northwestern University Press.

Kines, Gary Bret. 1988. "Chief Man-Of-Many-Sides: John Murray Gibbon and His Contributions to the Development of Tourism and the Arts in Canada." MA thesis, Carleton University.

King, Bill. 2002. "The Midas Touch: An Interview with Jeff Healey." *Jazz Report* 15, no. 2: 10–3.

Kingman, Daniel. 1990. *American Music: A Panorama*. 2nd ed. New York: Schirmer.

Klassen, Doreen. 1989. *Singing Mennonite*. Winnipeg: University of Manitoba Press.

Klump, Brad. 1999. "Origins and distinctions of the 'World Music' and 'World Beat' Designations." *Canadian University Music Review* 19, no. 2: 5–15.

Klymasz, Robert B. 1970. *An Introduction to the Ukrainian-Canadian Immigrant Folksong Cycle*. National Museums of Canada Bulletin 234, Folklore Series 8. Ottawa.

Koch, Eric. 1997. *The Brothers Hambourg*. Toronto: Robin Brass.

Kohl, Johann Georg. 1860. *Kitchi-Gamic: Life among the Lake Superior Ojibway*. London: n.p.

Kolstee, Anton Frederick. 1982. *Bella Coola Indian Music: A Study of the Interaction between Northwest Coast Indian Musical Structures and Their Functional Context*. Mercury Series, Canadian Ethnology Service Paper 83. Ottawa: National Museum of Man, National Museums of Canada.

Kopstein, Jack, and Ian Pearson. 2002. *The Heritage of Canadian Military Music*. St Catharines: Vanwell.

Korndorf, Nikolai. [n.d.]. "Brief Statement About My Work." http://mypage.direct.ca/k/korndorf/. (accessed 5 Jan. 2002).

Koskoff, Ellen, ed. 2001. *The United States and Canada*. Vol. 3 of *Garland Encyclopedia of World Music*. New York: Garland.

Krassen, Miles. 1974. "An Analysis of a Jean Carignan Record." *Canadian Folk Music Journal* 2: 40–4.

Krims, Adam. 2000. *Rap Music and the Poetics of Identity*. Cambridge: Cambridge University Press.

Lacoursière, Jacques, and Hélène-Andrée Bizier, eds. 1980. *Un pays à développer*. Vol. 4 of *Nos Racines: L'histoire vivante des Québécois*, Montréal: Robert Laffont.

Laforte, Conrad. 1976. *Poétiques de la chanson traditionelle française*. Québec: Presses de l'université Laval.

– 1977/87. *Le catalogue de la chanson folklorique française*. 6 vols. Québec: Archives de folklore, vols 18–23 [vol. 1 *Chansons en laisse* (1977); vol. 2 *Chansons strophiques* (1981); vol. 3 *Chansons en forme de dialogue* (1982); vol. 4 *Chansons énumératives* (1979); vol. 5 *Chansons brèves (Les enfantines)* (1987); vol. 6 *Chansons sur les timbres* (1983)].

Laforte, Conrad, and Robert Kelher. 1997. *Chansons de facture médiévale retrouvées dans la tradition orale: Répertoire recueilli de 1852 à nos jours précédé d'une analyse des mélodies canadiennes des chansons en laisse*. Cap-Saint-Ignace, QC: Nuit Blanche Éditeur.

Lamothe, Maurice. 1994. *La chanson populaire ontaroise de 1970 à 1990: ses produits, sa pratique*. Ottawa: Le Nordir; Montreal: Triptyque.

Lamb, Krista. 2001. "The Tea Party." *Canadian Musician* 23, no. 5: 34–37.

Lanza, Alcides, with Andrés Lewin-Richter. 2002. "On Hugh LeCaine: First-hand Memories of a Canadian Legend, by a Composer Who Met Him and Worked with His Inventions." *Musicworks 83* (Summer): 42–51.

Laterrière, Pierre de Sales. 1830. *A Political and Historical Account of Lower Canada*. London: W. Marsh and A. Miller.

Lazarevich, Gordana. 1988. *The Musical World of Frances James and Murray Adaskin*. Toronto: University of Toronto Press.

Leach, MacEdward. 1965. *Folk Ballads and Songs of the Lower Labrador Coast*. National Museum of Canada Bulletin 201, Anthropological Series 68. Ottawa: Queen's Printer.

Leavitt, Robert M. 1995. *Maliseet Micmac: First Nations of the Maritimes*. Fredericton, NB: New Ireland Press.

LeCaine, Hugh. www.hughlecaine.com (accessed 11 Feb. 2005).

Lederman, Anne. 1987. *Old Native and Métis Fiddling in Manitoba*. CD notes for Falcon FP-286.

– 2001a. "Anglo-Ontarian Music." In *Garland Encyclopedia of World Music*, 3: 1188–91. New York: Garland.

– 2001b. "Atlantic Canada: Anglo Music." In *Garland Encyclopedia of World Music*, 3: 1123–6. New York: Garland.

– 2001c. "Atlantic Canada: African Canadian Music." In *Garland Encyclopedia of World Music*, 3: 1169–70. New York: Garland.

– 2001d. "Franco-Ontarian Music." In *Garland Encyclopedia of World Music*, 3: 1192–4. New York: Garland.

– 2001e. "Métis." In *Garland Encyclopedia of World Music*, 3: 404–11. New York: Garland.

– 2001f. "Ontario: African Canadian Music." In *Garland Encyclopedia of World Music*, 3: 1211–14. New York: Garland.

– 2001g. "Québec: African Canadian Music." In *Garland Encyclopedia of World Music*, 3: 1169–70. New York: Garland.

Leeper, Muriel. 1981. *Sounds of Music 1931–1981: A Fifty-Year History of the Saskatoon Symphony Orchestra*. Saskatoon: Houghton Boston.

Lees, Gene. 1995a. "A Catalyst: A Profile of Gil Evans." *Jazz Report* 9, no. 1 (Fall): 20–3.

– 1995b. "A Crown Jewel: A Profile of Robert Farnon." *Jazz Report* 8, no. 4 (Summer): 20–2.

Lefebvre, Marie-Thérèse. 1986. *Serge Garant et la révolution musicale au Québec*. Montréal: Louise Courteau.

– 1991. *La création musicale des femmes au Québec*. Montréal: Éditions du remue-ménage.

– 1996. "The Role of the Canadian Pacific Railway in Promoting Canadian Culture." In *A Celebration of Canada's Arts 1930–1970*, ed. G. Carruthers and G. Lazarevich, 15–28. Toronto: Canadian Scholars' Press.

– 2001. "Overview of Québec." In *Garland Encyclopedia of World Music*, 3: 1146–53. New York: Garland.

Legras, Marc, ed. 1996. "Panthéon: Gilles Vigneault." *Chorus: cahiers de la chanson* 16, no. 3: 121–46.

Lehr, John. 1994. "As Canadian As Possible ... Under the Circumstances: Regional Myths, Images of Place and National Identity in Canadian Country Music." In *Canadian Music: Issues of Hegemony and Identity*, ed. Beverley Diamond and Robert Witmer. Toronto: Canadian Scholars' Press, 1994, 269–82. Orig. publ. 1985.

Lenoir, Yves. 1980. "Violet B. Archer: une élève canadienne de Béla Bartók." *Revue des archéologues et historiens d'art de Louvain, Belgium* 13: 148–53.

Lescarbot, Marc. 1968. *The History of New France*. 3 vols. Repr. New York: Greenwood Press. Orig. publ. 1907.

Levine, Lawrence W. 1988. *Highbrow/Lowbrow: The Emergence of Cultural Hierarchy in America*. Cambridge: Harvard University Press.

Levine, Victoria Lindsay. 2001. "Northeast." In *Garland Encyclopedia of World Music*, 3: 461–5. New York: Garland.

Lewis, Thane with Steven Staryk. 2000. *Fiddling With Life: The Unusual Journey of Steven Staryk*. Oakville, ON: Mosaic Press.

L'Herbier, Benoît. 1992. "André Gagnon" in *The Encyclopedia of Music in Canada*, ed. Helmut Kallmann et al., 509–10. 2nd ed. Toronto: University of Toronto Press.

Lipsitz, George. 1994. *Dangerous Crossroads: Popular Music, Postmodernism and the Poetics of Place*. London and New York: Verso.

Lobaugh, Bruce. 1997. "Henry Walker, Pioneer Musician in the Canadian Prairie West 1870–1906." In *Kanada-Studien: Music in Canada/La musique au Canada*, ed. Guido Bimberg, 77–90. Bochum: Brockmeyer.

Locat, Raymond. 1994. *La tradition musicale à Joliette: 150 ans d'histoire*. Joliette: MédiaPresse.

Logan, J. D. 1913a. "Canadian Creative Composers." *Canadian Magazine of Politics, Science, Art and Literature* 41 (Sept.): 490–8.

– 1913b. "Musical Tendencies in Canada: A Review and a Forecast." *Canadian Magazine of Politics, Science, Art and Literature* 41, no. 2: 142–9.

Lombardo, Guy, with Jack Altshul. 1975. *Auld Acquaintance: An Autobiography*. Garden City, N Y: Doubleday.

Lopez, Bernard F. 1996–2001. "Spotlight on Disco DJ Jimmy Yu." www.disco-music.com (accessed 10 Nov. 2001).

Lwin, Nanda. 2000. *Top 40 Hits: The Essential Chart Guide*. Mississauga: Music Data Canada.

Lyon, George W. 1999. *Community Music in Alberta: Some Good Schoolhouse Stuff!* Calgary: University of Calgary Press.

Lyon, James. 1761/1974. *Urania: A Choice Collection of Psalm-tunes, Anthems, and Hymns*. Repr. New York: Da Capo Press. Orig. publ. Philadelphia, n.p.

MacCormac, Sylvi. 1999. "Conversing with Nature: Reflections on Hildegard Westerkamp's *Talking Rain*." *Musicworks* 74, no. 2: 8–13.

MacDonald, Keith Norman. 1887/1979. *The Skye Collection of the Best Reels & Strathspeys*. Repr. Sydney, N S: College of Cape Breton.

MacKenzie, Kirk Loren. 1991. "A Twentieth-Century Musical/Theatrical Cycle: R. Murray Schafer's 'Patria.'" Ph D diss., University of Cincinnati.

Mackenzie, William Lyon. 1833. *Sketches of Canada and the United States*. London: n.p.

MacKenzie, William Roy. 1909. "Ballad Singing in Nova Scotia." *Journal of American Folklore* 22: 327–31.

MacMillan, Keith. 1988. "Ernest MacMillan: The Ruhleben Years." In *Musical Canada: Words and Music Honouring Helmut Kallmann*, ed. J. Beckwith and F. Hall, 164–82. Toronto: University of Toronto Press.

MacMillan, Rick. 1978. "Schafer Sees Music Reflecting Country's Characteristics." *Music Scene* 300 (Sept.–Oct.): 4.

Mactaggart, John. 1829. *Three Years in Canada: An Account of the Actual State of the Country in 1826–7-8*. 2 vols. London: n.p.

Maître, Manuel. 1993. *La vie d'un vrai patriote Abbé Charles-Émile Gadbois*. Montreal: Fondation Abbé Charles-Émile Gadbois.

"Make a Joyous Noise...": The Music of the Children of Peace. 1992. Sharon Temple Study Series 4. Sharon Temple, Ontario.

Malone, Bill C. 1993. *Singing Cowboys and Musical Mountaineers: Southern Culture and the Roots of Country Music*. Athens: University of Georgia Press.

Maloney, S. Timothy, ed. 2001. *Musicanada 2000: A Celebration of Canadian Composers*. Montreal: Liber.

Marest, Gabriel. 1931/1968. Letter from Father Marest. In *Documents Relating to the Early History of Hudson Bay*. ed. J. B. Tyrrell, 103–42. Repr. New York: Greenwood Press.

Markoff, Irene. 2001. "Ontario: Other European Music." In *Garland Encyclopedia of World Music,* 3: 1195–2000. New York: Garland.

Marshall, William. 1978. *William Marshall's Scottish Melodies: 1781, 1800, 1822, 1845.* Harrisville, NH: Fiddlecase.

Marshall, Joyce, ed. 1967. *Word from New France, the Selected Letters of Marie de l'Incarnation.* Toronto: Oxford University Press.

Martin, Denis-Constant. 1995. "The Choices of Identity." *Social Identities* 1, no. 1: 5–20.

Massignon, Geneviève. 1962. "La Chanson populaire française en Acadie." Thèse complémentaire non publiée. Paris.

Matejcek, Jan V. 1996. *History of BMI Canada Ltd. and PROCAN: Their Role in Canadian Music and in the Formation of SOCAN (1940–1990).* 2nd ed. Toronto: Copygraph.

Mates, Julian. 1962. *The American Musical Stage before 1800.* New Brunswick, NJ: Rutgers University Press.

McAllester, David P. 1980. "North American Native Music." In *Musics of Many Cultures: An Introduction,* ed. Elisabeth May, 307–31. Berkeley: University of California Press.

McCook, James. 1958. "Some Notes on Musical Instruments among the Pioneers of the Canadian West." *Canadian Music Journal* 2, no. 2: 21–24.

McFarlane, Matthew. 2004. "Learning to Listen: The Rich Aural Art of Francis Dhomont," *Musicworks* 88: 26–39.

McGee, Timothy J. 1985. *The Music of Canada.* New York: Norton.

McGregor, Gaile. 1985. *The Wacousta Syndrome: Explorations in the Canadian Landscape.* Toronto: University of Toronto Press.

McIlroy, Randal. 1997. "Glenn Buhr: Musician of Eclectic Range." *Classical Music Magazine* 26, no. 1 (March): 21–5.

McIntosh, Robert Dale. 1981. *A Documentary History of Music in Victoria, British Columbia,* vol. 1: *1850–1899.* Victoria: University of Victoria.

– 1989. *The History of Music in British Columbia 1850–1950.* Victoria: Sono Nis.

– 1994. *A Documentary History of Music in Victoria, British Columbia,* vol. 2: *1900–1950.* Victoria: Beach Holme.

McLauchlan, Murray. 1998. *Getting Out of Here Alive: The Ballad of Murray McLauchlan.* Toronto: Viking.

McMillan, Alan D. 1995. *Native Peoples and Cultures of Canada: An Anthropological Overview.* 2nd ed. Vancouver: Douglas & McIntyre.

McMillan, Barclay. 1983. "Music in Canada 1791–1867: A Travellers' Perspective." MA thesis, Carleton University.

McNeilly, Kevin. 1996. "Listening, Nordicity, Community: Glenn Gould's The Idea of North." *Essays on Canadian Writing* 59: 87–104.

McPhee, Colin. 1935. "The Absolute Music of Bali." *Modern Music* 12 (May–June): 163–9.

– 1966/1976. *Music in Bali.* New Haven: Yale University Press. Repr. New York: Da Capo Press.

Mealing, F. Mark. 2001. "Music of the Doukhobors." In *Garland Encyclopedia of World Music*, 3: 1267–71. New York: Garland.

Megill, Donald D. and Richard S. Demory. 2001. *Introduction to Jazz History.* New Jersey: Prentice-Hall.

Melhuish, Martin. 1983. *Heart of Gold: 30 Years of Canadian Pop Music.* Toronto: CBC Enterprises.

– 1996. *Oh What a Feeling: A Vital History of Canadian Music.* Kingston: Quarry Press.

Metropolitan Museum of Art. *A Checklist of Viole da Gamba (Viols).* New York: Metropolitan Museum of Art, Department of Instruments, 1979

Michaud, Irma. 1933. "Antonin Dessane (1826–1873); Madame Dessane, née Irma Trunel de la Croix Nord (1828–1899)." *Le bulletin des recherches historiques* 39, no. 2: 73–9

Miles, Colin. 2001. [On Nikolai Korndorf] http://www.musiccentre.ca/CMC/CMCNews/CMCNews.html (accessed 5 Jan 2002).

Miller, Mark. 1992. "Blue Rodeo" in *The Encyclopedia of Music in Canada*, 2nd ed., ed. H. Kallmann et al., 134. Toronto: University of Toronto Press.

– 1988. "Memories of a Beboper's Dream Band." *Globe and Mail*, 14 May: C5.

– 1997. *Such Melodious Racket: The Lost History of Jazz in Canada, 1914–1949.* Toronto: Mercury Press.

– 2001. *The Miller Companion to Jazz in Canada and Canadians in Jazz.* Toronto: Mercury Press.

Mishler, Craig. 1993. *The Crooked Stovepipe: Athapaskan Fiddle Music and Square Dancing in Northeast Alaska and Northwest Canada.* Urbana: University of Illinois Press.

Montreal Music Network. <www.sle.com> (accessed 6 Apr. 2001).

Moogk, Edward B. 1975. *Roll Back the Years: History of Canadian Recorded Sound and Its Legacy.* Ottawa: National Library of Canada.

Moore, Sarah. 2002. "Re-Articulating Canadian Popular Music through a Local Lens: Examining 'Great Big Sea' and Issues of Locality, Regionalism and Nationalism." MA thesis, Carleton University.

Moquin, Yves. 1980. *De la guerre à la crise, nos racines*, vol. 21. Montreal: Laffont Canada.

Morey, Carl, ed. 1984. "The Beginnings of Modernism in Toronto." In *Celebration*, ed. G. Ridout and T. Kenins, 80–6. Toronto: Canadian Music Centre.

– 1988. "Orchestras and Orchestral Repertoire in Toronto before 1914." In *Musical Canada: Words and Music Honouring Helmut Kallmann*, ed. John Beckwith and Frederick A. Hall, 100–14. Toronto: University of Toronto Press.

– 1997a. *MacMillan on Music: Essays on Music by Sir Ernest MacMillan.* Toronto: Dundurn.

– 1997b. *Music in Canada: A Research and Information Guide.* New York: Garland.

– 1998. "Nationalism and Commerce: Canadian Folk Music in the 1920s." *Canadian Issues* 20 (1998): 34–44.

Morris, Peter. 1978. *Embattled Shadows: A History of Canadian Cinema 1895–1939*. Montreal: McGill-Queen's University Press.

Morrison, Val. 2001. "Quebec: Intercultural and Commercial Musics." In *Garland Encyclopedia of World Music,* 3: 1154–62. New York: Garland.

Mountain, Rosemary. 2005. "Creating and Contributing: The Expansive Spirit of Marcelle Deschênes," *Musicworks* 86: 14–21.

Mueller, Richard. 1983. "Imitation and Stylization in the Balinese Music of Colin McPhee." PhD diss., University of Chicago.

MusicCanadaMusique 2000. 1999. Schedules <http://www.mc2m.com/schedules.htm> (accessed 10 Nov. 2000).

Myers, Helen, ed. 1993. *Ethnomusicology: Historical and Regional Studies*. New York: Norton.

Nahachewsky, Andriy. 1991. "The Kolomyika: Change and Diversity in Canadian Ukrainian Folk Dance." PhD diss., University of Alberta.

Nash, Peter Hugh. 1968. "Music Regions and Regional Music." *Deccan Geographer* 6: 1–24.

National Post. 2000. "Tommy Reilly: Canadian Elevated Status of the Harmonica." 3 October, copied from *The Daily Telegraph*.

Nattiez, Jean Jacques. 1983. "The *Rekkukara* of the Ainu (Japan) and the *Katajjaq* of the Inuit (Canada): A Comparison." *World of Music* 25: 33–44.

Neal, J. David. 1995. "The Politics of Pop Music in Canada." *Culture & Tradition* 17: 13–24.

Nettl, Bruno. 1954. *North American Indian Musical Styles*. Memoirs of the American Folklore Society, vol. 45. Philadelphia: American Folklore Society.

Oesterle, Michael. 2000 "Bridging Sonic Cultures: Tibetan Opera in Winnipeg." *BorderCrossings* 19, no. 4: 52–4.

Oh, Susan. 1999. "Deborah Cox, The Queen of R & B." *Maclean's* 112, no. 29: 38–40.

Oja, Carol. 1984. "Colin McPhee: A Composer Turned Explorer." *Tempo* 148: 2–6.

– 1990. *Colin McPhee: Composer in Two Worlds*. Washington: Smithsonian Institution Press.

O'Neill, Francis. 1913. *Irish Minstrels and Musicians*. Chicago: Regan Printing House.

Osborne, Evelyn. 2002. "'We Never Had a Bed Like That for a Violin! We Had a Bag!': Exploring Fiddlers and Dance Music in Newfoundland: Red Cliff, Bonavista Bay and Bay de Verde, Conception Bay." MA thesis, Carleton University.

Ostick, Stephen. 1995. *Superman's Song: The Story of Crash Test Dummies*. Kingston: Quarry Press.

Overhill, Daphne. 2002. *Sound the Trumpet: The Story of the Bands of Perth 1852–2002*. Toronto: Coach House.

Padfield, Marsha. 1991. "Cannibal Dancer in the Kwakiutl World." *Canadian Folk Music Journal* 19: 14–9.

Pantchenko, Daniel. 1997. "Robert Charlebois." *Chorus: les cahiers de la chanson* 21, no. 4: 87–108.

Pâquet, Sonia. 2003. "Mémoire – Jazz à Montréal: Dans les pas de Charlie Biddle." *Au Québec* 6: 42–54.

Paquin, Robert. 1980. "Ballad: Ballade, complainte, chanson tragique, chanson lyrico-épique ou chanson narrative?" *Canadian Folk Music Journal* 8: 3–13.

Parlow, Kathleen. 1961 "Student Days in Russia." *Canadian Music Journal* 6, no. 1: 13–20.

Parsons, David G. H. 1990. "The History of 'The Frog's Courtship': A Study of Canadian Variants." *Canadian Folk Music Journal* 18: 39–48.

– 1987. "Landscape Imagery in Canadian Music: A Survey of Composition Influenced by the Natural Environment." M A research essay. Carleton University, Ottawa.

Patterson, Michael. 1996. "Native Music in Canada: The Age of the Seventh Fire." *Australian-Canadian Studies* 14: 41–54.

Paul, Hélène. 1989. "La vie musicale Montréalaise en 1917–1918: Grandeurs et vicissitudes." *Cahiers de l'ARMUQ* 11: 36–48.

Payant, Robert. 1998. *Les chanteux: la chanson en mémoire: Anthologie de 50 chansons traditionnelles.* Montréal: Triptyque.

Peacock, Kenneth. 1965. *Songs of the Newfoundland Outports.* 3 vols. Ottawa: National Museum of Man. Bulletin 197, Anthropological Series 65. Ottawa: Queen's Printer.

Peacock, Kenneth, ed. 1970. *Songs of the Doukhobors: An Introductory Outline.* Ottawa, Queen's Printer.

Pearson, Tina. 1987. "Making a Cree Drum with Albert Davis." *Musicworks* 37: 17–22.

Pegley, Karen. 2000. "'Simple Economics?' Images of Gender and Nationality on MuchMusic (Canada) and MTV (United States)." *Women and Music* 4: 3–17.

– 2002. "Multiculturalism, Diversity and Containment on MuchMusic (Canada) and MTV (US)." *Canadian University Music Review* 22, no. 2: 93–112.

Pelinski, Ramon. 1981. *La musique des Inuit du Caribou.* Montreal: Presses de l'Université de Montréal.

Perlman, Ken. 1995. "A Lovely Sweet Music: Old-Time Fiddling on Prince Edward Island." *Sing Out* 39, no. 3 (Jan.): 32–44.

– 1996. *The Fiddle Music of Prince Edward Island: Celtic and Acadian Tunes in Living Tradition.* Pacific, MO: Mel Bay.

Perry, Shirley. 1998. "Doukhobor Singing through the Twentieth Century: A Legacy." In *Spirit-Wrestlers' Voices: Honouring Doukhobors on the Centenary of Their Migration to Canada in 1899,* ed. Koozma J. Tarasoff. New York: Legas.

Petrone, Penny, ed. 1983. *First People First Voices.* Toronto: University of Toronto Press.

Pevere, Geoff, and Greig Dymond. 1996. *Mondo Canuck: A Canadian Pop Culture Odyssey.* Scarborough, ON: Prentice-Hall Canada.

Pfeiff, Margo. 2000. "Fiddler on the Roof of the World." *Reader's Digest* 156, no. 937 (May): 101–6.

Pichette, Marie-Hélène. 2001. *Musique populaire et identité franco-ontariennes: la nuit sur l'étang.* Sudbury: Prise de parole.

Pinson, Jean-Pierre. 1989. "Le plain-chant à Québec, des origines au milieu du XIXᵉ siècle: pour une musicologie de l'interprétation." *Cahiers de l'ARMUQ* 11: 3–13.

– 1996. "La vie musicale dans les églises paroissiales de Nouvelle-France, des origines à 1800." *Cahiers de l'ARMUQ* 18: 25–42.

Plamondon, Luc. *La légende de Jimmy* <www.jimmy.fr.fm/> (accessed 22 Dec. 2001).

Poirier, Lucien. 1994. "A Canadian Music Style: Illusion and Reality." In *Canadian Music: Issues of Hegemony and Identity,* ed. B. Diamond and R. Witmer, 239–68. Toronto: Canadian Scholars' Press.

Pollock, Bruce, ed. 1998. *Popular Music,* vol. 23. Detroit: Gale Group.

Portugais, Jean, and Olga Ranzenhofer. 2000. "Îles de la Nuit: Parcours dans l'oeuvre pour quatuor à cordes de R. Murray Schafer." *Circuit* 11, no. 2: 15–54.

Posen, I. Sheldon. 1992. "English-French Macaronic Songs in Canada – A Research Note and Query." *Canadian Folklore Canadien* 14, no. 2: 35–43.

Potter, Greg. 1999. *Hand Me Down World: The Canadian Pop-Rock Paradox.* Toronto: Macmillan.

Potvin, Gilles. 1984. *Orchestre symphonique de Montréal: les cinquante premières années / The First Fifty Years.* Canada: Stanké.

– 1988. "Maurice Ravel au Canada." In *Musical Canada: Words and Music Honouring Helmut Kallmann,* ed. J. Beckwith and F. Hall, 149–163. Toronto: University of Toronto Press.

– 2000. "The Canadian Opera Career of Emma Albani." *La Scena musicale* 6, no. 2: 10–13. Orig. publ. 1980, *Aria* 3, no. 1.

Primos, Kathy. 1994. "A Life Experience: The Orchestral Works of Malcolm Forsyth." *Soundnotes* 6 (Spring–Summer): 12–21.

Prociuk, Paula. 1981. "The Deep Structure of Ukrainian Hardship Songs." *Yearbook for Traditional Music* 13: 82–96.

Proctor, George A. 1980. *Canadian Music of the Twentieth Century.* Toronto: University of Toronto Press.

Proulx, Gilles. 1987. "Les Québécois et le livre 1690–1760; loisirs québécois: des livres et des cabarets 1690–1760." Rapport interne. Québec: Parcs Canada.

– 1992. *Ma petite histoire de la Nouvelle-France.* Boucherville: Proteau.

Prower, Sylvia. 1964. "Dear Sir." *CBC Times* (14–20 Mar.), n.p.

Quebec popular musicians. <www.adisq.com> <www.slfa.com> <www.theagencygroup.com> <www.dkd.com> (accessed 12 Jan. 2001).

Qiu, Huai Sheng. 2005. "Chinese Traditional Music in Greater Vancouver." *Canadian Folk Music Bulletin* 39, no. 1: 1–5.

Quigley, Colin. 1985. *Close to the Floor: Folk Dance in Newfoundland.* St. John's: Memorial University of Newfoundland.

– 1995. "Anglo-American Dance in Appalachia and Newfoundland: Toward a Comparative Framework." In *Communities in Motion: Dance, Community, and Tradition in America's Southeast and Beyond*, ed. Susan Eike Spalding and Jan Harris Woodside, 73–86. Westport, CT: Greenwood.

Qureshi, Regula. 1972. "Ethnomusicological Research among Canadian Communities of Arab and East Indian Origin." *Ethnomusicology* 16, no. 3: 381–96.

Rahn, Jay. 1988 "*M'en revenant de la joli' Rochelle*": A Song from ca. 1500 in the Current French-Canadian Repertoire." *Canadian Folk Music Journal* 16: 16–31.

Rand, Silas T. 1850. *A Short Statement of Facts Relating to the History, Manners, Customs, Language, and Literature of the Micmac Tribe of Indians, in Nova Scotia and P.E. Island*. Halifax: James Bowes & Son.

– 1888. *Dictionary of the Language of the Micmac Indians Who Reside in Nova Scotia, New Brunswick, Prince Edward Island, Cape Breton and Newfoundland*. Halifax: Nova Scotia Printing Co.

– 1894. *Legends of the Micmac*. New York and London: Longmans, Green.

Rasmusssen, Knud. 1927. *Report of the Fifth Thule Expedition, 1921–1924*, vols. 7–9. Copenhagen: Gyldendal.

Raudsepp, Karl. 1999. "The Warrens." *Tracker* 1: 9–26.

Regenstreif, Mike. 1997. "Kate & Anna McGarrigle: On Their Own." *Sing Out!* 41, no. 4: 42–53.

Reid, Jamie. 2002. *Diana Krall: The Language of Love*. Markham: Quarry Press.

Reid, Jeanne Martine. 1981. "La ceremonie hamatsa des Kwagul: approche structuraliste des rapports mythe-rituel." PhD diss., University of British Columbia.

Report of the Royal Commission on National Development in the Arts, Letters and Sciences 1949–1951 [Massey Report] 1951. Ottawa: King's Printer.

Reynolds, Simon. 1999. *Generation Ecstasy: Into the World of Techno and Rave Culture*. New York: Routledge.

Rice, Timothy. 2000. "The Music of Europe: Unity and Diversity." In *Garland Encyclopedia of World Music*, 8: 2–15. New York: Garland.

Rice, Timothy, and Tammy Gutnik. 1995. "What's Canadian about Canadian Popular Music? The Case of Bruce Cockburn." In *Taking a Stand: Essays in Honour of John Beckwith*, ed. Timothy McGee, 238–58. Toronto: University of Toronto Press.

Robert, Véronique. 2000. "Le saga de l'opéra fantôme." *Actualité* (1 mars): 68, 70.

Roberts, Helen H. 1936. *Musical Areas in Aboriginal North America*. Yale University Publications in Anthropology 12. New Haven, CT: Yale University Press. Repr. 1970 New Haven, CT: Human Relations Area Files Press.

Roberts, Helen H., and Diamond Jenness. 1925. *Report of the Canadian Arctic Expedition, 1913–18*, vol. 14: *Eskimo Songs: Songs of the Copper Eskimos*. Ottawa: F.A. Acland.

Roberts, Helen H., and Morris Swadesh. 1955. *Songs of the Nootka Indians of Western Vancouver Island.* Transactions of the American Philosophical Society, New Series, vol. 45, part 3: 199–327.

Robbins, James. 1990. "What Can We Learn When They Sing, Eh? Ethnomusicology in the American State of Canada." In *Ethnomusicology in Canada,* ed. R. Witmer, 47–56. CanMus Documents 5. Toronto: Institute for Canadian Music.

Robinson, Gwendolyn, and John W. 1989. *Seek the Truth: A Story of Chatham's Black Community.* n.p.: n.p.

Robbins, Vivian. 1969. *Musical Buxton.* n.p.: n. p.

Robertson, William. 1992. *k.d. lang: Carrying the Torch.* Toronto: ECW Press.

Roger, Charles. 1871. *Ottawa Past and Present.* Ottawa: Time Print and Publishing.

Rolland, Pierre. 1980. Interview with François Morel. *Anthologie de la musique canadienne: François Morel.* CBC Radio Canada International.

Romero, Brenda M. 2001. "Great Lakes." In *Garland Encyclopedia of World Music,* 3: 451–60. New York: Garland.

Roper, E. 1891. *By Track and Trail: A Journey Through Canada.* London

Rosenberg, Neil V. 1974. "'Folk' and 'Country' Music in the Canadian Maritimes: A Regional Model." *Journal of Country Music* 5, no. 2: 84–8.

– 1994. "Don Messer's Modern Canadian Fiddle Canon." *Canadian Folk Music Journal* 22: 23–35.

Ross, James Andrew. 1994. "'Ye Olde Firme' Heintzman & Company, Ltd. 1885–1930: A Case Study in Canadian Piano Manufacturing." MA thesis, University of Western Ontario.

Rumson, Gordon. 2000. "A True Renaissance Man: The Vision of R. Murray Schafer." http://www.mvdaily.com/articles/2000/07/schafer3.htm (accessed 15 Aug. 2000)

Russell, Dale R. 1991. *Eighteenth Century Western Cree and Their Neighbours* Archaeological Survey of Canada Mercury Series Paper 143. Hull: Canadian Museum of Civilization.

Ryan, Thomas. 1899/1996. "Jenny Lind's 1850 American Tour As Recalled in 1899 by Thomas Ryan (1827–1903)" *Classical Music Magazine* 19, no. 2: 20–3.

Sale, David. 1968. "Toronto's Pre-confederation Music Societies." MA thesis, University of Toronto.

Salzman, Gregory. 2000. "Regarding Landscape." *Canadian Art* 17, no. 3: 61–7.

Sargent, Margaret. 1950. "Seven Songs from Lorette." *Journal of American Folklore* 63: 175–80.

Sawa, George. 2001. "Middle Eastern Music." In *Garland Encyclopedia of World Music,* 3: 1218–22. New York: Garland.

Schabas, Ezra. 1994. *Sir Ernest MacMillan: The Importance of Being Canadian.* Toronto: University of Toronto Press.

Schabas, Ezra, and Carl Morey. 2000. *Opera Viva: Canadian Opera Company: The First Fifty Years,* Toronto: Dundurn.

Schafer, Murray. 1977. *Music in the Cold*. Toronto: Coach House.

– 1993. *Voices of Tyranny: Temples of Silence*. Indian River: Arcana Editions.

– 2000. "La 'quaternité' et le quatuor." *Circuit* 11, no. 2: 11–4.

– 2002. *Patria: the complete cycle*. Toronto: Coach House.

Schaffer, Barbara. 1997. "Sing Out Spotlight: Moxy Früvous." *Sing Out!* 41, no. 3: 24–7.

Schuster, John. 1992. "Compositional Process in Clermont Pépin's *Quasars*." *Sonus: A Journal of Investigations into Global Musical Possibilities* 12, no. 2: 28–43.

Schau, Barbara Ann. 1983. "Sacred Music at Sharon, A Nineteenth-Century Canadian Community." M A thesis, Carleton University.

– 1985. "Sharon's Musical Past." *York Pioneer* 80: 17–31.

Schloss, Joseph. 1997. "A Handshake Business: The Ethics of Hip-Hop Mix Tapes." Paper given at the Society for Ethnomusicology conference, Pittsburgh, 25 October.

Schmidt, David L., and Murdena Marshall, eds. 1995. *MI'KMAQ Hieroglyphic Prayers*. Halifax: Nimbus.

Schrauwers, Albert. 1993. *Awaiting the Millennium: The Children of Peace and the Village of Hope 1812–1889*. Toronto: University of Toronto Press.

Schuster, John. 1992. "Compositional Process in Clermont Pépin's 'Quasars.'" *Sonus: A Journal of Investigations into Global Musical Possibilities* 12, no. 2: 28–43.

Schwandt, Erich. 1981. "The Motet in New France: Some 17th- and 18th-century Manuscripts in Québec." *Fontes Artis Musicae* 28, no. 3: 194–219.

– 1988. "*Musique spirituelle* (1718): Canada's First Music Theory Manual." In *Musical Canada: Words and Music Honouring Helmut Kallmann*, ed. John Beckwith and Frederick A. Hall, 50–9. Toronto: University of Toronto Press.

– 1996. "Some Motets in Honour of St. Joseph in the Archives of the Ursulines of Québec." *Canadian University Music Review* 17, no. 1: 57–71.

Schwandt, Erich, ed. 1981. *The Motet in New France: 20 Motets, Antiphons, and Canticles from the Archives of the Ursulines and the Archives of the Hotel-Dieu of Québec*. Victoria: Jeu Éditions.

Scott, Jay. 1988. "Yippee-I-O k.d.!: *Chatelaine*'s Woman of the Year." *Chatelaine* (Jan.): 54–5, 130–2.

Seeger, Charles. 1977. "Music and Class Structure in the United States." In *Studies in Musicology 1935–1975*, 222–36. Berkeley: University of California.

Sellick, Lester. 1969. *Canada's Don Messer*. Kentville, N S: Kentville Publishing.

Shepherd, John. 2001. "Government, Politics, and Popular Music in Canada." In *Garland Encyclopedia of World Music*, 3: 313–4. New York: Garland.

Sherinian, Zoe C. 2001. "k.d. lang and Gender Performance." In *Garland Encyclopedia of World Music*, 3: 107–11. New York: Garland.

Shive, Clyde S. 1997. "The 'First' Band Festival in America." *American Music* 15, no. 1: 446–58.

Silliman, Benjamin. 1822. *A Tour to Quebec in the Autumn of 1819*. London: n.p.

Sioui, Georges E. 1992. *For an Amerindian Autohistory: An Essay on the Foundations of a Social Ethic*. Montreal: McGill-Queen's University Press.

Simcoe, Elizabeth. 1965. *Mrs Simcoe's Diary*. Ed. M.Q. Innis. Toronto: Macmillan.

Small, Christopher. 1998. *Musicking: The Meanings of Performing and Listening*. Hanover: University Press of New England.

Smiderle, Wes. 2002. "Broadening the Audience for Hip-hop Music." *Ottawa Citizen*, 20 April: J10.

Smith, Dorothy Blakey. 1958. "Music in the Furthest West a Hundred Years Ago." *Canadian Music Journal* 2, no. 4: 3–14.

Smith, Gordon E. 1989. "Ernest Gagnon on Nationalism and Canadian Music: Folk and Native Sources." *Canadian Folk Music Journal* 17: 32–9.

– 1995. "Ernest Gagnon's *"Chansons populaires du Canada"*: Processes of 'Writing Culture.'" *World of Music* 37, no. 3: 36–65.

– 2001a. "Place." In *Garland Encyclopedia of World Music*, 3: 142–52. New York: Garland.

– 2001b. "Québec: Folk Musics." In *Garland Encyclopedia of World Music*, 3: 1163–8. New York: Garland.

Smith, Jerrard, and Diana Smith. 2000. "The Patria Design Project," <http://www.patria.org/pdp/ORDER/OVERVIEW.HTM> (accessed 15 Aug. 2000).

Snider, Roxanne. 1999. "Sounding a Fanfare for Canadian Music." *Opus* 22, no. 3: 14–7.

Snow, Hank, with Jack Ownbey and Bob Burris. 1994. *The Hank Snow Story: Hank Snow, the Singing Ranger*. Urbana: University of Illinois Press.

Solitudes. <www.solitudes.com/about.html> (accessed 15 Sept. 2001).

Southam, Ann. 1998. "If Only I Could Sing: Ann Southam in Conversation with Kalvos and Damian." *Musicworks* 71, no. 2: 20–8.

Southesk, James Carnegie, Earl of. 1875/1969. *Saskatchewan and the Rocky Mountains: A Diary and Narrative of Travel Through the Hudson's Bay Company's Territories in 1859*. Edmonton: Hurtig.

Sparling, Heather. 2003. "'Music is Language and Language is Music': Language Attitudes and Musical Choices in Cape Breton." *Ethnologies* 26, no. 2: 145–72.

Spencer, Jon Michael. 1991. *The R. Nathaniel Dett Reader: Essays on Black Sacred Music*. Black Sacred Music 5, no. 2. Durham, NC: Duke University Press.

Stambler, Irwin. 1977. *Encyclopedia of Pop, Rock & Soul*. New York: St Martin's Press.

Stanfield, Norman. 2001. "British Columbia: Overview." In *Garland Encyclopedia of World Music*, 3: 1254–59. New York: Garland.

Stanley, Shelagh, and Lee Anne Nicholson. 1989. "Country Music Sings a New Tune." *Canadian Living* (Nov.): 38–9, 41, 43, 45.

Stansbury, Philip. 1822. *A Pedestrian Tour of Two Thousand Three Hundred Miles, in North America ... in ... 1821*. New York: n.p.

Stephens, W. Ray. 1993. *The Canadian Entertainers of World War II*. Oakville, ON: Mosaic Press.

Stern, Percy. 1988. "k.d. lang Opens Up." *Canadian Musician* (Dec.): 48–9.

Stewardson, Richard. 1992. "Altered Guitar Tunings in Canadian Folk and Folk-Related Music." *Canadian Folk Music Journal* 20: 19–32.

Stocking, George W. 1968. *Race, Culture, and Evolution: Essays in the History of Anthropology*. New York: Free Press.

Stokes, Martin, ed. 1994. *Ethnicity, Identity and Music: The Musical Construction of Place*. Oxford, UK; Providence, RI: Berg.

Straw, Will. 1991. "Systems of Articulation; Logics of Change: Communities and Scenes in Popular Music." *Cultural Studies* 5, no. 3: 368–88.

– 1993. "The English Canadian Recording Industry Since 1970." In *Rock and Popular Music: Politics, Policies, Institutions*, ed. Tony Bennett, Simon Frith, Lawrence Grossberg, John Shepherd, and Graeme Turner, 52–65. New York: Routledge.

– 1996. "Sound Recording." In *The Cultural Industries in Canada*, ed. Michael Dorland, 95–117. Toronto: Lorimer.

– 2000. "In and Around Canadian Music." *Journal of Canadian Studies* 35, no. 3: 173–83.

Stuart, Wendy Bross. 1972. *Gambling Music of the Coast Salish Indians*. Mercury Series, Ethnology Division Paper 3. Ottawa: National Museum of Man.

Stybr, David. 1997. "Michael Conway Baker: Canada's Radical Romantic." *Classical Music Magazine* 20, no. 3 (Sept.): 16–19.

Sultzman, Lee. Huron History: http://www.tolatsga.org/hur.html (accessed 8 Aug. 2000).

Sutherland, Richard. 2002. "Canadian Content at 32." *Canadian Issues / Thèmes canadiens* (June): 13–7.

Sykes, Debra. 1996. "Henry Brant: Spatialman." *Musicworks* 64, no. 1: 42–8.

Taddie, Daniel. 1991. "Solmization, Scale, and Key in Nineteenth-Century Four-Shape Tunebooks: Theory and Practice." *American Music* 14, no. 1: 42–64.

Taft, Michael. 1990. "The Bard of Prescott Street Meets Tin Pan Alley: The Vanity Press Sheet Music Publications of John Burke." *Newfoundland Studies* 6, no. 1: 56–73.

– 1993. "Syncretizing Sound: The Emergence of Canadian Popular Music." In *The Beaver Bites Back? American Popular Culture in Canada*, ed. David H. Flaherty and Fred E. Manning, 197–208. Montreal: McGill-Queen's University Press.

Taylor, Kate. 1993. "Native Music Is a Hot Ticket These Days" *Globe and Mail* (Toronto), 20 March: C-1–2.

Teit, James A. 1900. *The Thompson Indians of British Columbia*. Ed. Franz Boas. Memoirs of the American Museum of Natural History, vol. 2, part 4.

– 1914. "Indian Tribes of the Interior." *Canada and its Provinces* 21: 283–312.

– 1915–21. Fieldnotes on Interior Salish Songs, Ethnology Division, Canadian Museum of Civilization, Gatineau, QC.

Teskey, Nancy, and Gordon Brock. 1995. "Elements of Continuity in Kwakiutl Traditions." *American Music Research Center Journal* 5: 37–56.

Tétu de Labsade, Françoise. 2001. *Le Québec: un pays, une culture*. Montreal: Boréal.

Théberge, Paul. 1997. *Any Sound You Can Imagine: Making Music / Consuming Technology*. Hanover, NH: University Press of New England.

Thirlwall, Stephen Lawrence. 1992. "Musical Landscape: A Definition and a Case Study of Musical Landscape in its Contribution to the Development of Quebecois Identity." MA thesis, Carleton University.

Thomas, Philip J. 1979. *Songs of the Pacific Northwest*. Saanichton, BC: Hancock House.

– 1993. "The 'Louis Riel Song': A Perspective." *Canadian Folk Music Journal* 21: 12–8.

– 1996. "*La lettre de sang / Chanson de Louis Riel*: Addenda." *Canadian Folk Music Journal* 24: 56–60.

Thwaites, Reuben Gold, ed. 1959. *The Jesuit Relations & Allied Documents*. 73 vols. New York: Pageant Book. Orig. publ. 1896–1901; available online at www.puffin.creighton.edu/jesuit/relations.

Tippett, Maria. 1990. *Making Culture: English-Canadian Institutions and the Arts before the Massey Commission*. Toronto: University of Toronto Press.

Tooker, Elisabeth. 1978. "Iroquois Since 1820." In *A Handbook of North American Indians*, vol. 15: *Northeast*, 449–65. Washington: Smithsonian.

Torrington, Frederick H. 1898. "Musical Progress in Canada." In *Canada: An Encyclopedia of the Country*, ed. J. Castell Hopkins, 4: 383–86. Toronto: Linscott.

Tremblay, Danielle. n.d. Le développement historique et le fonctionnement de l'industrie de la chanson québécoise (1917–1995). <http://www.filtronique-son-or.com/chanson/danielle/danielle.htm> (accessed May 2001).

Tremblay, Jacques. 2000. "L'écriture à haute voix: *Lonely Child* de Claude Vivier." *Circuit* 11, no. 1: 45–68.

Tyson, Ian, with Colin Escott. 1994. *Ian Tyson: I Never Sold My Saddle*. Vancouver: Greystone.

Vachon, Pierre. 2000. *Emma Albani*. Célébrités / Collection biographique. Montreal: Lidec.

Vastokas, Joan M. 1992. *Beyond the Artifact: Native Art as Performance*. North York: Robarts Centre for Canadian Studies, York University.

Vézina, Lyse. 2000. *Quarante ans au coeur de l'Orchestre symphonique de Montréal*. Montreal: Éditions Varia.

Vermazen, Bruce. 2004. *That Moaning Saxophone: The Six Brown Brothers and the Dawning of a Musical Craze*. New York: Oxford University Press.

Vincent, Odette. 2000. *La vie musicale au Québec: art lyrique, musique classique et contemporaine*. Saint-Nicolas, QC: Éditions de l'IQRC.

Virga, Patricia H. 1982. *The American Opera to 1790*. Studies in Musicology 61. Ann Arbor, MI: UMI Research Press.

Vogan, Nancy. 1991. "The Musical Traditions of the Planters and 'Mary Miller Her Book.'" In *Making Adjustments: Change and Continuity in Planter Nova Scotia 1759–1800*, ed. Margaret Conrad, 247–52. Fredericton: Acadiensis Press.

Voorvelt, Martijn. 1997. "The Environmental Element in Barry Truax's Compositions." *Journal of New Music Research* 26, no. 1: 48–69.

Voyer, Simone. 1986. *La danse traditionnelle dans l'est du Canada: quadrilles et cotillons*. Quebec: Presses de l'université Laval.

Voyer, Simone, and Gynette Tremblay. 2001. *La danse traditionelle québécoise et sa musique d'accompagnement*. Quebec: Éditions de l'IQRC.

Wagner, Anton, and Richard Plant. 1978. *Canada's Lost Plays*, vol. 1: *The Nineteenth Century*. Toronto: CTR Publications.

Walker, Klive. 1990. "Broken Arrow Mojah Verse to Vinyl Records." *Fuse* 14, no. 1–2 (Fall): 46.

Walser, Robert. 1993. *Running with the Devil: Power, Gender, and Madness in Heavy Metal Music*. Hanover, NH: University Press of New England.

Walton, Ivan H., with Joe Grimm. 2002. *Windjammers: Songs of the Great Lakes Sailors*. Detroit: Wayne State University Press.

Waterman, Ellen. 2005. Sounds Provocative: Experimental Music in Canada. University of Guelph. http://www.experimentalperformance.ca/pages/contact.shtm (accessed 29 Jan. 2006).

Warner, Jay. 1992. *The Billboard Book of American Singing Groups: A History 1940–1990*. New York: Billboard.

Warren, Richard S. 2002. *Begins with the Oboe: A History of the Toronto Symphony Orchestra*. Toronto: University of Toronto Press.

Warwick, Jacqueline. 1996. "Can Anyone Dance to this Music? Bhangra and Toronto's South Asian Youth." MA thesis, York University.

– 2000. "'Make Way for the Indian': Bhangra Music and South Asian Presence in Toronto." *Popular Music and Society* 24, no. 2: 25–44.

Waterman, Ellen. 1998. "Confluence and Collaboration *Patria the Epilogue: And Wolf Shall Inherit the Moon*." *Musicworks* 70, no. 1: 6–10.

Watmough, David. 1985. *The Unlikely Pioneer: Building Opera from the Pacific through the Prairies*. Oakville, ON: Mosaic Press.

Weber, William. 1994. "The Intellectual Origins of Musical Canon in Eighteenth-Century England." *Journal of the American Musicological Society* 47: 488–520.

Weinzweig, John. 1996. "The Making of a Composer." In *A Celebration of Canada's Arts 1930–1970*, ed. G. Carruthers and G. Lazarevich, 77–86. Toronto: Canadian Scholars' Press.

Wheeler, David E. 1914. "The Dog-Rib Indian and His Home." *Bulletin of the Geographical Society of Philadelphia* 12: 47–69.

Whidden, Lynn. 1993. *Métis Songs: Visiting Was the Métis Way*. Saskatoon, SK: Gabriel Dumont Institute.

Whitbread, Donald H. 1953. "The Eskimo Violin." *The Canadian Forum* 33, no. 390: 82–83.

Whitburn, Joel. 1986. *Pop Memories 1890–1954: The History of American Popular Music*. Memomonee Falls WI: Record Research.

Whitcomb, Ed. 1990. *Canadian Fiddle Music*, vol. 1. Ottawa: author.

– 2001 *Canadian Fiddle Music*, vol. 2. Ottawa: author.

White, Laurie. n.d. [1998?]. *First You Dream, Portia White*. CD with liner notes. PW 001–2.

Whitehead, Ruth Holmes. 1991. *The Old Man Told Us: Excerpts from Micmac History*. Halifax: Nimbus.

Wickwire, Wendy Cochrane. 1983. "Cultures in Contact: Music, the Plateau Indian, and the Western Encounter." PhD diss., Wesleyan University.

Wilburn, Gene. 1998. *Northern Journey 2*. Teeswater, ON: Reference Press; available at www.northernjourney.com/ with links to other sites (accessed 30 Jan. 2006).

Wildermuth, Kurt. 2002. "Mary Margaret O'Hara in Ecstasy." www.furious.com/perfect/marymargaretohara.html.

Williamson, Patricia. 1991. "Barbara Where Are You?" *Canadian Folk Music Journal* 18: 3–13.

Winnipeg Folk Festival. <www.wpgfolkfest.mb.ca> (accessed 18 Aug. 2001).

Wissler, Clark. 1912. *Ceremonial Bundles of the Blackfoot Indian*. Anthropological Papers of the American Museum of Natural History, vol. 7, no. 2.

Wood, Christopher. 1937. "Music Across Canada: The History and Career of the Toronto Symphony Orchestra." *Curtain Call* (Nov.): 9–10.

World Soundscape Project. 2000. http://www.sfu.ca/~truax/wsp.html (accessed 30 Jan. 2006).

Young, Gayle. 1989. *The Sackbut Blues: Hugh LeCaine, Pioneer in Electronic Music*. Ottawa: National Museum of Science and Technology.

Young, Kevin. 2001. "Quebec's Music Scene." *Canadian Musician* 23, no. 4 (Jul.–Aug.): 42–6.

INTERNET SITES

Canadian Electroacoustic Community: http://www.sonus.ca

Canadian Music Centre: www.musiccentre.ca

Canadian University Music Society. http://www.cums-smuc.ca/resources/links.html

Clifford Ford Publications: for the "Inventory of Canadian Notated Music" and publications such as the *Historical Anthology of Canadian Music*: clifford-fordpublications.ca.

Dictionary of Canadian Biography Online: http://www.biographi.ca.

For Quebec's popular music scene: www.quebecinfomusique.com

For Canadian popular music generally: http://www.canehdian.com/links.html

The availability of recordings is constantly changing; the following list concentrates primarily on traditional musics and pre-1950 Canadian works. For First Peoples' Music Arbor Records, Sunshine Records, Sweet Grass Records, and Festival Distribution have extensive offerings of powwow and contemporary artists. Contemporary materials are available from the Canadian Music Centre (www.music-centre.ca) and the Canadian Broadcasting Corporation (www.cbc.ca). The CBC's online independent music site (www.newmusiccanada.com) features information and clips about independent popular artists: Canadian popular recordings are available for purchase from the New World site (www.vaxxine.com/newworldcds/homepage.htm). Of particular note is the ongoing series Canadian Composers Portraits on the Canadian Music Centre's Centredisc label; releases as of early 2006 include Murray Adaskin, István Anhalt, Violet Archer, John Beckwith, Norma Beecroft, Jean Coulthard, Malcolm Forsyth, Harry Freedman, Jacques Hétu, Talivaldis Kenins, Oskar Morawetz, Phil Nimmons, Barbara Pentland, Jean Papineau-Couture, R. Murray Schafer, Ann Southam, Gilles Tremblay, Robert Turner, John Weinzweig, along with four corresponding sets of recordings in the CBC's Ovation series.

À la claire fontaine: Music in Krieghoff's Quebec. Opening Day ODR 9321.

Alys Robi Diva. Gala Records 101.

The Best Cree Fiddle Players of James Bay. Ozone Records, HB01CD.

"By a Canadian Lady": Piano Music 1841–1997. Carleton Sound CSCD 1006.

La Bonne Chanson. XXI-CD 2 1438.

Canada: the Rough Guide to the Music of Canada. RGNET 1125 CD.

Canadian Sounds: Deirdre Piper, Composer and Organist. Carleton Sound CSCD 1007.

Le Chant de la Jerusalem des terres froides: Québec – Montréal Indiens Abenakis. Les chemins du Baroque Nouvelle France K 617052.

Chief Jimmy Bruneau School Drummers: Drum and Dance Music of the Dogrib. Canyon Records 16260.

Diana Gilchrist Sings Songs of Canada. Carleton Sound CSCD 1003.

Earth Songs: Ohwejagehká: Gae:nashó:oh. For information: see www.ohwejagehka.com/artlyle/ or telephone Art Johnson and Lyle Anderson at 519-445–0887.

L'Époque du Julie Papineau (1795–1852): Musiques du Québec. ORCD-4108.

From Molt to McPhee: A Century of Canadian Piano Music. Carleton Sound CSCD 1004.

Heartbeat 2: More Voices of First Nations Women. Smithsonian Folkways SF CD 40455.

Hearts of the Nations: Aboriginal Women's Voices ... in the Studio 1997. Banff/97 [Sweet Grass].

Here and Now: A Celebration of Canadian Music. CDSP 4513.

Introduction to Canadian Music. Naxos 8.550171–2.

Inuit Iglulik Canada. Museum Collection Berlin CD 19.

Katutjatut Throat Singing: Alacie Tullaugaq, Lucy Amarualik. Inukshuk
    Records IPCD0798.

Laxwe'gila: Gaining Strength. U'mista Cultural Society.

Le Livre d'orgue de Montréal. FL 2 3022–3.

Noël: Early Canadian Christmas Music. Marquis Classics 77471 81227 2 8.

Northern Lights: Walter Bonaise. Abha Music 0004.

Oh What a Feeling 1 and *Oh What a Feeling 2* [31445208852]

Prima Donna on a Moose. Opening Day ODR 9310.

Rising from the Ashes. U'mista Cultural Society.

Romance: Early Canadian Chamber Music. Carleton Sound CSCD 1009

Songs and Stories of Canada. CD-ROM by Jon Bartlett and Rika Ruebsaat
    includes sixteen 26-minute programs with 87 folksongs/instrumentals.
    http://www3.telus.net/jonbartlett-rikaruebsaat/index.html

Songs of the Inuit II (Canada): Drum Dance Songs in Inuvik. VICG-5460–2.

Songs of the Newfoundland Outports and Labrador. 2003. Canadian Museum of
    Civilization.

Le Souvenir: Songs from Canada. CMC-CD 6596.

20 Years of Stony Plain. SPCD 1230.

Victoires et réjouissances à Québec (1690–1758). ORCD 4109.

We're from Canada. Opening Day ODR 9901/2.

Wolastoqiyik Lintuwakonawa: Maliseet Songs. 2004. Canadian Museum of Civi-
    lization.

SELECTIVE FILMOGRAPHY

Barrage The World On Stage. 2000. Madacy 2 Label Group.

Brébeuf and the Huron Carol. 2002. Redbark Productions, video 7292/1840;
    DVD 7648.

Dances of the Northern Plains. 1987. Saskatchewan Indian Cultural College.

Eternal Earth [on Alexina Louie]. 1987. National Film Board of Canada C 0187
    020 (www.nfb.ca/homevideo).

Glenn Gould: The Russian Journey. 2002. Atlantic Productions.

John Arcand and His Métis Fiddle. 2004. Gabriel Dumont Institute
    (www.gdins.org).

In the Key of Oscar: One Man's Journey Home [Oscar Peterson]. 2004. National
    Film Board.

Lonely Child: The Imaginative World of Claude Vivier. 1988. Silverfilm.

Mariposa Under a Stormy Sky. 1994. Lynx Images Releasing.

Métis Dance Instructional Video. Gabriel Dumont Institute.

Métis Summer, produced by L. Freeman and D. Breland-Fines, Winnipeg, MA;
    Culture and Heritage.

Musicanada. 1975. National Film Board of Canada C 0175 120.

One Warm Line: The Legacy of Stan Rogers. 1989. Lynx Images Releasing.

Potlatch: A Strict Law Bids Us Dance. 1975. U'mista Cultural Society (www.umista.org).

Pow Wow Canadian Style – Live at SIFC 1997. Turtle Island Music.

Richard Lafferty The Muskey Fiddler. 2002. Gabriel Dumont Institute.

A Sigh and a Wish: Helen Creighton's Maritimes. 2001. National Film Board of Canada (www.nfb.ca/homevideo).

The Travellers: This Land Is Your Land. 2001. National Film Board of Canada.

Unitas Fratrum: The Moravians in Labrador. 1983. National Film Board of Canada.

Wandering Spirit (2003) [with Cree elder Walter Bonaise]. Wandering Spirit Productions (no. 2, 8207–123 Ave., Edmonton, AB T5B 1B5)

Weinzweig's World. 1991. National Film Board of Canada.

With Glowing Hearts: A Canadian Musical Celebration. 2000. Canadian Broadcasting Corporation.

Index

An italic *f* following a page reference indicates the presence of an illustration; an italic *t* indicates a table

Canadian Recording Industry
Association, 245
Canadian Record Manufacturer's
Association, 245
Canadian Snapshots (CBC), 171
Canadian Society of Musicians, 385n29
Canadian soundmark, distinctive, 184,
252–3, 267–9, 296–7, 347–59; axes of
articulation in, 246–7; and Canadian
environment, 252; Canadian references in texts, 82f, 104, 300, 301,
414n8; defined by society, 311; "easy
listening" or "middle-of-the-road,"
186, 196–7, 207, 316; eclecticism,
267–9; folk and traditional roots of,
247, 303; as gaunt and lonely, 303–4;
harmonic elements, 243; of historical
sounds, 319; impact outside Canada,
311–13, 317; individual and group
solidarity, 240; nationalism, 301–2; as
personal vs national, 252; as process,
253; in Quebec, 306–10; recognition
of in Canada, 244, 312, 317. *See also*
landscape (of Canada)
*Canadian Ten Cent Ball-Room
Companion and Guide to Dancing*,
75, 118
Canadian University Music Society,
208
Canadien errant, Un, 146, 231
Canayens sont la!, Les, 146
CanCon policy (of CRTC), 245, 247,
412n27
Cantate Domino, 54, 55f
cantique de missions, 138
Cantique des Acadiens, La, 67, 68f
cantiques, 52, 99, 100
Cape Breton fiddling, 77, 78
Capitol Records of Canada, 225, 401n1
Capitol Theatre Symphony Orchestra
(Vancouver), 170
Capture of the Albert Johnson, The
(Carter), 201
Cardy, Patrick, 252; *Virelai*, 255
Caribbean music, 274, 313; Caribana,
246

Caribou Inuit, 16f, 40, 413n5
Carignan, Jean, 198–9, 227, 229f, 234
Carleton University, 4, 228, 399n10
Carmichael, Beatrice (née van Loon),
212
Caron, Alan, 410n2
Carpenter, Carole Henderson, 12
Carr, Emily, 128, 305
Carter, George E.: *Canada, mon pays*,
301
Carter, John, 378n8
Carter, Wilf, 172, 201–2, 232, 244, 311,
415n24
Cartier, Jacques, 37, 47, 49, 368n33,
381n30
Casals, Pablo, 177
Casavant, Joseph, 127
Casavant Frères, 127, 143
Cass-Beggs, Barbara, 325f
Catch and Glee Club (Saint John), 101
categorization of music, 5–9; as amateur
vs connoisseur, 6–7; as "classical,"
363n11; in Europe, 6–7, 8; as false vs
real, 362n8; as highbrow vs lowbrow,
144, 186, 361–2n5; as legitimate,
363n11; of opera, 362n7; as popular vs
refined, 7, 363n11; in the US, 7–8
Catholic church and Catholicism:
liturgical music and practices of, 48,
93, 138, 369n2, 370n5, 370n8, 370n9;
mass, 47, 48, 49, 53f, 175, 371n12;
opposition to popular entertainments, 61, 66, 75, 198, 397n29; *Rituel
du diocèse de Québec*, 370n5; schools
run by, 122
Cavaliers des Plaines, 232
CBC (Canadian Broadcasting
Corporation): creation of, 170–1; government funding for, 171, 249; jazz
programs, 236; Music Library, 4. *See
also* radio
CBC (Canadian Broadcasting
Corporation): radio and television
programs: *Canadian Snapshots*,
171; *Country Hoedown*, 232, 412n35;
Countrytime, 412n35; *Don Messer's*

electronic music, 265, 266; studios, 208, 224

Elleston, Art, 237

Elliott, Robin, 387n48

Elmdale Harmonic Band, 398n6

Elmes, Barry, 272

Empress Hotel (Victoria), 176, 392n12

Encyclopedia of Music in Canada, 5, 120, 361n1

Engagé de Bytown, L', 146

English Dancing Master, The (Playford), 71, 72*f*, 374n8

English Opera Company of Boston, 119

Enman, Angus, 146

Eno, Brian, 292

Ensemble de musique improvisée de Montréal, 272

environmental recordings, 274

environmental sounds, 250, 265, 306; in First Peoples' music, 297–8, 304

Equipe spectra, L', 283–4

erhu, 157, 158*f*, 263, 314

Erickson, John M., 395n6

Erlendson, Bob, 237

Essig, David, 269

Estacio, John: *Filomena*, 264

ethnomusicology, 208

Etidloiee, Etulu, 288

European conservatory system, 8, 123

European music, 6, 302, 303, 313, 362n9; melodic patterns, 59, 81, 156, 298–9, 376n22

European Sound Diary (Schafer), 250

Evans, Gil, 237, 319

Expresso S.V.P., 282

Fabian, Lara, 283

fado, 278

Faith, Percy, 196, 270; *Cheerio*, 196; *Summer Place*, 196; *Theme for Young Lovers*, 196; *A World of Whispers*, 196

Fallis, Mary Lou, 396n10

Fan, Sheng-E, 314

Fang, Liu, 314

Farewell Dance (Kwakwaka'wakw), 18

Farmer's Song (McLauchlan), 243

Farnon, Robert, 196, 237, 270, 311, 397n23; *Jumping Bean*, 196; *Lake of the Woods*, 196; *Symphonette*, 392n11; Symphonies nos. 1 and 2, 397n23

Fate of Old Strawberry Roan, The (Carter), 202

Fauset, Arthur, 162

Faux plaisirs, vains honneurs (La cantique des Acadiens), 67, 68*f*

Feast Song (Kwakwaka'wakw), 18

Federal Cultural Review Committee, 249

Feldbrill, Victor, 218, 400n20

Félix awards, 281

Feneboque, Abe, 169

Fenwick, G. Roy, 172

Ferguson, Maynard, 236, 244

Ferland, Jean-Pierre, 235, 271

Festival Canada, 406n8

Festival of the Sound, 251

festivals, 251, 406n2, 406n7, 406n8; African music, 313; blues, 271; choral, 132, 340–2, 406n8; CPR Festivals, 174–7; First Peoples' music, 286; folk, 227–8, 234, 290, 402n6; seasonal, 251, 406n8

Festival Singers, 400n21

Feux follets, 199

Feycock, Merry, 72

Fialkowska, Janina, 398n1, 410n40

Fiddle Album (Cormier), 285

fiddling, 75–9, 76*f*, 151*f*, 152–5; Ash Manuscript, 105; bowing, 78, 79; clogging, 78–9; competitions, 78, 385n29; electrified instruments, 285; irregular forms, 154, 232; in minstrel shows, 163; ornamentation, 79; piping tunes for, 79; scordatura, 77, 79, 398n30; as source for notated compositions, 181–2, 394n28; tunes played on accordion, 154, 318. *See also* folk songs; string instruments

fiddling styles: Down East, 77, 78, 375n16; First Peoples', 43–4, 77, 155, 286, 288, 299–300; French Canadian

(Quebec), 77, 154, 181–2, 198–9, 232, 234, 394n28; Irish, 77, 78, 198, 199; Métis and Red River, 74, 76f, 77, 149–50, 155, 200; Prince Edward Island, 77, 78–9; Scottish and Celtic, 77, 262, 299–300

fife and drums, 61, 69

Figgy Duff, 284

film industry, 281; film scores and soundtracks, 207, 236, 243, 262, 279, 284, 291, 292, 317, 407n12; musicians for silent films, 167, 169, 170, 188, 189, 391n2

Finkelstein, Bernie, 243, 247

Fiori, Serge, 281

First Nations. *See* First Peoples

First Peoples, 15–46, 187; arts training for, 262; attraction to European religious music, 50; Banff Centre Arts Program, 184, 263; ceremonial bundles, 22, 28, 298; ceremonies on white holidays, 165, 238; country music, 201, 238; elements of musical traditions, 44, 46; environmental sounds in, 297–8, 304; fiddling traditions, 43–4, 77, 155, 286, 288, 299–300; field recordings of traditional songs, 35, 185, 187; flutes, 22, 28, 33–4, 287, 288f, 298, 413n2; geographical regions, 15, 16f, 364n1–2; high pitchless "whoop," 36, 91, 299, 300; influence on Canadian composers, 268; initiation ceremonies, 20, 23–4, 25, 26; J.M. Gibbon's interest in, 172, 176; language families, 15, 16f, 364n1–2; percussion instruments, 21–2, 28, 32, 34, 39, 365n9; polyphonic singing, 21, 40, 299, 413n5; popular music of, 238–41, 245–6, 286–9; powwow movement, 165, 238, 239–40; rap, 289; rattles, 21–2, 28, 32, 34, 39, 365n9; representation of in refined music, 139, 140–1, 220, 263, 407n14; rhythmical accompaniments, 286; rock bands of, 286; roles in Western or refined music genres, 48, 50–2, 93,

262, 408n23; shamans, 21, 26–7, 29, 35, 38, 44; songs to control natural forces, 298; of South America, 263; terminology for, 364n1; Western religious materials in languages of, 50, 52, 98; in Wild West shows and rodeos, 164–5, 391n25, 404n34. *See also* specific nations or groups

First Peoples: drums: to accompany songs, 19, 286, 299; Cree, 29, 30; Dogrib, 23, 365n11; Inuit, 40–1, 43; Kwakwa̱ka'wakw, 18, 19, 21; Mi'kmaq and Maliseet, 39; Ojibwe, 32, 34; Plateau region, 28; for powwows, 239–40; snare drums, 23, 30, 32, 34, 286–7, 365n11; water drum, 32, 36, 287. *See also* percussion instruments

First Peoples: songs and dances: Buffalo Dance, 239; Buffalo Song and Dance, 176f; Calumet Dance, 31; Contest Dances, 239; Crow Hop, 239; Deer Dance, 176f; Dream Songs and Woman's Dance, 326f, 367n26; Drum Dance (Ojibwe), 32; Farewell Dance (Kwakwa̱ka'wakw), 18; Ghost (Spirit) Dance, 29; Hoop Dance, 239; Jingle Dance, 239; Little Woman Doctor Song, 323f; Medicine Dances, 29, 32; Medicine Song, 176f; Mourning Song, 18; Peace Dance Song, 18, 21; at powwows, 239–40; Prairie Chicken Dance, 29, 176f, 239; Ptarmigan Dance, 23; Rabbit Dance, 155, 239; Round Dance (Cree), 30; round dances, 238, 287; Shawl Dance, 239; Sneak-up, 239; Song of the Sun, 176f; Stick Dance, 25–6; Sun (Thirst) Dance, 28–9, 165, 176f, 238; Tea Dance (Toghà Dagowo), 23, 25, 29, 324f; Two-Step, 239; Victory Song, 239; War Dance, 328f; Wolf Songs (Siksika), 298

First World War, 135, 137, 179, 187, 190, 192–3, 387n45

Fisher, A.E., 385n29, 387n46

Fisher, Edward, 124

Fisher, Fred, 187

Fjellgaard, Gary, 284

Flaherty, Robert J., 384n26

Fléché, Jessé (priest), 50

Fleming, Robert, 398n3, 399n17, 399n18

Flotow, Friedrich: *Martha*, 118

flutes: Chinese, 237; fifes, 61; of First Peoples, 22, 28, 33–4, 287, 288*f*, 298, 413n2 (*See also* whistles); Hotteterre treatise on, 62, 64, 65; in jazz, 237; Longueil manuscript, 116; in New France, 51; in Sharon Band, 97

Flying Bulgar Klezmer Band, 291

folk festivals, 227–8, 234, 290, 402n6

folk-rock, 242

folk songs: anglophone, 147–8, 151–2, 199–200, 241; arrangements of, 70, 172–3, 174, 221, 393n17; ballads, 81, 82*f*, 148, 151, 152, 375n19, 375n20, 389n11; British, 80–3, 80*f*, 82*f*; broadsides, 81–3, 112, 160, 376nn22, 24, 27, 389n8; Canadian references in, 104, 300, 414n8; collections of, 146, 152, 226, 307; in concert hall setting, 173; effect of urbanization on, 104, 197, 226, 302; European views of, 6, 8, 300, 362n9; field recordings of, 173, 343–4; French Canadian, 57–61, 66, 83, 145–6, 198, 371n14; classification of, 57, 59, 329–31; *coureurs-de-bois* and voyageurs, 59–60, 83; J.M. Gibbon's interest in, 172, 174; origins of, 57–9, 174; as home entertainment, 83, 104; journalistic function of, 81, 148; in lumber camps, 104, 146–8, 151, 201, 388n5, 389n8, 414n8; macaronic, 148–51; and national identity, 302; in notated compositions, 138, 175, 179, 221, 222, 386n42; popular, 226–9, 247; singer-songwriters, 247, 272–3, 307, 309; working song traditions, 146. *See also* fiddling

Folk Songs of French Canada (Sapir and Barbeau), 393n18

folk song transcriptions, 152

Folkways Recordings (of Canadian music), 227, 228, 343–4, 364n14

Follow the Drinkin' Gourd, 390n18

Ford, Clifford, 4, 5

Forestier, Louise, 234

For Lovin' Me (Lightfoot), 232

Forrester, Maureen, 409n33

Forsyth, Amanda, 269

Forsyth, Malcolm, 253, 415n18; *Sketches from Natal*, 253

Forsyth, W.O., 120, 125, 141, 301; *Mon bouquet*, 141; *Prelude*, 143; *Romanza*, 136

Fort Garry (Manitoba), 93

For the Glory of the Grand Old Flag, 187

Fortier, Achille, 393n19; *O Salutaris hostia*, 138

Foster, David, 279, 292, 416n38

Foster, Stephen, 139, 159, 192, 390n17; *Old Folks at Home*, 145, 388n2

Four Lads, 230, 402n10

Four Strong Winds (I. Tyson), 231, 246

Four the Moment, 285

Fowke, Edith, 226, 227, 231, 241, 401n2

Francofolies, 284

Frankenstein, Alfred, 217–18

Frechette, Joey, 403n13

Frederick Harris Music, 407n9

Freedman, Harry, 215, 217, 221, 303–4, 399n17, 399n18, 400n20, 414n12; *Toccata for Flute and Soprano*, 221

Freeman, Stan, 196

Free Spirit, 98

Free Trade, 272

French language: musical impact of, 223, 232

Fresh-Wes, Maestro, 276–7

Fricker, Herbert A., 179

Friedman, Sam, 204*f*

From New York to L.A. (Gallant), 276

Frost, Henry, 121

Full Circle (McKennit), 290

Fuller, William Henry, 386n43; *H.M.S. Parliament*, 139

Fumbling towards Ecstasy (McLachlan), 294

funerals, music for, 69

Fung, Vivian, 408n21

Raminsch, Imant, 254; *Ave, verum corpus*, 254

Rand, Silas, 38, 39

Ranganathan, Lakshmi, 416n33

Rankin Family, 244, 272, 285

Ranville, Errol, 286

rap, 276, 289, 417n40

Rascalz, 277

Rasmussen, Knud, 40

rasps, 28

rattles (First Peoples), 21–2, 28, 32, 34, 39, 365n9

Raudot, Antoine-Denis, 63

Raudot, Jacques, 63

Ravel, Maurice, 178, 179

Real McKenzies, the, 286

Recoletts, 48

recorder, 97*t*, 266

recordings, 201, 235; Canadian labels, 243–5, 270, 275, 416n39; concept albums, 226, 242, 272, 284; development of, 130, 185, 223, 226, 235, 238, 273, 384n25; distinctive Canadian sound in, 312; folk music, 35, 173, 175, 185, 187, 227, 318, 343–4; on the Internet, 317; MAPL logo, 245; played at music clubs, 120; radio broadcast of, 397n21; recording as an art, 235; studios, 244, 416n39

Redbird, Duke, 12–14, 364n18

Red River fiddling, 200

Red River Jig, 76*f*, 77

Reed, Angelo, 385n29

Reed, Bill, 402n11

Reel de Tadoussac, 397n27

reels, 71–3, 73, 74, 78, 154, 198, 318

reference books, 4, 291, 301

refined music, 8, 363n11, 406n9

reggae, 274–5, 278, 411n12

Regina, 134, 135, 176

Regina Orchestra, 134

Regnard Duplessis de Sainte-Hélène, Mère Marie-Andrée, 54; *Musique spirituelle où l'on peut s'exercer sans voix* (1718), 54

Reich, Steve, 255

Reid, Ellen, 290

Reilly, James, 398n6

Reilly, Tommy, 207

Reiner, Fritz, 167

religious music, 48–57, 84–6, 112–14; Anglo-Catholic, 180, 394n24; anthems, 85, 97–8, 113–14, 137–8, 138, 190, 408n23; choral tradition, 102–3; congregational singing, 84, 102–3, 113–14; lining out, 84, 85*f*; liturgical (Catholic), 48, 93, 138, 369n2, 370nn5, 8, 9; motets, 53–5, 55*f*, 113, 137–8, 180, 369n2, 372n21; as popular music, 188, 319; role of organ, 114; singing schools, 84–5, 99, 103, 144, 376n25; trained musicians for, 84, 113–14. *See also* hymn tunes

Relyea, Gary, 398n2

Renaud, Emiliano, 186

Renaud, Louis, 64

Reno, Ginette, 281

Reno, Mike, 279

Repas dans les chantiers, Les, 414n8

research and studies: of Canadian music, 4–5

Rèvolution française, La, 282

revues, 164, 193

Rheostatics, 279

Rhumba Boogie, The (Snow), 202

rhythm and blues (R&B), 225, 226, 230, 231, 275, 276, 289, 292

Rhythme du monde, 313

Rhythm Pals, 229

Ribon-Lully, 62

Rice, Gitz, 187–8

Rice, Timothy, 144, 311

Richard, Zachary, 282

Ridder, Allard de, 170

Ridout, Godfrey, 180*f*, 184, 399n9, 400nn18, 20; *A Comedy Overture*, 392n11; reconstruction of Quesnel's *Colas et Colinette*, 91

Riel, Louis, 139, 220

Riley, Terry, 255

Rise Up (Parachute Club), 278

Rituel du diocèse de Québec, 370n5